Proceedings

Graphics **Interface** 2002

Wolfgang Stürzlinger and Michael D. McCool
Program Co-Chairs

www.graphicsinterface.org

Calgary, Alberta
27–29 May 2002

Papers are reproduced here from electronic files prepared by the authors.

ISSN 0713-5424
ISBN 1-56881-183-7

Proceedings Graphics Interface 2002, Wolfgang Stürzlinger and Michael D. McCool (Program Co-Chairs), Calgary, Alberta, 27–29 May 2002. Published by the Canadian Human-Computer Communications Society and A K Peters Ltd.

Graphics Interface is sponsored by:
The Canadian Human-Computer Communications Society (CHCCS)

Membership Information for CHCCS is available from:
Canadian Information Processing Society (CIPS)
2800 Skymark Avenue, Suite 402
Mississauga, Ontario L4W 5A6
Canada
Telephone: (905) 602-1370
Fax: (905) 602-7884
Web: `http://www.cips.ca/`

Additional copies of the proceedings are available from:
A K Peters Ltd.
63 South Avenue
Natick, MA 01760
Web: `http://www.akpeters.com/`

Published by the Canadian Human-Computer Communications Society and A K Peters Ltd.
Distributed by A K Peters Ltd.
Printed in Canada by Graphics Services at the University of Waterloo, Waterloo, Ontario.

Cover Credits

Wireframes: Front cover, Kevin Moule. Back cover: Marco Tarini, Hitoshi Yamauchi, Jörg Haber, and Hans-Peter Seidel (89); Hendrik Kück, Christian Vogelgsang, and Günther Greiner (81). Computer Program: Kevin Moule. Colour images: Left to right (starting on back left): Yefei He, James Cremer, and Yiannis Papelis (151); Hendrik Kück, Christian Vogelgsang, and Günther Greiner (81); Eric Paquette, Pierre Poulin, and George Drettakis (59); Brendan Lane and Przemyslaw Prusinkiewicz (69); Marco Tarini, Hitoshi Yamauchi, Jörg Haber, and Hans-Peter Seidel (89); Oleg Veryovka (9); Sageev Oore, Demetri Terzopoulos, and Geoffrey Hinton (133); Victor Ng-Thow-Hing and Eugene Fiume (107). Top to bottom (skipping joint): Michael Meißner, Stefan Guthe, and Wolfgang Straßer (209); John McDonald, Karen Alkoby, Roymieco Carter, Juliet Christopher, Mary Jo Davidson, Dan Ethridge, Jacob Furst, Damien Hinkle, Glenn Lancaster, Lori Smallwood, Nedjla Ougouag-Tiouririne, Jorge Toro, Shuang Xu, and Rosalee Wolfe (99); Michael McGuffin, Nicolas Burtnyk, and Gordon Kurtenbach (35); Robert Jagnow and Julie Dorsey (125). Design: Christine Goucher and Abby Van Dongen.

Message from the Program Co-Chairs

Wolfgang Stürzlinger
Department of Computer Science
York University

Michael D. McCool
School of Computer Science
University of Waterloo

Welcome to Graphics Interface (GI) 2002, a conference that combines coverage of original research results in both Human-Computer Interaction and Graphics. The conference took place in Calgary, Alberta, over 27–29 May 2002, and was held in conjunction with the Artificial Intelligence 2002 and Vision Interface 2002 conferences. GI 2002 is the 28th instance of the longest running conference series in human-computer interaction and computer graphics. This event has previously been held two times in Calgary: in 1977 and in 1991.

The program co-chairs received 96 submissions in all areas of human-computer interaction and computer graphics. The large number of submissions was a pleasant surprise; however, the number of submissions also necessitated an enlargement of the program committee on short notice. We are very grateful to all the additional program committee members who agreed to take time out of their busy schedules late in 2001. By agreeing to serve, these additional members reduced the workload on other committee members and permitted us to maintain our high reviewing standards.

The overall quality of the submissions was very high, which made the selection process difficult. After considerable deliberation, the program committee selected 25 papers for publication. The international program committee consisted of 20 people from around the world. Each paper received at least 4 reviews, two of which were from members of the program committee. The reviewing process was double-blind, and the identity of the authors was known only to program co-chairs and the program committee member responsible for choosing external reviewers for each submission. The program committee members were often able to solicit reviews from some of the topmost experts in a particular area of research. We greatly appreciate the effort of the members of the program committee. We would like to extend additional thanks to the 13 members of the program committee who attended the meeting at York University, Toronto, Canada on 16 February 2002 and funded their own travel.

Graphics Interface customarily has several invited speakers. This year three invited speakers were: Saul Greenberg, Professor at the University of Calgary; John Buchanan, Electronic Arts Canada and Adjunct Professor at the University of Alberta; and David Kirk, Chief Scientist at NVIDIA. We extend our gratitude to them for sharing their inspiration in their respective fields.

We would like to thanks James Stewart for his work on the PCS electronic submission and reviewing system. His help behind the scenes made our job a lot easier! We would also like to thank Pierre Poulin and Kelly Booth for handling the liaison with AI and VI conference organizers, and Kelly Booth again for additional valuable advice. We thank further all referees for their voluntary work, Ravin Balakrishnan for handling the posters, Sara Diamond for organizing the video show, and Fred Peet, treasurer of the Canadian Human-Computer Communication Society, for keeping the finances straight, and Graphics Services at the University of Waterloo for doing such an excellent job on the proceedings. Last but not least, we send a very big thanks to Camille Sinanan, Sheelagh Carpendale, Mario Costa-Sousa, and Joerg Denzinger for the local organization of the joint conferences at the University of Calgary. Without their work, this conference would simply not have been possible.

For further information about the conference series we invite you to visit our web site:

`http://www.graphicsinterface.org/`

Organization

Conference and Program Chairs
Wolfgang Stürzlinger, York University
Michael McCool, University of Waterloo

Local Organizers
Sheelagh Carpendale, University of Calgary
Mario Costa-Sousa, University of Calgary
Joerg Denzinger, University of Calgary
Camille Sinanan, University of Calgary

Posters Chair
Ravin Balakrishnan, University of Toronto

Videos Chair
Sara Diamond, Banff Arts Centre

Student Volunteer Organizer
Oliver St. Cyr, University of Waterloo

Online Services
James Stewart, Queen's University

Proceedings Editor
Michael McCool, University of Waterloo

Program Committee
Ravin Balakrishnan, University of Toronto
Gladimir Baranoski, University of Waterloo
Thomas Ertl, University of Stuttgart
Michael Garland, University of Illinois at Urbana-Champaign
Craig Gotsman, Technion
Carl Gutwin, University of Saskatchewan
Christopher Healey, North Carolina State University
Wolfgang Heidrich, University of British Columbia
Jessica Hodgins, Carnegie Mellon University
Ted Kirkpatrick, Simon Fraser University
Yoshifumi Kitamura, Osaka University
Paul Lalonde, Electronic Arts Canada
Hanspeter Pfister, MERL Cambridge Research
Pierre Poulin, Université de Montréal
Holly Rushmeier, IBM T.J. Watson Research Center
Peter-Pike Sloan, Microsoft Research
Thomas Strothotte, University of Magdeburg
Michiel van de Panne, University of British Columbia

CHCCS Treasurer
Fred G. Peet, Canadian Forest Service

Referees

Johnny Accot
John Amanatides
Nina Amenta
Alexis Angelidis
Ian Ashdown
Ravin Balakrishnan
Gladimir Baranoski
Gill Barequet
Lyn Bartram
Rui Bastos
Thomas Baudel
Ben Bederson
Ian Bell
Thomas Berlage
Jules Bloomenthal
Kellogg Booth
Kadi Bouatouch
Stefan Brabec
Chris Bregler
John Buchanan
Chris Buehler
Tom Calvert
Sheelagh Carpendale
Anthony Chee-Hung Fang
Min Chen
Yiorogs Chrysanthou
Mary Czerwinski
Luiz Henrique de Figueiredo
Leila De Floriani
Ralph Deters
Oliver Deussen
Prasun Dewan
Jean-Michel Dischler
Michael Doggett
Julie Dorsey
Sarah Douglas
Steven Drucker
Mark Duchaineau
Fredo Durand
Phil Dutre
Gershon Elber
Thomas Ertl
Irfan Essa
Anath Fischer
George Fitzmaurice
Eugene Fiume
Michael Garland
Michael Gleicher
Stephane Gobron
Michael Goesele
Craig Gotsman
François Guimbretiere
Stefan Gumhold
Damrong Guoy
Igor Guskov
Carl Gutwin
Jörg Haber
James Hahn
Eric Haines
Jason Harrison
John Hart
Knut Hartmann
Helwig Hauser
Li-wei He
Christopher Healey
Wolfgang Heidrich
Ken Hinckley
Koichi Hirota
Jessica Hodgins
Kenneth Hoff
Masahiko Inami
Poorang Irani
Jan Kautz
Ted Kirkpatrick
Yoshifumi Kitamura
Reinhard Klein
James Klosowski
Leif Kobbelt
Kevin Kreeger
Tomohiro Kuroda
Gordon Kurtenbach
Hideaki Kuzuoka
David Laidlaw
Paul Lalonde
Hugh Lauer
Jed Lengyel
Hendrik Lensch
Peter Lindstrom
David Luebke
I. Scott MacKenzie
Paolo Magillo
Tom Malzbender
Regan Mandryk
Dinesh Manocha
Steve Marschner
Masood Masoodian
Toshiyuki Masui
Nelson Max
Dave McAllister
Michael McCool
Joanna McGrenere
Ann McNamara
Michael Meißner
Stan Melax
Mark Meyer
Tim Miller
Jun-yong Noh
Haruo Noma
Manuel M. Oliveira
Dan Olsen
Sageev Oore
Victor Ostromoukhov
Eric Paquette
Sergey Parilov
Valerio Pascucci
Mark Pauly
Hanspeter Pfister
Jeff Pierce
Nancy Pollard
Jean Ponce
Stuart Pook
Pierre Poulin
Gilles Pouliquen
Simon Premoze
Werner Purgathofer
Andreas Raab
Patrick Ratto
Soraia Raupp Musse
Lionel Reveret
Christof Rezk-Salama
Penny Rheingans
Theresa-Marie Rhyne
Thomas Rist
Stefan Roettger
Jon Rokne
Jarek Rossignac
Holly Rushmeier
Annette Scheel
Eric Schenk
Stefan Schlechtweg
Alla Sheffer
Mikio Shinya
Peter Shirley
Maryann Simmons
Peter-Pike Sloan
Michiel Smid
A. Augusto Sousa
Milos Sramek
Robert St. Amant
Marc Stamminger
James Stewart
Lisa Streit
Norbert Streitz
Thomas Strothotte
Wolfgang Stürzlinger
Kelvin Sung
Haruo Takemura
Roger Tam
Hai Tao
Russell Taylor
Greg Turk
Michiel van de Panne
Nicolas Vidot
Vadym Voznyuk
Andrew Walenstein
Jason Walter
Marcelo Walter
Justin Wan
Greg Ward
Benjamin Watson
Ruediger Westermann
Stephen Westin
Jane Wilhelms
Craig Wittenbrink
David Wong
Yin Wu
Granier Xavier
Yasuyuki Yanagida
Michal Young
Michael Young
Qinxin Yu
Yizhou Yu
Matthias Zwicker

Table of Contents

Layered Environment-Map Impostors for Arbitrary Scenes

Stefan Jeschke
Institute of Computer Graphics and Algorithms
Vienna University of Technology

Michael Wimmer
Institute of Computer Graphics and Algorithms
Vienna University of Technology

Heidrun Schumann
Institute of Computer Graphics
Department of Computer Science
University of Rostock

Abstract

This paper presents a new impostor-based approach to accelerate the rendering of very complex static scenes. The scene is partitioned into viewing regions, and a layered impostor representation is precalculated for each of them. An optimal placement of impostor layers guarantees that our representation is indistinguishable from the original geometry. Furthermore the algorithm exploits common graphics hardware both during preprocessing and rendering. Moreover the impostor representation is compressed using several strategies to cut down on storage space.

Key words: virtual environments, walkthroughs, image-based rendering, impostors, environment maps

1 Introduction

The real-time display of very large and complex virtual environments has been one focus of computer graphics research for a considerable amount of time already. Although many advances have been made, the goal of displaying arbitrary (i.e., without restrictions on scene structure or navigation methods) scenes of high complexity at frame rates above 30 or even 60 Hz has consistently eluded any approach.

For instance, visibility calculations [25] can dramatically reduce the geometry to be rendered in walkthroughs of densely occluded environments. However, many scenes do not provide sufficient occlusion, and even for densely occluded scenes, switching to a different navigation behavior (like flyovers) can render visibility culling ineffective. In such cases, image-based rendering (IBR) [7] methods are usually called for, because their rendering complexity only depends on the output resolution of the image, not on the total number of primitives in the scene.

In this paper, we present a new algorithm that uses several optimally placed layers of image-based primitives—so-called *impostors*—to represent distant geometry. Each layer is arranged in a fashion similar to a cubic environment map. The layered impostors are generated in a preprocessing step for individual regions of space called *view cells*, and further optimized so that they take up little storage space and can be processed efficiently by current graphics hardware. A new error metric guarantees that the representation is practically indistinguishable from the original geometry it replaces, avoiding cracks and popping artifacts. Geometry near the viewer will be displayed using polygonal rendering.

Figure 1 shows an example of our impostor technique.

Figure 1: Example for layered environment-map impostors: (a) observer's view, (b) same scene from a bird's eye view.

The main contribution of this paper is an image-based geometry representation method that offers several advantages over previous methods:

1. It can deal with arbitrary static models with diffuse illumination, even if no scene structure is available. This is especially important because most available models consist of unstructured "polygon soups", which cannot be dealt with satisfactorily in most other methods.

2. High output image quality. The optimal layer place-

ment shown in this paper guarantees that the differences between impostor and the geometry it represents are practically imperceptible. In particular, it avoids image cracks due to missing information about hidden geometry and popping artifacts when switching between different impostors.

3. Compact impostor representation. Although the precalculated impostors for all view cells need to be stored on hard disk, the specific layer arrangement allows using special-purpose algorithms that dramatically reduce memory requirements both on harddisk and in texture memory.

4. Fast rendering. The method naturally supports conventional graphics hardware. Additionally, since no online calculations are necessary, optimal runtime efficiency is achieved.

The remainder of the paper is organized as follows: after a short review of previous work in section 2, an overview of the impostor system is given in section 3. Section 4 introduces the error metric used to calculate the optimal layer placement, and section 5 presents the techniques used to compress the impostor textures. Results of the system are given in section 6, and section 7 presents final conclusions.

2 Previous work

A huge amount of literature deals with methods to accelerate the real-time rendering of highly complex environments, including level-of-detail rendering [10], visibility culling [25], point-based rendering [24], light-field rendering [14], or image warping [7], to name just a few. Many of them share similar problems: they are not general enough for arbitrary scenes (e.g., visibility culling, see the introduction), or are not amenable to hardware acceleration, as is the case for most image-based rendering methods. We will review here only a subset of image-based methods that are directly related to our work.

The idea of using image-based representations to replace complex geometric objects in virtual walkthroughs was first introduced by Maciel in 1995 [15]. A particular object is rendered into a texture map with transparency information, and then mapped onto a quadriliteral placed into the scene in place of the object. The resulting primitive is called an *impostor*. Schaufler et al. [20] and Shade et al. [22] used this idea to build a hierarchical image cache for an online system, with relaxed constraints for image quality.

When using only one quadriliteral, the object is represented poorly by the impostor if the observer moves too far away from the reference viewpoint. Therefore, several authors have presented methods that use varying levels of geometric information to overcome this drawback. Starting from a planar impostor, depth information can be added using triangles [8, 16, 23], with the resulting primitive sometimes called textured depth mesh (TDM). TDMs are, however, prone to distortion and disocclusion artifacts. Depth can also be added per point sample—in particular, layered depth images (LDI) [17, 21] provide greater flexibility by allowing several depth values per image sample. However, LDIs contain more information than necessary for a good representation of parallax effects, and are not amenable to hardware acceleration. TDMs [1] and LDIs [2] can also be used to represent distant geometry for a whole view cell.

Finally, in a way closely related to our work, depth information can be added using layers [13, 18, 19]. There, an object is sliced into several impostors, each of them representing a different depth range. However, this technique was only used to simplify individual objects in a scene, and it is based on equidistant layers.

In this paper, we show how to use layered impostors to simplify distant geometry, and how to optimally place the layers so as to provide the highest possible image quality [5], while at the same time keeping storage cost to a tolerable level using an image-based visibility algorithm which is conceptually related to the extended projections technique [9].

3 Overview

Our system consists of two stages: a preprocessing stage in which layered impostors are calculated and optimized for all view cells in the scene, and a runtime component in which the compressed impostors are prefetched on demand and displayed in place of the original geometry. Each layer is arranged similar to a cubic environment map around the view cell.

More specifically, the *preprocessing stage* consists of the following steps:

1. The user needs to decide on the size of the view cells, on the number of layers, and on the display resolution the impostors should be calculated for.

2. Partition the space of possible viewing positions into view cells.

3. Generate the layered impostors in the following steps:

   (a) Determine the distance to the individual impostor layers (section 4.2) and the regions for which the impostors are used.

   (b) Render the geometry for each impostor layer into a texture using conventional graphics hardware.

(c) Compress the impostor textures by exploiting the special structure of the problem (section 5):
   i. Erase those parts of every impostor texture that are always occluded by impostor layers closer to the view cell (section 5.2).
   ii. partition the impostor polygon into smaller polygons that are well filled.
   iii. combine the textures for the smaller polygons into larger textures for efficient graphics hardware treatment.
   iv. compress those textures using PNG for efficient storage on disk.

(d) Finally, a list of the near geometry that is not represented by impostors is generated.

The *runtime component* is a simple 3D viewer where the user can freely navigate through the 3D model. Since most of the work was already done during preprocessing, the runtime component only has to:

1. Determine the current view cell of the observer.
2. Prefetch the geometry and impostors of adjacent view cells in order to avoid varying frame rates [11] (assuming—as is common for most prefetching schemes—a limited observer speed). To amortize the cost of texture downloads over several frames, prefetched impostor textures are downloaded to texture memory in smaller chunks.
3. Render the near geometry not represented by impostors.
4. Render the impostor polygons for the current view cell.

Note that the last two steps are done using graphics hardware.

4 Optimal impostor-layer placement

This section explains how the impostor layers are arranged around a view cell and how the optimal placement is calculated.

4.1 Layer arrangement

Figure 2 shows how impostor layers are arranged as *impostor cubes* around a particular view cell. Note that each impostor layer represents geometry within a certain depth range to the front and to the back of the layer. The *borders* show where the transition between two layers takes place: objects in front of a particular border are represented by the impostor nearer to the view cell, objects to the back are represented by the impostor farther from the view cell.

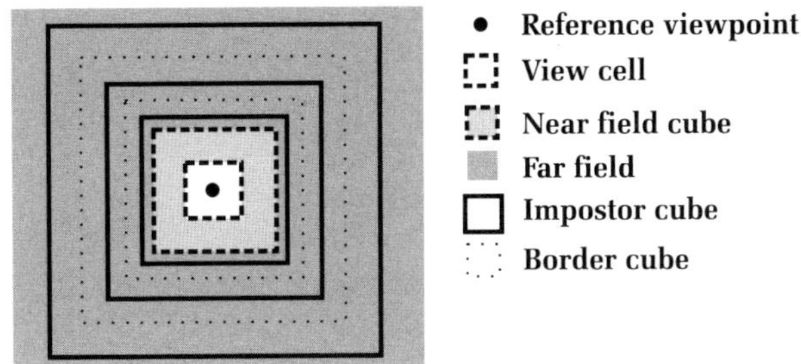

Figure 2: Layout of the impostors around a view cell.

When generating an impostor layer, each side of its impostor cube is rendered from the *reference viewpoint*, i.e., the center of the view cell, with the near and far clipping planes set to the appropriate sides of the adjacent border cubes.

The innermost border cube (near field cube in figure 2) is especially noteworthy: it defines the border between the *near field* and the *far field*. All geometry in the near field will be rendered using polygonal rendering, whereas geometry in the far field is represented by impostors.

While the size of the view cell is defined by the user directly, the placement of the impostor layers and their corresponding depth ranges (i.e., position of the borders) will be calculated automatically. The only user inputs to this calculation are the desired number of impostor layers and the desired image resolution.

4.2 Layer placement calculation

Two errors have to be taken into account when calculating an optimal placement of the layers: parallax errors and gaps between texels of consecutive layers.

Parallax errors: The impostor layers need to be placed so that every layer "faithfully" represents the geometry it replaces as long as the observer stays within the associated view cell. In order to quantify "faithfully", we characterize the error that occurs when viewing the impostor from a position different from the reference position using the *parallax angle* α (see figure 3). This is the angle between the true 3D position of a point F and its projection F' to the impostor, when seen from a position V different from the reference viewpoint V_r (see also [22]).

The goal is to find out in which configuration the maximum parallax error occurs, so that we can calculate from this the maximum possible depth range that guarantees that a given parallax angle will not be exceeded. Therefore, while the parallax angle can be calculated for any viewing position and any point on an object, we are actually only interested in the extremal case where the viewpoint is moved to a corner of the view cell, and we only

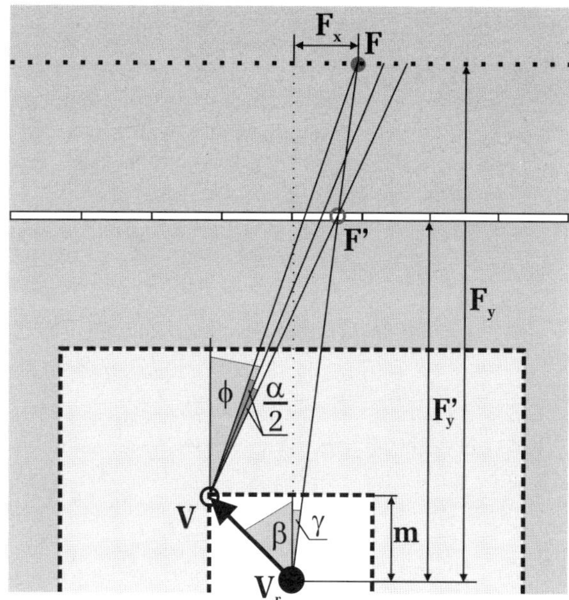

Figure 3: Maximum parallax angle within a view cell.

consider points on a border cube, i.e., points on a plane parallel to the impostor. For this case, a very intriguing result can now be shown[1]:

> Assume a given view cell, an impostor layer and a border cube. Then the maximum parallax angle between a point on the border cube and its projection to the impostor, when seen from the corner of the view cell, *always* occurs for a viewing direction of $\phi = \frac{\pi}{4} - \frac{\beta}{2}$ from the view cell corner, where $\beta = \frac{\pi}{4}$ for the 2D case and $\beta = \arctan(\sqrt{2})$ for the general 3D case (see figure 3).

The following equations show how to calculate from a known border F_y the next closer layer F'_y (or respectively from a known layer F_y the next closer border F'_y):

$$\begin{aligned} m &= \frac{size_{viewcell}}{2}; \\ F_x &= \tan(\phi - \frac{\alpha}{2})(F_y - m) - m\tan(\beta); \\ \gamma &= \arctan(\frac{F_x}{F_y}); \\ F'_y &= \frac{m\cos(\gamma)\sin(\phi + \frac{\alpha}{2} + \beta)}{\cos(\beta)\sin(\phi + \frac{\alpha}{2} - \gamma)}. \end{aligned} \quad (1)$$

When calculating the following border (or respectively layer), F_y must simply be set to F'_y from the previous step. To obtain the distance to the first impostor layer, F_y can be set infinitely far away, where γ becomes $\phi - \frac{\alpha}{2}$.

Gaps between texels: Two successive impostor layers should not move more than one texel against each other because visibility gaps might appear in a continuous surface represented in both layers.

As can easily be shown, the maximum texel movement appears when the observer looks from one corner of the view cell to texels at the opposite border of the impostor as shown in figure 4.

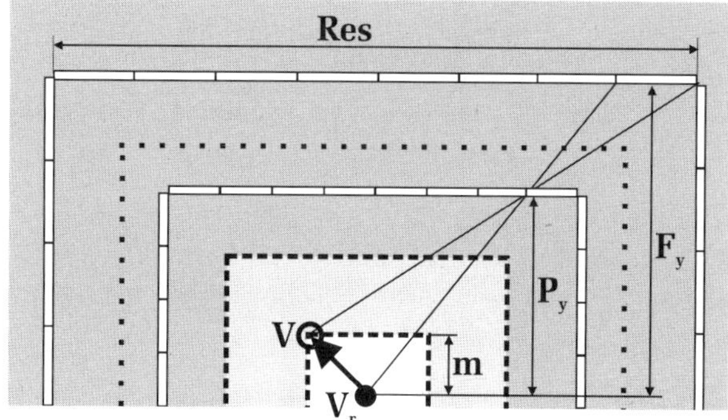

Figure 4: Maximum pixel movement within a view cell.

The minimum allowable distance to the next closer impostor layer, P_y, is then

$$P_y = \frac{F_y\, m\, Res}{m\, Res + F_y - m}, \quad (2)$$

where *Res* is the resolution of an impostor layer. This value is compared to the value F'_y obtained by two successive evaluations of equation 1. The larger of the two defines the actual distance of the impostor layer. If P_y is chosen, then the border between the two layers can be recalculated using equation 1 by setting α to

$$\alpha = 2\arctan\left(f\cos(\beta)\sqrt[4]{\frac{P_y(F_y - m)}{F_y(P_y - m)}} - \tan(\beta)\right) - 2\phi.$$

Here $f = 2$ in the 2D case and $f = 3$ in the 3D case.

4.3 Discussion

Choosing α: An obvious choice for α is the minimal angle subtended by a pixel in the output image.

Choosing the number of layers: Using only one impostor for the far field is equivalent to a conventional cubic environment map, except that the error incurred by using the environment map is a maximum of one pixel. The resulting near field is too large for most practical purposes, however. For example, an output resolution of 512x512

[1]For a detailed proof of this statement see [12].

pixels and a view cell size of 10x10 m would result in a near field distance of 1738 m.

Using more layers, which represent different depth ranges of the far field, dramatically reduces the size of the near field because the parallax movements are "split" and assigned to different layers. For example, with the same output resolution of 512x512 pixels and a view cell size of 10x10 m, using 64 layers will place the near field distance already at 42 m.

5 Impostor compilation

The layered impostors generated for each view cell need to be compressed before they can be used. For example, the impostors for a single view cell would require 384 MB at a resolution of 512x512 texels and using 64 layers. Therefore, we apply several methods to reduce the storage requirements of impostors on harddisk and, even more importantly, in texture memory. Finally, before generating the impostor geometry, it is necessary to close one-pixel visibility gaps that might arise between two impostor layers.

The methods presented here exploit the fact that all impostor layers use the same resolution, and that two adjacent layers only move by a maximum of one pixel against each other in any view. This allows us to use fast image processing techniques as described in the following sections.

5.1 Gap filling

The aim of gap filling is to prevent holes from appearing in continuous surfaces represented by different layers. Figure 5 (left) shows the problem in 1D: The line

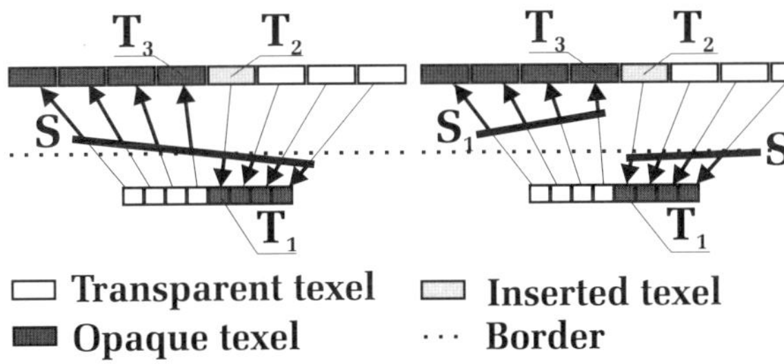

Figure 5: Filling the appearing gap between T_1 and T_3 by copying the texel T_1 to T_2. This may result in correct (left) or incorrect (right) visibility.

S is sampled so that the texel T_2 is not opaque. If the viewer now moves from the center of the view cell to the left, a hole of one texel appears between the near and the far layer. To avoid such undesirable artifacts, we fill the texel T_2 by copying the color information from texel T_1 to it. Thus we can always guarantee that continuous surfaces will have no holes.

The right side of figure 5 shows a case where the filling of T_2 results in incorrect visibility, but the error introduced thereby is usually not noticeable. It is not possible to avoid this problem, since after sampling the geometry, it is not possible to distinguish between the two cases.

In practice, the hole-filling operation is done easily by copying opaque texels that have at least one transparent neighbor (*opaque border texels*) of the current (closer) layer to texels at the same position in the next (more distant) layer, that are either opaque texels or *transparent border texels* (transparent texels that have at least one opaque neighbor).

5.2 Removing invisible texels

Normally, many texels in each layer are occluded by closer layers[2]. Therefore, we remove texels that are never visible because they are always hidden by texels of closer layers.

The algorithm for doing that proceeds by repeating the following operations for each pair of adjacent layers (see figure 6 for the problem in 1D, (a) shows the initial configuration):

Mark texels in the more distant layer as hidden if they are behind opaque texels of the closer layer which are not border texels (see figures 6 (b) or (c)). If texels in the closer layer were already marked as hidden in the previous iteration, they must be interpreted as opaque in this iteration (see figure 6 (c)) and set as transparent before proceeding to the next pair of layers (this can be seen in figure 6 (d)).

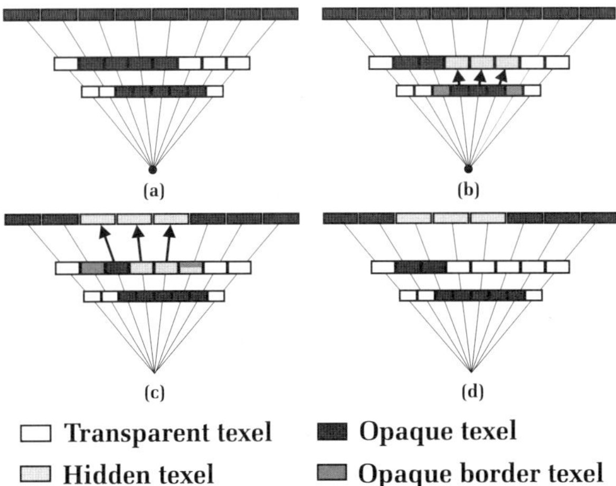

Figure 6: Removing texels in the layers that are hidden behind layers closer to the viewpoint.

[2]Note that occlusion due to near-field geometry is very complex and not addressed in our system.

After removing invisible texels, the layers contain exactly the information that might become visible when the viewer walks within the associated view cell.

5.3 Generation of impostor polygons

Since occluded texels have been removed in the previous step, most layers will contain a large amount of transparent texels that actually need not be stored at all. Therefore, we extract the opaque texels of every layer by splitting the texture into a number of smaller textures (*micro textures*) that tightly cover the opaque regions in the impostor texture, and creating corresponding rectangular impostor polygons (see the example in figure 7). The goal is to find a good tradeoff between minimizing the number of impostor polygons and the number of transparent texels in the microtextures.

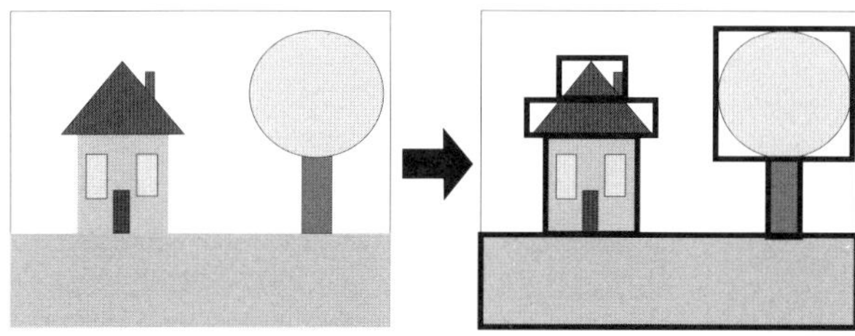

Figure 7: Representation of an impostor layer with only few covering polygons.

Since this problem is NP-complete, we employ a fast, greedy algorithm to find a good solution. First, overlay the impostor texture with a regular grid—with smaller grid size giving preference to a more accurate solution, but creating more polygons (we used an 8x8 grid). Then, as long as there is such a cell left, we choose a cell that is not completely transparent and try to grow it until the percentage of opaque pixels in the cell falls below a user-defined threshold. The cell can be grown in any direction (including diagonals), but is constrained to maintain rectangular shape. In each growing step, the direction that gives the best percentage of opaque pixels is chosen. If the cell cannot be grown further (either because there are no non-transparent cells in any direction, or because the threshold is reached), a microtexture and its corresponding impostor polygon is created, and all its grid cells are set to transparent.

Even tighter packing might be achieved using more involved algorithms [4] at the expense of longer preprocessing time.

5.4 Microtexture packing

As the number of microtextures created for a view cell in the previous step can be quite large (hundreds or even thousands, depending on the parameters), we try to pack microtextures into larger *macrotextures*. This reduces the general overhead involved in handling a large number of textures, and especially favors current graphics hardware which penalizes textures switches. Furthermore, we can account for the fact that graphics hardware can usually only handle textures with resolutions of powers of two (this restriction can be lifted for newer hardware).

Again, since the 2D rectangle packing problem is NP-complete [3], we use a fast, greedy algorithm that tries to generate very few macrotextures, while achieving a good coverage of the textures with opaque texels. First, all microtextures are rotated so that they are top-down. Afterwards they are sorted into a list by decreasing height and—for equal heights—by increasing width. The height of a new macrotexture is then determined using the height of the first microtexture in the list enlarged to the next power of two. The width of the macrotexture is calculated by dividing the summed area of all microtextures by the determined height and also enlarge this value to the next power of two (assuming the first microtexture will fit).

For filling the new macrotexture with microtextures, a bottom-left placement rule [6] is used beginning with the first in the sorted list, until the right border of the macrotexture is reached. The remaining space is filled by the remaining microtextures using a left-bottom placement rule beginning with the last (smallest) microtexture in the list.

After all microtextures are tested and possibly placed, the algorithm resumes by constructing the next macrotexture. This is repeated until there is no microtexture left.

The final result is a low number of relatively well-filled macrotextures that can be sent directly to graphics hardware. For storing them on disk, they are compressed using PNG compression.

6 Results

We have implemented the methods presented in this paper in C++ and OpenGL, and applied them to a 3D model of the ancient Aztec city of Tenochtitlan (which is freely available on the Internet). In order to provide adequate complexity, we replicated the model 3x3 times for a total of 854586 polygons. The Aztec model demonstrates the performance of the method in a scene with wide open spaces and sparse buildings, and shows that the method performs equally well for walkthrough situations and flyovers. A PC with an Athlon 1.2 GHz processor, 512 MB of main memory and a GeForce 3 graphics card was used for all tests.

Table 1 shows some statistics for the model. A corridor of 11x27 view cells (i.e., 154x378 m) was selected for preprocessing, which took slightly above 12 hours in our unoptimized implementation. Preprocessing the whole model would have taken prohibitively long, so—as is usual for methods involving preprocessing—it is advisable to carefully select the areas where the observer is expected to move around.

Polygons of whole model	854586
Side length of whole model	1350 m
Side length of view cell	14 m
Side length of near field cube	118 m
Avg. preproc. time per view cell	2.5 min

Table 1: Model statistics

Size of impostor layers	256 MB
Size of macrotextures	6018KB
Size of macrotextures after PNG	288 KB

Table 2: Effect of compression on avg. per view cell

The selected output resolution was 512x512 pixels, and the number of layers was set to 64. Note that since we move relatively near to the ground plane and the sky is not complex enough to warrant an efficient impostor representation, we only calculated impostors for the 4 directions orthogonal to the ground plane. Table 2 shows the compression achieved on average when going from the layers of a view cell to macrotextures, and after PNG compression of the macrotextures, for these selected parameters.

In order to test the runtime performance of the system, we have recorded a path (with both walkthrough and flyover characteristics) through the preprocessed part of the model, containing 2197 frames. Figure 8 shows the frame rates our system achieves for each frame of the path, and for comparison, the frame rates of an unaccelerated system using only OpenGL display lists. It can be seen that

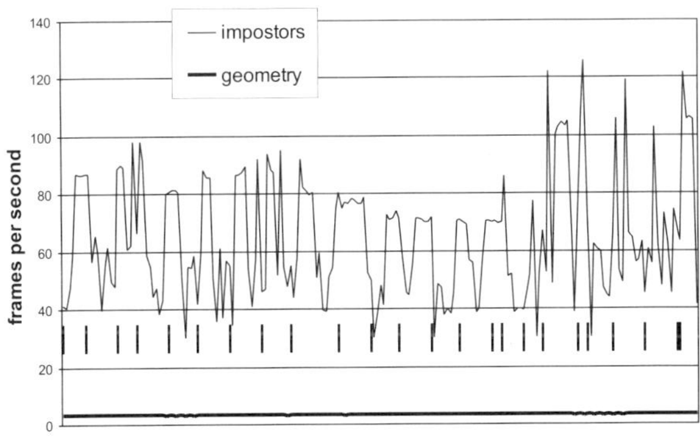

Figure 8: Frame rates for the recorded path containing 2197 frames. The vertical lines indicate where the view cell changed.

while the unaccelerated system never exceeds 3 frame per second (fps), our layered impostor system consistently reaches 40 fps, with an average of of more than 60 fps. This means that our system achieves a speedup of more than one order of magnitude over the unaccelerated system.

Finally, figure 9 shows the number of polygons used for impostors, the number of polygons remaining in the near field, and the total number of polygons for each frame of the same walkthrough.

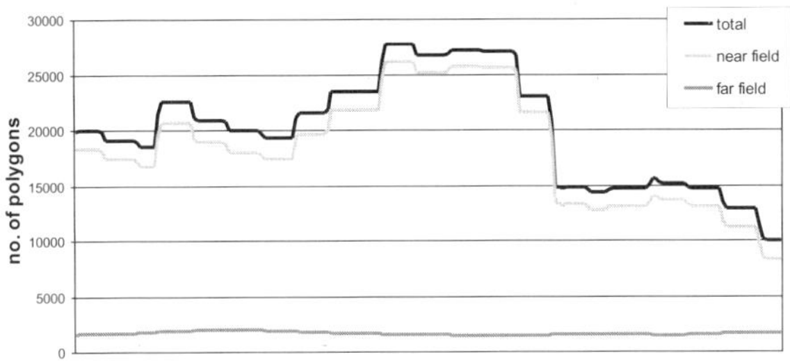

Figure 9: Complexity of the near field and far field for the recorded path.

Reconstruction quality is limited to the sampling provided by OpenGL at the moment, and includes an additional bias towards the reference viewpoint, which is however negligible in practice due to our error metric. While it would theoretically be possible to improve reconstruction quality by storing view-dependent information in the textures and using multiple rays for filtering [24], the expected preprocessing times and space required for the additional texture information would be prohibitively high.

7 Conclusions

We have presented a novel approach to render very complex, arbitrary virtual environments. The system represents distant geometry as layered textured polygons arranged similar to environment maps. The major contributions of the paper are twofold:

First, the impostor layers are optimally placed so that the parallax error remains bounded. This is particularly advantageous for distant geometry, since the layers can be placed increasingly farther apart. In addition, this placement guarantees that the output image never differs by more than a pixel from an image obtained with the original geometry.

Second, the special-purpose algorithms for compressing the generated impostor textures achieve a significant reduction in storage space. In particular, these algorithms also reduce the amount of texture memory required for impostor textures on the graphics hardware, which is crucial insofar as this allows textures for several view cells to be held in texture memory simultaneously, allowing prefetching.

In general, the method can be said to decouple the rendering speed of the far field from its geometric complexity. Note especially that the placement of the farthest layer—and therefore the number of layers required—does not depend on the extent of the scene (which can be arbitrarily large), but only on the desired output resolution. It also exploits the considerable polygon-rendering and texture-mapping capabilities of today's graphics hardware by using standard polygonal rendering for the near field (where using impostors would not be feasible because of the large parallax errors), and impostor polygons for the far field, which would overwhelm the graphics hardware if rendered using geometry alone.

We believe that layered environment-map impostors can be used to render models of hitherto unseen complexity. The method is especially interesting in applications where conventional acceleration methods such as visibility culling, level-of-detail rendering or previous image-based rendering methods fail due to the nature of the scene (e.g., only little occlusion), the navigation metaphor (e.g., flyovers), or missing structure information about the scene (e.g., polygon soups). However, since complexity is basically shifted into the preprocessing phase, some attention should be given to the choice of the possible viewing region. While the preprocess can be trivially parallelized to run on multiple PCs, a large possible viewing region can take prohibitively long to compute on a single computer.

In terms of future research, it is desirable to have an automatic method for choosing the size and the arrangement of the view cells. Furthermore, as is typical of preprocessing methods, the algorithm partly shifts the necessary processing-power for rendering a model from the pure polygon throughput of the graphics hardware towards the bandwidth of the bus between main memory and graphic system, and to the CPU. We are therefore investigating novel prefetching algorithms to make best use of this tradeoff.

Acknowledgements

This work was supported by the German Research Foundation (DFG) in the frame of the postgraduate program "processing, administrating, visualization and transfer of multimedia data—technical basics and social implications", and the Austrian Science Fund (FWF) contract no. P13867-INF.

References

[1] D. Aliaga, J. Cohen, A. Wilson, E. Baker, H. Zhang, C. Erikson, K. Hoff, T. Hudson, W. Stürzlinger, R. Bastos, M. Whitton, F. Brooks, and D. Manocha. MMR: An interactive massive model rendering system using geometric and image-based acceleration. In *1999 Symposium on interactive 3D Graphics*, pages 199–206, 1999.

[2] D. Aliaga and A. Lastra. Automatic image placement to provide a guaranteed frame rate. In *SIGGRAPH 99 Conference Proceedings*, pages 307–316, 1999.

[3] B. S. Baker, E. G. Coffman, Jr., and R. L. Rivest. Orthogonal packings in two dimensions. In *Proc. 16th Annual Allerton Conf. on Communication, Control, and Computing*, pages 626–635, 1978.

[4] Becker, Franciosa, Gschwind, Ohler, Thiemt, and Widmayer. An optimal algorithm for approximating a set of rectangles by two minimum area rectangles. In *CGMAA: Computational Geometry–Methods, Algorithms and Applications*, 1991.

[5] J. Chai, X. Tong, S. Chan, and Heung-Yeung Shum. Plenoptic sampling. In *SIGGRAPH 2000 Conference Proceedings*, pages 307–318, 2000.

[6] B. Chazelle. The bottom-left bin-packing heuristic: An efficient implementation. *IEEE Transaction on Computers C-28(8)*, pages 697–707, 1983.

[7] S. Chen. QuickTime VR – an image-based approach to virtual environment navigation. In *SIGGRAPH 95 Conference Proceedings*, pages 29–38, 1995.

[8] L. Darsa, B. Costa Silva, and A. Varshney. Navigating static environments using image-space simplification and morphing. In *1997 Symposium on Interactive 3D Graphics*, pages 25–34, 1997.

[9] F. Durand, G. Drettakis, J. Thollot, and C. Puech. Conservative visibility preprocessing using extended projections. In *SIGGRAPH 2000 Conference Proceedings*, pages 239–248, 2000.

[10] R. Scopigno E. Puppo. Simplification, lod and multiresolution - principles and applications. In *Eurographics'97 Tutorial Notes PS97 TN4*, pages 31–42, 1997.

[11] T. A. Funkhouser, C. H. Sequin, and S. J. Teller. Management of large amounts of data in interactive building walkthroughs. In *1992 Symposium on Interactive 3D Graphics*, volume 25, pages 11–20, March 1992.

[12] S. Jeschke and M.Wimmer. An error metric for layered environment-map impostors. Technical Report TR-186-2-02-04, Vienna University of Technology, 2002.

[13] P. Lacroute and M. Levoy. Fast volume rendering using a shear-warp factorization of the viewing transformation. In *SIGGRAPH 94 Conference Proceedings*, pages 451–458, 1994.

[14] Marc Levoy and Pat Hanrahan. Light field rendering. In *SIGGRAPH 96 Conference Proceedings*, pages 31–42, 1996.

[15] P. Maciel and P. Shirley. Visual navigation of large environments using textured clusters. In *1995 Symposium on Interactive 3-D Graphics*, pages 95–102, 1995.

[16] W. Mark, L. McMillan, and G. Bishop. Post-rendering 3D warping. In *1997 Symposium on Interactive 3D Graphics*, pages 7–16, 1997.

[17] N. Max and K. Ohsaki. Rendering trees from precomputed Z-buffer views. In *Rendering Techniques '95*, pages 74–81, 1995.

[18] A. Meyer and F. Neyret. Interactive volumetric textures. In *Rendering Techniques '98*, pages 157–168, 1998.

[19] G. Schaufler. Per-object image warping with layered impostors. In *Rendering Techniques '98*, pages 145–156, 1998.

[20] G. Schaufler and W. Stürzlinger. A three-dimensional image cache for virtual reality. *Computer Graphics Forum*, 15(3):227–235, 1996.

[21] J. Shade, S. Gortler, L. He, and R. Szeliski. Layered depth images. In *SIGGRAPH 98 Conference Proceedings*, pages 231–242, 1998.

[22] J. Shade, D. Lischinski, D. Salesin, T. DeRose, and J. Snyder. Hierarchical image caching for accelerated walkthroughs of complex environments. In *SIGGRAPH 96 Conference Proceedings*, pages 75–82, 1996.

[23] F. Sillion, G. Drettakis, and B. Bodelet. Efficient impostor manipulation for real-time visualization of urban scenery. *Computer Graphics Forum*, 16(3):207–218, 1997.

[24] M. Wimmer, P. Wonka, and F. Sillion. Point-based impostors for real-time visualization. In *Rendering Techniques 2001*, pages 163–176, 2001.

[25] P. Wonka, M. Wimmer, and F. X. Sillion. Instant visibility. *Computer Graphics Forum*, 20(3):411–421, 2001.

Animation with threshold textures

Oleg Veryovka†
Mainframe Entertainment

†Currently with Electronic Arts cluster
New Media Innovation Center (NewMIC),
Vancouver, BC

Abstract

We present a method for frame coherent texturing and hatching of 3D models with a discrete set of colors. Our technique is inspired by various artistic styles that use a limited set of colors to convey surface shape and texture. In previous research discrete color shading was produced by modifying smooth shading with a threshold function. We extend this approach and specify threshold values with an image or a procedural texture. Texture values and mapping coordinates are adapted to surface orientation and scale. Aliasing artifacts are eliminated by the modified filtering technique. The threshold texturing approach enables an animator to control local shading and to display surface roughness and curvature with a limited set of colors.

Key words: non-photorealistic rendering, texture mapping, filtering, animation

1 Introduction

Artistic rendering is the process of presenting visual information through the *" selection of significant and suppression of non-essential"*[26]. An artist emphasizes important features and minimizes extraneous details in the pursuit of visually effective representation. In cartoon style rendering, visual details are reduced in order to draw the audience into the story and to add humor and emotional appeal[15]. Cartoonists draw silhouette lines and provide visual cues of surface shading using minimal variations of colors. Hatching and texturing is an effective method of suggesting surface properties and materials. Unfortunately, drawing frame coherent animated hatching lines by hand is an extremely laborious process and thus hatching is often limited to rendering of static objects and backgrounds.

Frame coherent non-photorealistic rendering (NPR) is one of the most challenging problems of computer graphics research[2]. Current approaches enable digital animation in pen-and-ink, oil and water color painting styles using particle-based systems[17, 12, 5], graftals[14, 16], tonal art maps[22], and generalized mip-maps[8]. A texture mapping approach was used in the past to assist in cel animation[6] but was not applied to rendering with a limited set of colors.

Recent NPR research had successfully approximated the style of cartoon rendering. A silhouette detection problem was investigated by Buchanan and Sousa[3], Northrup and Markosian[18] and Gooch et. al. [11]. A system for real time cartoon shading was developed by Lake et. al. [15]. Commercial and public domain "toon" shaders are offered for most common animation systems[24]. Unfortunately, the issue of texturing and hatching with a limited set colors has not been sufficiently investigated.

The goal of our research is the development of a frame coherent rendering algorithm for the display of textures using a discrete set of colors. Our approach is based on threshold textures and is closely related to stylistic halftoning area of NPR. We review stylistic halftoning results in the following section.

1.1 Stylistic halftoning

Halftoning is the process of image approximation with a limited set colors. A texture is often introduced as a result of this approximation. Research in conventional halftoning attempts to hide this texture[28].

Non-photorealistic halftoning uses this texture to create a stylized rendering of an image and to convey additional information. Ostromoukhov and Hersch[19] modified ordered dithering and enabled artists to design single screen elements. This technique was later extended to multi-color halftoning[20]. Buchanan[4] introduced a variety of halftoning textures by altering various parameters in a clustered error diffusion method. Veryovka and Buchanan[29] generated dither matrices by processing a texture image with the clipped adaptive histogram equalization (CLAHE) algorithm. This technique enables designers to emboss a halftoned image with a desired texture or to imitate traditional illustration styles.

A number of algorithms adapt halftoning texture to the rendered image thus enhancing its display. Streit and Buchanan[27] developed an importance driven halftoning system and controlled the placement of graphics elements by an importance function. Ostromoukhov[21] presented an interactive digital facial engraving system based on halftoning. Durand et. al.[7] extended this halftoning approach to other styles of traditional drawing. Veryovka and Buchanan[30] investigated an algorithm for automatic control of halftoning texture using image buffers that store 2D and 3D information.

All the previous stylized halftoning techniques worked in image space and are not applicable to frame coherent animation. We extend stylized dither matrix approach to digital animation. Our method is based on a mapping of threshold textures onto 3D models. We introduce procedural and image based textures that enhance rendering, highlight important model features, suggest surface textures, and approximate traditional rendering styles. Our technique allows an animator to control the number of colors and their appearance depending on lighting and viewing conditions. Threshold textures evolve with changes in surface scale and orientation. We address aliasing problems by modifying previous texture filtering methods. In conclusion, we discuss advantages and limitation of the texture thresholding approach.

2 Discrete color shading with a step function

A cartoon rendering style is associated with shading of surfaces with a limited set of colors. In computer graphics this shading effect can be approximated by augmenting a conventional illumination Equation 1 with a step function. Consider the following illumination equation:

$$\begin{aligned} I &= m_a l_a + \sum_i m_d f_d(N, L_i) l_i + \\ &\qquad \sum_i m_s f_s(N, L_i, V) l_i. \end{aligned} \tag{1}$$

where V is the eye vector, N is a surface normal, L_i is the direction to the i-th light of color l_i, m_a, m_d, m_s are ambient, diffuse and specular colors of the material; l_a is an ambient light of the scene. Functions $f_d(N, L_i)$ and $f_s(N, L_i, V)$ are continuous diffuse and specular components that produce continuous shading values. We modify the result of f_d and f_s by a step function T (Equation 2), thus limiting shading values to a set of discrete colors.

$$\begin{aligned} I &= m_a l_a + \sum_i m_d T(f_d(N, L_i)) l_i + \\ &\qquad \sum_i m_s T(f_s(N, L_i, V)) l_i, \end{aligned} \tag{2}$$

In the previous research[15, 24] a threshold function $T(x, t)$ was used as a step function:

$$T(x,t) = \begin{cases} 0 & \text{if } x < t \\ 1 & \text{otherwise} \end{cases} \tag{3}$$

where t is a threshold. A single threshold of $t = 0.5$ was suggested. Diffuse shading with a single threshold will produce only 2 colors. Multi-color shading with $n + 1$ discrete colors can be achieved by modifying a step function as follows:

$$T_n(x,t) = \frac{1}{n}(\lfloor xn \rfloor + T(Frac(xn), t)), \tag{4}$$

where $Frac(x)$ denotes a fractional-part function $Frac(x) = x - \lfloor x \rfloor$. A modification of the diffuse shading component with a step function T_n, where $n = 2$ results in a discrete three color shading (Figure1).

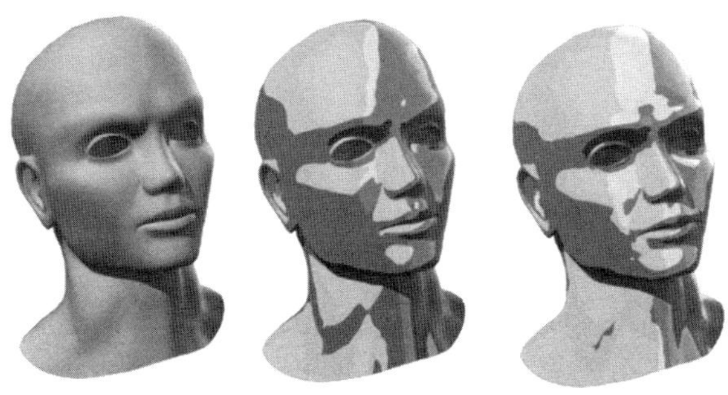

Figure 1: Thresholding components of the smooth shading model (left) introduces discrete tone shading (center). Threshold values vary across the surface controlling local shading and enhancing surface display (right).

The style of discrete color shading produced thus far approximates cartoon style rendering found in hand-drawn cel animation. We extend the thresholding technique and introduce a threshold texture to vary threshold values in the step function T (Equation 4).

3 Threshold textures

A variation of threshold values in the shading equation (Equation 2) modifies the resulting color locally. We use this property to control local shading highlighting model geometry and creating surface texturing.

Discrete color shading may hide important details of the geometry and exaggerate others. For example, the forehead surface of a head model (Figure 1, center) appear disconnected, muscles of the neck seem overly exaggerated. A threshold texture is constructed to highlight forehead bones, eyes, and lips (Figure 1, right).

In the rest of the section we present techniques for the creation of threshold textures that can be used to convey surface roughness and to imitate line hatching. The following considerations are important in the design of threshold textures.

Threshold textures modify surface shading and may significantly alter perception of an object shape. For ex-

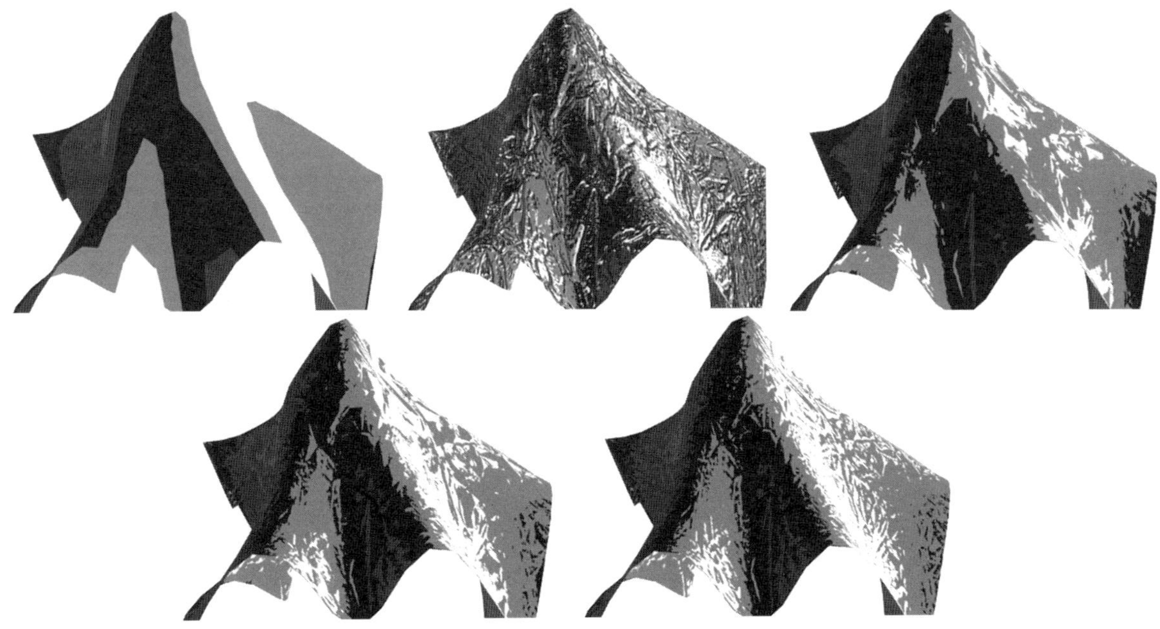

Figure 2: Discrete color shading with a single threshold (top-left) is enhanced by texture mapping. One approach is to use a texture as a bump map (top-center). When an unprocessed texture is used as thresholds its non-uniform distribution of values may distort display of the surface shape (top-left). We apply clipped histogram equalization algorithm (CLAHE) thus approximating uniform and homogeneous distribution of thresholds. The scale of texture features is controlled by CLAHE window parameter w. Smaller w produce softer textures ($w = 16$ pixels, bottom-left; $w = 8$ pixels bottom-right).

ample, the wrinkled paper texture distorts shading of the patch hiding surface folds ((Figure 2, top-right). Thus, texturing should approximate the overall shading of the model. Previous research suggests the use of threshold textures with uniform and homogeneous distribution of values[29]. These properties enable similar discrete approximation of continuous shading values across a 3D surface.

Artists vary surface details depending on surface scale, orientation, distance from the viewer, etc. Thus, it is important to control the level of texture details. Moreover, texture details should gradually evolve with changes in the scene. We found that texture features "attach" to the surface at multiple scales only if local minima and maxima points at lower resolution correspond to the minima and maxima at the higher resolution level.

3.1 Surface texture

We use threshold texturing to convey roughness of a 3D surface. Color texturing and bump mapping is traditionally used for this purpose. However, these methods may be hard to control or not be suitable for rendering with a limited set of colors (Figure 2).

We construct threshold textures from texture images using the adaptive histogram equalization algorithm with clipping of values (CLAHE). Veryovka and Buchanan[29] demonstrated that CLAHE processed images approximate uniform and homogeneous distribution of threshold values. The level of texture detail is controlled by window size and clipping parameters of the algorithm. When processed with a window $w = 8$ the wrinkled paper texture produced softer shading (Figure 2, bottom row). However, static control of the details is not sufficient for the use in animation. The same texture will appear at different scales and orientations and has to be controlled locally (Figure 3, right wall).

One approach is to compute threshold values dynamically and vary histogram equalization window according to the surface normal and distance from the camera. In this case histogram equalization will be recomputed for every texture sample. We approximate dynamic computation of threshold values using a mip-map filtering approach. In a pre-process step, we construct the mip-map texture pyramid and apply the CLAHE algorithm to every level of the pyramid. The resulting rendering smoothly adapts surface texturing depending on surface orientation and scale (Figure 3, floor and left wall).

The smooth transition between texture scales is achieved by tri-linear interpolating between pixel values

Figure 3: The mip-map filtering reduces the range of threshold values resulting in reduced texture definition (right wall). We apply CLAHE algorithm to every mip-map level to maintain sharp texturing across multiple scales (floor and left wall).

of the closest two mip-map levels. The CLAHE algorithm ensures that dark pixels at one level are mapped to the locally dark pixels at the other level.

Overall, our algorithm constructs threshold textures with the necessary distribution of thresholds and gradually adapts to local texture scale. We believe that discrete shading with image based threshold textures introduces texturing effects and conveys shape and roughness of the surface.

3.2 Line hatching

Line hatching is a widely used method of illustrating surface curvature. Hatching often appears in conjunction with discrete color shading in printed images but is rare in hand-drawn animation. Previous research[9] concludes that the use of textures and line hatching aligned with surface curvature enhances perception of 3D shapes.

We generate procedural line textures and introduce hatching effects of line drawing to digital animation. A similar approach was suggested before[1], however, the proposed textures did not satisfy threshold distribution properties necessary for uniform shading approximation. Procedural line textures with uniform and homogeneous value distribution were developed for comprehensive halftoning of rendered scenes by Veryovka and Buchanan[30]. We extend this previous work to account for multiple scales.

In order to guarantee the approximately constant size of lines we re-map texture coordinates according to the diadic scale of the projected texture[1]. Let us assume that procedural lines are generated by a function of the v texture coordinate and therefore are parallel to the u coordinate. We compute diadic texture scale using the following equation:

$$s = \log_2 \frac{d}{w}, \tag{5}$$

where d is the screen distance between u and $u+1$ texture iso-lines, and w is the desired scale of the procedural texture. Thus, the v texture coordinates are re-mapped as follows:

$$\bar{v} = Frac(v\lfloor s \rfloor) \tag{6}$$

Unfortunately, the use of the integer part of the diadic scale $\lfloor s \rfloor$ in coordinate re-mapping (Equation 6) introduces texture discontinuities. We achieve a smooth transition between texture scales by accounting for the fractional-part of the diadic scale $Frac(s)$. Let $F(v, Frac(s))$ be the multi-scale texture function, and $F(v,0) = f(v)$ represents a texture at an integer diadic scale $\lfloor s \rfloor$. Then, $F(v,1)$ denotes texture at the next scale $\lfloor s \rfloor + 1$ and is constructed as follows:

$$F(v,1) = \begin{cases} F(2v,0) & \text{if } v < 0.5 \\ F(2v-1,0) & \text{otherwise} \end{cases} \tag{7}$$

We generate texture at the intermediate scale $t = Frac(s)$ as a linear combination of $F(v,0)$ and $F(v,1)$:

$$F(v,t) = (1-t)F(v,0) + tF(v,1). \tag{8}$$

Similar to the previous research[30], a base function $f(v) = v$ is used. This function provides uniform distribution of values at all intermediate scales and its local minima and maxima match at consecutive levels. Note, that the $sin(v)$ suggested in [1] does not satisfy this property. The multi-scale textures can be modified by a noise

Figure 4: Procedural line textures adapt to surface curvature and orientation. Composition of multiple line textures approximates various styles of cross-hatching.

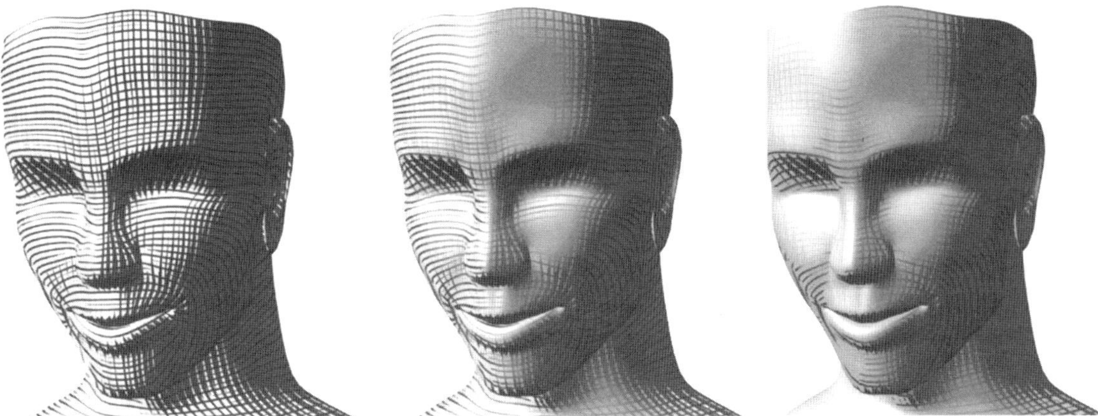

Figure 5: The strength of threshold texturing effects (left) vary depending on surface orientation (center) and illumination (right).

function or composed together to approximate various styles of line drawings: single line, cross-hatching, stippling (Figure 4).

4 Texture filtering

A thresholding process creates sharp discontinuities of the shading intensities. If not accounted for properly these discontinuities create strong aliasing artifacts. It turns out that filtering threshold values does not eliminate these artifacts. This is explained by the fact that smooth variations in threshold texture do not prevent large shading variations.

The conventional approach is filtering the final result with multiple samples per pixel. However, due to the large number of shading discontinuities, a large number of rays is needed making this approach very computationally expensive.

Durand et. al. [7] use "soft thresholding" to eliminate sharp shading transitions. We found that soft thresholding can be used to modify the overall look of the shading but is not sufficient for anti-aliasing in animation.

Our technique is similar to the percentage-closer filtering[23] solution for antialiased shadow rendering with depth maps. We threshold smooth diffuse and specular components with multiple texture samples. Thus, we filter not the texture itself but the result of thresholding. The sampling method depends on the texture used. Analytical filtering is possible for the procedural line textures. In the case of image textures we compute a discrete shading value as a weighted sum of thresholding results with threshold values from two levels of the mip-map pyramid. The resulting filtering combined with multiple rays per pixel is sufficient for elimination of most aliasing artifacts for both procedural and image based textures.

5 Implementation

The discrete shading with threshold texture mapping approach is implemented as a collection of shaders in the Softimage/MentalRay environment.

Texture shaders compute a set of threshold values and their filtering weights. An image texture shader applies CLAHE algorithm and samples mip-map pyramid levels. A procedural line shader re-maps texture coordinates depending on the diadic scale and samples texture in pseudo-random fashion.

A material shader computes soft illumination values first and then thresholds them using texture samples. Multiple samples are filtered according to their precomputed weights. We control the strength of texturing effects by blending between the original and thresholded illumination values. An artist can vary the amount of blending depending on surface orientation and/or illumination level. For example, in Figure 5, the intensity of hatching lines is reduced on the surfaces facing the camera (center). The lines disappear in darkest and brightest areas of the model (right) when the intensity level control is added.

An artist can vary textures for the display of the same model. Wide cross hatching texture was used to display general shading of a vase (Figure 6), while thin lines suggested specular highlights.

Our threshold texturing approach was combined with a contour rendering software implemented in MentalRay (Figure 7). The contours are computed through sampling of geometry and are not affected by the discrete color shading. The use of contours highlighted silhouette edges of the model and complemented the cross-hatching texture (Figure 7).

6 Discussion

The main advantage of the threshold texture mapping approach is its ability to produce frame-coherent rendering in a variety of styles (Figure 6). Textures and lines attach to 3D surfaces and gradually evolve with changes in scale and orientation (Figure 7). Unlike previous techniques[13, 22], the texture display always remains sharp and is not blurred at intermediate mip-map levels. The use of textures with a uniform and homogeneous distribution of values allows a fine control of the overall shading of the model. The threshold texture mapping algorithm can be combined with various illumination models [10, 25] and contour detection algorithms [3, 18].

Our technique has a number of limitations. Unlike tonal art maps [22] the same texture is used for various shading intensities. Particle-based algorithms [17] separately place every brush stroke or a hatch line. We have limited control over line placement through texture coordinates.

7 Conclusions

Artists often use a limited number of colors to represent shading and texturing of surfaces. The main contribution of this research is the threshold texture mapping technique that enables approximation of these artistic styles in digital animation (Figure 6).

Our approach is based on the thresholding of a conventional illumination model. Unlike previous research, threshold values are specified by a procedural or an image-based texture. We found that uniform and homogeneous distribution of thresholds is necessary for a good shading reproduction. Thus, image-based textures were processed with the clipped adaptive histogram equalization algorithm (CLAHE). We modified the mip-map filtering to maintain uniform texture effects regardless of surface orientation and scale. Similarly, procedural line textures are constructed with the necessary distribution of values. In order to maintain constant spacing between the lines, our algorithm recomputes coordinates of procedural textures depending on surface position. The aliasing artifacts were addressed by filtering shading values produced with multiple threshold samples.

The use of threshold texture mapping approach enhanced stylistic rendering in animation. Artists applied image based textures to highlight important features and to suggest surface roughness. Application of procedural textures approximated artistic hatching and helped to convey surface curvature.

Acknowledgements

We thank Chris Welman, Dave Fraccia, Tim Belsher and the entire crew at Mainframe Entertainment for the insightful comments of technical and artistic nature, and for making this publication possible.

References

[1] Larry Gritz Anthony A. Apodaca. *Advanced RenderMan: Creating CGI for Motion Pictures*. Morgan Kaufmann Publishers, 1999.

[2] Amy Ashurst Gooch Bruce Gooch. *Non-Photorealistic Rendering*. A K Peters Ltd, 2001.

[3] John W. Buchanan and Mario C. Sousa. The edge buffer: A data structure for easy silhouette rendering. In *Non-Photorealistic Animation and Rendering 2000 (NPAR '00)*, Annecy, France, June 5-7,2000.

[4] John W. Buchanan. Special effects with half-toning. *Computer Graphics Forum*, 15(3):97–108, August 1996. ISSN 1067-7055.

[5] Derek Cornish, Andrea Rowan, and David Luebke. View-dependent particles for interactive non-photorealistic rendering. *Graphics Interface 2001*, pages 151–158, June 2001. ISBN 0-96888-080-0.

[6] Wagner Toledo Corrêa, Robert J. Jensen, Craig E. Thayer, and Adam Finkelstein. Texture mapping for cel animation. *Proceedings of SIGGRAPH 98*, pages 435–446, July 1998. ISBN 0-89791-999-8. Held in Orlando, Florida.

[7] Fredo Durand, Victor Ostromoukhov, Mathieu Miller, Francois Duranleau, and Julie Dorsey. Decoupling strokes and high-level attributes for interactive traditional drawing. *Eurographics Workshop on Rendering*, 2001.

[8] Bert Freudenberg, Maic Masuch, and Thomas Strothotte. Walk-through illustrations: Frame-coherent pen-and-ink style in a game engine. *Computer Graphics Forum*, 20(3), 2001. ISSN 1067-7055.

[9] Ahna Girshick, Victoria Interrante, Steven Haker, and Todd Lemoine. Line direction matters: An argument for the use of principal directions in 3d line drawings. In *Non-Photorealistic Animation and Rendering 2000 (NPAR '00)*, Annecy, France, June 5-7,2000.

[10] Amy Gooch, Bruce Gooch, Peter Shirley, and Elaine Cohen. A non-photorealistic lighting model for automatic technical illustration. *Proceedings of SIGGRAPH 98*, pages 447–452, July 1998. ISBN 0-89791-999-8. Held in Orlando, Florida.

[11] Bruce Gooch, Peter-Pike Sloan, Amy Gooch, Peter Shirley, and Richard Riesenfeld. Interactive Technical Illustration. *Interactive 3D Conference Proceedings*, April 1999.

[12] Matthew Kaplan, Bruce Gooch, and Elaine Cohen. Interactive artistic rendering. In *Non-Photorealistic Animation and Rendering 2000 (NPAR '00)*, Annecy, France, June 5-7,2000.

[13] Allison W. Klein, Wilmot Li, Misha Kazhdan, Wagner Toledo Corra, Adam Finkelstein, and Thomas Funkhouser. Non-photorealistic virtual environments. *Proceedings of SIGGRAPH 2000*, July 2000. Held in New Orleans, Louisianna.

[14] Michael A. Kowalski, Lee Markosian, J. D. Northrup, Lubomir Bourdev, Ronen Barzel, Loring S. Holden, and John Hughes. Art-based rendering of fur, grass, and trees. *Proceedings of SIGGRAPH 99*, pages 433–438, August 1999. ISBN 0-20148-560-5. Held in Los Angeles, California.

[15] Adam Lake, Carl Marshall, Mark Harris, and Marc Blackstein. Stylized rendering techniques for scalable real-time 3d animation. *NPAR 2000 : First International Symposium on Non Photorealistic Animation and Rendering*, pages 13–20, June 2000.

[16] Lee Markosian, Barbara J. Meier, Michael A. Kowalski, Loring S. Holden, J.D. Northrup, and John F. Hughes. Art-based rendering with continuous levels of detail. In *Non-Photorealistic Animation and Rendering 2000 (NPAR '00)*, Annecy, France, June 5-7,2000.

[17] Barbara J. Meier. Painterly rendering for animation. *Proceedings of SIGGRAPH 96*, pages 477–484, August 1996.

[18] J.D. Northrup and Lee Markosian. Artistic silhouettes: A hybrid approach. In *Non-Photorealistic Animation and Rendering 2000 (NPAR '00)*, Annecy, France, June 5-7,2000.

[19] Victor Ostromoukhov and Roger D. Hersch. Artistic screening. *Proceedings of SIGGRAPH 95*, pages 219–228, August 1995. ISBN 0-201-84776-0. Held in Los Angeles, California.

[20] Victor Ostromoukhov and Roger D. Hersch. Multicolor and artistic dithering. *Proceedings of SIGGRAPH 99*, pages 425–432, August 1999. ISBN 0-20148-560-5. Held in Los Angeles, California.

[21] Victor Ostromoukhov. Digital facial engraving. *Proceedings of SIGGRAPH 99*, pages 417–424, August 1999. ISBN 0-20148-560-5. Held in Los Angeles, California.

[22] Emil Praun, Hugues Hoppe, Matthew Webb, and Adam Finkelstein. Real-time hatching. *Proceedings of SIGGRAPH 2001*, pages 579–584, August 2001. ISBN 1-58113-292-1.

[23] William T. Reeves, David H. Salesin, and Robert L. Cook. Rendering antialiased shadows with depth maps. In *Computer Graphics (Proceedings of SIGGRAPH 87)*, volume 21, pages 283–291, Anaheim, California, July 1987.

[24] Craig Reynolds. Stylized depiction in computer graphics. http://www.red3d.com/cwr/npr/.

[25] Peter-Pike Sloan, William Martin, Amy Gooch, and Bruce Gooch. The lit sphere: A model for capturing npr shading from art. *Graphics Interface 2001*, pages 143–150, June 2001. ISBN 0-96888-080-0.

[26] Harold Speed. *The Practice and Science of Drawing*. Steeley, Service and Co. Ltd., London, 1917.

[27] Lisa Streit and John Buchanan. Importance driven halftoning. *Computer Graphics Forum*, 17(3):207–218, 1998. ISSN 1067-7055.

[28] Robert Ulichney. *Digital Halftoning*. MIT Press, 1987.

[29] Oleg Veryovka and John Buchanan. Texture-based dither matrices. *Computer Graphics Forum*, 19(1):51–64, March 2000. ISSN 1067-7055.

[30] Oleg Veryovka and John Buchanan. Comprehensive halftoning of 3D scenes. *Computer Graphics Forum*, 18(3):13–22, September 1999. ISSN 1067-7055.

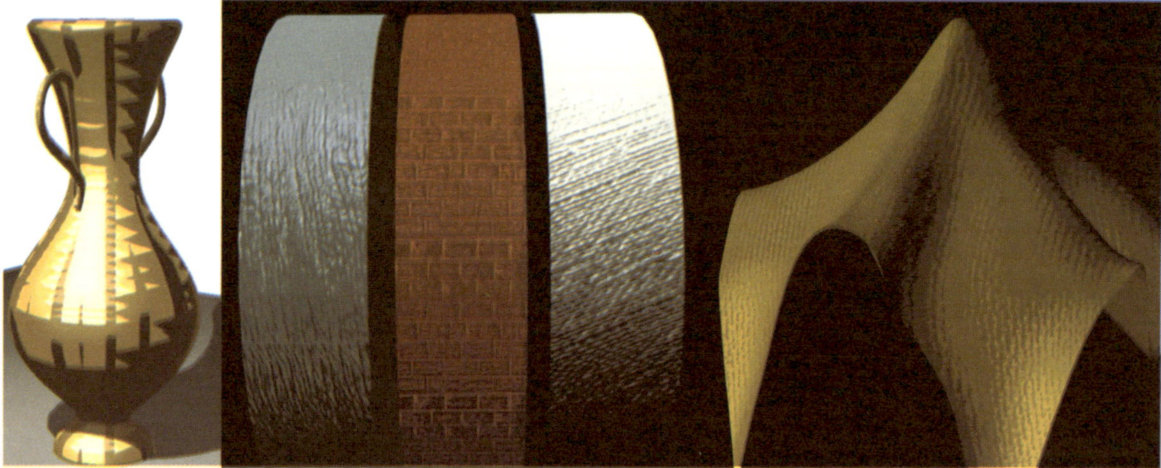

Figure 6: Image-based and procedural textures modify shading suggesting surface materials (wood, brick, textile) or traditional art media (brush strokes, pencil drawing).

Figure 7: Procedural line hatching is used to convey discontinuities of the hair surface. The spacing of hatching lines adapts to orientation, scale, and deformation of the face model.

A Fresh Perspective

Karan Singh

Department of Computer Science
University of Toronto

Abstract

"Painting is an activity, and the artist will therefore tend to see what he paints rather than to paint what he sees."

E.H. Gombrich.

While general trends in computer graphics continue to drive towards more *photorealistic* imagery, increasing attention is also being devoted to painterly renderings of computer generated scenes. Whereas artists using traditional media almost always deviate from the confines of a precise linear perspective view, digital artists struggle to transcend the standard pin-hole camera model in generating an envisioned image of a three dimensional scene. More specifically, a key limitation of existing camera models is that they inhibit the artistic exploration and understanding of a subject, which is essential for expressing it successfully. Past experiments with non-linear perspectives have primarily focused on abstract mathematical camera models for raytracing, which are both non-interactive and provide the artist with little control over seeing what he wants to see. We address this limitation with a cohesive, interactive approach for exploring non-linear perspective projections. The approach consists of a new camera model and a toolbox of interactive local and global controls for a number of properties, including regions of interest, distortion, and spatial relationship. Furthermore, the approach is incremental, allowing non-linear perspective views of a scene to be built gradually by blending and compositing multiple linear perspectives. In addition to artistic non-photorealistic rendering, our approach has interesting applications in conceptual design and scientific visualization.

Key words: Non-Photorealistic rendering, Multiprojection, Non-linear Perspective, Camera model.

1 Introduction

Before a user can express a digital 3D scene using a 2D projection, he must obtain a good perception of the scene himself. 2D projections, however, are the only common way a user can currently explore a digital 3D scene. While a linear perspective view certainly constitutes a robust and well understood medium for exploring and visualizing localized regions of an object, the model can be restrictive for the visualization of complex shapes. The user could then simply use many such disjoint exploratory images to express a 3D scene. It is, however, neither spatially efficient nor aesthetically desirable to expect a viewer to percieve detail from multiple images: it takes time and skill to understand such a scene since the eye has to jump between the images and mentally stitch them together. Industrial designers often have to take recourse to turntable animations to display or draw attention to parts of their models, which could have been captured effectively in a single non-linear perspective view.

The goal of this work is to allow artists to explore, understand, and subsequently express 3D shapes in 2D imagery. To motivate this objective, we will consider three pictures utilizing non-linear perspective projections.

Figure 1: Femme nue accroupie (P. Picasso,1959), ©2002 Estate of Pablo Picasso / Artists Rights Society (ARS), New York.

Figure 1 shows a painting by Pablo Picasso, which typifies his style of compositing different views of different parts of a scene into a single projection. It is a perfect example of a scene that can be visually thought of as broken into disjoint parts that are viewed from different linear perspectives and then patched back together. The choice of view directions is entirely at the artist's mercy. Note the region around the hands that provides a continuous transition of perspective from one arm to the other. In contrast, the line down the middle of the face is a discontinuous transition between the two sides of the face.

Figure 2: Tetrahedral Planetoid (M.C. Escher), ©2002 Cordon Art B.V. - Baarn - Holland. All rights reserved.

Figure 3: Pearblossom Hwy. No. 2 (D. Hockney 1986), ©1986, D. Hockney, The J. Paul Getty Museum, Los Angeles.

In keeping with the mathematical leanings of M.C. Escher's art, Figure 2 shows a continuous change in perspective across the scene. In contrast to the Picasso painting, the transition between the different projections are gradual and continous, with localized regions of the image adhering to an almost linear perspective.

Figure 3 shows a photomosaic by David Hockney, where many linear perspective views capturing parts of a scene have been patched together with intentional stylistic discontinuity. Hockney has even described Pearblossom Hwy. as "a panoramic assault on Renaissance one-point perspective." Hockney suggests that our actual experience of looking is better expressed by a collage of photographs than by a single image: "If you put six pictures together, you look at them six times. This is more what it's like to look at [something]."

Most visualizations of a scene, scientific or artistic, are compositions of regions that locally have linear perspective[1]. While the three pictures represent very different projective techniques, they all showcase the significance of non-linear perspective projections as an expressive artistic tool. They bring to light the importance of linear perspective as a powerful way to explore and present parts of a scene, as well as the inability of a single linear perspective to visually capture all aspects of a complex scene. Using these images as our guideline, we propose the usage of multiple linear perspective views to explore a scene, as well as the construction of nonlinear perspective visualizations of the scene from these views.

1.1 Related work

Non-linear perspective projections have been applied in computer generated imagery for a variety of purposes, that can be divided into the following main categories: image warping, 3D projections, and multi-perspective panoramas.

Image warping [3, 7, 22] is a popular technique for manipulating digital images. Since this approach is inherently 2D, however, it limits the ability to explore different viewpoints and the spatial relationship between objects. View morphing as presented by Seitz and Dyer [19] attempts to automate the interpolation of a viewpoint in images to provide more natural morphs that have a compelling 3D look to them. The problem of compensating for the distortion introduced by a perspective projection onto a curved object (such as an OMNIMAX screen) [14] or planar screens for off-axis viewing [5] has been researched. Zorin and Barr [24] have developed an approach to correct the perceived geometric distortion seen in many photographic images by reprojection. Research in the area of nonlinear magnification for the purpose of visualization is well documented by Carpendale [4].

As an alternative, 3D deformations [9, 18] are widely used for manipulating 3D geometry. For some applications, however, it is preferable to modify the camera

[1] There are exceptions to this, such as historical Japanese prints done using an inverse linear perspective.

transformation rather than to change the 3D shape of the object being depicted. Barr [2] used non-linear ray tracing to render deformed objects; an idea also applied by Gröller [10]. View dependent distortions to scene geometry for animation and illustration have also been explored [13, 17]. The distortion associated with 3D projections has been utilized for artistic purposes by Inakage [11] and Levene [12]. Inakage developed a library of esoteric projection tools, and this work was extended by Levene with an interactive system for editing a non-linear 3D projection surface and the warped space around it. Further, Levene explored the spatial relationship in a 3D scene by allowing different projections to be associated with individual objects. The main limitations of these approaches, however, are that they rely on a single center of projection, which can lead to severely distorted control lattices (for example if the artist wishes to direct the viewer's attention towards a region of an object far from the center of interest), and that the results of associating different projections with different objects can be unpredictable.

Recently, non-linear projections have also used in conjunction with *multi-perspective* panoramas. Inspired by the compelling illusion of depth in classic Disney animations, Wood et al. [21] generated 2D panoramas for predescribed 3D camera paths, achieving the effect of 3D perspective as the camera panned across the panorama. In a related technique, albeit with a very different motivation, Rademacher et al. [16] generated *multiple-center-of-projection images* by moving a camera along a 3D path, sampling a 1-dimensional slice of a 2D panorama at each point on its way. The aim of this work was to provide a more flexible and efficient representation for image based data sets. Peleg et al. [15] have generalized the creation of mosaic panoramas from camera motion by allowing them to be mapped on to an adaptively changing 2D manifold. Panoramas are an effective way of visualizing landscapes with a wide angle of view, or for unfolding the detail of an object. These approaches are catered to capturing imagery using real cameras. They are also, unfortunately, not well suited to interactive manipulation.

The research of most relevance to this paper is work on abstract camera models by Wyvill and McNaughton [23] and the approach to multiprojection rendering by Agrawala et al. [1].

Wyvill and McNaughton define an abstract camera model using a surface in 3D from which rays emanate in arbitrary directions. While the general model is very powerful and conceptually simple, it is hard to specify and control intuitively by a user and is difficult to implement interactively.

Agrawala et al. [1] use multiple linear perspectives to define a scene. In their approach each object in the scene is assigned to some camera in the scene and rendered based on the linear perspective of that camera. The rendering of all cameras in the scene are composited to generate the final image. A visibility ordering is created for the objects using a master camera and this is used during the compositing stage. Conflicts in a clear visibility ordering of objects are resolved at the pixel level by simple depth comparison. The use of linear perspective to both explore the scene and to construct the nonlinear image makes their system both interactive and easy to use. While the approach works well for scenes with disjoint objects with different linear perspectives, it would be difficult to construct scene visualizations of the kind shown in Figures 2 and 3. The main reasons are the continuous transitions of linear perspective seen in Figure 2 and collage like compositing of camera images in Figure 3. Figure 1 could be generated with the technique if the woman in the scene were carefully segmented into distinct objects that could then be viewed from different linear perspectives and composed to construct the image. Our approach will also use multiple linear perspective cameras but objects in our framework are potentially influenced by all cameras, yielding an interpolated virtual camera whose parameters often vary across different points on the object.

In summary, non-linear projections have been used in a variety of contexts for visualizing 3D shapes, but existing techniques are limited with respect to our goal of allowing artists and scientists alike to intuitively explore, understand, and subsequently express or visualize 3D models in 2D images.

1.2 Overview

The rest of this paper is organized as follows. Section 2 presents our model for the construction of a non-linear perspective projection of objects in a scene using a number of linear perspective cameras. Section 3 describes the implementation details and the user interface framework that is crucial to the success of this model. Section 4 concludes with a discussion of the results obtained and provides directions for future research.

2 Model for non-linear perspective

Let C_i represent the camera parameters[2] [6], for exploratory view $i \in 1,..,n$. Let M_i represent the perspective projection matrix built from the parameters C_i. $<x,y,z>= PM_i$ represents the linear projection of P into canonical space $x \in [-1,1], y \in [-1,1], z \in [0,1]$.

Given a viewport specification represented by matrix V_i the resulting point in two dimensional screen space

[2]Example parameters that specify a linear perspective camera are eye position, center of interest, up-vector, hither/yon clip planes and focal length.

$< x_s, y_s >$ is $< x_s, y_s, z_s >= PM_iV_i$. Usually, $z_s = z$ is the depth value of the point P, unchanged by V_i. We extend the viewport transformations V_i so that the canonical depth of a point $z \in [0, 1]$ is linearly mapped to z_s in an arbitrary, user specified range. While the relative depth values are preserved with respect to a single perspective view, this allows the powerful visual capability of intuitively altering the relative depths of points in a scene as one transitions between the mutiple linear perspectives. It is through the depth mapping that visibility in the nonlinear projection of the scene is controlled, both automatically [1] and with user interaction. This will be illustrated in Section 3.3 (Case Study II).

Now suppose that a normalized weight vector $< w_{1P}, w_{2P}, .., w_{nP} >$ is specified for any point P in the scene. We define the projection of P to be PM_PV_P, where M_P is the perspective projection of a virtual linear perspective camera C_P. The parameters of C_P are obtained as an average of the parameters of cameras $C_1..C_n$, weighted by $w_{1P}..w_{nP}$. Similarly V_P is generated by weight averaging the affine components of viewport transformations $V_1..V_n$ with the weights $w_{1P}..w_{nP}$.

The rationale for generating an interpolated camera and an interpolated viewport independently, rather than simply weight averaging the projected points resulting from applying each linear perspective camera projection to P, is twofold. First and foremost, a number of camera parameters are angular and are best interpolated individually using quaternions. Secondly, the camera parameters have intuitive physical manifestations and their interpolation can be better understood and controlled by a user.

We now have an abstract conceptual model for the generation of a non-linear perspective projection from multiple linear perspective views. One can observe that the multiprojection setup of Agrawala et al. [1] is a special case of this model where:

- The $< x, y >$ viewport transformations of all cameras are the same.
- The $< z >$ mapping for all viewport transformations can be set based on the visibility ordering of a master camera.
- $w_{kP} = 1$, for all points P on an object, where the object is being visualized by the kth camera, C_k.

In the next section we look at techniques and controls that provide a compelling and interactive user interface to the model described above. The generation of non-linear perspective visualizations of a scene from multiple linear exploratory views is thus made fast and easy to control.

3 Implementation

This section describes an implementation written as a plug-in to the animation system *Maya 1.5*. The exploratory linear perpective cameras are rendered using OpenGL. These are composited into a non-linear perspective projection that is calculated and then displayed in an orthographic GL view along with multiple translucent red boxes that represent the multiple viewports in the scene. The scene is lit in perspective space with the surface normal at a point P transformed using the projection matrices computed at P.

3.1 User Interface

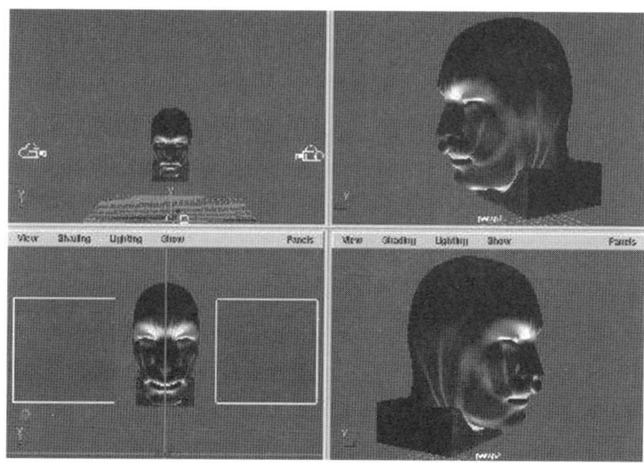

Figure 4: UI Framework (equal camera weight)

The basic user interface framework can be seen in Figure 4. A global linear perspective view (*top-left* panel) shows the object in the scene as well as two exploratory cameras. The views through the exploratory cameras can be seen in the *top-right* and *bottom-right* panels. The *bottom-left* panel shows two square viewports for the two exploratory cameras and the composite non-linear perspective view. The weights are set to be equal for all points in the scene and thus the composite view is a linear perspective projection as viewed through a virtual camera placed halfway between the two exploratory cameras and mapped to a viewport that is right in the middle of the viewports of the exploratory cameras.

Exploratory cameras can be added and deleted at will. Their parameters can be accessed by selecting the camera from its icon in the global perspective view or directly from its own view panel. The camera parameters can be interactively manipulated directly using various camera tools. The viewports are represented by boxes in the composite view (*bottom-left* panel of Figure 4). These can be interactively selected and transformed and the depth of the boxes defines the range to which the cannonical z value of points is mapped.

We now calculate the weight vector $< w_{1P}, .., w_{nP} >$ for a point P in the scene.

3.2 Computing the relative influence of cameras

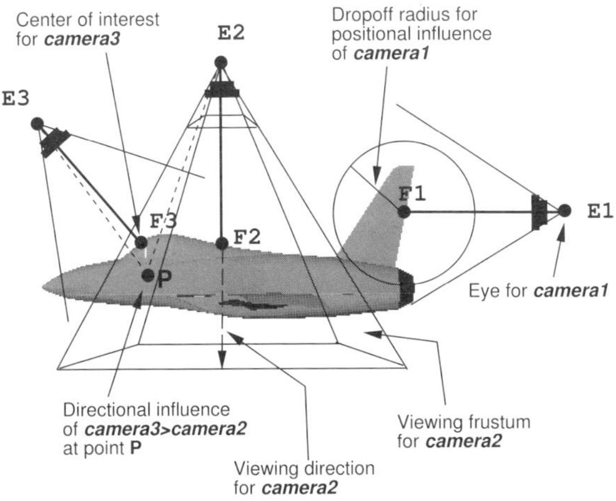

Figure 5: Camera parameters

We use two heuristics that result in smoothly varying weight vectors for points in the scene.

- **Positional influence :** is based on the observation that a local region around the center of interest or focus of an exploratory camera is likely to be visualized using that camera. This is computed as a radial dropoff function around the center of interest; the intensity, radius of influence and decay rate of which are under user control (See Figure 5).

- **Directional influence :** similarly notes that points in the scene that are along the viewing direction of an exploratory camera are more likely to be visualized by that camera than points on the fringes of the camera's viewing frustum [6]. We compute this as a prismatic dropoff function that decays from the view direction axis to the extent of the trapeziodal frustum that is obtained from the viewing parameters of the camera [6] (See Figure 5). Once again the intensity, radius of influence and decay rate of the dropoff function are under user control.

Directional influence provides a number of useful scientific projections like panoramas. Figure 6 shows the same exploratory camera configuration as Figure 4 with directional influence activated. The resulting non-linear projection is a smooth panoramic transition from the view of the *bottom-right* panel to the *top-right* panel as the viewport moves from left to right. Fish eye views can also be obtained using directional influence for a planar

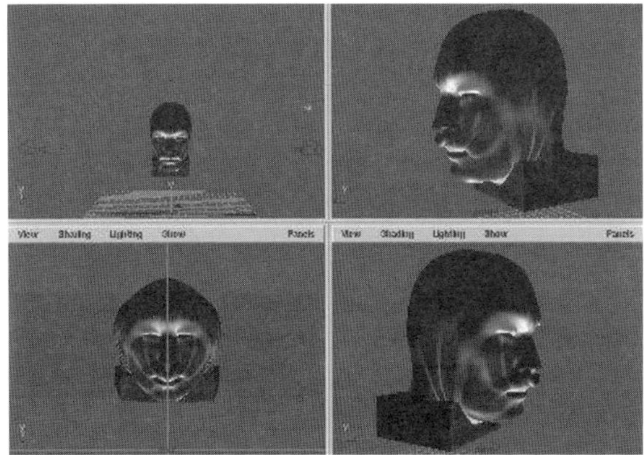

Figure 6: UI Framework (directional influence)

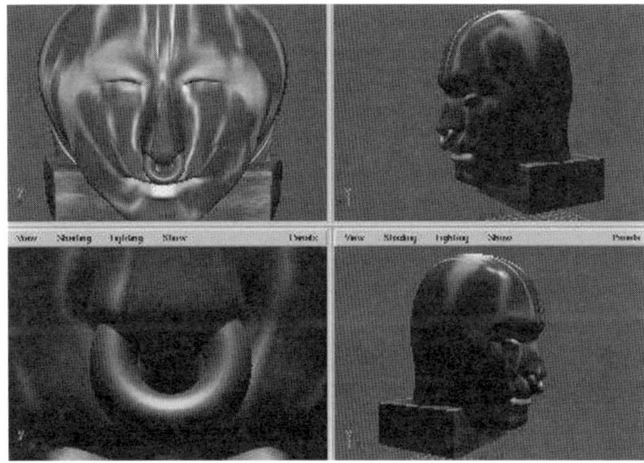

(a) Nose camera active

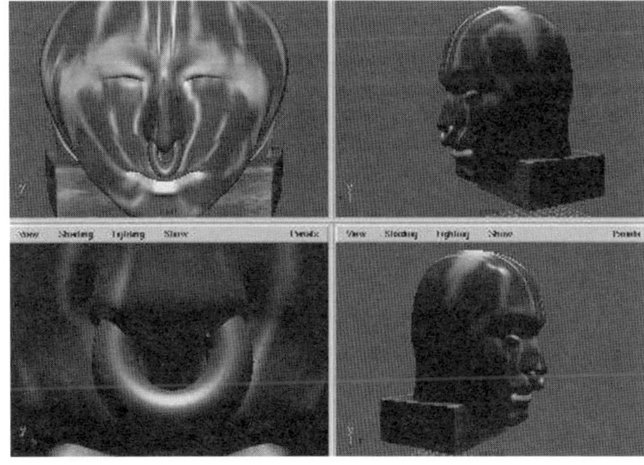

(b) Nose camera inactive

Figure 7: Refining the visualization (positional influence)

grid of exploratory cameras with parallel viewing directions (to simulate a real lens whose area is the size of the grid). The distorted view of Figure 2 is a strong example of perspective changing from principal exploratory views based on positional and directional influence.

Positional influence provides strong local control and is ideal for incremental local refinements of a non-linear perspective using additional cameras. This is well illustrated in Figure 7, where adding a camera trained on the nose corrects an otherwise flattened nose-ring.

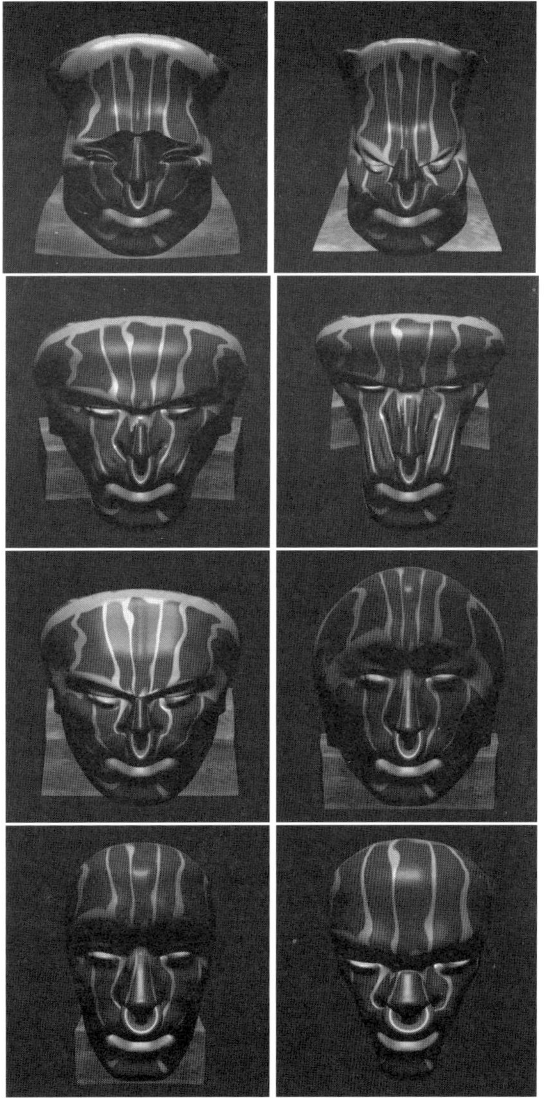

Figure 8: Non-Linear perspective animation stills

In general, however, it is difficult to computationally anticipate an artists intention for more stylistic visualizations (See Figure 1). The user is therefore able to paint weight values for the various exploratory cameras on the objects in the scene directly, using interactive brush tools such as *Maya-Artisan*. User painted weights and other heuristic influences are simply blended together and normalized to generate the weight vector for any given point. Figure 8 has examples of user painted weights applied using a stripe texture to the cheeks that causes the creases above the mouth in the fourth image of the sequence.

For interactivity of the system we only project the control vertices of the objects. While this is an analytically precise operation for linear perspectives and polygon based objects it is clearly a discrete approximation for a non-linear perspective projection. The accuracy of the projection can be simply improved by using subdivided geometry that has a denser sampling of control points. The implementation shows interactive update rates while animating the camera parameters for objects with thousands of polygons.

We now look at two example case studies that illustrate some of the controls described for the generation of a non-linear perspective view.

3.3 Case Studies

Case Study I : We begin with a two camera panorama of the head in Figure 9a, using a setup like the one shown in Figure 6. The panorama is then stretched in Figure 9b as a result of interactively moving the viewports of the two cameras further apart. In Figure 9c a third camera focused on the nose is added and its viewport stretched horizontally. In Figure 9d this viewport is shrunk horizontally and translated down. Note how the upper lip pouts over the lower lip by reducing the z-depth of the camera on the nose relative to the other two cameras. This can be seen even better in Figure 9e where the viewport for the nose camera is pulled out further and off-center. Figure 9f shows the diversity of visualization that non-linear perspectives bring. A fourth camera is added above the head looking down with a strong directional influence and weak positional influence. This makes most of the head shown as viewed straight down the forehead, except the eyes. Each eye is visualized by one of the side cameras that focuses on them with a strong positional influence. The two ear like projections are regions of the head on the fringes of the viewing frustum of the overhead camera. The side cameras thus have more of an influence on them. The nose is picked up by the camera trained on the nose and the projection of the mouth is a more equal contribution of all 4 cameras. Finally Figure 9g shows the same camera configuration with a lowered intensity of the various influences used.

Case Study II : Figure 10 shows a cube with 8 cameras located at its origin and aimed at the corners of the cube. Figure 11a shows a non-linear perspective projection with the positional influence turned up. The translu-

(a) (b) (c) (d)

(e) (f) (g)

Figure 9: Case Study I

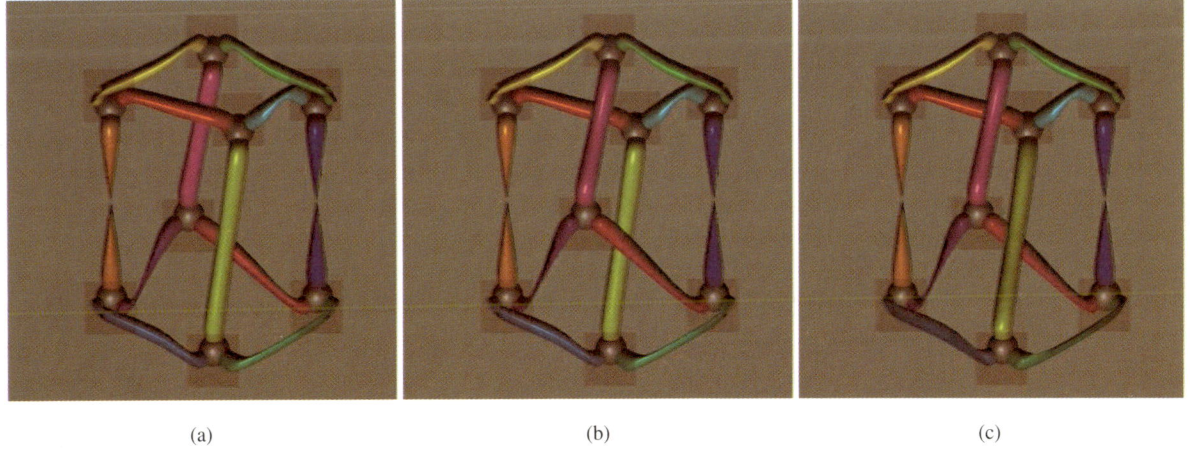

(a) (b) (c)

Figure 11: Case Study II

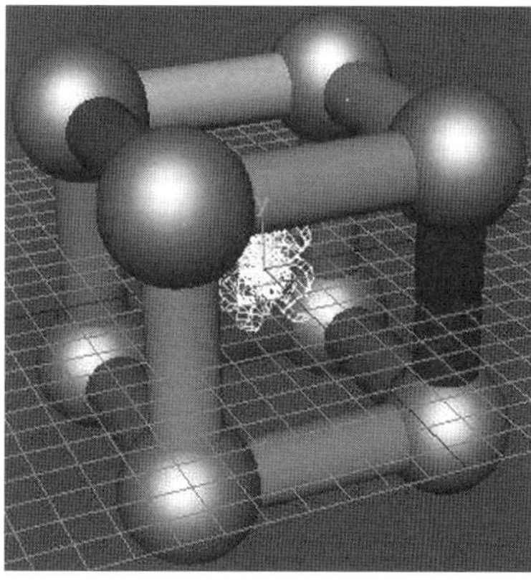

Figure 10: Case Study II: Camera configuration

cent squares are the 8 viewports. Some of them are horizontally scaled by -1 to unravel the object better but are also responsible for the twisted behavior of the orange and royal blue edges. The relative depth of the *purple-magenta-pink* corner's viewport is changed to make the cube projection appear turned inside out in Figure 11b. Note that the silhouette of the edges remains unchanged. Changing the depth on the *green-limegreen-blue* corner's viewport in Figure 11c results in a 2D projection of a 3D projection of a tesseract (a common Escher motif, held by the jester in his work titled Belvedere).

4 Conclusion

We have presented a new interactive approach for exploring and rendering 3D objects. Our chief contribution is an intuitive way for artists to experiment with a 3D subject and subsequently convey it expressively in a 2D rendering. Aside from its applicability to non-photorealistic and painterly rendering, the model has wider applications in scientific visualization, where the limitations of the traditional linear perspective are well recognized [20]. Interaction of illumination models with such non-linear projections is fertile area for future research. In conclusion, the approach presented in this paper marks a step towards overcoming the limited expressive potential of existing projection models. We hope that this work will motivate further discussion and open the door to an interesting new type of computer generated imagery.

References

[1] M. Agrawala, D. Zorin and T. Munzner. Artistic Multiprojection Rendering. *Eurographics Rendering Workshop*, 125–136, 2000.

[2] A. Barr. Ray Tracing Deformed Surfaces. *Computer Graphics*, 20(4):287–296, 1986.

[3] T. Beier and S. Neely. Feature based image metamorphosis. *Computer Graphics*, 26(2):35–42, 1992.

[4] S. Carpendale. A framework for elastic presentation space. *PhD. Dissert., Simon Fraser University*, 1999.

[5] J. Dorsey, F. Sillion and D. Greenberg. Design and Simulation of Opera Lighting and Projection Effects. *Computer Graphics*, 25(4):41–50, 1991.

[6] J. Foley, A. van Dam, S. Feiner, J. Hughes. Computer Graphics, Principles and practice. *Addison-Wesley*, Chapter 6:229–284 ,1990.

[7] C. Fu, T. Wong, P. Heng. Warping panorama correctly with triangles. *Eurographics Rendering Workshop*,1999.

[8] E. H. Gombrich. Art and Illusion. Phaidon, 1960.

[9] J. Gomez, L. Darca, B. Costa and L. Velho. Warping and Morphing of Graphical Objects . *Morgan Kaufmann, San Francisco, California*, 1998.

[10] E. Gröller. Nonlinear ray tracing: visualizing strange worlds. *The Visual Computer*, 11(5):263–276, 1995.

[11] M. Inakage. Non-Linear Perspective Projections. *Proceedings of the IFIP WG 5.10)*, 203–215, 1991.

[12] J. Levene. A Framework for Non-Realistic Projections. *Master of Engineering Thesis, MIT*, 1991.

[13] D. Martin, S. Garcia and J. C. Torres. Observer dependent deformations in illustration. *Non-Photorealistic Animation and Rendering 2000* , Annecy, France, June 5-7, 2000.

[14] N. Max. Computer Graphics Distortion for IMAX and OMNIMAX Projection. *Nicograph '83 Proceedings* 137–159.

[15] S. Peleg, B. Rousso, A. Rav-Acha and A. Zomet. Mosaicing on Adaptive Manifolds. *IEEE Transactions on Pattern Analysis and Machine Intelligence*, 22(10):1144–1154, 2000.

[16] P. Rademacher and G. Bishop. Multiple-Center-of-Projection Images. *SIGGRAPH*, 199–206, 1998.

[17] P. Rademacher. View-Dependent Geometry. *Computer Graphics*, 439–446, 1999.

[18] T. Sederberg and S. Parry. Free-form deformation of solid geometric models. *Computer Graphics*, 20:151–160, 1986.

[19] S. Seitz and C. Dyer. View Morphing: Synthesizing 3D Metamorphoses Using Image Transforms. *Computer Graphics*, 21–30, 1996.

[20] Edward Tufte. Envisioning Information. *Graphics Press*, 1990.

[21] D. Wood, A. Finkelstein, J. Hughes, C. Thayer and D. Salesin. Multiperspective Panoramas for Cel Animation. *Computer Graphics*, 243–250, 1997.

[22] George Wolberg. Digital Image Warping. *IEEE Computer Society Press*, 1992.

[23] G. Wyvill and C. McNaughton. Optical models. *Proceedings CGI*, 1990.

[24] D. Zorin and A. Barr. Correction of Geometric Perceptual Distortion in Pictures. *Computer Graphics*, 257–264, 1995.

Constraint-based Automatic Placement for Scene Composition

Ken Xu
University of Toronto

James Stewart
Queens University

Eugene Fiume
University of Toronto

Abstract

The layout of large scenes can be a time–consuming and tedious task. In most current systems, the user must position each of the objects by hand, one at a time. This paper presents a constraint–based automatic placement system, which allows the user to quickly and easily lay out complex scenes.

The system uses a combination of automatically–generated placement constraints, pseudo–physics, and a semantic database to guide the automatic placement of objects. Existing scenes can quickly be rearranged simply by reweighting the placement preferences. We show that the system enables a user to lay out a complex scene of 300 objects in less than 10 minutes.

1 Introduction

Object layout is an important and often time consuming part of modeling. It takes six degrees of freedom to fully lay out an object, while standard input devices have only two degrees of freedom (DOF). In addition, the layout must satisfy physical constraints such as non-interpenetration and physical stability. As a result of the high cost of object layout, computer graphics scenes are often unrealistically simple or overly tidy.

Previous efforts to facilitate object placment have resulted in better input devices and more efficient object manipulation techniques, which allow individual objects to be placed more quickly and accurately. However, the layout of large, complex scenes remains a difficult problem because users must still manually place objects into the scene one at a time.

In this paper we present CAPS, a Constraint-based Automatic Placement System. CAPS makes feasible the modeling of large, complex scenes: A scene consisting of more than 300 objects can be laid out in less than 10 minutes, as shown in Figure 1. The system uses a set of intuitive placement constraints to allow the manipulation of large numbers of objects simultaneously. Through the use of pseudo–physics, objects can automatically be placed in physically stable configurations, once their placement constraints have been set. A user need not be concerned with the details of placement, unless he or she wishes to. In addition, CAPS attaches semantic information to objects, which allows placement constraints to be generated automatically. As a result, CAPS can place hundreds of objects into a scene and can quickly redistribute them into semantically meaningful locations with absolutely no user intervention.

2 Related Work

A number of researchers have addressed the issue of object placement in 3D environments. These techniques can be broadly categorized into four groups:

1. techniques which attempt to reduce the number of DOF to which users are exposed;
2. techniques which abandon low DOF input devices altogether in favor of more complicated devices — some with as many as six DOF — in order to facilitate direct object manipulation;
3. techniques which employ pseudo–physics to automatically compute a physically stable position and orientation for an object, after having dropped it from some spot in the scene; and
4. techniques which use semantic information to guide object placement.

The vast majority of existing approaches have treated object placement as a purely geometric problem. However, more recent approaches have begun to utilize semantic information in the layout process.

2.1 DOF Reduction Techniques

Some DOF–reduction methods attempt to compensate for the two DOF of common input devices by mapping 2D input vectors to higher dimensional vectors [20, 32]. Others ease object placement with "snap to" constraints, such as snapping to grids, object faces, or auxiliary helper geometry [1]. A final group of methods makes the assumption that surfaces are planar, and tends to restrict object motion along those surfaces, thereby reducing the DOF to which users are exposed [11, 6, 27].

2.2 Input Devices and Manipulation Techniques

The limited DOF available on standard input devices has motivated much research on higher DOF input devices. Such devices include the Space Ball (a six DOF joystick), the bat (a six DOF mouse) [34], the Roller Mouse (a three DOF mouse) [32], and the Data Glove (a six DOF device which can encode the position of each of the user's fingers) [36]. These devices are often used in conjunction with other specialized hardware, such as head mounted displays, to completely immerse the user in a virtual environment. A number of existing VR systems [15, 14, 33, 7, 18, 22] make use of these specialized input devices.

The new six DOF devices allow users to reach out a hand, grab an object, and manipulate it as one would in the real world [25]. This direct mapping metaphor has some problems. First, the physical arm is confined to a small space around the user, so many objects cannot be directly reached and the user must travel to the location of the object before being able to handle it. Second, manipulation of large objects is difficult, not because they are heavy, but because they obscure the user's view during the placement task.

Techniques which overcome these problems include World In Miniature [29], Automatic Scaling [19], Go-Go [24], and ray casting techniques [18, 9, 22]. Bowman [4] and Poupyrev [23] provide very nice categorizations of existing techniques.

Other research using specialized hardware includes object manipulation techniques in Augmented Reality, where virtual and real objects appear together in a scene. As an example, Kitamura [12] discussed ways of using haptic feedback to make object manipulation feel the same as in the real world.

2.3 Pseudo–Physical Techniques

The use of pseudo–physics can help to automatically place objects in physically stable positions, without incurring the computational cost of a full physical simulation. In systems which use pseudo–physics, users need not be concerned about the details of placement; they need only to drag the object into an approximate location, drop it, and let the pseudo–physics do the rest. There are many implementations of pseudo–physics, including those of Shinya and Forgue [26], Snyder [28], Breen [5], and Milenkovic [16, 17].

2.4 Semantic Techniques

The vast majority of layout systems consider only geometry. A few layout systems also exploit semantic information about the objects that they manipulate, including Houde's system [11] and the MIVE system [27]. Houde attaches to objects "narrative handles," which are positioned and shaped to indicate their manipulation capability. MIVE attaches semantic information to objects in the form of labels, "binding areas," and "offer areas." If the labels of two objects are compatible, objects are placed together by connecting binding areas to offer areas. The binding and offer areas are specified manually by the user. To assist in scene manipulation, grouping of objects is automatically performed [30].

Semantic information in the form of *constraints* has long been used in editing complex objects. Examples include Sutherland's original Sketchpad system [31], Borning's ThingLab system [2], and the Cassowary constraint solver [3].

Recently, Coyne and Sproat [8] demonstrated the power of semantic information in assisting scene composition. Their WordsEye system uses a text description to gather semantic information about the scene. From a pre–existing database, three dimensional (3D) objects are matched to the objects described in the text, and are placed in locations consistent with the text description. WordsEye allows prototype scenes to be quickly generated, based on a few lines of text.

2.5 Issues to Address

The various techniques described above have significantly improved user manipulation of individual objects. Nearly all of these techniques eliminate the need for multiple projected views. Certain techniques, such as that of Bier [1] and Smith *et al.* [27], can make very accurate object placements. Six DOF input devices have the advantage that manipulation feels more natural, and pseudo–physical techniques eliminate the need for users to be concerned about the details of placement. Finally, the Wordseye system demonstrates that layout can be made trivial if the system in question considers the *semantic information* associated with the objects that it manipulates.

Despite these advances, however, weaknesses still exist. Techniques such as those by Nielson [20] and Venolia [32] suffer from lack of control, and it may be quite troublesome to define the alignment manifolds as suggested by Bier [1]. Six DOF manipulation techniques have the disadvantages that the specialized hardware is expensive, is not universally accessible, and can cause noticeable physical fatigue.

While the Wordeye system demonstrated the power of semantic information for object layout, it may not be appropriate as a general layout tool because of the inherent ambiguity of natural language: The system could easily misinterpret the intent of the user. Many systems (with the exception of pseudo–physical techniques, of course) have no sense of the physical constraints that govern object placement, while others have only limited pseudo–physical support, and assume that objects are to be placed in an upright position only.

Most importantly, nearly all of the techniques examined here manipulate *only one object at a time*. A realistic scene having hundreds or thousands of objects cannot be efficiently laid out one object at a time.

Figure 1: A scene of 300 objects which was laid out in less than 10 minutes with CAPS.

3 Constraint–based Automatic Placement

CAPS, which is the subject of this paper, allows users to create and manipulate large scenes quickly and easily. CAPS can lay out large numbers of objects simultaneously. It has a rich pseudo–physics which allows objects to be placed in arbitrary, stable configurations. It exploits semantic information to aid in the placement. It permits objects to be placed randomly (within the limits of their placement constraints and pseudo–physical constraints), which results in scenes that exhibit a high degree of visual richness and realism.

In the sections that follow, each of pseudo–physics, placement constraints, and semantics will be discussed in turn.

3.1 Pseudo–physics

CAPS uses the pseudo–physics engine of Shinya and Forgue [26], which provides several features: non–interpenetration of objects, object stability (using a support polygon), and a limited form of friction. Using this model, objects that are dropped from above a surface will come to rest in a physically realistic position on the surface. Figure 2 shows a scene created using the pseudo–physics engine in CAPS.

3.2 Placement Constraints

CAPS uses constraints to facilitate the placement of objects. A set of constraints is associated with each object to define where the object may or may not be placed. The constraints can be as precise or as vague as the user requires.

3.2.1 Constraints

A **surface constraint** indicates how the object is to be placed on the surface of another. The constraint is specified by

- The supporting surface.
- A boolean flag indicating whether the placement is to be exact.
- If placement is exact, the exact placement location on the surface; otherwise, one or more *container polygons* and zero or more *forbidden polygons* on the surface.

If placement is exact, the object must be placed at the exact location specified. Otherwise, the object must be placed inside one of the containing polygons and outside all of the forbidden polygons.

A **proximity constraint** indicates how close the object should be placed to relative to another object, and is specified by a *proximity polygon*. The NEAR constraint causes placement within the polygon; the AWAY constraint causes placement outside the polygon.

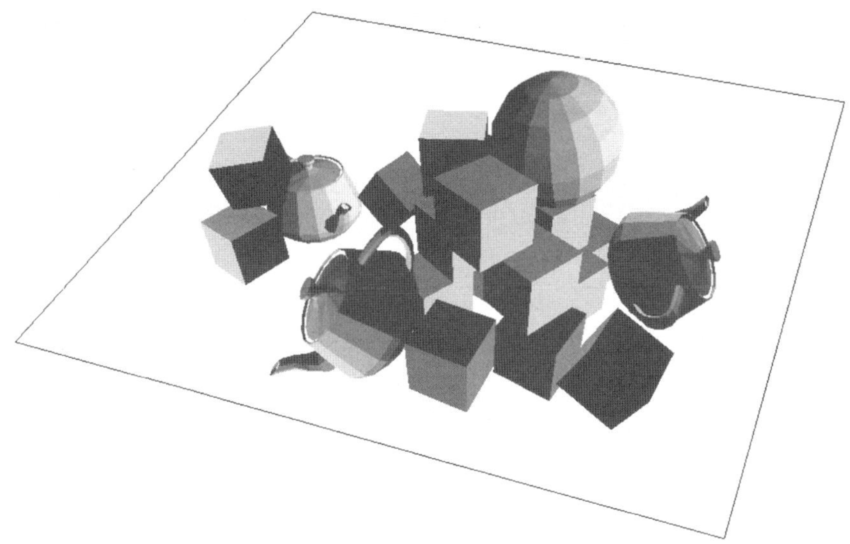

Figure 2: Pseudo–physics in CAPS automatically ensures the stability and non–interpenetration of objects.

A **support constraint** indicates whether the object can support others and whether it can be supported by others. The CANSUPPORT boolean flag is true if and only if the object can have others on top of it. The CANBESUPPORTED boolean flag is true if and only if the object can be on top of others.

3.2.2 Spatial Planning with Constraints

Given the constraints on an object's placement, two dimensional spatial planning [10] is used to find the set of allowable placements: Let S, F, and O be point sets representing, respectively, a surface, forbidden areas on that suface, and an object. Let O^t be the translation of O from its default position by the vector t. Then the problem is to find a t such that O^t is entirely inside of S (i.e. $O^t \subseteq S$) and entirely outside of F (i.e. $O^t \cap F = \emptyset$).

To use 2D spatial planning for the 3D objects in a scene, we use the *footprint* of each object: The footprint is the convex hull of the projection of the object directly downward onto the ground plane. Only the footprints are used to plan where an object is to be placed (an extension to 3D spatial planning is discussed in section 5). The constraints are implemented as follows:

- **Surface constraints:** Let S be the union of the container polygons, F be the union of the forbidden polygons, and O be the object.
- **Proximity constraints:** For a proximity polygon P, the NEAR constraint causes S to be restricted to P (i.e. $S \leftarrow S \cap P$) and the AWAY constraint causes P to be used as a forbidden polygon (i.e. $F \leftarrow F \cup P$).
- **Support constraints:** If an object's CANSUPPORT flag is false, that object's footprint is viewed as a forbidden polygon when placing any other object. If an object's CANBESUPPORTED flag is false, the footprints of all other objects are treated as forbidden polygons when placing that object.

All constraints are thus reduced to an instance of the spatial planning problem.

3.2.3 Solving the Spatial Planning Problem

The spatial planning problem has classically been solved using the theory of Minkowski sums and differences. The Minkowski sum of two point sets A and B is defined as

$$A \oplus B = \bigcup_{b \in B} A^b,$$

where A^b is A translated by b. The Minkowski difference of two point sets A and B is defined as

$$A \ominus B = \bigcap_{b \in B} A^{-b}.$$

Given two point sets, A and B, it has been shown [13] that Minkowski sums can be used to compute the set of *forbidden translations* T_f such that $B^t \bigcap A \neq \emptyset$ for $t \in T_f$. It has also been shown [10] that Minkowski differences can be used to compute set of *permitted translations* T_p such that $B^t \subseteq A$ for $t \in T_p$.

The spatial planning problem can thus be solved using Minkowski sums and differences. Given point sets S, F, and O (as defined in the preceding section), we can find the set of safe translations of O as follows: First, compute the set of permitted translations T_p such that $O^t \subseteq S$ for $t \in T_p$. Second, compute the set of forbidden translations T_f such that $O^t \bigcap F \neq \emptyset$ for $t \in T_f$. Then the set of safe translations is $T_p - T_f$.

It is not feasible to compute Minkowski sums and differences for arbitrary point sets. However, algorithms do exist to compute the Minkowski sum and difference for simple polygons. Even so, the general algorithm for simple polygons is slow and complicated to implement. Fortunately, algorithms for Minkowski sums and differences are simpler and faster for a number of special cases. In CAPS, we take advantage of these special cases, and restrict all forbidden polygons to be convex, and all container polygons to be simple. Thus, we need to compute the Minkowski sum for only the convex-convex case, and the Minkowski difference for the simple-convex case, using techniques by O'Rourke [21] and Ghosh [10] respectively.

3.3 Semantics–based Constraints

In a realistic scene, object layout is governed not only by physical constraints, but also by semantic ones including function, fragility, and interactions with other objects. Semantic properties of objects are often independent of the geometry, and are constant over the vast majority of scenes. CAPS therefore maintains a *semantic database* of information about objects, and uses it to generate *default placement constraints* for objects.

3.3.1 Semantic Database

With CAPS, the user assigns each object to a *class*, which represents the real–world classification of the object. For example, there might be a class for all tables, and another for all chairs. For the purpose of layout, it is useful to know the set of plausible placements that objects of one class can take relative to objects of each other class. To this end, each class C stores the following information:

- A list of *parent classes*: Objects of the parent class typically appear *under* objects of C. For example, if the current object class is a plate, parent classes might be tables and counters. These are denoted "parent classes" because the supporting object is the parent of the supported object in the CAPS scene graph.
- A list of *child classes*: Objects of the child class typically appear *on top of* objects of C. For example, if the current object class is a bookshelf, child classes might be books and plants. (The child and parent classes are symmetric; we use the two, instead of just one, to make the placement algorithm more efficient.)
- A CANSUPPORT flag, which is true if and only if objects *other than* those in C's child classes may appear on top of objects of C.
- A CANBESUPPORTED flag, which is true if and only if objects *other than* those in C's parent classes may appear under objects of C.
- For each parent class, an *orientation constraint* to control the orientation of objects of C with respect to objects of the parent class.

The child and parent classes determine the surfaces on which an object O can be placed. If such a surface already supports other objects, the CANSUPPORT and CANBESUPPORTED flags determine whether O can be "piled" on top of those objects.

For example, a book is typically placed upon a table, but if a lamp appears on that table already the book should not be placed upon the lamp. But if other books appear on that table, the new book could reasonably be placed upon the others. In terms of the semantic database: tables are in the parent class of a book; lamps have a false CANSUPPORT flag; and books have a true CANSUPPORT flag (used to allow the books on the table to support other objects), and a true CANBESUPPORTED flag (used to allow the book currently being placed to be piled upon other objects).

3.3.2 Default Placement Constraints

For a particular object O, placement constraints are automatically generated by CAPS from the semantic database, as follows:

- A default surface constraint is defined for each supporting object in O's parent classes. The default constraint has a single container polygon which is the boundary of the object's upward–pointing surface, and has no forbidden polygons.
- For each supporting object, the CANSUPPORT and CANBESUPPORTED flags, as well as any orientation constraints, are taken from the semantic database.

Automatic generation of default placement constraints greatly simplifies the scene layout task: The user can populate a scene with hundreds of objects in a matter of minutes, and can then refine the placements by modifying the constraints or by repositioning objects manually.

3.3.3 Classes vs. Instances

Surface constraints, proximity constraints, support constraints, and orientation constraints apply to object instances, while semantic constraints such as parent class and child class apply to object classes. The values for CANSUPPORT, CANBESUPPORTED, and orientation constraints, as stored in the semantic database, may be thought of as default values that are given to new object instances of a particular class. These default values are assigned to the initial instance, and may later be changed by the user.

3.4 Scene Layout with CAPS

CAPS automatically lays out a scene by placing objects into the scene, one object at a time. As each new object is placed, the object finds a feasible position which satisfies its placement constraints. The placement algorithm for a single object O is as follows (see Figure 3 for an example):

1. Choose a surface S from amongst those objects in O's parent classes. This choice is made randomly according to user–defined probability distribution over the available surfaces (or according to a uniform distribution if the user has defined none).

2. Identify all the forbidden regions on the surface S. The set of forbidden regions includes any forbidden polygons specified with the surface constraint of S, as well as the footprints of all objects that have already been placed on S and that have a false CANSUPPORT flag. If O has a false CANBESUPPORTED flag, the footprints of *all* objects currently on S will be considered forbidden regions.

3. Perform spatial planning as described in Section 3.2.3, using the forbidden polygons calculated above, and using a container polygon which defaults to the boundary of S. (The user may have explicitly defined the container polygon to be smaller by editing the automatically–generated surface constraint.)

4. If no safe positions exist for O, go back to Step 1 and attempt to place O on one of the other available surfaces. Note that CAPS does not attempt to undo previous placements of other objects in order to place O. If there is no surface on which to safely place O, nothing is done.

5. Of the safe positions calculated for O in Step 3, choose one at random.

6. Since there may be other objects (which have a true CANSUPPORT flag) at the chosen position, move O *above* the chosen position and drop it, using the pseudo–physics engine to compute a physically stable configuration.

3.4.1 Object Placement by the User

The user may place objects into the scene by selecting a surface and selecting multiple objects to be placed on that surface. This process is considerably simplified by the semantic database: Once the user has selected a surface, a list is presented of objects that can appear on that surface. The user may choose any number of any type of those objects, which CAPS will then place on the surface in positions that satisfy all placement constraints (using Steps 2 through 6 above). For example, each bookshelf in Figures 1 and 4 was populated simply by selecting it and instructing CAPS to add a certain number of books to it.

CAPS thus provides the user with a means of very quickly increasing the visual richness of the scene.

3.4.2 Adjustable Level of Control

CAPS provides users with the precise level of control that they require. At the highest level, users may rely on the automatically generated placement constraints. Should those prove unsatisfactory, the user may replace any automatically generated constraint with user defined ones. For example, the user can replace a default surface constraint by sketching the container and forbidden polygons on the surface. If precision is required, the user can restrict object placement to a single point, thus providing as much control as any previous method. CAPS never forces a user to make placements that are more precise than is required, which saves time in the layout process and produces a more realistic and visually rich scene.

3.4.3 Fast Object Redistribution using Scenarios

An object of class C may be placed on objects of its parent classes. A weight is assigned to each parent class of C, and the objects of C are placed on the objects of the parent classes in proportion to these weights. By default, these weights are all equal, yielding a uniform distribution.

These weights are called *scenarios* because they vary with the situation that is being modelled. Before supper, for example, plates are likely to be on the table; after supper, they are more likely to appear beside the sink. The weights of the plate's parent classes (the table and sink classes) may be modified to reflect these two situations.

CAPS permits objects to be *redistributed* in the scene simply by changing the scenarios. Upon such a change, the objects are removed from their current positions — any supported objects being settled with pseudo–physics — and are redistributed according to the new scenarios.

Objects of class C are distributed amongst the parent classes in proportion to the scenario weights. But amongst the *objects* of each parent class, a *secondary distribution* may be used (if desired) to favour placement on

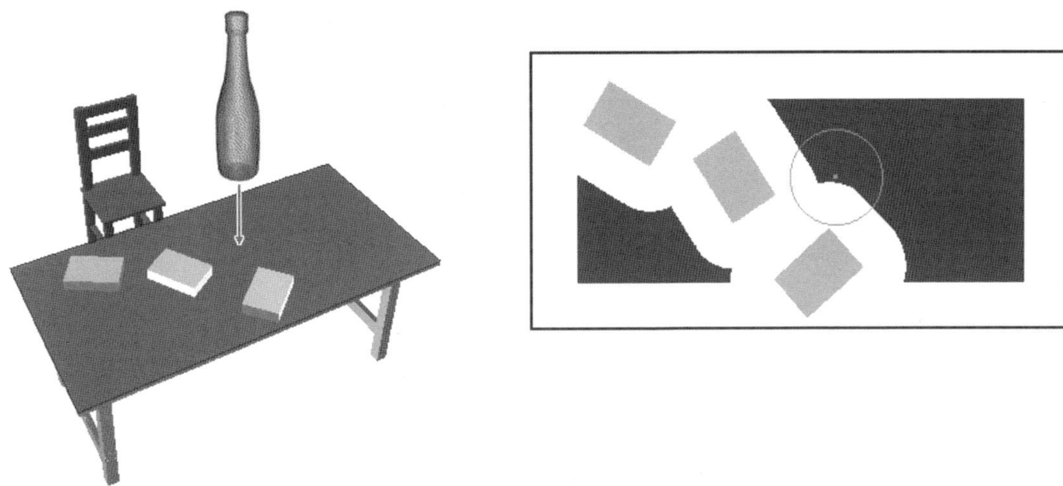

Figure 3: Left: *Positioning a carafe on a tabletop which already supports three books. The carafe has a false* CanBeSupported *flag, so it cannot be placed on any of the books.* Right: *The two dark areas, computed with Minkowski sums and differences, represent the set of safe positions for the carafe, whose circular footprint is shown.*

certain objects of the same parent class. As with the primary distribution (i.e. the scenarios), the secondary distribution is, by default, uniform.

Objects may thus be redistributed quickly and easily by simply adjusting the scenario weights and, if more control is desired, by adjusting the weights of the secondary distributions.

3.4.4 Direct Object Manipulation by the User

In addition to its automatic layout capabilities, CAPS permits the direct user manipulation of already–placed objects. Direct manipulation could be a tedious task due to the need to explicitly group objects and to restore physical stability once changes have been made. For example, to move a table that supports other objects — without explicitly grouping the table and objects — could result in the objects floating in space. Also, moving the bottom book from a pile of books requires adjustments to all the books above it. CAPS provides dependency tracking and implicit grouping to assist direct user manipulation.

Dependency tracking maintains the physical dependences between objects: For each object, CAPS keeps a list of all the other objects that might affect the stability of that object if they are moved. When a physical instability arises, CAPS can quickly determine which objects need to be re–stabilized, and can use the pseudo–physics engine to calculate new, stable positions for them.

Implicit grouping is achieved by moving as a group all dependency–connected objects: Such a group is called a **pile**. For example, if the user moves a bookshelf that supports several books, the books will automatically move with the bookshelf.

To move objects from one surface to another, the automatic placement mechanism is used to initially place the object on the new surface, after which direct user manipulation may be done. During direct manipulation, semantic constraints are purposefully disabled to allow users full freedom of manipulation. Visual feedback from the manipulation is instantaneous. Collision detection is enabled to prevent piles from interpenetrating. Dependency tracking and implicit grouping are both implemented using a novel data structure called the "Footprint Based Dependency Graph" [35], which is updated during the automatic placement process.

4 Results

The combination of pseudo–physics and the semantic database proves to be quite powerful for purposes of scene layout. Pseudo–physics ensures that physical constraints are satisfied, while the semantic database provides plausible layouts which may easily be modified.

CAPS permits the user to act as a director, since the details of object placement are handled by the computer. For example, the user can select a bookshelf, ask that 100 books be placed on the shelf, and CAPS will do the rest. A user can thus very quickly populate a scene with hundreds of objects, which brings a visual richness to the scene not otherwise achievable in a limited amount of time. Manual refinement (with the mouse or a six DOF input device) can then be used to fine–tune the scene to its exact desired form.

Figure 4: A scene of 500 objects which was laid out in 25 minutes with CAPS. Most of the time was spent by the user in exactly positioning monitors and chairs. (Consider that a traditional modeling system would require the user to exactly position the 479 other objects.)

Once the scene has been populated, the objects can be quickly redistributed to semantically acceptable locations using the various scenarios. This is especially useful where many variants of a certain scene are required. Where the automatically generated placement constraints prove unsatisfactory, placement constraints can be quickly refined by attaching a new, user–specified placement constraint to the affected objects. Since placement constraints can be attached to multiple objects simultaneously, adjusting initial object placements is quite efficient.

Figure 1 showed a scene crafted using CAPS. That particular scene has 300 objects and was laid out in less than 10 minutes: 5 minutes to get a skeletal layout, and 5 minutes to populate and redistribute the rest of the objects. Figure 4 shows a scene with 500 objects, which required 25 minutes to lay out due to the many monitors and chairs which required exact placements. Although more extensive user tests are required to validate these productivity gains, these initial results are very encouraging.

5 Future Work

5.1 Three Dimensional Planning

Because we use footprints to plan object placements, certain effects, such as placing chairs under tables, are currently not achievable (since, in this example, the footprints would overlap). However, this *can* be achieved by performing the spatial planning simultaneously on several horizontal slices of the space. For example, we could take a horizontal slice at the foot of the chair, another in the midsection of both chair and table, and a final slice at the top of the table. CAPS would enforce the 2D constraints within each slice in the usual manner. Placement of an object would be considered safe if and only if placement is safe in each of the slices.

Although it seems natural that an extension to using 3D Minkowski sums and differences could be made, this doesn't seem to be worthwhile. Because objects tend to rest on surfaces, the layout problem is more 2D than 3D in nature. For this reason — and due to their efficiency — we favor 2D techniques over 3D ones. (However, 3D

Minkowski sums and differences could be useful in certain situations, such as detecting the free space under the table where chairs may be placed.)

5.2 Generalized Distributions

Currently, objects are distributed uniformly randomly on a surface once placement constraints are satisfied. Under this scheme, we can view forbidden regions as having zero placement probability density, while safe regions have uniform probability density. A more general probability distribution would provide more control. For example, we could use a Gaussian distribution for the NEAR constraint in order to more heavily weight closer placement. As another example, we could model the placement of forks on one side of a plate by making the probability density of the NEAR constraint very high on that side of the plate. This would permit a fork to be placed in approximately the right position, with a bit of leeway (depending upon the distribution) to add some real–world sloppiness in the fork's placement.

5.3 Semantic Database

When a new class of objects is defined in the semantic database, its CANSUPPORT relations with each already–existing class must be checked. A more powerful formal representation — using abstract classes and inheritance, for example — would be appropriate in a future extension to CAPS. We also need to extend the use of semantic information to deal with functional and non–local dependencies that are currently not considered. A simple example of such a dependency is the strong relationship that exists between the position and the direction of the monitors and the position of the chair in Figure 4.

6 Conclusion

The combination of physics, semantics, and placement constraints permits us to quickly and easily lay out a scene. We have shown that the layout task can be substantially accelerated with a simple pseudo–physics engine and a small amount of semantic information. Future work into generalized distributions and a richer set of semantic information might lead to a new modeling technique, where users can create scenes by specifying the number and distribution of each class of object to be included in the scene.

References

[1] E.A. Bier. Snap-dragging in three dimensions. *ACM Symposium on Interactive 3D Graphics*, pages 193–204, 1990.

[2] A. Borning. The programming language aspects of thinglab, a constraint oriented simulation laboratory. *ACM Transactions on Programming Languages and Systems*, (3):353–387, 1981.

[3] A. Borning, K. Marriott, P. Stuckey, and Y. Xiao. Solving linear arithmetic constraints for user interface applications. In *ACM Symposium on User Interface Software and Technology (UIST)*, pages 87–96, 1997.

[4] D. Bowman and L. Hodges. An evaluation of techniques for grabbing and manipulating remote objects in immersive virtual environments. *ACM Symposium on Interactive 3D Graphics*, pages 35–38, 1997.

[5] D.E. Breen, R.T. Whitaker, E. Rose, and M. Tuceryan. Interactive occlusion and automatic object placement for augmented reality. *Eurographics*, 15(3):11–22, 1996.

[6] R. Bukowski and C. Sequin. Object associations. *ACM Symposium on Interactive 3D Graphics*, pages 131–138, 1995.

[7] J. Butterworth, A. Davidson, S. Hench, and T. Olano. 3DM: a three-dimensional modeler using a head-mounted display. *ACM Symposium on Interactive 3D Graphics*, 25(2):135–138, 1992.

[8] B. Coyne and R. Sproat. Wordseye: An automatic text-to-scene conversion system. *ACM SIGGRAPH*, pages 487–496, 2001.

[9] A. Forsberg, K. Herndon, and R. Zeleznik. Aperture based selection for immersive virtual environment. *ACM Symposium on User Interface Software and Technology (UIST)*, pages 95–96, 1996.

[10] P.K. Ghosh. A solution of polygon containment, spatial planning, and other related problems using minkowski operations. *Computer Vision, Graphics, and Image Processing*, (49):1–35, 1990.

[11] S. Houde. Iterative design of an interface for easy 3-d direct manipulation. *ACM SIGCHI*, pages 135–142, 1992.

[12] Y. Kitamura and F. Kishino. Consolidated manipulation of virtual and real objects. *Proceedings of virtual reality software and technology*, pages 133–138, 1997.

[13] Z. Li. *Compaction algorithms for non-convex polygons and their applications.* PhD thesis, Harvard University, Cambridge, Massacusettes, 1994.

[14] J. Liang. Jdcad: A highly interactive 3D modeling system. *Computers and Graphics*, 18(4):499–506, 1994.

[15] D.P. Mapes and J.M. Moshell. A two handed interface for object manipulation in virtual environments. *Presence*, 4(4):403–416, 1995.

[16] V.J. Milenkovic. Position-based physics: simulating the motion of many highly interacting spheres and polyhedra. *ACM SIGGRAPH*, pages 129–136, 1996.

[17] V.J. Milenkovic. Optimization-based animation. *ACM SIGGRAPH*, pages 37–46, 2001.

[18] M.R. Mine. Isaac: a meta-cad system for virutal environments. *Computer Aided Design*, 29(8):547–553, 1997.

[19] M.R. Mine, F.P. Brooks, and C.H. Sequin. Moving objects in space: Exploiting proprioception in virtual-environment interaction. *ACM SIGGRAPH*, pages 19–26, 1997.

[20] G.M. Nielson and D.R. Olson. Direct manipulation techniques for 3D objects using 2D location devices. In *WorkShop on Interactive 3D Graphics*, pages 175–182, 1986.

[21] J.O. O'Rourke. *Computational Geometry in C.* Cambridge University Press, 1998.

[22] J. Pierce, A. Forsberg, M. Conway, S. Hong, R. Zeleznik, and M. Mine. Image plane interaction techniques in 3D immersive environments. *ACM Symposium on Interactive 3D Graphics*, pages 39–43, 1997.

[23] Poupyrev, S. Weghorst, M. Billinghurst, and T. Ichikawa. Egocentric object manipulation in virtual environments: Emperical evaluation of interaction techniques. *Computer Graphics Forum*, 17(3):41–52, 1998.

[24] I. Poupyrev, M. Billinghurst, S. Weghorst, and T.Ichikawa. Go-go interaction technique: Non-linear mapping for direct manipulation in VR. *ACM Symposium on User Interface Software and Technology (UIST)*, pages 79–80, 1996.

[25] W. Robinett and R. Holloway. Implementation of flying, scaling and grabbing in virtual worlds. *ACM Symposium on Interactive 3D Graphics*, pages 197–208, 1992.

[26] M. Shinya and M.C. Forgue. Laying out objects with geometric and physical constraints. *The Visual Computer*, (11):188–201, 1995.

[27] G. Smith, T. Salzman, and W. Stuerzlinger. 3D scene manipulation with 2D devices and constraints. *Graphics Interface*, pages 135–142, 2000.

[28] J.M. Snyder. An interactive tool for placing curved surfaces without interpenetration. *ACM SIGGRAPH*, pages 209–217, 1995.

[29] R. Stoakley, M.J. Conway, and R. Pausch. Virtual reality on a wim: interactive worlds in miniature. *ACM SIGCHI*, pages 265–272, 1995.

[30] W. Stuerzlinger and G. Smith. Efficient manipulation of object groups in virtual environments. In *IEEE Virtual Reality*, 2002. to appear.

[31] I. Sutherland. Sketchpad: a man-machine graphical communication system. In *Proceedings of the IFIP Spring Joint Conference*, 1963.

[32] D. Venolia. Facile 3D direct manipulation. *ACM SIGCHI*, pages 31–36, 1993.

[33] C. Ware. Using hand position for virtual object placement. *Visual Computer*, 5(6):245–253, 1990.

[34] C. Ware and D.R. Jessome. Using the bat: a six-dimensional mouse for object placement. *IEEE Computer Graphics & Applications*, 8(6):65–70, 1988.

[35] K. Xu. Automatic object layout using 2D constraints and semantics. Master's thesis, University of Toronto, 2001.

[36] T.G. Zimmerman, J. Lanier, C. Blanchard, S. Bryson, and Y. Harvill. A hand gesture interface device. *Proceedings of CHI and GI*, pages 189–192, 1987.

FaST Sliders: Integrating Marking Menus and the Adjustment of Continuous Values

Michael McGuffin[2], Nicolas Burtnyk[2], and Gordon Kurtenbach[1,2]

[1] Alias|wavefront
210 King Street East
Toronto, Ontario
Canada M5A 1J7

[2] Dept. of Computer Science
University of Toronto
Toronto, Ontario
Canada M5S 3G4

mjmcguff@cs.toronto.edu, n.burtnyk@toronto.edu, gordo@aw.sgi.com

Abstract

We propose a technique, called FaST Sliders, for selecting and adjusting continuous values using a fast, transient interaction much like pop-up menus. FaST Sliders combine marking menus and graphical sliders in a design that allows operation with quick ballistic movements for selection and coarse adjustment. Furthermore, additional controls can be displayed within the same interaction, for fine adjustments or other functions. We describe the design of FaST Sliders and a user study comparing FaST Sliders to other transient techniques. The results of our user study indicate that FaST Sliders hold potential. We observed that users found FaST Slider easy to learn and made use of and preferred its affordances for ballistic movement and additional controls. A sample program demonstrating our technique can be downloaded at http://www.dgp.toronto.edu/~mjmcguff/research/FaSTSlider/

Keywords: marking menus, control menus, flowmenus, gestures, sliders, fast slider, interaction design

Introduction

The adjustment of continuous values is a common transaction in many computer applications. Adjustment generally involves the setting of a value within a range of values with a certain degree of precision. For example, many GUI desktops use a graphical slider to control the computer's audio output level.

Many applications allow users to adjust numerous continuous values. Audio mixing applications, like physical audio mixing consoles, present users with a myriad of adjustable continuous values. Other applications with similar rich functionality like 3D modeling and animation applications may also make heavy use of continuous values (Figure 1).

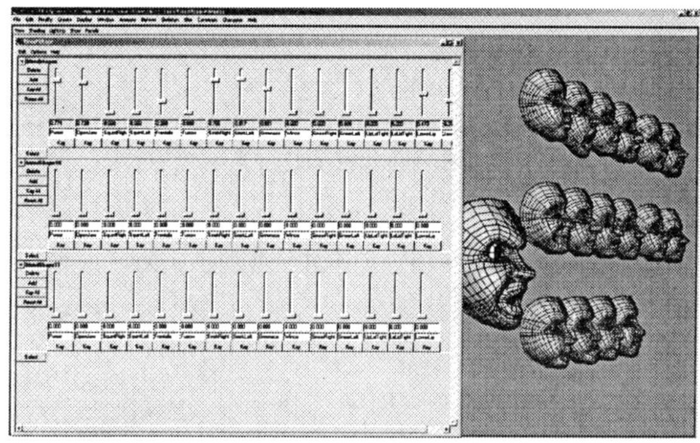

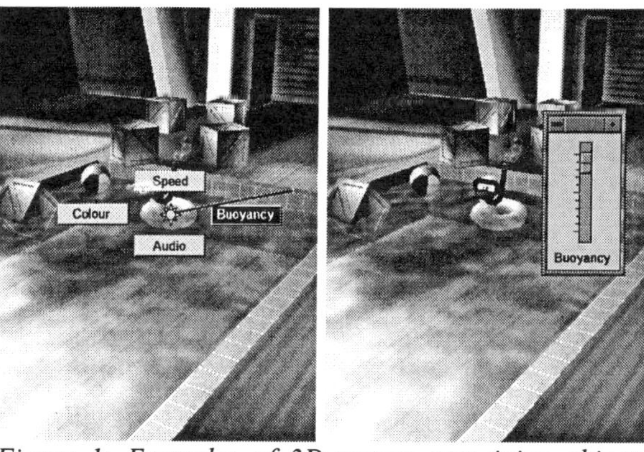

Figure 1: Examples of 3D scenes containing objects where each object has many associated parameters. The top screen shot, of a UI for controlling facial expressions, shows how the sliders consume screen space if they are all displayed simultaneously. In the bottom sequence, a user invokes a marking menu over a duck object to select and adjust one of its parameters. The slider that appears can be dismissed after the adjustment is complete.

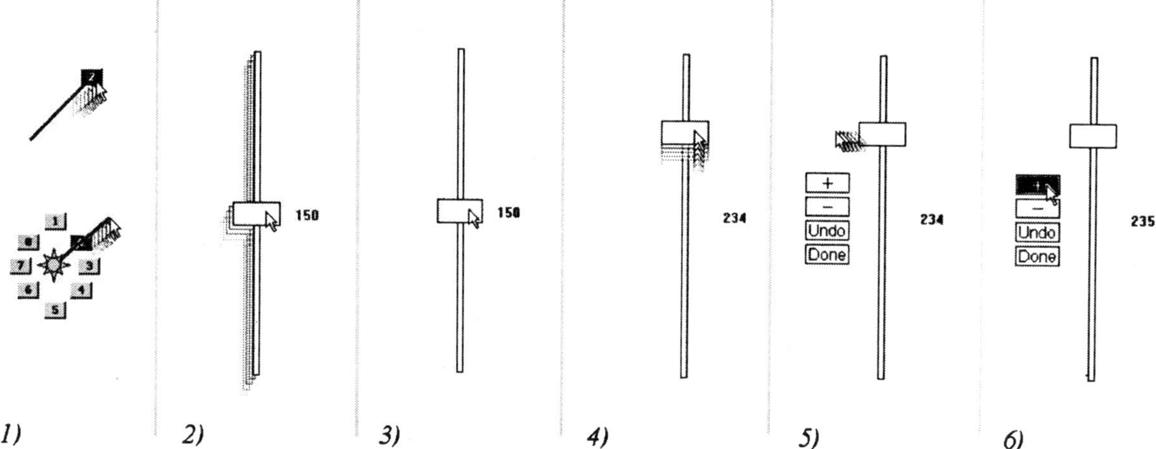

Figure 2: FaST Slider interaction 1) The user does a drag-release using either a menu or a quick "flick" gesture. This displays a slider. 2) With the mouse button released the entire slider follows the cursor. 3) When the mouse button is pressed the slider is "glued" to the screen. 4) Dragging adjusts the wiper (releasing at this point would dismiss the slider). 5) Dragging perpendicular to the slider posts the slider and some additional controls 6) these controls can then be used. Clicking on "Done" completes the interaction.

A popular approach to representing adjustable continuous values is the common graphical slider. Typically a graphical slider is presented to a user in a window, perhaps grouped with other related sliders. This arrangement can work well since it allows a user to see the relative settings of values and adjust them directly by dragging a slider's "wiper" with the cursor.

However, there are many situations in which it is not important to see the relative settings of sliders side-by-side. In these cases, a significant drawback of displaying multiple sliders at once is the consumption of screen space. As the top image in figure 1 shows, this can become an acute problem as the number of adjustable values grows. Another potential drawback of displaying multiple sliders grouped in a window can be the dissociation between sliders and the objects they control. While there has been much work on designing space saving small widgets to adjust values [3][7], another avenue of exploration is to make slider interaction transient to save space, as suggested by the bottom sequence in figure 1.

In addition to trying to save screen space, we are also interested in basing our transient slider design on some of the successful properties of marking menus [8]. Over the past six years we have gained extensive experience in deploying and using marking menus in commercial software made by Alias|wavefront. We have found that marking menus' property of "scale independence"—interpreting marks based on their shape and not their size—allows users to select very quickly and casually, and has become extremely popular with expert users. For example, some experts are so proficient with marking menus that they can perform an entire product demonstration without displaying a single menu. Thus our goal is to design a transient slider interaction technique that allows fast and casual operation consistent with marking menus.

The interaction technique we propose is a combination of marking menus and graphical sliders. Other interaction techniques have proposed similar combinations of radial menu techniques and dragging to control values [9][10][5]. These techniques use a single drag to perform both the selection of a value and its adjustment. Our technique differs in that we use two distinct drags to perform value selection and value adjustment. This decoupling produces some important differences in the resulting interaction.

In this paper we describe the design of our technique, the design principles it is based on, how it compares with other similar techniques, and users' reactions to the technique relative to other techniques. We conclude with a discussion of the overall merits of the technique.

FaST Sliders

We call our technique FaST Sliders, which stands for "Flick and Slide or Tweak". Our technique has three distinct steps: the first step ("Flick") is the selection of the value to be adjusted and the second step ("Slide") is the actual adjustment of the value. The third step ("Tweak") is optional and allows for additional kinds of adjustments of the value. The technique is a combination of a marking menu and a one-dimensional graphical slider (Figure 2). It works as follows:

Flick Step – Selection of a value The user pops up a marking menu by holding down a mouse button. This menu contains menu-items which represent adjustable values. Like a regular marking menu, an item can be selected by moving into the radial area for the menu item to highlight it and releasing the mouse button. The menu is then popped down. Since the menu is a marking menu, selection can also be accomplished quickly without displaying the menu by performing a "flicking" drag movement.

Slide Step – Adjustment of the value Once selection is complete the system goes into "follow-mode". In this mode, a slider appears with its wiper directly under the cursor. If the cursor is moved, the entire slider follows the cursor, keeping the wiper located directly under the cursor. To adjust the slider value, the user presses down the mouse button and this "glues" the slider to the screen, allowing the user to drag the wiper to adjust the value. This drag is called "adjust-mode". When the mouse button is released the slider disappears and the interaction is complete.

Tweak Step – Additional controls If the mouse button is not released in adjust-mode, and the user drags the cursor off of the wiper by moving it perpendicular to the sliders' trough, this results in additional controls appearing (Figure 2.5). If the user releases the mouse button in this state (outside of the wiper), the wiper and additional controls stay posted. Now the user is free to move over and activate any of these controls as many times as needed. Once the user is satisfied with the adjustment they can dismiss the slider and the controls by clicking on the "Done" button. This ends the interaction.

Discussion of Design

In the design of FaST Sliders we have attempted to support several design properties. The first principle is to allow and exploit ballistic cursor motion. Ballistic motion is based on the concept of a *motor program* in motor control studies. A motor program is "a set of muscle movements structured before a movement begins, which allows the entire sequence to be carried out uninfluenced by peripheral feedback" [6]. Ultimately we want our technique to allow for ballistic movement and therefore require a minimum amount of user attention to system feedback.

Ballistic movement is supported in several ways. First, since we use a mouse up event to signal the selection step of the interaction, this is compatible with marking menus' "scale independence" property. Because of this, users can make marks of arbitrary size to select menu-items thus making selection fast and casual, generally a "flicking" ballistic movement. Second, because the entire slider follows the cursor after this ballistic flick, a user does not need to move the cursor over the wiper before starting to drag/adjust the value. This is especially important when ballistic mouse movements cause the cursor to move far away from the point where the mouse button was released. Essentially this design allows a user to "flick and slide"--using two very fast and casual mouse drags to display, select, adjust, and undisplay adjustable values.

Another important design property is what we call "distinct engagement"—that is, a distinct user gesture (mouse down) is used to engage the actual adjustment of the slider. We believe this may be an improvement over other techniques that use the less explicit event of dragging past some activation threshold (for example, past the outer edge of the radial menu). This property produces a subtle but important effect. Imagine a user is making an audio recording and wants to adjust a recording level slider. It is critical in this case that the slider be moved gently either up or down so that no "spikes" or "dips" occur in the recorded material. If an activition threshold is used, the user must be very attentive as to when they cross the threshold and once they cross the threshold their movement must be very controlled. Note that the difficultly of this situation increases as the user increases the speed of their initial selection movement. Thus this approach does not bode well with our goal of fast and casual movement.

However, the use of an explicit user trigger event eliminates this interference between selection and adjustment. Once a user releases the mouse button following a selection, they enter an interim mode (follow-mode) where they have a chance to stabilize their movements before engaging the adjustment of slider. This allows a quick ballastic selection movement followed by a controlled adjustment movement. One additional benefit of following-mode is that it also allows the user to reposition the cursor or input device before beginning to adjust the slider. This can be used to move into a more comfortable position or to position the slider away from or close to a particular part of the display.

Another important design principle is to allow in the design the incorporation of additional methods for modifying a value. For example, many applications have graphical sliders which, in addition to having a wiper for adjustment by dragging, may also have increment/decrement controls, numeric entry, default values, etc. Ultimately, a slider control could be a dialog box with a variety of common GUI controls.

Given this requirement, we allow additional controls to be accessed through the tweak step. It is important to note that once the user has dragged out of the wiper, the additional controls are posted and the mouse button can be released. This essentially leaves the user free to move to and click on any of these additional controls. Thus, in addition to the controls shown in our example of FaST Slider in Figure 2.5, any sort of dialog element could be available. Essentially, each invocation of a FaST Slider is capable of evolving into interaction with a full blown dialog box. Conceptually, this works out nicely since a UI designer has the option of encapsulating all of the controls associated with a value into a single "interaction location" in a user interface.

Comparison with Other Techniques

Two other interaction techniques that are similar to FaST Sliders have been proposed in previous work. Perhaps the most similar are Control Menus [9]. Control Menus, like FaST Sliders, use a marking menu to select the value to adjust. However, rather than using a mouse up event to signal the end of the selection step, Control Menus enter adjustment mode the moment the cursor is dragged beyond a fixed threshold distance from the center of the menu. Figure 3 shows an example of a Control Menu. As described earlier, we believe this approach can make ballistic motion difficult and carefully controlled engagement of adjustment difficult. However, this cost comes at the benefit of being able to perform the entire interaction in a single drag. Our user testing section discusses users' reactions to this cost/benefit trade-off.

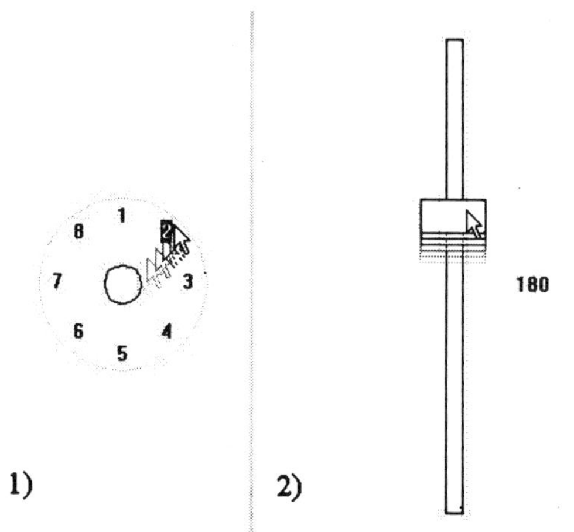

Figure 3: Using a Control Menus. 1) the user drags to select a value to adjust. When they drag past the edge of the menu, the selected slider is displayed. 2) Continuing to drag immediately adjusts the slider.

Another difference between FaST Sliders and Control Menus is that, with the latter, dragging is the only means available to adjust a value. FaST Sliders provide a method to escape dragging adjustment and access additional controls via its tweak-step. However, this benefit comes at the cost of limiting our current design of FaST Slider to only adjusting one-dimensional values. For example, Control Menus easily support two-dimensional panning, while dragging in the second dimension of a FaST Slider is used to post additional controls.

FlowMenus [4] are another radial menu based technique that is comparable to FaST Slider. FlowMenus, like FaST Sliders, are capable of supporting value selection, adjustment, and other controls. However, the interaction style to support this functionality has some significant differences. First, while FlowMenus use a radial menu layout like marking menus, item selection is performed by dragging into an item then back to the center of the menu. This "return to center" design allows a user to navigate through a hierarchy of menus without moving all over the screen. Second, continuous adjustment is supported by a special menu item, which affords adjustment by circular motion (Figure 4). Finally, like Control Menus, FlowMenus afford selection, adjustment, and other controls in a single drag.

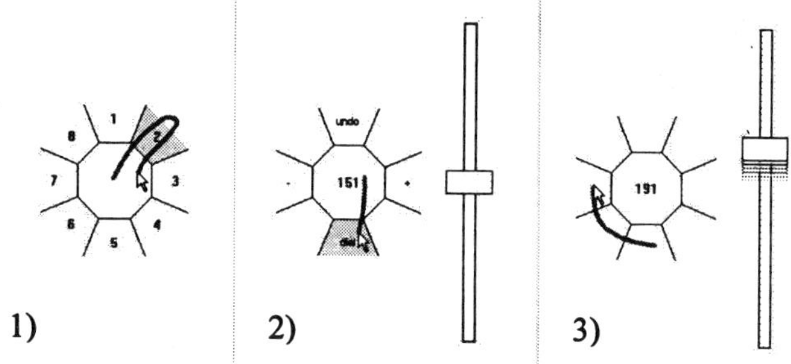

Figure 4: Example of using a FlowMenu to adjust a value. 1) a value is selected by dragging in and out of an item. This causes the display of a submenu with adjustment controls shown in 2) Moving into the dial menu item causes the display of a "rotary dial" shown in 3) where rotation adjusts the slider.

User Testing

To get a better understanding of the advantages and disadvantages of our FaST Slider design, we performed informal user tests. Specifically, we were interested in what effect the major design differences between FaST Sliders, Control Menus, and FlowMenus would have on users' impressions and performance with these techniques. Our intention was to use this information to further refine the FaST Slider design.

We implemented the three techniques such that each one could be used to adjust eight continuous parameters in a test program. The parameters ranged in value from 0 to 300. Since the study focused on adjustment of parameters rather than their selection, we used non-hierarchical menus for the Control Menu and the FaST Sliders (Figures 2 and 3). Similarly, the FlowMenu only had one menu level to select a parameter, followed by an additional level containing adjustment controls (Figure 4).

For all three techniques we attempted to provide the same level of functionality within the limits of the technique. For example, while fine-tuning functions could be provided in FaST Slider and FlowMenus, Control Menus have no obvious way of supporting these additional functions. Furthermore, FlowMenus as described in [4] have many additional ways to adjust a value. To be fair, we designed our own FlowMenu layout, which we thought would be effective but with functionality equivalent to the FaST Slider.

We tested 12 users, all of whom were familiar with Marking Menus. Most of them had 2-8 years of experience using complex 3D modeling software such as Alias|wavefront's Studio or Maya, and some were heavy users of Marking Menus, hotkeys, and other techniques for fast interaction.

To avoid confounding variables, no feedback was shown to the user other than that which the adjustment techniques provided; i.e., except for when a technique was engaged, the screen was blank. The tester controlled which technique was currently available to the user. A mouse was used for input, and the screen was 19" with a resolution of 1024x768.

Initially, users were told that each of the techniques would first present them with a menu for selecting one of eight parameters, and then allow them to adjust the selected parameter in some fashion. We then asked each user to try out and explore the techniques on their own, while talking aloud, to see if they could learn how to use them. The order of presentation of the techniques was permuted for each user. After about five minutes of exploration, if the user had still not completely understood the techniques, the tester explained how they work. (Note, however, that once this explanation was given, no further assistance or coaching was given during the tasks to follow.)

After the exploratory phase, the user was asked to perform a set of tasks using each of the techniques. The first task was *inspection*, where the user had to find out the current values of some of the parameters without changing them. The second was *extremal assignment*, where the user had to quickly set the parameters to their minimal or maximal value. The third was *rough assignment*, where the user had to assign a mid-way value of roughly 150 (10) to the parameters. Fourth was *exact assignment*, where the user was asked to assign a given value to various parameters. The fifth task was *fine-adjustment*, where the user was asked to increase or decrease a given parameter by 1 or 2 units.

Test Observations

Control Menus and FaST Slider were easy to learn. FlowMenu was more difficult.

We observed in the exploratory phase that all the users were able to learn how to roughly operate both the Control Menus and FaST Slider without coaching, although Control Menus' undo feature was only discovered by one user and went unnoticed by the others. The FlowMenu, on the other hand, generally required coaching. For example, one user commented that it "wasn't intuitive at all". Users seemed to be especially confused by the dial menu item, because, first, selection of all other items in the FlowMenu requires users to move out to the item and then *back* to the center, whereas dialing requires moving out and around, and, second, nothing in the FlowMenu's shape or feedback suggests rotary movement to the users.

This created many problems using the FlowMenu. For example, two users, intending to increment a value, moved over the increment menu item and released instead of moving back to the center to complete the selection. Even after users were given an explanation of how to operate the menu, mistakes were made. Some users often started to dial in the wrong direction and had to correct their motion. One user performed dialing not in the intended way, but by leaving the menu center in an arbitrary direction and traveling around until they accidentally hit the dial menu item. The user did this many times without noticing that anything was wrong.

Inspection and Fine-tuning were very difficult with Control Menus

The Control Menu was found to be almost impossible to use for inspection, since the user modified the parameter as soon as they traveled more than one pixel beyond the gray threshold circle. One user commented "that really bugs me [...] to me that makes this [technique] unusable". However, two users discovered that by performing undo, they could successfully inspect values with the Control Menu without having to gingerly "just cross" the threshold circle. The Control Menu was also difficult to use for fine-adjustment, for similar reasons.

In terms of the other techniques, the FlowMenu easily supported inspection and fine-adjustment. The FaST Slider also allowed fast inspection, as the user only had to "flick" to go into "follow-mode" and see the value. The FaST Slider could then be dismissed simply by click-releasing over the wiper. Unfortunately, the mouse often moved one or two pixels between the click and release, causing the value to change. For fine-adjustment and exact assignment, a similar problem occurred if the user moved off of the wiper to post the additional controls for fine adjustment: as the cursor moved off, it slightly nudged the wiper up or down by an unintended amount. However, we believe simple modifications could correct this problem.

We observed a similar problem with the FlowMenu. Our implementation of FlowMenu allows the user to release immediately after dialing a new value. However, users sometimes tried to return to the center of the menu after dialing, presumably because they either assumed it was necessary (since all the other menu items require a return to center) or because they wanted to access the fine-tuning menu items. Unfortunately, because the return trajectory did not follow an exactly straight, radial line, the value was inadvertently changed along the way. It is not clear how to correct this problem, other than to avoid returning to the centre after dialing.

Users often ran out of screen space using the Control Menu.

Because Control Menus' slider is not movable once popped up, users often started their interaction close to the screen edge and ran out of screen space to complete a adjustment. To recover from this required re-invoking the menu at a different location. Note this is not a problem with FaST Slider, since the follow-mode allows a user to relocate the slider to a better screen location before adjusting. Many users commented positively about this feature, stating how they could use it to their advantage, for example, not only to avoid running out of screen space but to locate the slider as to not obscure their work.

In terms of rough and extremal assignment, apart from Control Menu's problem with screen space, all the techniques performed well.

Other observations

When asked which method they preferred, five chose the FaST Sliders, four users chose the FlowMenu, two were tied between these two techniques, and only one user preferred the Control Menu.

The users who preferred the FlowMenu stated that they enjoyed the challenge of learning how to use it. They described it as "cool", "smart" and "nice". Two users explicitly stated that they preferred it because it was "different". On the other hand, those who didn't prefer the FlowMenu described the circular dialing motion as a "little weird" or "unnatural", or that it "seems like a lot of extra work".

Users who preferred FaST Sliders reported they liked the ability to release and tweak, saying that FaST Sliders were the "safest" and "most stable" of the techniques, or that they were "familiar [...] like a popup menu".

The sole user who preferred the Control Menu reported that it required the least work to adjust values.

Finally, one user was observed to make many selection errors with the Control Menu. For example, when the user wanted to quickly select a lower menu item and increase the corresponding parameter, he would stroke down in the appropriate direction (but not far enough) and then stroke up, unwittingly selecting and adjusting the parameter for an upper menu item. This lends support for our belief that scale-invariant interpretation of Marking Menu strokes is important.

Discussion & Conclusions

Our user study gives evidence to the effectiveness of some of our original design principles. In terms of ballistic motion and distinct engagement, we believe that part of the success of FaST Slider is due to careful attention to these design aspects. Evidence for this is given by the problems observed when using Control Menus to perform inspect and fine adjustment. An additional benefit of designing for ballistic motion is the "follow-mode" design feature in FaST Slider. Not only did this allow users to inspect values safely, but also allowed for repositioning of the slider to the user's advantage. In our study, users repositioned the slider to avoid running out of screen space to complete a drag. Users also acknowledged the potential usefulness of repositioning the slider to avoid obscuring their work, e.g. a 3D model, or to place it relative to objects in a scene, e.g. using it as a ruler.

Our other design principle of supporting additional controls proved effective. The additional controls present in FaST Slider and the FlowMenu were used in our study, and the lack of these proved to be a weakness for Control Menu. Furthermore, by allowing users to post the additional controls of the FaST Slider, we open the design to potentially support the complete range of standard controls available in a dialog box. In contrast, it is not clear how to integrate standard controls in the FlowMenu's design. Furthermore, it is important to note that because FaST Sliders can be posted, our design could allow for multiple sliders to be displayed simultaneously, behaving as modeless dialog boxes.

Despite FlowMenus and FaST Sliders scoring very closely in terms of preference in our user study, we believe a UI designer may prefer FaST Sliders since FlowMenus are a much more unconventional style of interaction and therefore require additional user learning and may not appear to be consistent with other standard GUI techniques.

Future Work

Our current design of FaST Slider deals only with one-dimensional dragging. Extending the technique to two-dimensional adjustment, while still retaining the tweak step, is still an unsolved problem.

Based on some user's preference for the circular dragging in FlowMenus, replacing FaST Slider's linear slider with a rotary slider is an interesting future research topic. One useful property of rotary adjustment is that users can continuously control the C:D ratio by varying the radial distance of the cursor to the dial's center. Furthermore, rotary motion naturally lends itself to relative adjustment.

While the focus of this paper has been on the control of numerical values, future research could be done to adapt FaST Slider to adjust non-numerical data using techniques such as the AlphaSlider [1].

Although our design does not adhere to the concept of physical tension proposed in [2], requiring more than one drag for an interaction phrase did not seem to cause a problem. We believe this is due to the "follow-mode" providing sufficient visual feedback to keep users aware of the current state. It may be that this type of feedback (the entire slider following the cursor) provides a kind of "visual tension" analogous to physical tension. The issue of physical versus visual tension in user interface design bears further investigation.

Our work has not compared the relative speed of operation of each technique. Because FaST Sliders require at least two drags for an interaction, a naïve keystroke model analysis suggests that our design should be slower compared to the other techniques. However, we suspect that the improved support for ballistic motion designed into FaST Sliders may more than offset the penalty incurred by an extra button press. A formal study is required to test this hypothesis, and could contribute to a deeper understanding of the role of gesture design in supporting high quality interaction.

Acknowledgements

We thank George Fitzmaurice, Ravin Balakrishnan, Azam Khan, and Scott Guy for design comments and suggestions. We also thank the participants in our user study.

References

1. Ahlberg, C., and Shneiderman, B., (1994) The Alphaslider: A Compact and Rapid Selector. *Proceedings of CHI '94*, ACM Press, 365-371
2. Buxton, W. (1986). Chunking and phrasing and the design of human-computer dialogues. In Kugler, H. J. (Ed.) *Information Processing '86, Proceedings of the IFIP 10th World Computer Congress*, 475-480, Amsterdam: North Holland Publishers.
3. Buxton, W., Reeves, W., Fedorkow, G., Smith, K. C., & Baecker, R. (1980). A Microcomputer-Based Conducting System. *Computer Music Journal* 4(1), 8-21.
4. Guimbretiere, F. & Winograd, T. (2000) FlowMenu: Combining Command, Text, and Data Entry. *Proceedings of UIST 2000*, ACM, 213-216
5. Hopkins, D. (1991) The design and implementation of pie menus. *Dr. Dobb's Journal*, 16(12), 16-26.
6. Keele, S. W. (1968) Movement control in skilled motor performance, *Psychological Bulletin*, 70, 387-403.
7. Kurtenbach, G. (1988) Hierarchical Encapsulation and Connection in a Graphical User Interface: a Music Case Study, MSc thesis, University of Toronto
8. Kurtenbach, G. & Buxton, W. (1993) The limits of expert performance using hierarchical marking menus. *Proceedings of the CHI '93 Conference on Human Factors in Computing Systems,* New York: ACM., pp. 482-487
9. Pook, S., Lecolinet, E., Vaysseix, G., and Barillot, E. (2000) Control Menus: Execution and Control in a Single Interactor. *CHI 2000 Extended Abstracts*, ACM, pp. 263-264.
10. Reinhardt, A. (1991). First Impression: Momenta Point to the Future. *Byte Magazine*.

Traces: Visualizing the Immediate Past to Support Group Interaction

Carl Gutwin

Department of Computer Science, University of Saskatchewan
57 Campus Drive, Saskatoon, SK, S7N 4J2
carl.gutwin@usask.ca

Abstract

Virtual embodiments of people in groupware systems provide a wealth of information to others in the group. They allow for explicit gestural communication, and they provide implicit awareness information about people's locations and activities. However, the constraints of current networked groupware limit the effectiveness of these kinds of communication. This paper investigates how embodiments can be augmented with traces – visualizations of past movements – to help others perceive and interpret bodily communication more clearly and more accurately. The paper presents a case study of traces applied to telepointers, and gives several examples of how the concept can be used to improve interaction effectiveness in groupware.

Key words: Synchronous groupware, groupware usability, awareness, interaction histories, edit wear.

1 Introduction

Shared workspace groupware allows people who are in different locations to work together in a visual task space. In these systems, people are often represented by some form of visual embodiment – a visible representation that stands in for the actual person in the computational workspace. Embodiments can take many forms, from telepointers and view rectangle in a 2D workspace [9] to fully-rendered humanoid avatars in a virtual world [2].

Groupware uses embodiments because the real bodies that they are modeled on are so useful in collaboration, as a vehicle for communication and group awareness. In real world collaborative situations, bodies provide other group members with a great deal of information: either explicitly, through gestural communication; or implicitly, by simply "giving off data" about what the person is doing [20].

However, groupware embodiments are poor approximations of their real-world counterparts. They provide only a small fraction of the information that would be provided by a real body, and display and network constraints make them harder to notice and harder to interpret than a real body.

Telepointers are a good example of this problem. Telepointers are not nearly so obvious as a real body in a physical workspace: they are small visual objects in a workspace filled with other small visual objects. Where actions or gestures by a real person in a physical space are readily noticeable, even through peripheral vision, telepointer motion often become lost in the clutter of the workspace. In addition, system factors such as processor load and network traffic further reduce the intelligibility of the telepointer, by making its motion erratic and jittery [8].

How can the usefulness of user embodiments be improved upon? One approach is to increase the expressiveness and realism of the embodiment by increasing the number of input sensors and the complexity of the rendered image. This direction is an established area of groupware research (e.g. [26]); however, these techniques are often difficult to implement using current desktop technology, and do not solve (and in fact add to) the problems caused by processor and network load.

A second approach is to augment embodiments using information that is not available in physical settings. This approach is complementary to that of making embodiments more realistic, and can address some of the specific problems that arise in the artificial world of a groupware workspace.

This paper investigates one such augmentation called traces: visualizations of an embodiment's past movements that make gestures and actions easier to see and interpret in a shared workspace. The following sections outline the foundations of the idea, and then present a case study of the application of traces to telepointer embodiments. Adding a trace to the telepointer that shows the path and motion of the pointer over the past few moments can smooth out jerky motion caused by network delays, can help people to understand what is going on when they glance at another person's work, and can allow for more concrete gestural communication. Other applications of the idea are also discussed; experience with the technique thus far suggests that it is a good example of how the "informational physics" [13] of groupware embodiments can be exploited to improve the usability of shared workspaces.

2 Motivation: How Bodies Communicate

Bodies (and embodiments) are a primary mechanism for conveying communication and awareness information: "whenever activity is visible, it becomes an essential part of the flow of information fundamental for creating and sustaining teamwork" ([20] p. 24). Bodies communicate in two main ways: through explicit gestures, and through consequential communication.

Explicit and intentional gestures are ubiquitous in face-to-face collaboration, and gesture has been often studied in CSCW research [1,24,21,25]. People use gestures to point to objects (e.g. "this one"), to indicate areas of the workspace, to demonstrate an action without really doing it, to illustrate concepts (e.g. using the gap between finger and thumb to show size), to indicate paths in the workspace, to communicate symbols (e.g. "thumbs up"), or to generate actual utterances in a language such as American Sign Language.

Bodies also convey information implicitly. Since most things that people do in a workspace are done through some bodily action, the position, posture, and movement of heads, arms, eyes, and hands provide a wealth of information to others about what's going on. This is *consequential communication*: information transfer that emerges as a consequence of a person's activity within an environment [20]. Although it is completely unintentional, consequential communication provides a great deal of information. Norman [17] provides an example from commercial aviation:

> When the captain reaches across the cockpit over to the first officer's side and lowers the landing-gear lever, the motion is obvious: the first officer can see it even without paying conscious attention. The motion not only controls the landing gear, but just as important, it acts as a natural communication between the two pilots, letting both know the action has been done. ([17] p. 142)

Gestures and consequential communication have certain requirements in order to be seen and interpreted correctly. First, the actions must be noticeable: the large motions of arms and hands draw attention to the fact that something is happening, attention that is needed before communication can take place. Second, the information contained in gestures and consequential communication is based on motion over time, and so has temporal requirements for intelligibility. That is, a gesture must be distinguishable from events before and after it, and must be shown smoothly without too many stops and starts, in order to be successfully interpreted by another person.

These requirements are well met in the real world, where the constraints of body mechanics ensure that motions are large, and where visual information flow is instantaneous and smooth. However, in the artificial world of a groupware workspace, where embodiments are small and where system factors get in the way of information flow, these necessities are rarely provided.

3 Solution Approach: Interaction Histories and Informational Physics

Our approach to solving these problems is based on Hill and colleagues' work on information physics and interaction histories [13,14]. Their overall motivation is the question of how computation can be used to improve "the reflective conversation with work materials" ([13] p. 3). Their research in this area arises from an important distinction between the real world and a virtual one – that each has a set of rules and physical laws that govern how people perceive information and interact with objects. The real world's laws are not negotiable, but the "informational physics" of an artificial world are completely up to the designer. Although there are advantages to duplicating the real world's laws – namely that people already have extensive knowledge of how they work – there are situations where changing the rules can be beneficial for the user:

> These same techniques also allow us to create virtual worlds that give concrete existence to abstract entities operating according to a physics of our choice. The entities and their physics can be designed to highlight aspects of phenomena not normally available to us but that are important for supporting understanding and task performance." ([13], p. 7)

Thus, information in a virtual world can behave in ways that are appropriate to its meaning and importance, rather than ways determined by its physical properties. Hill et al. propose an alternate informational physics for work artifacts that bends time and shows the past in the present:

> The basic idea is to maintain and exploit object-centered interaction histories: record on computational objects...the events that comprise their use...and display useful graphical abstractions of the accrued histories as part of the objects themselves." ([13], p. 3)

This idea leads to a number of innovative displays, such as a scrollbar that shows how often each line of a file has been read or edited. Others have followed this lead and proposed other techniques and displays [6,15,23]. However, researchers in this area have focused on work artifacts and the interactions that people have with them, and do not consider the objects in the workspace that represent people – i.e. embodiments – and the interactions that happen between people in collaboration. The intention of our research is to extend the idea of informational physics and interaction histories to embodiments, in order to make gestures and consequential communication more understandable.

The problems that we are trying to solve are ones of motion over time, and real-world physics do not hold well enough in groupware to meet their requirements. However, it may not be necessary to invent a completely new information physics for embodiments, for several alternates already exist in the worlds of the visual arts. In particular, there are art forms where movement is regularly augmented in order to assist comprehension: the cartoons and the comics.

4 Inspiration: Motion Lines in the Comics

Cartoon and comic artists have long had to address the problem of showing movement convincingly and comprehensibly in a static medium. The depiction of motion in a single image has a long history (summarized in [16]) beginning with Duchamp's and Marey's experiments with overlaid representations and with lines to trace the path of the moving object. These ideas were taken up by comic illustrators, and evolved into three distinct techniques for showing motion: motion lines, motion blur, and stutter blur. These are shown in Figure 1. Motion lines are the simplest, with one or more lines tracing the path of the moving object; motion blur adds the optical effect of streaks along the path; and stutter blur shows several intermediate representations of the object along the path.

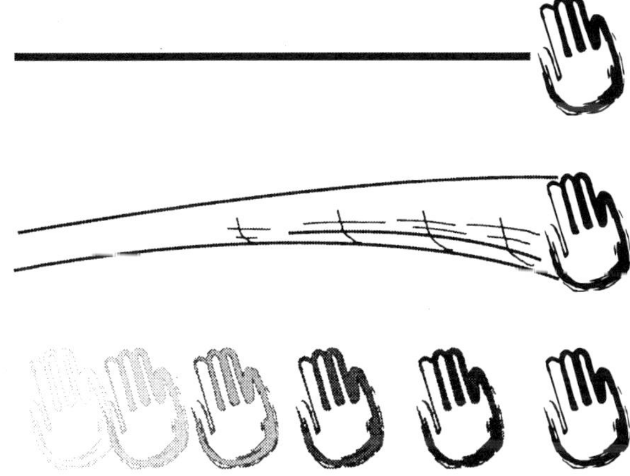

Figure 1. Motion lines, motion blur, and stutter blur in comic strip art (adapted from [16]).

Cartoonists and animators also have to deal with the problem of motion depiction. Even though cartoons depend partially on the illusion of motion created by the sequence of still frames, they generally have a much lower frame rate than film, and so must find ways to make movement seem smooth and understandable. Cartoonists regularly use both motion blur and stutter blur—not necessarily to show the path of a moving object, but more to emphasize certain movements and to make objects and characters more convincing and real to the viewer. Chang and Ungar [3] state a rule of thumb that if an object moves more than half its own size between two frames, motion blur must be used to convey the illusion of continuous movement.

In emphasizing certain aspects of a character's motion, the cartoonist provides visual cues to assist comprehension. As Chang and Ungar state, the techniques work extremely well, allowing even impossible motions and events to be easily understood. In groupware, we also want to assist understanding of others' motion and activity. The techniques used in comics and cartoons for depicting and emphasizing motion appear to be a useful alternative physics for embodiments, a way of augmenting the basic representation to better convey motion-based information. The next sections describe a case study of applying the idea of traces and the visualization techniques described above to groupware telepointers.

5 Designing Telepointer Traces

Telepointer traces are visualizations of the previous motion and location of a remote mouse cursor. Our goals in adding traces to telepointers are to make gestures easier to see, to make motion easier to interpret, and to provide a bit of context that helps people understand what is going on when they look at the telepointer. These goals, however, cannot be met at the expense of people's ability to carry out their individual work; in particular, telepointer trails cannot be distracting or annoying to the people in the workspace.

We designed several representations for telepointer trails and demonstrated them to users who had experience with synchronous groupware. The different representations used different values for the following variables:

- technique: motion lines, motion blur, stutter blur, or a combination of techniques
- trace length: the amount of motion that the trace will capture and display
- trace area: the number of pixels required for the total visualization at any one time (e.g. width of the motion lines, width of the blur, size of the stutter images)
- contrast: how clearly the trace stands out from the background
- fading: whether old sections of the trace fade out and disappear

Five examples are shown in Figure 2. Motion lines were implemented simply by joining up each of the points that the telepointer passed through, and motion blur by using a rectangle the same height as the telepointer (essentially a thick motion line). Stutter blur was implemented by drawing a copy of the telepointer at each point. Fading was implemented by making the older sections of the trail more and more transparent until they disappeared from view.

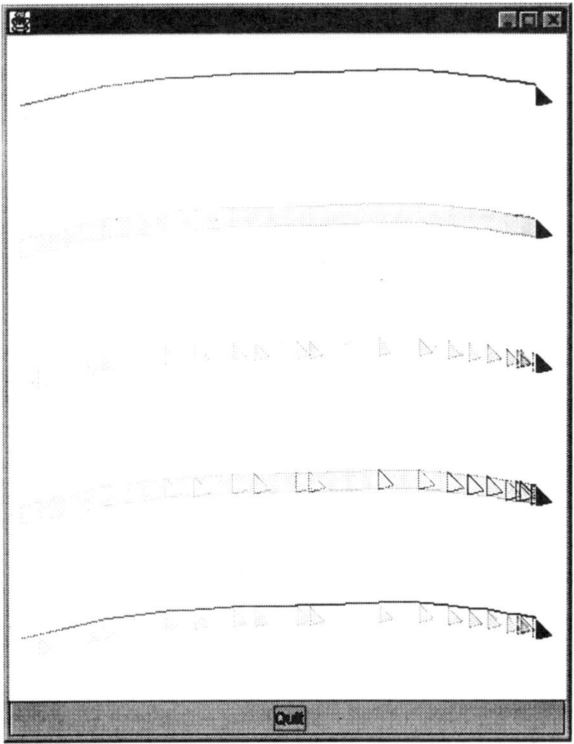

Figure 2. Example telepointer-trace representations From top: motion line, motion blur, stutter blur, motion blur plus stutter, motion line plus stutter. The actual telepointers are at right, coloured black.

Although we were more interested in simply exploring the representation space than we were in choosing the best representation, there was a general preference for short, low-contrast, fading trails that used either the motion line or motion blur technique. Some of our specific findings were:

- Traces that captured more than about one second of motion quickly cluttered the screen with lines (the "scribble effect"), reducing the clarity of the more recent lines. Many gestures and movements take less than a second to produce, and there seems to be little value in showing more than the latest one.
- Low contrast traces were seen as less distracting than high-contrast trails. However, low-contrast traces were still surprisingly easy to see, even when the darkest part of the trail was 90% transparent.
- Fading trails seem much more natural than solid trails (those of uniform colour for the entire length of the trace). Since trails are added to at one end and removed at the other, solid trails appear to be distinct objects that moves as a unit. This gives the odd impression of a worm chasing the telepointer.
- Stutter blur on its own does not do a good job of showing the path traveled. Especially when the telepointer is moving quickly, stutter blur leaves gaps that can be difficult to interpret. However, stutter blur does record changes in pointer speed, which lines or blur alone do not.
- Many of the representations were computationally intensive, a distinct disadvantage in something intended to offset the effects of processor load. Single lines were predictably the cheapest to draw, and the combination representations (e.g. motion blur plus stutter) were most expensive. However, transparency appeared to be the biggest drain on the CPU, regardless of which technique it was used with.

6 Example Applications of Telepointer Traces

We have added telepointer traces to a variety of simple groupware systems in order to explore the concept further and to determine whether traces assist group interaction. Two of these investigations are described below: using traces to combat jitter, and using traces in realistic groupware applications.

6.1 Using traces to smooth network jitter

Network jitter is the intermittent delay due to variance in the arrival times of a stream of messages (such as telepointer position messages). These intermittent delays cause the telepointer to momentarily freeze on the screen, and also cause messages to pile up, with several arriving at the receiver at once instead of being correctly spread out. When the receiver processes the multiple messages, several telepointer moves are collapsed into a single screen update. The telepointer looks as if it is jumping from position to position, and the end result is a frame rate so low that the illusion of smooth motion is impossible to maintain [8].

We implemented a telepointer trace using a motion line to smooth out this jittery movement. Since all of the telepointer positions are received (but not all are shown), it is possible to recreate the actual motion of the pointer using the trace. Thus, a viewer should get a more complete representation of the gesture than without the trace. An example of the effect is shown in Figure 3.

We are currently comparing people's abilities to recognize basic pre-recorded gestures (such as the outlines of number and letter shapes, paths, and enclosure of areas) at various levels of network jitter, both with and without the telepointer trail. The trail was designed so that about one-third of the gesture was visible in the trail at any one time. Our initial results show that at high jitter magnitudes, the trail makes an enormous difference in interpreting gestures. The reason is simple: without the trail, the viewer sees only a few frames of the gesture – that is, the telepointer jumps to only a few points and no smooth motion is apparent at all. With the trail, all of the intermediate points that were skipped are drawn as trail segments, and the viewer sees all of the movement (although not smoothly). The gesture is essentially drawn on the screen, and the viewer is simply to look at it, rather than attempt to interpolate between a few isolated frames. More details on this study can be found in [7].

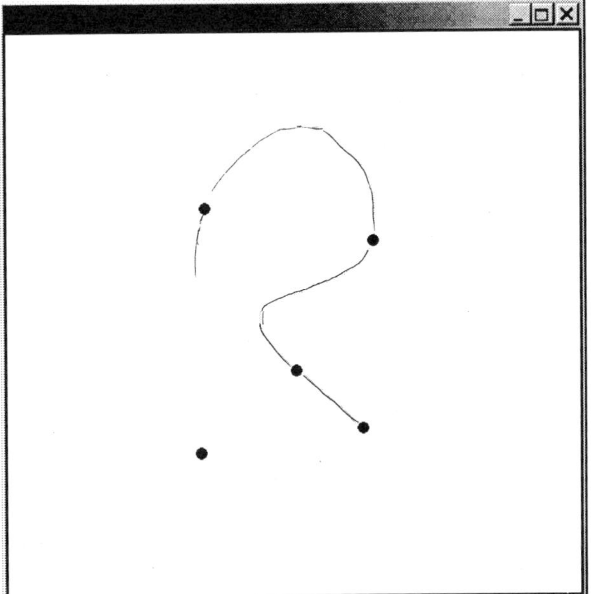

Figure 3. Telepointer gesture with trail. The dots indicate the only telepointer positions that the viewer would see in a high-jitter situation.

6.2 Trails in realistic groupware applications

We implemented telepointer trails in a group file viewer and in a real-time multiplayer game, both of which are Groupkit applications [18]. In these examples, we were interested in finding out how the traces were used in a more naturalistic setting. We have tested the applications informally with several groups, both with people in our lab and with outsiders.

We again used the motion line representation to reduce computation load. In addition, Tcl/Tk (the language underlying Groupkit) does not allow transparency, so we implemented fading by gradually changing the line colour to match the background, and applying a bit-mask to gradually remove the line.

Figure 4 illustrates the shared file viewer. People are represented in the document workspace with telepointers (the system also includes a multi-user scrollbar to show out-of-view location). This system is intended for use as a discussion tool (such as in a code review); therefore, people will generally have a shared focus on the document. In the figure, one person is indicating a variable declaration and where in the file it should be moved.

Second, Figure 5 shows a multi-player game similar to the Pipedreams arcade game. The object of the game is to connect an inlet valve to an outlet by dragging pipe pieces from storehouses and attaching them to the end of the pipeline. The players must work quickly, since after a certain amount of time water begins flowing through the pipe, and will flood the workspace if it reaches the open end of the pipe. This system provides a large workspace and gives more opportunity for independent work in different parts of the workspace. In the figure, one participant has just dragged a pipe from the stack at lower left to the end of the partially completed pipeline, and has moved back towards the left side of the screen.

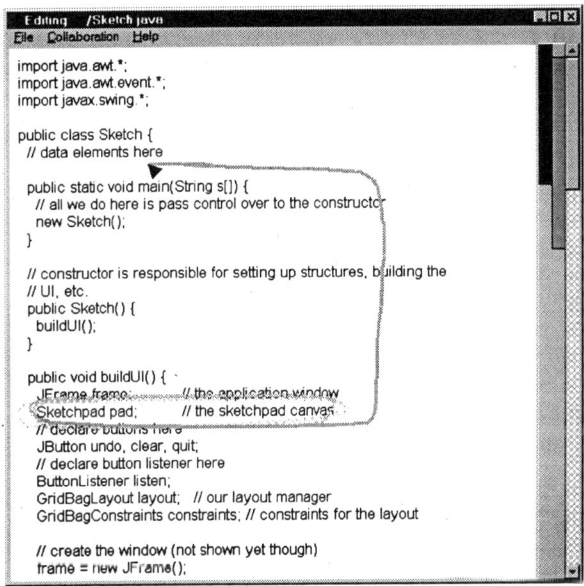

Figure 4. Telepointer traces in a code browser.

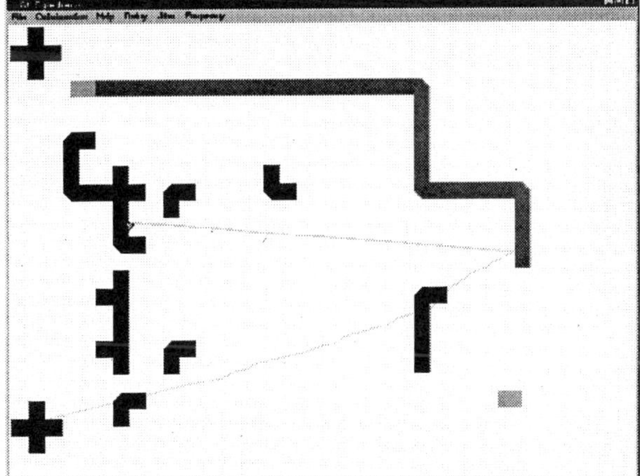

Figure 5. Telepointer traces in a multi-player game.

7 User Experiences

We discussed the traces with participants after they had used the groupware systems both with and without the telepointer traces. Our evaluations were unstructured and opportunistic; our goal was to see whether traces would be useful for helping people maintain awareness and for assisting them in communicating with gestures.

People in general liked the idea of telepointer traces, and had no difficulty understanding what they were for. Furthermore, none of the participants found the traces to be particularly distracting in any of the applications. In the multi-user game (where people have to concentrate on their individual tasks), players said that it was quite easy to ignore their partner's trail when they were concentrating on their own work. A few people suggested, however, that putting the representation under the control of the viewer would allow people to reduce distraction when it did occur.

7.1 Using Traces for Awareness

Our intention was that telepointer traces would assist awareness of where people were and what they were doing. In our discussions with people after they used the systems, some participants said that they had a better sense of what activities the other person was carrying out. For example, one person used the line of the trail to predict where the other person was moving in the pipedreams game. A second person said that they used the traces as a general indicator of activity – that is, he could see "out of the corner of his eye" if the other group members were active

However, people did not often recall situations where they gathered awareness information by watching the traces. On reflection, it seems that for many tasks, the basic telepointer alone provides enough consequential communication to support the collaboration adequately. The realistic groupware systems were run on a fast network, however, and we believe that there are certainly situations where the normal telepointer will not be able to convey enough information for adequate awareness. In addition, certain types of tasks have greater requirements for keeping track of people's precise actions. For example, design work or instructional situations often require keeping a closer eye on others' activities. Finally, one participant suggested that if the application itself involved gestural input (e.g. [12]), the trails would be extremely helpful in understanding what another person was doing.

7.2 Using Traces for Gesturing

In contrast, almost all of the participants used the traces for gestural communication. People found that gestures were much easier to see, and people liked the way that their gestures were made more persistent by the telepointer trace. Several participants said in particular that indicating objects in the workspace was easier with the traces. For example, people would circle lines of code in the file browser, or would draw out a path for the pipeline in the multi-user game. We were initially surprised at the number of positive comments about *creating* the gestures (instead of viewing them). However, communicative acts require both that the receiver interprets the message successfully, *and* that the sender gets confirmation that the message has been received. We believe that telepointer traces assist this confirmation process, in that the creator of the gesture had greater confidence that the receiver was actually seeing the gestures correctly.

The "persistent gestures" that are afforded by telepointer traces blur the line between gesturing and drawing. Many kinds of gestures are really "drawings in the air" in the first place, and adding a trace to the pointer simply builds on the idea. Drawing makes it easy to see an entire gesture at once and allows relationships to be shown over a larger distance, while the gradual fading prevents the workspace from becoming cluttered with marks. Using traces for drawing is similar to a groupware feature that has appeared in several systems, that of providing an annotation layer for drawing on the workspace without changing it [19]. We consider traces as a very lightweight version of this annotation layer, and traces could easily be extended to produce permanent marks as well. However, it seems clear that the transitory nature of traces has a place in collaborative communication. People liked being able to mark up the workspace in an impermanent way, although they wanted more control over how long the traces stayed around.

Overall, people felt that traces improved gestural communication for both the creator and the viewer of the gesture. Since mice are imprecise and telepointers are small, the lines drawn by the telepointer trace helped people to indicate objects, show paths, and draw associations.

8 Extending the Idea Beyond Telepointers

Telepointers are only one type of embodiment, and there are other possibilities for interaction histories with other types. In addition, there are other kinds of informational physics that could be used with other representations. Two examples are described below.

8.1 Viewport rectangles

A second common type of embodiment in 2D shared workspaces is the viewport. This is simply a rectangle superimposed on the workspace indicating the bounds of each person's view, and is useful for knowing when an object can be seen by another person. View rectangles are often implemented in miniature overviews of the entire workspace (called radar views [22]).

Interaction histories can also be maintained for viewports; although the viewport is not involved in gestural communication, it is often useful for group members to know where another person has been working in the workspace. An example radar view where viewports are augmented with traces is shown in Figure 6. As with the telepointer trace, a fading trail shows the past locations and movements of the viewport. The informational physics of viewports are slightly different that those of telepointers, however: the time scale of interest for a viewport is much larger, since they change position much more slowly than telepointers. Therefore, a trace would show the previous minutes or hours of viewport movement, rather than only the past few moments. Viewport traces are another example where allowing user to control the time period shown in the trace could be valuable. For example, a person might wish to extend the coverage of the visualization backwards in time to see whether a person had ever visited a particular region of the workspace.

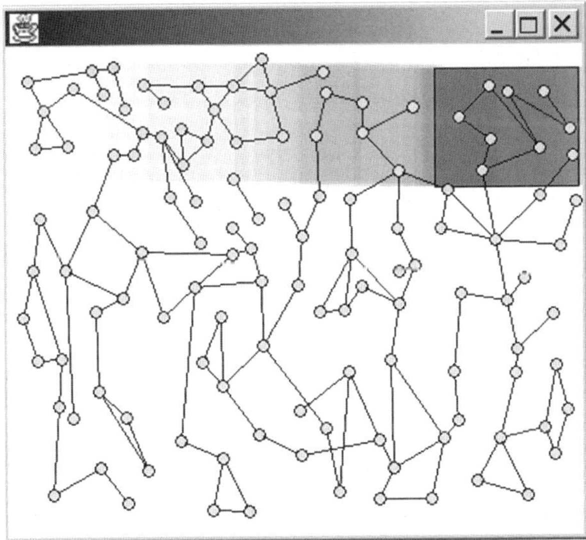

Figure 6. Radar view on a graph browser, with fading trail on viewport (colours darkened for printing). Main view is not shown.

8.2 Casual awareness with video

In video-based collaboration systems, people are represented by video images of themselves, rather than by a graphical embodiment. Nevertheless, we can apply the idea of traces to add information about past activities. For example, consider an awareness server that lets a workgroup see regularly-updated video snapshots of each others' offices, to help maintain casual awareness of who is around and who is available for collaboration (e.g. [4]). Since people only look at the pictures sporadically, they may miss useful events, such as someone returning from lunch but then leaving their office again.

Adding a trace to each person's video image provides information about activities and presence over a particular time period. For example, Figure 7 shows how a system could composite the last five snapshots from a webcam to provide awareness of the past five minutes in a person's office. Previous images appear as ghosts overtop the current snapshot; in the example situation given above, a co-worker would now be able to tell that the person had at least been in the office, even though they were no longer there.

Figure 7. Composite image with stutter blur, achieved by overlaying multiple images. Current image is of the empty office, previous images appear as ghosts.

9 Conclusions

CSCW research usually attempts to support the interaction techniques and mechanisms that people already know from face-to-face collaboration. This approach is a necessary one, but the traces project suggests that there are also situations where computation can be used to augment reality and help overcome the drawbacks and limitations of distributed groupware environments.

This paper has shown examples of how embodiments can be augmented using an informational physics that visualizes the past along with the present. The past is visualized as traces of movement and activity. When applied to telepointers, traces can have significant impact on people's ability to see and interpret gestures, and can provide people with a new means of marking and annotating the workspace in a clear but temporary fashion.

Future work will include further explorations of how traces support consequential communication in longer-term tasks, more focused studies of traces in situations of high network latency and jitter, and continued development of other types of traces such as the viewport and video prototypes discussed above. In addition, there are interesting usage issues to be explored further, such as how to protect against misuse of the information summarized in a trace, how to easily control the length and duration of a trail, and how the viewer and the producer can negotiate a length and duration that are acceptable to both parties.

Acknowledgments

This research was supported by the Natural Sciences and Engineering Research Council of Canada.

References

[1] Bekker, M., Olson, J., and Olson, G. Analysis of Gestures in Face-to-Face Design Teams Provides Guidance for How to Use Groupware in Design CSCW. *Proceedings of DIS'95 Symposium on Designing Interactive Systems*, 1995, 157-166.

[2] Benford, S., Bowers, J., Lennart, E.F., Greenhalgh, C., Snowdon, D. User embodiment in collaborative virtual environments. *Proc. ACM CHI'95*, 1995, 242 – 249.

[3] Chang, B., and Ungar, D., *Animation: From Cartoons to the User Interface*. Sun Microsystems Technical Report TR-95-33, March 1995.

[4] Dourish, P., and Bly, S., Portholes: Supporting Awareness in a Distributed Work Group, *Proc. ACM CHI'92*, Monterey CA, 1992, 541-547.

[5] Dourish, P., and Bellotti, V. Awareness and Coordination in Shared Workspaces, *Proc. ACM CSCW'92*, Toronto, 1992, 107-114.

[6] Eick, S.G., J.L. Steffen, and E.E. Sumner, SeeSoft: A Tool for Visualizing Software, *IEEE Trans. on Software Engineering*, Vol. 18, No. 11, Nov. 1992, 957-968.

[7] Gutwin, C. and Penner, R. (in preparation). The Effects of Telepointer Trails on Gesture Recognition in Jittery Groupware. In preparation, 2001.

[8] Gutwin, C. The Effects of Network Delays on Group Work in Real-Time Groupware. *Proc. 7th European Conference on CSCW*, Bonn, 2001, 299-318.

[9] Gutwin, C., and Greenberg, S. A Descriptive Framework of Workspace Awareness for Real-Time Groupware. In press, *Journal of CSCW*.

[10] Gutwin, C. and Greenberg, S. Design for Individuals, Design for Groups: Tradeoffs between power and workspace awareness. *Proceedings of ACM CSCW'98*, Seattle, ACM Press, 1998, 207-216.

[11] Gutwin, C., and Greenberg, S. Effects of Awareness Support on Groupware Usability. *Proceedings of ACM CHI'98*, Los Angeles, 1998, 511-518.

[12] Hardock, G., Kurtenbach, G., and Buxton, W. A Marking Based Interface for Collaborative Writing. *Proceedings of the ACM Symposium on User Interface Software and Technology*, 1993, 259-266

[13] Hill, W.C. & Hollan, J.D. Edit wear and read wear. *Proc. ACM CHI'92*, 1992, ACM Press, 3-9.

[14] Hill, W.C. & Hollan, J.D. History-enriched digital objects: prototypes and policy issues. *The Information Society*, 10(2), 1994, 139-145.

[15] Ishii, H. "The Last Farewell": Traces of Physical Presence, *interactions*, 1998, 5 (4), 56-57.

[16] McCloud, S. *Understanding Comics*. Kitchen Sink Press, 1994.

[17] Norman, D., *Things That Make Us Smart*, Addison-Wesley, Reading, Mass., 1993.

[18] Roseman, M. and Greenberg, S. Building Real Time Groupware with GroupKit, A Groupware Toolkit. *Transactions on Computer-Human Interaction*, 1996, 3(1), 66-106.

[19] Roseman, M. and Greenberg, S. GroupKit: A groupware toolkit for building real-time conferencing applications. In *Proc ACM CSCW'92*, 43-50.

[20] Segal, L. Designing Team Workstations: The Choreography of Teamwork, in *Local Applications of the Ecological Approach to Human-Machine Systems*, P. Hancock, J. Flach, J. Caird and K. Vicente ed., Erlbaum, Hillsdale NJ, 1995, 392-415.

[21] Short, J., Williams, E., and Christie, B., Communication Modes and Task Performance, in *Readings in Groupware and Computer Supported Cooperative Work*, R. M. Baecker ed., Morgan Kaufmann, Mountain View CA, 1976, 169-176.

[22] Smith, R. What You See Is What I Think You See, *SIGCUE Outlook*, 21(3), 1992, 18-23.

[23] Tam, J., McCaffrey, L, Maurer, F. and Greenberg, S. *Change Awareness in Software Engineering Using Two Dimensional Graphical Design and Development Tools*. Report 2000-670-22, Department of Computer Science, University of Calgary.

[24] Tang, J. Findings from Observational Studies of Collaborative Work, *International Journal of Man-Machine Studies*, 34(2), 1991, 143-160.

[25] Tatar, D., G. Foster, and D. Bobrow. Design for Conversation: Lessons from Cognoter, *International Journal of Man-Machine Studies*, 34(2), 1991, 185-210.

[26] Weimer, D., and Ganapathy, S. K. A Synthetic Visual Environment with Hand Gesturing and Voice Input. *Proc ACM CHI'89*, 1989, 235-240.

Image-Based Hair Capture by Inverse Lighting

Stéphane Grabli, *i*MAGIS -GRAVIR
François X. Sillion, *i*MAGIS -GRAVIR
Stephen R. Marschner, Stanford University
Jerome E. Lengyel, Microsoft Research

Abstract

We introduce an image-based method for modeling a specific subject's hair. The principle of the approach is to study the variations of hair illumination under controlled illumination. The use of a stationary viewpoint and the assumption that the subject is still allows us to work with perfectly registered images: all pixels in an image sequence represent the same portion of the hair, and the particular illumination profile observed at each pixel can be used to infer the missing degree of directional information. This is accomplished by synthesizing reflection profiles using a hair reflectance model, for a number of candidate directions at each pixel, and choosing the orientation that provides the best profile match. Our results demonstrate the potential of this approach, by effectively reconstructing accurate hair strands that are well highlighted by a particular light source movement.

Key words: Hair Reflectance, Hair Modeling, Reflectance Analysis, Shape from Shading.

1 Introduction

More and more computer graphics applications, for instance video games or teleconferencing, require virtual models of people. For this reason, recently, a great amount of effort has gone toward digitizing people. However although hair plays a significant role in a person's appearance, the efficient acquisition of hair geometry remains an important unsolved problem.

Indeed, the usual digitization techniques fail in the face of the complex geometry of human hair, which is an intricate gathering of tens of thousands of thin elements, that are nearly invisible at human scale.

This article presents a method for retrieving the geometry of hair strands by analyzing images. We investigate how to extract as much information as possible from a series of images of a subject's hair, taken under a single known viewpoint and a moving light source. Each lit hair strand reflects light according to its orientation; the idea is then to infer this orientation using a hair reflectance model from the observed images. Although the discussed method is complete as itself, it does not pretend to solve the problem of hair acquisition. It must rather be viewed as an innovative approach to this arduous task, that still needs to be exploited. Furthermore, as we will see in section 6, it must be combined with other more classical approaches to become practical.

After a brief overview of previous work, we outline the approach in section 3. Then, in section 4, we detail a possible implementation. Lastly, in sections 5 and 6, we present our results and conclude with directions for future work.

2 Related work

Although a large body of work deals with modeling [9, 5, 20, 18, 21], animating [9, 5, 18] and rendering [15, 14, 19, 13] human hair, few articles treat the question of its acquisition. Likewise, the extensive research on "Shape from Shading" [3, 16] only addresses the case of relatively continuous surfaces, and doesn't offer techniques suited to hair.

With [17], Nakajima is the only one, to our knowledge, having considered hair modeling from pictures. His approach is purely geometric and consists of building a 3D hair volume from pictures showing the subject's hair from various viewpoints. Hair strands are then generated inside this volume, without any mechanism to ensure faithfulness in their directionality. This simple method presents several limitations: in particular, it seems unlikely to work well on complex hairstyles.

Our method requires a reliable model of reflectance for hair. Kajiya and Kay [11] first introduced a lighting model for hair, to render their "Teddy Bear". It includes two components: diffuse and specular. The diffuse component is derived from the Lambertian model applied to a very small cylinder, considering a hair strand to be lit on the whole half-cylinder facing the light source. Goldman, in [8], improved it by solving its lack of directionality. This improvement is particularly interesting in the case of backlighting simulation. Furthermore, in [1], Banks, also aiming at rendering fur, adds a self-shadowing term to the Kajiya-Kay model. The integration of a shadowing treatment in the model is interesting, but, as we will see in section 4, hardly applicable in our case.

3 Approach

Our approach consists of capturing the geometry of the hair strands geometry by studying images taken under controlled lighting conditions. We chose to observe the hair from a few viewpoints, and, for each viewpoint, to move the light source along a specific path, taking pictures for many light source positions along this path. The light source locations as well as the intrinsic camera parameters are known and controlled. The images produced are organized in sequences, each corresponding to a single camera position and a specific light source path. Figure 1a shows a sample of pictures from one sequence.

The main hypothesis concerns the chosen reflectance model and the hair material. Our system is a pipeline, taking sequences of hair pictures as input, and producing the geometry of the hair strands as output. We describe each step of this pipeline here in general terms, and provide implementation details in section 4.

3.1 Construction of a Sequence Mask

One of the main goals of this image analysis stage is to detect the hair strands that are best highlighted in the sequence, and to characterize their direction in image space. This step relies on the following assumption: for a given pixel position, all pictures in the sequence show projections of the same hair strand.

First, on each image of the sequence we create a mask indicating the pixels for which strands outlines are the most visible. Each pixel of each mask has an associate vector defined in the image plane. The vector's direction gives the direction of the hair strand projecting onto that pixel, and its magnitude is proportional to the contrast intensity of this hair strand in the picture. We then have, for a given pixel position, a collection of vectors, the size of which is at least equal to zero and at most equal to the number of images in the sequence. All these vectors are assumed to represent the projection of the same hair strand. Figure 1a shows a sample of these masks.

In order to determine the orientation of the hair strand, all the vectors of a single collection must agree. Therefore, in a second step, we identify the relevant vectors in each collection by an election mechanism. Then we extract from each chosen collection a single representative vector and store it into a new mask, which we call the sequence mask. This mask contains the pixels corresponding to the most visible hair strands in the whole sequence, as well as the associated 2D vectors. Figure 1b shows such a sequence mask. A possible implementation for this construction is given in section 4.2

3.2 Construction of a Pixel Profile

The resolution of the input images must be good enough to consider that we have a single hair strand projecting onto one pixel (in order to have only one direction related to a given pixel position). The system's basic idea is that, for a given pixel position, the color sequence observed across the picture sequence can be related to the reflectance map of the hair strand projecting onto that pixel position. The set of these three curves (for red, green and blue) forms what we will call the "measured pixel profile", illustrated in Figure 1c.

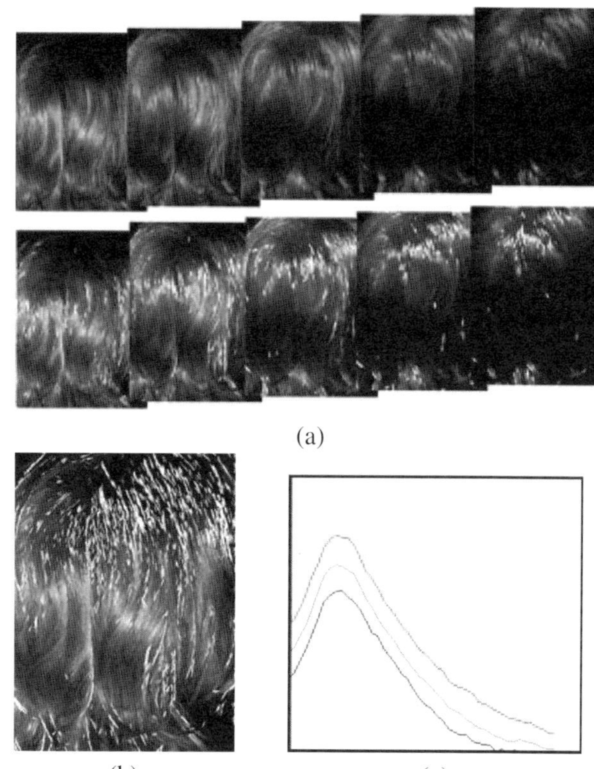

Figure 1: a) For each picture in the sequence, a mask is computed. b) The data set mask. It is displayed by drawing the vector associated to each pixel marked in the mask. c) A measured pixel profile. It shows the RGB components (in picture, R:highest, G:middle, B:lowest) of the colors taken on by on pixel through the sequence.

3.3 Computing 3D vectors in the sequence Mask

We now have a set of 2D vectors defined in image space. Each of these 2D vectors is the projection of a 3D vector indicating the orientation of the corresponding hair strand in space. From each 2D vector $\vec{t}$ we want to infer the corresponding 3D vector $\vec{T}$. We use, for that, the geometric information given by the 2D vector and the camera parameters as well as the observed reflectance. This step can be divided into three parts:

Generation of 3D candidate vectors

Let us consider a 2D vector $\vec{t}$. Basic geometric considerations show that the corresponding 3D vector $\vec{T}$ lies in the plane containing $\vec{t}$ and the camera's optical center. This plane's equation can thus be derived from the camera parameters. The idea is then to generate a dense set of 3D candidate vectors lying in that plane, and finding the one closest to the real hair strand. Figure 2 illustrates this process.

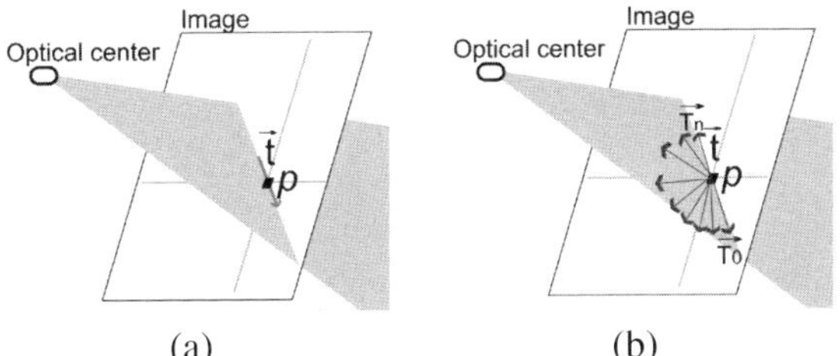

Figure 2: a) $\vec{T}(p)$ necessarily lies in the plane containing the optical center of the camera and $\vec{t}(p)$ b) A collection of 3D vectors $(\vec{T}_k(p))_k$ is generated in that plane.

Synthesis of Pixel Profiles

Using a hair reflectance model, we compute, for each 3D candidate vector, a reflectance map according to the lighting and observing conditions of the sequence. These maps are stored as pixel profiles, called "synthesized pixel profiles". For each pixel of the mask, we then have a set of 3D candidate vectors, and for each of these 3D vectors, a synthesized pixel profile. Section 4.3 provides more details about the chosen illumination model, and the synthesis of pixel profiles.

Election of a 3D candidate vector

Let us again consider a pixel of the mask. The real reflectance of the hair projecting onto that pixel is represented in the corresponding measured pixel profile. We now search among the synthesized pixel profiles, for the one that looks most like the measured one; the associated 3D vector will provide the hair strand orientation. The analysis of the correlation between pixel profiles curves is detailed in section 4.3 This stage finally extracts a mask of 3D vectors from the sequence mask of 2D vectors.

3.4 Hair Strands

By chaining the resulting 3D vectors, we finally build hair strands.

4 Implementation

4.1 Data Sequence Acquisition

Our approach requires viewpoints and light positions under which the subject is observed and lit, to be known and controlled. Furthermore, we need to keep the subject still for the duration of each sequence acquisition. Concerning the subject's immobility, we decided to work with a synthetic wig[1], so that we could focus on the image processing itself. To control the light source and camera positions, we used the Stanford Spherical Gantry [4] as our acquisition apparatus. It consists of two arms which carry a light source and a camera, and a turntable on which the subject rests. Both arms and the turntable move under computer control, allowing the subject to be viewed and illuminated under practically any configuration.

The camera we used was a 3CCD video camera, and to eliminate noise in the images, we combined images taken using several different exposure times at each position [6].

[1]This allows a proof of concept, but naturally in the long term we will have to work with human subjects.

4.2 Sequence Mask building

Image analysis

The main visible phenomena concerning hair are due to lighting, such as specular reflections or shadowing. We chose to use the Sobel contrast detector [10] to characterize the most visible hair strands in each picture. This gradient-type filter detects contrasts in a particular direction. The result's magnitude is proportional to the contrast. In our case, we apply the filter horizontally and vertically in order to obtain a 2D vector in the image plane. The resulting vector has the direction of maximum contrast, and is therefore perpendicular to the curve delimiting the hair strand projecting there.

We finally get a vector per pixel, with direction perpendicular to the outline and magnitude proportional to the contrast. Pixels showing an insufficient contrast are of low magnitude, and are associated with uncertain directions. Therefore, we set a threshold in order to keep only vectors with high enough magnitude. By rotating all the remaining vectors by 90 degrees, we produce, for each image, a vector field giving the hair strand's directions for high contrast pixels. This step results in a sequence of masks of pixel positions, with a 2D vector associated with each position (see figure 1b). Afterwards, let N refer to the number of images contained in a sequence and p to the (x, y) coordinates of a point in image space. p will be called "pixel" or "position". The mask sequence produced previously is denoted $(L_i(p))_{i\in\{0,\dots,N\}}$. $L_i(p) = 1$ means that the pixel p of image i succeeded the magnitude test, we then say that p is "marked" in L_i. Lastly, the collection of 2D vectors associated with a position p is referred to as $(\vec{t}_i(p))_{i\in\{0,\dots,N\}}$. We consider that $L_i(p) = 0 \Rightarrow \vec{t}_i(p) = \vec{0}$.

Election of relevant vectors

As mentioned before, each collection $(\vec{t}_i(p))_i$ represents the projection of a single hair vector. Although in theory all the vectors of a same collection should be similar, in reality some noise might appear, making difficult the task of representing a collection by a single vector. Our implementation uses two tests to check each collection's validity. Let us consider the collection $(\vec{t}_i(p))_i$ associated with the pixel position p.

- Collection size We consider that a collection must contain a sufficient number of samples in order to avoid noise and to be relevant. Therefore, we count the number $\mathcal{N}_p$ of masks L_i for which $L_i(p) = 1$ and set up a threshold indicating the minimum number of pictures, $\mathcal{N}_{min}$, in which a pixel p must be marked in order to be selected. Thus, p passes the test if and only if $\mathcal{N}_p = card\{L_i(p), \forall i \in \{0, .., N\} / L_i(p) = 1\} \geq \mathcal{N}_{min}$ This test helps eliminate noise as well as pixels that are shadowed for too many pictures of the sequence, making their pixel profile unusable.

- Homogeneity in the vector directions Each collection is supposed to clearly indicate a single vector. For that reason, this test concerns the direction of the vectors $(\vec{t}_i(p))_i$ associated with a pixel position p. We calculate the angle variance $v_\theta(p)$ of the $\vec{t}_i(p)$ vectors through the whole sequence, and we set a threshold $v_{\theta_{max}}$, to give the maximum variance. So, p passes the test if and only if $v_\theta(p) \leq v_{\theta_{max}}$. For each selected pixel p a single vector $\vec{t}(p)$ is obtained for the entire sequence by summing and then normalizing the vectors of the corresponding collection.

In this way we obtain the sequence mask as well as its associated vectors field $(\vec{t}(p))_p$(see figure 1b).

4.3 Retrieving 3D vectors

Generation of 3D candidate vectors

We showed in section 3.3 how a set of 3D candidate vectors was generated for each pixel marked in the sequence mask. Let $(\vec{T}_k(p))_k$ be the 3D candidate vectors associated to each pixel p of the mask.

Synthesis of Pixel Profiles

The synthesis of reflectance maps using the candidate vectors $\vec{T}_k(p)$, for a pixel p, requires a reliable hair reflectance model. We chose the one introduced by Kajiya and Kay in [11], improved by including the backlighting treatment presented by Goldman in [8]. Letting $\vec{T}$ be the hair tangent unit vector, $\vec{L}$ the unit vector pointing from the hair position P to the light position and $\vec{E}$ the unit vector pointing to the eye from this same position, this hair reflectance model can be written as:

$$\Psi_{hair} = f_{dir} \times (\textit{diffuse} + \textit{specular})$$

where f_{dir} is the directionality term introduced by [8], characterizing the reflection and the transmission properties, where *diffuse* is the model diffuse component,

$$\textit{diffuse}(P) = K_d \times sin(\vec{T}, \vec{L})$$

K_d being the diffuse reflection coefficient and where *specular* is the model specular component,

$$\textit{specular}(P) = K_s \times cos^\alpha(\vec{E}, \vec{E'})$$

K_s being the specular reflection coefficient, E' the vector of the reflection cone the nearest to E, and α the Phong coefficient. Consider again a pixel p, supposing that we wish to compute the reflectance map of the candidate vector $\vec{T}_k(P)$. $\vec{E}$ is the unit vector lying on the ray joining p to the optical center. In order to compute the vector $\vec{L}$, we need to know the hair position P in space. This position necessarily lies on the line joining the optical center to the pixel. If the hair volume was precisely known, we could determine the exact hair position by computing the intersection of this voulme with the line previously defined. For the moment, as we do not have a model of the hair volume, we use as first approximation a semi-ellipsoid, to simulate long hair. This choice does not penalize our result insofar as the distance between P and the light source is much greater than the distance between the real P's position and the approximated one and as thus, the computed $\vec{L}$ is close to the real one. The vector $\vec{L}$ is then set, using the known and light position.

K_d and K_s remain to be determined. They depend on the hair material, whose definition constitutes our second hypothesis. The model used to define a material distinguishes its diffuse, specular and ambient properties. Each of them corresponds to a color, which can be extracted from pictures using image segmentation[2][7]. K_d and K_s are set using the diffuse and specular color thus obtained.

We can then calculate the reflectance profile for each 3D vector, under the experiment's lighting and viewing conditions. We finally have, for each pixel p of the mask, a synthesized pixel profile $f^{(k)}_{t_p}(x)$ for each candidate vector $\vec{T}_k(p)$, $k \in \{0, ..., m\}$. Figure 3 shows a sample of synthesized pixel profiles. It is important to notice that these profiles only consider the interactions between a hair strand and the light source. The interactions with neighboring hairs such as indirect reflections or shadowing, are not taken into account.

Electing a 3D vector by studying correlation

The election of a vector among the candidate vectors is done by studying the correlation between the measured pixel profile and each of the synthesized pixel profiles.

[2] More precisely, using the k-mean algorithm with $k = 3$, we extract three colors from the images. One color stands for a shadowed hair, the second one represents the hair diffuse color and the last one corresponds to the hair specular color.

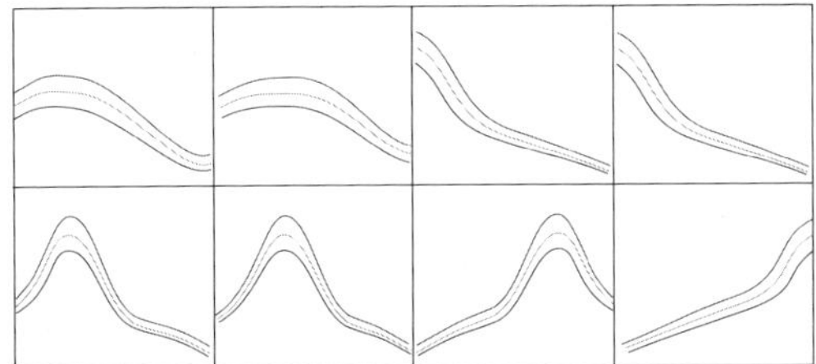

Figure 3: A sample of synthesized pixel profiles (Intensity versus light source position) for different candidate vectors.

Each pixel profile is composed of three curves (R, G and B), and we study the correlation component by component. Because the technique is the same for each of them, we will describe our method for a single component. Let $f_m(x)$ and $f_t(x)$ be the measured and synthesized pixel profiles. In the previous section, we stressed out that the synthesized curves did not include any interaction with the hair's environment. Although inter-reflection is important in the case of hair, the phenomenon which most perturbs our data is the shadowing due to the hair volume itself. Goldman in [8] and Banks in [1] include this phenomenon in their model by specifying a term $\vec{N}.\vec{L}$, $\vec{N}$ being the vector normal to the underlying surface at the hair position, and $\vec{L}$ the vector pointing to the light from this same position. This term requires a precise knowledge of the hair surface. Although this knowledge can be available in the case of hair synthesis, this can hardly be assumed in the analysis case. We first focus on unshadowed regions, leaving the issue of shadowed areas for future work. We identify in the pictures a color s_o, corresponding to hair lying in the shadow. s_o is called the "shadow threshold" and represents an intensity below which a pixel is considered to be in shadow and is not processed. This thresholding is equivalent to setting up shadow maps in the pictures. When we process a measured pixel profile, curve points lying below the threshold are ignored. Valid abscissas form valid intervals I_v:

$$I_v = \{x \in [0, N] / f_{m_p}(x) \geq s_o\}$$

The correlation computation between a measured pixel profile and a synthesized one only involves these valid intervals.

Setting up an Energy function for Correlation study

We now have to determine the most similar synthesized curve, on the valid interval. We do not expect candidate curves to match exactly the measured one, but to be similar in terms of shape. For example, a difference in amplitude is not a valid criterion to dismiss a candidate curve. Classic norms such as L_2 norm would not be adapted to this correlation study insofar as it is not invariant to an amplitude difference. Thus, we need to define a measure suited to the evaluation of curves shape likeness. We use two criteria, dealing with positions of extrema and shape of the curves (first order derivatives). We introduce a distance energy E_{dist}, made of two terms $E_{extrema}$ and E_{shape}, to quantify the similarity according to these criteria.

$E_{extrema}$: **distance energy measured at maxima.** The curves are such that the number of maxima is, except in particular cases, equal to zero or one[3]. Our energy expression applies to two curves, each of them having one maximum. Let x_{max1} and x_{max2} be these two maxima abscissa. We define:

$$E_{extrema} = K_e \times (|x_{max1} - x_{max2}|)^r$$

where K_e is a constant which includes parameters such as the interval's size and insures $E_{extrema} \in [0, 1]$, and r is the polynomial degree. $E_{extrema}$ is defined as a polynomial rather than as a linear curve so as to penalize very distant maxima more than closer ones. $r = 3$ proved to work well in our experiments.

E_{shape}: **distance energy measured on the curve's shape.** E_{shape} is supposed to measure the difference between the shapes of the two curves. Two curves having the same shape show a constant gap between them. We thus chose to first center each curve by substracting its mean value, then to calculate the mean value $\overline{d}$ of the distance between these two centered curves. Let us consider the two curves f_m and f_t defined on the valid interval $[x_{min}, x_{max}]$. $\overline{f}_m$ and $\overline{f}_t$ are the mean values calculated on this interval. Let $\tilde{f}_m(x) = f_m(x) - \overline{f}_m$ and $\tilde{f}_t(x) = f_t(x) - \overline{f}_t$ be the centered curves. We define $d(x) = |\tilde{f}_m(x) - \tilde{f}_t(x)|$, the distance between $\tilde{f}_m$ and $\tilde{f}_t$. E_{shape} is defined as the L_1 norm of $d(x)$:

$$E_{shape} = \overline{d} = \frac{1}{(x_{max} - x_{min})} \times \int_{x=x_{min}}^{x_{max}} d(x)dx$$

Electing and measuring trust

We now select, for each pixel p, the profile with the lowest energy and elect the associated candidate vector. In other words, if we let $f_{dist_p}(k)$ be the value of $(E_{dist}^{(k)}(p))_k$ as a function of k, we choose, for a pixel p, the absolute minimum of $f_{dist_p}(k)$, if it exists. Unfortunately, many cases are problematic. They can be grouped into two families:

1. The cases where determining an absolute minimum for f_{dist} is impossible or ambiguous:

[3] A real continuous function on a compact set admits at least one maximum, but we exclude the case where the maximum is realized on one of the interval's limits, making possible the case for which there is no maximum.

   (a) If there is more than one local minimum for f_{dist}, and if the two lowest minima values are too close, choosing one of them is ambiguous.

   (b) When f_{dist}'s variation in amplitude is too low, choosing a minimum is not necessarily significant.

2. The cases where measured distance energies are not significant, because of a bad quality of the measured pixel profile:

   (a) If the amplitude of a measured pixel profile is too low, it has a higher noise sensitivity resulting in bad quality data.

   (b) If the valid interval's size is too small, the amount of data used to compare the two profiles is insufficient to produce reliable results.

These different cases are illustrated in figure 4.

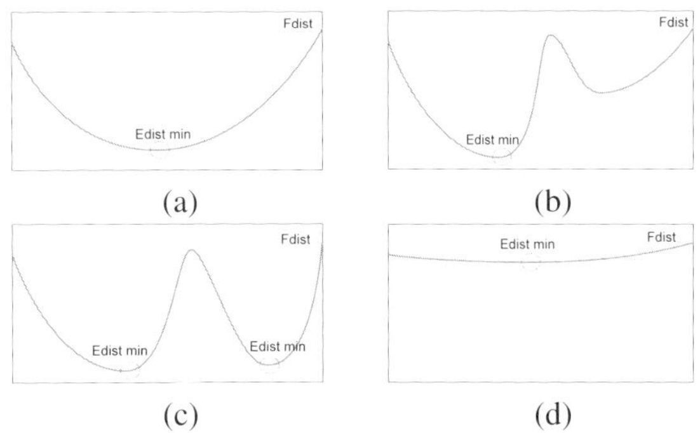

(a) (b) (c) (d)

Figure 4: (a) and (b): two curves examples for f_{dist} where the determination of a minimum is not ambiguous. (b) and (c): two cases where this determination is ambiguous or not significant.

It is essential to identify these cases and to have a measure of the certainty with which a candidate vector has been elected. Therefore, we introduce a trust coefficient c_{trust} such that $c_{trust} \in [0, 1]$ and $c_{trust} = 0$ in case 1a. In the other cases, its value is proportional to the area of the part of the measured curve located above the shadow threshold and to f_{dist}'s variation in amplitude. Let n_{minima} be the number of minima found for f_{dist}, $E_{dist}^{(min)}$ be f_{dist}'s minimum and $E_{dist}^{(max)}$ its maximum and x_{max} and x_{min} be the upper and lower limits of the valid interval. Then c_{trust} equals 0 if $n_{minima} \neq 1$, and

$$\frac{\lambda}{2} \times \int_{x_{min}}^{x_{max}} (f_m(x) - s)dx + (E_{dist}^{(max)} - E_{dist}^{(min)})$$

if $n_{minima} = 1$. λ is a multiplicative term such that the valid area contribution of f_m is equal to one when this one equals half of $(x_{max} - x_{min}) \times (f_m^{(max)} - f_m^{(min)})$. In practice, we ensure that this contribution never exceeds 1. Thus, for each mask pixel p, we elect a 3D candidate vector $\vec{T}(p)$, and we attribute to it a trust coefficient $c_{trust}(p)$, giving the certainty with which it has been chosen. Figure 5a shows an example of 3D vector sequence.

4.4 Thresholding the 3D vector mask

Since the trust $c_{trust}(p)$ tells how certain each 3D vector election was, it is easy to refine a mask by selecting only vectors having a high enough trust coefficient:

$$L_{3D} = \{p \in \{0, ..., w \times h\} / L_{2D}(p) = 1, c_{trust}(p) \geq c_{trust}^{(min)}\}$$

c_{trust}^{min} being the threshold parameter, and w and h the width and height of the images. With $c_{trust}^{min} = 0.5$, we obtain masks of good quality. Figure 5 shows a 3D vector mask before and after thresholding.

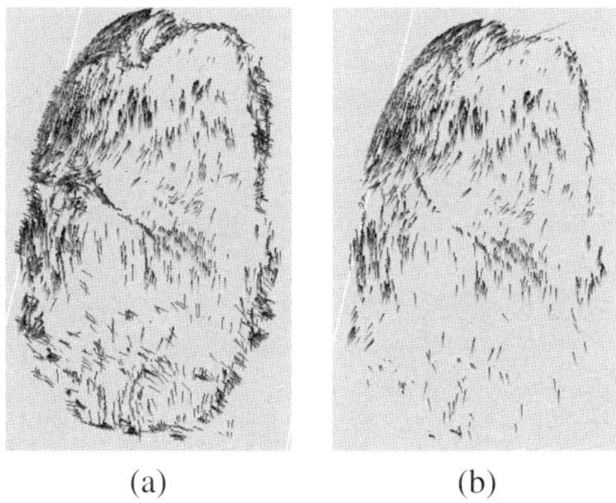

(a) (b)

Figure 5: a) 3D vector mask before thresholding. Colors assigned to vectors indicate their trust coefficient (red standing for low and green for high). b) 3D vector mask after thresholding.

4.5 Building 3D strands

We chose to build the final 3D hair strands in two steps. First, we build chains of pixels in image space, using the 2D vector field of the sequence mask and using the "snakes" technique [12, 2]. Each node of each pixel chain is related to a 2D vector, itself associated to a 3D vector (see section 3.3). We finally get the third dimension, in the building process, by using the information given by 3D vectors of each node.

5 Results

Our system allows the extraction of hair strand geometry from picture sequences. The number of pictures in a sequence varies between 48 and 81, according to the light path. Image resolution is 486x720. The number of pixels left in the sequence mask depends both on the chosen viewpoint and light path. Indeed, the better the viewpoint and light path, the greater the number of well contrasted hair strands on pictures. For example, a hair strand which is parallel, in image space, to the light path produces good-quality data whereas pixel profiles obtained for hair strands perpendicular to the light path can rarely be exploited.

Figure 6a shows hair strands produced with one sequence, made of 81 images, with a vertical light path. This configuration produces reliable pixel profiles since a high number of hair strands are vertical, and therefore, parallel to the light path. The number of pixels left in the mask of that sequence is about 6,300 pixels before thresholding, and about 3,900 after thresholding. Computing of hair strands for a sequence takes time $O(n \times k \times N)$, where n is the number of pixels marked in the sequence mask, k is the number of 3D candidate vectors per pixel of the mask, and N is the number of pictures in a sequence. Computing of this 2D sequence mask took approximately 9 minutes on a Pentium III 800 MHz with 256 Mb of RAM. The extraction of a 3D mask from this 2D mask lasts about 1 hour.
One can notice that the rebuilt hair strands distribution is quite sparse with one sequence; indeed, one couple viewpoint/light path exploits only part of the hair. However, whatever the direction of a hair strand may be, there is a light source path exploiting it. Thus, by combining the hair strands built from complementary sequences, we expect to reconstruct most of the hair. This combination is straightforward since our method produces hair strands defined in world coordinates. The rebuilt strands that are common to two or more sequences proved to match properly in 3D.

Figures 6b and 6c show hair strands obtained by combining five sequences. We can validate our reconstruction's accuracy using a set of pictures showing the wig from various viewpoints, which ones are different from the viewpoints used for the hair strands building process. Thus, in figure 6, under each picture of rebuilt hair strands is a picture showing the wig from the same viewpoint, proving that the main hair strands directions are correctly recovered. These results are partial inasmuch as other data sequences, with different light source paths, are needed in order to build hair strands on the whole head.

Furthermore, this work serves to demonstrate the accuracy of the reflectance model used for hair. Indeed, the synthesized pixel profiles which were elected match precisely the measured ones and produced, in most of the cases, correct 3D vectors.

6 Summary and future work

We have shown that the method of analyzing reflectance to retrieve shape is a particularly interesting approach to the problem of modeling a specific subject's hair. This work suggests a number of areas for future research, such as:

Developing a complementary geometric method As said previously, our method is rather a contribution to the problem of hair acquisition than its complete solution, and therefore need to be used in addition to other approachs. In particular, our technique shows some limitation in the global positioning of hair strands in space. An ideal solution to the problem of 3D hair model acquisition could result from the joining of a purely geometric method, such as the one presented in [17], together with a reflectance analysis approach like ours. Indeed, a preliminary reconstruction of the hair volume would lead to a significant increase in the accuracy of our results.

References

[1] David C. Banks. Illumination in diverse codimensions. Computer Graphics Proceedings, Annual Conference Series, pages 327–334. ACM SIGGRAPH, ACM Press, July 1994.

[2] A. Blake and M. Isard. *Active Contours*. Springer-Verlag 1998, 1998.

[3] M. J. Brooks and B. K. P. Horn. Shape and source from shading. In B. K. P. Horn and M. J. Brooks, editors, *Shape from Shading*, pages 53–68. MIT Press, Cambridge, MA, 1989.

[4] Custom Scanner Spherical Gantry CyberWare. http://www.cyberware.com/products/sphereinfo.html.

[5] A. Daldegan, N. M. Thalmann, T. Kurihara, and D. Thalmann. An integrated system for modeling, animating and rendering hair. *Computer Graphics Forum*, 12(3):C211–C221, 1993.

[6] Paul E. Debevec and Jitendra Malik. Recovering high dynamic range radiance maps from photographs. *Computer Graphics*, 31(Annual Conference Series):369–378, 1997.

[7] Keinosuke Fukunaga. *Introduction to Statistical Pattern Recognition, Second Edition*. Academic Press, Boston, MA, 1990.

[8] Dan B. Goldman. Fake fur rendering. In Turner Whitted, editor, *SIGGRAPH 97 Conference Proceedings*, Annual Conference Series, pages 127–134. ACM SIGGRAPH, Addison Wesley, August 1997.

[9] Ken ichi Anjyo, Yoshiaki Usami, and Tsuneya Kurihara. A simple method for extracting the natural beauty of hair. *Computer Graphics*, 26(2):111–120, July 1992.

[10] B. Jahne. *Digital image processing*. Springer-Verlag New York, Incorporated, 1991.

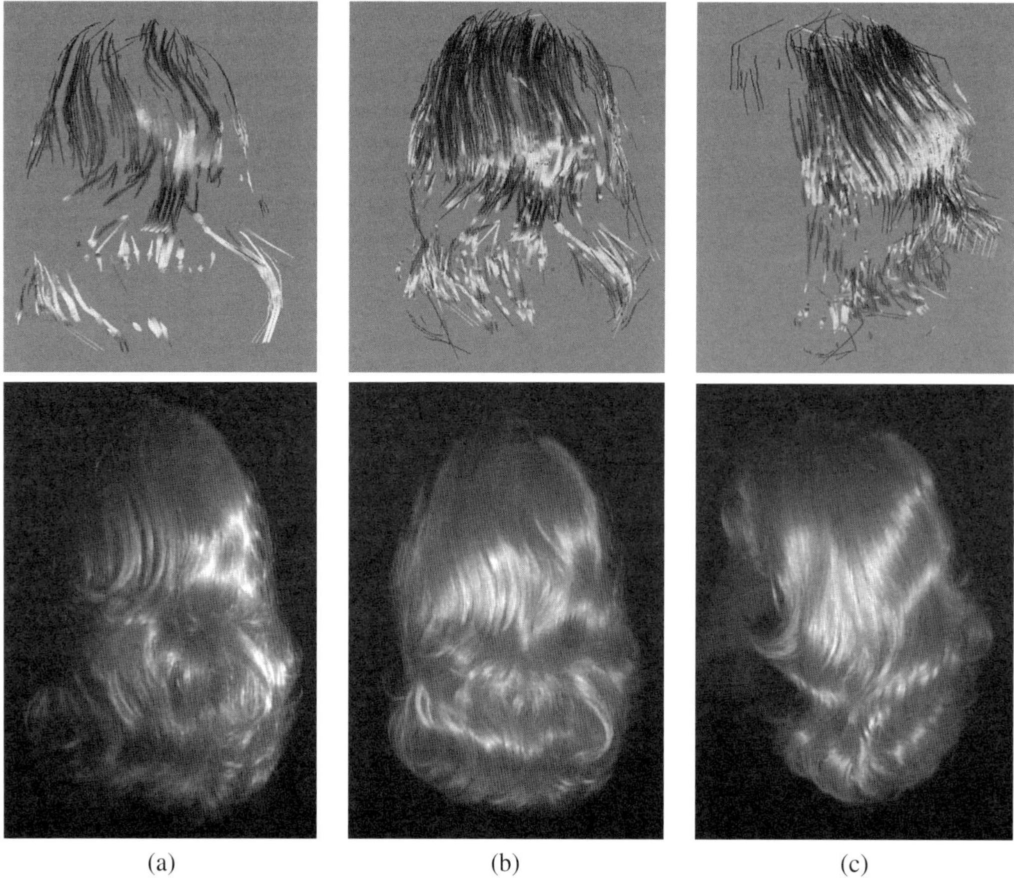

(a) (b) (c)

Figure 6: a) Up: hair strands rebuilt with a single picture sequence and rendered using broad strands for visualization convenience. Down: picture of the sequence (same viewpoint). b) and c) Up: hair strands rebuilt with five sequences, observed from two different viewpoints and rendered using broad strands for visualization convenience. Down: pictures showing the wig from the same respective viewpoints.

[11] James T. Kajiya and Timothy L. Kay. Rendering fur with three dimensional textures. In Jeffrey Lane, editor, *Computer Graphics (SIGGRAPH '89 Proceedings)*, volume 23, pages 271–280, July 1989.

[12] M. Kass, A. Witkin, and D. Terzopoulos. Snakes: Active contour models. In *Proc. of IEEE Conference on Computer Vision*, pages 259–268, 8-11 1987.

[13] W. Kong and M. Nakajima. Hair rendering by jittering and pseudo shadow. In *Proceedings of the Conference on Computer Graphics International (CGI-00)*, pages 287–294, Los Alamitos, CA, June 19–24 2000. IEEE.

[14] A. M. LeBlanc, R. Turner, and D. Thalmann. Rendering hair using pixel blending and shadow buffers. *The Journal of Visualization and Computer Animation*, 2(3):92–97, July–September 1991.

[15] Jerome Edward Lengyel. Real-time fur over arbitrary surfaces. In *ACM 2001 Symposium on Interactive 3D Graphics*, 2000.

[16] S. Magda, D. Kriegman, T. Zickler, and P. Belhumeur. Beyond lambert: Reconstructing surfaces with arbitrary brdfs. In *ICCV01*, pages II: 391–398, 2001.

[17] Masayuki Nakajima, Kong Wai Ming, and Hiroki Takashi. Generation of 3d hair model from multiple pictures. In *IEEE Computer Graphics & Applications (12) 1999 Multimedia Modeling'97*, 1999.

[18] R. E. Rosenblum, W. E. Carlson, and E. Tripp, III. Simulating the structure and dynamics of human hair: modelling, rendering and animation. *The Journal of Visualization and Computer Animation*, 2(4):141–148, October–December 1991.

[19] Nadia M. Thalmann, Stephane Carion, Martin Courchesne, Pascal Volino, and Yin Wu. Virtual clothes, hair and skin for beautiful top models. In *Computer Graphics International 1996*, 1996.

[20] Allen Van Gelder and Jane Wilhelms. An interactive fur modeling technique. In Wayne A. Davis, Marilyn Mantei, and R. Victor Klassen, editors, *Graphics Interface '97*, pages 181–188. Canadian Human-Computer Communications Society, May 1997.

[21] Watanabe Y. and Suenaga Y. Drawing human hair using wisp model. In *Computer Graphics International, 1989*, 1989.

The Simulation of Paint Cracking and Peeling

Eric Paquette
Dép. I.R.O., Université de Montréal
REVES/INRIA Sophia Antipolis and *i*MAGIS-GRAVIR/IMAG-INRIA Rhône-Alpes
Pierre Poulin
Dép. I.R.O., Université de Montréal
George Drettakis
REVES/INRIA Sophia Antipolis

Abstract

Weathering over long periods of time results in cracking and peeling of layers such as paint. To include these effects in computer graphics images it is necessary to simulate crack propagation, loss of adhesion, and the curling effect of paint peeling. We present a new approach which computes such a simulation on surfaces. Our simulation is inspired by the underlying physical properties. We use paint strength and tensile stress to determine where cracks appear on the surface. Cracks are then propagated through a 2D grid overlaid on the original surface, and we consider elasticity to compute the reduction of paint stress around the cracks. Simulation of the adhesion between the paint and the underlying material finally determines how the paint layer curls as it peels from the surface. The result of this simulation is rendered by generating explicit geometry to represent the peeling curls. We provide user control of the surface properties influencing the propagation of cracks. Results of our simulation and rendering method show that our approach produces convincing images of cracks and peels.

Key words: Deteriorations, surface imperfections, paint, cracks, multi-layer surfaces, natural phenomena.

1 Introduction

Cracks and peels in paint are a common everyday phenomenon. For example, after a few years of exposure to the elements, cracks appear on painted wooden doors, often resulting in peeling of the paint layer away from the underlying wood. These visual effects can be very significant (see for example the left images of Figures 8, 9, and 10), and we believe that it is important to include them in computer generated images. As with all aging and weathering effects, simulating and rendering such phenomena results in images which have a much higher degree of realism. In typical synthetic environments, used for example in films or video games, many painted objects exist as well as objects which are made from layered surfaces, and thus it is important that they include the simulation of cracking and peeling.

Previous approaches in computer graphics have either only simulated cracks and their propagation without treating multi-layer phenomena and peeling [7, 8], or presented tools to control the location of detached paint areas without treating the creation and propagation of cracks [18]. Consequently, no complete method currently exists, which allows a user to simply request the generation of cracks and peels on a surface.

Our approach is inspired by the underlying physical phenomena, but uses a simplified model. It allows a fast and simple simulation process, provides good control to obtain the desired effects, and gives convincing results.

Our current implementation operates on a planar surface, and assumes that the outer paint layer is infinitesimally thin. We generate cracks on the surface, based on the simulation of tensile stress in the paint layer. Cracks are created and propagated on the surface using a 2D grid to access local surface properties. These properties can be represented in different ways, either procedurally, as a constant, or a texture. For example, if we wish to reproduce a specific type of crack pattern, textures can be used to define surface properties. The cracks are then guided by texture value and gradient. Simple intersection of cracks is handled, and fine details of cracks are maintained separately, thus increasing simulation speed. The simplicity of our crack propagation algorithm allows us to compute a simulation efficiently, giving the user fine control and the ability to easily experiment to obtain the desired result.

In addition to crack propagation, we generate and render the curling effect of peeling on our two-layer representation based on the simulation of adhesion between these layers. To our knowledge this is the first treatment of adhesion and curling for peeling in computer graphics. This effect adds important and convincing visual detail. Curling is computed at an appropriate level of detail of the crack path as paint loses its adhesion with the underlying surface. As a result, peeling can occur in different directions as simulation proceeds, which corresponds to observed physical reality. It is important to note that we do not modify the underlying geometry to add this curling effect, but simply superimpose additional geometry on the underlying object.

The entire approach, crack propagation and peeling, is relatively simple to use with standard rendering packages.

2 Previous Work

Simulating "imperfections" or "weathering" is a relatively young area in computer graphics. To our knowledge, the first such approach was that of Becket and Badler in 1990 [2] which described a general system treating scratches, stains, splotches, and rust.

Dorsey and colleagues have developed a series of methods treating a number of different phenomena, such as patinas, weathering due to flow of liquids, and weathering of stone (a survey is presented in [5]). These models are typically based on involved physical simulations, with relatively expensive computation times and the need to determine physical parameters. Such models are indispensable for correct and accurate simulation of weathering phenomena, and have produced images of striking realism and beauty. Nonetheless, their usage can be cumbersome for some applications, and more simplistic, albeit less accurate, approaches can also be useful. Approximate models can often be more appropriate, for the computer graphics industry [17] for example.

In this paper we treat generation and propagation of cracks on a two-layer model. Dorsey and Hanrahan [4] developed a model based on multiple layers to simulate metallic patinas, in the context of texture generation tools. Sophisticated shading models were used, resulting in great realism. Merillou *et al.* [10] presented a two-layer model to simulate scratches on a surface. Their approach does not add geometry to represent the scratches, but simply defines an appropriate anisotropic reflectance function to give the correct visual impression of scratches.

Another aspect of our work deals with the formation and propagation of cracks which can then peel. Terzopoulos and Fleischer [16] developed an early physically-based model of fracture, as part of the treatment of inelastic behavior in general. O'Brien and Hodgins [12] developed a model for fracture on an adaptively subdivided tetrahedral mesh. A more complete physically-based simulation is used, and cracks are propagated in 3D. This model concentrates on the dynamics and the motion of fracture, yielding impressive visual results, but at a non-negligible computational cost.

Hirota *et al.* [8] simulated cracks on a surface caused by surface contraction. Their approach is based on physics to a certain extent, and is modeled as a network of springs. Cracks appear as springs break, and thus their paths are constrained by the spring network. The nodes are squares or hexagons, resulting in different types of crack shapes. The visual quality of the cracks is directly affected by aliasing across the network cells. Neff and Fiume [11] simulated the generation of cracks due to a blast wave. A seed crack is used and cracks are propagated, releasing energy as they proceed. This enables the creation of new crack branches. A simple random variation scheme on the branching direction generates visually convincing results.

For our crack propagation method, we have been inspired by the ideas presented in Gobron and Chiba [7]. Their method however deals only with cracks and does not simulate adhesion or peeling. As with our approach, cracks are propagated across a 2D grid, using a relaxation method. Certain aspects however of their simulation are more simplistic, as their approach does not treat peeling (adhesion, curling, etc.). Since between 100,000 to a million cells are required for the simulation of their cracks, computation time is quite expensive, ranging from 20 minutes to several hours.

Finally, in the general system presented by Wong *et al.* [18], peeling is treated along with rust and dust. This approach simply modifies the surface color based on a threshold function for the choice of the appropriate layer color, and thus the geometric effect of cracks, loss of adhesion, and surface curling are not simulated. No simulation of crack creation and propagation is performed, and the user must manually position "peeling light sources".

3 Physical Basis

Paint and other thin layers are applied on many surfaces for both decorative and protective purposes. The condition of the paint layer over years of exposure depends on many factors including the paint itself (*e.g.*, latex or oil), the surface on which it is applied (*e.g.*, material such as wood or metal, roughness, penetration [9]), as well as environmental factors (*e.g.*, UV light, oxygen, pollutants). All these factors affect paint differently during its lifespan [6]. Four properties are of major importance to paint cracking and peeling: stress, strength, elasticity, and adhesion to the base surface.

One factor is inherent to every kind of paint: as paint dries, it shrinks, producing *stress* in the paint layer [13]. In this context, thinner paint layers are preferable to thicker ones since they induce less stress. A dirty or wet base surface and insufficient stirring of the paint also results in weaker paint layers [3]. The method of application (*e.g.*, brush, spray, roller) also affects the layer quality [3]. Even after paint has dried, its properties are not fixed as it will slowly become weaker because of interaction with the elements of its environment. The principal cause of damage is moisture [15], but many other environmental factors [1, 3] such as water, UV light, temperature variations (contraction or dilation of the base surface), pollutants, abrasion, and impacts all weaken the paint layer.

When paint is weakened, the physical properties of the layer change. Paint is to some extent *elastic*, that is it can be stretched thus redistributing surface stress. As years pass, the elasticity of paint is likely to decrease. Long term exposure to pollutants for example can greatly decrease elasticity. The paint also has a specific *strength*, which determines the greatest stress it can handle before it starts to break. As is the case for elasticity, exposure to harsh elements or UV light can reduce the strength of the paint, making it prone to develop cracks and peels. When a crack forms, it is readily visible since it enables the paint on either side to shrink back to a state with less stress. This release of tensile stress occurs perpendicularly to the crack [7]. *Adhesion* is the most important property of paint. We define it as the ability of paint to attach itself to the underlying surface. Moisture, base surface contraction, or rust can all greatly reduce the adhesion of paint. When the paint shrinks as cracks release tensile stress, a shearing force is introduced at the interface between the paint and the base surface, pulling the paint away from its initial position. As paint loses adhesion with the base surface, it can either peel by slowly curling away [6, 3], or flake [3] and eventually fall off the base surface.

As we can see, peeling is a complex phenomenon that spans over years. It is not fully understood, since most of the (physical) research focuses on preventing its occurrence [6]. Moreover, most of its parameters are difficult to measure. In this paper, we develop a model inspired by, rather than strictly simulating, the physics of the phenomenon. Our goal is ease of control, allowing the user to obtain effects that are visually appealing. In our simulation process, the paint strength and stress determine where cracks appear on the surface. Reduction of stress around the cracks is computed by considering the elasticity. Finally, curling of the paint layer as it peels from the surface is computed with the adhesion. In the next two sections, we detail the structures and algorithms of our empirical peeling model.

4 Simulation

4.1 Overview

Our simulation model is simple and summarized in Figure 1. A surface is defined by two layers that we will refer to as *base layer* and *paint layer*.[1] When tensile stress (Figure 1-i) is too high compared to the paint strength,

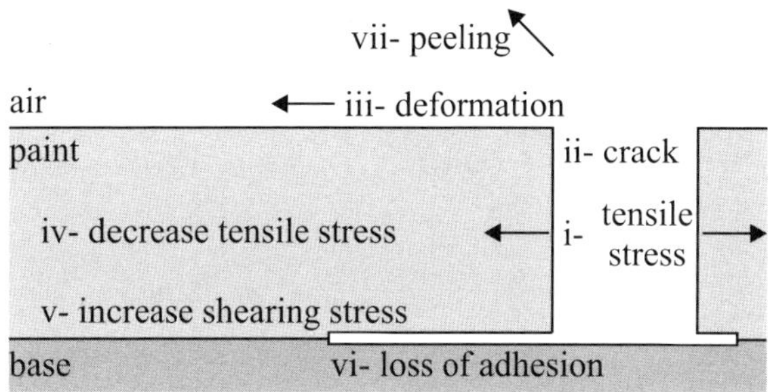

Figure 1: Peeling model.

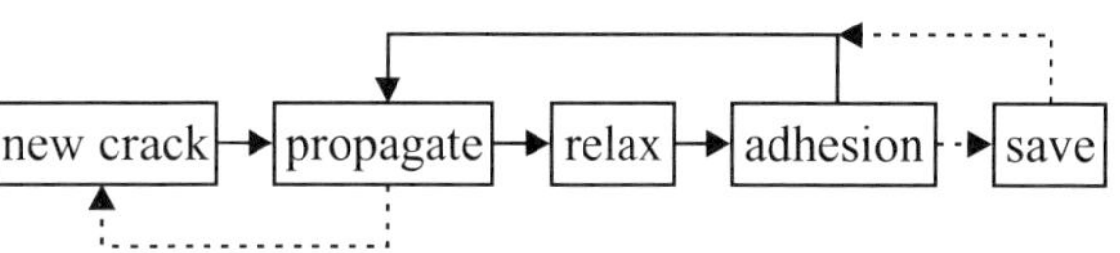

Figure 2: Simulation cycle.

a crack can appear (Figure 1-ii) and expand on the paint layer according to the local surface properties. By allowing the paint to shrink (Figure 1-iii) to a lower energy state, cracks reduce the tensile stress (Figure 1-iv) in the paint layer, producing an increase in shearing stress (Figure 1-v), and can cause adhesion to the base layer to be lost (Figure 1-vi). Thereafter, the paint is free to peel away from the base layer (Figure 1-vii).

Our simulation process is presented in Figure 2. Several cracks evolve on a surface and can intersect each other. To produce an image, the cracks and their parameters are passed to the rendering module (described in Section 5) where their shape is computed and rendered. This can be done at the end of the simulation or at time step intervals.

The surface properties are represented by a 2D grid structure. Each grid cell stores its local paint properties (adhesion, stress, etc.) and bilinear interpolation is used to compute properties for any location on the surface. Every surface property can have a value that varies with respect to direction on the surface. We represent such directional variations by storing samples for a predefined number of directions.[2] The resolution of the grid is responsible for many features (propagation speed, crack details, efficiency, etc.) that will be explained in the next sections.

Cracks propagate on the surface and are represented

[1] While the top layer can be of a different material than paint (*e.g.*, wallpaper), it is simpler to refer to it as paint.

[2] Since these properties are symmetrical, they need to be stored only within 180°. We typically use four directions ($0^o, 45^o, 90^o, 135^o$).

Paint Properties	Units	Source	Use
σ Tensile stress	force / length	user specified	creation, propagation, relaxation
S_b Tensile break strength	force / length	user specified	creation
S_c Tensile crack strength	force / length	user specified, $S_c < S_b$	propagation
δ Tensile deformation	length	$\delta = \sigma.cellSize.(1 - \frac{distance}{D_r})$	relaxation
D_r Elastic relaxation distance	length	user specified	relaxation
τ Shearing stress	force / length	$\tau = \delta / cellSize$	adhesion
S_a Adhesion strength	force / length	user specified	adhesion
Crack Properties			
W_c Crack width	length	$\sum \delta_i$	rendering
W_a Adhesion width	length	$distance$	merging, rendering

Table 1: Paint and crack properties. The equations are simple so their effect is intuitive to understand. All the user specified properties can be constant or vary over the surface. Constant terms should be added in the equations of δ and τ so that the units match, but were not included for clarity.

by connected segments forming piecewise linear curves. They are independent of the 2D grid representation which only serves to query the local surface properties. Typically, crack segments are smaller than the grid cell size. The surface and crack properties used throughout Sections 4 and 5 are presented in Table 1.

4.2 New Cracks and Propagation

We assume that if nothing else held it in place (*e.g.*, neighbor cells, adhesion to base layer), the paint layer in a cell would shrink to a stable lower energy state. The *tensile stress* σ is the difference in energy (force) between the current state and the stable state of the paint layer. The *tensile break strength* S_b is the maximal force the paint layer can handle before it breaks. Thus, if the stress σ exceeds the strength S_b, the paint will break. A new crack appears within the grid cell with the highest stress to strength ratio σ/S_b (Figure 3(a)).

The creation and propagation of cracks are strongly influenced by the stress and strength properties of paint. These properties can be dependent on the direction on the surface. For instance, wood fibers in the base layer can induce directional variations in stress and strength. When creating a crack, the orientation of the initial segment is perpendicular to the orientation of the maximal stress to strength ratio σ/S_b. Since we represent the directionality with samples for fixed directions, we use random distributions based on the sample values to compute the orientation of the maximal value of a property.

A propagation step moves each crack end point by a linear segment of length smaller or equal to the grid size, thus guaranteeing that we do not miss any grid cell contribution along this segment (we typically use a uniform distribution between 0.5 and 1.0 times the grid cell size). This propagation defines the path followed by a crack (Figure 3(b)). When propagating cracks, the stress σ is compared to another paint property, the *tensile crack strength* S_c. A crack stops when the local stress σ is below the strength S_c, or when it intersects another one (see Section 4.5). As when computing the orientation of new cracks, each of the two end points of a crack has a tendency to propagate in the direction perpendicular to the local highest stress to strength ratio σ/S_c. We also mix the computed orientation with the previous crack direction to prevent changes in direction which are too abrupt.

The top arrow in Figure 2 presents the main simulation loop, showing how the cracks and paint are adjusted in each step. We propagate the cracks until extinction of movement, before creating a new crack (bottom arrow in Figure 2). This simulates the fact that it often requires less energy to propagate a crack than to create a new one [14]. It also prevents the creation of many separate cracks within regions of high stress, and results in more continuous and realistic cracks. This strategy also greatly reduces the number of intersections that must be computed. In the same spirit, our crack strength S_c is lower than the break strength S_b to ensure that cracks will not stop after only a few propagation steps (we typically use a S_b that is equal to 1.5 times S_c).

4.3 Relaxation of Tensile Stress

As we saw in Section 3, cracks reduce tensile stress in the paint layer. We simulate this relaxation process by reducing the tensile stress of the cells close to each crack segment.

The *elastic relaxation distance* property D_r determines how far from the segment we should release stress. A *tensile deformation* δ of the paint layer, corresponds to the release in tensile stress. This is shown in Figure 4(a) for each cell. The amount of deformation (and stress re-

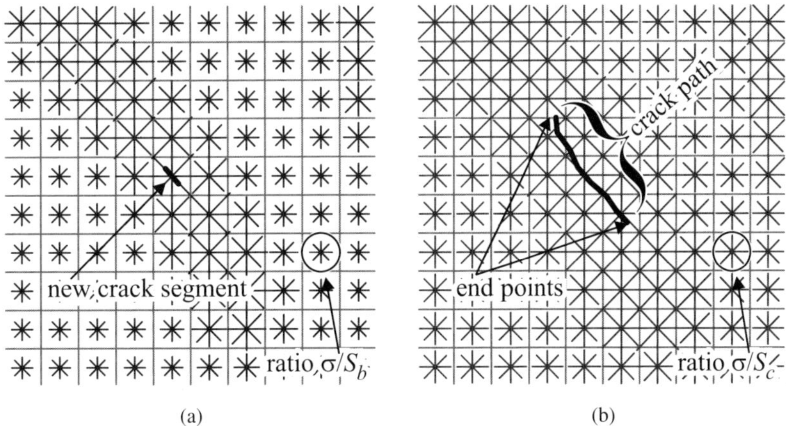

Figure 3: Snapshots from our system for creation and propagation of cracks. (a) The initial stress to strength ratio σ/S_b scaled such that a ratio of 1.0 corresponds to the size of a cell and presented as lines for the four sampled orientations. A new crack is created perpendicular to the maximal ratio. (b) The propagation of a crack (note that $\sigma/S_c > \sigma/S_b$ and that no relaxation was computed on the stress σ used to compute the presented ratios).

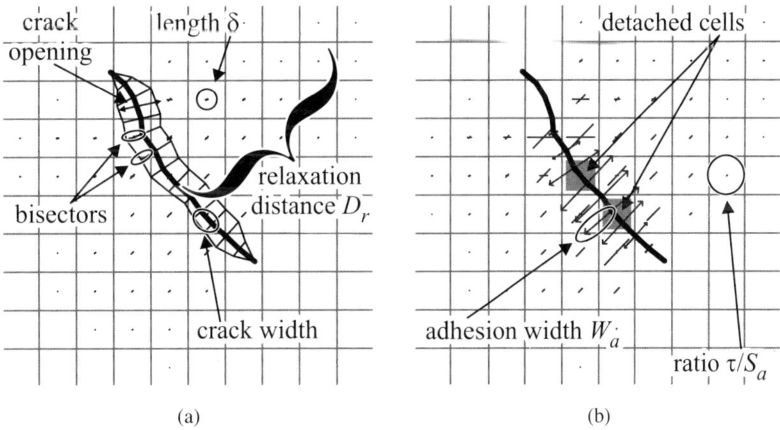

Figure 4: Snapshots from our system for relaxation and adhesion. (a) The cumulated deformation lengths δ caused by the relaxation. The bisectors on both sides of the crack represent the crack width and determine the region affected by each segment. (b) The shearing stress to adhesion strength ratio τ/S_a. Grey cells have lost adhesion to the base layer, and arrows on each side of the crack represent how far adhesion to the base layer is lost with respect to the crack.

lease) decreases linearly from the crack segment to the user specified relaxation distance D_r.

The paint tensile stress released by a crack should be roughly perpendicular to the crack. The direction of relaxation for a point on the paint layer is interpolated from the two bisector vectors for each segment (see Figure 4(a)). Compared to Gobron and Chiba [7] where only the direction perpendicular to the segment is considered, our approach avoids unwanted overlap (when consecutive segments form a concave curve) or cells that can receive no relaxation (in the convex case).

The set of cells close to the crack end points will be used to compute the paint tensile stress on the next propagation step. Since they will serve in the crack propagation computation, relaxing their stress would cause the crack to release stress ahead of itself. This would be incorrect with respect to the real physical phenomenon, and could cause the crack to stop for no apparent reason. These cells are thus excluded from the relaxation computation.

As described so far, the crack propagation has resulted in a set of piecewise linear segments indicating the central path of the crack. However a crack is an opening in the paint layer. As the paint layer is relaxed by the cracks, it shrinks locally by the deformation lengths δ. This causes the crack to widen, and the base layer to become visible. The deformation length δ of each relaxed cell is added to the *crack width* property of the crack segment(s) responsible for this relaxation. For each crack segment, an independent width is computed for each side of the crack. This results in two sets of corresponding piecewise linear segments with independent crack width values defining the crack sides. The crack widths are displayed in Figure 4(a) as segments on both sides of the crack path; linear interpolation is used to ensure continuity from one segment to the next.

4.4 Adhesion Modification

We next explain how we determine when curling of the peels can occur. As the paint layer shrinks by relaxation, it causes a lateral deformation of the layer, which induces a *shearing stress* τ counteracted by the paint adhesion. The *adhesion strength* S_a represents the maximal force (due to shrinking) that the paint layer can tolerate before adhesion to the base layer is broken. If the shearing stress τ increases above the adhesion strength S_a in any direction, the paint layer in this cell is considered as "detached" from its base layer for all directions. This computation only accounts for deformation local to the cell, without considering deformation of adjacent cells. It also is a binary operator, so even if adhesion to the base layer would be lost in the vicinity of the crack, when considering the whole cell, adhesion to the base layer can remain.

It should be noted that when the relaxation of tensile stress (Section 4.3) encounters cells detached from the base layer, it sums the deformation lengths δ, but extends the relaxation to a larger region by considering the detached cells as having a null size. The linear decrease of the relaxation deformation is thus moved further away from the crack, due to the loss of adhesion.

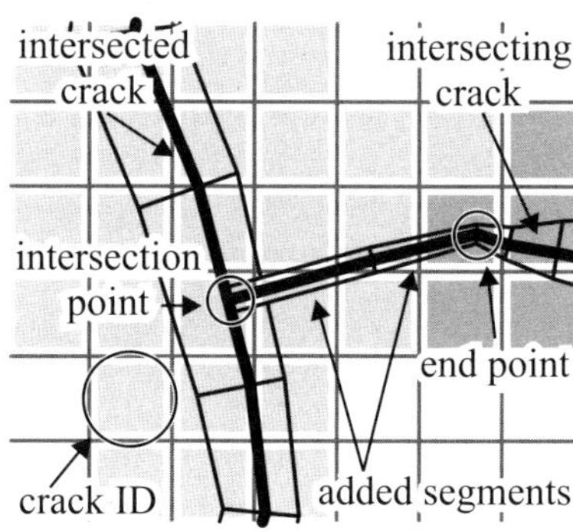

Figure 5: Intersection between two cracks, the intersected (previous) crack and the intersecting (new) crack. The identified end point corresponds to the intersecting crack end point before the intersection is detected. Cells with a light grey background are those marked by the intersected crack ID, while the cells with a dark grey are those marked by the intersecting crack.

When adhesion is lost, the paint can curl away from the base layer. To compute this peeling, each crack segment keeps, in an *adhesion width*, the distance to the closest cell (with respect to the region defined by its bisectors) that is still attached to the base layer (Figure 4(b)).

4.5 Intersection

As a crack propagates through the grid, every cell within a distance of half a cell is marked with its crack ID. We do not allow two cracks to traverse the same cell. Independent cracks are therefore always separated by a minimal distance related to the grid resolution. Self-intersection of a crack cannot be detected by the crack ID but can be handled by separately testing for intersection of the crack with itself.

When a crack enters a previously marked cell, the new segment is guaranteed not to cross over a previous crack segment. At this point the *intersecting* crack has not yet reached the *intersected* (previous) crack (see Figure 5) but we force the new crack to intersect the previous crack, as if the weakened paint layer suddenly broke. We thus need to connect the two cracks. The intersection point is the "closest" point on one segment of the intersected crack. First we eliminate the segments of the intersected crack for which the intersecting segment end point is not contained in the space confined within the intersected segment and bisector directions. For the remaining segments, we identify their respective intersection point and keep the segment with the closest intersection point.

We then add two segments to the intersecting crack to connect it to the intersected crack. Elastic relaxation of tensile stress is computed with respect to the added segments to determine the crack width of the intersecting crack where the intersection occurred. After relaxation, the intersected crack is split at the intersection point with respect to the intersecting crack width. The newly formed (opened) crack smoothly joins each side of the intersecting segment.

4.6 Segment Merging and Crack Detail

As the paint loses adhesion to the base layer, elastic relaxation reaches further away from the crack and the peels also curl further. Similarly to elastic relaxation, the peels curl away from the base layer in the direction perpendicular to the crack path (in our case, the directions of the interpolated bisectors of Figure 4(a)). As the relaxation or peeling reach further away from the segment, they should consider a larger portion of the crack. The computations thus have to consider the crack at a coarser level of detail as the adhesion width increases.

As explained earlier, the crack path traverses the paint layer with changes in direction that are not too abrupt. When little adhesion is lost, the adhesion width W_a vectors (Figure 4(b)) are short and the peel will curl very locally. When the loss of adhesion extends much further, the adhesion width W_a vectors are much longer and they can even intersect each other, yielding unexpected results as illustrated in Figure 6(a). It will also be difficult to create geometry for curling such peels. We solve these problems by merging together adjacent segments. This is similar to considering the crack path at a coarser level of detail, disregarding high frequency variations of the crack path (see Figure 6(b)). Merge operations are controlled by a set of metrics that determine if segments should be merged or not. These metrics consider different factors such as the segment lengths with respect to their adhesion width, and the difference in direction between consecutive segments.

Of course, we still want to keep the high frequencies of the crack path to compute the geometry of the peels, even though we do not use them to compute the relaxation or the peels curling directions. We do this by keeping *detail* records that store the difference (in crack and adhesion widths, as well as position) between the merged segments and the coarser level segment (see Figure 6(b)). This information is used when generating the geometry and for rendering the final peels.

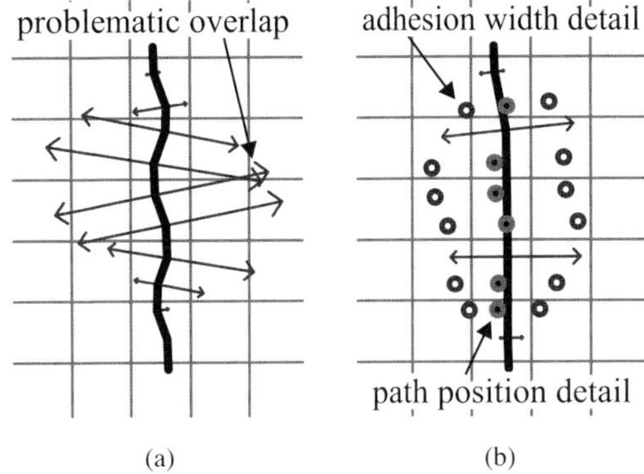

Figure 6: Merge of segments at a coarser level of detail. (a) Before merging, the peeling regions of some segments overlap. (b) After merging and recomputation of the adhesion widths, peeling regions respect the linear behavior of the crack path. The detail records for the crack path position (black dot on grey circle) and the adhesion width (white dot on grey circle) are also shown.

4.7 Interaction

We implemented this technique in an interactive system in which the user can specify the different properties and simulation parameters. Running on an Octane2 with a MIPS R12k 400 MHz CPU, the propagation is interactive (many new segments per second) for up to about 30 cracks. This enables the user to observe the evolution and change the parameters early in the simulation process.

The specification of paint layer parameters can be done with properties constant over the entire surface, isotropic properties, or directional properties. We found that textures to control the location of high and low strength are particularly useful (in Figures 9 and 10, the second image is the texture used to define the tensile strength property). To guide the crack to higher stress regions and to retrieve directional information from the texture, gradient operators are computed.

5 Rendering

Once the paths and widths of the cracks have been determined by the simulation, we pass this information to the rendering phase. It generates the peeling geometry on top of the original geometry, locally along the crack paths, and computes the final image with proper shading. The final rendering phase could be done with any high-quality renderer; we use Alias|Wavefront's Maya™.

After the crack is formed, new portions of the paint layer (sides and underneath the crack) get exposed to environmental attacks (*e.g.*, oxygen, UV light). The differential stress between the top and the bottom within the

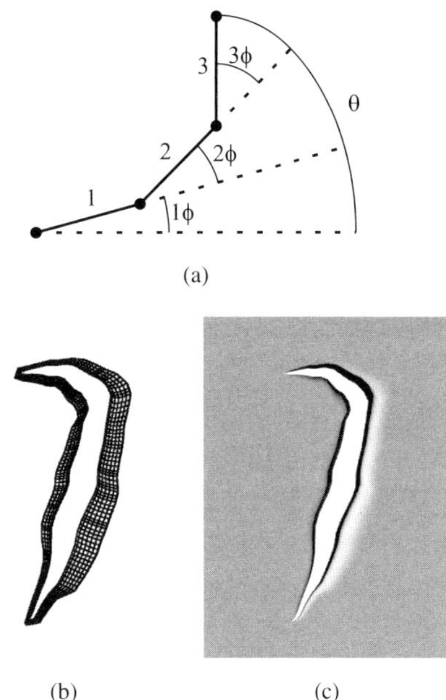

Figure 7: Geometry of the peels. (a) Cross-section of the curling geometry with three sections and angles $\theta = 90^o$, $\phi = 90^o/(1+2+3) = 15^o$. (b) Generated mesh. (c) Rendered result.

paint layer will cause this layer to curl. Instead of simulating this process in detail, we simply rely on a controllable approximation shown in Figure 7.

We compute the outward curling of the paint layer using a spiral-shaped geometry. The end of the curl forms an angle θ with the base surface (Figure 7(a)). This angle is user controlled and vanishes to zero at the end points of a crack.

To generate and render the effect of peeling, we create a mesh of micro-polygons with elements smaller than a user specified size (Figure 7(b)). A crack segment is subdivided in as many sub-segments as needed to respect this maximal size. It is also subdivided at each location where detail information is available (Section 4.6). Along the crack, the geometry is built generating one quadrilateral strip per sub-segment. To ensure smooth shading of the peels (Figure 7(c)), the surface normals of the micro-polygons are averaged and stored at every mesh vertex location.

This technique is simple and efficient, and can thus be generated on the fly in most standard rendering environments such as Maya™, or could be generated in a preprocess to create the peels geometry into a file added to the final scene. The approach has the advantage that the additional geometry is "glued" to the base surface,

	Door	Shutters	Wall
Simulation time†	75 min	20 min	3 min
Number of cracks	200	200	30
Number of segments	2900	1500	700
After merge	1200	850	250
Grid resolution	50 k	36 k	30 k
Rendering time‡	3 min	3 min	3 min
Number of polygons	400 k	150 k	130 k

Table 2: Statistics for the scenes of Figures 8, 9, and 10. † Simulations were computed on an Octane2 with a single MIPS R12k 400 MHz CPU. ‡ Rendering was done using the multiprocessing capabilities of Maya™ on an Onyx 3400 with 16 MIPS R12k 400 MHz CPUs.

and thus does not require remeshing or modifying the objects. Some care must however be taken to add a small offset with respect to the original surface to avoid "surface acne" artifacts.

In the rendering process we also need to compute the shading of the base geometry. It must show the base layer color inside a crack and the paint color outside. This corresponds to evaluating if the point to be rendered is inside or outside a crack. We use a 2D grid structure to accelerate this test. We implemented this inside a plugin shader with user input for paint and base layer shaders and output of the appropriate color for the point being shaded. This is very flexible, allowing the use of any shader, 2D/3D texture, or other utilities to send the desired color to our shader. Shadows and other illumination effects are handled by the renderer.

6 Results

Figures 8, 9, and 10 present real photographs (left) and synthetic results (rightmost two) of our system for a garage door, wood shutters, and an indoor wall. When the peels are viewed from a closer viewpoint (right), the shading and shadowing clearly show how both the curl geometry and the base layer appearing inside the crack are important to the visual quality of the results. In Figures 9 and 10, the second image from the left shows the tensile break strength S_b texture used, with darker representing lower strength and lighter representing higher strength.

Table 2 summarizes the statistics for these three scenes. Our simulation system is time and memory efficient, requiring about 35 MB of memory for the presented simulations. The computation of the elastic relaxation is the most time consuming part (about 80% of the total simulation time). The synthetic images were rendered with high quality anti-aliasing at a resolution of 640×480 pixels.

7 Conclusion and Future Work

We have presented a simple, fast, and easy to use approach for crack generation and peeling on layers such as paint. If desired, the user may control the generation of cracks with textures to describe the different surface properties. The crack propagation is performed on the surface, with a 2D grid to query and update the various surface properties. As cracks propagate, they remove constraints in the paint layer, allowing it to slightly shrink. We simulate both this shrinking and the related loss of adhesion between the paint and the base layer. The result of the crack propagation simulation is passed to the rendering phase, which generates geometry to represent the curling process of peeling and uses the appropriate shader when inside or outside of the cracks. Our approach produces visually appealing results, which are close to observed phenomena.

In future work, we will treat pieces of peels which break off, as often happens in reality. To add further realism, we should be able to treat more than two layers, for example when paint is added over wallpaper, etc. Another important direction is the treatment of curved surfaces, which complicates both the crack propagation algorithm, in particular the determination of the directions of propagation, and the generation and rendering of curl geometry.

Finally, our overall goal is a complete system to treat a wide variety of deterioration effects, in an integrated and easy to control manner. This will require careful determination of parameter choices, which will undoubtedly be a combination of automatic and user-assisted solutions.

Acknowledgements

Our work was supported by grants and scholarships from FCAR, NSERC, and MRI-MEQ. We thank Alias |Wavefront for the Maya™ system, the reviewers, and everyone from LIGUM, REVES, and *i*MAGIS. We would like to thank A. Reche for his help with the photography.

References

[1] D.J. Alner, editor. *Aspects of Adhesion – proceedings*. CRC Press; University of London Press, Cleveland, Ohio; London, 1965.

[2] W. Becket and N.I. Badler. Imperfection for realistic image synthesis. *Journal of Visualization and Computer Animation*, 1(1):26–32, August 1990.

[3] T. Cyril and J.A. Marks. *Paint Technology Manuals*. Oil and Colour Chemists Association, Chapman and Hall, London, 1961.

[4] J. Dorsey and P. Hanrahan. Modeling and rendering of metallic patinas. In *Proceedings of SIGGRAPH 96*, pages 387–396, 1996.

[5] J. Dorsey and P. Hanrahan. Digital materials and virtual weathering. *Scientific American*, 282(2):46–53, February 2000.

[6] W. Von Fischer and E.G. Bobalek. *Organic Protective Coatings*. Reinhold Pub. Corp., New York, 1953.

[7] S. Gobron and N. Chiba. Crack pattern simulation based on 3D surface cellular automata. *The Visual Computer*, 17(5):287–309, 2001.

[8] K. Hirota, Y. Tanoue, and T. Kaneko. Generation of crack patterns with a physical model. *The Visual Computer*, 14(3):126–137, 1998.

[9] J.S. Long and R.R. Myers. *Treatise on Coatings*. M. Dekker, New York, 1967.

[10] S. Merillou, J.-M. Dischler, and D. Ghazanfarpour. Surface scratches: Measuring, modeling and rendering. *The Visual Computer*, 17(1):30–45, 2001.

[11] M. Neff and E. Fiume. A visual model for blast waves and fracture. In *Graphics Interface 99*, pages 193–202, 1999.

[12] J.F. O'Brien and J.K. Hodgins. Graphical modeling and animation of brittle fracture. In *Proceedings of SIGGRAPH 99*, pages 137–146, August 1999.

[13] Society of Chemical Industry, editor. *Adhesion and Adhesives Fundamentals and Practice*. Wiley, New York, 1954.

[14] J. Smith, A. Witkin, and D. Baraff. Fast and controllable simulation of the shattering of brittle objects. In *Graphics Interface 2000*, pages 27–34, 2000.

[15] G.G. Sward, editor. *Paint Testing Manual – physical and chemical examination of paints, varnishes, lacquers, and colors*. American Society for Testing and Materials, Philadelphia, 1972.

[16] D. Terzopoulos and K. Fleischer. Modeling inelastic deformation: Viscoelasticity, plasticity, fracture. In *Computer Graphics (SIGGRAPH '88 Proceedings)*, volume 22, pages 269–278, August 1988.

[17] R. Warniers. Dirty pictures. *Computer Graphics World*, 21(6):50–60, June 1998.

[18] T.T. Wong, W.Y. Ng, and P.A. Heng. A geometry dependent texture generation framework for simulating surface imperfections. In *Eurographics Workshop on Rendering 1997*, pages 139–150. Springer Wien, 1997.

Real Synthetic Synthetic

Figure 8: Garage door with six wood panels having different crack properties.

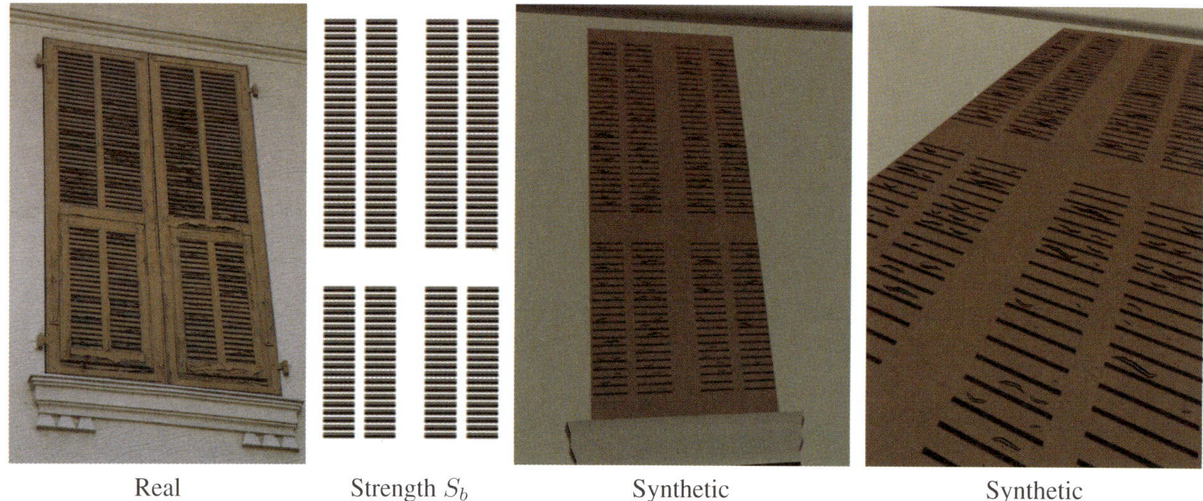

Real Strength S_b Synthetic Synthetic

Figure 9: Wood shutters with peeling on the small lamina plates.

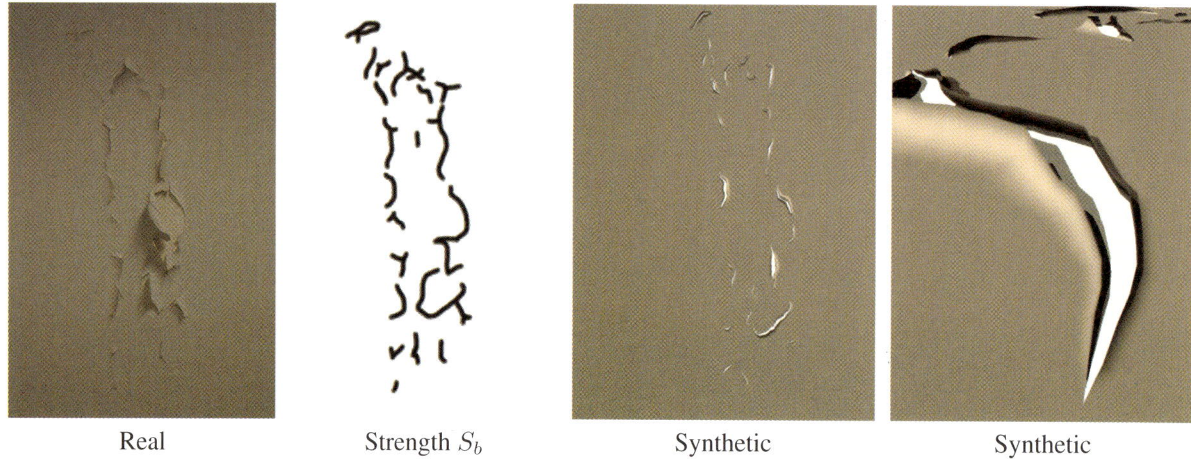

Real Strength S_b Synthetic Synthetic

Figure 10: Large peels over a painted plaster wall.

Generating Spatial Distributions for Multilevel Models of Plant Communities

Brendan Lane Przemyslaw Prusinkiewicz

Department of Computer Science
University of Calgary
laneb | pwp @ cpsc.ucalgary.ca

Abstract

The simulation and visualization of large groups of plants has many applications. The extreme visual complexity of the resulting scenes can be captured using multilevel models. For example, in two-level models, plant distributions may be determined using coarse plant representations, and realistic visualizations may be obtained by substituting detailed plant models for the coarse ones. In this paper, we focus on the coarse aspect of modeling, the specification of plant distribution. We consider two classes of models: local-to-global models, rooted in the individual-based ecosystem simulations, and inverse, global-to-local models, in which positions of individual plants are inferred from a given distribution of plant densities. We extend previous results obtained using both classes of models with additional phenomena, including clustering and succession of plants. We also introduce the formalism of multiset L-systems to formalize the individual-based simulation models.

Key words: realistic image synthesis, multilevel modeling, plant ecosystem, spatial distribution, clustering, succession, multiset L-system

1 Introduction

The simulation and visualization of plant ecosystems has many theoretical and practical applications. They include fundamental research in ecology, visual impact analysis of forestry practices, and synthesis of complex scenery for computer animations, among others. The inherent complexity of the scenes resulting from the ecosystem simulations can be managed using the multilevel approach to modeling [3]. Rather than model the entire ecosystem at the detailed level of plant organs, such as leaves, flowers, apices, and internodes [13], the multilevel approach employs a hierarchy of models. For example, in the simplest, two-level case, a high-level model determines the distribution of the plants, and lower-level models determine the plants' shapes. The models are coupled so that information created at a higher level can affect the outcome of the model at the lower level.

In this paper, we focus on the generation of the spatial distribution of plants. Specifically, we extend the methods reported in [3] with the ecologically and visually important phenomena of clustering and succession of plants. We also introduce the formalism of *multiset L-systems* to formalize some of these models.

Previous work on multilevel modeling of plant ecosystems is summarized in Section 2. Following the approach introduced there, we distinguish the *local-to-global* approach, in which the distribution of plant densities is determined by a simulation of interactions between the individual plants, and the *global-to-local* approach, in which positions of individual plants are inferred from given large-scale density distributions. In Section 3.1, we introduce multiset L-systems as an extension of the L-system modeling framework. This extension allows us to use L-systems, long an individual plant modeling paradigm, to express local-to-global algorithms for generating plant distributions as well. Sample applications of multiset L systems are given in Sections 3.2 to 3.4. The concept and examples of the global-to-local modeling of plant distribution are presented in Section 4, which extends preliminary results reported in [7]. Conclusions are presented in Section 5.

2 Previous work

Multilevel modeling of plant communities for image synthesis purposes was introduced in [3], although related techniques had been used earlier, *e.g.* [1]. The main concept was to consider the generation of a plant ecosystem as a hierarchy of tasks: specification of the terrain, generation of plant distribution using coarse plant models, synthesis of detailed plant models as needed to populate the scene, and the rendering of the final scene using instances of these detailed models.

Two different methods were used in [3] to create plant distributions. The first one was an individual-based ecosystem simulation, based on a model of Firbank and Watkinson [4]. Following that model, simulated plants were placed in the field at random, then iteratively 'grown', and 'killed' when dominated by larger plants. The resulting distribution fit the *self-thinning curve* of plant ecology [8], a relationship between the average mass and average density in a monoculture of plants of the same age. The individual-based approach was also used in [3] to produce a hierarchy (distribution) of plant sizes (*c.f.* [8]), similar to that observed in nature.

The second method was intended to allow more user control in defining the local density of plants. The input was a greyscale image representing a map of the density of plants throughout the field. The Floyd-Steinberg error diffusion algorithm [5] was used to create the positions of individual plants conforming to these densities. The points produced by this algorithm were slightly jittered to make the distribution appear more random.

These two methods exemplify two different approaches to ecological modeling. The individual-based simulation is representative of the local-to-global approach. It is characterized by the emergence of global features from the local interactions of individual plants. In contrast, the error diffusion method is an example of the inverse, global-to-local approach, in which local characteristics are derived from global properties of the distribution. This distinction is similar to the distinction between local-to-global and global-to-local methods used to model individual plants [14].

The methods described in [3] tend to create uniform plant distributions. In reality, however, plants often are clustered. *Clustering*, also known as *clumping* or *underdispersion* [2], is a common phenomenon, caused by environmental factors (plants of the same type tend to cluster in the areas favorable to their growth), propagation (seeds fall close to their parent plants, or plants propagate by runners), as well as other mechanisms. It has a significant impact on the appearance of plant distributions, which is why we are seeking to model it.

The effect of clustering can be quantified using several statistical measures. We use the *Hopkins index* [6], which is defined as the average distance from a randomly chosen point to its nearest plant within a given region, divided by the average distance from a randomly chosen plant to its nearest plant:

$$H = \frac{\langle min_i(\|x - p_i\|)\rangle_x}{\langle min_i(\|p_j - p_i\|)\rangle_j}.$$

Distributions that are completely uncorrelated ('random') have an H value of 1. Distributions that are more dispersed than random ('regular') have an H value less than 1, and distributions that are clustered have an H value greater than 1. For example, Figure 1 compares an overdispersed distribution with a Hopkins index of 0.4 and a clustered distribution with a Hopkins index of 2.4.

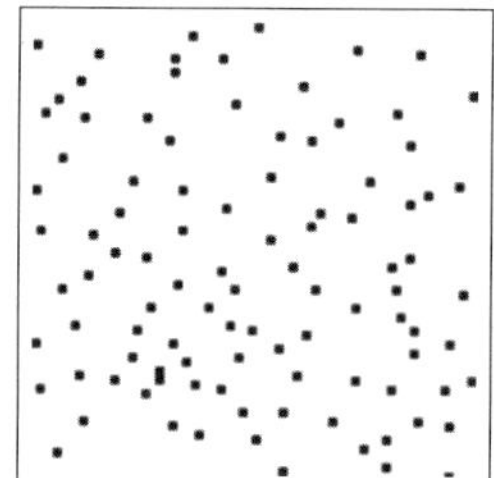
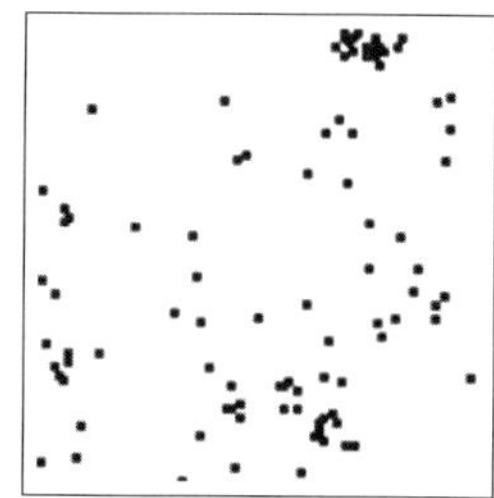

Figure 1: The effect of clustering on plant distribution. Left: an overdispersed distribution with H = 0.4. Right: a clustered distribution with H = 2.4.

3 Local-to-global modeling of plant distribution

3.1 Multiset L-systems

We model the individual plants using L-systems [13] and a related technique based on Chomsky grammars [14]. In addition, we extend the L-system formalism to generate plant distributions using the local-to-global approach. To this end, we introduce the notion of *multiset L-systems*.

An L-system model generates plants represented as strings of symbols [9] with optional parameters [13]. These strings define both the topology and the geometry of the resulting structures. An L-system specification consists of three components: the *alphabet*, which is the set of symbols that represent distinct components of the plant; the *axiom*, which represents the initial state of the modeled structure; and a list of *productions*, which define the development of the plant's components over steps of time. The alphabet may be defined implicitly, as the set of symbols that appear in the productions. The development of a plant is simulated in a sequence of *derivation steps*. In any step, each symbol is rewritten using the first applicable production on the list (or rewritten into itself if no production applies), yielding a new string. An extension of L-systems called *pseudo-L-systems* [11] makes it possible to rewrite two or more symbols using a single production. Another extension, called *open L-systems* [10], makes is possible to capture the interactions between the modeled plants and their environment.

Multiset L-systems unify and extend to branching structures two previously defined notions of the L-system theory: developmental systems with finite axiom sets [16] and L-systems with fragmentation [17]. In multiset L-systems, the set of productions operates on a multiset of strings that represent many plants, rather than a single string that represents an individual plant. New strings can be dynamically added to or removed from this multiset, representing organisms that are added to or removed from the population.

Formally, a context-free non-parametric multiset L-system is a four-tuple $G = \langle V, \%, \Omega, P\rangle$ where V is the *alphabet* (a finite set of symbols), $\% \notin V$ is a reserved *fragmentation symbol*, $\Omega \subset V^\star$ is a finite set of words over V called the *axiom*, and $P \subset V \times (V \cup \{\%\})^\star$ is a finite set of *productions*. The alphabet V may contain, in particular, a pair of brackets, [and], which are used to delimit branches in the *bracketed string* notation of tree structures [13].

A derivation step in a multiset L-system consists of two sub-steps. First, all words x_i in the predecessor multiset are replaced by the intermediate successor words y_i using productions in P. The individual derivations $x_i \rightarrow y_i$ are performed as in an ordinary L-system. Second, the words y_i that contain one or more fragmentation symbols % are subdivided. In this process, symbol % acts as the marker of positions at which branches y_{ik} are cut off the tree y_i. The remaining part of the tree y_i and the cut off branches y_{ik} become the members of the successor multiset.

For example, let us consider the multiset L-system specified below.

Alphabet: {A, B, I, [,] }
Axiom: { A, B }
Productions: 1. A $\rightarrow$ I[B]A
2. B $\rightarrow$ B%A

Starting with the axiom, the first two derivation steps yield the multisets listed in the Table 1.

step	intermediate multiset	final multiset
0	{A, B}	{ A, B }
1	{ I[B]A, B%A }	{I[B]A, B, A }
2	{I[B%A]I[B]A, B%A, I[B]A }	{ I[B]I[B]A, A, B, A, I[B]A }

Table 1: Operation of a sample multiset L-system

Extensions of L-systems, such as pseudo-L-systems and open L-systems, also apply to the multiset L-systems. In particular, in the simulations of ecosystems we rely extensively on the *communication symbols* ?E, introduced in [10] as a part of the open L-system formalism. The communication symbol is a vehicle for information exchange between plant models and their environment. It can be associated with one or more parameters, which are set by the environmental program interfaced with the L-system-based simulator.

The plant models used in the ecosystem simulations are extremely simplified, in order to accommodate a large number of plants. We have used the L-system-based plant modeling software `L-studio/cpfg` [12], extended with multiset capabilities, to both generate plant distributions and model the individual plants.

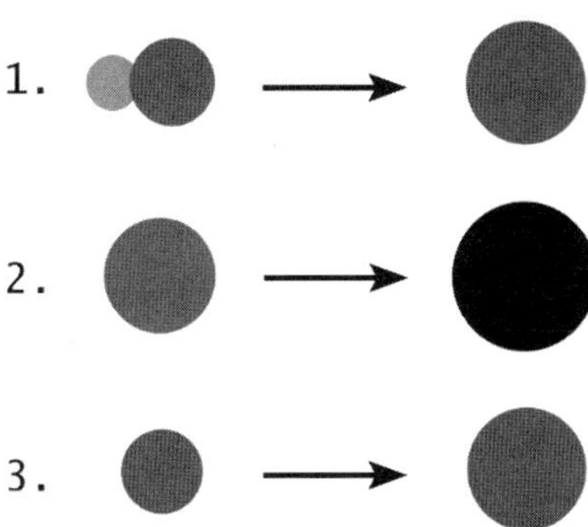

Figure 2: Diagrammatic representation of a model of self-thinning. Dark grey circles represent growing plants, the light grey circle represents a dominated plant, and the black circle represents a mature plant that no longer grows.

3.2 Self-thinning

As the first illustration of the concepts described above, let us consider a multiset L-system implementation of the individual-based self-thinning model outlined in [3]. Self-thinning takes place among a group of plants of the same species and age. As the plants grow and compete with each other for resources, smaller and weaker plants become *dominated* by larger, stronger plants, and eventually die. The essence of this process can be captured using the set of rules shown in Figure 2. The corresponding L-systems is given below:

Axiom: { T($\vec{x}_1$,r_1)?E(1) ,
T($\vec{x}_2$,r_2)?E(1) ,
... ,
T($\vec{x}_n$,r_n)?E(1) }

1. T($\vec{x}$,r)?E(c) : $c == 0 \rightarrow \epsilon$
2. T($\vec{x}$,r) : $r \geq R \rightarrow$ T($\vec{x}$,R)
3. T($\vec{x}$,r)?E(c) $\rightarrow$ T($\vec{x}$,r + grow(r, Δt))

Each plant is described by module T($\vec{x}$,r) followed by the communication module ?E(c). Vector $\vec{x}$ and number r represent position and size (shoot radius) of the plant. Parameter c is used for communication with the environmental process, which sets c to 1 if the plant is not dominated and to 0 if it is dominated. The environmental process considers each plant as a circle of a radius r, and determines which circles are intersecting. The smaller of any pair of intersecting circles is considered dominated.

The axiom introduces n plants with random positions and sizes (the initial distribution of plants could also be generated algorithmically). The first production, guarded

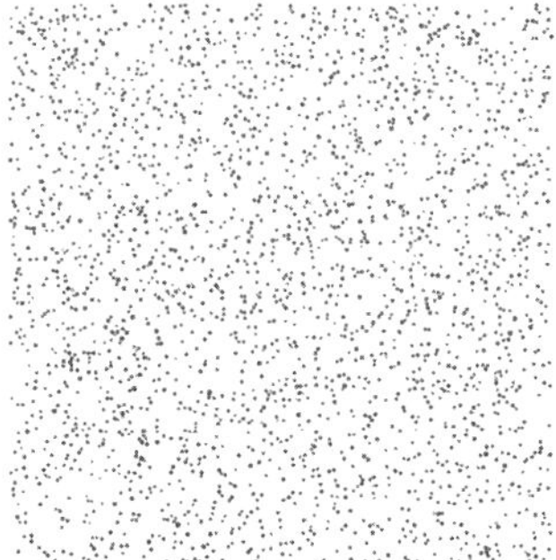
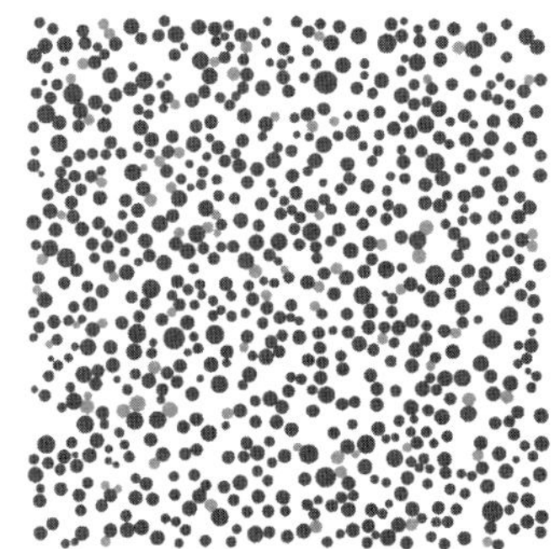
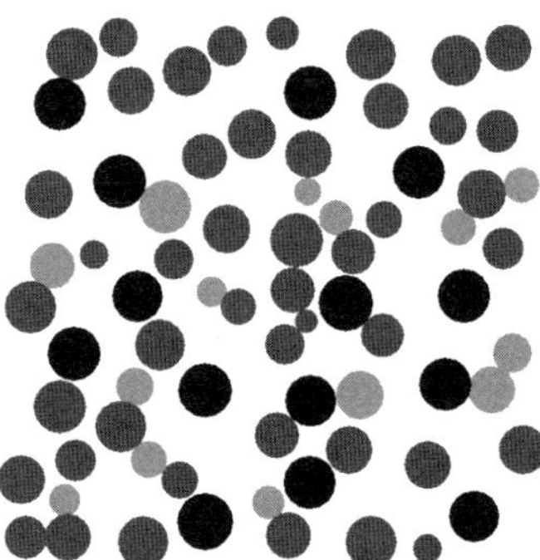

Figure 3: Three stages of simulation of the self-thinning process. Dark grey circles are growing plants, light grey circles are dominated plants, and black circles are mature plants, as in Figure 2.

by the condition $c == 0$, removes any dominated plant and its associated communication module from the population. Production 2 stops the growth of a plant that has reached its the maximum size R. Finally, production 3 increases the size of a plant that is neither dominated nor mature. The user-defined function grow(r, Δt) captures growth of a plant of radius r over time interval Δt.

Figure 3 shows three stages of a self-thinning process simulated using this L-system. As the plant community develops over time, dominated plants gradually disappear and thin out the distribution. Sample visualizations obtained by substituting realistic plant models for the individual circles are shown in [3].

3.3 Plant succession

An extension to the previous L-system transforms it into a model of interaction between two plant species:

Axiom: { X }

1. X $\rightarrow$ T($\vec{x}_1$,r_1,1)?E(1) %
   ...
   T($\vec{x}_n$,r_n,1)?E(1) %
   T($\vec{x}_{n+1}$,r_{n+1},2)?E(1) %
   ...
   T($\vec{x}_{n+m}$,r_{n+m},2)?E(1) % X

2. T($\vec{x}$,r,sp) > ?E(c) : c == 0 &&
   random(1) < shaded[sp] $\rightarrow$ T($\vec{x}$,r,sp)
3. T($\vec{x}$,r,sp) ?E(c) : c == 0 $\rightarrow \epsilon$

4. T($\vec{x}$,r,sp) : $r \geq R$ && random(1) < oldage[sp]
   $\rightarrow$ T($\vec{x}$,R,sp)
5. T($\vec{x}$,r,sp) : $r \geq R \rightarrow \epsilon$

6. T($\vec{x}$,r,sp) $\rightarrow$ T($\vec{x}$,r + grow(r,sp, Δt),sp)

In this model a plant is represented by the module T($\vec{x}$,r,sp). Parameters $\vec{x}$ and r denote the plant's position and radius, as in the previous model. Parameter sp is the plant's species identifier, either 1 or 2. Production 1 adds n new plants of species 1 and m new plants of species 2 to the population. The production predecessor X reappears in the successor multiset, thus new plants are added in every simulation step. Productions 2 and 3 remove a dominated plant with probability $1 - \text{shaded}[sp]$[1]. The value shaded[sp], called the *shade tolerance* of the plant, is a measure of how likely it is to survive in shadow.

Productions 4 and 5 model the senescence of plants. Once a plant has reached the radius R, it survives with the probability oldage[sp]; a plant that does not survive dies and is removed from the community. Production 6 uses the growth function grow(r,sp,Δt) to simulate the growth of plants that are neither dominated nor old, according to their size and species.

With the right parameterization, this model captures the phenomenon of *succession* [8]. If species 1 has a higher growth rate but lower shade tolerance and old-age survivorship than species 2 (grow(r,1Δt) > grow(r,2,Δt), shaded[1] < shaded[2], oldage[1] < oldage[2]), then an initially empty field will be populated in stages. First, the field will be dominated by species 1. As the largest members of species 1 die, smaller members of species 2, which have survived due to their greater shade tolerance and now have a size advantage over young seedlings of species 1, will fill in the gaps. Eventually, the field will be dominated by members of species 2. A straightforward extension of this model to three plant species is illustrated in Figure 4.

[1] Recall that the production list is ordered, thus the string rewriting mechanism will first attempt to apply production 2, and only use production 3 if the condition of production 2 is not satisfied.

Figure 4: Four stages of ecosystem simulation using the plant succession model. Left: results of coarse-level simulation, using pink circles to indicate position of herbaceous plants (fireweed), orange circles to indicate positions of the early-succession deciduous trees, and green circles to indicate positions of the late-succession coniferous trees. Right: synthetic images obtained by placing tree models at the locations generated by the coarse-level simulation.

3.4 Plant propagation

The evaluation of the Hopkins index for the distributions shown in Figure 3 yields values of H equal to 0.8, 0.4, and 0.4, respectively. Similarly, the evaluation of the Hopkins index for the distributions in Figure 4 results in H values of 0.6, 0.7, 0.7, and 0.6. This shows that the competition for space leads to overdispersed plant distributions.

We can see why this is the case. If any two plants so much as touch each other, one of them will become dominated. In our self-thinning model, the dominated plant immediately dies; in the succession model, it dies with some probability per derivation step. In either case, the competition for space drives the plants apart, and there is no opposite mechanism encouraging plants to cluster.

One clustering mechanism observed in nature is local propagation. We can capture it, for instance, by 'sowing' new plants near the parent plants of the same species, instead of making them appear at random throughout the field. The resulting alteration of the succession model is given below.

Axiom: { T($\vec{x}_1$,r_1,1)?E(1) ,
... ,
T($\vec{x}_n$,r_n,1)?E(1) ,
T($\vec{x}_{n+1}$,r_{n+1},2)?E(1) ,
... ,
T($\vec{x}_{n+m}$,r_{n+m},2)?E(1) }

1. T($\vec{x}$,r,sp) > ?E(c) : c == 0 && random(1) < shaded[sp] $\rightarrow$ T($\vec{x}$,r,sp)
2. T($\vec{x}$,r,sp) ?E(c) : c == 0 $\rightarrow \epsilon$
3. T($\vec{x}$,r,sp) : $r \geq R$ && random(1) > oldage[sp] $\rightarrow$ T($\vec{x}$,R,sp)
4. T($\vec{x}$,r,sp) : $r \geq R \rightarrow \epsilon$
5. T($\vec{x}$,r,sp) ?E(c) $\rightarrow$ T($\vec{x}$,r + grow(sp,r,Δt),sp) ?E(c) % T($\vec{x} + \Delta\vec{x}$,r_0,sp) ?E(c)

The axiom defines the initial state of the model by placing n plants of species 1 and m plants of species 2 at random in the field. The subsequent productions are the same as in the succession model, except for production 5. According to it, a plant that is not dominated creates a new plant at position $\vec{x} + \Delta\vec{x}$, where $\Delta\vec{x}$ is a small random vector. Since the new plant is in close proximity to its parent, this propagation mechanism encourages clustering in the distribution.

Figure 5 illustrates the operation of this model. At the beginning, plants are randomly distributed. As the ecosystem develops, the two species become spatially segregated, creating large clusters of plants of each species. For example, the Hopkins indices of species 1 at the three stages shown are equal to 1.1, 4.2, and 11, respectively.

4 Global-to-local modeling of plant communities

4.1 The deformation-kernel method

The effect one plant in the self-thinning model (Section 3.2) has on the probability of finding another plant nearby is shown diagramatically in Figure 6. Within the reference plant radius r_t, the probability of finding another plant is very small; outside that radius, the probability is not affected by the reference plant.

The function K shown in Figure 6 is an example of a *deformation kernel*. If we suppose there is a field of values that characterizes the probability of placing a new plant at various locations, the deformation kernel captures the impact of an existing plant on this field. Various interactions between plants can be described using deformation kernels of different shapes, as suggested in Figure 7.

A simple plant placement algorithm can now be developed using this deformation kernel idea. We maintain a *joint probability density function* [15] $f(x,y)$, which characterizes the probability $f(x,y)dxdy$ of placing a new plant in the area $dxdy$ centered at point (x,y). The plants are placed one at a time; as each is placed, its deformation kernel modifies the probability function f that will be used to determine the position of the next plant. In this manner, a distribution of plants will eventually be formed.

Formally, the joint density function f defines a probability field, where the probability of a new plant growing in the rectangle $[0,x_s] \times [0,y_s]$, with $0 \leq x_s \leq x_{max}$ and $0 \leq y_s \leq y_{max}$, is given by the cumulative probability distribution function

$$F(x_s,y_s) = P\{x_t \leq x_s, y_t \leq y_s\} = \int_0^{x_s}\int_0^{y_s} f(x,y)\,dx\,dy.$$

Obviously, the probability that the plant will be found in the whole field is one, thus the density function must satisfy the normalizing equation

$$\int_0^{x_{max}}\int_0^{y_{max}} f(x,y)\,dx\,dy = 1. \tag{1}$$

We find the position (x_t,y_t) of the plant to be added by calculating first its y, then its x coordinate. To this end, given the two-dimensional density function $f(x,y)$, we create the *marginal distribution function* $F_Y(y_s)$. That

Figure 5: Three stages of ecosystem development simulated using the plant propagation model. Left: results of coarse-level simulation, using orange circles to indicate positions of poplar trees and green circles to indicate positions of spruce trees. Right: synthetic images obtained by placing tree models at the locations generated by the coarse-level simulation.

distribution function describes the probability that $y_t \leq y_s$ independently of the choice of x_t [2] :

$$F_Y(y_s) = P\{x_t \leq x_{max}, y_t \leq y_s\} = F(x_{max}, y_s).$$

We choose the y_t coordinate for the plant using the *inverse transformation method* [15]. To this end, we generate a random number u from the uniform distribution on $[0, 1]$. We then perform a binary search on $F_Y(y)$ to find the value y_t such that $F_Y(y_t) = u$. As F_Y is monotone and continuous, y_t exists and is unique. This is our plant's y coordinate.

Once we have chosen y_t, we calculate the *conditional distribution* $F_{X|Y}(x_s \mid y_t)$, which describes the probability that $x_t \leq x_s$ for a given a y value y_t:

$$F_{X|Y}(x_s \mid y_t) = P\{x_t \leq x_s \mid y_t\} = \frac{\int_0^{x_s} f(x, y_t)\, dx}{\int_0^{x_{max}} f(x, y_t)\, dx}.$$

We then apply the inverse transformation method to find coordinate x_t, given $F_{X|Y}(x_s \mid y_t)$.

[2] There is a corresponding marginal distribution function $F_X(x_s)$, which describes the probability that $x_t \leq x_s$, independent of what is chosen for y_t.

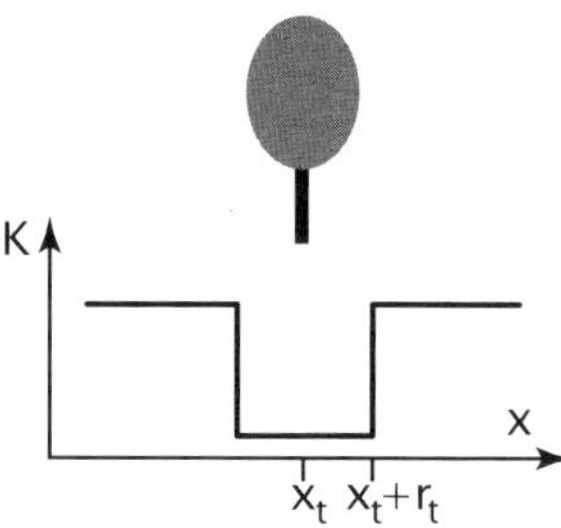

Figure 6: The effect of a reference plant on the probability of finding neighboring plants

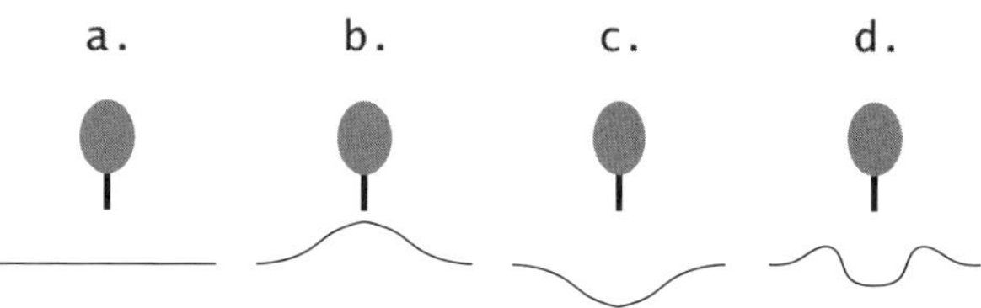

Figure 7: Examples of deformation kernels: a) kernel that has no effect on the neighboring plants, b) kernel that has a promotional effect, c) kernel that has an inhibitory effect, d) kernel that has an inhibitory short-range effect and promotional longer-range effect.

Having placed a plant of size r_t at position (x_t, y_t), we now deform the probability density function $f(x, y)$ in order to simulate the effects of that plant on the placement of nearby plants. To this end, we first multiply the probability density function $f(x, y)$ by the plant's deformation kernel $K(x, y)$,

$$f_{temp}(x, y) = f(x, y)K(x, y),$$

then renormalize the function $f_{temp}(x, y)$ to satisfy Equation 1. The deformation kernel typically is a function of the form

$$K(x, y) = \kappa\left(\frac{\sqrt{(x - x_t)^2 + (y - y_t)^2}}{r_t}\right),$$

where the function $\kappa(r)$ measures the effect a unit-sized plant has on the formation of plants at a distance r from it.

An obvious way to implement the above concepts is to represent values of the probability density function $f(x, y)$ using an n by n array of samples f_{ij}. To calculate position of a new plant, we create a vector **R** of partial sums of the rows, where

$$R_k = \sum_{i=0}^{k}\sum_{j=0}^{n-1} f_{ij}, \quad k = 0, 1, \ldots, n-1.$$

We determine the coordinate y_t of the newly placed plant using the inverse transformation method. To this end, we pick a random number u from the uniform distribution on the interval $[0, R_{n-1}]$, then perform a binary search to locate R_i such that $R_i \leq u < R_{i+1}$. We then linearly interpolate between (i, R_i) and $(i+1, R_{i+1})$ to find (y_t, u).

Now a vector **C** of values representing the conditional distribution $F_{X|Y}(x_s \mid y_t)$ is computed by interpolating rows i and $i + 1$ of the array f_{ij}.

$$C_k = (y_0 - i)\sum_{j=0}^{k} f_{(i+1)j} + ((i+1) - y_0)\sum_{j=0}^{k} f_{ij},$$

Given the values C_k, $k = 0, 1, \ldots, n-1$, we choose a value from the uniform random distribution on the interval $[0, C_{n-1}]$, and use the inverse transformation method to find x_t.

The kernel is applied by simply calculating the distance d of every sampling point (i, j) from (x_t, y_t), then multiplying the value f_{ij} of the distribution function f at that point by $\kappa(\frac{d}{r_t})$.

If there are m plants to be placed and the function f is represented using n^2 values f_{ij}, the above algorithm will take $O(mn^2)$ time to run, since the sums R_k must be recalculated each time a new plant is placed. We improve on this result by updating the array **R** incrementally. When a kernel is applied to the distribution, the differences between f_{ij} and $\kappa(\frac{d}{r_t})f_{ij}$ are summed for each (i, j) within the range of the plant, and the differences are applied to the array **R**. Assuming that the kernel is only applied to a small fraction of the cells in the grid, this operation can be performed in $O(n)$ time per plant.

The operation of the kernel method is illustrated in Figure 8. The deformation kernel is that of Figure 7d. The initial distribution is uniform; $f(x, y) = c$. In the middle, a single plant has been added to the field; the density function has been altered in the plant's neighborhood. On the bottom, four more plants have been added; the density function has been modified near each of them.

Figure 9 shows point patterns generated using this algorithm with different deformation kernels. The Hopkins indices of these patterns are 0.4, 1.0, 1.2, and 2.4, confirming the visual observation that the kernel method is capable of creating a range of distributions, from overdispersed to random and clustered.

In Figure 10 points have been replaced by simple models of daisies, created using an L-system. The overdispersed pattern at the top of Figure 10 looks less realistic than the clustered pattern at the bottom, which justifies the introduction of clustering into the model.

The distributions shown in Figure 10 have been generated after initializing the probability density function

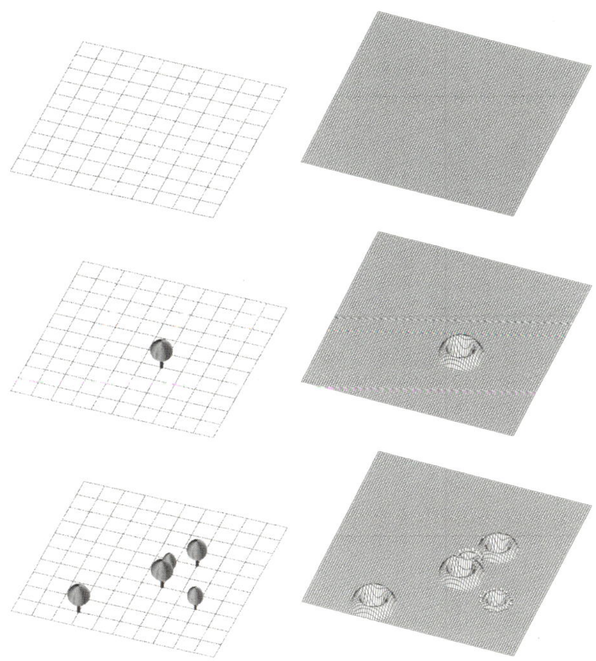

Figure 8: An example of the deformation kernel algorithm, using the kernel of Figure 7d. Left: the plant distribution. Right: the joint probability density function f. From top to bottom: the initial state, the state after placing the first plant, and the state after placing four more plants.

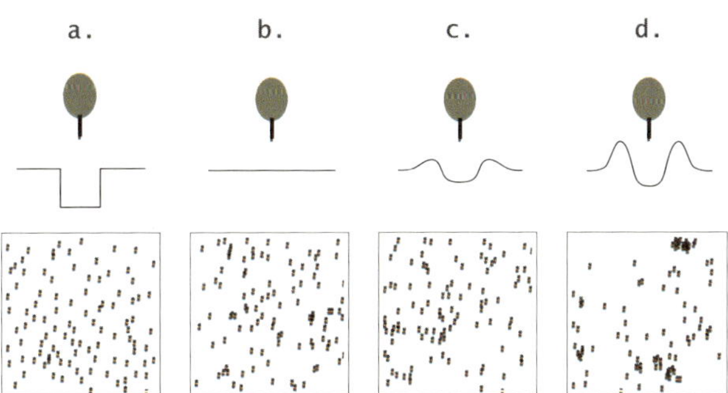

Figure 9: Some kernels and the point patterns they generate. The kernels are drawn at a larger scale than the point patterns.

f to a constant value. If, instead, we initialize f to a user-defined field (with a paint program, for example), we can generate spatial distributions of plants that conform to this field, as shown in Figure 11.

This result improves on the methodology described in [3], which allowed for the application of a user-specified density map, but did not make it possible to control the degree of plant clustering.

Figure 10: Point patterns corresponding to Figures 9a and 9c, rendered as fields of daisies.

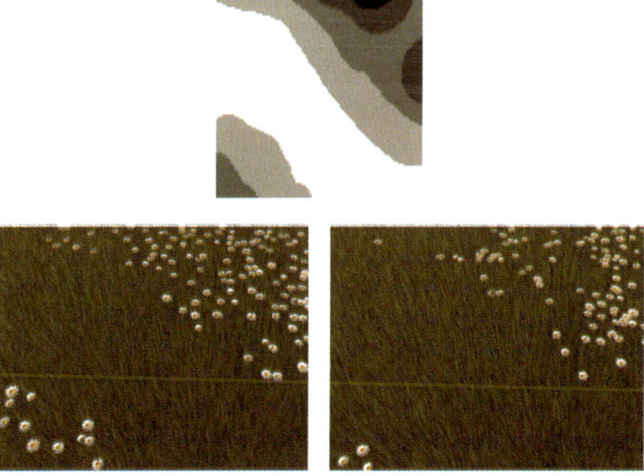

Figure 11: Plant distributions created from the user-defined density map, shown at the top. The Hopkins index values are $H \approx 1.2$ (left) and $H \approx 1.9$ (right).

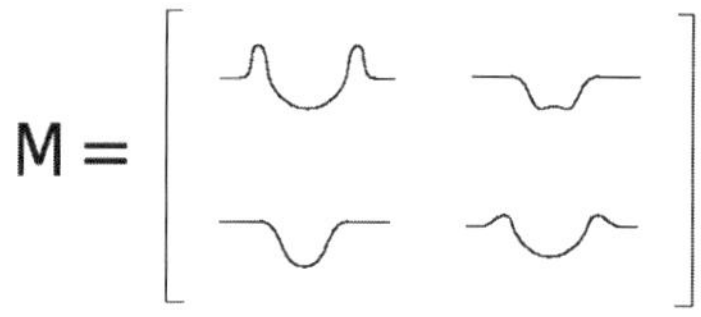

M =

Figure 12: The concept of the kernel matrix M for two species

4.2 Extensions

The kernel-based method can be extended to include information about the plants' sizes, as well as to model the interaction of several species.

Size information is taken into account by placing plants in order of size, largest first. Larger, older plants then affect the positioning of smaller, younger plants, as it is to be expected. The actual sizes may be drawn from a distribution that gives few large plants, more plants of medium size, and still more small plants.

Plants of species 1 may have a different effect on other plants of species 1 than they do on plants of species 2. Different kernels are thus required to capture these effects. In fact, for two species, the total of four kernels is required: one for the effects species 1 has on itself, one for the effects species 1 has on species 2, one for the effects species 2 has on species 1, and one for the effects species 2 has on itself. This leads, in the general case, to a *kernel matrix* M (Figure 12), which defines the effects that each species has on itself and on each other species.

In an extension of the kernel placement method to n species, we keep track of n different probability density functions f_i. As plants are placed, each probability density function is deformed by the relevant kernel; thus if a plant of species j is placed, each function f_i is deformed by kernel $M_{i,j}$, where $i = 1, 2, \ldots, n$. This process is illustrated in Figure 13.

A sample application of the above method is presented in Figure 14. The modeling of trees incorporated in this scenes was discussed in [14].

5 Conclusions

We formalized and extended the methods for defining plant distributions that had originally been proposed in [3]. To this end, we introduced multiset L-systems, an extension of the L-system formalism, to model groups of plants, rather than single plants alone. We then applied these L-systems to simulate the essence of self-thinning, succession, and clustering of plants in an ecosystem.

We also improved the interactive techniques for generating plant distributions, making is possible to specify not only global densities, but also levels of clustering. The resulting kernel deformation method can produce plant distributions with a wide range of clustering values, from overdispersed to random to highly clustered. We have illustrated the use of this method using several models of plant communities.

Fig.	Number of			Time taken[a]		
	plants	different plants	primitives (millions)	distribution generation[b]	plants	rendering
4a	2688	20	34	9 sec	30 sec	8 min
b	1593	20	18	72 sec	27 sec	8 min
c	1409	20	30	2 min	30 sec	9 min
d	834	20	78	3 min	40 sec	11 min
5a	5584	24	141	2 min	30 sec	15 min
b	5526	24	147	22 min	30 sec	14 min
c	3427	24	100	44 min	30 sec	12 min
10	100	8	1.5	0.05 sec	2 sec	2 min
14	1599	36	147	0.5 sec	65 sec	11 min

[a] Times recorded on a 733 MHz Pentium III processor.

[b] For Figures 4 and 5, the times given show how long the simulation took to reach the given frame.

Table 2: Statistics pertinent to Figures 4, 5, 10, and 14

Both methods make it possible to generate plant ecosystems at the speeds required for their practical applications to realistic image synthesis. Statistics pertinent to the scenes included in this paper are given in Table 2.

We believe that the proposed methods can be applied to model diverse plant ecosystems and have various practical applications, such as scene dressing for computer animation purposes, and visual impact analysis of tree cutting and regrowth on the landscape. The realism of the resulting scenes can be further improved using more accurate models of the underlying biological processes, and more sophisticated rendering methods.

Acknowledgments

We thank Martin Fuhrer for the model of fireweed used in Figure 4, Lars Mündermann for the model of grass used in Figures 10 and 11, and the referees for their insightful comments. We acknowledge Radoslaw Karwowski and Radomir Měch for the development of the `L-studio/cpfg` plant modeling software, and Craig Kolb for the development of the `rayshade` ray tracer, which we used to render the scenes. The partial support of this research by grants from the Natural Sciences and Engineering Research Council of Canada is also gratefully acknowledged.

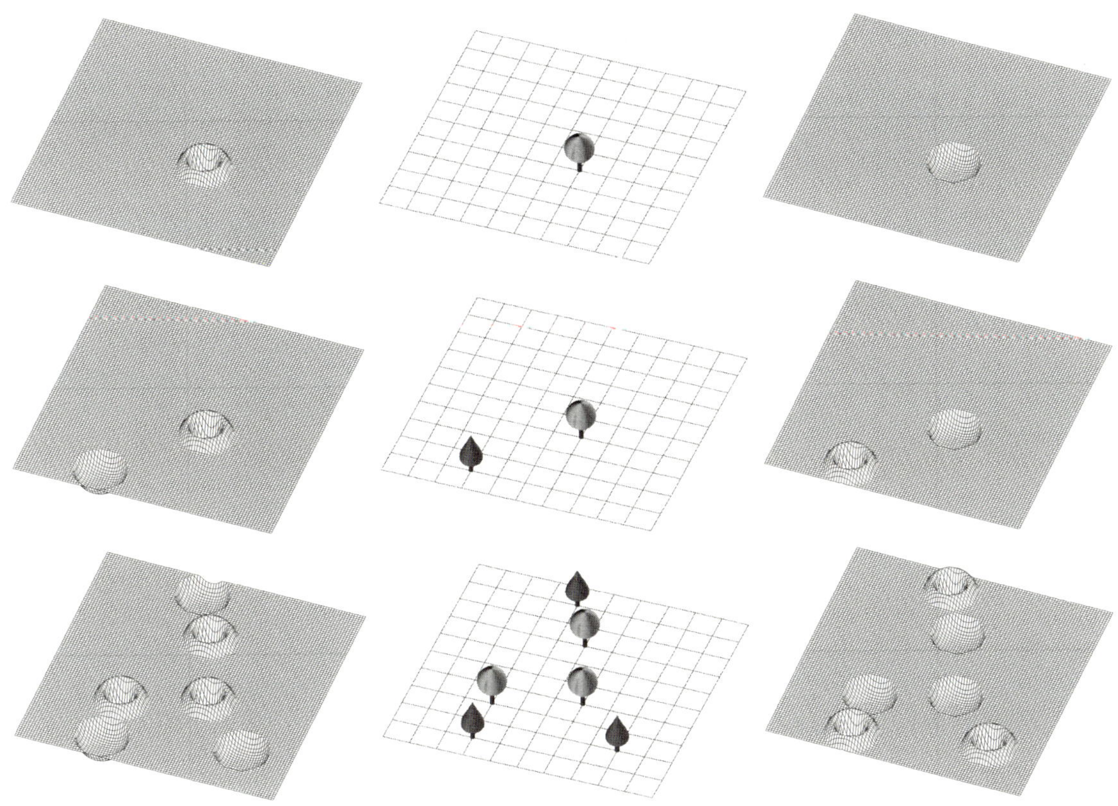

Figure 13: Generation of a two-species distribution using the deformation kernel algorithm with the kernel matrix shown in Figure 12. On the left, the probability density function of species 1; on the right, that of species 2. From top to bottom: the state of the system after placing the first plant of species 1, after placing the first plant of species 2, and after placing several plants of each species.

Figure 14: A forest model consisting of four species of trees. Left: distribution of plants. Right: realistic visualization of the model.

References

[1] N. Chiba, K. Muraoka, A. Doi, and J. Hosokawa. Rendering of forest scenery using 3D textures. *Journal of Visualization and Computer Animation*, 8(4):191–199, 1997.

[2] M. R. T. Dale. *Spatial Pattern Analysis in Plant Ecology*. Cambridge Studies in Ecology. Cambridge University Press, Cambridge, UK, 1999.

[3] O. Deussen, P. Hanrahan, B. Lintermann, R. Měch, M. Pharr, and P. Prusinkiewicz. Realistic modeling and rendering of plant ecosystems. *Proceeding of SIGGRAPH 98 (Orlando, Florida, July 19-24, 1998)*, pages 275–286, 1998.

[4] F. G. Firbank and A. R. Watkinson. A model of interference within plant monocultures. *Journal of Theoretical Biology*, 116:291–311, 1985.

[5] R. W. Floyd and L. Steinberg. An adaptive algorithm for spatial greyscale. *Proceedings of the Society for Information Display*, 17:75–77, 1975.

[6] B. Hopkins. A new method for determining the type of distribution of plant individuals. *Annals of Botany*, XVIII:213–226, 1954.

[7] B. Lane and P. Prusinkiewicz. Randomized generation of nonuniform plant distributions. *Proceedings of Western Computer Graphics Symposium 2000*, pages 61–66, 2000.

[8] L. Legendre and P. Legendre. *Numerical Ecology*. Elsevier, Amsterdam, 1983.

[9] A. Lindenmayer. Mathematical models for cellular interaction in development, Parts I and II. *Journal of Theoretical Biology*, 18:280–315, 1968.

[10] R. Měch and P. Prusinkiewicz. Visual models of plants interacting with their environment. *Proceedings of SIGGRAPH 1996*, pages 397–410, August 1996.

[11] P. Prusinkiewicz. Graphical applications of L-systems. In *Proceedings of Graphics Interface '86 — Vision Interface '86*, pages 247–253, 1986.

[12] P. Prusinkiewicz, R. Karwowski, R. Měch, and J. Hanan. L-studio/cpfg: A software system for modeling plants. In M. Nagl, A. Schürr, and M. Münch, editors, *Applications of graph transformation with industrial relevance*, Lecture Notes in Computer Science 1779, pages 457–464. Springer-Verlag, Berlin, 2000.

[13] P. Prusinkiewicz and A. Lindenmayer. *The Algorithmic Beauty of Plants*. Springer-Verlag, New York, 1990. With J. S. Hanan, F. D. Fracchia, D. R. Fowler, M. J. M. de Boer, and L. Mercer.

[14] P. Prusinkiewicz, L. Mündermann, R. Karwowski, and B. Lane. The use of positional information in the modeling of plants. *Proceeding of SIGGRAPH 2001 (Los Angeles, California, August 11-17, 2001)*, pages 289–300, 2001.

[15] S. M. Ross. *Introduction to Probability Models*. Academic Press, 1997.

[16] G. Rozenberg and K. P. Lee. Developmental systems with finite axiom sets. Part I. Systems without interactions. *International Journal of Computer Mathematics*, 4:43–68, 1974.

[17] G. Rozenberg, K. Ruohonen, and A. Salomaa. Developmental systems with fragmentation. *International Journal of Computer Mathematics*, 5:177–191, 1976.

Simulation and Rendering of Liquid Foams

Hendrik Kück[a] Christian Vogelgsang[b] Günther Greiner[b]

[a] Department of Computer Science
University of British Columbia
Vancouver, Canada
kueck@cs.ubc.ca

[b] Institut für Informatik
Friedrich Alexander Universität Erlangen-Nürnberg
Erlangen, Germany
{vogelgsang,greiner}@cs.fau.de

Abstract

In this paper we present a technique for simulating and rendering liquid foams. We are aiming at a functional realism that allows our simulation to be consistent with the physical effects in real liquid foam while avoiding the prohibitive computational cost of a physically accurate simulation. To this end, we have to recreate two important attributes of foam. The dynamic behaviour of the simulated foam must be based on the physics of real foam, and the characteristic interior structures of foam and their optical properties must be reproduced. We tackle these requirements by introducing a two part hybrid rendering approach. The first stage is geometric and determines the dynamic behaviour of the foam by simulating structural forces on a set of spheres, which represent the foam bubbles. In the second stage we render these spheres using a special surface shader that implicitly reconstructs the foam surfaces and performs the shading calculations. This two step approach allows us to easily integrate our technique into existing ray-tracing systems. We include images of an example animation to demonstrate the visual quality.

Key words: liquid foam, simulation, rendering, natural phenomena, shading techniques

1 Introduction

The simulation of natural phenomena is an important and fascinating research field in computer graphics. Convincing simulations and renderings of these phenomena add greatly to the realism of computer generated imagery.

Liquid foams are natural phenomena that are prominent in everyday life. On most carbonated beverages, for example, there will be at least a small amount of froth. While techniques have been developed to simulate and render liquids and their dynamics very realistically, the addition of foam would significantly increase the realism of animations.

Another point motivating the need for realistic computer generated foam is that foam is quite difficult to handle, as it tends to disintegrate over time. Also, its internal structure changes due to effects such as film rupture and diffusion. Such changes alter the visual appearance of the foam. Thus, filming scenes featuring foam is a difficult task and using computer animations is an effective alternative. Due to the complex dynamical and optical properties of foams, it is very hard or even impossible to achieve sufficiently believable animations of foam at various scales using existing modelling and rendering techniques such as particle systems or texturing. Thus, a specialized technique for simulation and rendering of foam is needed.

The rest of the paper is structured as follows. The next section describes previous work in the field of foam simulation and rendering. Section 3 gives an overview of the physical and geometric properties of liquid foams. In Section 4 we describe our model for the simulation of foam structure and dynamics. Our rendering method is explained in Section 5. Section 6 contains implementation details and presents some results. We end with concluding remarks and ideas for future work.

2 Previous Work

Soap films and bubbles have fascinated children and researchers from many different disciplines for centuries. While children are fascinated by the fragility and beauty of the iridescent soap bubbles, mathematician's interest in soap film structures is mainly due to the surface minimizing property of these films [11]. Although this theoretic research on minimal surfaces has produced various insights in the geometry of foams [23, 2], many problems still remain unsolved [24].

Analytical solutions for the geometry of soap bubble clusters exist for clusters of up to three bubbles. The liquid films are spherical in these cases. Glassner models such clusters using CSG operations and renders them using a special shader that takes Fresnel reflection and interference effects at the soap films into account [13].

As the geometry of larger bubble clusters cannot be computed analytically, numerical methods have to be used. The Surface Evolver program by Brakke evolves triangular meshes towards a state of minimal energy, taking surface tension and other forces into account [5]. It can be used to numerically compute the geometry of bubble clusters in equilibrium [19]. However, due to its computational expense, this approach is not feasible for large numbers of bubbles. Almgren and Sullivan [1] render bubble cluster geometries produced by Surface Evolver simulations using a shading model very similar to the one used by Glassner.

Icart and Arquès restrict their simulation of soap froth to two-dimensional foam, i.e. bubbles in a common plane [14]. They use spherical and planar films to approximate the foam structure. As for Almgren, Sullivan and Glassner, the main focus of their work is on the simulation of the interference effects at the liquid films.

In contrast, Durikovic does not address optical properties at all and focuses instead on the simulation of the geometry and the dynamic behaviour of soap bubbles [10]. He uses particles connected by springs to approximate the bubble surface and its deformation in response to forces caused by wind or contact with other bubbles or objects.

None of the published research dealing with the rendering of soap bubbles or foam takes the junctions of the liquid films into account, although these are of great importance for the visual appearance of foams.

Physicists have been studying foams for a long time to investigate their dynamic properties. Although there is a great deal of published research in soft condensed matter physics on many aspects of foams [26, 3, 15, 25, 21], foam dynamics is still far from completely understood. Due to the instability of liquid foam, many foam experiments tend to be very difficult to perform. This is one reason why physicists developed and used computer simulations of foam structure and dynamics. Most of the approaches restrict themselves to the simulation of two-dimensional foams. This reduction in dimensionality significantly decreases the complexity of the problem and most insights gained from these 2D simulations can be transferred to the 3D case. There are two different types of models for the foam structure that researchers have used in their simulations. Kermode and Bolton both developed computer programs for the simulation of two-dimensional foam. They model the foam as a network of curved liquid films. Kermode's simulation program 2D-Froth (described in [26]) assumes the films to be infinitely thin circular segments joined at vertices. For given pressures in the enclosed cells, the structure is equilibrated by moving the vertices. Bolton [4] extends this model by allowing the junctions of films to have spatial extents, which allows for the simulation of foam with higher liquid fractions.

The other type of model, used by Durian [7, 8] represents the foam as a collection of interacting gas bubbles. In comparison with network based approaches, this greatly simplifies the simulation of the dynamic behaviour of foam since one does not have to deal with topological changes as bubbles move.

3 Foam Physics

3.1 Foam Structure

Liquid foams are two phase systems consisting of a liquid enclosing bubbles of gas. Depending on the liquid content, the structure of the foam can vary greatly. In an extremely wet foam, the gas bubbles are spherical and separated by large amounts of liquid. At the other extreme, a very dry foam consists of extremely thin films of liquid separating the gas bubbles. Foams encountered in everyday life such as beer foam or dish washing foam are quite dry, featuring liquid films with thickness ranging from a few to several tens of microns.

Where the films meet, small tubes with a triangular cross-section are formed (see Figure 3). Known as *Plateau borders*, these tubes are where most of the water in a foam is contained. They are responsible for some of the characteristic visual properties of liquid foams.

The surface tension in liquids causes contracting forces along the surface of the liquid. As a result, liquids always try to minimize their surface area. The reason why a bubble remains stable and does not collapse into a drop of liquid is that there is an excess pressure inside the bubble. This produces forces acting on the bubble surface that exactly cancel the forces owing to the surface tension.

3.2 The Laplace-Young Law

Laplace and Young derived an equation relating the radius of curvature R of a liquid film with surface tension γ to the pressure difference Δp between the gas cells it separates [3]:

$$R = 4\frac{\gamma}{\Delta p}.$$

This law can be used to compute the radius of individual soap bubbles, as well as the radius of curvature of films separating two gas cells. According to this law, such a separating liquid film will be curved toward the cell with the smaller pressure. It also follows from this law that smaller bubbles have higher pressure than larger bubbles and thus the separating film between two different size bubbles will be curved towards the larger bubble.

3.3 Law of Plateau

In the 19th century, Plateau performed experiments with soap films and frameworks [20]. He experimentally established rules about the geometric properties of soap films that were later theoretically proven. These rules

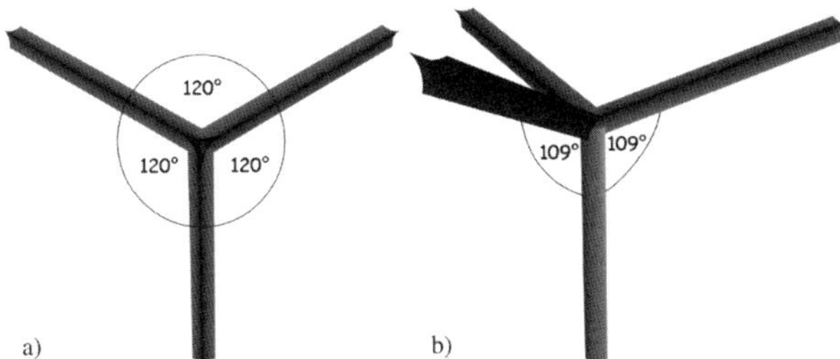

Figure 1: Angles formed by films and Plateau borders

state that the liquid films in a foam always meet in groups of three. At these junctions (the Plateau borders) the films always form angles of 120° (see Figure 1a). The Plateau borders themselves meet in groups of four in the tetrahedral angle of 109.5° (Figure 1b).

3.4 Dynamic Effects in Liquid Foams

The structure of foam changes over time for several reasons. Gravity exerts forces on the liquid, resulting in a drainage of the foam. Thus, the films get thinner over time, and the probability of film rupture increases. As more and more films break, the foam gets coarser and finally disintegrates. Additionally, in the case of froth on a liquid, new bubbles could rise from the liquid and add to the foam from below.

3.5 Optical Effects

Liquid foam has fascinating optical properties. For example, it is intriguing, that a transparent liquid can form a bright white foam that seems to be completely opaque. These properties are caused by the effects of refraction and reflection at the liquid/gas boundaries of the complex foam structures. In this section we take a closer look at these interactions of light with the foam structures.

If we follow a ray of light into the foam, we have to distinguish between collision with a film and a Plateau border. As the liquid films are extremely thin, their two

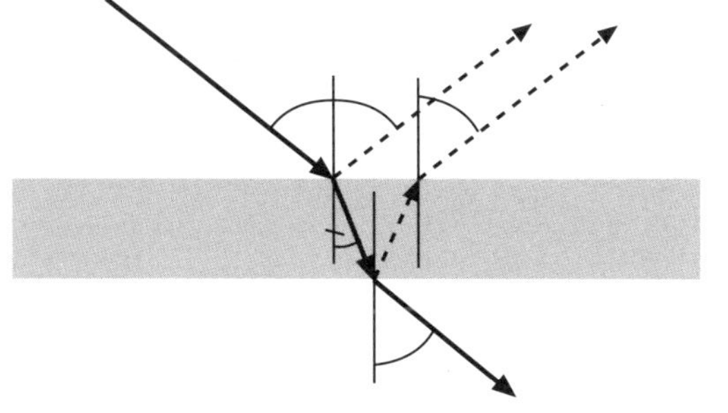

Figure 2: Light ray refracted and reflected at liquid film

boundary surfaces are almost perfectly parallel to each other. As illustrated in Figure 2, a ray of light passing through a film is refracted according to Snell's law at the first boundary. However, because the boundaries are parallel, the change in direction will be reversed at the second interface. Thus the ray leaves in the same direction as it entered but with a small positional offset.

Part of the light is reflected at the interfaces. The fraction of the light that is reflected is given by the Fresnel reflection coefficient [12], a value which depends on the indices of refraction of liquid and gas and also on the incident angle of the light ray. A fraction of the light entering the liquid will also be reflected inside the liquid one or more times. This results in light leaving the liquid in the same direction as the directly reflected light (see figure 2) but with a phase shift due to the different path lengths and the additional phase shift occurring when the light enters the liquid. Due to the interference of the light waves taking these different paths, some wavelengths are reinforced, while others are cancelled [6]. If the thickness of the films is sufficiently close to the wavelength of visible light (0.5 to about 2 microns), these interferences cause only a few maxima and minima in the visible spectrum and thus produce the characteristic iridescent colours of soap bubbles. However, for all but extremely dry foams, the liquid films are thicker and thus do not exhibit visible interference effects [3].

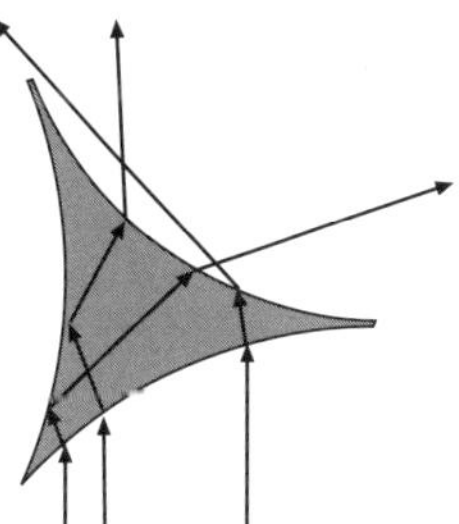

Figure 3: Refraction and total refraction at Plateau border

While the effect of refraction on light rays passing through liquid films is negligible, the effect is significant at Plateau borders. Due to refraction and total reflection at the interfaces, the direction of the rays leaving the Plateau border can vary greatly for the same incident angle and only a small positional offset (see Figure 3). Due to these refraction effects and the additional Fresnel reflections at films and Plateau borders, the light is scattered inside the foam and its direction is randomized. To what extent the direction of light entering the foam is randomized, depends on the 'optical thickness' of the foam and on the distance that the light travels through the foam. The optical thickness determines the frequency of scattering events in a medium and it can be characterized in terms of the transport mean free path, i.e. the average distance a photon will travel before it is scattered into a random direction [16]. Measurements show that in the

case of liquid foams this value is proportional to the average bubble diameter [9]. The randomization of light directions due to multiple scattering results in the nearly uniform white appearance of dense liquid foams.

4 Simulation

The model we use for the simulation is very similar to the one proposed by Durian [7]. However, there are important differences. Durian's model is restricted to the simulation of two-dimensional foams in the wet regime. We extended it to three dimensions and also generalized it to simulate foams with arbitrary liquid content by allowing attractive forces between bubbles. The only external influence on the simulated foam in Durian's work is exerted by moving the topmost bubbles with constant velocity. We allow for interaction of the simulated foam with the environment by taking forces due to contact with external objects into account.

During the simulation, we do not compute the exact geometry of the foam structure or how the bubbles are deformed as they come into contact with other bubbles or external objects. Instead, we represent the bubbles by spheres with fixed radii and move them according to assumed forces.

4.1 Bubble - Bubble Forces

If we take a look at two bubbles in an extremely wet foam, we see that the bubbles are spherical gas cells surrounded by water. When these bubbles touch each other, they deform into non-spherical shapes. As a sphere has minimal surface area, this deformation increases the surface of the bubbles and thus gives rise to a repulsive force due to surface tension. According to Durian [7], these forces are close to harmonic and can thus be approximated by spring forces between touching bubbles.

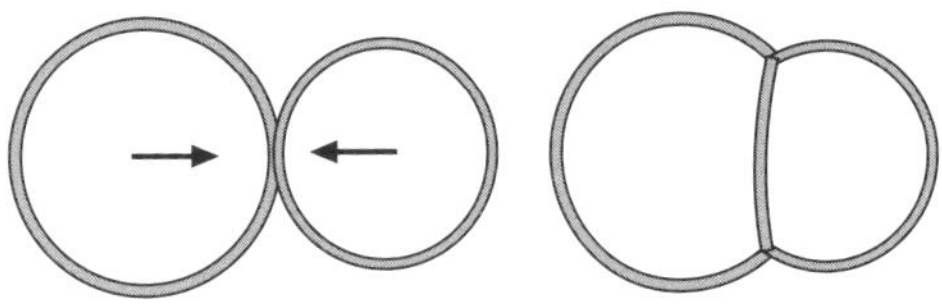

Figure 4: Attracting force acting on touching bubbles

The situation is more complicated in a dry foam. If two bubbles surrounded by air touch each other as shown in Figure 4 they can share the separating film and thus decrease the overall surface by moving closer together. This causes an attractive force which drags the bubbles toward each other. The surface area is minimized when the Plateau condition is met, i.e. when the films meet at 120° angles as on the right side of Figure 4.

We use a combination of attractive and repulsive spring forces acting on touching bubbles to model this behaviour. Ideally, these forces will cancel each other exactly when the Plateau conditions are met.

The repulsive force $\mathbf{F}^r_{ij} (= -\mathbf{F}^r_{ji})$ acting on bubble i due to contact with bubble j in our model is given by

$$\mathbf{F}^r_{ij} = k_r \left(\frac{1}{||\mathbf{p}_i - \mathbf{p}_j||} - \frac{1}{rad_i + rad_j} \right) (\mathbf{p}_i - \mathbf{p}_j),$$

where k_r is a user-defined coefficient that models the surface tension in the liquid. $\mathbf{p}_i$ and $\mathbf{p}_j$ are the positions of the sphere centres for the spheres representing bubbles i and j and rad_i and rad_j are the radii.

The attractive force between two bubbles depends on the surface area that these bubbles can share when moving closer together. Obviously, if additional other bubbles touch both bubbles, the possible common surface area will be smaller, resulting in a smaller pairwise attractive force. To approximate this, we take the number of neighbours of the spheres into account when computing the attractive force $\mathbf{F}^a_{ij}$ acting on bubble i due to contact with bubble j. More specifically,

$$\mathbf{F}^a_{ij} = k_a \, c_{nb} \, c_{dist} \frac{\mathbf{p}_j - \mathbf{p}_i}{||\mathbf{p}_j - \mathbf{p}_i||}$$

with

$$c_{nb} = \frac{\frac{1}{|NB_i|} + \frac{1}{|NB_j|}}{2}$$

$$c_{dist} = \frac{||\mathbf{p}_j - \mathbf{p}_i|| - max(rad_i, rad_j)}{min(rad_i, rad_j)}.$$

Again, k_a is a user-defined coefficient. The ratio $\frac{k_a}{k_r}$ models the liquid content (i.e. the wetness) of the simulated foam. $|NB_i|$ is the cardinality of the set of neighbours of sphere i, i.e. all the spheres that are overlapping with that sphere in the current configuration.

For gas bubbles to change their position relative to each other, liquid must flow through the films and Plateau borders. As the bubbles move with respect to their neighbours, they experience a force opposed to this movement due to viscosity of the liquid. We assume the force F^v_i to be proportional to the velocity at which bubble i moves relative to the bubbles touching it. That is,

$$\begin{aligned} \mathbf{F}^v_i &= k_v(\overline{\mathbf{v}_i} - \mathbf{v}_i) \\ &= k_v \left(\left[\sum_{j \in NB_i} \frac{\mathbf{v}_j}{|NB_i|} \right] - \mathbf{v}_i \right), \end{aligned}$$

where k_v is a user-defined parameter modelling the viscosity of the liquid, $\mathbf{v}_i$ is the velocity of bubble i and $\overline{\mathbf{v}_i}$ is the mean velocity of the bubbles in contact with i, i.e. the bubbles in NB_i.

4.2 Object - Bubble Forces

We want the foam to react to objects in the scene. We must therefore compute the forces acting on the bubbles due to contact with those objects. The forces we take into account here are very similar to the ones between bubbles. Again, we assume attractive and repulsive spring forces for bubbles touching the objects. Additionally, we also consider forces due to friction at the object surface:

$$\mathbf{F}_i^{of} = k_{of}(\overline{\mathbf{v}^o}_i - \mathbf{v}_i), \tag{1}$$

where $\overline{\mathbf{v}^o}_i$ is the mean velocity of the scene objects touching bubble i and k_{of} is the friction coefficient, which can be adjusted by the user on a per-object basis.

4.3 Other Forces

An additional constant force $\mathbf{F}_g$ acts on all forces and models the effect of gravity. Another frictional force in our model is the force $\mathbf{F}_i^{air}$ acting on bubble i due to air resistance. We assume the air to be static, so that this force is proportional to the velocity of the bubble:

$$\mathbf{F}_i^{air} = -k_{air}\,\mathbf{v}_i,$$

where the user-defined parameter k_{air} models the air resistance.

4.4 Deriving an ODE System

The total force $\mathbf{F}_i^{total}$ acting on bubble i is given by

$$\begin{aligned}
\mathbf{F}_i^{total} &= \mathbf{F}_i^{ra} + \mathbf{F}_i^{fr} + \mathbf{F}^g, \\
\text{with} & \\
\mathbf{F}_i^{ra} &= \sum_{j \in NB_i} (\mathbf{F}_{ij}^{r} + \mathbf{F}_{ij}^{a}) + \sum_{k \in NO_i} (\mathbf{F}_{ik}^{or} + \mathbf{F}_{ik}^{oa}); \\
\mathbf{F}_i^{fr} &= \mathbf{F}_i^{v} + \mathbf{F}_i^{of} + \mathbf{F}_i^{air},
\end{aligned}$$

where $\mathbf{F}_i^{ra}$ represents all the repulsive and attractive forces acting on bubble i due to contact with adjacent bubbles (NB_i) and objects (NO_i). $\mathbf{F}_i^{fr}$ represents the frictional forces acting on bubble i due to movement relative to its neighbour bubbles, objects and the surrounding air.

Like Durian [7], we assume that the bubbles have no mass. A consequence of this assumption is, that the forces acting on a bubble have to sum up to $\mathbf{0}$, that is,

$$\mathbf{F}_i^{total} = \mathbf{0}.$$

Using this, we can relate the velocity of a bubble to the position and the velocities of adjacent bubbles and objects. Solving for $\mathbf{v}_i$ gives

$$\mathbf{v}_i = \frac{1}{k_v + k_{of} + k_{air}} \left(k_v \overline{\mathbf{v}}_i + k_{of} \overline{\mathbf{v}^o}_i + \mathbf{F}_i^{ra} + \mathbf{F}^g\right).$$

Since $\mathbf{v}_i = \dot{\mathbf{p}}_i$, we have a first-order ODE system. We use numerical integration to solve for the positions of the bubbles at the current animation frame. The result of this simulation is then used as start configuration for the simulation for the next frame.

Unlike most physical models involving spring forces, the springs in our model are not statically assigned, but depend instead upon the position of the bubbles. Thus, for each step of the numerical integration scheme, it has to be determined which spheres overlap with which other spheres and which external objects, as this information is needed for the computation of the forces acting on the bubbles. We exploit the temporal coherence of sphere overlaps to accelerate these computations using a scheduling approach similar to the one described in [17].

4.5 Other Dynamic Effects

Our simulation also models the rupture of liquid films and the creation of bubbles rising from a supporting liquid (or appearing from any other source) by simply removing random bubbles during the simulation and adding new random bubbles according to a set of user-defined parameters specifying the distribution of positions and radii of new bubbles as well as the rate of additions and film rupture.

4.6 Generating Geometry

Using the result of the simulation, we create simple geometry consisting of overlapping spheres with the computed centres and radii. The spheres are flattened at the intersection with scene objects. The resulting geometry is passed to the ray-tracer for rendering using the shading approach described in the next section.

5 Shading

The main purpose of our shading algorithm is to transform a set of spheres into the visual appearance of a contiguous foam structure. The existing geometry is a sphere structure like the one on the left side of Figure 5. Our shader then tries to mimic the look of real foam, as depicted on the right side.

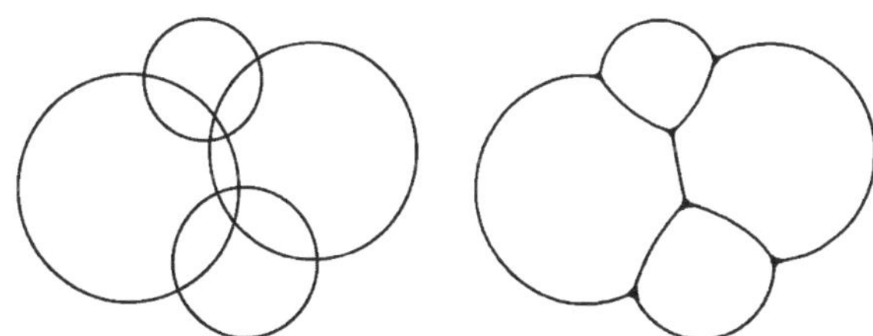

Figure 5: Sphere representation (left) and corresponding foam structure (right)

We use a special surface shader, which is called at every intersection of a viewing ray with one of the gener-

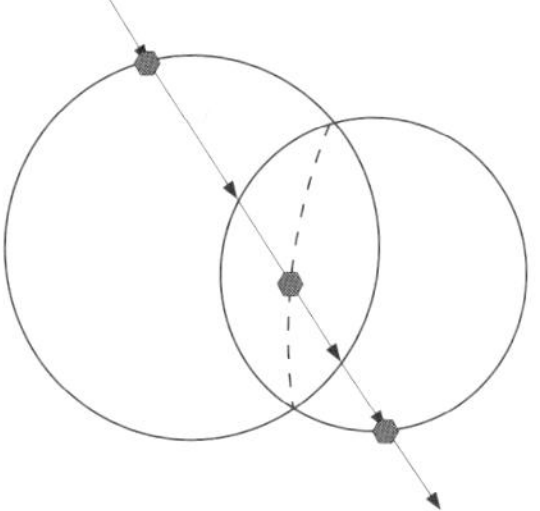

Figure 6: Ray intersecting overlapping spheres

ated spheres. For each such intersection, we must decide if there is a liquid film or Plateau border at this position in the corresponding foam structure, for which local shading has to be performed. Otherwise, no shading calculations are carried out at this intersection. In the example shown in Figure 6 we only want to perform local shading at the three marked positions. As can also be seen in this example, the surface of an assumed liquid film separating two or more bubbles does not necessarily coincide with the surfaces of the spheres. Thus, in such cases, we have to somehow approximate the intersection with this separating film from the information we get for the ray's intersections with the spheres. The basic idea is to make all these decisions depending on the order in which a ray enters and leaves the overlapping foam spheres. To do this, we associate a data structure with a ray that keeps track of which spheres the ray currently is inside, as well as the order in which it entered these spheres.

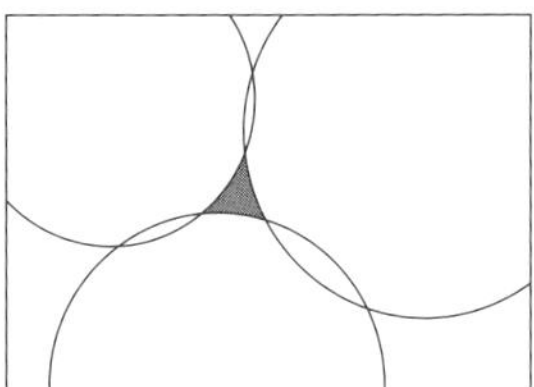

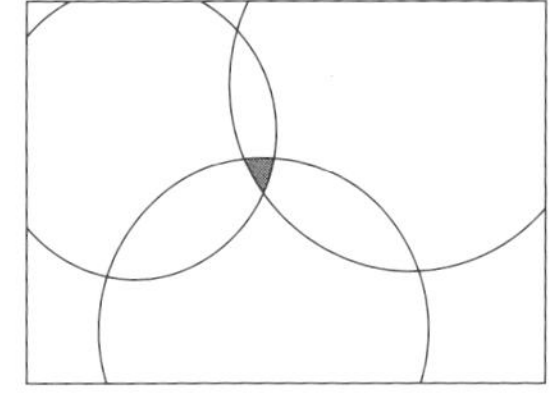

Figure 7: Two sphere configurations in which a Plateau border is assumed

Given this information at a ray/sphere intersection, we decide to assume a Plateau border in the foam structure in both cases shown in Figure 7. The grey areas indicate where Plateau borders would be assumed by our algorithm. In the left case, a ray passing through the grey area travels through a small amount of free space between spheres. We detect this case when the ray enters a sphere from free space and the distance to the last intersection with another sphere is smaller than a user-defined upper bound for the width of Plateau borders. As shown in the right case in Figure 7, we also assume a Plateau border when the ray traverses the intersection of at least three overlapping spheres. The condition to detect this case at an intersection is that the ray was in exactly three spheres and at this intersection leaves the one sphere out of the three that it entered the first. If a plateau border is detected using one of these conditions, we perform the local shading as described in Section 5.2.

If the current intersection does not meet the conditions for a Plateau border, we check if it represents an intersection with a liquid film. This will be the case if *a)* a sphere is entered from empty space or *b)* the ray leaves a sphere into empty space and neither at this nor at the next intersection along the ray are the conditions for a Plateau border met. The local shading calculations for the intersection are then performed using the shading model for liquid films described in Section 5.1. There is one other case when local shading for liquid films must be performed. It deals with the assumed liquid films separating touching bubbles such as at the second marked point in Figure 6. Such a separating liquid film is assumed when the ray was in exactly two spheres and leaves the sphere it entered first. Since the assumed separating film does not coincide

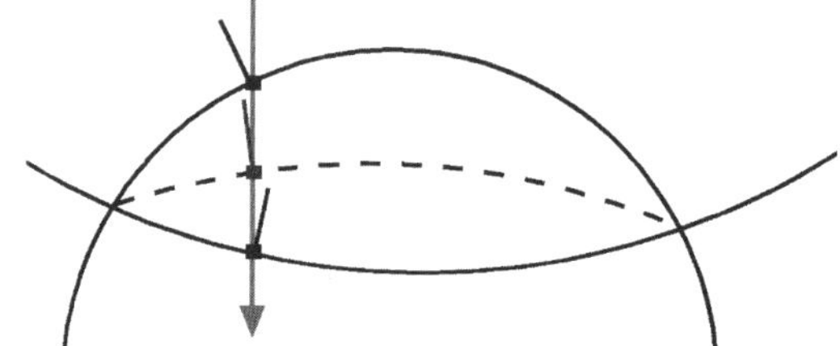

Figure 8: Approximation of intersection with separating liquid film

with the sphere surfaces, we must approximate the intersection with that film. We do this by simply averaging the positions and normal vectors of the intersections with the two overlapping spheres as shown in Figure 8. As the smaller bubble has a higher curvature, the averaged normal vectors will give the visual impression of a surface curved towards the larger bubble, which is consistent with the shape of liquid films in real foams (see Section 3.2). It has to be mentioned however, that this does not necessarily hold for grazing viewing angles. Thus, this simple and somewhat crude approximation manages to qualitatively recreate the curvature of the liquid films quite well and at low computational cost for most viewing angles.

5.1 Local Shading for Liquid Films

As described in Section 3.5 refraction does not change the direction of rays passing through the liquid films. The mentioned positional offset of the ray is so small (a few microns at most) that it can be safely ignored. So when a ray hits a liquid film, we perform the local shading and continue to follow the ray further into the scene. For the local shading of the films we use a simple shader that approximates Fresnel reflection [12]. Currently we do not take interference effects into accounts. However, a shader that simulates these effects using the techniques described in [6, 22] could be used instead for the rendering of extremely dry foams.

5.2 Local Shading for Plateau Borders

As mentioned in section 3.5, the high curvature shapes of the Plateau borders cause incident light to be scattered in many different directions through Fresnel reflection, refraction and total reflection. In our shading approach for the Plateau border we model both the scattering of direct incident light towards the camera at a single Plateau border, as well as the diffusion of light due to multiple scattering in the foam.

We approximate the diffusion as the sum of the intensities of all light sources illuminating the foam, weighted by a user-defined parameter. This parameter represents the diffusive properties of the foam. To determine the amount of direct incident light, that is scattered towards the camera at a Plateau border, we first approximate the Plateau border's principal direction $\mathbf{d}$. We construct $\mathbf{d}$ as being maximally close to perpendicular to the normal vectors of the adjacent sphere surfaces. The direction $\mathbf{r}$ of an incoming light ray can be split up into a component parallel to $\mathbf{d}$ and a perpendicular one. We then make the simplifying assumption that Fresnel reflection, refraction and total reflection have the effect of completely randomizing the component perpendicular to $\mathbf{d}$ while leaving the parallel component almost unchanged. The only change to the parallel component is due to refraction because the Plateau border surfaces are perpendicular to $\mathbf{d}$ and thus reflections have no effect on this component. As the change that occurs due to refraction when the ray enters the liquid is counteracted by the change occurring when it exits, the assumption of a small change is valid.

The contribution of a single light source according to this model is then taken to be the intensity of that light source weighted by $cos^n\theta$, where n is a user-defined parameter and θ is the minimum angle between any light ray from this light source scattered at the Plateau border according to the assumptions stated above and the direction from the Plateau border to the camera. The cos^n distribution models the small possible change of the component parallel to $\mathbf{d}$ due to refraction.

6 Implementation

We implemented our approach as a combination of a geometry and material shader for Mental Ray from Mental Images, a commercial ray-tracing system. The implementation includes a geometry shader responsible for the simulation calculation and sphere creation. A material shader was implemented to perform the shading in the rendering stage.

In our implementation, we support two different types of objects that can interact with the simulated foam. The first object type is convex polygonal objects. The foam is restricted to the interior of these objects. The other supported shapes are spheres. They can be placed as foam obstacles. These types of objects were chosen based on the ease and efficiency of intersection tests with the foam spheres. The objects used to affect the foam need not appear in the rendering. Using invisible spheres and convex objects, arbitrary object shapes can be approximated.

6.1 Results

Figure 9 contains three frames of a simple animation. In this animation, a small amount of foam consisting of about 700 bubbles slides down a slant and around a spherical obstacle. The resulting animation is quite convincing, featuring plausible foam dynamics. The interaction with external objects greatly increase the realism.

The simulation computations for this scene took about 4 seconds per frame. The time spent in the rendering itself was 40 seconds per frame (for 800x630 images on a dual PII/400). For larger numbers of bubbles, the simulation and rendering times stay reasonable. A scene with 3000 foam bubbles resulted in a per-frame simulation time of 28 seconds and a rendering time of 90 seconds.

7 Conclusion and Future Work

We have developed a rendering technique that allows high quality foam simulation and rendering in reasonable time. The simulation stage uses a physically-based 3D simulation with foam bubbles represented by fixed-size spheres. With this approach, we avoid the explicit construction of the complex interior surfaces of foam. To achieve visually convincing results, we use a custom surface shader to approximate these structures in the rendering stage. Although not physically accurate, this combination leads to a rendering method that is consistent with the physical effects in real foam and reasonably fast for production use.

Previous work on the rendering of bubbles and liquid foams in computer graphics has mainly focused on the modelling and rendering of single bubbles or small clusters of bubbles. The other extreme, a dense foam viewed from a large distance, could be rendered using multiple scattering techniques as described in [18], thus ignoring the internal structure of the foam completely. Our work lies somewhere between these extreme cases. The compromise between physics and heuristics we take in our model works quite well for foams with several thousand bubbles, viewed from moderate distance.

A promising area for future research could be the extension of our technique to allow arbitrary numbers of

Figure 9: Foam of approximately 700 bubbles sliding past a hemisphere on an inclined plane

bubbles viewed from arbitrary distances. This could be achieved using a level of detail approach. For close-ups, the internal structure of the foam should be explicitly modelled and rendered with more suitable shading models. For dense foams, computation of bubble positions in the interior may be avoidable. At the same time, our approximation of light transport inside dense foam needs to be replaced by an actual simulation of the multiple scattering effects. Such an integrated technique would allow efficient simulation and rendering of convincing animations of a wide variety of liquid foams.

Acknowledgements

We want to thank the Animation/VFX department at SZM Studios, Munich, Germany, who sponsored this project by providing both hardware and software. Special thanks must go to Horst Hadler and Michael Kellner at SZM Studios for their support in many ways and especially for answering numerous technical questions. We would also like to thank the anonymous reviewers for their detailed and valuable comments.

References

[1] F. Almgren and J. Sullivan. Visualization of soap bubble geometries. In M. Emmer, editor, *The Visual Mind*, pages 79–83. MIT Press, 1993.

[2] F. J. Almgren, Jr. and J. E. Taylor. The geometry of soap films and soap bubbles. *Scientific American*, 235(1):82–93, 1976.

[3] J. J. Bikerman. *Foams*. Springer-Verlag, Berlin, 1973.

[4] F. Bolton. A computer program for the simulation of two-dimensional foam, 1990. www.tcd.ie/Physics/Foams/plat.html.

[5] K. Brakke. The surface evolver. *Experimental Mathematics*, 1:141–165, 1992.

[6] M. L. Dias. Ray tracing interference color. *IEEE Computer Graphics and Applications*, pages 54–60, 1991.

[7] D. J. Durian. Foam mechanics at the bubble scale. *Physical Review Letters*, 75(26):4780–4783, 1995.

[8] D. J. Durian. Bubble-scale model of foam mechanics: Melting, nonlinear behaviour and avalanches. *Physical Review*, E(55):1739–1751, 1997.

[9] D. J. Durian, D. A. Weitz, and D. J. Pine. Multiple light-scattering probes of foam structure and dynamics. *Science*, 252(5006):686–688, 1991.

[10] R. Durikovic. Animation of soap bubble dynamics, cluster formation and collision. *Computer Graphics Forum*, 20(3), 2001.

[11] M. Emmer. Soap bubbles in art and science: From the past to the future of math art. In M. Emmer, editor, *The Visual Mind*, pages 135–142. MIT Press, 1993.

[12] J. Foley, A. van Dam, S. Feiner, and J. Hughes. *Computer graphics - Principles and Practice*. Addison-Wesley, 2nd edition, 1990.

[13] A. Glassner. Soap bubbles. *IEEE Computer Graphics and Applications*, 20(6):99–109, 2000.

[14] I. Icart and D. Arquès. An approach to geometrical and optical simulation of soap froth. *Computers and Graphics*, 23(3):405–418, 1999.

[15] C. Isenberg. *The Science of Soap Films and Soap Bubbles*. Dover Publications, 1987.

[16] A. Ishimaru. *Wave Propagation and Scattering in Random Media*. Wiley-IEEE Press, 1999.

[17] D. J. Kim, L. J. Guibas, and S. Y. Shin. Fast collision detection among multiple moving spheres. *IEEE Transactions on Visualization and Computer Graphics*, 4(3):230–242, 1998.

[18] F. Pérez, X. Pueyo, and F. X. Sillion. Global illumination techniques for the simulation of participating media. In Julie Dorsey and Philipp Slusallek, editors, *Eurographics Rendering Workshop 1997*, pages 309–320, New York City, NY, 1997. Eurographics, Springer Wien.

[19] R. Phelan, D. Weaire, and K. Brakke. Computation of equilibrium foam structures using the surface evolver. *Experimental Mathematics*, 4:181–192, 1995.

[20] J. A. F. Plateau. *Statique Expérimentale et Théorique des Liquides soumis aux seules Forces Moléculaires*. Gauthier-Villars, Paris, 1873.

[21] R. K. Prud'homme and S. A. Khan, editors. *Foams: Theory, Measurements and Applications*. Marcel Decker, Inc., 1995.

[22] B. E. Smits and G. Meyer. Newton's Colors: Simulating Interference Phenomena in Realistic Image Synthesis. In K. Bouatouch and C. Bouville, editors, *Photorealism in Computer Graphics*, pages 185–194, 1992.

[23] J. M. Sullivan. The geometry of bubbles and foams. In J.-F. Sadoc, editor, *Foams, Emulsions, and Cellular Materials*, pages 379–402. NATO ASI, 1998.

[24] J. M. Sullivan and F. Morgan. Open problems in soap bubble geometry. *Int. J. Math.*, 7(6):833–842, 1996.

[25] D. Weaire and J. Banhart. *Foams and Films*. MIT Verlag Bremen, 1999.

[26] D. Weaire and S. Hutzler. *The Physics of Foams*. Oxford University Press, 1999.

Texturing Faces

Marco Tarini[1,2] Hitoshi Yamauchi[1] Jörg Haber[1] Hans-Peter Seidel[1]

[1] Max-Planck-Institut für Informatik, Saarbrücken, Germany
[2] Visual Computing Group, IEI, CNR Pisa, Italy
mtarini@di.unipi.it, {hitoshi,haberj,hpseidel}@mpi-sb.mpg.de

Abstract

We present a number of techniques to facilitate the generation of textures for facial modeling. In particular, we address the generation of facial skin textures from uncalibrated input photographs as well as the creation of individual textures for facial components such as eyes or teeth. Apart from an initial feature point selection for the skin texturing, all our methods work fully automatically without any user interaction. The resulting textures show a high quality and are suitable for both photo-realistic and real-time facial animation.

Key words: texture mapping, texture synthesis, mesh parameterization, facial modeling, real-time rendering

1 Introduction

Over the past decades, facial modeling and animation has achieved a degree of realism close to photo-realism. Although the trained viewer is still able to detect minor flaws in both animation and rendering of recent full-feature movies such as *Final Fantasy*, the overall quality and especially the modeling and texturing are quite impressive. However, several man-years went into the modeling of each individual character from that movie. Trying to model a real person becomes even more tricky: the artistic licence to create geometry and textures that "look good" is replaced by the demand to create models that "look real".

A common approach towards creating models of real persons for facial animation uses range scanners such as, for instance, Cyberware scanners to acquire both the head geometry and texture. Unfortunately, the texture resolution of such range scanning devices is often low compared to the resolution of digital cameras. In addition, the textures are typically created using a cylindrical projection. Such cylindrical textures have the drawback to introduce visual artifacts, for instance on top of the head, behind the ears, or under the chin. Finally, there is no automatic mechanism provided to generate textures for individual facial components such as eyes and teeth.

In this paper, we present an approach to generate high-resolution textures for both facial skin and facial components from several uncalibrated photographs. The generation of these textures is automated to a large extent, and the resulting textures do not exhibit any patch structures, i.e. they can be used for mip-mapping. Our approach combines several standard techniques from texture mapping and texture synthesis. In addition, we introduce the following contributions:

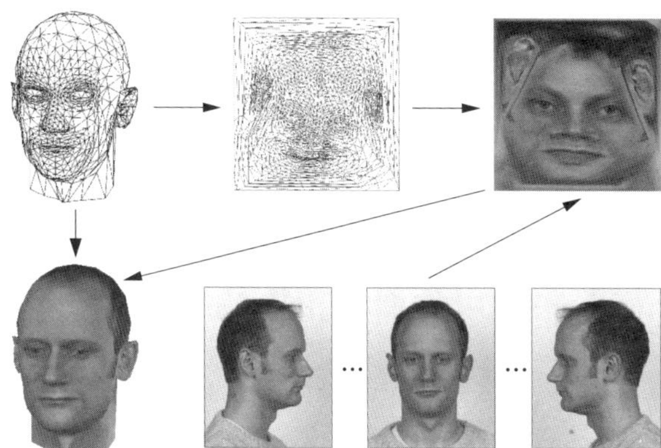

Figure 1: Overview of our skin texture generation process: the 3D face mesh is parameterized over a 2D domain and the texture is resampled from several input photographs.

- a view-dependent parameterization of the 2D texture domain to enhance the visual quality of textures with a fixed resolution;
- a texture resampling method that includes color interpolation for non-textured regions and visual boundary removal using multiresolution splines with a fully automatic mask generation;
- a radial texture synthesis approach with automatic center finding, which robustly produces individual eyeball textures from a single input photograph;
- a technique that uses a single natural teeth photograph to generate a teeth texture, which is applied to an appropriate 3D model to resemble the appearance of the subject's mouth.

All of these techniques are fully automated to minimize the construction time for creating textures for facial modeling. However, we do not address the topic of facial modeling itself in this paper. We apply the textures generated by the techniques presented in this paper in our facial animation system [12], which has been designed to produce physically based facial animations that perform in real-time on common PC hardware. Thus the focus of our texture generation methods is primarily on the applicability of the textures for OpenGL rendering and a simple but efficient acquisition step, which does not require sophisticated camera setups and calibration steps.

2 Previous and Related Work

Research on either texturing or facial animation has provided a large number of techniques and insights over the years, see the surveys and textbooks in [13, 6] and [25] for an overview. Texturing in the context of facial animation is, however, an often neglected issue. Many sophisticated facial animation approaches, e.g. [32, 18, 19], simply use the textures generated by Cyberware scanners. In [35], Williams presents an approach to generate and register a cylindrical texture map from a peripheral photograph. This approach is meanwhile superseded by the ability of Cyberware scanners to acquire geometry and texture in one step. The method presented in [1] generates an individual head geometry and texture by linear combination of head geometries and textures from a large database that has been acquired using a Cyberware scanner in a costly preprocessing step. Marschner *et al.* describe a technique that uses several input photographs taken under controlled illumination with known camera and light source locations to generate an albedo texture map of the human face along with the parameters of a BRDF [23]. Several other approaches such as [26, 11, 16, 17] are image-based and use a small number of input photographs (or video streams) for the reconstruction of both geometry and texture. Although these approaches could potentially yield a higher texture quality compared to the Cyberware textures, they typically suffer from a less accurate geometry reconstruction, limited animation, and reduced texture quality by using cylindrical texture mapping.

Creating textures from multiple, unregistered photographs has been addressed in the literature by several authors [28, 3, 24]. First, they perform a camera calibration for each input photograph based on corresponding feature points. Next, a texture patch is created for each triangle of the input mesh. The approaches differ in the way these texture patches are created, blended, and combined into a common texture. However, the resulting textures always exhibit some patch structure, which makes it impossible to generate mip-maps from these textures. Creating textures that can be mip-mapped requires to construct a parameterization of the mesh over a two-dimensional domain. To this end, generic techniques based on spring meshes have been presented in [10, 15, 7]. Special parameterizations that minimize distortion during texture mapping for different kinds of surfaces have been investigated by several authors, see for instance [27, 29, 22, 21].

Texture synthesis [9, 33] has become an active area of research in the last few years. Recent publications focus on texture synthesis on surfaces [34, 31, 36] or on texture transfer [8, 14]. All of the methods presented so far use a Euclidean coordinate system for the synthesis of textures. In contrast, we use a polar coordinate system to synthesize textures that exhibit some kind of radial similarity.

3 Texturing Facial Skin

To generate a skin texture for a head model, we first take about three to five photographs of the person's head from different, uncalibrated camera positions. All photographs are taken with a high-resolution digital camera (3040×2008 pixels). The camera positions should be chosen in such a way that the resulting images roughly cover the whole head. During the acquisition, no special illumination is necessary. However, the quality of the final texture will benefit from a uniform, diffuse illumination. In addition, we acquire the geometry of the head using a structured-light range scanner. As a result, we obtain a triangle mesh that consists of up to a few hundred thousand triangles. After the texture registration step, this triangle mesh is reduced to about 1.5k triangles for real-time rendering using a standard mesh simplification technique. Each photograph is registered with the high-resolution triangle mesh using the camera calibration technique developed by Tsai [30]. Since the intrinsic parameters of our camera/lens have been determined with sub-pixel accuracy in a preprocessing step, we need to identify about 12–15 corresponding feature points on the mesh and in the image to robustly compute the extrinsic camera parameters for each image. This manual selection of feature points is the only step during our texture generation process that requires user interaction.

Next, we automatically construct a parameterization of the 3D input mesh over the unit square $[0, 1]^2$. This step is described in detail in the following Section 3.1. Finally, every triangle of the 2D texture mesh is resampled from the input photographs. A multiresolution spline method is employed to remove visual boundaries that might arise from uncontrolled illumination conditions during the photo session. Details about this resampling and blending step are given in Section 3.2. Figure 1 shows an overview of our texture generation process.

3.1 Mesh Parameterization

We want to parameterize the 3D input mesh over the 2D domain $[0,1]^2$ in order to obtain a single texture map for the whole mesh. To obtain a mip-mappable texture, the texture should not contain individual patches (*texture atlas*) but rather consist of a single patch. Clearly, this goal cannot be achieved for arbitrary meshes. In our case, the face mesh is topologically equivalent to a part of a plane, since is has a boundary around the neck and does not contain any handles. Thus we can "flatten" the face mesh to a part of a plane that is bounded by its boundary curve around the neck. We represent the original face mesh by a spring mesh and use the L^2 stretch norm presented in [29] to minimize texture stretch. In our simulations, this L^2 norm performs better than the L^∞ norm that is recommended by the authors of [29].

By applying the texture stretch norm, texture stretch is minimized over the whole mesh. In the following step, we introduce some controlled texture stretch again. Since the size of textures that can be handled by graphics hardware is typically limited, we would like to use as much texture space as possible for the "important" regions of a head model while minimizing the texture space allocated to "unimportant" regions. Obviously, the face is more important for the viewer than the ears or even the back of the head. To accomplish some biased texture stretch, we have introduced an additional weighting function ω into the L^2 stretch norm presented in [29]:

$$L^2(M) := \sqrt{\frac{\sum_{T_i \in M} \left(L^2(T_i)\right)^2 \omega(T_i) A'(T_i)}{\sum_{T_i \in M} \omega(T_i) A'(T_i)}}$$

with

$$\omega(T_i) := \frac{1}{\langle N(T_i), V\rangle + k},$$

where $M = \{T_i\}$ denotes the triangle mesh, $A'(T_i)$ is the surface area of triangle T_i in 3D, $N(T_i)$ is the triangle normal of T_i, V is the direction into which the head model looks, and $k > 1$ is a weighting parameter. The weighting function ω thus favors the triangles on the face by diminishing their error while penalizing the triangles on the back of the head by amplifying their error. As a consequence, triangles on the face become larger in the texture mesh while backfacing triangles become smaller. Useful values for k are from within $[1.01, 2]$.

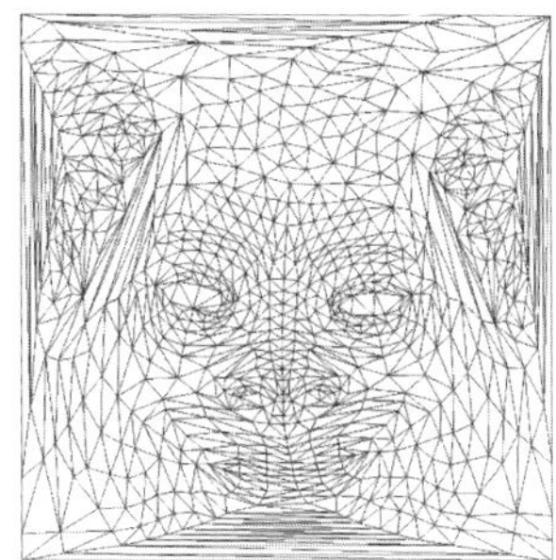
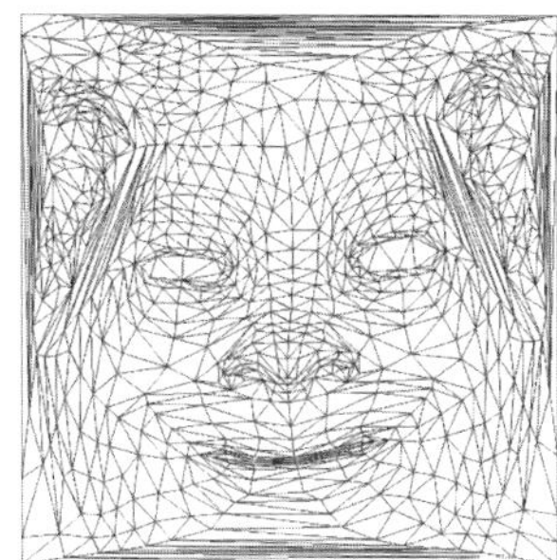

Figure 2: Comparison between a view-independent texture mesh parameterization according to [29] (left) and our view-dependent parameterization (right).

Figure 2 shows a view-independent texture mesh parameterization obtained with the original L^2 stretch norm as well as a view-dependent parameterization with our modified stretch norm for $k = 1.2$.

The difference between our *view-dependent texture mesh parameterization* and the *view-dependent texture mapping* proposed in [5, 26] is the following: the latter performs an adaptive blending of several photographs for each novel view, whereas we create a static texture that has its texture space adaptively allocated to regions of different visual importance.

3.2 Texture Resampling

After having created the 2D texture mesh from the 3D face mesh, we resample the texture mesh from the input photographs that have been registered with the face mesh. First, we perform a vertex-to-image binding for all vertices of the 3D face mesh. This step is carried out as suggested in [28]: Each mesh vertex v is assigned a set of *valid photographs*, which is defined as that subset of the input photographs such that v is visible in each photograph and v is a non-silhouette vertex. A vertex v is visible in a photograph, if the projection of v on the image plane is contained in the photograph **and** the normal vector of v is directed towards the viewpoint **and** there are no other intersections of the face mesh with the line that connects v and the viewpoint. A vertex v is called a silhouette vertex, if at least one of the triangles in the fan around v is oriented opposite to the viewpoint. For further details see [28]. In contrast to the approach in [28], we do not require that all vertices of the face mesh are actually bound to at least one photograph, i.e. the set of valid photographs for a vertex may be empty.

Let $\triangle = \{v_1, v_2, v_3\}$ denote a triangle of the face mesh and $\widetilde{\triangle} = \{\tilde{v}_1, \tilde{v}_2, \tilde{v}_3\}$ be the corresponding triangle in the texture mesh. For each triangle $\triangle$, exactly one of the following situations might occur (see also Figure 3):

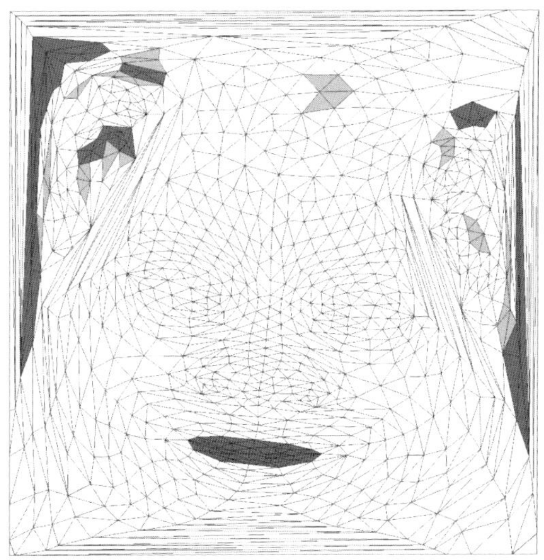

Figure 3: Greylevel-coded triangles of the texture mesh: each white triangle has at least one common photograph to which all of its vertices are bound; the vertices of light grey triangles don't have a common photograph, but they are all bound; dark grey triangles have at least one unbound vertex.

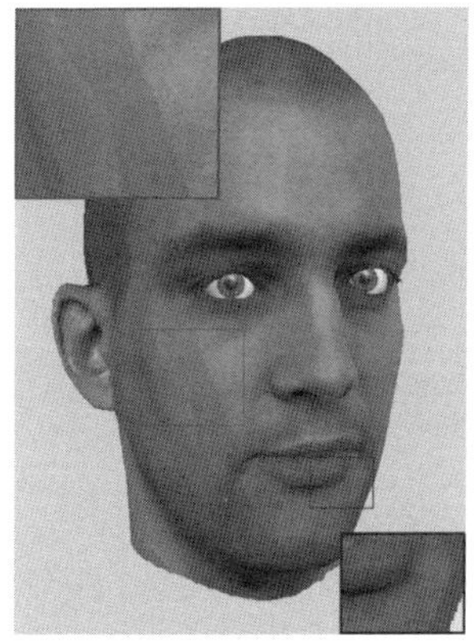

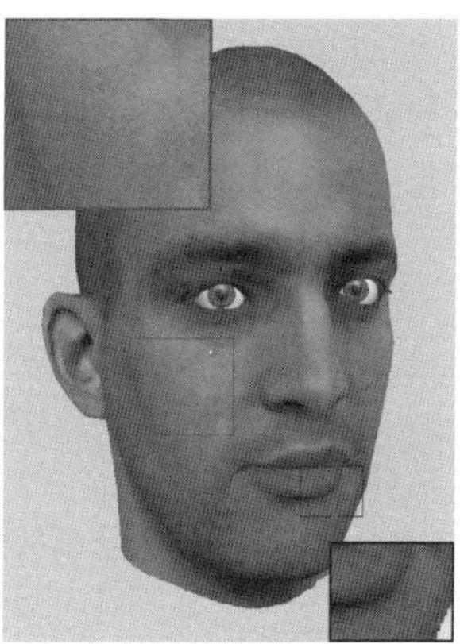

Figure 4: Boundaries in the skin texture (left) are removed using multiresolution spline techniques (right).

1. There exists at least one common photograph in the sets of valid photographs of the three vertices v_1, v_2, v_3 of $\triangle$ (white triangles).

2. All of the vertices of $\triangle$ are bound to at least one photograph, but no common photograph can be found for all three vertices (light grey triangles).

3. At least one vertex of $\triangle$ is not bound to any photograph (dark grey triangles).

In the first case, we rasterize $\widetilde{\triangle}$ in texture space. For each texel T, we determine its barycentric coordinates ρ, σ, τ w.r.t. $\widetilde{\triangle}$ and compute the corresponding normal N by interpolating the vertex normals of $\triangle$: $N = \rho N(v_1) + \sigma N(v_2) + \tau N(v_3)$. For each common photograph i in the sets of valid photographs of all vertices of $\triangle$, we compute the dot product between N and the viewing direction V_i for the pixel P_i that corresponds to T. Finally, we color T with the color obtained by the weighted sum of pixel colors $\sum_i \langle N, V_i \rangle \cdot \text{Color}(P_i) \;/\; \sum_i \langle N, V_i \rangle$.

In the second case, we color each vertex $\tilde{v}_j$ of $\widetilde{\triangle}$ individually by summing up the weighted pixel colors of the corresponding pixels in all valid photographs i of $\tilde{v}_j$ similarly as in the first case: $\text{Color}(\tilde{v}_j) := \sum_i \langle N(v_j), V_i \rangle \cdot \text{Color}(P_i) \;/\; \sum_i \langle N(v_j), V_i \rangle$. The texels of the rasterization of $\widetilde{\triangle}$ are then colored by barycentric interpolation of the colors of the vertices $\tilde{v}_1, \tilde{v}_2, \tilde{v}_3$. Alternatively, we tried to use as much information as possible from the input photographs if, for instance, the vertices v_1, v_2 of $\triangle$ share a photograph and the vertices v_2, v_3 share another photograph. However, we found that this second case does not occur very often (cf. Figure 3) and that the difference between plain color interpolation and a more sophisticated approach is almost invisible.

Since we do not require that each vertex of the face mesh is bound to at least one photograph, there might exist some vertices that cannot be colored by any of the previously described schemes. We address this problem in a two-stage process: First, we iteratively assign an interpolated color to each unbound vertex. Next, we perform the color interpolation scheme from the second case for the remaining triangles of $\widetilde{\triangle}$ that have not yet been colored. The first step iteratively loops over all unbound and uncolored vertices of the face mesh. For each unbound vertex v, we check if at least $p = 80\,\%$ of the vertices in the one-ring around v are colored (either by being bound to a photograph or by having an interpolated color). If this is true, we assign to v the average color of all the colored vertices around v, otherwise we continue with the next unbound vertex. We repeat this procedure until there are no further vertex updates. Next, we start the same procedure again, but this time we only require $p = 60\,\%$ of the vertices in the one-ring around v to be colored. As soon as there are no more updates, we repeat this step twice again with $p = 40\,\%$ and $p = 20\,\%$. Finally, we update each unbound vertex that has at least one colored neighbor. Upon termination of this last step, all vertices of the face mesh are either bound or colored and the remaining triangles of $\widetilde{\triangle}$ can be colored.

If the input photographs have been taken under uncontrolled illumination, the skin color might differ noticeably between the images. In this case, boundaries might appear in the resampled texture. We then apply a multires-

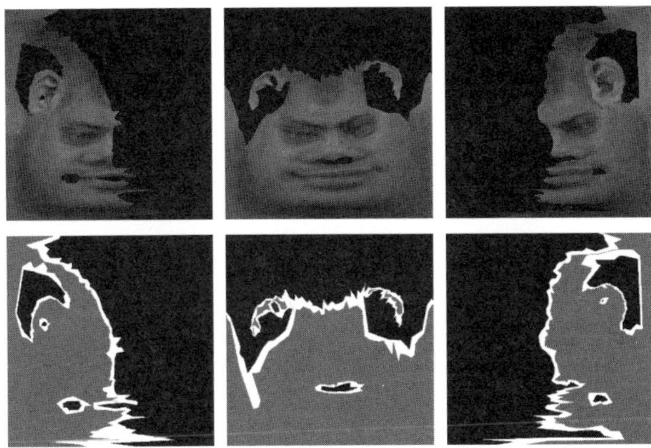

Figure 5: Multiresolution spline masks: three different regions in the texture mesh resampled from different input photographs (top) and their corresponding masks shown in grey (bottom).

olution spline method as proposed in [2, 17] to remove visual boundaries. Figure 4 shows a comparison between a textured head model with and without multiresolution spline method applied. To smoothly combine texture regions that have been resampled from different input photographs, we automatically compute a mask for each region by removing the outmost ring of triangles around the region, see Figure 5. Such a shrinking is necessary to ensure that there is still some valid color information on the outside of the mask boundary, because these adjacent pixels might contribute to the color of the boundary pixels during the construction of Gaussian and Laplacian pyramids. In addition to the masks for each input photograph, we create one more mask that is defined as the complement of the sum of all the other masks. This mask is used together with the resampled texture to provide some color information in those regions that are not covered by any input photograph (e.g. the inner part of the lips). As described above, these regions have been filled by color interpolation in the resampled texture. By blending all of the masked input photographs and the masked resampled texture with a multiresolution spline, we obtain a final texture with no visual boundaries and crispy detail.

4 Texturing Facial Components

Both human eyes and teeth are important for realistic facial animation while, at the same time, it is difficult to acquire data from a human being to precisely model these facial components. Thus we use generic models of these components as shown in Figure 8. The design of our generic models has been chosen such that they look convincingly realistic when inserted into a face mesh while still being rendered efficiently using OpenGL hardware.

On the other hand, both eyes and teeth (especially the more visible middle ones) are crucial features to visually differentiate one individual from another. Hence, it would be very desirable to use individual models for each person. Luckily, texturing can do the trick alone: indeed it is sufficient to apply a personal texture to a generic model to get the desired effect. Moreover, it is possible to automatically and quickly generate these textures each from a single input photograph of the subject's eye and teeth, respectively. Details about this process will be given in the next two subsections.

4.1 Texturing Eyes

In order to realistically animate our head model, we must be able to perform rotations of the eyeball and dilation of the pupil. While the latter can be achieved by transforming the texture coordinates, we need an eye texture that covers the whole frontal hemisphere of the eyeball for the rotations.

Our goal to generate such an eyeball texture from a single input photograph is complicated by several factors such as the presence of occluding eyelids, shadows of eyelashes, highlights, etc. Still, all these factors are local and can be detected and removed. A new texture can then be synthesized from an input image consisting of the surviving pixels. In our current approach, we focus our effort on the iris, since it is obviously the most characteristic part of the eye.

Both the detection and the synthesis phase rely on the simplicity of the eye structure, i.e. an almost perfect point symmetry about the center, assuming our photograph represents an eye looking at the camera. To take advantage of this symmetry, we must first know precisely where the center of the eye is located. Since this would encumber the user, the center finding is done automatically by refining a rough estimation to sub-pixel precision using the following heuristic: we progressively enlarge an initially point-sized circle while checking the pixels on the circle at every iteration. If these pixels are too bright, they are assumed to be outside the iris and we thus move the center of the circle away from them. When most of the circle is composed by too bright pixels, we assume its center is the eye center and its radius is the iris radius. This approach runs robustly as long as the initial estimation is inside the pupil or the iris.

At this point, removal of occluded, shadowed, and highlighted pixels is done by:

- removing pixels with a color too similar to the skin;
- removing pixels with a color too dissimilar to the pixels at the same radial distance from the center.

For the second case, we compute the average color and standard deviation of the pixels at the same radial dis-

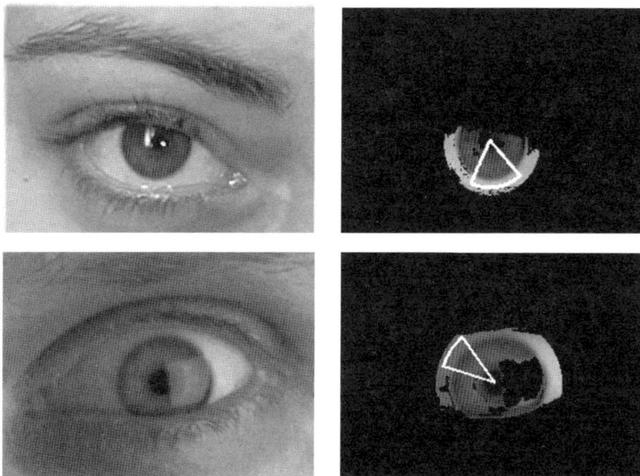

Figure 6: Two input photographs (left) and the resulting reference patches outlined by white sectors (right). Occluded, shadowed, highlighted, and skin-colored pixels (shown in black) have been removed automatically.

tance and remove those pixels that are at least α times the standard deviation away from the average. The parameter α should be chosen within $[2, 3]$. We typically use a rather small value of $\alpha = 2.3$, as it empirically proved to remove the problematic (occluded, shadowed, highlighted, etc.) pixels in most cases. In addition, we remove pixels too close to the skin to better take into account small shadows cast by eyelids. Actually, the decision of which pixel to remove does not need excessively fine tuning: due to the regularity of the eye, we can be pretty conservative and remove many pixels, since the reconstruction phase requires only a small zone of pixels in order to synthesize more. Figure 6 shows the remaining set of pixels for two different input photographs.

For the reconstruction phase it is natural to resort to some texture synthesis from samples approach like e.g. [33]. In our case, we need to work in polar coordinates, because the eyeball texture behaves like a texture as defined in [33] only along the *angle* axis. This means that subregions of the eyeball texture are perceived to be similar if their *radius* coordinates are the same, cf. Figure 10. To take this into account, when choosing a candidate pixel p in the input image for filling a pixel p' in the output texture, we constrain the radius coordinate of p to be within a small threshold of the radius coordinate of p'.

A robust approach for texture synthesis is to use only a small patch of the original input image as the reference image and synthesize the texture from scratch. Although larger reference images theoretically result in more faithful textures, we obtained very good results with small reference patches covering a sector of about 30 degrees around the pupil. Small reference patches have the advantage of being more uniform and thus bypassing problems related to uneven lighting in the original photograph. In our approach, we simply use the largest sector of valid pixels of at most 60 degrees as the reference patch. In the rare cases where the largest sector is too small, e.g. spanning less than 20 degrees, the entire set of valid pixels with a valid neighborhood is used as the reference image.

Since the detail frequencies of human irises are roughly the same, it is sufficient to use a texture synthesis scheme with a fixed neighborhood size rather than a multiresolution approach. In our case, the size of the neighborhood mask depends only on the resolution of the input image. For instance, for an image of an iris with a diameter of approximately 80 pixels, we use a 3×6 pixel mask (radius $\times$ angle). For other iris diameters, the pixel mask is set proportionally. Depending on the value of the radius coordinate, a neighborhood with a fixed size in polar coordinates covers areas of different sizes in the input image. Our simulations showed, however, that no correction is needed, since the human iris usually exhibits higher frequency detail towards the center. Thus an iris resampled in polar coordinates shows quite uniform frequency distribution. Figure 9 shows several input photographs together with the resulting eye textures for various individuals.

To speed-up the reconstruction step, we use a one-dimensional texture synthesis approach along the angle axis alone, modeling the texture as a Markov chain rather than a Markov random field. Each symbol of the chain is an entire row of texels at a given angle coordinate. We output each new row accordingly to the previous rows. This approach gives similar results (even if it requires slightly larger reference textures) and is much faster, not even requiring any vector quantization for finding the best neighborhood row. If, however, the size of the reference patch is very small, we apply a two-dimensional texture synthesis approach as described earlier in this section.

4.2 Texturing Teeth

Geometry and color of teeth are difficult to capture and, at the same time, crucial to reflect personal appearance. We address this problem by distinguishing between

- the six middle teeth (incisors and canines) and
- the rest of the teeth (4–5 on each side).

The middle teeth are much more visible than the other teeth. This means that they account for most of the visual appearance of an individual person, but also that it is much easier to reconstruct them from a photograph. In addition, the middle teeth have an almost two-dimensional structure: they are shaped to have the function of a blade. Their small width allows us to model

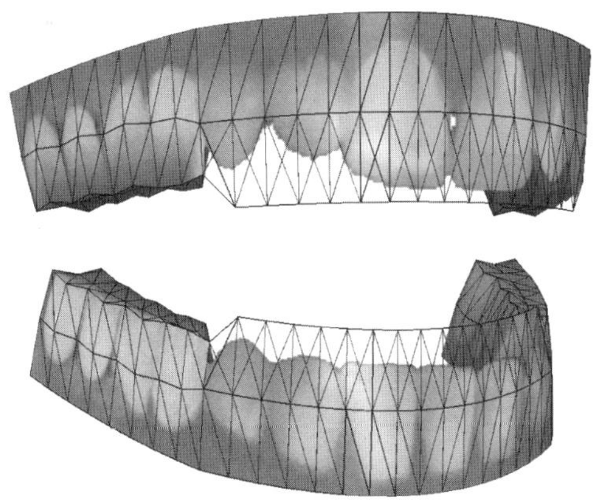

Figure 7: Teeth arch model using the texture shown in Figure 11. The wireframe shows the geometry of the teeth model, which consists of 384 triangles.

them using a billboard (impostor). Being a 2D data structure, the billboard can be easily extracted directly from a normal photograph of the subject exposing the teeth in a similar way as shown in Figure 11 (left). Using local transparency, it is straightforward to make the texture embed the teeth shape and size including gaps between teeth. This approach allows us to use the same (billboarded) 3D model for every face model and just change the texture from person to person.

The rest of the teeth, while being more voluminous and less accessible and visible, do not allow this useful shortcut. But, for the same reason, it is also less important to model them faithfully and individually for each single person. Thus it seems reasonable to use a standard 3D model and a standard texture (up to recoloring, see below) for this part of the teeth arch.

Following these considerations, we have built a generic 3D model for the teeth, which is non-uniformly scaled according to the individual skull and jaw geometry to fit into every head model. For each individual head model, we only need to vary the texture (including the billboard), which is created fully automatically. The generic teeth model is constructed such that the transition between the billboard (in the middle) and the 3D structure (left and right) is smooth, see Figure 7. The billboard, which is bent for better realism, could cause undesired artifacts when seen from above. To avoid this, only the upper part of the lower teeth and the lower part of the upper ones is actually modeled as a billboard. The remaining parts of the upper and lower middle teeth smoothly gain some width as they go up and down, respectively.

To automatically create a texture for the teeth, we start from a normal photograph of the subject showing his/her teeth. Several stages of the whole process of generating a teeth texture are shown in Figure 11. We color-code dark parts that represent voids with a blue color, which is replaced by a transparent alpha value during rendering. Similarly, we identify and remove gums, lips, and skin, recoloring it with some standard gums color. To make this color-coding more robust, we identify the different regions using threshold values, which are obtained by finding the biggest jumps in the histograms of the color distances to the target color (red for gums and black for voids). In addition, we expand teeth into those parts of the gums that have been covered by the lips in the input photograph. We use some simple heuristics to include the missing part of the tooth roots, cf. Figure 11.

During rendering, our teeth model is shaded using a Phong shading model, which means that we have to deshade our teeth texture. In order to do so for uncontrolled illumination, we equalize the color of the teeth, supposing they have approximately the same albedo. First, we define a target color by computing the average color of all teeth pixels and setting its brightness (but not the hue) to a predefined value. Next, we subdivide the texture in six vertical stripes and compute the average color of each stripe. We then add to the pixels in each column the difference between the target color and the stripe average, taking care of enforcing continuity in this correction by using a piecewise linear function. Similarly, we use the target color to correct the color of the "generic" part of the texture, which is applied to the side teeth. Finally, we composite the middle teeth texture into our generic texture using a curved boundary that follows the silhouettes of the canines.

5 Results

We have created facial textures for several individuals who have also been range-scanned to acquire their head geometry. Rendering of our head model is performed in real-time using OpenGL hardware (about 100 fps on a 1.7 GHz PC with a GeForce3 graphics board). A physics-based simulation is used to control the facial animation. Several images of our head models are distributed over this paper, see for instance Figures 1, 4, 8, and especially Figure 12. For each skin texture, the only interactive step is the initial identification of corresponding feature points. This step takes about five minutes per input photograph, which sums up to about 15–25 minutes spent interactively for three to five photographs. Computing an optimized parameterization of the face mesh (approx. 1600 triangles) takes about 80 minutes on a fast PC (1.7 GHz Pentium 4). Resampling a 2048×2048 texture from five input photographs takes about one minute, additional multiresolution spline blending (if necessary)

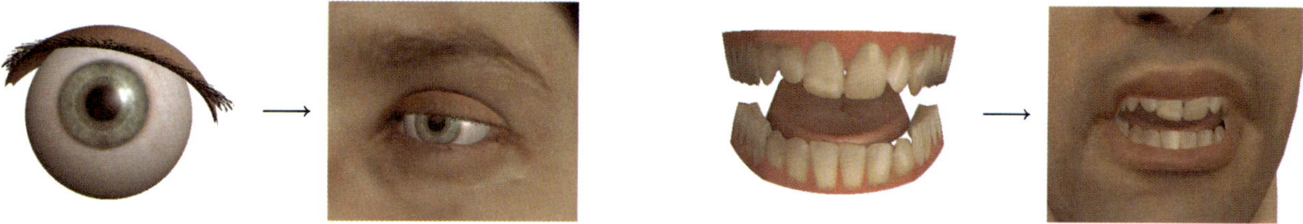

Figure 8: Generic models of eyes, teeth, and tongue are fitted into individual face meshes.

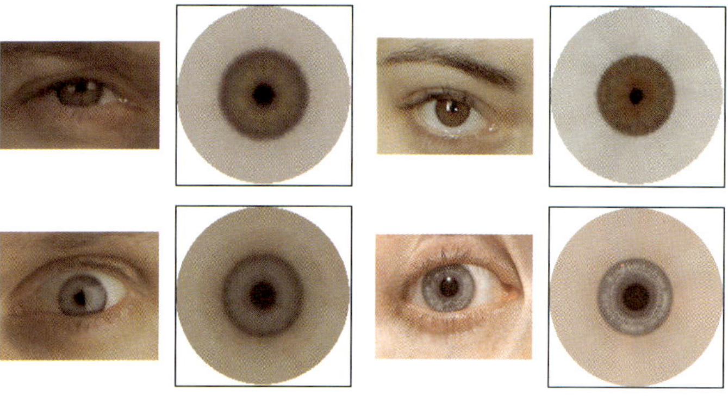

Figure 9: Input photographs and resulting eye textures: the input images have been taken under various illumination conditions with different resolutions. The size of the resulting textures changes from 128×128 (top left) to 1024×1024 (bottom right).

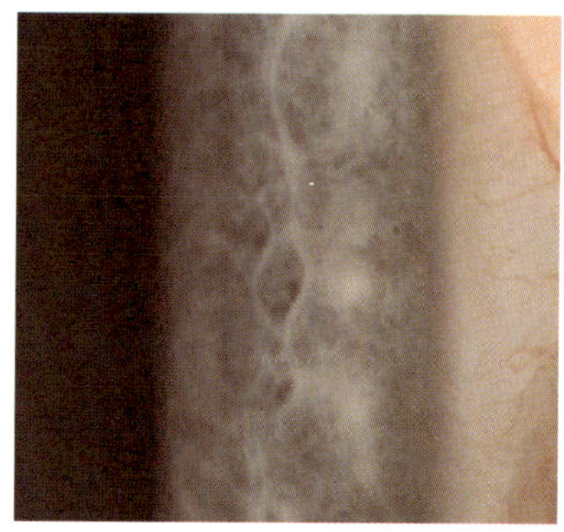

Figure 10: A detail of the texture from Figure 9 (bottom right) shown in polar coordinates. The abscissa represents the radius axis and the ordinate represents the angle axis.

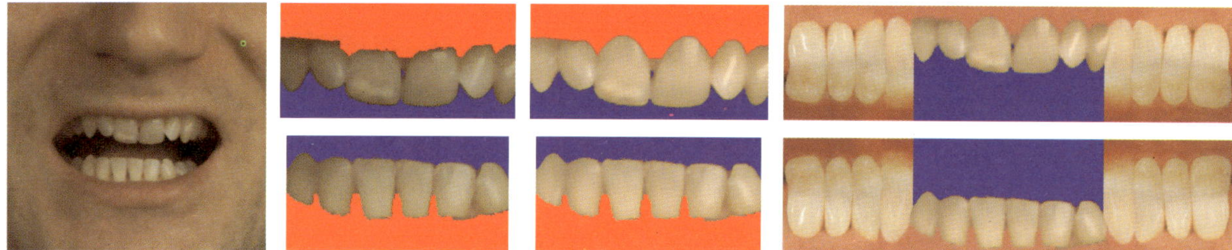

Figure 11: Teeth texture generation. Left to right: starting from an input photograph, we extract the upper and lower middle teeth, fill in missing parts and adjust the color, and composite the new image with a generic teeth texture. The blue pixels in the final texture (right) will be rendered transparently.

Figure 12: Side-by-side comparison of photographs (left) and head models (right) for plain OpenGL rendering.

takes about ten minutes. Currently, our algorithms are optimized with respect to robustness but not to speed.

Generating the teeth and eye textures takes only a few seconds even for large textures using the 1D Markov chain method for the texture synthesis. If a full Markov field is used, construction time may go up to several minutes, depending on the size of the texture being created.

6 Conclusion and Future Work

We have introduced a number of techniques that help to minimize the time and effort that goes into the creation of textures for facial modeling. With the exception of the initial feature point selection for the skin texturing, our methods are fully automated and do not require any user interaction.

For the generation of skin textures from uncalibrated input photographs, we propose a view-dependent parameterization of the texture domain and a texture resampling method including color interpolation for non-textured regions and multiresolution splining for the removal of visual boundaries. Using our methods, both eye and teeth textures can be created fully automatically from single input photographs, adding greatly to a realistic appearance of individual subjects during facial animation.

One of the main goals of ongoing research is to get rid of the interactive camera calibration step for skin texturing. Given that the resulting texture should contain fine detail, this is a tough problem, indeed. Automatic approaches such as [20] fail simply due to the fact that the silhouette of a human head looks more or less identical when viewed from within a cone of viewing directions from the front or the back. Furthermore, it would be desirable to account for lighting artifacts in the input photographs. Although a uniform, diffuse illumination during the photo session helps a lot, there are still contributions from diffuse and specular lighting in the photographs. Approaches to overcome these problems have been suggested [4, 23], but they require sophisticated camera setups and calibration steps. Finally, it would be very helpful to speed-up the computation time of the current bottleneck, namely the mesh parameterization, using a hierarchical coarse-to-fine approach.

Acknowledgments

The authors would like to thank their models Letizia, Claudia, and Kolja for all the smiles during the photo sessions. Many thanks also to our colleagues, who gave helpful comments during the development of our techniques, and to the anonymous reviewers for their suggestions.

References

[1] V. Blanz and T. Vetter. A Morphable Model for the Synthesis of 3D Faces. In *Computer Graphics (SIGGRAPH '99 Conf. Proc.)*, pages 187–194, August 1999.

[2] P. J. Burt and E. H. Adelson. A Multiresolution Spline with Application to Image Mosaics. *ACM Transactions on Graphics*, 2(4):217–236, October 1983.

[3] P. Cignoni, C. Montani, C. Rocchini, R. Scopigno, and M. Tarini. Preserving Attribute Values on Simplified Meshes by Resampling Detail Textures. *The Visual Computer*, 15(10):519–539, 1999.

[4] P. E. Debevec, T. Hawkins, C. Tchou, H.-P. Duiker, W. Sarokin, and M. Sagar. Acquiring the Reflectance Field of a Human Face. In *Computer Graphics (SIGGRAPH '00 Conf. Proc.)*, pages 145–156, July 2000.

[5] P. E. Debevec, C. J. Taylor, and J. Malik. Modeling and Rendering Architecture from Photographs: A Hybrid Geometry- and Image-based Approach. In *Computer Graphics (SIGGRAPH '96 Conf. Proc.)*, pages 11–20, August 1996.

[6] D. S. Ebert, F. K. Musgrave, D. Peachey, K. Perlin, and S. Worley. *Texturing & Modeling: A Procedural Approach*. Academic Press, London, 2 edition, 1998.

[7] M. Eck, T. DeRose, T. Duchamp, H. Hoppe, M. Lounsbery, and W. Stuetzle. Multiresolution Analysis of Arbitrary Meshes. In *Computer Graphics (SIGGRAPH '95 Conf. Proc.)*, pages 173–182, August 1995.

[8] A. A. Efros and W. T. Freeman. Image Quilting for Texture Synthesis and Transfer. In *Computer Graphics (SIGGRAPH '01 Conf. Proc.)*, pages 341–346, August 2001.

[9] A. A. Efros and T. K. Leung. Texture Synthesis by Non-parametric Sampling. In *IEEE Int'l Conf. Computer Vision*, volume 2, pages 1033–1038, September 1999.

[10] M. S. Floater. Parametrization and Smooth Approximation of Surface Triangulations. *Computer Aided Geometric Design*, 14(3):231–250, 1997.

[11] B. Guenter, C. Grimm, D. Wood, H. Malvar, and F. Pighin. Making Faces. In *Computer Graphics (SIGGRAPH '98 Conf. Proc.)*, pages 55–66, July 1998.

[12] J. Haber, K. Kähler, I. Albrecht, H. Yamauchi, and H.-P. Seidel. Face to Face: From Real Humans to Realistic Facial Animation. In *Proc. Israel-Korea Binational Conf. on Geometrical Modeling and Computer Graphics*, pages 73–82, October 2001.

[13] P. S. Heckbert. Survey of Texture Mapping. *IEEE Computer Graphics and Applications*, 6(11):56–67, November 1986.

[14] A. Hertzmann, Ch. E. Jacobs, N. Oliver, B. Curless, and D. H. Salesin. Image Analogies. In *Computer Graphics (SIGGRAPH '01 Conf. Proc.)*, pages 327–340, August 2001.

[15] K. Hormann and G. Greiner. MIPS: An Efficient Global Paramctrization Method. In *Curve and Surface Design: Saint-Malo 1999*, pages 153–162. Vanderbilt University Press, 2000.

[16] W.-S. Lee, J. Gu, and N. Magnenat-Thalmann. Generating Animatable 3D Virtual Humans from Photographs. In *Computer Graphics Forum (Proc. EG 2000)*, volume 19, pages C1–C10, August 2000.

[17] W.-S. Lee and N. Magnenat-Thalmann. Fast Head Modeling for Animation. *Image and Vision Computing*, 18(4):355–364, March 2000.

[18] Y. Lee, D. Terzopoulos, and K. Waters. Constructing Physics-based Facial Models of Individuals. In *Proc. Graphics Interface '93*, pages 1–8, May 1993.

[19] Y. Lee, D. Terzopoulos, and K. Waters. Realistic Modeling for Facial Animations. In *Computer Graphics (SIGGRAPH '95 Conf. Proc.)*, pages 55–62, August 1995.

[20] H. P. A. Lensch, W. Heidrich, and H.-P. Seidel. Automated Texture Registration and Stitching for Real World Models. In *Proc. Pacific Graphics 2000*, pages 317–326, October 2000.

[21] B. Lévy. Constrained Texture Mapping for Polygonal Meshes. In *Computer Graphics (SIGGRAPH '01 Conf. Proc.)*, pages 417–424, August 2001.

[22] J. Maillot, H. Yahia, and A. Verroust. Interactive Texture Mapping. In *Computer Graphics (SIGGRAPH '93 Conf. Proc.)*, pages 27–34, August 1993.

[23] S. R. Marschner, B. Guenter, and S. Raghupathy. Modeling and Rendering for Realistic Facial Animation. In *Rendering Techniques 2000 (Proc. 11th EG Workshop on Rendering)*, pages 231–242, 2000.

[24] P. J. Neugebauer and K. Klein. Texturing 3D Models of Real World Objects from Multiple Unregistered Photographic Views. In *Computer Graphics Forum (Proc. EG '99)*, volume 18, pages C245–C256, September 1999.

[25] F. I. Parke and K. Waters, editors. *Computer Facial Animation*. A K Peters, Wellesley, MA, 1996.

[26] F. Pighin, J. Hecker, D. Lischinski, R. Szeliski, and D. H. Salesin. Synthesizing Realistic Facial Expressions from Photographs. In *Computer Graphics (SIGGRAPH '98 Conf. Proc.)*, pages 75–84, July 1998.

[27] D. Piponi and G. D. Borshukov. Seamless Texture Mapping of Subdivision Surfaces by Model Pelting and Texture Blending. In *Computer Graphics (SIGGRAPH '00 Conf. Proc.)*, pages 471–478, July 2000.

[28] C. Rocchini, P. Cignoni, C. Montani, and R. Scopigno. Multiple Textures Stitching and Blending on 3D Objects. In *Rendering Techniques '99 (Proc. 10th EG Workshop on Rendering)*, pages 119–130, 1999.

[29] P. V. Sander, J. Snyder, S. J. Gortler, and H. Hoppe. Texture Mapping Progressive Meshes. In *Computer Graphics (SIGGRAPH '01 Conf. Proc.)*, pages 409–416, August 2001.

[30] R. Y. Tsai. An Efficient and Accurate Camera Calibration Technique for 3D Machine Vision. In *Proc. IEEE Conf. on Computer Vision and Pattern Recognition*, pages 364–374, June 1986.

[31] G. Turk. Texture Synthesis on Surfaces. In *Computer Graphics (SIGGRAPH '01 Conf. Proc.)*, pages 347–354, August 2001.

[32] K. Waters and D. Terzopoulos. Modeling and Animating Faces Using Scanned Data. *J. Visualization and Computer Animation*, 2(4):123–128, October–December 1991.

[33] L.-Y. Wei and M. Levoy. Fast Texture Synthesis Using Tree-Structured Vector Quantization. In *Computer Graphics (SIGGRAPH '00 Conf. Proc.)*, pages 479–488, July 2000.

[34] L.-Y. Wei and M. Levoy. Texture Synthesis over Arbitrary Manifold Surfaces. In *Computer Graphics (SIGGRAPH '01 Conf. Proc.)*, pages 355–360, August 2001.

[35] L. Williams. Performance-Driven Facial Animation. In *Computer Graphics (SIGGRAPH '90 Conf. Proc.)*, volume 24, pages 235–242, August 1990.

[36] L. Ying, A. Hertzmann, H. Biermann, and D. Zorin. Texture and Shape Synthesis on Surfaces. In *Rendering Techniques 2001 (Proc. 12th EG Workshop on Rendering)*, pages 301–312, 2001.

A Direct Method for Positioning the Arms of a Human Model

John McDonald, Karen Alkoby, Roymieco Carter, Juliet Christopher, Mary Jo Davidson, Dan Ethridge, Jacob Furst, Damien Hinkle, Glenn Lancaster, Lori Smallwood, Nedjla Ougouag-Tiouririne, Jorge Toro, Shuang Xu, Rosalee Wolfe

jmcdonald@cs.depaul.edu, asl@cs.depaul.edu

School of CTI
DePaul University

Abstract

Many problems in computer graphics concern the precise positioning of a human figure, and in particular, the positioning of the joints in the upper body as a virtual character performs some action. We explore a new technique for precisely positioning the joints in the arms of a human figure to achieve a desired posture. We focus on an analytic solution for the IK chains of the model's arms and an interface for conveniently specifying a desired targeting point, or articulator, on the model's hand. Also, we consider the problem of specifying a target for that articulator in space or in contact with the model's own body. These methods recast the seven degrees of freedom in the arm to provide a more intuitive interface for animation. We demonstrate the efficacy and efficiency of these techniques in positioning a virtual American Sign Language interpreter.

Key words: Analytic Algorithms, Inverse Kinematics, Human Arm, ASL.

1 Introduction

Many applications in Computer Graphics (CG) require the positioning and animation of articulated figures containing joints with multiple degrees of freedom [1]. In the case of the human body, the animator must coordinate the positioning of dozens of joints. The two arms of a virtual human may contain over 30 joints in the shoulder, elbow, wrist and knuckles [6]. Animators use a range of techniques to manage this complexity, of which the many Inverse Kinematics (IK) methods are among the most widely used [2].

IK techniques were first used in robotics to position a series of joints, so as to place an end-effector on the robot's arm at a position and orientation necessary to perform some task [7]. Compared to robotics, character animation requires finer nuances in a character's motion.

Another application requiring fine nuances in motion is animating American Sign Language (ASL) [6]. ASL is a natural language used by the North American Deaf community and is the fourth most widely used language in North America [8]. The purpose for animating ASL is to support the development of a synthetic interpreter for cases when human translators are unavailable or too expensive [12].

In ASL, subtleties in motion, position and configuration of the arms can make an enormous difference in meaning. One example is the differences between the signs for EYEGLASSES and GALLAUDET UNIVERSITY. See Figure 1 in Appendix A. They both have the same hand configuration (handshape) and both have the same basic movement, but EYEGLASSES happens on the front of the face around the eye, while GALLAUDET happens just to the side of the eye, pulling back towards the ear [10].

There is always a tradeoff between the amount of accuracy and control an application achieves, on one hand, and the speed at which an animator can express their intent, on the other. Applications such as character animation and ASL require computational methods and interfaces that make such fine control easy and intuitive, so that the animator can produce precise and expressive animations.

This paper describes a direct, analytic IK technique that supports an interface allowing animators to transcribe signs in ASL quickly and precisely. This same technique could also be incorporated into any general animation system for specifying arm movements.

2 Description of the Problem

Building a general system for animating ASL requires highly complex and intuitive controls for the model, two goals that are often at odds. In particular, ASL signs often require that the model's hand be in contact with the other hand or some part of the body or face. For more information on the linguistics of ASL, see [5] or [9].

It is imperative that the positions recorded by the animator be precise enough that the model's fingers do not wind up in collision with the model's own body. Moreover, the specific part of the hand contacting the body will vary from sign to sign. In Figure 2 of Appendix A, the sign for IDEA places the tip of the index finger in contact with the face, whereas the sign for CHOCOLATE uses the lower part of the thumb as the point of contact [10]. We define an *articulator* to be a point on the hand used for targeting.

Since we wanted the computational methods to be as efficient and as stable as possible we rejected the more traditional inverse Jacobean and iterative IK methods. Certainly, other applications call for specifying a target position for the wrist in space, but these can be handled by current analytic IK methods [3] [4]. However, for our application, in addition to the simple case, we also needed to

1. Allow the user to specify several key global orientations for the wrist (such as up, down, in, out, etc.) that are specified at times in ASL grammar, both in spatial positioning and in contact situations.
2. Specify a target for an articulator on the hand, while giving the user complete control over the local rotation at the wrist joint, and then, allow the user to manipulate the local wrist orientation without affecting the position of the articulator.

Problem 1 can be handled quite easily with an application of the techniques in [4]. But an extension of these techniques is necessary to solve problem 2. Tolani, Goswami and Badler [11] considered a problem related to 2, but stopped short of a full direct solution, relying instead on optimization techniques to calculate the elbow's bend angle.

The key difference between problems 1 and 2 is how the user specifies the orientation of the wrist. Case 1 is identical to the grasping task problem encountered in robotics and ergonomics studies. In many grasping tasks the orientation of the palm is specified relative to the object being grasped, i.e. in world coordinates [4]. Given this orientation, the solution is a simple matter of subtracting a vector aligned along the palm to calculate where the wrist must be placed. After this, one can solve the triangle formed by the shoulder, elbow and wrist to get the complete orientation of the arm, see Figure 1.

In animating ASL signs, the primary focus is slightly different, as specified in case 2. Of primary importance is how the wrist and shoulder look in relationship to the rest of the body. Neither joint must look unduly strained. To make such subtle relationships easy to achieve, an animator must be given direct control over the orientation of the wrist relative to the forearm. For the purposes of the IK calculation, we consider the wrist as a fixed rotation relative to the forearm and calculate rotations for the shoulder and elbow necessary to place the articulator in the desired position.

This is similar to the aiming task considered in [11], the key difference being that there they do not specify the distance to the target point. As previously mentioned, their technique requires iterative optimization to calculate the elbow's bend angle in the most general case. However, it turns out that an extension of Kondo's geometric method solves our problem completely and directly.

3 Analytic IK Solutions

Two popular IK methods are the inverse Jacobean and optimization approaches, each of which requires the calculation of a series of approximations converging to the desired solution. Such algorithms are quite effective for general IK problems, but when confronted with a simpler problem such as the orientation of the arm, with only three joints, a more stable, direct solution may be achieved depending on the specific problem and constraints. For more information, [11] has a nice overview of classical analytic and numerical algorithms for IK.

One of the key problems with iterative solutions is their unpredictability and instability in the presence of an underdetermined system, such as the human arm. Consider that, even when placing the wrist at a desired point in space, there are an infinite number of solutions parameterized by the rotation of the system about an axis through the shoulder and wrist, see Figure 1.

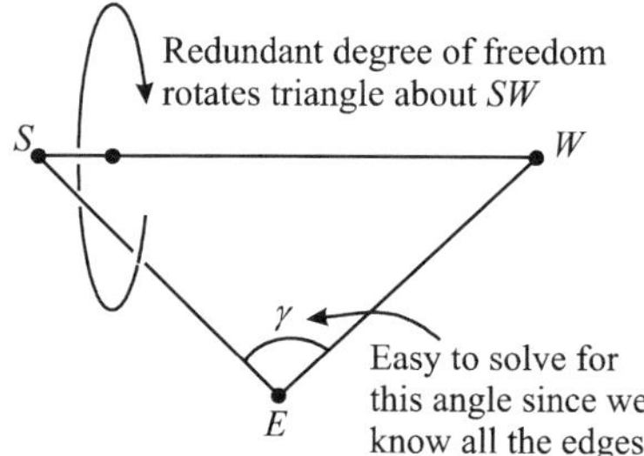

Figure 1: Triangle for Placing Wrist

In a system for positioning a human model, the animator should be given an intuitive set of controls for choosing a desired configuration amongst all of the available solutions. This is not provided by general iterative methods, which most often give unpredictable results for redundant degrees of freedom.

Another key problem is that such techniques can be highly unstable near targets where the iterative solution is ill conditioned. For example, when the Jacobean matrix fails to have full rank or near targets for which there is no solution, iterative methods can become highly unstable, causing the system to fluctuate wildly and never reach an optimal solution [11].

Lastly, iterative methods are computationally inefficient compared to analytic solutions. Therefore, we desired a direct analytic solution that was stable, easy to control and which would allow the user to explore the redundant degrees of freedom in an intuitive manner.

As mentioned previously, there have been several efforts in this direction, for analytic solutions including

1. Traditional IK chains where the shoulder and elbow joints control the positioning of the wrist and the palm is simply an end-effector which will be placed in a desired orientation. It does not affect the IK chain unless the desired position would violate a rotational constraint [2].
2. Grasping tasks where the global orientation of the end-effector is known, and therefore, also is the wrist position [4]. Solving this problem requires solving a triangle, whereas when specifying a *local* orientation of the wrist, the solution requires calculating the angles of a general tetrahedron, as we shall see momentarily.

We achieved our goals by extending the methods of Kondo to place an arbitrary point on the hand at a given position, and given parameters for the redundant degrees of freedom defined by the animator. In addition, the redundant degrees of freedom correspond to intuitive motions of the shoulder and wrist.

4 Our Solution

Consider the IK chain displayed in Figure 2 representing the human arm. This chain has three joints: the shoulder S, the elbow E and the wrist W. The articulator A lies on the hand, but does not necessarily lie on the central axis of the hand, as shown in the Figure. This must be taken into account in our calculation, but does little more than add a fixed rotation into the kinematic chain. The articulator may be placed anywhere on the hand, or at the wrist, which then reduces to Kondo's case.

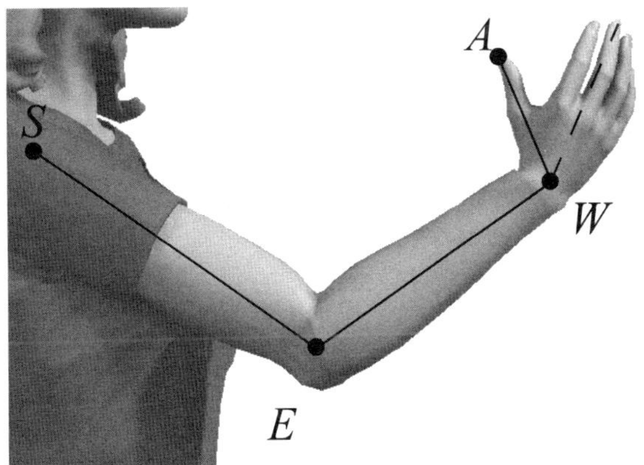

Figure 2: The IK Chain for the Human Arm

The shoulder S is a ball joint with 3 degrees of rotational freedom including a radial twist. The elbow is a hinge joint with only one rotational direction, while the wrist has two degrees of freedom, flexion/extension, and abduction/adduction. The radial twist of the forearm-wrist complex happens as the two forearm bones, the radius and ulna, rotate with respect to each other. In our model, we actually place this rotation at the elbow to facilitate deformations in the forearm mesh, but for this discussion we will place that radial twist at the wrist.

When considering the placement of the articulator A at an arbitrary target point P in space, our system has several redundant degrees of freedom. The first is a rotation ψ of the arm about a line from the shoulder through the articulator A. See **Figure 3**. The other degrees we will discuss later. For now, we will assume that we have chosen a fixed orientation R for the wrist. With the choices of R and ψ, the system is no longer underdetermined.

Thus, given an orientation R of the wrist, and a chosen rotation ψ of the system about the shoulder-articulator axis, SA, we wish to calculate the rotations of the shoulder and elbow that will place the articulator A at the chosen target P. We will represent the orientation of the upper arm SE in spherical coordinates, which can be converted from there into Euler angles if the application so dictates. Also, we will initially calculate the orientation of the system in a chosen default orientation of $\psi = 0$.

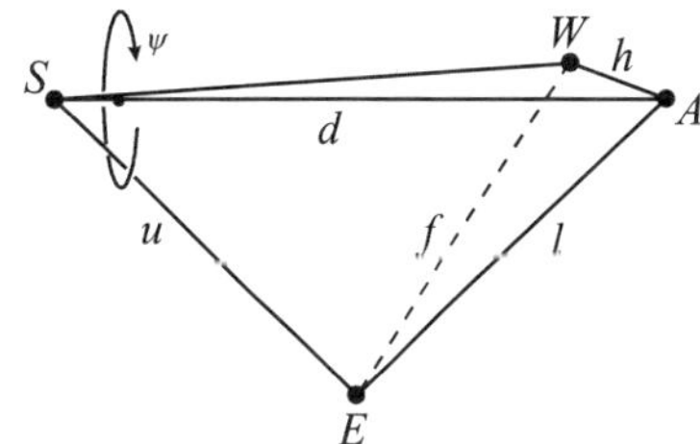

Figure 3: The Tetrahedron Formed by the Arm

To facilitate the definition of a spherical coordinate system for the upper arm, define a local coordinate system with origin at S, and with z-axis pointing towards the negative vertical in the world system. This choice is compatible with the physiology of the arm because the rest position of the arm places the elbow and wrist below the shoulder in a vertical line against the body. From here, we define two spherical angles ϕ_s, θ_s as shown in Figure 4. The third degree of freedom for the shoulder is then the radial twist τ_s, which doesn't enter this calculation until we consider the rotation ψ.

The solution follows in several steps by basic trigonometry, since the points in this system define a tetrahedron formed by the convex hull of the four points $\{S, E, W, A\}$. Figure 3 displays this tetrahedron with the original arm chain in bold. The solution of this problem amounts to solving for the dimensions and orientation of this tetrahedron in space. The main degenerate case we need to worry about is if the tetrahedron collapses to a line.

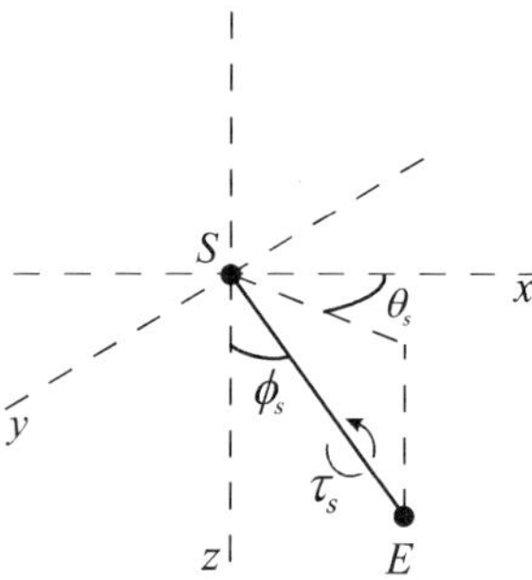

Figure 4: The Shoulder Coordinate System

4.1 Calculating the Elbow Bend Angle

Since we are given the dimensions of the arm's components, the fixed position of A relative to W, and the desired location of the articulator, $A = P$, we know the following five lengths

$$u = |SE| \qquad f = |EW|$$
$$h = |WA| \qquad d = |SA|$$
$$l = |EA|$$

From now on, we will not distinguish between A and P. Since we know all sides of the front triangle SEA, we can solve for its angles with the law of cosines

$$\alpha = \arccos\left(\frac{u^2 + l^2 - d^2}{2ul}\right)$$

Note that we are not given the position of W, nor do we yet know the orientation of the tetrahedron, so we do not know the global direction of the vector $A - W$. More importantly, we do not know the key angle $\gamma = SEW$, shown in Figure 5, which is the desired elbow rotation.

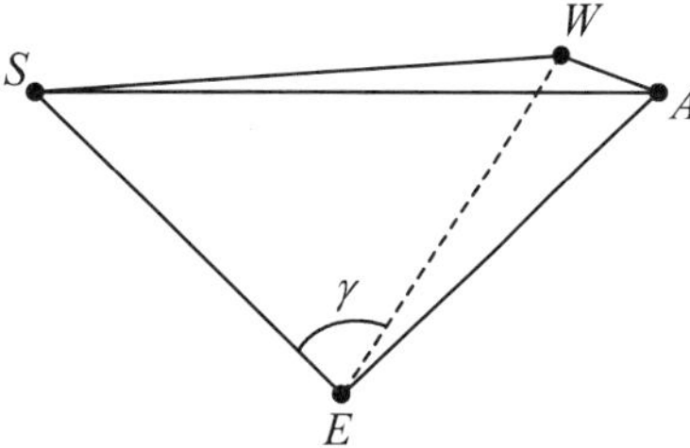

Figure 5: The elbow rotation γ

To find γ we must first reorient the tetrahedron to facilitate certain calculations. Rotate the tetrahedron so that EW lies on the vertical z-axis and S lies in the positive x portion of the x,z-coordinate plane, as indicated in Figure 6. Thus we are looking at the tetrahedron in the coordinate system of the elbow joint, a system that allows us to effectively leverage the given information.

We are given the fixed orientation of the wrist and position of the articulator. Combining this into a single transformation, we can calculate the coordinates of A in the local coordinate system of the elbow

$$\begin{aligned} A &= (h\cos\theta_w \sin\phi_w, h\sin\theta_w \sin\phi_w, h\cos\phi_w + f) \\ &= (x, y, z) \end{aligned}$$

where θ_ω, ϕ_ω are the spherical coordinates of A with respect to the wrist, and h is the length of the hand. Let $A' = (x, 0, z)$ be the projection of A to the x,z-plane, which means that the angle $\varepsilon = \angle$ WEA' = arctan(x/z).

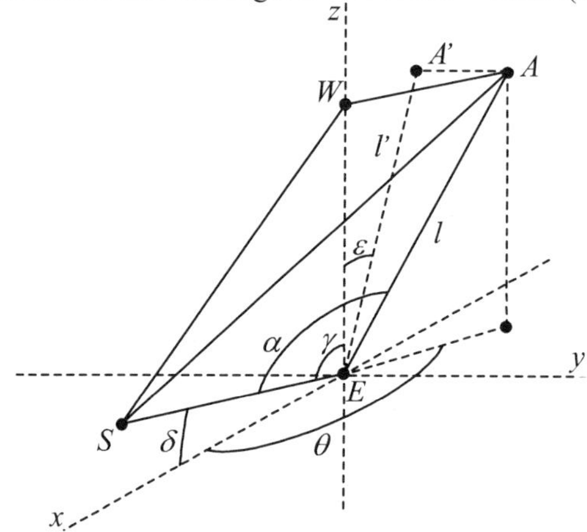

Figure 6: Solving for γ

Let δ be the angle that SE makes with the x-axis, and notice that the desired elbow angle $\gamma = \pi/2 - \delta$. So, we solve this problem by calculating δ. To this end, notice that whatever δ is, we have the following relationships by trivially rewriting the given lengths.

$$|SE| = u = \sqrt{u^2\cos^2\delta + u^2\sin^2\delta}$$
$$|SA| = d = \sqrt{(u\cos\delta - x)^2 + (u\sin\delta - z)^2 + y^2}$$
$$|EA| = l = \sqrt{x^2 + y^2 + z^2}$$

Now using the expression for α given by the law of cosines, and a few trigonometric manipulations

$$\begin{aligned} \cos\alpha &= \frac{u^2 + x^2 + y^2 + z^2 - (u\cos\delta - x)^2 - y^2 - (u\sin\delta - z)^2}{2u\sqrt{x^2 + y^2 + z^2}} \\ &= \frac{u^2 - u^2(\cos^2\delta + \sin^2\delta) + 2u(x\cos\delta + z\sin\delta)}{2ul} \\ &= \frac{x\cos\delta + z\sin\delta}{l} \end{aligned}$$

We can use the expression which calculated ε to write x

and y in terms of ε. Let l' be the length of EA' as shown in the figure, then

$$A' = (x, 0, z) = (-l'\sin\varepsilon, 0, l'\cos\varepsilon)$$

and therefore, by the angle difference identity for sin

$$\cos\alpha = \frac{l'\sin\delta\cos\varepsilon - l'\cos\delta\sin\varepsilon}{l}$$
$$= \frac{l'}{l}\sin(\delta - \varepsilon)$$

which then can be rewritten as

$$\delta = \arcsin\left(\frac{l}{l'}\cos\alpha\right) + \varepsilon$$

Since $\gamma = \pi/2 - \delta$, this completes the construction of the elbow's bend angle. Note, however, that this calculation can fail in one of two situations.

1. If $l' = 0$, then the orientation of the wrist combined with the location of the articulator relative to the wrist has placed A at the elbow. Since this is impossible given the physiology of a normal human arm, we ignore this case.
2. Second, is the possibility that

$$\text{abs}\left(\frac{l}{l'}\cos\alpha\right) > 1$$

   This happens when the target is unreachable, and if we clamp this value to 1, we will get the closest attainable position for A.

4.2 Calculating the Shoulder Orientation

At this point we have calculated the angles of the tetrahedron. From here, we just need to calculate the orientation of this tetrahedron in space to determine the necessary orientation of the shoulder joint S. Note that we have two fixed points on the tetrahedron: S and A. So, the only degree of freedom we have left is that of rotating the tetrahedron about the edge SA. This angle is the control angle ψ specified in the statement of the problem.

Remember, that we begin by finding the orientation of the tetrahedron in a standard position where $\psi = 0$, and then rotate the system by ψ about SA from there. As a default reference orientation, we have three possibilities:

1. If S, E and W are not collinear, then we orient the tetrahedron so that S, E and W are all in the vertical plane formed by S, W and the z-axis. See **Figure 7**.
2. If $\gamma = \pi$ or $\gamma = 0$, meaning that S, E and W are collinear, then we set the default orientation to be when S, W, E and A are all coplanar with the z-axis.
3. If all four points are collinear, then the system is completely independent of ψ and so the system is already completely determined, and we just orient the shoulder to the same spherical coordinates, relative to S, as A itself.

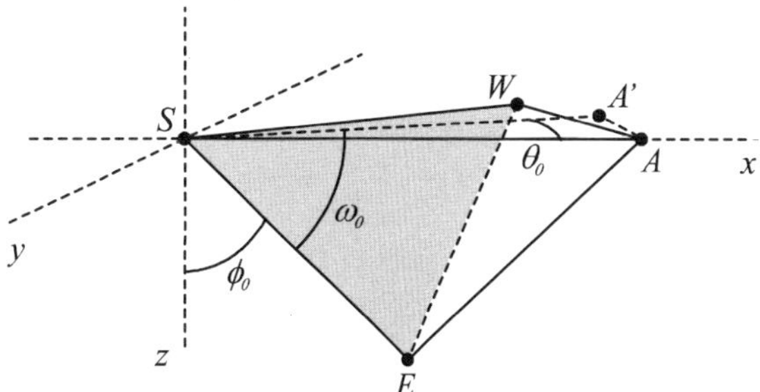

Figure 7: The Spherical Coordinates of SE in the Default Position

Also, we make the simplifying assumption that A lies along the x-axis in the shoulder's coordinate system so that the spherical orientation of A relative to S becomes $\phi_A = \pi/2$, $\theta_A = 0$. Once we find the orientation of the shoulder, (ϕ_0, θ_0) in this default case, we can simply add the spherical orientation of A to that of SE to obtain the final orientation: ϕ_s, θ_s.

The setup of this calculation is displayed in **Figure 7**. Notice that W may be above or below the x,y-plane, but that E lies directly below the line SW. As indicated in the figure, ϕ_0 is the angle formed by the z-axis and SE, which is $\pi/2 - \omega_0$, as shown. To obtain these angles, we appeal, once again, to the projection A' of A to the plane formed by SEW. Thus,

$$\phi_0 = \pi/2 - \arccos\left(\frac{SE \bullet SA'}{|SE||SA'|}\right)$$

$$\theta_0 = \arccos\left(\frac{SA \bullet SA'}{|SA||SA'|}\right)$$

The only problem being that we don't know the position of E, or the position of W in this base coordinate system. But we do know their positions in the elbow's coordinate system, displayed in Figure 8. In this coordinate system,

$$S = (u\cos\delta, 0, u\sin\delta)$$
$$E = (0,0,0)$$
$$A = (x, y, z)$$
$$A' = (x, 0, z)$$

Since we just calculated δ in the last section, we know the positions of each of these points, and so we can calculate all of the vectors required to determine ϕ_0, θ_0. Then if ϕ_A, θ_A are the spherical angles of A in the base coordinate system, we finish the construction by setting

$$\theta_S = \theta_0 + \theta_A$$
$$\phi_S = \phi_0 + \phi_A$$

Notice that this part of the construction will fail if

1. $|SA| = 0$, in which case the target is at the shoulder. Thus, the tetrahedron collapses to a triangle and simpler methods may be used. Physiologically, it is painful to place part of the hand in the center of the shoulder joint.
2. $|SA'| = 0$, in which case the target and the wrist lie on perpendicular axes through the shoulder. An example would be if the wrist lies on the x-axis in the shoulder's coordinate system and the wrist lies in the y,z-plane. Thus $\phi_0 = \pm\pi/2$, depending on the orientation of A with respect to W. This corresponds to a physical action of placing your wrist directly in front of your shoulder and the articulator on the line coming horizontally out of the shoulder. This position would certainly put strain on both the shoulder and the wrist.

As long as we take care of these two exceptional cases, the construction is complete. Note that the entire construction is analytic and completely determined up to four redundant degrees of freedom, which we leave at the control of the user.

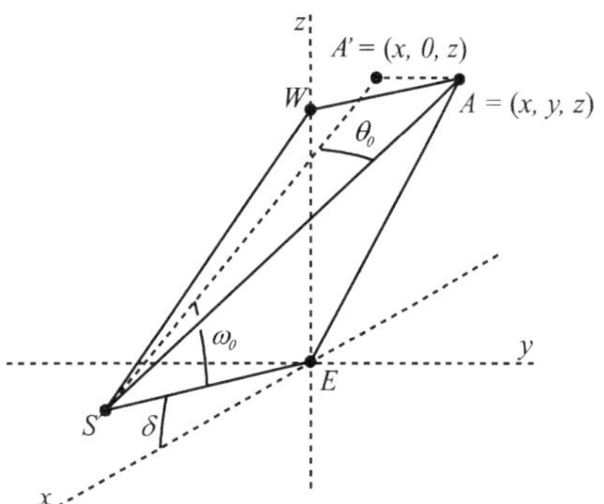

Figure 8: Angles in the Elbow's Coordinate System

4.3 Degrees of Freedom

In our complete kinematic chain for the human arm, there are a total of seven degrees of rotational freedom: three angles in the shoulder, one in the elbow, and three in the wrist. Positioning the articulator gives the animator three degrees of freedom for working with the model. There are four more degrees of freedom in the model, which the above algorithm conveniently parameterizes for the animator.

We have already discussed the fact that the rotation of the system about the axis through the shoulder and articulator is a redundant degree of freedom that the animator may use to achieve a desired posture.

The rotation of the wrist provides the remaining three degrees. If the user changes the wrist orientation, but leaves the articulator target fixed, then the above algorithm can adjust the rest of the angles in the system to compensate, leaving the articulator position unchanged. This compound operation forms three degrees of freedom for the system parameterized by the three angles of rotation for the wrist. Note the difference between this and the usual forward kinematic treatment of wrist rotations.

Thus, the user has full control over an intuitive parameterization of the seven degrees of freedom in this model, including the position of the articulator.

5 Applying the Technique

We applied this technique in a general system for transcribing ASL signs. First consider the positioning of the articulator. This action forms the first three degrees of freedom described above.

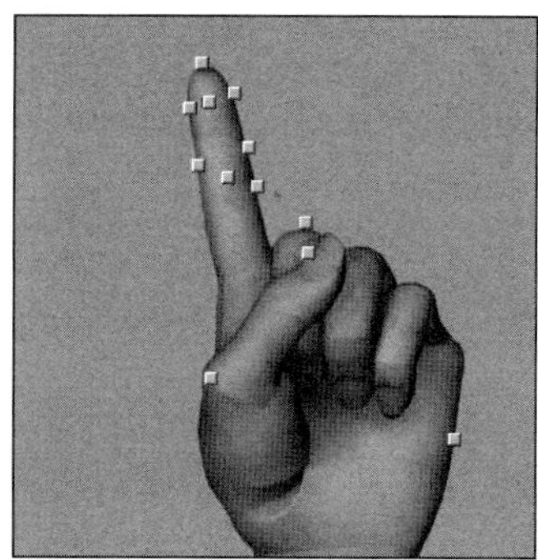

Figure 9: Choosing Articulators on a Handshape

In ASL, each specific configuration of the hand, or handshape has a number of different legal articulators defined by ASL linguistics. See Figure 9. Also, each articulator may be placed in contact with various points on the body, the face or the other hand. This works for positioning either hand. Figure 10 shows the interface for choosing such sites on the face. These sites are also predetermined by the linguistics of ASL. Our system also contains a method for specifying a spatial position when the articulator is not in contact with the body.

Once a target (either spatial or contact) has been chosen, the user is free to adjust the orientation of the wrist and the height of the elbow (our angle ψ) with the control panel displayed in Figure 3 of Appendix A. This figure displays the results obtained by flexing the wrist when the tip of the index finger is in contact with the model's cheek.

As the user is adjusting these controls, the above IK method automatically adjusts the orientation of the shoulder and elbow so that the articulator stays in place. This eliminates a process of successive refinements that would be necessary if the system used an ordinary IK chain where the wrist is set as an end-effector. The user would have to successively rotate the wrist and then adjust the wrist's position to compensate, an operation automated by our IK technique.

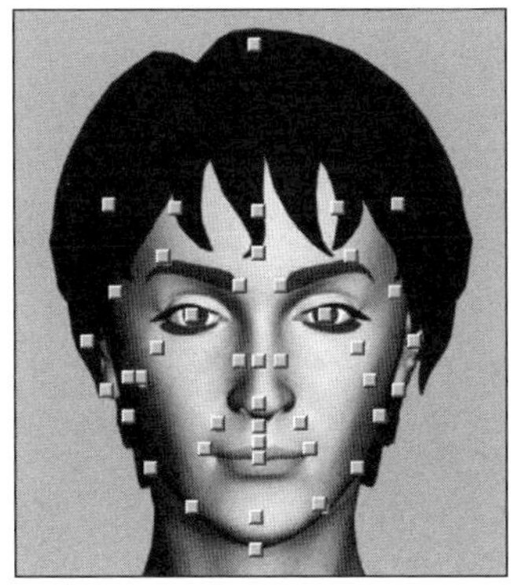

Figure 10: Choosing Targets on the Face

6 Conclusion and Future Work

The calculations of the shoulder and elbow angles θ_s, ϕ_s and ψ, detailed in section 4.2, provide an analytic parameterization of the seven degrees of freedom present in the wrist and arm of the human body. Using these parameters, we obtain an intuitive set of controls for choosing key positions for the arms of a human model. These key positions can include hand/body contact, and can be easily interpolated to display animations of the character's motion.

We are currently integrating this system into a complete model of the upper body, including the spine, neck and collarbone. In particular, the model described in this paper assumes that the shoulders are fixed with respect to the torso, which is simply not true in a human model. Nor is the motion of the shoulders a trivial one. It accounts for much of the expressiveness of the upper body especially for motions like shrugging and slumping. A complete, expressive human model must include such motions.

To make the animator's job easier we are currently working to create an automatic algorithm to coordinate some of the shoulder's motion with the arm's reach. For example, when the model reaches for a target far from the body, the shoulder should automatically move forward to extend the reach of the model.

References

[1] Badler N, Phillips C, Webber B. Simulating Humans: Computer Graphics Animation and Control. *Oxford University Press*. New York, NY. 1993.

[2] Girard M, Maciejewski A. Computational Modeling for the Computer Animation of Legged Figures. *Computer Graphics*. 19(3), July 1985, Pages 253-270.

[3] Koga Y, Kondo K, Kuffner J, and Latombe J. "Planning Motions with Intentions," *Proc., SIGGRAPH'94,* Orlando, FL, July 24-29, 1994. Pages 395-407.

[4] Kondo K. Inverse Kinematics of a Human Arm. *Technical Report STAN-CSTR-94-1508*, Dept. of Computer Science, Stanford University.

[5] Liddel S, Johnson R. American Sign Language: The Phonological Base. *Sign Language Studies.* 64, 1989, Pages 195-277.

[6] McDonald J, Toro J, et. al. An Improved Articulated Model of the Human Hand. *Proceedings of the 8th International Conference in Central Europe on Computer Graphics, Visualization and Interactive Digital Media*. 2000. Pages 306 – 313.

[7] Murray R, Li Z, and Sastry S. A Mathematical Introduction to Robotic Manipulation. *CRC Press, Inc.*, 1994.

[8] National Institute on Deafness and other Communication Disorders, Website. Current as of March 2002. http://www.nidcd.nih.gov/health/pubs_hb/asl.htm.

[9] Sandler W. Phonological Representations of the Sign: Linearity and Nonlinearity in American Sign Language. *Foris Publications*, Dordrecht, Holland. 1989.

[10] Tennant R, Brown M, Nelson-Metlay V, The American Sign Language Handshape Dictionary, *Clerk Books*, Washington, DC, 1998, pages 74-75.

[11] Tolani D, Goswami A, and Badler N. Real-time inverse kinematics techniques for anthropomorphic limbs. *Graphical Models* 62 (5), September 2000, Pages 353-388.

[12] Wolfe R, et al. An Interface for Transcribing American Sign Language. SIGGRAPH 99 Sketches, August 11, 1999, Page 229.

Appendix A: Signs and Controls

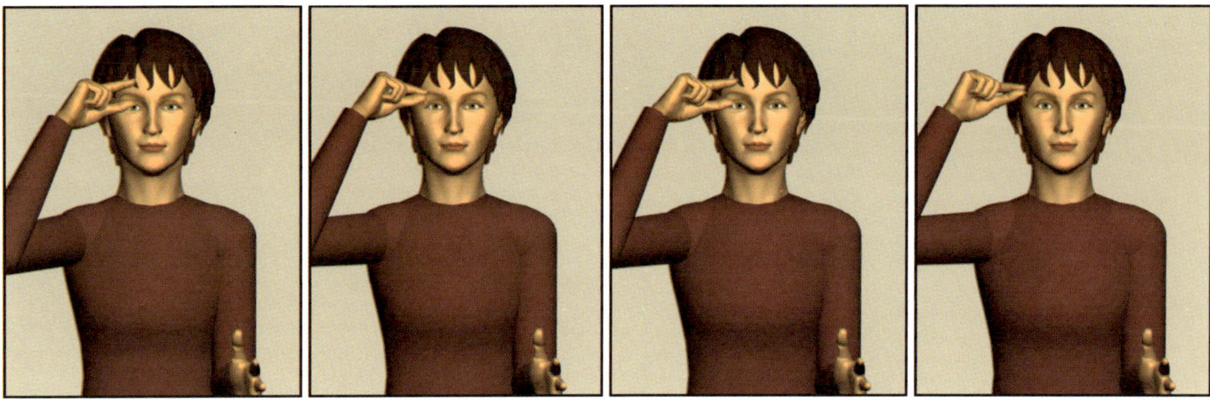

Figure 1: Sign for GLASSES (left two frames) and GALLAUDET UNIVERSITY (right two frames)

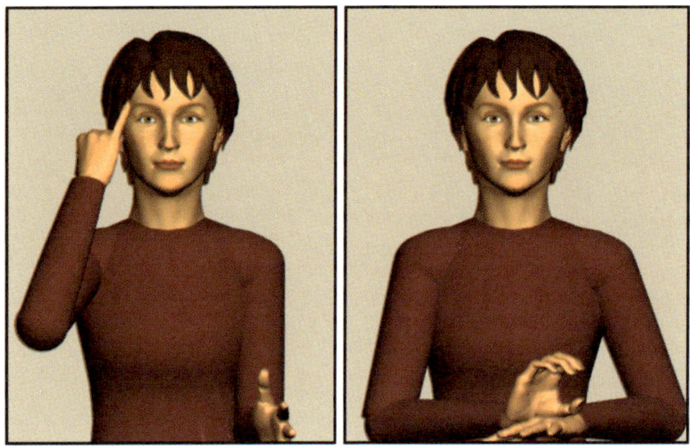

Figure 2: Signs for IDEA (left) and CHOCOLATE (right)

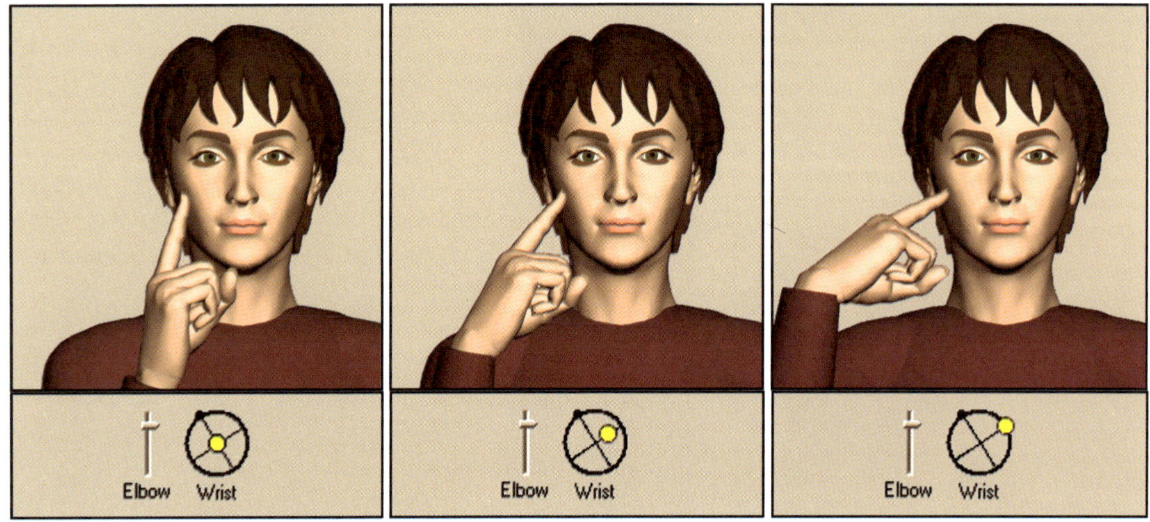

Figure 3: Moving the Wrist Controls with an Articulator in Contact with the Face

Application-specific muscle representations

Victor Ng-Thow-Hing
Fundamental Research Laboratories
Honda R&D Americas, Inc.
vngthowhing@hra.com

Eugene Fiume
Department of Computer Science
University of Toronto
elf@dgp.toronto.edu

Abstract

The need to model muscles means different things to artistic and technical practitioners. Three different muscle representations are presented and the motivations behind their design are discussed. Each representation allows unique capabilities and operations to be performed on the model, yet the underlying mathematical foundation is the same for all. This is achieved by developing a data-fitting pipeline that allows samples that are generated from different data sources to be used in the guided construction of a B-spline solid. We show how B-spline solids can be used to create muscles from contour curves extracted out of medical images, digitized fibre sets from dissections of muscle specimens, and profile curves that can be interactively sketched and manipulated by an anatomical modeller.

Key words: Anatomical modelling, muscles, data-fitting, B-spline solid

1 Introduction

The concept of modelling muscles means different things to different communities. When modelling humans and other animals for use in film animation, the intention is to emulate the effects of superficial muscle anatomy that can be seen to contract and stretch through the skin. For biomechanists, the functional aspects of muscle have greater importance. Muscle models are developed based on controlled experiments with real muscle specimens to create parameterized models that relate generated force with muscle length, velocity of shortening, and neural activation. Simulations use these muscle models as actuators to exert forces on mechanical skeletons to study and reproduce motor tasks. At the structural level, anatomists seek to discover the internal fibre arrangements of muscle and how this *muscle architecture* determines the functional role the muscle plays in the overall context of the body's locomotion system.

The development of muscle models has progressed relatively independently in the animation and biomechanics industries. Justifiably, the trend has been to only model what is needed and to avoid unnecessary complexity. Animation applications stress the need for body physiques to appear adequately realistic while biomechanical applications only model the functional aspects of muscle, such as muscle force generation.

Of the many modelling primitives available for such representations, parametric solid representations are particularly convenient. Previously, the B-spline solid model has been used to demonstrate that a large variety of muscle shapes can be compactly represented by a model based on B-spline basis functions[7]. The model's volumetric properties allows internal structures to be specified and scalar field functions to be defined over the entire solid's domain. A data-fitting pipeline has been described that allows deformable muscle models to be built from medical images of transverse slices of muscle anatomy[6]. In this work, the same mathematical framework is used to create entirely different muscle representations that each enable new visualizations and phenomena to be depicted.

The purpose of this work is to demonstrate how considerations of application and user interface drive the development of very different muscle models and that this design process is essential to the success of the model's utility. The next section reviews the previous work in muscle modelling in the fields of animation and biomechanics. In Section 3, the data-fitting pipeline for B-spline solids is reviewed, followed by separate sections for each of the three models developed with their unique applications. We conclude with discussion of current and future applications of these models.

2 Previous work

The idea of anatomical models for human and animal construction was introduced to the computer graphics community using geometric primitives such as ellipsoids, and parametric surfaces[14, 15, 12]. The emphasis on these models was the modelling of general approximations of anatomic muscle groups. As these muscles would never be directly seen because of an obscuring skin surface, there is no need to correctly model exact muscle shapes. Indeed, since the introduction of these methods, many film production houses have implemented their own proprietary systems to incorporate an anatomical layer of muscles in the modelling pipeline of digital characters[11, 13]. In these applications, secondary dynamic phenomena such as muscle "jiggles" are added to simulate inertial effects. The muscles themselves are used for shape definition and have no functional role in the creation of the motions. Shape changes are mainly driven by joint motion of an underlying kinematic skeleton.

In biomechanics, the venerable Hill model[16] is used ubiquitously to describe force magnitudes of muscle as a function of various parameters such as muscle length, activation and rest length. In combination with a musculoskeletal system that represents muscle lines of action as piecewise line segment actuators on the skeleton[4], simulations have been made with muscles as active actuators driving tasks such as jumping and walking[9]. As the emphasis is on the functional role of muscle, the volumetric representation of muscle is ignored. Assumptions are made that simplify muscle architecture and inter-muscular interactions that may lead to inaccuracies for some motions. Finite element models that represent both shape and physical function of muscles are usually restricted to single muscles simulated in isolation[3]. The use of the finite-element method generally requires lengthy computational times for detailed simulation that limits the scalability of the technique to large, multiple muscle systems.

One of the goals of using a common mathematical foundation for modelling different muscle representations is the ability to adapt to different levels of complexity using the same set of routines for tasks such as display tessellation and volume calculation. Selective emphasis can be made to focus on graphical, structural, or physical characteristics of muscle contraction.

3 Data-fitting pipeline

The B-spline solid model allows smooth shapes to be defined with a compact set of control point parameters, $\boldsymbol{q}$:

$$\boldsymbol{x}(u,v,w) = \sum_i \sum_j \sum_k B_i^u(u) B_j^v(v) B_k^w(w) \boldsymbol{q}_{ijk}, \quad (1)$$

where i, j, k index the control point lattice and basis functions of the triple B-spline tensor product. The degree of the basis functions, and thus the resulting solid, can be chosen arbitrarily to meet the smoothness and metric properties demanded by the application. The evaluated points, $\boldsymbol{x}(u,v,w)$ are the Cartesian coordinates that compose the boundary and volume of the solid being modelled. Given n control points, $\boldsymbol{q}$, we can select n material coordinates $\boldsymbol{u}_i^{max} = (u,v,w)_i, i = 0, \cdots, n-1$, that map to a set of n spatial points, $\boldsymbol{x}$:

$$\boldsymbol{x} = \boldsymbol{B}(\boldsymbol{u}^{max})\boldsymbol{q}. \quad (2)$$

The matrix $\boldsymbol{B}$ contains the triple tensor products of Equation 1 while the coordinates of $\boldsymbol{u}^{max}$ are chosen with sampled values of u, v, and w that produce the maxima of each of their corresponding B-spline basis functions. The position of a spatial point, $\boldsymbol{x}$, would be most influenced by its corresponding control point, $\boldsymbol{q}$, in the same row of Equation 2, providing intuitive control over the solid's shape as the spatial point is moved.

The data-fitting pipeline requires that spatial points be ultimately provided for each of the known material coordinates, $\boldsymbol{u}^{max}$ to solve the system in Equation 2. In many cases, the original samples drawn from various muscle sources may not be uniformly distributed. If these data points were directly used as spatial points, the resulting B-spline solid's control points would be unevenly clustered near the original data. A *continous volume sampling function* (CVSF) is created from the original data samples of each different muscle representation. A uniform sampling of the CVSF's domain generates a distribution of spatial points that produces B-spline solids with a uniform arrangement of control points. Furthermore, we can directly solve for any number of control points by generating as many samples as we need from the CVSF.

3.1 CVSF pipeline

The data-fitting process can described as follows:

1. From various raw data sources, extract 3-D coordinate data that samples the physical object we wish to represent. Samples can occur within the volume of the object as well as on its boundary.

2. Using the 3-D data, construct a *continuous volume sampling function* (CVSF). The CVSF can be described as: $CVSF(\tilde{u}, \tilde{v}, \tilde{w})$, such that $(\tilde{u}, \tilde{v}, \tilde{w}) \in [0,1]^3$.

3. We uniformly sample the parameter space of the CVSF to generate the same number of spatial points as we have control points in our model. The material coordinates, $\boldsymbol{u}_{max}$ are assigned to these spatial points.

4. Using the sampled data points as spatial points, $\boldsymbol{x}$, solve the linear system described in Equation 2.

Once the B-spline solid is created with an initial shape based on the data points, we can subsequently manipulate the shape or animate global changes through physically-based modelling or deformation.

Of the four stages in the CVSF data-fitting schema, Stages 3 and 4 are independent of the original form of the data. Stages 1 and 2, however, must be designed to accommodate each new muscle representation and application. Equations 1 and 2 provide extremely general ways in which to effect this. While this level of generality is needed to accommodate the different forms of input that different muscle modelling applications may need, there is a clear structure in the way that each application both gathers and represents discrete data. That structure defines a specific traversal of an otherwise very complex volume as well as having semantic importance to the application. We have isolated three structures: contour curves, fibre sets, and profile curves. In the next three sections, we demonstrate how each can be used both to define a novel muscle representation and to accommodate the forms of data sources that are available in that application.

4 Contour curves

Medical imagery containing transverse anatomical cross-sectional slices can be used to perform reconstruction of muscles. For example, portions of the Visible Human data-set[8] in the lower leg region can be used to isolate the boundary form of muscles (Figure 8). Full details of this process are described in [7]. Once muscles have been successfully segmented from the image slices, they can be selectively displayed and examined in relation to neighbouring anatomy.

4.1 Creating the CVSF

Given a set of n contour curves extracted from the transverse slices: $\boldsymbol{C}_0, \cdots, \boldsymbol{C}_{n-1}$, we wish to design a CVSF that produces a uniform sampling of points throughout the volume spanned by these image contour curves. The contour curves are represented as B-spline curves created by interpolating sample points taken along muscle cross-sectional boundaries. The sample points are re-indexed to minimize the distance between corresponding samples on adjacent slices sharing the same index. This step will reduce rotational distortions in the B-spline solid. The CVSF is designed to interpolate the contour curves such that traversing the parameters will span the solid in an intuitive manner. We select parameter $\tilde{u}$ to increase radially outward from a central axis of the solid to its contour boundaries. Parameter $\tilde{v}$ will traverse the perimeter around the axis and $\tilde{w}$ will range from the bottom of the stack to the top (Figure 1).

A curve, $\mathbf{axis}(\tilde{w}), \tilde{w} \in [0,1]$ through the centroids of the contours is defined to travel along the length of the muscle. Given a specific set of parameters, $(\tilde{u}_0, \tilde{v}_0, \tilde{w}_0)$, a second B-spline curve, $\mathbf{profile}_{\tilde{v}_0}(\tilde{w})$ is created on the outer boundary of the muscle that interpolates all of the

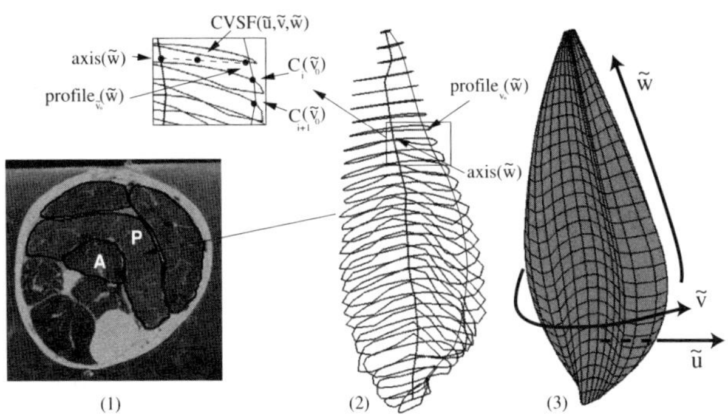

Figure 1: CVSF construction from contour curves

points $\boldsymbol{C}_i(\tilde{v}_0), i = 0, \cdots, n-1$ from each contour. The $\tilde{w}_0$ parameter generates two points, $\mathbf{axis}(\tilde{w}_0)$ and $\mathbf{profile}_{\tilde{v}_0}(\tilde{w}_0)$, along the length of each of the two curves and these points are linearly interpolated by $\tilde{u}_0$ to produce the final spatial point.

Using an arclength parameterization for $\mathbf{axis}(\tilde{w}_0)$ and $\mathbf{profile}_{\tilde{v}_0}(\tilde{w}_0)$ ensures that the iso-parametric curves in the $\tilde{w}$ direction of the solid do not undergo excessive twisting and iso-parametric curves in the $\tilde{v}$ around the muscle's axis are evenly distributed along the muscle's length instead of being aligned with the original image slices. Degree 2 B-spline basis functions were used in the v and w domains to reduce unwanted oscillations in the surface yet still produce smooth surfaces. A degree 1 B-spline basis was used for the parameter u to model an even distribution of material from the inner axis to the boundary of the muscles.

By transforming the original static images from the Visible Human data-set to a deformable B-spline solid model, we have animated its shape to simulate contractions[6] and generated muscle fibres as streamlines in the solid's volume. Unfortunately, from an anatomical standpoint, the fibres reconstructed from a B-spline solid derived from medical images do not match muscle architecture observed in real muscle (Figure 2). The contour curves inherently contain only boundary information, losing all internal muscle architectural information. This restricts the use of muscles obtained in this manner to only external muscle visualizations, volume and mass computation, or modelling of general anatomical shapes of muscle groups. It is extremely difficult if not impossible to track individual fibres between adjacent transverse sections. As muscle contracts in the direction of its fibre arrangement, correct modelling of shape changes during muscle activation cannot be obtained for muscles reconstructed from only its boundary surface.

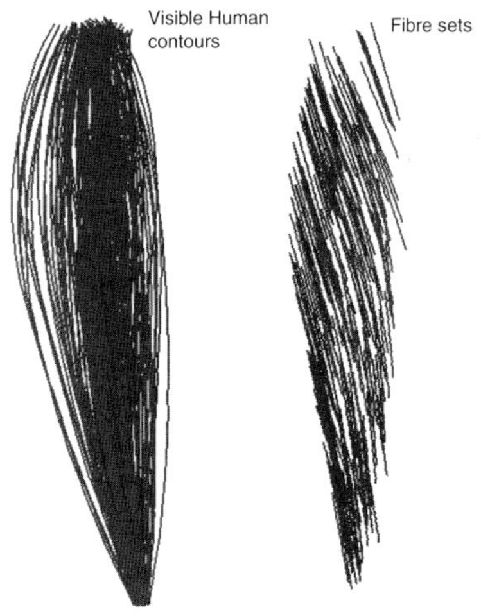

Figure 2: Comparison of generated fibres for the posterior soleus region from different data sources. The image on the left shows fibres incorrectly running from top to bottom in a side view of posterior soleus derived from contour stacks. The right image shows the correct fibre arrangement in a solid generated from fibres obtained by serial dissections.

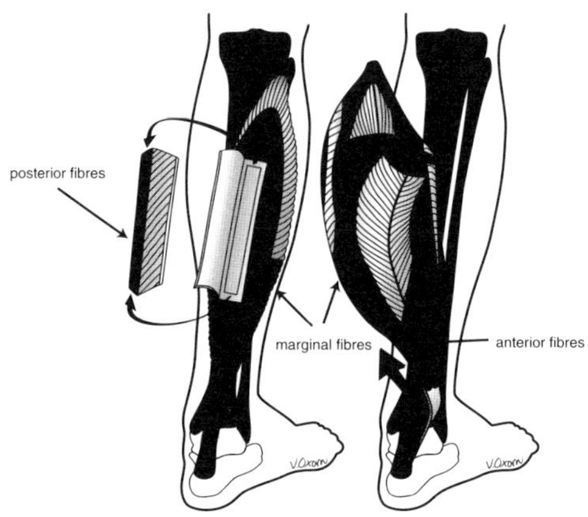

Figure 3: There are three architecturally-distinct regions in the human soleus: marginal, posterior and anterior fibres. Images courtesy of Valerie Oxorn, Copyright 1998-1999.

5 Fibre sets

In order to depict the correct arrangement of fibres that make up muscle tissue, we digitized fibre positions from serial dissections of cadaveric muscle specimens.

5.1 Specimen preparation for serial dissection

The human soleus muscle has three architecturally, distinct regions: posterior, marginal and anterior (Figure 3). In serial dissection, the layers of muscle tissue are removed one at a time from the most superficial layers to the deeper, interior ones (Figure 5). At each layer, representative fibres are selected and digitized to obtain fibre arrangements throughout the entire volume of the muscle as shown in Figure 4. In contrast to previous muscle fibre reconstructions using B-spline solids [6], we have designed a CVSF that incorporates all available fibre data throughout the muscle volume instead of a limited subset of fibres located only on the boundaries of the muscle. This increases the fidelity of the fibre arrangement visualization.

5.2 Fibre set CVSF construction

For each architecturally distinct muscle region, a muscle fibre is represented as a B-spline curve, $\mathbf{fibre}_{i,j}(\tilde{w})$, by interpolating the corresponding digitized 3-D points obtained for each fibre during serial dissection. The index i refers to the layer of muscle the fibre resides in and j indexes the fibres within that layer. The curve is arclength parameterized to ensure spatial points are selected evenly along the physical length of the fibre. For fibres consisting of two endpoints only, degree 1 B-spline curves are used (i.e., line segments). For all other fibres, degree 2 curves are used. Cubic curves introduced unwanted oscillations with overly long fibre lengths.

The other two parameters, $\tilde{u}$ and $\tilde{v}$, define the index range that selects four fibre curves to bilinearly interpolate to obtain the final spatial point. Given $(\tilde{u}_0, \tilde{v}_0, \tilde{w}_0)$, we let $\tilde{u}_0$ travel down through the layers of a muscle and **numLayers** be the number of layers obtained with serial dissection. Parameter $\tilde{v}_0$ travels along the $\mathbf{numFibres}_i$ muscle fibres in layer i. Using floor functions, we compute:

$$\begin{aligned} i &= \lfloor \tilde{u}_0(\mathbf{numLayers} - 1) \rfloor, \\ j &= \lfloor \tilde{v}_0(\mathbf{numFibres}_i - 1) \rfloor. \end{aligned}$$

A bilinear interpolation between the space spanned by the four points,

$$\begin{aligned} \mathbf{p}_{00} &= \mathbf{fibre}_{i,j}(\tilde{w}_0), \\ \mathbf{p}_{01} &= \mathbf{fibre}_{i,j+1}(\tilde{w}_0), \\ \mathbf{p}_{10} &= \mathbf{fibre}_{i+1,j}(\tilde{w}_0), \\ \mathbf{p}_{11} &= \mathbf{fibre}_{i+1,j+1}(\tilde{w}_0), \end{aligned}$$

is performed using the interpolation parameters:

$$\begin{aligned} \hat{u} &= \tilde{u}_0(\mathbf{numLayers} - 1) - i, \\ \hat{v} &= \tilde{v}_0(\mathbf{numFibres}_i - 1) - j \end{aligned}$$

to get the final spatial point with the following steps:

$$\begin{aligned} \mathbf{p}_0 &= \mathbf{p}_{00}(1 - \hat{v}) + \mathbf{p}_{01}\hat{v}, \\ \mathbf{p}_1 &= \mathbf{p}_{10}(1 - \hat{v}) + \mathbf{p}_{11}\hat{v}, \\ \mathbf{CVSF}(\tilde{u}_0, \tilde{v}_0, \tilde{w}_0) &= (1 - \hat{u})\mathbf{p}_0 + \hat{u}\mathbf{p}_1. \end{aligned}$$

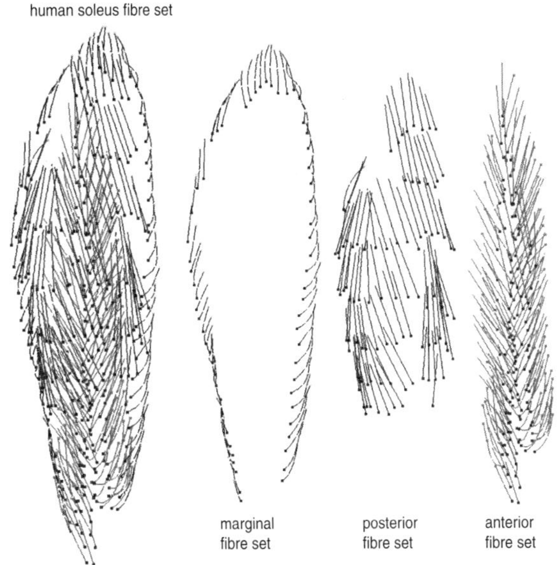

Figure 4: Digitized fibre sets for the three regions of human soleus

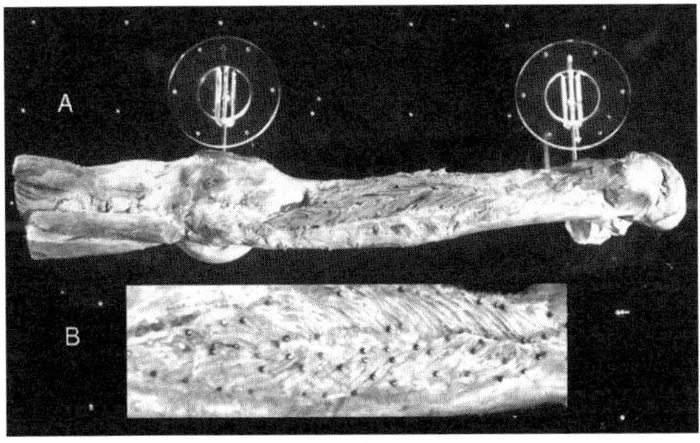

Figure 5: Serial dissection of human soleus muscle with marked fibre points

Figure 6 illustrates this process.

With the generated fibres, we can obtain virtual measurements of fibres and their angles of insertion to the tendon region of muscle. These can be used to obtain estimates of muscle force that take into account the finer details of muscle architecture. An arbitrary number of fibres can be visualized within the solid by generating streamlines represented as 3-D space curves. Sampling using parameter values at uniform intervals produces an unnaturally, regular grid-like distribution of fibres. On the other hand, a random sampling of fibres produces uneven clumps of fibres in the muscle. We have found a two-dimensional Sobol sequence[10] guarantees a more even distribution of fibres (Figure 7).

By embedding viscoelastic links with Hill muscle

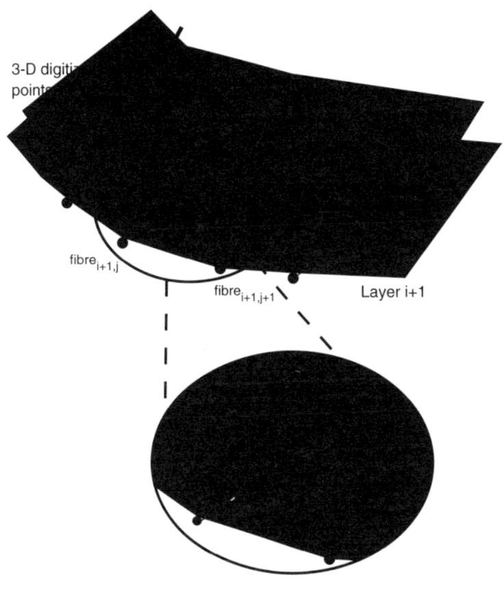

Figure 6: CVSF construction for fibre sets. The CVSF sample point is the result of a bilinear interpolation process on the fibre set data.

force models[16], muscle contraction under volume preservation has been simulated (Figure 9). Full details of this process are described in [5]. These fibre set models allow biomechanists to study muscle function to a greater level of detail than previously offered. Cadaver studies on soleus muscle have demonstrated that pennation angles can vary throughout the volume of muscle[1]. Models that account for pennation effects as a single parameter only describe average force production for muscle fibres, losing any information about local regional effects within a muscle. Furthermore, the activation of muscle fibres is not simultaneous. The parameterization of the B-spline solid model permits local fibre regions to be delineated and assigned different activation values. The combination of this ability to model detailed fibre architecture and the provision of a data-fitting pipeline to create models from real specimens makes our model a suitable candidate for extensive functional studies of different muscles.

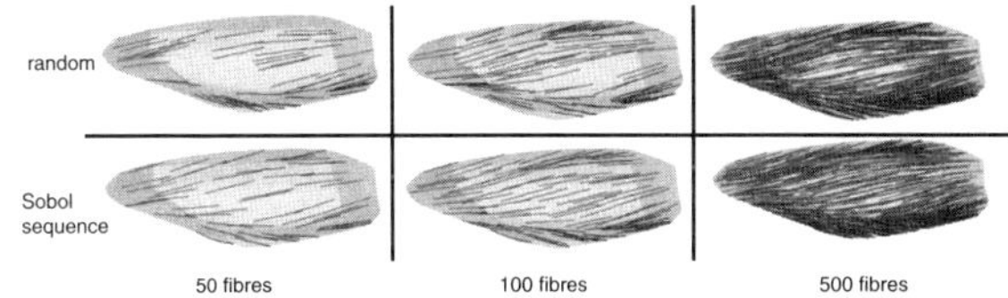

Figure 7: Generation of fibres. 50, 100, and 500 fibres were generated in a model of the posterior soleus using uniform pseudorandom number generation and Sobol sequences. The Sobol sequence produced better distribution of fibres.

6 Profile curves

Contour curves and fibre sets offer a migration path from sources of actual anatomical muscle data to the construction of a virtual B-spline solid model. However, there are occasions where interactive creation of solid shapes is desirable. For example, for an application involving muscle reconstruction of extinct animals, it would be impossible to obtain soft tissue specimens of real anatomy. A computer artist may wish to design a novel creature with a unique musculoskeletal system that does not exist. Generally, a creature designer will use comparative anatomy to guide where major muscle groups are placed on a fictional animal. These applications need to be able to interactively design the shapes of B-spline solids, with visual guidance from a human designer.

In creature modelling applications, the artist needs only approximate shapes of muscle groups because the underlying anatomy will be covered by a layer of skin. Manipulating the individual control points of a B-spline solid would be too tedious. Using multiple *profile curves*, a modeller could capture important features and the overall muscle shape at a higher level of abstraction than through control points.

The attachment of musculotendon onto a skeleton can be characterized by three important curves: *origin*, *insertion* and *axial*. The origin and insertion curves indicate the attachment areas of the tendon portions of a musculotendon to the bony surfaces of the skeleton. The axial curve indicates the direction the muscles takes from one end of the curve to the other - its line of action. If the axial curve connects the centroids of the cross-sections of the muscle, biomechanists can use this curve to calculate the moment arm of the muscle about a joint. Additional curves could be added along the axial curve to further refine the muscle's shape by creating a swept surface of these curves. In our application, a single mid-sectional curve is defined. We have designed a CVSF that constructs the solid muscle using these profile curves (see Figure 10).

The origin and insertion curves are represented as two closed, periodic B-spline curves, $\mathbf{origin}(\tilde{v})$ and $\mathbf{insertion}(\tilde{v})$. The axial curve is an open, aperiodic B-spline, $\mathbf{axial}(\tilde{w})$. We have used degree 2 B-spline curves, but higher order curves can be used. In practice, quadratic curves provide a good compromise between smooth curves and reduced oscillations in the curve. We would like the CVSF to have the following properties that guarantee the solid will interpolate the profile curves on its boundaries:

$$\begin{aligned} CVSF(1,\tilde{v},0) &= \mathbf{origin}(\tilde{v}), \\ CVSF(1,\tilde{v},1) &= \mathbf{insertion}(\tilde{v}), \\ CVSF(0,\tilde{v},\tilde{w}) &= \mathbf{axial}(\tilde{w}), \forall \tilde{v} \in [0,1]. \end{aligned}$$

The mid-sectional curve, $\mathbf{middle}(\tilde{v})$, is generated automatically by averaging the local coordinates of the insertion and origin curves (see Section 6.1 for the calculation of local frames of reference for each curve) and can be initially positioned anywhere along the axis. We chose the halfway point on the axial curve for a balanced weighting between the two end curves. The mid-sectional curve along with the end curves influence the shape of the musculotendon along its length. Rather than linearly interpolating between the sections directly, a nonlinear weighting is made to account for the observation that the shape does not uniformly change from the midsection to the extremal sections. Each cross-section of the solid is desired to be approximately oriented perpendicular to the local tangent of the axial curve.

6.1 Reference frames for the axial curve

To generate points that deform as the axial curve moves, we need to define a local reference frame that can be centred on any $\tilde{w}$ of $\mathbf{axial}(\tilde{w})$. We use Bloomenthal's rotation minimizing frame[2] to avoid sudden large changes in orientation of the local frames along the axial space curve. This reference frame can be represented as a 3×3 matrix, $L_{rotmin,\tilde{w}}$ with the origin located at the point, $\mathbf{axial}(\tilde{w})$. Having developed a local coordinate system for these profile curves, we will describe an interactive user interface to allow an artist to directly sketch and deform muscle shapes on a skeleton.

6.2 Profile curve sketching with direct manipulation

The user sketches 3-D muscles by selecting points directly on the visible bone surface geometry through which profile curves should interpolate, allowing direct manipulation and editing of points. A musculotendon shape designer would proceed to select points to sketch out the curves for the origin, insertion and axial profiles of the muscle (Figure 10). If the user is using a 2-D pointing device to pick points on an image of a 3-D skeleton, the problem is to find the corresponding 3-D points of the picked geometry.

One alternative is to locate the intersection of a projected ray from the picked screen coordinate with the surface geometry. The computational expense involved in locating the geometric intersection point of this ray in a complex scene may be too high for interactive applications. Furthermore, the original picked point is at pixel precision, which is already a discrete approximation of the true point on the viewing plane.

Instead, taking advantage of current depth buffer-based graphics hardware, the screen coordinates (x, y, z) are extracted, where x and y are image coordinates and $z \in [0, 1]$ contains the depth buffer value for that pixel. With these coordinates, inverse transformations of the modelling, camera and projection matrices are performed to determine in real-time the corresponding world coordinates for the picked point on the screen.

As we are dealing with discretized representations of the geometry, there is always the danger of imprecision. To minimize this potential inaccuracy, we closely bound the geometry with the near and far clipping planes to increase the dynamic range of the depth buffer. Current depth buffers have 16 to 32 bits of precision, providing enough significant digits for finding adequate world coordinates. A nice side-effect of using this method is that if more precision is required, the designer can zoom the camera closer to the bone geometry, so that accuracy is bound to the discretization error of the picked visible pixel.

6.3 CVSF construction

Having created a local reference frame for our axial curve and having obtained point samples for the origin, insertion and mid-section curves, we now describe how to compute spatial points from these profile curves given the sampling parameters $(\tilde{u}_0, \tilde{v}_0, \tilde{w}_0)$.

The interpolating curves, $\textbf{origin}(\tilde{v})$, $\textbf{insertion}(\tilde{v})$, and $\textbf{middle}(\tilde{v})$ are created from point samples obtained interactively from the user. We evaluate the points:

$$\begin{aligned} \boldsymbol{p}_O &= \textbf{origin}(\tilde{v}_0), \\ \boldsymbol{p}_I &= \textbf{insertion}(\tilde{v}_0), \\ \boldsymbol{p}_m &= \textbf{middle}(\tilde{v}_0). \end{aligned}$$

and express them in terms of the axial local frame of references, $L_{rotmin,0}$, $L_{rotmin,1}$, and $L_{rotmin,0.5}$ respectively, to get:

$$\begin{aligned} \boldsymbol{p}'_O &= \boldsymbol{p}_O L^T_{rotmin,0} \\ \boldsymbol{p}'_I &= \boldsymbol{p}_I L^T_{rotmin,1} \\ \boldsymbol{p}'_m &= \boldsymbol{p}_m L^T_{rotmin,0.5}. \end{aligned}$$

The parameter $\tilde{w}$ is used to determine a point, $\boldsymbol{p}'$ on the muscle's surface through interpolation of the points in Equation 3. Although we can use linear interpolation to get a point, $\boldsymbol{p}'$ on the muscle's surface, the resulting swept surfaces are not satisfactory and there is only C^0 continuity on the mid-section curve. Rather, we nonlinearly bias the swept surfaces towards the mid-section curve by using a quadratic function. This creates a wider region of influence in the middle of the muscle that follows the shape of $\textbf{middle}(\tilde{v})$ before tapering off to the origin and insertion curves. Depth in the muscle from the surface to the axis is controlled by scaling the point $\boldsymbol{p}'$ by $\tilde{u}_0$ before transforming $\boldsymbol{p}'$ back to its position in world coordinates:

$$CVSF(\tilde{u}_0, \tilde{v}_0, \tilde{w}_0) = \textbf{axial}(\tilde{w}_0) + \tilde{u}_0 L_{rotmin,\tilde{w}_0} \boldsymbol{p}'. \tag{3}$$

By allowing a muscle shape designer to interactively modify the origin, insertion and axial curves, we can completely specify a new B-spline solid which interpolates these profile curves. This technique allows a larger number of control points of the solid to be completely specified by a smaller set of points that make up the curve. Profile curves can be considered a deformation technique to define solid shapes because the points of the solid are referenced and transformed relative to a local coordinate system based on the profile curves. The technique of modelling from profile curves is suitable for high-level design of musculature on a human or animal model as seen in Figure 11, but lacks the fine muscle architectural detail needed for accurate muscle simulations.

7 Conclusion

The development of a consistent framework for data-fitting of B-spline solids allows the flexibility of designing volumetric geometric representations that are tailored to different available data sources. In all cases, careful consideration of how the model will be used plays a major role in the construction of its CVSF. The three applications we presented range from detailed muscle architectural studies to intuitive profile curves for interactive sketching of muscles onto a skeleton. The variety of muscle representations displayed attests to the versatility of the B-spline solid model. However, a significant shortcoming of using B-spline solids is the inability to inherently model branching structures. Although it is possible to create a branched muscle through a union of several B-spline solid muscles, subdivision solids may provide a more elegant method to inherently support branching.

The various muscle models presented here can also be combined to take advantage of the strength of each model's representation. For example, multiple fibre-set muscles can be nested within a single muscle derived from contour curves to visualize intricate fibre arrangements within the boundaries of a muscle extracted from medical imagery. The control points of the enveloping solid can be used directly as a free-form deformation, ensuring the nested solids deform with the solid that contains them. A unified B-spline solid framework can be used to construct a digital library of muscle models containing various levels of detail from general muscle groups to detailed muscle fibre arrangements.

Acknowledgements

We would like to thank Anne Agur and Nancy McKee from the University of Toronto's Department of Anatomy for motivating the need to model accurate muscle fibre architecture and for performing the data collection of muscle fibres from cadaveric specimens. We thank Honda R&D Americas for their continued support of this work and the anonymous paper reviewers for their useful suggestions and comments.

References

[1] A.M.R. Agur and N.H. McKee. Soleus muscle: Fiber orientation. *Clinical Anatomy*, 10:130, 1997. Abstract.

[2] J. Bloomenthal. Calculation of reference frames along a space curve. In Andrew S. Glassner, editor, *Graphics Gems*, pages 567–571. Academic Press, Inc., 1990.

[3] D. T. Chen and D. Zeltzer. Pump it up: Computer animation of a biomechanically based model of muscle using the finite element method. In *Computer Graphics (SIGGRAPH '92 Proceedings)*, volume 26, pages 89–98, July 1992.

[4] S. L. Delp, J. P. Loan, M. G. Hoy, F. E. Zajac, E. L. Topp, and J. M. Rosen. An interactive graphics-based model of the lower extremity to study orthopaedic surgical procedures. *IEEE Transactions on Biomedical Engineering*, 37(8):757–767, 1990.

[5] V. Ng-Thow-Hing. *Anatomically-based models for physical and geometric reconstruction of humans and other animals*. PhD thesis, University of Toronto, 2001.

[6] V. Ng-Thow-Hing, A. Agur, K. Ball, E. Fiume, and N. McKee. Shape reconstruction and subsequent deformation of soleus muscle models using b-spline solid primitives. In S.L. Jacques, editor, *Laser-Tissue Interaction IX, SPIE proceedings 3254*, pages 423–434, 1998.

[7] V. Ng-Thow-Hing and E. Fiume. Interactive display and animation of b-spline solids as muscle shape primitives. In *Computer Animation and Simulation '97*, pages 81–97. Springer-Verlag/Wien, 1997.

[8] U.S. National Library of Medicine. The visible human project. MRI, CT, and axial anatomical images of human body, October 1996.

[9] M. G. Pandy and F. C. Anderson. Three-dimensional computer simulation of jumping and walking using the same model. In *VIIth International Symposium on Computer Simulation in Biomechanics*, pages 92–95, 1999.

[10] William H. Press, Saul A. Teukolsky, William T. Vetterling, and Brian P. Flannery. *Numerical Recipes in C*. Cambridge University Press, second edition, 1992.

[11] H. Rijpkema and B. J. Green. Skinning cats and dogs using muscle deformations. In *Siggraph 2001 Conference abstracts and applications*, page 262, 2001.

[12] F. Scheepers, R. E. Parent, W. Carlson, and Stephen F. May. Anatomy-based modeling of the human musculature. In *Computer Graphics (SIGGRAPH '97 Proceedings)*, pages 163–172, August 1997.

[13] D. Turner and S. Marino. Dynamic flesh and muscle simulation: Jurassic park iii. In *Siggraph 2001 Conference Abstracts and Applications*, page 173, 2001.

[14] J. Wilhelms. Animals with anatomy. *IEEE Computer Graphics and Applications*, 17(3):22–30, 1997.

[15] J. Wilhelms and A. Van Gelder. Anatomically based modeling. In *Computer Graphics (SIGGRAPH '97 Proceedings)*, pages 173–180, August 1997.

[16] F. E. Zajac. Muscle and tendon: Properties, models, scaling, and application to biomechanics and motor control. *Critical Reviews in Biomedical Engineering*, 17(4):359–411, 1989.

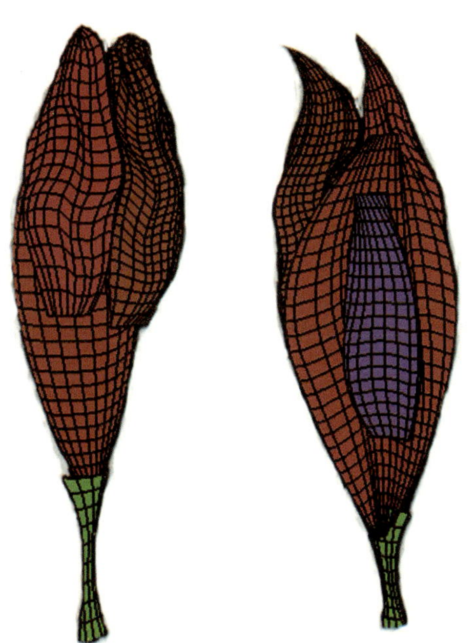

Figure 8: Soleus and gastrocnemius muscle reconstructed from Visible Human data

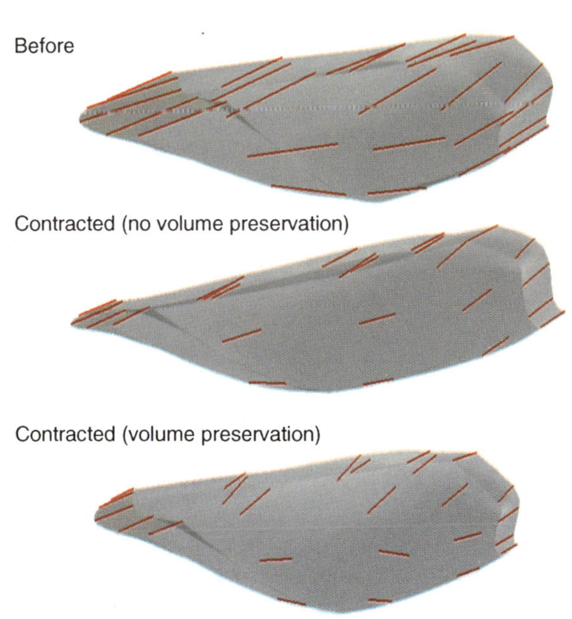

Figure 9: Detailed simulations of muscle contraction can be performed on muscles derived from fibre sets.

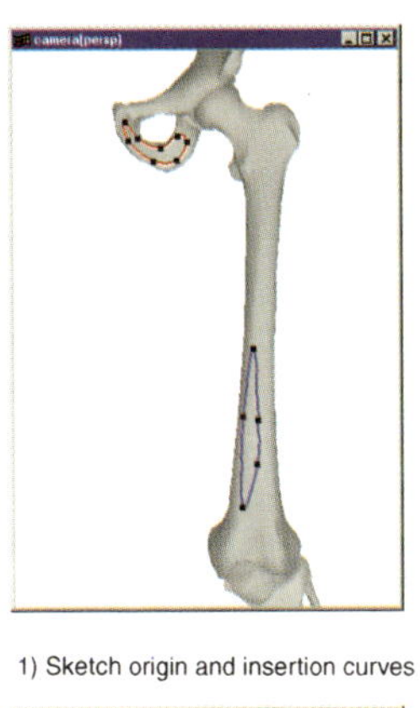

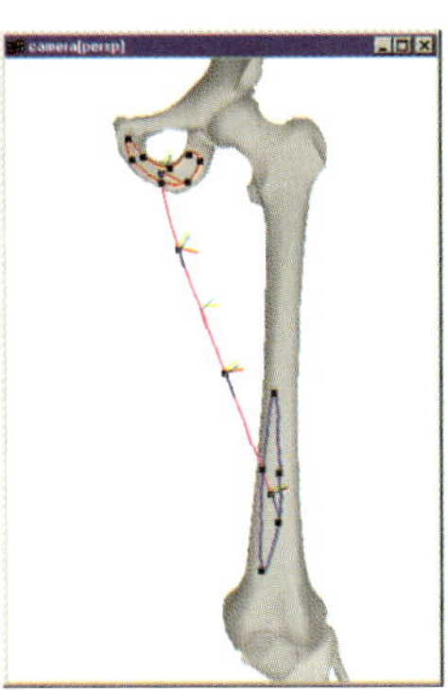

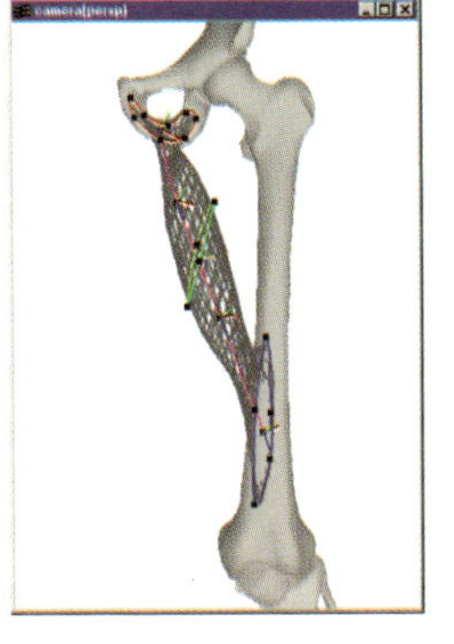

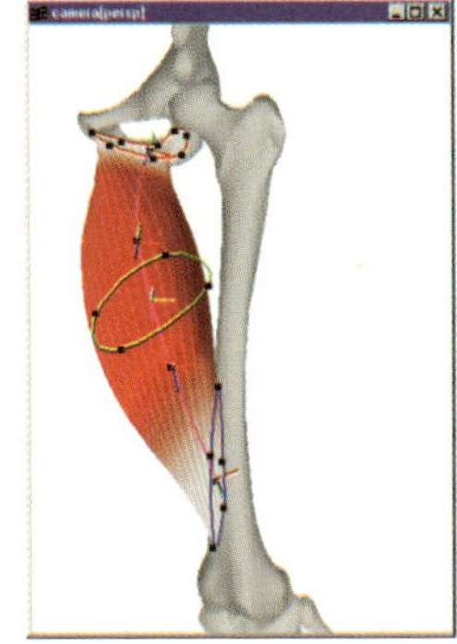

Figure 10: Stages of development of B-spline solids from profile curves. The middle curve is generated automatically in step 3. In the fourth step, the solids can be shaded and textured with striation patterns.

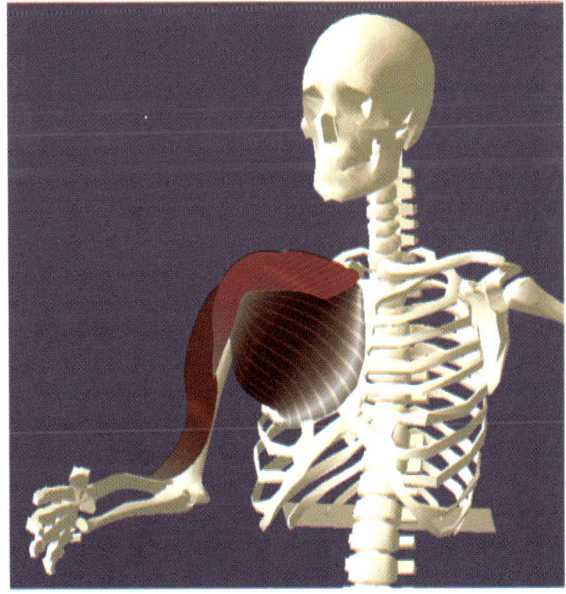

Figure 11: Anatomy-based modeller using profile curves to sketch muscles on a skeleton

A Model of Two-Thumb Text Entry

I. Scott MacKenzie & R. William Soukoreff

Dept. of Computer Science
York University
Toronto, Ontario, Canada M3J 1P3
smackenzie@acm.org, will@acm.org

Abstract

Although text entry has been extensively studied for touch typing on standard keyboards and finger and stylus input on soft keyboards, no such work exists for two-thumb text entry on miniature Qwerty keyboards. In this paper, we propose a model for this mode of text entry. The model provides a behavioural description of the interaction as well as a predicted text entry rate in words per minute. The prediction obtained is 60.74 words per minute. The prediction is based solely on the linguistic and motor components of the task; thus, it is a peak rate for expert text entry. A detailed sensitivity analysis is included to examine the effect of changing the model's components and parameters over a broad range (+/-50% for the parameters). The model demonstrates reasonable stability — predictions remain within about 10% of the value just cited.

1.1 Introduction

Current research in text entry includes significant interest in the use of small physical keyboards. Some devices allow text entry with as few as five keys, such as the *AccessLink II* by Glenayre Electronics (Charlotte, NC). Others sport a complete, but miniature, Qwerty keyboard, such as the *Blackberry* by Research In Motion (Waterloo, Canada). These are both examples of two-way pagers. As well, text entry using the mobile phone keypad has grabbed the attention of users and researchers. While most mobile phones support text entry via the conventional telephone keypad, Nokia has recently introduce the 5510, a mobile phone with a full Qwerty keyboard.

Much of the interest is spurred by the remarkable success of so-called *SMS messaging* on mobile phones (aka *text messaging*). The ability to discretely, asynchronously, and at very low cost, send a message from one mobile device to another has proven hugely successful, particularly in Europe. The statistics are staggering: Volumes are now approaching 1 billion messages per day! (Various SMS statistics are available at http://gsmworld.com/technology/sms.html) Given the limited capability of the mobile phone keypad for text input, it is not surprising, therefore, that the current wave of mobile text entry research includes numerous researchers and companies working on new ideas to improve text entry techniques for mobile phones or other anticipated mobile products supporting similar services.

In this article, we propose what we believe is the first model of two thumb text entry on small physical keyboards. The model provides both a behavioural description of the interaction plus a predicted peak text entry rate for expert users. In the following sections, the model is described and our prediction is given. This is followed by a detailed analysis examining the model's sensitivity to changes in the various components and parameters that affect the prediction.

Two-thumb text entry is depicted in Figure 1.

Figure 1. Two-thumb text entry

The device shown is a Sharp *EL-6810* organizer (also shown in Figure 2a). Other devices for which a similar interaction style is expected include the Motorola *PageWriter 2000* two-way pager (Figure 2b), the Research In Motion *Blackberry* two-way pager (Figure 2c), and the Nokia *5510* mobile phone (Figure 2d). These are all small devices bearing a complete, but miniature, Qwerty keyboard.

(a)

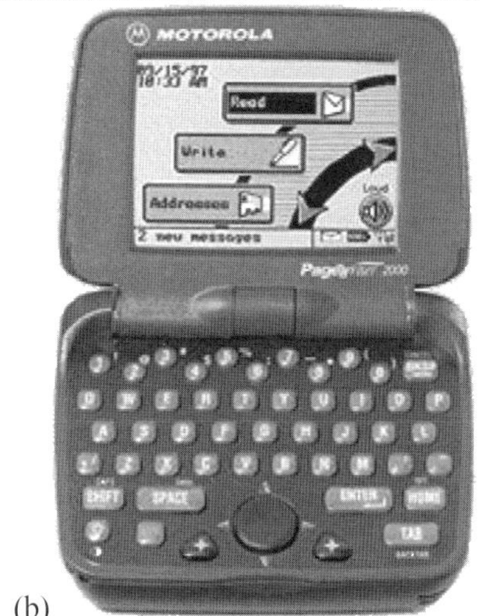

(b)

(c)

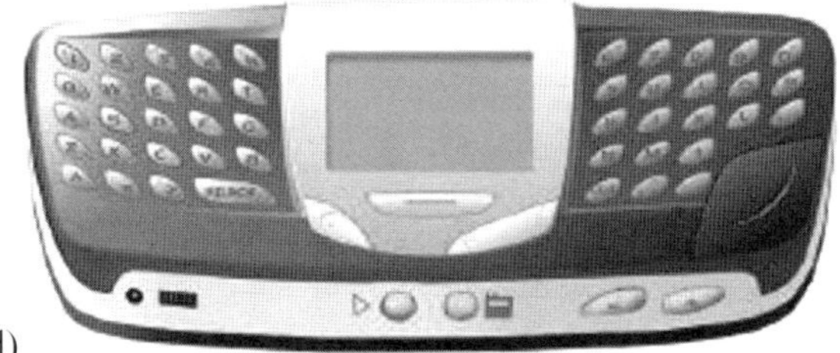

(d)

Figure 2. Devices with miniature Qwerty keyboards (a) Sharp *EL-6810* organizer (b) Motorola *PageWriter 2000* two-way pager (c) Research In Motion *Blackberry* two-way pager (d) Nokia *5510* mobile phone

1.2 Model Overview

To model two-thumb text entry, the following steps are proposed:

1. Obtain a word-frequency list derived from a language corpus.
2. Digitize the miniature keyboard of interest.
3. Determine the assignment of the left and right thumbs to letters and keys.
4. Given the information in steps 1-3, compute the predicted entry time for each word in the corpus, including the time to enter a terminating SPACE character after each word.
5. Multiply the predicted entry time for each word by the frequency of the word in the corpus, then sum the values. The result, t_{CORPUS}, is the time to reproduce the entire corpus.
6. Multiply the size of each word (including a terminating a SPACE character) by the frequency of the word in the corpus, then sum the values. The result, n_{CORPUS}, is the number of characters in the corpus.
7. Compute $t_{CHAR} = t_{CORPUS} / n_{CORPUS}$. The result, t_{CHAR}, is the mean time to enter each character in the corpus. The units are "seconds per character".
8. Compute $t_{WPM} = (1 / t_{CHAR}) \times (60 / 5)$. The result, t_{WPM}, is the text entry throughput in "words per minute". The scaling factor includes "second per minute" (60) and "characters per word" (5).

The steps above are similar to those in prior work on text entry on soft keyboards using a stylus [6, 7, 9, 10] and one-finger text entry on a mobile phone keypad [8]. There are two significant departures, however. First, the unit of linguistic analysis is the word. The models in prior work are based on digrams. Second, the motor component of the model works with two thumbs rather than a single finger or stylus. Thus, simple Fitts' law predictions for the time to press a key given a previous key are not possible — at least, in the case where the two keys are pressed by different thumbs.

Each step above is detailed in the following sections.

1.3 Word-Frequency List (Step 1)

Our word-frequency list contains the 9022 most-frequent words in the British National Corpus. It is the same list used by Silfverberg et al. [8] in developing their text entry model for mobile phone keypads. The frequencies total 67,962,112. The shortest word is "a" (frequency = 1,939,617), while the longest word is "telecommunications" (18 letters, frequency = 1221). The average word size is 7.088 characters if a simple mean is calculated, or 4.427 characters if weighted by the word frequency.

Although our model's predictions are generated using a word-frequency list, digram-frequency and letter-frequency lists are also useful to facilitate certain analyses, for example, on SPACE key usage and word transitions. Both are easily built from the word-frequency list, with the added assumption that each word is followed by a space. The letter-frequency list has 27 letters (A-Z, SPACE) with frequencies totaling 368,832,032. The digram-frequency list has 27 x 27 = 729 digrams, with frequencies again totaling 368,832,032. Some statistics from these lists are now given.

Letters	Frequency	% of Letters
SPACE	67,962,112	18.43%
All others	300,869,920	81.57%
Total	368,832,032	100.00%

Figure 3. Frequency of the SPACE character

As seen in Figure 3, spaces constitute about 18.43% of all letters. Similarly, 18.43% of all digrams are of the form SPACE-letter (start of word), and an additional 18.43% of all digrams are of the form letter-SPACE (end of word). We can split the start-of-word and end-of-word digrams by "side-of-keyboard". This refers simply to the position of "letters" in SPACE-letter or letter-SPACE digrams as per the conventional left- and right-hand keypresses for touch typing. These results are shown in Figure 4 and Figure 5.

Digrams at Start of Word	Frequency	% of Start-of-word Digrams	% of Digrams
SPACE-left	44,686,347	65.75%	12.12%
SPACE-right	23,275,765	34.25%	6.31%
Total	67,962,112	100.00%	18.43%

Figure 4. Digrams at start of word

Digrams at End of Word	Frequency	% of End of-word Digrams	% of Digrams
left-SPACE	47,905,787	70.49%	12.99%
right-SPACE	20,056,325	29.51%	5.44%
Total	67,962,112	100.00%	18.43%

Figure 5. Digrams at end of word

As seen in Figure 4, about 65.75% of words begin with a letter on the left side of the keyboard, with the remaining 34.25% beginning with a letter on the right side. A similar breakdown for word endings is seen in Figure 5. 70.49% of words end with a letter on the left, while 29.51% end with a letter on the right. Thumb-to-key assignments are discussed in more detail shortly.

1.4 Digitized Keyboard (Step 2)

Digitizing a keyboard is straight-forward. Working with an image of a keyboard, the *x-y* coordinate and the size of each key is measured and entered into a table along with the letter assigned to the key. For rectangular or elliptical keys, the smaller of the width and height dimensions is entered as the size of the key, as suggested in prior Fitts' law research [4]. The units are arbitrary. Our measurements were gathered using the pixel coordinates of an image processing application.

We used the Sharp *EL-6810* as a representative keyboard for testing our model (see Figure 2a). The digitized rendering is shown in Figure 6.

Letter	*X* Position	*Y* Position	Size
q	46.0	314	35
w	119.4	314	35
e	192.8	314	35
r	266.2	314	35
t	339.6	314	35
y	413.0	314	35
u	486.4	314	35
i	559.8	314	35
o	633.2	314	35
p	706.6	314	35
a	80.0	366	35
s	153.4	366	35
d	226.8	366	35
f	300.2	366	35
g	373.6	366	35
h	447.0	366	35
j	520.4	366	35
k	593.8	366	35
l	667.2	366	35
z	118.0	418	35
x	191.4	418	35
c	264.8	418	35
v	338.2	418	35
b	411.6	418	35
n	485	418	35
m	558.4	418	35
_	416	470	35

Figure 6. Digitized Sharp *EL-6810* miniature Qwerty keyboard (Note: '_' represents the SPACE key)

1.5 Assignment of Thumbs to Letters and Keys (Step 3)

To determine the assignment of thumbs to letters and keys, a few assumptions are necessary. A reasonable assumption is that each thumb presses keys normally pressed by the corresponding hand during touch typing. This is illustrated in Figure 7.

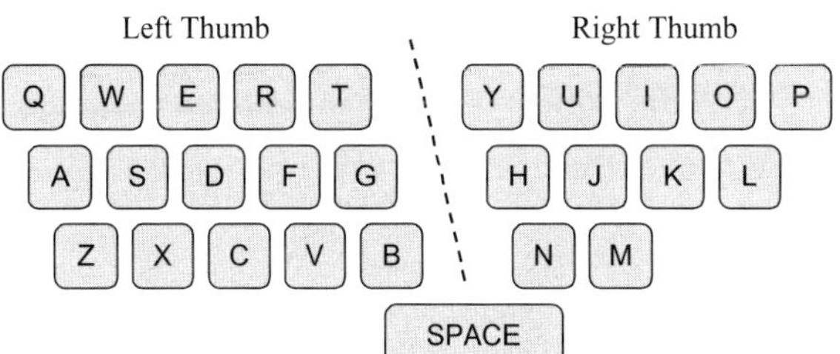

Figure 7. Assumed use of left and right thumbs for two-thumb text entry on a miniature Qwerty keyboard

Although it is uncertain whether the thumb assignments in Figure 7 occur in practice, this is a reasonable start. Changes are easily introduced later to accommodate different thumb-to-key assignments. Given the assignments in Figure 7, it is known which thumb is used to enter each letter. Figure 8 shows an example, where `L` is for the left thumb, `R` is for the right thumb.

```
Letter:  t h e _ q u i c k _ b r o w n _ f o x
Thumb:   L R L R L R R L R L L L R L R L L R L
```

Figure 8. Example phrase and thumb assignment for two-thumb text entry (see text for discussion on SPACE key usage)

1.5.1 Space Key Policy

SPACE key usage is problematic, since the size and position of the SPACE key varies among devices. If the SPACE key is centrally located, as with standard keyboards, then it is equally accessible to the right or left thumb. Since spaces constitute about 18% of English text entry, it is important to embed in our model an appropriate behavioural description of SPACE key usage. We call this the *Space Key Policy*. The following three SPACE key policies seem tenable.

Alternate Thumb. One possibility is that the SPACE key is activated by the *alternate thumb* to that used for the last letter in a word. This behaviour is shown for the example phrase in Figure 8. Viewed in isolation, this is optimal. For two-handed touch typing, for example, it is known that keying time is less when the preceding key is pressed by a finger on the opposite hand [3]. Arguably, the first letter in the next word should also be considered; however, this complicates the model and will not be considered at the present time.

Left Thumb. The *left thumb* space key policy assumes simply that the SPACE key is always pressed by the left thumb.

Right Thumb. With a *right-thumb* space key policy, the SPACE key is always pressed by the right thumb.

The left-thumb and right-thumb space key policies are particularly appealing if the SPACE key is positioned on either the left or right side or the keyboard, as seen, for example, in Figure 2b and Figure 2d where the SPACE key is on the left. In these cases, the model should likely adopt a left-thumb space key policy.

1.5.2 Thumb Transitions

Given our three space key policies and the earlier assumptions on the assignment of thumbs to letters and keys, it is possible to categorize two-thumb text entry by thumb transitions for each digram in our corpus. This is shown in Figure 9.

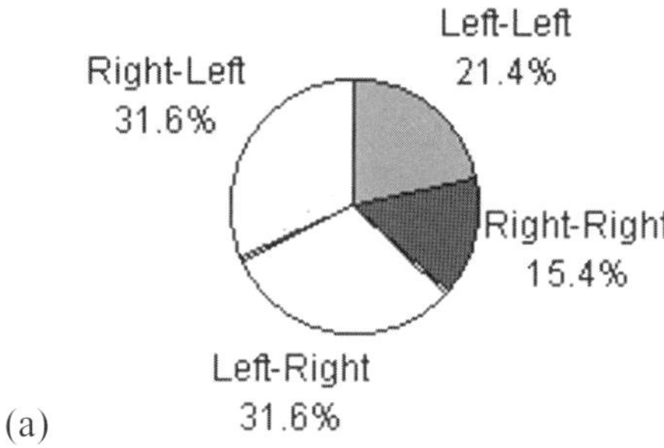

(a)

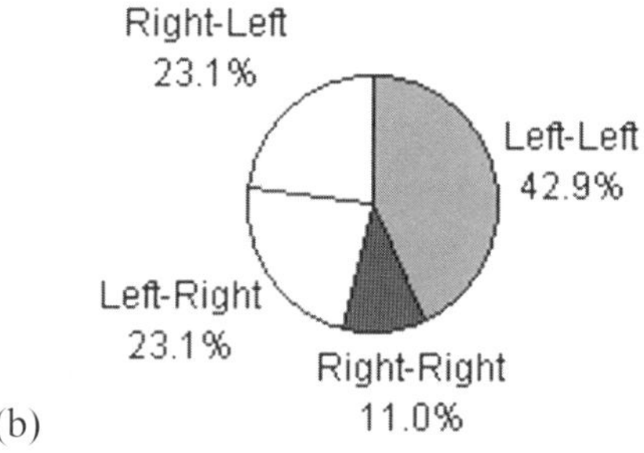

(b)

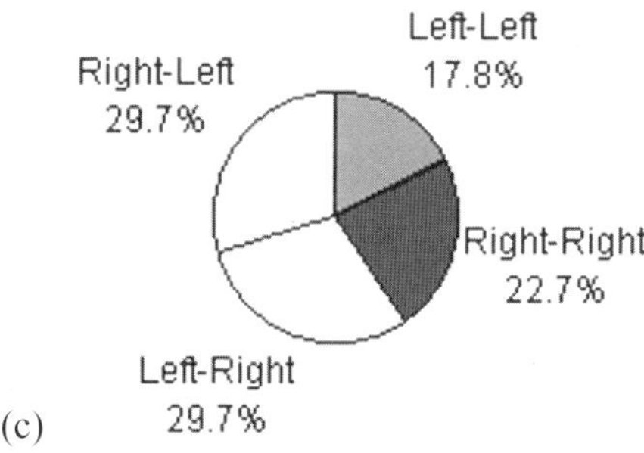

(c)

Figure 9. Thumb transitions by space key policy (a) alternate thumb (b) left thumb (c) right thumb

The ratios in Figure 9 are of 368,832,032 total frequencies in the digram-frequency list cited above. Among the insights in Figure 9 is the identification of key actions characterized by Fitts' law. These are the key sequences LEFT-LEFT or RIGHT-RIGHT. For the alternate thumb space key policy (Figure 9a), about 36.8% of the actions are of this type, whereas 63.2% of the key actions are of the form LEFT-RIGHT or RIGHT-LEFT. Our method of modeling the key actions and thumb transitions is explained in the next section.

1.6 Predicted Entry Times (Step 4)

Our next step is to determine the predicted entry time for each word in the corpus. Before giving a detailed analysis, we introduce t_{MIN}, the minimum time between keystrokes on alternate thumbs. We use

$$t_{MIN} = \frac{1}{2} \times t_{REPEAT} \quad (1)$$

where t_{REPEAT} is the time to press one key repeatedly with the same finger. The rationale is based on research in two-handed touch typing, as reported in Card et al. [1, p. 60]. The idea is depicted in Figure 10. The time between keystrokes when using one thumb to repeatedly type the same key is t_{REPEAT} (depicted in Figure 10a). When using two thumbs to repeatedly alternate between two keys, the keystroke rate almost doubles because the movement of the two thumbs overlaps (Figure 10b).

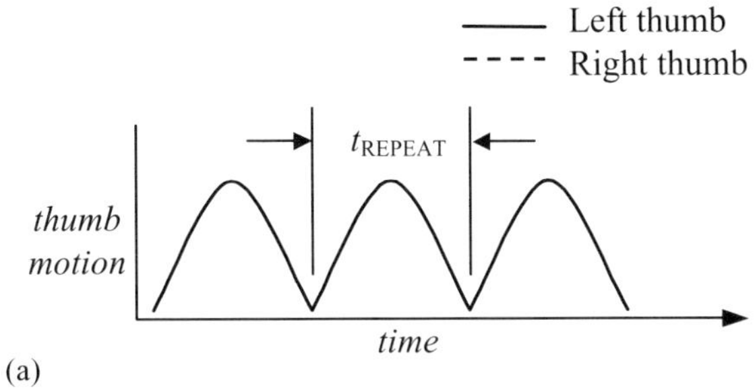

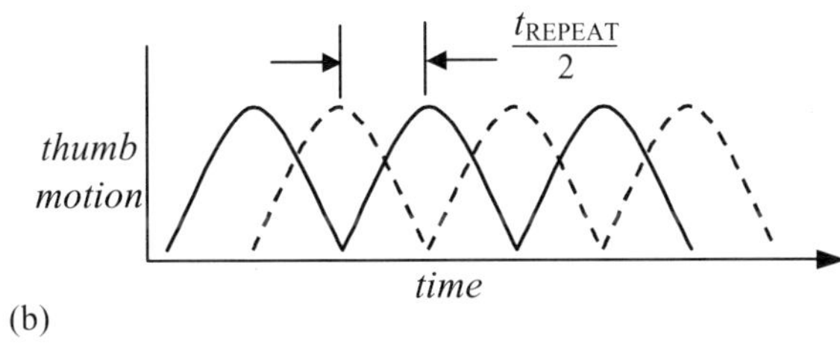

Figure 10. Illustration of key repeat time (a) single thumb (b) alternating thumbs

Our method to compute the predicted entry time for each word is explained through an example. Figure 11 illustrates an arbitrary sequence of letters followed by SPACE, entered as LLRLRL. Each circle represents a keystroke. Entry proceeds left-to-right as two separate coordinated streams of input, one for the left thumb (top line) and one for the right thumb (middle line). The combined effect is shown in the bottom line. The time to enter the word is t_6.

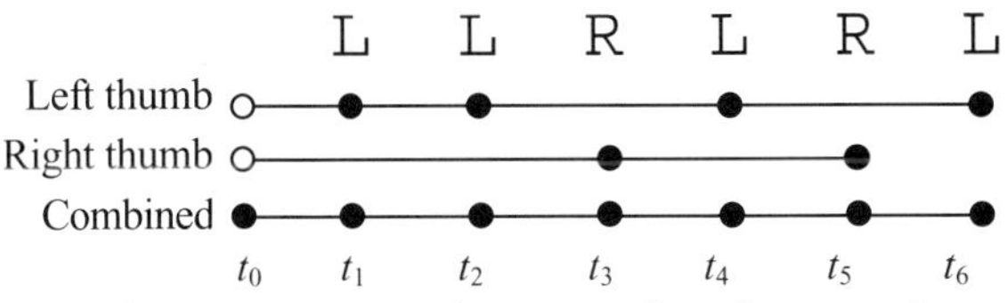

Figure 11. Computing entry time for a word

The open circles on the left represent the SPACE character terminating the previous word. Since our model considers words only, and is based on a specific space key policy (see above), we do not know which thumb was used for the SPACE key preceding a word. However, this uncertainty can be accommodated as now explained. Our earlier analysis of end-of-word digrams reveals that 70.49% of words end with a letter on the left side of the layout in Figure 7. Based on our SPACE key policy, this implies that 70.49% of the time, the SPACE key is pressed by the right thumb, and 29.51% of the time the SPACE key is pressed by the left thumb.

We use the values just cited as weighting factors in determining t_1. The example word in Figure 11 begins with a left-thumb keystroke. If the left thumb was used for the preceding SPACE, the movement time for first letter is t_{FITTS}, where t_{FITTS} is the time for the left thumb to move to and press the key bearing the first letter in the word, having just pressed the SPACE key. If the right thumb was used for the preceding SPACE, we assume the left thumb is poised to enter the first letter with negligible movement. In this case, movement time is t_{MIN}. We combine these descriptions with the weighting factors to accommodate uncertainty on which interaction takes place. Since the example word in Figure 8 begins with a left-thumb keystroke, we use

$$t_1 = 0.2951 \times t_{FITTS} + 0.7049 \times t_{MIN} \quad (2)$$

For words beginning with a right-thumb keystroke, we use the same formula, except the weighting factors are reversed.

Time t_2 in Figure 11 is simply

$$t_2 = t_1 + t_{FITTS} \quad (3)$$

where t_{FITTS}, in this case, is the time for the left thumb to move to and acquire the key bearing the second letter, having just entered the first. A similar calculation is used throughout a word if the same thumb is used for the preceding letter.

The third letter in the example is entered with the right thumb. There is again uncertainty on the preceding interaction. For the sequence in Figure 11, we use

$$t_3 = \max(t_2 + t_{MIN}, t_0 + t_{FITTS}) \quad (4)$$

In this case, t_{FITTS} is the time for the right thumb to press the key bearing the third letter having previously pressed the SPACE key (which occurs at t_0 in the example). At the very least, t_3 should be $t_2 + t_{MIN}$, so we choose the maximum of these two possibilities. A similar calculation is used throughout a word if a different thumb is used for the preceding letter.

To complete the example,

$$t_4 = \max(t_3 + t_{MIN}, t_2 + t_{FITTS}) \quad (5)$$

$$t_5 = \max(t_4 + t_{MIN}, t_3 + t_{FITTS}) \quad (6)$$

$$t_6 = \max(t_5 + t_{MIN}, t_4 + t_{FITTS}) \quad (7)$$

This completes our example walk-through for the key sequence in Figure 11. Let's re-state the procedure in general terms. For the first letter in a word, we use

$$t_1 = 0.2949 \times t_{FITTS} + 0.7051 \times t_{MIN} \quad (8)$$

if entered with the left thumb, or

$$t_1 = 0.7051 \times t_{FITTS} + 0.2949 \times t_{MIN} \quad (9)$$

if entered with the right thumb. For subsequent letters, we use

$$t_n = t_{n-1} + t_{FITTS} \quad (10)$$

if the same thumb is used for the previous letter, or

$$t_n = \max(t_{n-1} + t_{MIN}, t_{RECENT} + t_{FITTS}) \quad (11)$$

if the opposite thumb is used for the previous letter. The time stamp of the most recent use of the same thumb is represented by t_{RECENT}, which is at least two keystrokes before the current keystroke. Of the four equations above, equation 11 is used most often (about 57% of the time). It is for this reason — considering more than one preceding keystroke — that our model is based on words rather than digrams.

1.6.1 Model Coefficients

An important component of the model is missing. Fitts' law models have not been reported for pressing keys with thumbs, as shown in Figure 1. Two models are needed: one for the preferred hand, and one for the non-preferred hand. A related model is reported by Silfverberg et al. [8] for the thumb on the preferred hand pressing keys on a mobile phone keypad:

$$MT = 176 + 64 \times \log_2(A / W + 1) \quad (12)$$

where A is the amplitude of the movement and W is the width of the destination key. We can tentatively use this model for both thumbs. As well, t_{REPEAT} = 176 ms in Equation 1. So, a tentative value for t_{MIN} is

$$t_{MIN} = 88 \text{ ms} \quad (13)$$

1.7 Model Predictions (Steps 5-8)

With these model coefficients, and the behavioural description above, all the components of the model are in place. A Java program was written to generate a prediction, as per the procedure and coefficients just described. The program works with a space key policy, a word-frequency list and a digitized rendition of a keyboard. Our default invocation uses the alternate thumb space key policy, the 9022 word-frequency list from the British National Corpus, and a digitization of the Sharp *EL-6810* keyboard in Figure 2a. Our program provides the following prediction for two-thumb text entry:

$$t_{WPM} = 60.74 \text{ wpm} \quad (14)$$

Previous predictions for key-based mobile text entry are in the range of 20.8 wpm to 45.7 wpm [5, 8]. Although our prediction of 60.74 wpm seems quite high, it is important to remember that it is a peak rate for experts and it is for dual-stream input using two thumbs. Rates of 80 wpm, or beyond, are readily attained by expert touch typists on standard keyboards; so our prediction is not unreasonable.

1.8 Sensitivity Analysis

There are numerous factors influencing our model's prediction. A useful exercise, therefore, is to test the sensitivity of the model to changes in the components and parameters contributing to the prediction. Such an exercise is known as a *sensitivity analysis.* For examples, see [1, 8].

1.8.1 Slope Coefficient

A good start is to vary the slope coefficient in the Fitts' law model and observe the effect on the model's predictions. As noted earlier, we tentatively used Silfverberg et al.'s [8] model for pressing keys with the thumb, using the same model for both thumbs. The slope coefficient in their model is 64 ms/bit (see Equation 12). Figure 12 illustrates the effect of systematically altering the slope coefficient. For this, we generated six additional predictions: three with higher slope coefficients (+10%, +20%, and +50%) and three with lower slope coefficients (-10%, -20%, and -50%).

Slope Coefficient (ms/bit)		WPM Prediction	
Value	% of Nominal	Value	% of Nominal
32.0	50%	76.44	125.8%
51.2	80%	66.18	109.0%
57.6	90%	63.35	104.3%
64.0*	-	60.74*	-
70.4	110%	58.34	96.0%
76.8	120%	56.12	92.4%
96.0	150%	50.37	82.9%
* Nominal values			

Figure 12. Sensitivity to the Fitts' law slope coefficient

The relationship is inverse, as expected, since increasing the slope coefficient increases the predicted Fitts' law movement time which, in the end, reduces text entry throughput in words per minute. A 10% change in the slope coefficient, for example, yields a change of about 4%-5% in the word-per-minute prediction. This effect is readily seen in Figure 13. The 50% increase and decrease in slope coefficient values represent extremes that are presented for completeness. Reasonable (up to +/-20%) variation of the slope results in a less than 10% change in our nominal prediction.

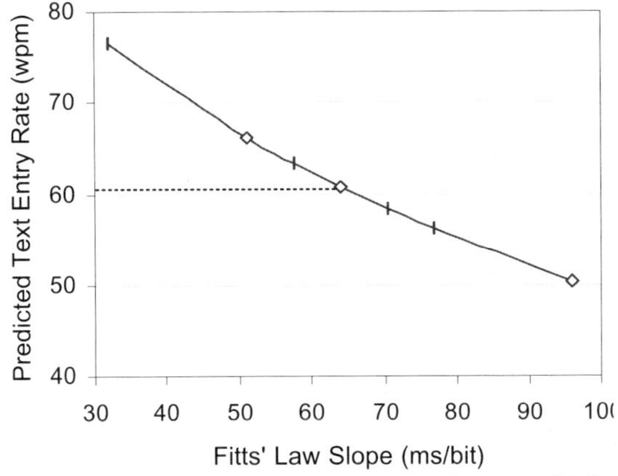

Figure 13. Sensitivity to the Fitts' law slope coefficient, chart form (dashed line shows nominal value)

1.8.2 t_{MIN}

Our model makes frequent use of t_{MIN}, the assumed minimum time between key presses with alternate thumbs. We nominally set t_{MIN} = 88 ms, or one half the intercept in the Fitts' law equation, as explained earlier. However, it is not clear that users will exhibit such behaviour during normal or high speed text entry. And so, examining the influence of t_{MIN} on the model is worthwhile. Figure 14 shows this influence, replicating the procedure in the preceding section.

t_{MIN} Coefficient (ms)		WPM Prediction	
Value	% of Nominal	Value	% of Nominal
44.0	50%	63.84	105.1%
70.4	80%	61.97	102.0%
79.2	90%	61.36	101.0%
88.0*	-	60.74*	-
96.8	110%	60.12	99.0%
105.6	120%	59.51	98.0%
132.0	150%	57.47	94.6%
* Nominal values			

Figure 14. Sensitivity to t_{MIN}

Clearly the influence is much less than for the slope coefficient. Changes of +/-10% yield just a 1% change in the word-per-minute prediction produced by the model. Even changes of +/-50% in the slope coefficient yield changes of only about 5% in the predicted text entry rate. The effects are more-clearly seen in Figure 15.

1.8.3 Key Widths

As well as sensitivity to the Fitts' law coefficients, our model is sensitive to the assumed width of the keys, which is confounded with the width of the thumb. Our model uses the key heights as W in the model, since key height is the smaller of the width and height dimensions of the keys. This assignment for target width was used by Silfverberg et al. [8] and is recommended in prior Fitts' law research [4]. However, the input "device" is a thumb, not a stylus, so the "effective key width" may be somewhat larger if we also consider the width of the thumb. This was noted by Drury [2] in a study of keying times on calculators with various inter-key gaps. If the assumed key widths are increased by 10%, 20%, and 50%, for example, the word-per-minute prediction increases by 1.9% (61.89 wpm), 3.7% (62.96 wpm), and 8.3% (65.76 wpm), respectively.

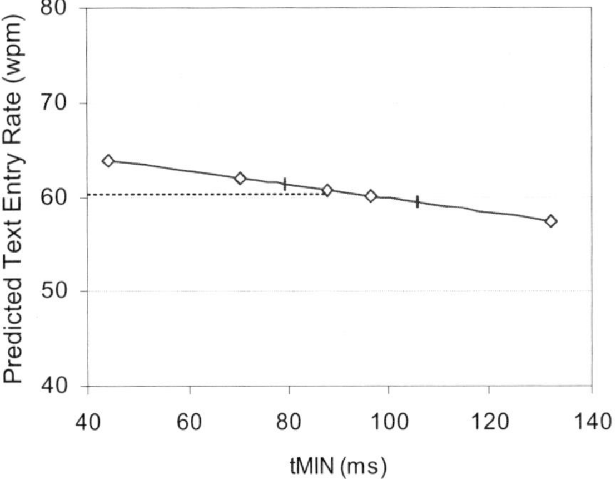

Figure 15. Sensitivity to t_{MIN}, chart form (dashed line shows nominal value)

1.8.4 Corpus Effect

We used the same word-frequency list as Silfverberg et al. [8]. To test for a possible "corpus effect" we also generated predictions with three other word-frequency lists. The first is a much larger list from the British National Corpus that inludes numerous additional low-frequency words. The second is a word-frequency list derived from the Brown Corpus (available from numerous on-line sites). The third is a word-frequency list derived from a set of 500 phrases constructed in-house for our text entry evaluations. These lists are available from the first author upon request. The results are given in Figure 16.

Corpus	Unique Words	Total Frequencies	WPM Prediction	% of Nominal
BNC1	9022	67,962,112	60.74*	-
BNC2	64,588	90,563,847	60.21	99.1%
Brown	41,532	997,552	60.18	99.1%
Phrases	1163	2712	59.81	98.5%
* Nominal value				

Figure 16. Model sensitivity to corpus

Clearly, the corpus effect is minimal. The first two additional predictions are extremely close to the original prediction of 60.74 wpm. Even the prediction generated with the very limited word-frequency list from our phrase set is within 1% of the nominal value.

1.8.5 Space Key Policy

Our nominal prediction assumes a specific policy on SPACE key usage; namely, that the user always presses the SPACE key with the alternate thumb from that used for the last letter in a word. Again, it is not clear that this will occur in practice. And so, we also generated word-per-minute predictions for the two other SPACE key policies described earlier. The results are shown in Figure 17.

SPACE Key Policy	WPM Prediction	% of Nominal
Alternate thumb	60.74*	-
Left thumb	49.92	82.19%
Right thumb	56.54	93.09%
* Nominal value		

Figure 17. Model sensitivity to SPACE key policy

Using the alternate thumb for the SPACE key is highly preferential to the policy of always using the same thumb. There are significant performance costs (7-18%) in the latter cases, depending of whether the left or right thumb is used. We consider these differences more the result of changes in user behaviour, rather than a sensitivity effect in the model. Importantly, this exercise demonstrates the utility of our model for a priori analyses.

The predictions in Figure 17 are for the Sharp *EL-6810* keyboard which includes a centrally located space key (see Figure 2a). If the space key is offset to the left or right, then the effect of SPACE key policy may be different. For example, the keyboards on the Motorola *PageWriter 2000* two-way pager (Figure 2b) and the Nokia *5510* mobile phone (Figure 2d) position the SPACE key to the left of centre. The effect of SPACE key positioning and SPACE key policy are the focus of continuing work in modeling two-thumb text entry.

1.9 Conclusions

This paper presents a model for two-thumb text entry on mobile keyboards. We have provided a detailed behavioural description of the interaction as well as a predicted rate for English text entry. Our prediction of 60.74 wpm is based solely on the linguistic and motor component of the interaction; thus, it is a peak rate for expert users.

Our model's prediction is relatively stable. In a sensitivity analysis, we examined the effect of changes in the various components and parameters that influence the predictions. We generated new predictions after changing corpora, assumed key widths (accounting for thumb width), the minimum time between keypresses by alternate thumbs, and slope coefficients in the movement time prediction equations. In most cases, the predicted text entry rate changed by less than 10%.

A change is text entry throughput of about 7-18% is expected if the user adopts a non-preferential space key policy, such as always using the left or right thumb to press the SPACE key. This expectation is coincident with a centrally located SPACE key. The effect may be somewhat different for other keyboard geometries.

Further work includes building the Fitts' law models for two-thumb text entry, directly observing thumb-to-key assignments and space key policies with users, and testing users on two-thumb text entry tasks with representative keyboards.

References

[1] Card, S. K., Moran, T. P., and Newell, A. *The psychology of human-computer interaction*, Hillsdale, NJ: Lawrence Erlbaum, 1983.

[2] Drury, C. G., and Hoffmann, E. R. A model for movement time on data-entry keyboards, *Ergonomics 35* (1992), 129-147.

[3] Kinkead, R. Typing speeds, keying rates, and optimized keyboard layouts, *Proc of the 19th Annual Meeting of the Human Factors Society*. Santa Monica: Human Factors Society, 1975, 159-161.

[4] MacKenzie, I. S., and Buxton, W. Extending Fitts' law to two-dimensional tasks, *Proc of CHI '92*. New York: ACM, 1992, 219-226.

[5] MacKenzie, I. S., Kober, H., Smith, D., Jones, T., and Skepner, E. LetterWise: Prefix-based disambiguation for mobile text input, *Proc of UIST 2001*. New York: ACM, 2001, 111-120.

[6] MacKenzie, I. S., and Zhang, S. X. The design and evaluation of a high-performance soft keyboard, *Proc of CHI '99*. New York: ACM, 1999, 25-31.

[7] MacKenzie, I. S., Zhang, S. X., and Soukoreff, R. W. Text entry using soft keyboards, *Behaviour & Information Technology 18* (1999), 235-244.

[8] Silfverberg, M., MacKenzie, I. S., and Korhonen, P. Predicting text entry speed on mobile phones, *Proc of CHI 2000*. New York: ACM, 2000, 9-16.

[9] Soukoreff, W., and MacKenzie, I. S. Theoretical upper and lower bounds on typing speeds using a stylus and soft keyboard, *Behaviour & Information Technology 14* (1995), 370-379.

[10] Zhai, S., Hunter, M., and Smith, B. A. The Metropolis keyboard: An exploration of quantitative techniques for graphical keyboard design, *Proc of UIST 2000*. New York: ACM, 2000, 119-128.

Virtual Sculpting with Haptic Displacement Maps

Robert Jagnow Julie Dorsey
Massachusetts Institute of Technology

Abstract

This paper presents an efficient data structure that facilitates high-speed haptic (force feedback) interaction with detailed digital models. Models are partitioned into coarse *slabs*, which collectively define a piecewise continuous vector field over a thick volumetric region surrounding the surface of the model. Within each slab, the surface is represented as a displacement map, which uses the vector field to define a relationship between points in space and corresponding points on the model's surface. This representation facilitates efficient haptic interaction without compromising the visual complexity of the scene. Furthermore, the data structure provides a basis for interactive local editing of a model's color and geometry using the haptic interface. We describe implementation details and demonstrate the use of the data structure with a variety of digital models.

Key words: Haptic, displacement map, sculpt, slab

1 Introduction

The pursuit of intuitive human-machine interfaces has led researchers to investigate the potential of haptic hardware – force-feedback devices capable of facilitating tactile interaction with digital models. This new generation of interface devices offers the promise of more immersive virtual environments that engage the tactual senses in much the same way that animation and sound engage the visual and auditory senses. But as with any fledgling technology, haptics comes with its own unique set of challenges.

Haptic devices require far faster update rates than visual output devices. For instance, the *PHANToM* system by Sensable Technologies Inc. requires updates at 1000 Hz – a constraint imposed by the inherent sensitivity of human tactile sensation. If this constraint is not met, unacceptable tactile artifacts, and possibly even hardware instability may result. Thus, the data structures that are useful for generating visually convincing scenes are often not efficient enough for haptic rendering.

The problem of generating an efficient haptic rendering system is exacerbated if we desire to modify the geometric data interactively, as it limits the amount of precomputation that we can perform on the model.

Figure 1: A familiar model, edited in a few minutes with a haptic device.

In this paper, we introduce a data structure that facilitates haptic rendering of complex scenes and accommodates local modifications to a model's surface characteristics, including, but not limited to, its geometry and color. We have implemented a system that uses the data structure for intuitive local editing of digital models.

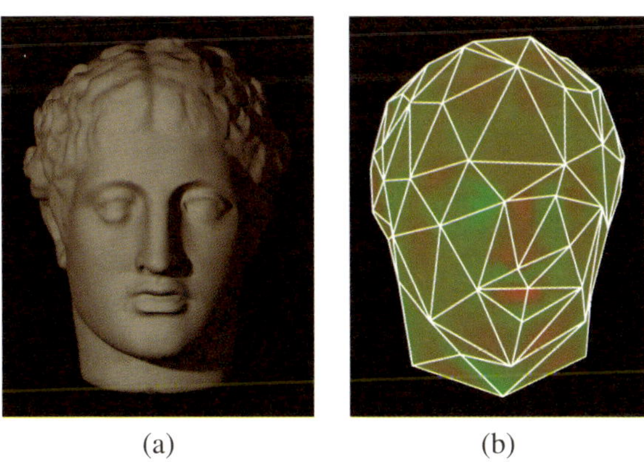

(a) (b)

Figure 2: A geometrically detailed object (a) and its slab representation (b). Red regions in the displacement maps represent the largest displacements from the interior slab boundaries.

1.1 Related Work

This paper builds on a foundation of related research for improving the efficiency and flexibility of haptic rendering, as well as the efficiency of graphic rendering. The simplest method for decreasing the computational burden on a haptic system is to decrease the complexity of the digital model. In some instances, this can be accomplished with minimal impact on the apparent complexity of the scene. Morgenbesser [10] demonstrated that in some situations, a coarse polygonal mesh can suffice to represent the tactile feedback of a more complex geometric surface. He uses a *force shading* algorithm to provide the tactile illusion of a smoothly curved surface in much the same way that Phong shading provides a visual illusion of smoothness [11]. Normal vectors are precomputed at each vertex in a coarse mesh so that a local normal can be calculated as a weighted average of the normals at adjacent vertices. Morgenbesser performed user experiments using simple models consisting of three or fewer polygons, but did not address the haptic rendering of models of arbitrary complexity.

Other researchers considered alternative haptic data structures. McNeely et al. [9] implemented a voxel-based system to accelerate haptic collision detection in complex environments, but their geometric models were not intended for interactive modification. SensAble Technologies, Inc. [14] commercially produces a volume-based modeling system. Their system is powerful and intuitive, but exhibits common voxel rendering artifacts. Other related data representations include voxel-based systems with isosurfaces extraction [5], B-spline surfaces [3], and subdivision surfaces [6], all of which are suitable for interactive geometric editing of models with low to moderate visual complexity.

Here, we explore the use of displacement maps [2] for representing visually complex surfaces in a manner that is amenable to high-speed haptic interaction with limited geometric modification. A similar data structure was used by Lee et al. [8] for displacing subdivision surfaces, but not for the purpose of haptic rendering. The most closely related data structure is the *volumetric surface*, introduced by Dorsey et al. [4], which consists of a set of extruded quadrilateral slabs that form a thick skin of varying depth around the surface of a model. Dorsey used this representation for simulation of surface erosion rather than for haptic editing.

1.2 Goals and Contributions

In this paper, we introduce a data structure that facilitates high-speed haptic interaction with visually complex models. A model is represented as a collection of extruded triangular *slabs* – small volumetric regions in which the local geometry is expressed as an array of scalar displacements embedded between the inner and outer extents of the slab. Adjacent slabs are seamlessly stitched together to provide both visual and tactile continuity.

The advantage of this representation lies in its simplicity and flexibility. The natural hierarchical division between coarse and fine features allows for rapid computation of local surface features, making the data structure ideal for rapid collision detection for a haptic interface. Furthermore, since local features are represented by an array of scalar values, limited editing of the local geometry can be done rapidly by modifying the values in the displacement map.

In addition to the displacement values, supplementary arrays may be used to represent surface properties such as color, friction, hardness, or specularity. Other fields may represent the depth of various materials underneath or above the visible surface – materials that may be exposed or added by an edit operation.

In the remainder of this paper, we provide an overview of haptic displacement maps (Section 2), introduce a method for high-speed haptic collision detection and response (Section 3) and discuss methods for modifying the local geometry and color of the model (Sections 4 and 5). We then address graphic rendering concerns (Section 6) and describe our implementation, showing some example models (Section 7). Finally, we discuss the limitations of the algorithm and directions for future research (Section 8).

2 Haptic Displacement Maps

In the haptic displacement map data structure, slabs are arranged to completely and unambiguously enclose features of a detailed mesh while maintaining the full detail of the model by representing local features as displacements between the interior and exterior slab boundaries. This hybrid data structure offers the detail of a surface representation with the flexibility and physical intuition of a volumetric representation. Unlike many voxel representations, haptic displacement maps avoid common artifacts by orienting the slabs to coincide with the orientation of the local surface.

Figure 2 shows an object that appears to be highly tessellated with fine geometric details; however, the underlying representation is a simple slab mesh with the detailed features stored as displacement maps at each surface.

Each slab is defined as a region of space enclosed by six vertices: three on the interior of the model, and three on the exterior. The interior and exterior faces of the slab are planes defined by the three interior and exterior vertices respectively. The three other faces of the slab are bilinear patches defined by linearly interpolating between two interior and two exterior vertices. This results in a consistent definition of boundaries between slabs as shown in Figure 3.

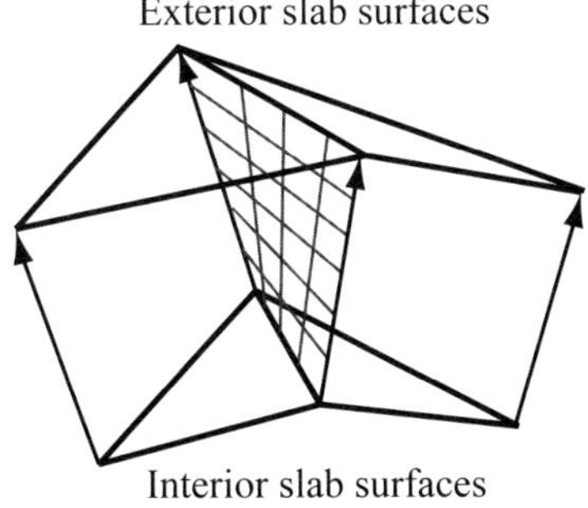

Figure 3: A bilinear patch between adjacent slabs.

Within each slab, displacement values are stored in a uniform triangular grid. In practice, this triangular grid is stored in the lower triangular region of a two-dimensional array, as shown in Figure 5c. The direction of surface projection is interpolated between the three rays at the corners of the slab, forming a detailed *submesh* as shown in Figure 4. Each displacement value along the edge of a slab is duplicated in the adjacent slab. T-vertices are disallowed in the slab mesh to insure correspondence of submesh vertices along the edges of adjacent slabs.

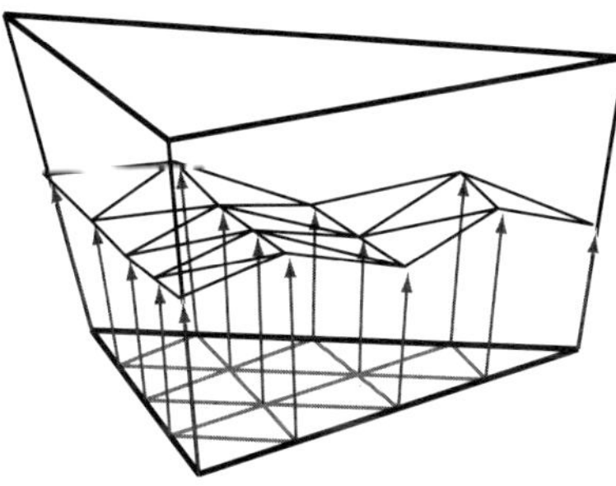

Figure 4: A detailed submesh formed by offsetting the interior slab surface.

3 Haptic Collision Detection and Response

One of the primary advantages of the displacement map data structure described in Section 2 is its efficiency for use with haptic collision detection. Within a slab, a continuous vector field directed from the interior plane to the exterior plane can be defined by linearly interpolating between the rays at the corners of the slab. At slab boundaries, this vector field remains continuous due to a consistent definition of the bilinear patches that separate adjacent regions. In this section, we demonstrate how this continuous vector field is used to define a relationship between arbitrary points in space and corresponding points on the model's surface – a mapping that can be used for efficient haptic collision detection and response.

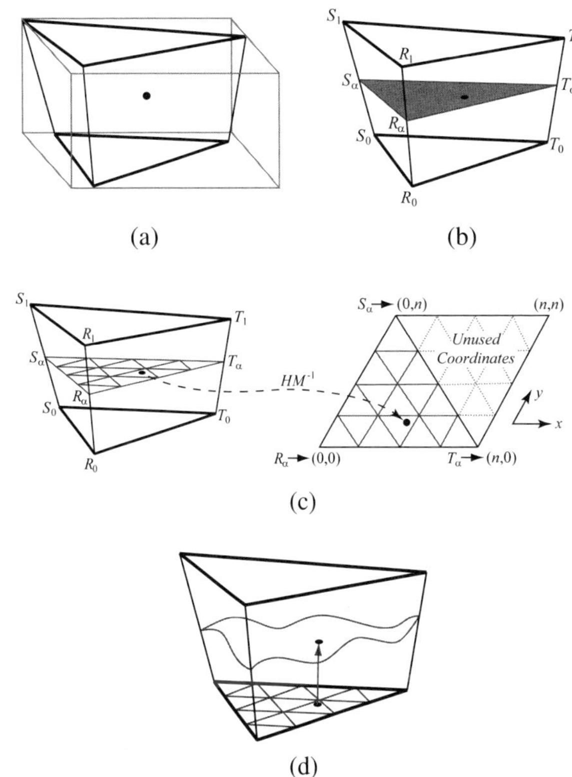

Figure 5: The haptic collision detection process: (a) Check the cursor against an axis-aligned bounding box. (b) Calculate the position of the interpolated plane containing the cursor. (c) Cast the cursor into a homogeneous coordinate space. (d) Reconstruct the surface.

3.1 Determining Slab Intersections

The first step in the haptic collision detection process is determining which slab, if any, contains the haptic cursor. Although the cursor is visualized as having volume, we treat it as a point for purposes of collision detection. The algorithm begins with a conservative check to see if the haptic cursor lies inside of an axis-aligned bounding box that encloses the slab (Figure 5a). If this succeeds, the next step is to determine how far the cursor has penetrated into the interior of the slab.

Each slab can be thought of as the region of space swept out by a triangle whose vertices are linearly interpolated from the interior slab plane to the exterior slab plane. At any distance between the interior plane, which has an interpolation value of zero, and the exterior plane, which has an interpolation value of one, this triangle denotes a surface of constant penetration α between zero and one. An example alpha-plane is shown in Figure 5b. To determine penetration, we solve for an α interpolation value that defines the plane at the same penetration depth as the haptic cursor.

Each alpha-plane is expressed in terms of its three corner vertices R_α, S_α, and T_α:

$$f(\alpha) = A_\alpha x + B_\alpha y + C_\alpha z + D_\alpha = 0, \qquad (1)$$

where

$$A_\alpha = \begin{bmatrix} 1 & R_{\alpha y} & R_{\alpha z} \\ 1 & S_{\alpha y} & S_{\alpha z} \\ 1 & T_{\alpha y} & T_{\alpha z} \end{bmatrix},$$

$$B_\alpha = \begin{bmatrix} R_{\alpha x} & 1 & R_{\alpha z} \\ S_{\alpha x} & 1 & S_{\alpha z} \\ T_{\alpha x} & 1 & T_{\alpha z} \end{bmatrix},$$

$$C_\alpha = \begin{bmatrix} R_{\alpha x} & R_{\alpha y} & 1 \\ S_{\alpha x} & S_{\alpha y} & 1 \\ T_{\alpha x} & T_{\alpha y} & 1 \end{bmatrix},$$

$$D_\alpha = -\begin{bmatrix} R_{\alpha x} & R_{\alpha y} & R_{\alpha z} \\ S_{\alpha x} & S_{\alpha y} & S_{\alpha z} \\ T_{\alpha x} & T_{\alpha y} & T_{\alpha z} \end{bmatrix}.$$

Each of R_α, S_α, and T_α are, in turn, defined as interpolants between the slab's extrema R_0, R_1, S_0, S_1, T_0, and T_1:

$$\begin{aligned} R_\alpha &= (R_1 - R_0)\alpha + R_0 \\ S_\alpha &= (S_1 - S_0)\alpha + S_0 \\ T_\alpha &= (T_1 - T_0)\alpha + T_0. \end{aligned}$$

When expanded, this series of equations yields quadratic expressions for A_α, B_α, and C_α, and a cubic expression for D_α:

$$\begin{aligned} A_\alpha &= A''\alpha^2 + A'\alpha + A \\ B_\alpha &= B''\alpha^2 + B'\alpha + B \\ C_\alpha &= C''\alpha^2 + C'\alpha + C \\ D_\alpha &= D'''\alpha^3 + D''\alpha^2 + D'\alpha + D. \end{aligned}$$

Each of the terms A, through D''' depends only on the six points that define a slab boundary. Thus, these constants can be precomputed for each slab. Looking again at expression (1), we can redistribute the terms to express the alpha-plane as a cubic function in α:

$$\begin{aligned} f(\alpha) &= D'''\alpha^3 + [A''x + B''y + C''z + D'']\alpha^2 \\ &+ [A'x + B'y + C'z + D']\alpha \qquad (2) \\ &+ [A + B + C + D] = 0 \end{aligned}$$

Thus, given the location of the haptic cursor p, we can solve for α by using the general solution to the cubic or, more simply, by using an iterative approach.

To begin the iterative solution process, we check if the point p lies between the inner and outer extents of the slab, which have α-values zero and one respectively. If $f(0)$ and $f(1)$ have the same sign, then the haptic cursor lies outside of the slab. But if they have opposite signs, then p is bounded by the interior and exterior planes, in which case we can approximate a value for α by using a binary search algorithm. The search process repeatedly divides the search area in half, insuring that the upper and lower search bounds always yield opposite signs when entered into Equation 2. In practice, 15 iterations is sufficient, yielding an answer for α within an error of $1/2^{15}$.

Now that we have determined where the haptic cursor lies between the inner and outer slab boundaries, we can check its position against the bilinear patches at the other three slab faces. This is done by casting the point p into a homogeneous coordinate system where the boundary check becomes trivial. We begin by defining two matrices, M and H. The former transforms coordinates into a system with basis R_α S_α T_α. The latter transforms coordinates into the homogeneous displacement map coordinate system shown in Figure 5c. These matrices are defined as follows, where n is the width of the displacement map:

$$M = \begin{bmatrix} R_{\alpha x} & S_{\alpha x} & T_{\alpha x} \\ R_{\alpha y} & S_{\alpha y} & T_{\alpha y} \\ R_{\alpha z} & S_{\alpha z} & T_{\alpha z} \end{bmatrix}$$

$$\text{and } H = \begin{bmatrix} 0 & 0 & n \\ 0 & n & 0 \\ 0 & 0 & 0 \end{bmatrix}.$$

We can now use HM^{-1} to transform the point p from its position in the interpolated alpha-plane to the homogeneous coordinate system as illustrated in Figure 5c. M is invertible if R_α, S_α, and T_α are noncollinear, which should always be the case with a well-formed slab.

In the homogeneous coordinate system, a point $h = (h_x, h_y)^T$ is known to lie on the interior of the slab if it satisfies the following three conditions:

$$\begin{aligned} h_x &\geq 0 \\ h_y &\geq 0 \\ h_x + h_y &\leq n. \end{aligned}$$

All other points lie outside of the slab boundaries.

If no hierarchical optimization is desired, slabs are checked in sequence to determine the location of the haptic cursor, yielding a cost that scales linearly with the number of slabs in the model. Since slabs are designed to be nonoverlapping, the algorithm can terminate collision checks as soon as any intersecting slab is found. Since the haptic cursor only moves small distances between time steps, this search can be optimized by first checking the slab found in the previous time step and its immediate neighbors.

The following sections describe how the homogeneous coordinates recovered by this process are used to reconstruct the surface of the detailed mesh and to provide appropriate haptic feedback.

3.2 Reconstructing the Surface

In the final stage of the collision detection process, we transform the haptic cursor position into a homogeneous coordinate system. The resulting 2D coordinates are used to index into the displacement map to determine the local surface displacement. Since the homogeneous coordinates of the haptic cursor are unlikely to coincide directly with integral coordinate values in the displacement map, the algorithm calculates the displacement as a weighted average of the values at the three nearest coordinates. This simple interpolation scheme yields piecewise linear connectivity between adjacent displacement map coordinates.

For a known homogeneous coordinate $h = (h_x, h_y)^T$ with a known displacement δ, the world coordinate of the corresponding point on the surface of the detailed mesh can be computed as follows. First, determine the vertices at the corners of the alpha-plane:

$$\begin{aligned} R_\delta &= (R_1 - R_0)\delta + R_0 \\ S_\delta &= (S_1 - S_0)\delta + S_0 \\ T_\delta &= (T_1 - T_0)\delta + T_0. \end{aligned}$$

Then, interpolate between these three points using the interpolation weights:

$$\begin{aligned} T_{weight} &= h_x/n \\ S_{weight} &= h_y/n \\ R_{weight} &= 1 - T_{weight} - S_{weight} \end{aligned}$$

to yield the surface point:

$$R_{weight} * R_\delta + S_{weight} * S_\delta + T_{weight} * T_\delta.$$

3.3 Calculating Cursor Penetration

Displacement values are stored as normalized scalars that indicate the relative depth of the surface between the inner and outer extents of the slab. Thus, if the α value for the cursor position (Section 3.1) is greater than the corresponding surface displacement value δ (Section 3.2), then the haptic cursor has not penetrated the surface of the detailed mesh, and no force needs to be returned to the haptic device. If, however, the α value is less than the surface displacement value, then the cursor has penetrated the mesh by a magnitude equal to the distance between the cursor position and the corresponding point on the surface of the mesh. In this case, a response force should be applied proportional to the depth of penetration, as indicated in the following section.

3.4 Applying a Response Force

To return a force to the user, a haptic system requires knowledge of the *surface contact point* (SCP), or *proxy position* – the point of interaction constrained to the surface of the model – and the surface normal at the SCP. Given this information, the system can account for surface spring and damping characteristics, as well as the effects of static and dynamic friction [12, 13].

Every small triangle in the displaced submesh of a particular slab can be considered to have its own local normal. But if the haptic feedback loop applies a response force in the direction of this local normal, at a magnitude proportional to the penetration distance, we encounter problematic behavior near major concavities and convexities in the surface of the model. Figure 6a shows five adjacent vertices of a displaced surface. As the position of the haptic cursor is moved along the dotted line, a force is applied in the direction of the local surface normal. The resulting surface feels as though it has a discontinuity at the peak. Furthermore, the ambiguous forces at the concavity can cause instabilities in the haptic device as opposing forces alternately attempt to achieve an unattainable equilibrium state.

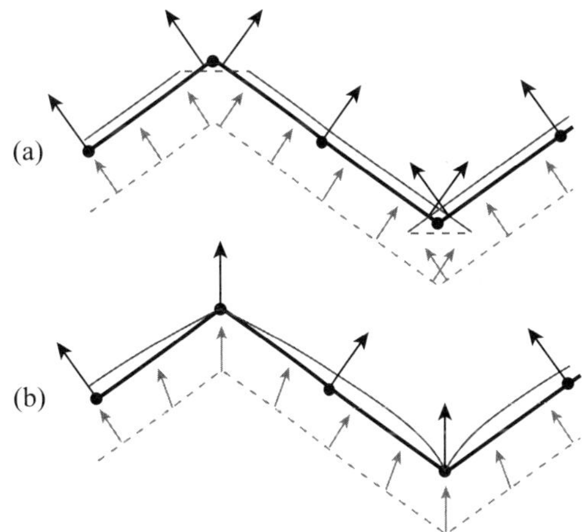

Figure 6: Surface reconstruction using (a) piecewise normals and (b) interpolated normals. Haptic cursor penetration through the model surface results in the reconstructed surface slightly above the polygons of the original mesh.

A better solution associates a normal vector with every vertex in the displaced mesh. This supplementary vector can be computed for each vertex as the average of the normals of the adjacent surfaces. At each point in the displacement map, an interpolated normal can be calculated as a weighted average of the normals of the three nearest vertices.

Using the penetration distance and the local surface normal, the collision response algorithm computes the surface contact point using a method similar to Morgenbesser's force shading algorithm. The surface contact point is offset from the haptic cursor position in the direction of the local surface normal, at a distance equal to the penetration depth. As can be seen in Figure 6b, the resulting point may not lie directly on the surface of the displaced mesh, but the magnitude and direction of the resulting force provide a convincing representation of the local geometry, as verified by Morgenbesser's user experiments [10].

4 Modifying Geometry

Since the coordinates of the displacement maps provide a uniform scaffolding that fully covers the surface of the model, they provide an ideal framework for locally modifying geometry or color attributes. The displacement maps within each slab have an inherent notion of adjacency and connectivity, and we can use precomputed adjacency relationships along slab boundaries to seamlessly span slabs as attributes are modified.

4.1 Removing Volume with Surface Clipping

3D sculpting or painting can be done by using a flood-fill method that walks from vertex to vertex within a constrained region of the surface, modifying geometry or color according to a desired function. To begin the sculpting process, our system first positions a tool that is used to modify the geometry, such as a simple sphere that clips away submesh vertices that intersect with its surface. As part of the collision detection process, the haptics algorithm already computes the local surface normal $\vec{n}$. To allow the tool to penetrate the surface by an amount proportional to the user-applied pressure, the sculpting routine positions the center of the tool as follows:

$$\vec{center} = \vec{cursor} + \vec{n} * (r + k),$$

where $\vec{cursor}$ designates the position of the haptic cursor, r is the desired tool radius, and k is the thickness of a resilient band of material at the model's surface. The resilience constant k allows the model surface to return feedback forces without being sculpted until sufficient force is applied (Figure 7).

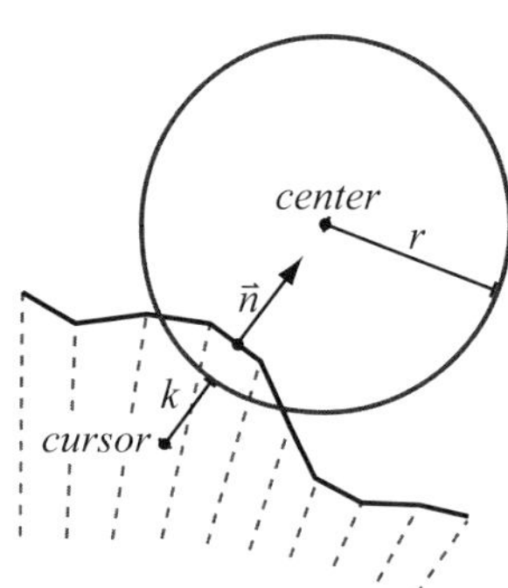

Figure 7: Positioning a spherical sculpting tool at the surface of a slab.

Once the tool is positioned, the sculpting algorithm clips the geometry that falls inside of the sphere. It begins by "seeding" a recursive process at the homogeneous coordinate nearest to the haptic cursor. At each point in the submesh, the algorithm computes the surface projection line that passes through the homogeneous coordinate at the interior and exterior slab boundaries. If this line intersects the spherical sculpting tool at a point on the interior of the mesh, then the surface is clipped at the sphere boundary. The procedure continues by recursing to all adjacent displacement map coordinates that fall inside of the spherical tool.

Since the sculpt routine adds some overhead to the basic collision-detection algorithm described in Section 3, the routine is not executed with each iteration of the haptic collision detection process. Instead, sculpting is performed at 10Hz – approximately once per every 100 iterations of the haptic loop – with minimal impact on the overall performance of the haptic rendering routine. The tactile artifacts that result from this temporal quantization can be reduced by increasing the frequency of the sculpting operations, at the expense of haptic rendering speed.

4.2 Adding Volume

By centering a spherical tool at the surface contact point, a similar routine can be used for *adding* material to the surface of the model. In this case, as the recursive algorithm marches along the surface of the mesh, a thin layer of material is deposited with a thickness linearly proportional to the distance from each submesh vertex to the center of the spherical tool. Thus, material is added in a conical shape, at a constant speed, regardless of pressure.

4.3 Limitations

Although haptic displacement maps are well-suited for limited local modification of a model's surface, the algorithms presented in this section are not intended for dramatic topological changes. For instance, slabs cannot be modified in such a way as to add a new undercut surface or to drill entirely through an object.

5 Haptic Painting

The challenge of precisely applying color to a three-dimensional model has been pursued for some time – initially using mouse-based interfaces [7], and more recently, using haptic interfaces [1, 6]. The advantage of the haptic interface is that it offers the intuitive simplicity of a paintbrush. With the haptic displacement map data structure, color can be applied to a surface by using a straightforward modification to the sculpting algorithm described in the previous section.

In our system, the virtual paintbrush is represented as a sphere, centered at the surface contact point. When the user touches the surface of the model, the paint process calculates the pressure p with which the paint should be applied. This is based on the penetration distance, normalized to a range between zero and one. Calculating the pressure as zero for small penetration distances allows the user to lightly touch the surface without modifying any surface properties.

As with the geometry modification routine, the recursive floodfill routine is "seeded" at the homogeneous coordinate nearest to the haptic cursor. At each iteration of the procedure, a new color c_n for the coordinate is calculated based on the old color c_o, the paintbrush color c_b, the pressure p, the brush radius r, and the distance δ between the center of the brush and the submesh vertex.

The color is applied with a normalized intensity k equal to $p*(1-\frac{\delta}{r})$. Thus, the most intense color is applied with greater pressure, nearest to the center of the brush, linearly decreasing out toward the edges of the sphere. The new color is computed by blending the existing color and the brush color as follows:

$$c_n = c_b * k + c_o * (1 - k).$$

The procedure continues by recursing to all adjacent texture coordinates that lie within the sphere of the paintbrush, as is done in the haptic sculpting algorithm. Like the sculpting algorithm, the paint routine is only executed 10 times per second to keep the basic collision detection routine unencumbered.

6 Graphic Rendering

Interactive visual feedback forms an important component of an effective haptic interface, so it is vital that the graphic rendering algorithm for the slab data be carefully optimized. Since the graphic and haptic routines require different rates of execution, each is run as a separate process to decouple the frame rate and haptic refresh.

Each slab maintains its own optimized display list to help accelerate graphic rendering. If the haptic process modifies a slab, a flag is set to indicate that the graphic process should generate a new display list for that particular region of geometry. Thus, the graphic process is concerned only with local updates for modified slabs while reusing display lists for unmodified regions of geometry. If graphic rendering is unacceptably slow, one alternative is to generate the visible mesh from a coarse subset of the coordinates in the displacement map.

Color is applied to the surface of each slab submesh using a texture map rather than by assigning per-vertex colors. This provides a speed advantage, and also decouples the resolutions of the geometric data and the texture data. Thus, color can be mapped to the surface of a slab at a higher density than the displacement data with negligible impact on rendering speed.

7 Implementation and Examples

We implemented our system on an SGI Octane with dual 250 MHz MIPS R10000 processors and 1.5 Gb memory, running IRIX 6.5. For the haptic interface, we used the A-model *PHANToM Premium* haptic device from SensAble Technologies, Inc. with the *GHOST* Software Development Toolkit, Version 3.0. Graphic rendering is done using OpenGL.

To initialize the slab data structure, we produced a decimated triangle mesh for each model. This mesh was grown inward and outward from the model surface to define the interior and exterior slab boundaries. For regions with thin features, like the ears in the bunny model, the resulting slabs were edited by hand to prevent overlap. The displacement maps were constructed by calculating where the projecting rays for the slab submesh intersect the original polymesh geometry.

Figures 1, 8, and 9 present polygonal models that were converted to the slab data structure and edited using the haptic sculpting system. The head and pumpkin models are formed with 200 slabs, and the bunny model with 150 slabs. Each slab stores displacement and color data with 16 values along each edge, forming a visually rendered mesh with 225 polygons per slab. All edited models were produced in approximately 15 minutes. In a typical editing session, the geometry modification routines perform 20,000 to 80,000 discrete edit operations on 1,000 to 3,000 individual slab vertices.

With the most complex of these models, the haptic system typically performs a single iteration of the collision detection and response process in under 0.65 milliseconds, thus utilizing 65% of the available processor time. The additional burden of performing sculpting or painting operations at 10Hz appears to have negligible impact on overall computational cost. With each of the example models, the graphic rendering system maintains a refresh rate of approximately 10 Hz, with minimal performance degradation during sculpting or painting operations.

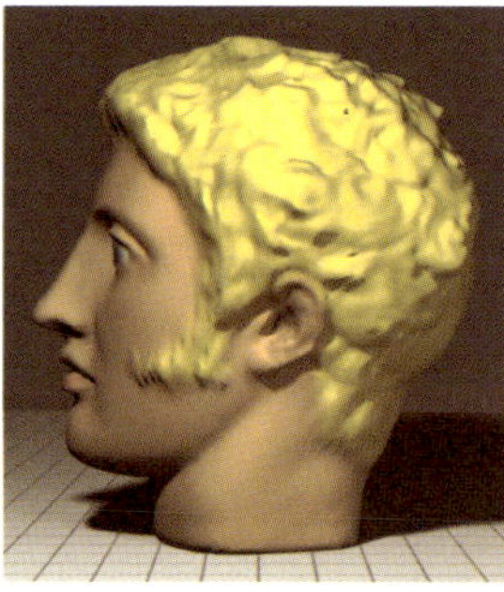

Figure 8: The head model is composed of 200 slabs, forming a visually rendered mesh with 45,000 triangles.

Figure 9: The pumpkin model is also formed with 200 slabs. The edited model was completed in approximately 15 minutes.

8 Conclusions and Future Work

Haptic displacement maps offer a step toward intuitive methods of interaction for rapid editing of complex models. Still, this data structure does not solve all the difficulties of digital editing. Slabs are effective for performing local modifications to a model in a thin region surrounding the surface of the initial mesh, but different techniques are needed for applying dramatic changes to the underlying topology of an object.

There are additional limits on the types of models that can be represented using haptic displacement maps. Slabs are designed to be used with "thick" models, with clear interior and exterior regions, and without thin or overlapping topological features.

Despite these restrictions, there are certain applications for which haptic displacement maps are particularly well suited. Many physical phenomena limit their influence to a thin region near the surface of a material, suggesting that a number of interesting effects might be produced via physical simulation or other forms of direct editing.

Other areas of future research include multiresolution meshes that can increase submesh detail where desired and multiple levels of detail obtained by rendering coarse subsets of submesh vertices.

Acknowledgements

We would like to thank Barb Cutler, Leonard McMillan, and Matthias Müller for helpful discussions. This work was supported by NSF grants CCR-9988535 and EIA-9802220 and by a gift from Pixar Animation Studios.

References

[1] Maneesh Agrawala, Andrew C. Beers, and Marc Levoy. "3D Painting on Scanned Surfaces," *1995 Symposium on Interactive 3D Graphics*, Monterey, CA, pp.145-150.

[2] Robert L. Cook. *Shade Trees*. In the Proceedings of *SIGGRAPH 1984*.

[3] Frank Dachille IX, Hong Qin, Arie Kaufman, and Jihad El-Sana. "Haptic Sculpting of Dynamic Surfaces," In the Proceedings of *Symposium on Interactive 3D Graphics 1999*, pp 103-110.

[4] Julie Dorsey, Alan Edelman, Henrik Wann Jensen, Justin Legakis, and Hans Kohling Pedersen. "Modeling and Rendering of Weathered Stone," In the Proceedings of *SIGGRAPH 1999*, pp 225-234.

[5] Eric Ferley, Marie-Paule Cani, and Jean-Dominique Gascuel. "Sculpture Virtuelle," In the Proceedings of *Les journées AFIG 99*, Reims, November 1999.

[6] A. Gregroy, S. Ehmann and M. C. Lin. "*inTouch*: Interactive Multiresolution Modeling and 3D Painting with a Haptic Interface," In the Proceedings of *IEEE Virtual Reality Conference 2000*.

[7] Pat Hanrahan and Paul Haeberli. "Direct WYSIWYG Painting and Texturing on 3D Shapes," In the Proceedings of *SIGGRAPH 1990*, pp.215-223.

[8] Aaron Lee, Henry Moreton, and Hugues Hoppe. "Displaced Subdivision Surfaces," In the Proceedings of *SIGGRAPH 2000*, pp 85-94.

[9] William A. Mcneely, Kevin D. Puterbaugh, and James J. Troy. "Six Degree-of-Freedom Haptic Rendering Using Voxel Sampling," In the Proceedings of *SIGGRAPH 1999*, pp 401-408.

[10] H. B. Morgenbesser. *Force Shading for Haptic Shape Perception in Haptic Virtual Envornments*. M.Eng. Thesis, Massachusetts Institute of Technology, September 1995.

[11] B. T. Phong. "Illumination for Computer Generated Pictures," *Communications of the ACM*, 18(6), pp 311-317, June 1975.

[12] Diego C. Ruspini, Krasimir Kolarov and Oussama Khatib. "The Haptic Display of Complex Graphical Environments," In the Proceedings of *SIGGRAPH 1997*, pp 345-352.

[13] SensAble Technologies, Inc. *GHOST SDK Version 3: General Haptic Open Software Toolkit*. January, 1999.

[14] SensAble Technologies, Inc. *FreeForm Modeling System*. http://www.sensable.com/freeform. 2001.

A Desktop Input Device and Interface for Interactive 3D Character Animation

Sageev Oore
Department of Computer Science
University of Toronto

Demetri Terzopoulos
Department of Computer Science
New York University

Geoffrey Hinton
Department of Computer Science
University of Toronto

Abstract

We present a novel input device and interface for interactively controlling the animation of graphical human character from a desktop environment. The trackers are embedded in a new physical design, which is both simple yet also provides significant benefits, and establishes a tangible interface with coordinate frames inherent to the character. A layered kinematic motion recording strategy accesses subsets of the total degrees of freedom of the character. We present the experiences of three novice users with the system, and that of a long-term user who has prior experience with other complex continuous interfaces.

Key words: Interactive character animation, Input device, Motion capture, Expert user interaction, Tangible interfaces

1 Background

Performance animation is the interactive creation of animation whereby the user manipulates an input device to continuously control the motion of a graphical character in real-time, and at the same time is provided with immediate feedback displaying the animation as it is being created [23, 21]. The animator is effectively a puppeteer; the computer graphics character is the puppet; and the mapping defines how the puppet is virtually strung. In principle, mappings can range from the simple triggering of scripted actions, to a continuous, low-level control over the character. It is in low-level control that we are interested, as that does not limit the animator to a specific set of pre-animated motions, and furthermore affords him with the opportunity to provide his own detailed human input.

The difficulty with this kind of control, however, is providing an interface to the very large number of degrees of freedom (DOF) of the graphical output. In fact, it has been claimed that performance animation

> [...] is particularly appropriate when the characters to be animated are simple and their range of movement limited [...] The great number of DOF that need to be controlled for complex human motion does not make [performance animation] a viable solution for realistic looking animation[19, pg.28].

For this reason, real-time animation of more complex 3D characters is typically done by motion capture [20], where an actor is covered in sensors, and her joints are mapped directly ("literally") onto the corresponding joints of the character. However, this requires a non-trivial post-processing stage to correct for the differences between the body proportions of the actor versus those of the character [6, 11]. In the case of an imaginary creature with a completely different body type, this issue becomes even more difficult or impossible. Furthermore, motion capture requires a costly, elaborate hardware studio setup, limiting its accessibility and making "retakes" inconvenient. Many of the bottlenecks stem from the essential limitation that, although this type of motion capture works in real-time, it is not interactive.

A fundamental characteristic of performance animation that differentiates it from the above approach is its highly interactive nature. The live continuous feedback of performance animation allows *non-literal* mappings, meaning that the motions of the user do not have to mirror those of the character. This non-literal approach has been used in a variety of interesting and creative ways, from having an actor's hands and feet control a cartoon worm character [7], to the impressive interactive control of a dynamic 2-D simulation by mouse and keyboard [16]. Furthermore, contrary to the claim quoted earlier regarding the limitations of performance animation, we contend and demonstrate that by capitalizing on the interactive feedback loop, it is even possible to design a real-time interface for low-level control of complex 3D character animation.

2 Approach

We achieve this within a desktop environment, using less than one tenth the number of sensors typically used for a motion capture session. By combining an appropriate input device design together with a multi-layered motion recording approach, we can use two 6-DOF Polhemus

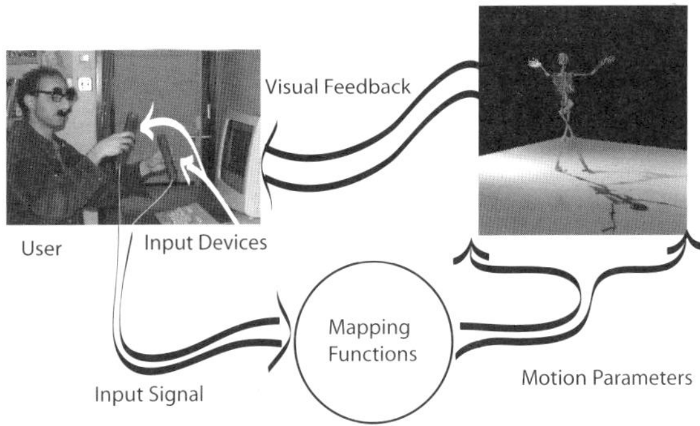

Figure 1: DIGITAL MARIONETTE*: Performance animation is a method of creating animation in real-time: The user manipulates real-time input devices to interactively drive the motion of a computer graphic (CG) character, and is provided with immediate feedback displaying the animation as it is being created. Our animation interface can be operated within a desktop environment.*

motion trackers [22, 18] to provide the user with real-time continuous interface to the 30-DOF joint angle space of an articulated 3D character. As will be described later, the multi-layered approach consists of partitioning the character's degrees of freedom into groups, e.g. left arm, right leg, etc., and designing bimanual mappings from the input device to the group. Most of these mappings are partially symmetric in the sense that they may have the same general task (e.g. during the leg mapping, each hand controls one of the legs), but different specific goals (e.g. each leg will have a different desired motion) [15]. Furthermore, the bimanual task has the advantage of being visually integrated [4] by the simple fact that each leg clearly belongs to the same character. On the other hand, the spine mapping makes use of asymmetric bimanual mappings in accordance with Guiard's Kinematic Chain theory [12] as applied within a computer graphics context [5]. In particular, as will be explained in more detail later, the left hand is used for the joint which is closest to the root of the hierarchy (the lower back), thus providing the reference frame for the joints controlled by the right hand (upper back and neck).

Together, these elements contribute to making our system extremely efficient, allowing an experienced user to create the motion parameters of a 1-minute long character animation in under 10 minutes (see Figure 5).

In designing this interface, two critical issues needed to be solved:

1. development of an effective way of acquiring user input, and
2. conception and specification of a strategy for mapping to the character's joint angles.

In the remainder of this paper we discuss our solutions to these issues, followed by a discussion of the resulting animations and user experience.

3 Input Device Design

The Polhemus sensors are small, oddly-shaped devices, about $2cm$ long, and very lightweight. Each tracker provides a 6-dimensional input vector consisting of positional and orientation information relative to a (fixed) source emitter.

Directly manipulating the translation and orientation of the sensors is awkward, as the small size and shape of the sensors makes them prone to slip, and hard to manipulate accurately over a continuous time window. Also, when the cables get too curled, then their stiffness usually causes the sensors to flip around, slipping on the user's fingers, unless the user grips really tightly. But gripping tightly makes it harder to maneuver fluidly.

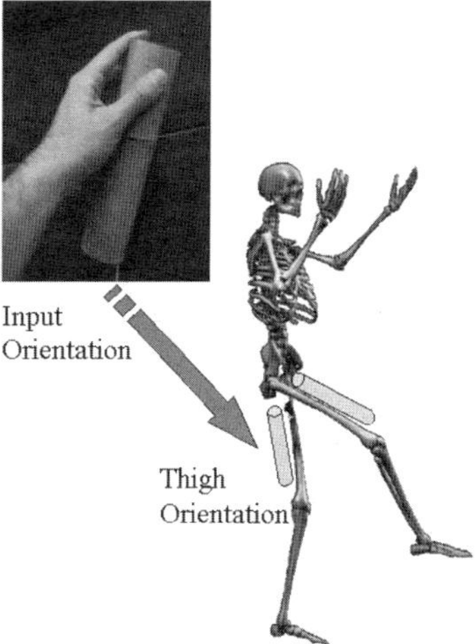

Figure 2: Bamboo Tubes For 3D Animation: The upper photo shows the user holding one of the two input tubes. Although not visible, the tracker is in the top of the tube, near the user's fingers. Below, cylinder icons next to the thigh bones illustrates the mapping from the input to the hip rotation, which keeps the thighs parallel to the tubes themselves.

We therefore redesigned the input device, with respect to both its geometry and physical characteristics, by embedding the trackers in cylindrical bamboo tubes, 15-$20cm$ in length, and about $5cm$ in diameter. The upper part of Figure 2 shows the user holding onto the bamboo stick input device. This is related to other approaches taken for embedding trackers in outer shells

[1, 10, 13, 14]. However, this new design provided essential advantages in making the system easier to use both accurately and, ultimately, in a more natural manner for the task of interactive character animation, as we now discuss.

3.1 Grip

Our tubes afford the user both *power* and *precision* grips [17, Ch.2][24]. Interestingly, we found that the inexperienced or untrained subjects would naturally hold the interface devices in a power grasp. As the primary test subject became more advanced, the precision grip was used more often, and still quite naturally; the sticks are sufficiently light that they can be held without needing to engage all five fingers. The same device design is well-suited to accommodate both phases, and the bamboo has been described as being very comfortable to hold. Note that adding buttons to the device, as is often done, can make it much harder to maintain a precision grip while moving it through the orientations necessary for the animation task.

3.2 Coordinate Frame: Cues

The cylindrical input device provides visual and tactile cues indicating a reference frame with a "long-axis," as well as axes of symmetry. These kinesthetic feedback cues [13] establish a tangible interface to coordinate frames inherent to the character. For example, rotating the input tube around its long axis can correspond to rotating a virtual object such as the humerus or thigh bone around its long axis as well, as shown in Figure 2. This modification was very helpful in the development and use of the mappings.

The mass of the bamboo also provides orientation feedback, by making the tubes naturally gravitate towards their neutral vertical orientation. Reorienting the axes so that the cable emerges from the bottom of the tube encourages holding the tube upright, again emphasizing a sense of the neutral orientation, as well as differentiating between the upwards and downwards directions, while visually retaining the existing symmetry along this axis.

3.3 Inertial Resistance and Smoothing

Hinckley points out that input tools with mass provide kinesthetic feedback due to gravity and inertial properties [13, Section 4.6]. This feedback— primarily the feeling that one was actually holding on to real object, rather than just waving one's hands around in space— did indeed make the input control a far more satisfying experience. The lightness of the cables relative to the weight of the heavier tubes made the cables themselves much less noticeable than before. Furthermore, the inertial properties of such an input device reduces hand jitter.

4 Filtering

Although the mass of the sticks can indeed dampen the physically generated jitter, another source of input noise comes from the sensor readings themselves, e.g. as caused by the presence of electromagnetic devices in the environment. It is therefore still very important to be able to filter the raw input signal in some way. Let x_i represent the value received for one of the input parameters at time step t_i. Then the corresponding filtered value $y_i = f(x_i, x_{i-1}, \ldots, x_0)$ we use is given by

$$y_i = y_{i-1} + (1-\alpha)(y_{i-1} - y_{i-2}) + \alpha(x_i - x_{i-1}). \quad (1)$$

We can interpret Eq (1) as forcing the output velocity to be an average of its previous velocity with the most recent input velocity, thus adding a "viscosity" term to the output motion. This has been found to work quite well for our purposes, though for different animations, a different filter might be more appropriate. Figure 3 shows a sample of raw and filtered input data. Setting a value for α will be discussed in Section 6.6.

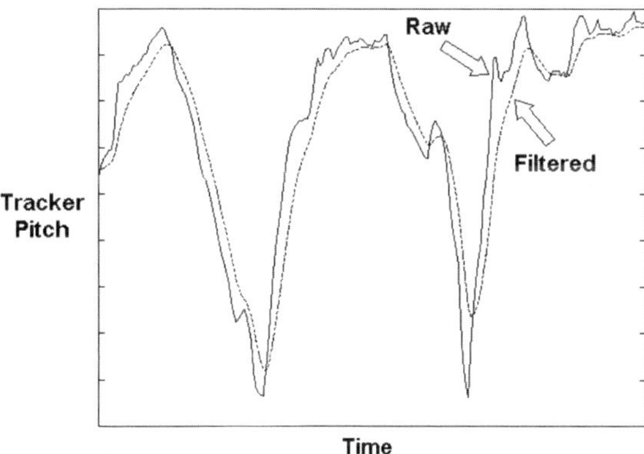

Figure 3: Filtered Input Signal: The solid line shows raw input data of one of the Polhemus tracker parameters. The dotted line shows the corresponding filtered data for $\alpha = 0.8$.

5 Layered Motion Recording

Multi-tracking— the recording and re-recording of various instruments in separate tracks— has been used in the music recording industry for many years. Applying this strategy to the animation problem, we control the articulated character in multiple layers, each layer controlling a subset of the output DOF.

We thus begin by subdividing the DOF of our character into layers as shown in Figure 4.

The multiple layers need to be accessible, to allow coordination of the playing and recording of multiple

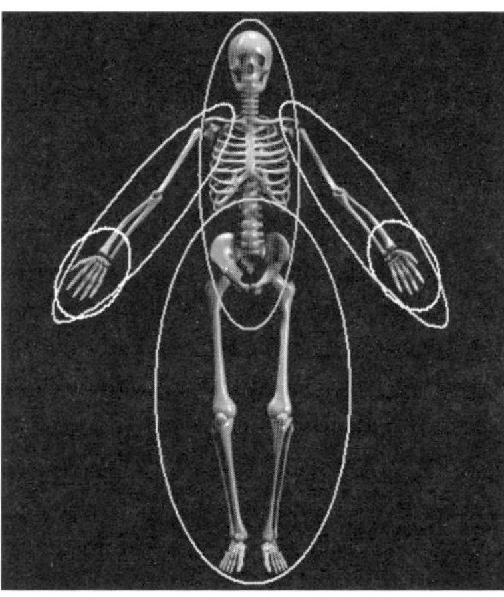

Figure 4: Kinematic Layering Strategy: Legs are usually recorded first, since they define the motion of the character's root. Spine and head are usually recorded simultaneously, followed by arms.

tracks. To create a functional recording studio environment for the animated motions, we therefore implemented modular components such as "Channel", "Mapping", and "Input Device", along with corresponding graphical user interfaces. Each channel includes its own clocking mechanism, and the user interface enables synchronization between clocks. This is crucial for layering motions in real time.

6 Kinematic Mappings

6.1 The Animated Character Output

The CG puppet we are controlling is a rigid articulated body consisting of a set of links connected by joints for a total of 33 controllable DOF, as summarized in Table 1.

Joint	D.O.F.	Child Link
Root	6	pelvis
Lower Back (L1)	3	back/torso
Lower Neck (C7)	3	neck
Head Nod (C1)	1	head
Left, Right Shoulders	3 each	upper arm
Left, Right Elbows	1 each	forearm
Left, Right Wrists	1 each	hand
Left, Right Hips	3 each	thigh
Left, Right Knees	1 each	lower leg
Left, Right Ankles	1 each	foot

Table 1: Output Degrees of Freedom

6.2 Legs

The hips, knees and ankles are all recorded simultaneously, and the mappings for each have been designed to facilitate this. The orientation of the graspable input tube is mapped onto that of the thigh bones, so that there is a direct correspondence between the tube and thigh orientation (as previously illustrated in Figure 2). That is, when the tube is held vertically, the thigh should be vertical as well, and similarly for rotations. The tracker height determines the orientation of the lower legs, or shins, relative to the world coordinate system. This is initially done by a linear mapping, and later modulated by a physics-based model (as will be described below). The tracker's z-translation is mapped to control the flexion at the ankle. Ankle and knee motion is also influenced by physics-based filters, which are beyond the current scope of discussion, but described in detail elsewhere[21].

6.3 Arms

The arms can be controlled similarly to the legs. That is, the tube containing the tracker is mapped to control the orientation of the humerus by rotating the shoulder. The height of the tracker controls the bend at the elbow, and the tracker's z-translation controls the flexion and extension of the wrists.

6.4 Spine

The spine is currently modeled by a 3 DOF joint at the lower back (vertebrae L5) which is attached to the root of the model, another 3 DOF joint at the upper back (vertebrae C7), and a hinge joint for the head (at C1). The ball and socket joints are controlled analogously to the hip control, while the head nod is controlled using a linear relationship as for the ankles and wrists. The left hand controls the lower back joint, nearest the root of the chain, while the right hand controls the upper back and head. Future models will use the same approach but allow a more flexible spine.

6.5 Root Motion and Ground Contact

A critical issue in achieving satisfying control of the puppet is keeping it grounded. This is also the basis for locomotion. Since the trackers translate freely in 3D space, it is virtually impossible to control the height of the pelvis directly without betraying the lack of any underlying ground constraint.

We solve this by imposing the constraint that one of the puppet's feet is touching the ground. Thus, as the character rotates at the hip, one foot is constrained to stay at a fixed position relative to the floor, hence becoming the center of rotation. Nailing a single foot to the floor will not let the character go very far, so a mechanism is provided for switching feet as the next foot touches the ground. By virtue of this ground contact, the puppet can be made to locomote in any direction. Our method can generalize to more contact points, and multiple ground levels of an uneven terrain. We currently use two contact points per foot— one at each of the heels and balls of the feet.

6.6 Setting Filter Viscosity Values

Adjusting the value of α between 0 and 1 in Eq (1) controls the smoothness of the input signal y_i (and therefore also of the resulting motion which depends directly on the input, as will be described in more detail in the next section). If α is too high (e.g. $\alpha = 1$ in the extreme case), then the input signal is essentially unfiltered, and the noise is very apparent in the animation. If α is too low, then the responsiveness is compromised, and significant lag is introduced as well. In the extreme case, for example, when $\alpha = 0$, the input value does not affect the output at all.

This leaves us with a range of possible values, with which we can control the smoothness quality of the resulting motion, to advantageous effect. For example, setting a high smoothness for the hip gives the character a certain appealing quality, related to what many viewers described as "very graceful motion". The local attenuation of higher frequency components can enhance what is seen as part of the character's "style" of motion. In contrast, for other joints such as head rotation, it is effective to use a much lower-smoothness filter, allowing more responsiveness to jerky motions such as quickly glancing over his shoulder.

The choice of a particular filter value helps emphasize corresponding qualities of the character's motion. This fact led us to try giving the user real-time control over the filter parameter α itself. Although doing so produced some interesting results, it was quite difficult to learn to control the interaction between this and the rest of the animated parameters (i.e. direct control of joint angle values), certainly when attempting to achieving realistically-based motion. In particular, changing the filter response in real-time can lead to highly non-linear effects, analogous to playing with delay, gain and various other parameters on effects pedals during a musical performance.

7 Results

A one-minute-long demonstration animation, "Digital Marionette Dance", was created by a fairly experienced user, having the character dancing alone to some music. Sample frames from the animation are shown in Figure 5. All of the animated parameters of this sequence were created at the desktop environment, using our interface, in a total of under 10 minutes, with no re-takes necessary. This is extremely efficient compared to traditional animation techniques. Images from another animation are shown in Figure 6

The expressiveness of the animation created with our system has been demonstrated in a wide variety of contexts, ranging from live television[2] to live theatre[3]. For the theatrical performance, the CG skeleton character was projected onto a very large movie-size screen. All tracks of the animation were created in front of the audience, together with live musical and vocal accompaniment when the fully layered animation was being played back. Projecting the character onto such a large screen involved the risk of finding and magnifying any weaknesses— perhaps subtle or otherwise unnoticeable in the screen-sized version— in his motion. However, the effect was quite strong, and audience and producer response was very positive.

8 User Learning & Experience

Like many complex control tasks, from playing a musical instrument to operating a physical marionette controller, this system, too, is designed with experienced users in mind; the goal is not to have an interface which makes each user an "instant animator", but a system which allows trained animators to create nearly instant animations. Hence, our discussion is based primarily on the observations of, and by, an experienced subject S—, as well those of some novice users[1].

S—'s learning experience involved three primary aspects: basic control tasks, refinement of complex motions, and general principles, including the importance of the overlap itself between the different learning stages.

8.1 Basic Control Tasks at the Initial Stage

The main motion chosen to be learned was walking, since it is a complex yet familiar motion, and leaves room for expressiveness. However, achieving a good, expressive walk right away was not possible, so initial simplifications and sub-tasks were necessary, leading to two main types of initial exercises: isolated motions and functional bipedal locomotion, which we discuss below.

Isolated Motions

Examples of isolation exercises included swinging one leg back and forth from the hip, and shifting support from one leg to the other. By isolating an output parameter, the user observed the specific combination, or *synergy*, of motions in his own body that lead to this constrained output, and thus focused his awareness on the relationship between his kinesthetic experience and the resulting effects.

[1] S— is also a musician, as well as being a user of the GloveTalkII system [8, 9], and thus has extensive prior familiarity learning complex, continuous interfaces. In this light, there are some interesting parallels between this learning experience with that of GloveTalkII and musical instruments, and these are discussed in considerable detail in [21]. S— was also the designer of the current system.

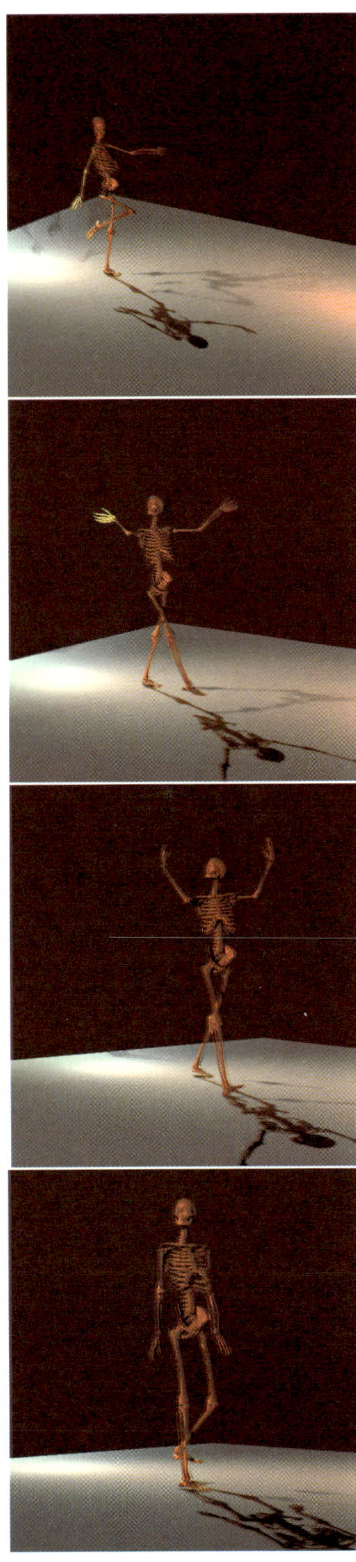

Figure 5: Digital Marionette Dance... Still Frames: These images were taken from an interactively-generated dance animation sequence created using our interface. All animated character parameters of the one-minute long sequence were generated in a total of 10 minutes at a desktop environment. The camera positions were set using a conventional mouse-based interface.

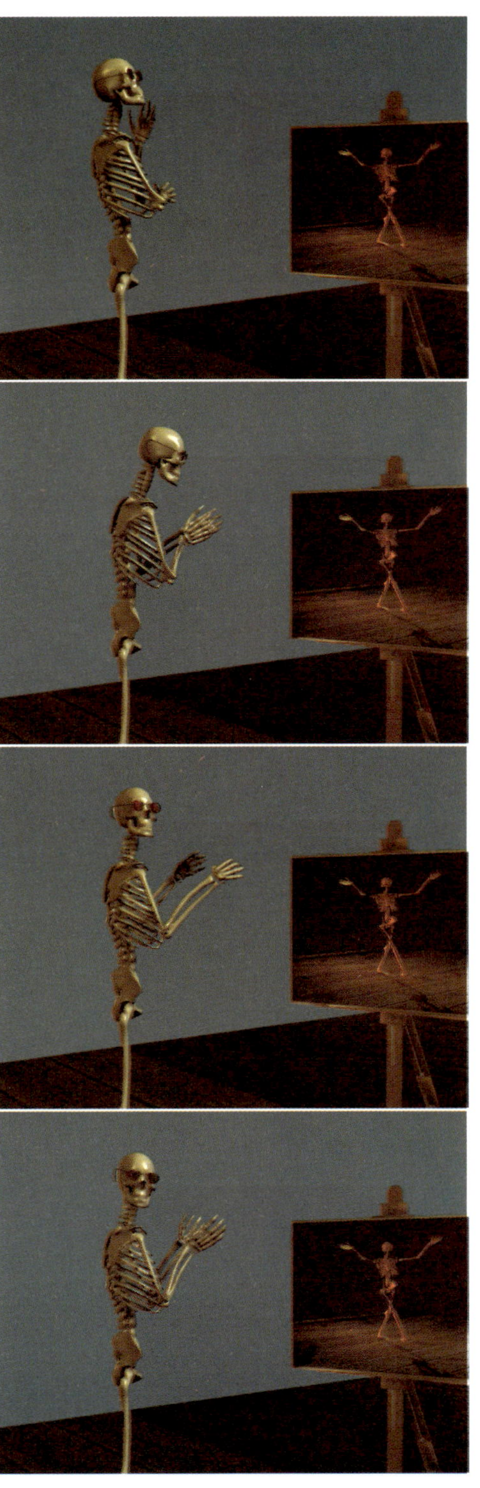

Figure 6: The Appreciator... Still Frames: Images taken from a short animation in which the character expresses his enjoyment of a painting. The frames shown here and in the previous sequence were sampled about one to four seconds apart (going down the columns), highlighting some of the postures achieved by the character.

Functional Bipedal Locomotion

"Functional locomotion" means that initially, the forward motion did not have to be graceful or even resemble conventional locomotion. Having first isolated concepts such as switching feet and swinging a leg, the user could now focus on getting the proper synchronization between them to propel forward. This often began as a "waddle", keeping the character's knees straight and just swinging his free leg out and around.

8.2 Refining Complex Motion: Walking

The exercise for functional locomotion was next refined in various ways to become a walking motion. Once the control of basic bipedal locomotion was "internalized" from the user's perspective (i.e. once the user became comfortable with the necessary coordination patterns), then most corrections and refinements were perceived as isolated details layered on top of a nearly automatic motion. The refinement tasks included aspects such as: controlling the arc of the swing; finding the right combination of "falling forward" and swinging the free leg; and velocity control.

8.3 Novice User Experience

Three novice users practised the system for about two hours each, over two or three separate sessions of 30-60 minutes in length. One of these users had minimal previous experience with animation, while the other two did not. None of them had any previous puppeteering experience. The format of these sessions consisted primarily of the users directly manipulating the CG character, occasionally commenting on the control, with interspersed short breaks of 5-15 minutes each. Due to the complexity of the task, it was essential for the sessions to be exploratory, and therefore structured more like *lessons* than *tests*[2].

Nevertheless, all three users were indeed able to achieve some form of basic bipedal locomotion within the first 20-30 minutes of practise, although after this brief practise time it was still quite inconsistent, and did not yet look like a realistic walk. By the end of the two hour period, all three test subjects had accomplished at least a couple of short walking sequences which, although not as refined as those achieved by the more experienced user, were clearly beyond the initial stages of "waddling". Some of these walking sequences showed early signs of refinement such as the leg swinging through with some smoothness.

[2]Although informal, a more formal approach would be analogous to (and similarly difficult as) attempting to evaluate the quality of "the piano" as a musical instrument based on the first few times some beginners sit down to try it out.

9 Conclusion

We achieved our primary goal of providing an efficient, powerful and satisfying interface for expressive character animation. In doing so, we have brought the power of the performance animation tool to the desktop environment.

One of the challenges in achieving this was indeed handling the large number of DOF of the output. By embedding the trackers in a physical tubing, we established a tangible interface with various coordinate frames inherent to the character, providing a valuable synergy between the physical input device and the underlying transformations from input to motion. Building on this compatibility, we constructed a multi-track motion recording framework and a feasible set of layered mappings from the two input trackers to the thirty three DOF of the graphics character.

By demonstrating an input and interface solution for continuous, low-level control over a dancing 3D articulated character, we have provided a foundation and reference point for numerous future directions. One such direction, in particular, is the exploration of motion layers comprised of greater numbers of parameters and more complex mapping functions, including layers sharing parameters. This would allow application of the system to increasingly refined character models with greater numbers of degrees of freedom, while maintaining a desktop usability, real-time efficiency, and interactively-generated expressiveness. It will be interesting to additionally apply our 3D interface for the control of camera motion.

One limitation of the system is in the ground contact model, wherein at least one foot is making contact with the ground. A more flexible model is being developed. Also, due to the nature of non-literal kinematic-based control, it is relatively easy to allow the character to recover from unstable positions (e.g. including positions in which he would be expected to fall down in a dynamic environment). However, this can occasionally look non-realistic; adding appropriate constraints to the system is an interesting area of research.

Finally, another aspect of future work is to develop systematic evaluation strategies for the task at hand. We thereby intend to provide comparisons to other animation tools, and make explicit the suitability of different approaches for different tasks. Such an approach will also allow for rigorous comparisons between different mappings.

Acknowledgements

We thank to Chakra Chennubhotla for numerous helpful discussions and feedback. We thank Petros Faloutsos and Victor Ng for providing the DANCE platform and support. We thank the referees for their helpful comments and suggestions.

References

[1] Wand/Wanda (TM) VR Input Devices. Input Device, http://evlweb.eecs.uic.edu/research/.

[2] Breakfast Television on City TV. Television program, May 2001.

[3] Subtle Technologies (Toronto, Canada). Conference and Artshow, May 2001.

[4] R. Balakrishnan and K. Hinckley. Symmetric bimanual interaction. In *Proceedings of the ACM Conference on Human Factors in Computing Systems (CHI'2000)*, pages 33–40, New York, 2000. ACM.

[5] Ravin Balakrishnan. *Issues in Bimanual Interaction for Computer Graphics*. PhD thesis, University of Toronto, 2001.

[6] B. Bodenheimer, C. Rose, S. Rosenthal, and J. Pella. The process of motion capture: Dealing with the data. In D. Thalmann and M. van de Panne, editors, *Computer Animation and Simulation '97 : Proceedings of the Eurographics Workshop in Budapest, Hungary*, Springer Computer Science, pages 3–18, NY, September 1997. Springer.

[7] B. deGraf. Protozoa. Company.

[8] Sid Fels. *Glove-TalkII: Mapping Hand Gestures to Speech Using Neural Networks – An Approach to Building Adaptive Interfaces*. PhD thesis, University of Toronto, 1994.

[9] Sid Fels and Geoffrey Hinton. Glove-talkII: An adaptive gesture-to-format interface. In *Proceedings of CHI'95 Human Factors in Computing Systems*, pages 456–463. ACM Press, 1995.

[10] George W. Fitzmaurice. *Graspable User Interfaces*. PhD thesis, University of Toronto, 1996.

[11] Michael Gleicher. Retargetting motion to new characters. In *Proceedings of SIGGRAPH 98*, pages 33–42. ACM SIGGRAPH, 1998.

[12] Yves Guiard. Asymmetric division of labor in human skilled bimanual action: The kinematic chain as a model. *Journal of Motor Behaviour*, 19(4):486–517, 1987.

[13] Ken Hinckley. *Haptic Issues for Virtual Manipulation*. PhD thesis, University of Virginia, 1996.

[14] Intersense. Is-900 precision motion tracker. www.isense.com.

[15] S. Kelso, D. Southard, and D. Goodman. On the coordination of two-handed movements. *Journal of Experimental Psychology: Human Perception and Performance*, 5(2):229–238, 1979.

[16] Joseph F. Laszlo, M. van de Panne, and E. Fiume. Interactive control for physically-based animation. In *Proceedings of SIGGRAPH 2000*. ACM SIGGRAPH, 2000.

[17] C. Mackenzie and T. Iberall. *The Grasping Hand*, volume 104 of *Advances in Psychology*. Amsterdam, 1994.

[18] I. Scott MacKenzie. Input devices and interaction techniques for advanced computing. In W. Barfield and T.A. III Furness, editors, *Virtual Environments and Advanced Interface Design*, pages 437–470. Oxford University Press, New York, 1995.

[19] Roberto Maiocchi. 3-D Character Animation Using Motion Capture. In Nadia Magnenat Thalmann and Daniel Thalmann, editors, *Interactive Computer Animation*. Prentice Hall Europe, London, 1996.

[20] A. Menache. *Understanding Motion Capture for Computer Animation and Video Games*. Morgan Kaufmann, 1999.

[21] Sageev Oore. *Digital Marionette: Augmenting Kinematics with Physics for Multi-Track Desktop Performance Animation*. PhD thesis, University of Toronto, Toronto, Canada, 2001.

[22] Polhemus. `www.polhemus.com`.

[23] David J. Sturman. Computer puppetry. *IEEE Computer Graphics and Applications*, 18(1):38–45, January/February 1998.

[24] S. Zhai, P. Milgram, and W. Buxton. The effects of using fine muscle groups in multiple degree-of-freedom input. In *Proc. ACM CHI'96*, pages 308–315, 1996.

Laser Pointers as Collaborative Pointing Devices

Ji-Young Oh, Wolfgang Stuerzlinger

Department of Computer Science, York University
http://www.cs.yorku.ca/~wolfgang

Abstract

Single Display Groupware (SDG) is a research area that focuses on providing collaborative computing environments. Traditionally, most hardware platforms for SDG support only one person interacting at any given time, which limits collaboration. In this paper, we present laser pointers as input devices that can provide concurrent input streams ideally required to the SDG environment.

First, we discuss several issues related to utilization of laser pointers and present the new concept of computer controlled laser pointers. Then we briefly present a performance evaluation of laser pointers as input devices and a baseline comparison with the mouse according to the ISO 9241-9 standard.

Finally, we describe a new system that uses multiple computer controlled laser pointers as interaction devices for one or more displays. Several alternatives for distinguishing between different laser pointers are presented, and an implementation of one of them is demonstrated with SDG applications.

Keywords: Single display groupware, hardware for collaboration, laser pointer, input devices.

1 Introduction

General computer systems are designed to support interaction with only one user at a time. When multiple users want to use a computer collaboratively, they are currently forced to take turns to control the system.

Single Display Groupware (SDG, see e.g. [8]) is defined as a system that can support collaborative work between people that are physically in relative proximity. Since users are sharing a display in the same room, they are free to interact face to face, which facilitates collaboration. Ideally, a SDG system should provide multiple *independent* input streams so that several users can control a display at the same time without waiting for their turn to use a the single input device. Even though the SDG software *may* still enforce taking turns, there are several scenarios and applications where allowing at least a degree of parallel interaction can be very beneficial.

As not all collaborators can stand in the same place in a SDG system, *remote* interaction devices become almost a necessity. Consider a planning session for rescue efforts with ten or more participants scattered around a room with an SDG system. If there is only one interaction device that is wired to the computer, the device can only be used in a limited range. If participants in the back of the room want to contribute, they have to come to the front to use the interaction device. Even worse, since there is only one input device available, people are forced to go through the process of acquiring the device before they can contribute their ideas. A system with multiple remote devices does not suffer from this drawback.

Another scenario is a presentation, where interested members of the audience are given the ability to control the slides in the question and answer part of the talk. Again, remote input devices facilitate participation by all people in the audience. Yet another illustration is a brainstorming session in any of a large number of design applications. Here designers can quickly and effortlessly try out their ideas if multiple remote interaction devices are available.

Last, but not least, games become much more compelling when one display is shared between multiple players, while still allowing independent input from each player. Inkpen *et al.* [10] beautifully illustrated the benefits of multi-user SDG in an experiment with children. A pair of children played a paper-based puzzle game on a computer with one display and one mouse, and then on a computer with one display and two mice. The result shows that children are much more engaged and active when two mice are available compared to the single mouse condition.

There are other cases when it can be advantageous to share a display between multiple users, each having an input device. Common to all above applications is that extremely precise pointing and selection are usually not required as users are sitting or standing at varying distances from the display. Consider that a user in the back of the room can see only a certain level of detail due to fundamental limitations of the human visual system. If we assume that a remote pointing device is used, similar limitations in pointing accuracy apply due to hand jitter (see e.g. [1]). Consequently, a SDG application needs larger icons, buttons, and labels to be usable for *all* participants. Note, however, that a user right in front of the display may obtain high accuracy by working directly on or close to the display surface. For this reason we believe that fine manipulation tasks are counterproductive in SDG settings, unless fine positioning is *the* focus of the meeting.

We argue that if precise alignment, etc. is required, the SDG application should provide helpful manipulation techniques such as automatically snapping objects together for ease of alignment or providing 'intelligent' objects that

place themselves according to context in a 3D environment [13].
Laser pointers have been favored in meeting rooms as participants can directly point to objects on the display from any distance. We build on this and also address one of the main limitations of most current SDG hardware, namely that only *one* user can interact with the system at any given time. A camera, pointed at the screen, is used to detect the position of the laser spot. This position is then communicated to the system for further processing.
This paper discusses issues related to using a laser pointer as an input device. Then a usability test is presented to address if the device is suitable for SDG applications. Finally, we propose an efficient method to detect and identify *multiple* laser pointers.

2 Previous Work

Kirstein and Muller [2] presented a system that uses a laser pointer as a pointing device. Their system acquires video frames at 20 fps. They report that they are able to detect the laser spot in only 50% of the frames.
A simple performance test of the laser pointer as an input device was presented in the Pebbles project [1]. Since the button press on a laser pointer is not communicated to the computer in their system, they ask the user to turn the laser pointer on or off to select objects. However, the results of the user test clearly show that users cannot reliably turn on or off the laser pointer at the position they intend. To combat this, the authors suggest using the first and last dwelling positions as selection events. Still the problem is that detecting precise dwell positions takes about 2.5 seconds. The paper concludes that the laser pointer is inappropriate for selecting precise positions on a screen. Consequently, the authors claim that the laser pointer is not suited for selecting targets such as buttons or menus. Instead they suggest that the laser pointer be used only to select a region of an object or a menu system and to copy the selected object to a hand-held device for further manipulation.
Olsen [3] proposes an inexpensive interaction technique by introducing a set of window events for the laser pointer such as laser-on/off, and laser-move/dwell. To make the user aware of errors, and noise of the laser pointer, it displays a cursor corresponding to the detected position of the laser spot on the screen. Winograd and Guimbretiere [9] propose a new kind of interaction techniques for large displays, which are based on "gesture and sweep" paradigm instead of the usual "point and click".
Chen and Davis [4] describe a system that can provide multiple laser pointer inputs with multiple cameras. The system identifies the strokes created by the laser pointers on the screen in the following way. A Kalman filter is used to smooth the readings, which in turn are used to predict where the laser pointer will appear in the future. In each frame all points that potentially correspond to the current position of each stroke are collected. Then, the system collects all points that are within a certain range of the prediction and chooses the closest one as the candidate. As no physical identification to distinguish strokes exists, wrong points can be selected as a part of the stroke and consequently the system cannot keep track of individual users.
Very few of the mentioned papers discuss the practical tradeoffs concerned with the detection of laser spots. None of the previously mentioned approaches can reliably support multiple users interacting with the system.

3 The laser pointer as a pointing device

In this section, we discuss several issues related to laser pointers. We mention laser spot detection, mechanisms to indicate selection, and a computer controlled laser pointer.
Laser spots appear whenever a laser pointer is held towards a screen. Similar to previous work the basic system utilizes a camera connected to a computer pointed at the screen to detect these laser spots. Note that depending on the setup, the camera can either be in front of the reflective screen or in the case of a transparent display, on either side of the screen. We recommend a back-projected screen where the camera is situated behind the screen, because it allows users to move more freely. Due to the space requirements of back-projected screens, one or more mirrors are often necessary to fold the optical path. We recommend using the same mirror to fold the optical path of the camera, too. Note that in this case, care has to be taken to avoid the direct reflection of the projection system, which usually saturates the image.
As in previous work, we perform a threshold operation to identify bright pixels for every frame acquired by the camera, and obtain the center of the laser spot from the weighed average of the bright pixels, which results in sub-pixel accuracy. This is also based on the observation that laser spots usually form the brightest pixels in the image. One reason for this is that many cameras are most sensitive in the red region of the spectrum. Consequently, a bright red laser spot often saturates the pixels in the video image.
One important advantage of using laser pointers is that there is no need to display a cursor, as the laser spot itself provides visual feedback of the selection.

3.1 Issues with laser spot detection

However, there are some issues that make it hard to perform reliable detection of laser pointer spots with this simple method that relies on contrast.
First, the camera must be focused on the screen. This can be difficult for large screens, especially if the camera is too close to the screen or mounted at a significant angle relative to the screen. This will cause a blurry and consequently dimmer image of the laser pointer spot in some regions of the screen. This also happens in the corners of a screen, if the screen is large relative to the distance of the camera as the brightness of the image diminishes with relative angle to the portion of the screen. The only solution here is to position the camera far enough from the screen and to make sure that the whole image is in reasonable focus.
The second issue is that the projected image and the image in the camera need to be registered. In other words, we

need to know for each pixel in the camera image, what the corresponding point on the display is. For a camera with good optics, a perspective mapping is enough. With cheaper optics, the barrel distortion of the image may also need to be compensated.
On the topic of image quality, the camera image as a whole might be too bright. One way to reduce the brightness is to reduce the aperture of the camera, but this changes the image geometry. Our preferred alternative is to reduce the shutter/exposure time of the image. With a relatively long exposure time the image of a fast moving laser spot is in general a blurred and dimmed trail. Consequently, we recommend the shortest shutter time possible.
A related topic is low contrast images due to a high level of incident illumination. The best solution is to make sure that there is not much light directly falling onto the screen. This can often be accomplished with appropriate baffles or similar devices. If there is a lot of ambient (undirected) illumination the only solution is to reduce the light level, which may necessitate using directed lighting for work surfaces. Another solution would be brighter laser pointers, but we hesitate to recommend this due to eye safety concerns. Last of all, we could use a more sensitive camera, but such devices are usually also much more expensive.
Users standing at an oblique angle to the screen also cause problems because the laser spot becomes progressively larger and dimmer. We observe this only to be a problem at angles greater than 85 degrees from the normal of the screen surface.
Another issue with camera based systems is latency. Latencies occur due to the time for the transmission of the image from the camera to the computer and the time for the computation to detect the laser point. Using grayscale images instead of color images can reduce the transmission time. Another alternative is to reduce image resolution, but this also reduces the effective resolution of the input device. Finally, we could use compression, but here compression artifacts are a concern.
Due to hand jitter, it is practically impossible to use a remote pointing device to indicate a small target for an extended period. Therefore, only lightweight remote pointing devices are recommended in practice to avoid fatigue issues. Another choice is to use supporting surface, such as e.g. the work surface in the case of a mouse. But in many SDG systems such a surface may not be available everywhere in a meeting environment.
To reduce the effects of jitter on the laser pointer position we use a Kalman filter to smooth out the readings similar to the approach described in [6]. With the described techniques we are able to reliably track a laser pointer with an NTSC camera at 60 Hz. If configured correctly a side benefit of the Kalman filter is that it smoothes out jitter due to the even and odd fields of the NTSC signal.

3.2 Selecting objects with laser pointers

For a person with a laser pointer there are multiple possibilities to indicate selection of an object. As discussed in the paper about the Pebbles project [1] one alternative is to use the on/off of the laser pointer as an indication of selection. In other words, whenever a laser spot appears this indicates selection. However, the authors report that the user cannot reliably make the laser spot appear where they intend with this method.
Another option explored in the Pebbles project is to use a threshold on the dwell time (e.g. 2.5 seconds). As reported there, this approach is problematic due to hand jitter and has the additional disadvantage that it is time-consuming to select an object. The authors of [1] abandoned this approach and used a handheld computer with an integrated laser pointer for their future work.
The last alternative is to directly use the button on the laser pointer without switching the laser pointer on or off. In our experience, most first-time users for the laser pointer believe that this is the natural way of doing things. To achieve this, it is sufficient to modify a laser pointer so that the button and laser power can be controlled separately. For all hand-held laser pointer devices an important question is if the button event should be transmitted on the up or down motion. Most desktop-based devices use the up-event to designate a click. For laser pointers this does not work, as each button press will cause a small 'dip down' in the position of the laser spot due to the force exerted onto the laser pointer case as the user holds the laser pointer in the air. Consequently, it is better to record the position for the button down event and to use this for selection purposes.
One way to separate power and button control is to mount a little power switch on the laser pointer and use the button to interrupt the laser power while it is pressed. However, with this method the laser may stay on for extended periods, which significantly shortens the lifetime of the laser diode. More seriously, a laser pointer that is always on may cause safety problems. A better realization is to put the laser pointer under computer control.

3.3 A computer controlled laser pointer

For a computer controlled laser pointer, there are two important issues: sensing button presses and switching the laser on or off from the computer.
There are several ways to connect a laser pointer to a computer. The simplest and most reliable approach is to use a cable. However, from our experience with Virtual Reality (VR) hardware, we know that cables are a major nuisance. People are limited in their range of operation or trip over cables, the cable often gets in the way, or the weight of the cable itself causes problems.
Wireless alternatives are to use infrared, ultrasonic or radio transmission. If the same mechanism is used to transmit button presses and the power signal, there is the potential for cross talk, which complicates things. If different mechanisms are used this issue is eliminated.
The alternative we recommend is to use infrared for the 'power-on' signal and to use ultrasound for transmitting the button press. As for the button press, the simplest alternative is to use an ultrasonic emitter, which is activated as

long as the button is pressed. For the 'power-on' signal infrared LED's should be mounted near the screen (preferably at the bottom or the top) to transmit the 'power-on' signal to the laser pointer. A little infrared sensor mounted on the front of the laser pointer then closes the circuit to the batteries as long as the signal is received. This is an application of the technology used to control so-called shutter glasses for VR. The benefit of using infrared is that the laser pointer may turn itself automatically off if the pointer is not pointed in the direction of the screen

4 User test of the laser pointer

In this paper, we are considering a laser pointer as an input device for a large-scale display. To see if a laser pointer can be used in practice, we have to assess its performance from the user's perspective. The best comparison point is the mouse, yet we have to address the issue of different screen sizes. Consequently, we choose to perform a baseline comparison that compares the laser pointer with a mouse, where the mouse is used on both a small and a large display.

4.1 The task and measurement

We have chosen to follow the methodology proposed by the ISO 9241 standard [5], which is based also on MacKenzie *et al.* [7] work. In this study we perform a "pointing and selecting" task (see the ISO standard) with the laser pointer and the mouse. A sketch of the display for the task is shown in Fig. 1. The task is designed to exercise many different directions of movement. The numbers marked on the circles define the order of the selections the participant has to perform. Selecting the target marked '0' starts a block of trials. Each trial starts after the selection of the current target, and ends at the selection of the next target. Consequently, there are 15 trials in each block. The movement time is measured on a per trial basis.

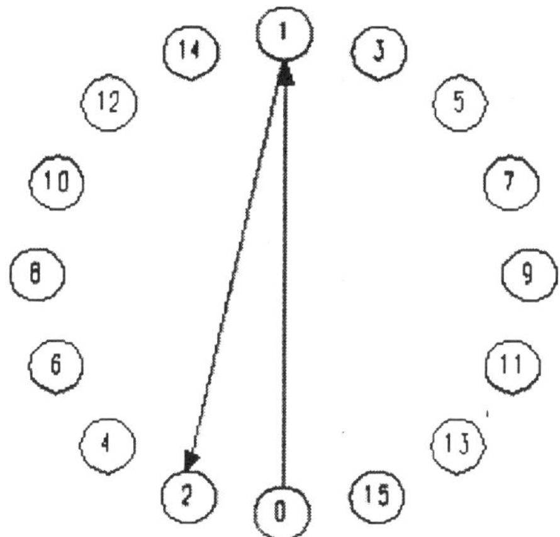

Fig. 1. Sketch of input device evaluation task.

As explained above we use the 'button-down' event for the laser pointer. For the mouse, we still use the 'button-up' event as in standard desktop applications. A cursor of the laser pointer on the screen is the laser spot itself, and no graphical cursor is displayed. An error is recorded when the participant misses a target.

According to the ISO standard, different indices of difficulty should be included in the test. The index of difficulty (ID) is a measure of the precision required from the user in a task. It is defined in bits as:

$$ID = \log_2(1 + \frac{D}{W}),$$

where D is the distance between targets, and W is the width of the target. In our user study, we asked participants to perform tasks at three different ID's.

Throughput as defined by ISO standard, is then calculated from the measured movement time (MT) in seconds and the recorded user events:

$$Throughput = \frac{ID_e}{MT},$$

where ID_e is the effective index of difficulty. Throughput is measured in bits per second (bps). The effective index of difficulty is defined as:

$$ID_e = \log_2(1 + \frac{D}{W_e}) \text{ with } W_e = 4.133 \times SD_x,$$

where W_e is the effective width of target and SD_x is the standard deviation in the selection coordinates measured along the axis of approach to the target. The use of the effective width and not the real width accounts for the fact that users sometimes miss the target by a small amount.

4.2 Installation and procedure of the test

We mounted a class I (output < 1mW) laser pointer into a small case and installed two buttons on top of this case. Only the foremost button was used in this test. See Fig. 2 for a picture, the head of the laser pointer is visible on the left side.

Fig. 2. The laser pointer used in the baseline comparison.

The computer controls the power of the laser pointer via a small circuit consisting mainly of an optical coupler mounted into a control box. For simplicity and speed, we choose to use the parallel port of the computer for I/O. The laser pointer itself is connected to the control box via lightweight telephone wire.

Depending on the condition the task either displayed on a back-projected 6' by 4' screen (using a 700 lumens projector) or a 19" desktop screen. For this study, we used a NTSC camera. The camera was installed behind the 6' by 4' screen. The camera captures the grayscale image of the screen at 60 Hz. A PC running Windows NT acquires the images. In all conditions participants were seated and we asked them not to move the chair during the test. To ensure that the apparent size and viewing angle of the screen were consistent during the test, we positioned the 19" screen so that the screen corners lined up with the corners of the 6'x4' screen from the participant's point of view. The test was performed under normal office lighting conditions.

Prior to the test, we gave a practice session to minimize learning effects and to familiarize the participant with the use of the laser pointer. In this practice period, each participant was required to repeat each task with each device at least three times and we gave them the option of further practice. For the test, participants were instructed to hit the targets as fast as possible. Between the trial blocks, we allowed participants to rest whenever they expressed a need to do so. After the test, participants were asked to answer questions assessing the comfort and ease of use, as specified in ISO9241-9 [5]. In our user study, participants took an average of 50 minutes for the total test including practice, test, and questionnaire fill-up time.

4.3 Design

The experiment is a (3 device conditions) x (15 trials) x (10 blocks) x (3 index of difficulty) x (12 participants) factorial design. Twelve participants (six male, six female, age ranging from 26 to 45, average 26.3) were recruited from graduate and undergraduate students at the local university. Each of participants performed a total of 1,350 trials according to the test configuration specified in table 1. We counterbalanced the device conditions to combat learning effects.

Table 1. Configuration of the experiment

Factor	Values
Device	Mouse with 19" screen Mouse with 6'x4' screen Laser pointer with 6'x4' screen
Index of difficulty	2.58 (300,60)* 3.17 (400,50) 3.75 (500,40)
Block	10 blocks of trials
Trial	15 trials in each block

* The pair of numbers in brackets indicates distance between targets and diameter of a target in pixel, respectively.

The above design was chosen based on the results of a small pilot study and the fact that we were primarily interested in a baseline comparison. Based on our observations in the pilot study the three indices of difficulty mentioned above correspond to an easy, medium and reasonably difficult task. Furthermore, we designed the experiment to keep the time per participant to less than one hour to limit fatigue effects. This imposed a maximum on the number of trials and on the different factors we could investigate in the test.

4.4 Results

Learning effect

First, we analyzed the results according to learning effects. A quick glance at the graph of average trial movement times grouped by block (see Fig. 3) shows that there are still learning effects in the first few trials. A more detailed analysis with a repeated-measures ANOVA by blocks shows that the blocks from 5 to 10 form one group ($F_{2,9}$=3.82, p<0.01).

We also observe that the movement time of the laser pointer is increasing towards the end of the user test. As far as we can tell this is because participants felt tired from holding the laser pointer in the air throughout the test. However, the difference between the blocks of laser pointer trials is not significant ($F_{9,350}$=0.97, p>0.05).

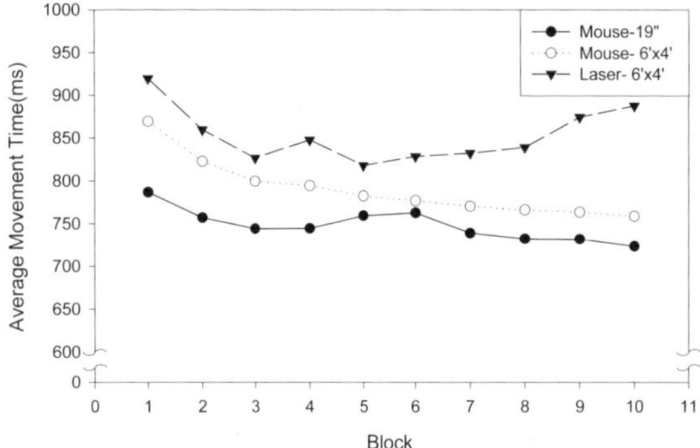

Fig. 3. Average movement time of device by block.

To exclude potential issues with learning effects, we choose to ignore blocks 1 to 4 and all results reported from now on are for block 5-10 only.

Movement time

The movement time by device is shown in Fig. 4 as a box plot. Boxes indicate the 25th to the 75th percentile range. The bars above and below the box indicate the 90th and 10th percentile. The line in the middle marks the median.

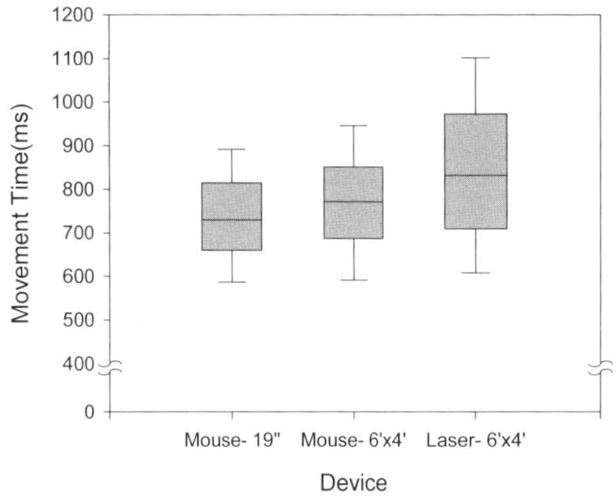

Fig. 4. Movement time by device.

The average movement time per trial for the laser pointer is 846.78 ms, the mouse with 6'x4' screen is 769.72 ms, and the mouse with 19" screen is 741.06 ms. The movement time of the laser pointer is significantly different from both mouse conditions at $F_{2,645}$=28.46, p<0.001. The difference between the two mouse conditions is statistically not significant. Consequently, we can conclude that the size of the screen is not important, but that there is a difference between the devices.

Analysis of the movement time according to the index of difficulty yields the unsurprising result that more difficult tasks take longer. The movement time of the laser pointer is significantly different from the rest of the device conditions with the first index of difficulty at $F_{2,213}$=7.15, p<0.001.

Error Rate

The average error rate for the laser pointer is 32.16%, the mouse with 6'x 4' screen is 20.46%, and the mouse with 19" screen is 20.31%. The difference of error rate between the mouse with 19" screen 6'x4' screen is not significant. The difference between the laser pointer and the mice conditions is significant at $F_{2,645}$=19.71, p<0.001.

A more detailed analysis of the error rate reveals that the error rate for the laser pointer increases stronger with increasing index of difficulty compared to the mouse. In other words the smaller the target the harder it is to select it with the laser pointer. In the most difficult condition, the error rate is approximately 40%.

Throughput

The average throughput of the laser pointer is 3.04 bps, the mouse with 6'x4' screen is 3.98 bps, and the mouse with 19" screen is 4.09 bps. The throughput of the laser pointer is significantly different from the mouse with 19" screen and with 6'x4' screen at $F_{2,645}$=67.50, p<0.001. In other words, the average throughput of the laser pointer is about 75% of the mouse. Fig. 5 shows the distribution of throughput of each device.

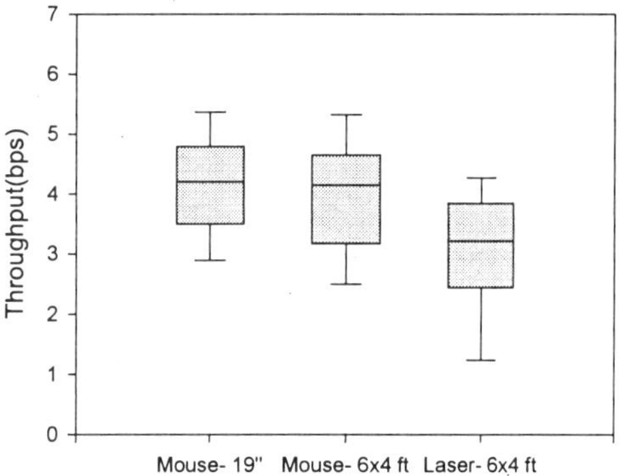

Fig. 5. Throughput by device.

Qualitative evaluation

After the test, participants answered the thirteen questions listed in the ISO standard. Those questions are designed to evaluate the comfort and difficulty of using device.

As shown in table 2, the averages of general comfort and overall difficulty of laser pointer are slightly lower than the mouse, but the difference is not statistically significant. The results for all other questions are not significant, as well.

Table 2. Evaluation of general comfort and overall difficulty for different conditions.

	Mouse-19"	Mouse-6'x4'	Laser-6'x4'
General comfort	3.92	3.83	3.42
Overall difficulty	4.67	4.58	4.17

Furthermore, we asked participants to freely comment on the devices. The most frequent comment was that the button on the box was hard to press and that this caused them difficulties in selecting targets. Another comment was that the contrast of the laser spot against the display was not high enough. In fact, we observed that participants sometimes completely lost track of the laser spot in fast movements. Both factors cause fatigue and discomfort, which may explain the rising times towards the end of the study.

On the positive side, participants commented that they would really like to use this device for giving presentations, as it is free of the desk surface, yet provides optical feedback of the current position via the laser spot. Asked about their first choice for a remote pointing device, participants clearly expressed a strong preference for the laser pointer.

4.5 Discussion

The most striking result of our baseline comparison is that the throughput of the laser pointer is significantly below that of the mouse, at approximately 75%. Since the laser pointer is held in the hand, whereas the mouse rests on the desktop, this result is not very surprising. In fact, we consider 75% compared to the mouse a relatively good result, considering the absence of a stabilizing surface. Since laser pointers have strong advantages over mice in SDG environment such as mobility and the ability to interact with the display from everywhere in a room (even *standing*), we see this result as an indication that laser pointers are very good input devices for SDG systems.

The size of the screen slightly affects mouse performance, but no statistical difference exists. Thus, we can say that the size of the display does not matter for mouse performance.

A side benefit of the laser pointer is that the bright spot caused by the laser pointer serves directly as the cursor. While it is physically smaller than a mouse cursor, it is still very noticeable. With our first prototype the laser spot was sometimes too dim during fast movements, which caused problems. Users effectively had to perform a visual search for the laser spot after a movement, which decreased performance.

If we compare our results with MacKenzie's experiments [7] we can see that the error rate is much higher. We attribute this to the fact that we instructed our participants only to complete the task as fast as possible – as opposed to achieving maximum speed while still hitting all the targets. This naturally led to a much higher error rate in our study.

The biggest technical problem in our baseline comparison was the button, which required a relatively large amount of force to be pressed. From our observations we believe that the button press itself took longer compared to a mouse button press, but we did not attempt to measure this. Sometimes participants involuntarily performed repeated button presses on the same target, which increased the error rate for the laser pointer by a significant amount

4.6 Modifications to the original design

Based on the user comments and our observations from the user study we modified our design for the laser pointers. The first modification was to use a common laser pointer case as enclosure, which also makes the device lighter. An added benefit is that the button in such laser pointers is connected to a microswitch similar to the ones used in mice. Furthermore, we replaced the laser diode with a model that conforms to class IIIa (output < 5mW), which increases the brightness of the laser pointer. We also took this modification as an opportunity to replicate the circuitry for one pointer to support multiple laser pointers, see the next section. Fig. 6 shows our current prototype with three laser pointers.

We also replaced the NTSC camera with a Firewire camera (Pyro Webcam) that can acquire images with 640x480 resolution at 30 Hz. While the lower frame rate somewhat degrades performance, the image quality is significantly better. Another major advantage of the new camera is that the shutter time can be controlled electronically, which greatly simplifies setup and adaptation to different lighting conditions.

In our experience, the modifications improved both the reliability of laser spot detection and the formfactor for the laser pointer. In addition, the new button allows for practically error free button press detection, which makes it much more responsive from the user's point of view. Although we have not performed a formal user study with this new version, we are confident that results will be better than for our first implementation.

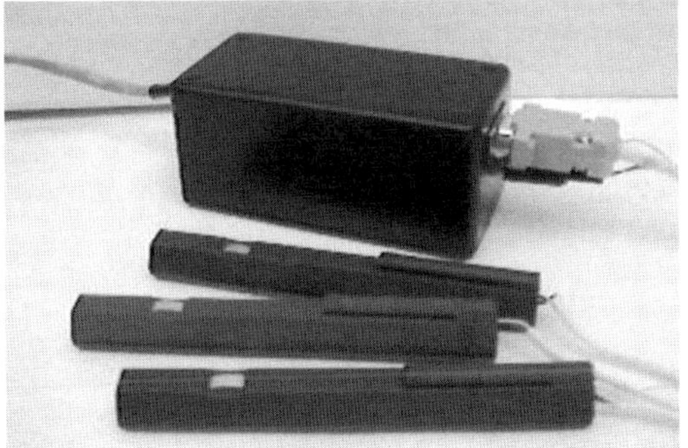

Fig. 6. Three computer controlled laser pointers and the box containing the electronics to control them.

5 Distinguishing multiple laser pointers

The basic idea in tracking multiple laser spots is to use prediction and to assign the laser spot that is closest to each predicted position to the corresponding laser pointer. This has been tried before [4]. However, as mentioned there, this scheme fails when multiple laser spots come in close proximity. Also, it is hard to reliably determine which user is manipulating which laser when laser pointers are turned on or off or leave the screen.

5.1 Identifying different laser pointers

To improve on this we discuss multiple ways of distinguishing between different laser pointers. We consider different colored lasers and blinking the lasers.

While different colored laser pointers make it easy for the users to distinguish them, there are a couple of problems. The biggest problem in using color as an identifier is that laser pointers outside the 650-680 nm range are relatively expensive. Moreover, as bright laser spots often saturate the CCD, it is relatively hard to reliably detect the color of a laser pointer from the image. An alternative is to use multiple cameras with different band-pass filters. This is more expensive and the use of filters makes the images much darker, which amplifies laser spot detection problems.

A better alternative is to use different patterns to blink the laser pointers. This necessitates that the blinking cycles are synchronized with the picture acquisition by the camera. This is easy to realize by modifying the state of the laser pointer directly *after* a frame was recorded. Please note that blinking standard laser diodes may shorten the lifetime of these devices significantly. We recommend using laser diodes that support modulated input signals.

The simplest approach is to power each laser pointer in turn in a cyclic pattern. The biggest disadvantage is that each laser pointer is only powered for a fraction of the time, which dims the laser spot for the user. Another approach is to blink the lasers in a binary or Gray code pattern, which maximizes the number of laser pointers that can be used. Note that the pattern 00…0 cannot be used. The downside to using binary patterns is that some laser pointers will be off most of the time (consider the pattern 0…01) and some will be on most of the time (e.g. 1…10). That means that each laser pointer has different number of measurements, which leads to different tracking behavior. The last approach is to turn each laser pointer *off* for only one cycle of a repeated pattern. Compared to the first alternative, every laser pointer will be on most of the time, and we have the benefit of equal number of measurements per time for each laser pointer. See Table 3 for a comparison of the different alternatives.

Table 3. Comparison between blink patterns of length 3.

Method	Blink-on	Binary	Blink-off
1st laser pointer	001	001	110
2nd laser pointer	010	010	101
3rd laser pointer	100	011	011
4th laser pointer	N/A	100	N/A
…	…	…	…
7th laser pointer	N/A	111	N/A
Percentage on	33%	Varies	66%

Regardless of the pattern used, the cycle length limits the frequency at which laser pointers can be identified reliably. Consequently, for a 60 Hz camera and cycle length three, we can get reliable identification of laser pointers at 20 Hz. Depending on the details of the algorithm, intermediate classifications may be correct or incorrect.

5.2 Proof of Concept

In our implementation, we use the blink-off approach to identify the laser pointers. In the following description we use a pattern length of three, but the algorithms generalize easily to more laser pointers.

For each frame, we predict the position where a laser pointer should currently appear with the help of a Kalman filter. As in [4] we initially assign to each laser pointer the spot that is closest to the prediction for this pointer. Simultaneously, the program records if the laser pointer has been assigned the detected spot.

Depending on the circumstances, at the end of this per-frame process there may be laser spots that cannot be associated with a laser pointer and laser pointers that cannot find a laser spot close to the predicted position. Unassociated laser spots are classified as starting points for a new laser pointer. If there is a laser pointer where no close enough laser spot exists, we assume that it has been turned off. Finally, each laser pointer updates its measurement if a current laser spot was found and record their pattern as on, otherwise they record their pattern as off.

After a number of frames corresponding to the length of the pattern have been recorded (i.e. 3 in our discussion), the method compares the recorded and predefined patterns. If the patterns do not match, we can say that one or more measurements were erroneous. In our current implementation we simply look for another laser pointer with wrong measurements (which must exist) and swap the last readings for these two pointers.

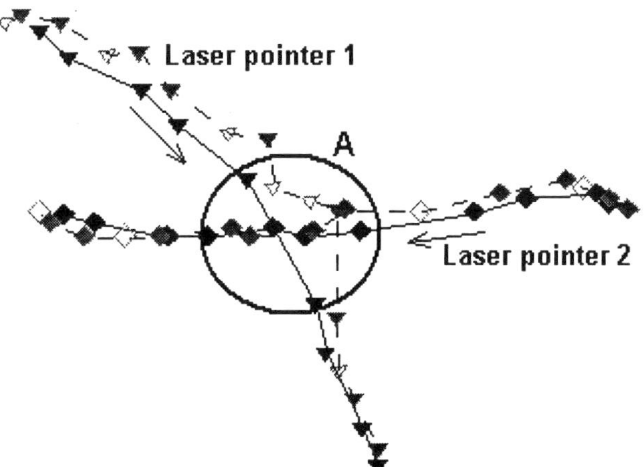

Fig.7. Recorded paths of two laser pointers.

Fig. 7 shows the path for two laser pointers recorded at 30 Hz. Solid lines with black points are measured points and dashed lines with gray points illustrate the prediction. Empty shapes stand for predictions without a corresponding measurement. The first laser pointer is designated by triangles and has the pattern 011, whereas the second is shown with diamonds and has the pattern 110. One can observe misclassifications in area A, but can also observe that the misclassification is quickly corrected. Note also how the prediction error increases after empty shapes due to the higher inaccuracy in prediction.

With this scheme, the classification of the acquired points depends only on the predictions for each frame and their recorded state pattern. Problems arise if a laser spot is not detected reliably e.g. due to very fast movements or when two laser spots coincide. Consequently, we cannot *guarantee* that each laser pointer is detected correctly in every frame. However, we can reliably identify laser pointers correctly at every third frame!

For a wireless implementation of our system, we need to separate signals for different laser pointers. For the buttons, this can be achieved by using transmitters with different frequencies. For the infrared transmission of the power-on signal, we can use the circuitry used in TV remotes to transmit different signals and to distinguish among them at the laser pointer side.

5.3 Extension for tiled displays

Large tiled displays are needed to display, annotate, and edit large amounts of information in a collaborative environment. For example, the i-Land system [11] presents the DynaWall, a wall sized touch sensitive display, as one of the components of the roomware prototype.

Without expensive equipment such as a touch sensitive display, laser pointers are a simple and cheap input alternative that supports multiple/parallel inputs for large-scale displays. Our current implementation uses only one display, but there's no reason why the system cannot be extended to multiple displays. In fact, one way to achieve this has been described in [4].

5.4 Discussion

We created two demonstration applications. One is a simple puzzle game, another is a 3D interior design application. When running the system we observe that users indeed use the opportunity to work in parallel if they are not focusing on a single object.

Surprisingly, although there is no visual identification of each laser pointer, users do not seem to experience problems identifying their laser pointer. A quick 'wiggle' of the laser pointer will usually give enough visual feedback to identify it.

6 CONCLUSIONS

In this paper, we presented a comprehensive discussion of laser pointers as input devices. Several issues regarding reliable detection of laser spots and selection techniques with laser pointers were mentioned. A new form of computer controlled laser pointer device was introduced. This implementation may be more expensive than using multiple

mice. However, the mobility and accessibility from remote distances are strong advantages over using mice.
Furthermore, we presented an initial baseline comparison of laser pointers with a mouse according to the ISO standard. Our results indicate that laser pointer performance is approximately 75% compared to a mouse. We interpret this as a good indication that laser pointers can indeed be used in applications where users may be standing or sitting in chairs. The results of the presented study also show an increased error rate for the laser pointer, which may be due to limitations in the first prototype. Based on this and other issues raised by the user study we discussed modifications to the prototype, which makes the device easier to use.
The refined system also supports multiple laser pointers as interaction devices on one or more displays. Consequently, the system affords seamless and parallel collaboration among several users. Several alternatives for distinguishing between different laser pointers were discussed, and one implementation was demonstrated with SDG applications.
For a wireless version of the system, we do not expect any major functional differences to the results presented here. We are currently working on such a system and will report about it in future work.
In addition, we plan to perform a more controlled user study of the performance of the modified laser pointer system. This study will explore a wider range of indices of difficulty and will also investigate the fatigue factor. Also we plan to inform participants better about the need to hit targets accurately, which should improve the error rates.
Furthermore, we are currently investigating way to make computer controlled laser pointers safer, as a class IIIa laser pointers can *potentially* cause at least temporary eye damage [12]. Finally, we intend to study of the multi-user aspects of our system with SDG applications.

Acknowledgements

We wish to thank Scott MacKenzie for helpful advice on our user test, Andrejs Vorozcovs for help with the video figure and hardware, and Max Garber for the first implementation of the system. The Natural Sciences and Engineering Research Council (NSERC) of Canada funded this research project.

REFERENCES

[1] Myers, B. A., Bhatnagar, R., Nichols, J., Peck, C. H., Kong, D., Miller, R., and Long, A. C., Interacting at a distance: measuring the performance of laser pointers and other devices, *Proceedings CHI'02*, to appear.

[2] Kirstein, C. and Muller, H., Interaction with a projection screen using a Camera-tracked laser pointer, *Multimedia Modeling '98 Proceedings*, pp. 191-192.

[3] Olsen, D. R. Jr. and Neilsen, T., Laser pointer interaction, *CHI'2001*, pp.17-22.

[4] Chen, X. and Davis, J., LumiPoint: Multi-user laser-based interaction on large tiled displays, *graphics.Stanford.edu/papers/multiuser.*

[5] ISO, ISO/TC 159/SC4/WG3 N147: Ergonomic requirements for office work with visual display terminals (VDTs) - Part 9 - Requirements for non-keyboard input devices, *International Organisation for Standardisation*, May 25, 1998.

[6] Azuma, R. T., Predictive Tracking for Augmented Reality, *Ph.D. Dissertation*, University of North Carolina at Chapel Hill, NC, USA.

[7] MacKenzie, I. S., Jusoh, S., An evaluation of two input devices for remote pointing. *EHCI 2001*, Heidelberg, Germany: Springer-Verlag.

[8] Stewart, J., Bederson, B. and Druin, A., Single display groupware: a model for co-present collaboration, *CHI'99 Conference Proceedings*, pp. 286-293.

[9] Winograd, T. and Guimbretiere, F., Visual Instruments for an Interactive Mural, *CHI'99 Abstracts*, 234-235.

[10] Inkpen, K M., Ho-Ching, W., Kuederle, O., Scott, S., Shemaker, G. B.D., "This is fun! We're all best friends and we're all playing", Supporting Children's Synchronous Collaboration, *Proceedings of Computer Supported Collaborative Learning (CSCL) '99*. Dec. 1999. Stanford, CA.

[11] Streitz, N.A., Geißler, J., Holmer, T., Konomi, S., Müller-Tomfelde, C., Reischl, W., Rexroth, P., Seitz, P., and Steinmetz, R., i-LAND: An interactive Landscape for Creativity and Innovation, *CHI '99*, pp. 120-127.

[12] http://www.sciam.com/askexpert/medicine/medicine38/medicine38.html

[13] Smith, G., Salzman, T., Stuerzlinger, W., 3D Scene Manipulation with 2D Devices and Constraints, *Graphics Interface 2001*, pp. 135-142, June 2001.

Real-time Extendible-resolution Display of On-line Dynamic Terrain

Yefei He
National Advanced Driving Simulator
& Simulation Center
The University of Iowa

James Cremer
Computer Science Department
The University of Iowa

Yiannis Papelis
National Advanced Driving Simulator
& Simulation Center
The University of Iowa

Abstract

We present a method for multiresolution view-dependent real-time display of terrain undergoing on-line modification. In other words, the method does not assume static terrain geometry, nor does it assume that the terrain update sequence is known ahead of time. The method is both fast and space efficient. It is fast because it relies on local updates to the multiresolution structure as terrain changes. It is much more space efficient than many previous approaches because the multiresolution structure can be extended on-line, to provide higher resolution terrain only where needed. Our approach is especially well-suited for applications like real-time off-road driving simulation involving large terrain areas with localized high-resolution terrain updates.

Key words: dynamic terrain, triangle bintree, multiresolution representation, view-dependent mesh, level of detail

1 Introduction

Many techniques have been developed for representation and efficient visualization of terrains and other surfaces. In particular, the recent development of view-dependent multiresolution methods has provided a strong advance over distance-based discrete level-of-detail and other simple methods aimed at minimizing rendered polygons.

Existing methods focus either on static terrains or on time-varying geometry where all changes are known prior to any rendering. In this paper, we present methods for representation and real-time visualization of *on-line dynamic* terrain. In on-line dynamic terrain, surface geometry, color, and material properties can change over time and the particular changes are not known *a priori*; this precludes the preprocessing approaches of many techniques, which build a multiresolution structure that is dependent on the initial terrain geometry.

Specifically, our approach to view dependent visualization on-line dynamic terrain is:

- *fast.* The approach extends the ROAM[6] algorithm, and is fast because local terrain updates require only local updates to the multiresolution structure.
- *space efficient.* Through on-line extension of the multiresolution structure only where needed, dynamic terrain applications can save an enormous amount of space over methods that "prepare for the worst" everywhere (even if they never need it).

Figure 1: A screenshot from an off-road driving simulation application using our dynamic terrain algorithm.

We do not claim to have developed major new algorithmic results. But, we believe that support for online changes to geometry, color, and texture, represents an very important challenge for multiresolution methods, and that we have demonstrated useful practical early results in the area.

Our work was initially motivated by off-road driving simulation applications for The National Advanced Driving Simulator[23] — automobile and agricultural vehicle industry, as well as military, applications requiring real-time on-line simulation and visualization of vehicle-terrain interaction. Real-time determination of the effects of vehicle-terrain interaction, computed via tire-soil dynamics simulation, is a challenging computational problem. Furthermore, integration and correlation between very high resolution (non-visual) terrain databases required for tire-soil dynamics, and visual databases used for rendering is itself a challenging software systems issue (see [1]). In this paper, we address only the visualization of terrain changes determined through real-time tire-soil simulation or other processes.

2 Background and Related Work

Several good surveys on multiresolution surface representations exist, including Garland and Heckbert [7, 11], De Floriani et al. [5], Luebke [17], etc.

A multiresolution, or multiple level-of-detail (LOD), representation of a surface typically contains a sequence of approximations of the input surface, each with a different level of detail. These approximations are organized into a hierarchical structure, such as a DAG, a tree, or a forest, where the nodes represent parts of the approximations of various detail, with nodes closer to the top having lower detail. Edges relate parts from different approximations. In addition to the hierarchical structure, an *error metric* is also given, to use in measuring the deviation, or error, of approximation meshes in the hierarchy from the input surface. In some *view dependent* algorithms, screen-space error is used, which measures the size of the geometric approximation error projected onto the screen. The world space error, from which the screen-space error is derived, is view independent. During each iteration, the hierarchy is "trimmed" to get a single approximation of the surface that satisfies the error criteria.

Multiresolution surface representations can be classified as either vertex hierarchies or face hierarchies.

- Face hierarchy models (FHMs) are constructed to indicate the relation between the faces from approximations of different LODs. Existing algorithms based on face hierarchies include Lindstrom and Pascucci [16], Lindstrom et al. [15], Scarlatos and Pavlidis [20], de Berg and Dobrindt [2], Gross, Gatti and Staadt [9], De Floriani et al. [4], Duchaineau et al. [6], etc. A general face hierarchy model, *multi-triangulation*, was presented in De Floriani [3].

- Vertex hierarchy models (VHMs) are built from the relation between vertices from different approximations. Usually, each node of the hierarchy corresponds to a set of vertices, and the set of vertices denoted by the children of that node are the vertices used to replace them in a more refined approximation of the input surface. Error measures can be associated to each node in the hierarchy. Since vertices alone cannot determine the approximation, additional information about how the surface is polygonalized is required. Vertex hierarchy methods include Rossignac and Borrel [19], Luebke and Erikson [18], Hoppe [12, 13, 14], Xia and Varshney [24], and Garland and Heckbert [8].

Shamir, Pascucci and Bajaj [22] presented an approach for multiresolution dynamic surface visualization. Their method uses a DAG as the hierarchical structure and incrementally modifies the DAG as the surface deforms. The result is a super hierarchy, T-DAG, that combines the DAGs at all time-steps. T-DAG is capable of visualizing dynamic surfaces with arbitrary changes, including changes in topology and connectivity. The approach is not well suited for on-line updates due to the relatively high cost of T-DAG modification.

3 Real-time Visualization of Dynamic Terrain

As mentioned above, many terrain visualization algorithms rely on an assumption of static surface geometry to create, during a preprocessing step, a multiresolution structure from which efficient rendering may be done at run time. The assumption is invalid in on-line dynamic terrain applications,

To support on-line dynamic terrain, one must construct the hierarchical structure from the initial input surface and then modify it to reflect any changes made to the input surface. In some algorithms, such as Schroeder et al. [21] and Hoppe [12], the approximation sequence or multiresolution structure is constructed through an optimization process so that each approximation simplifies the previous mesh in the sequence while increasing the approximation error as little as possible. When applied to height fields, such a process can be called data-dependent simplification because the organization of the precomputed multiresolution depends on the heights of the vertices. In data-dependent approaches, structure updates to account for terrain changes are generally quite costly.

In data-independent approaches, only the (x, y) values of the vertices affect the organization of the multiresolution structure. For example, sub-sampling a regular grid mesh is a data-independent process. Data-independent approaches are thus good for on-line dynamic terrain based on height fields; terrain updates do not necessitate multiresolution structure reorganization. The block-based face quadtree method presented in Lindstrom et al. [15] and the ROAM algorithm in Duchaineau et al. [6], both use data-independent hierarchies.

In the following section, we present the general idea of extendible resolution terrain representation. Sections 5 and 6 then present the details of our dynamic terrain representation and visualization approach.

4 DEXTER: Dynamic EXTEnsion of Resolution

The methods described in Section 2 pre-construct hierarchies from which meshes of various detail level can be derived at run time. Even in view dependent methods, the hierarchy itself is fixed, and the highest detail available to approximate any part of the surface is pre-determined.

In on-line dynamic terrain applications, greater interest may be put on the deformed regions, requiring higher resolution there than on untouched regions. In some cases, the particular maximum deformed resolution requirement may be known ahead of time. But, terrain deformation is often sparse and the precise location and degree of the deformation is not known until run time. A preconstructed "prepared for the worst" hierarchy that represents, everywhere in the terrain, the high resolution required by potential terrain modifications, can be prohibitively and unnecessarily space inefficient. When only a small portion of terrain will be modified, additional levels of the hierarchy in regions of untouched terrain waste memory that could better be used to represent important areas of dynamic modification in even better detail.

Thus, instead of a fixed-hierarchy, we use a dynamically extendible hierarchy for multiresolution terrain representation. The initial hierarchy is created so that it satisfies the resolution requirement of the initial non-deformed terrain. The finest mesh constructed from the hierarchy may have different detail at different parts of the terrain, depending on the local ruggedness of the initial terrain and other attributes such as the variation in color and texture, etc. The hierarchy is not fixed, however; as terrain deformation takes place, the hierarchy is extended only where necessary. The dynamic extension of resolution provides additional levels of detail at the modified regions without wasting memory space representing untouched terrain at unnecessarily high resolution.

DEXTER is a simple but general idea that can be applied to enhance many multiresolution surface representation methods. For different methods, there are different issues that need to be addressed in order to use DEXTER. In this paper, we demonstrate the necessary modifications for our real-time ROAM-based terrain visualization method.

5 Dynamic Terrain Extension to ROAM

A uniformly spaced, axis-aligned grid of terrain posts is a compact and efficient way of representing terrain surfaces. This grid is the foundation of the hierarchical structure built for the purpose of a multiple level-of-detail representation. Every grid point can be used as a vertex in the mesh that approximates the terrain surface. The finest approximation mesh is obtained when all the grid points are present in the mesh. All the elements that make up that mesh are considered to have zero approximation error.

The ROAM algorithm is well suited for the task of real-time visualization of terrain surfaces represented by a regular grid. In order to use ROAM for dynamic terrain visualization, two extensions of the algorithm were carried out. First, necessary updates of mesh data are added in each iteration to reflect the deformation of the terrain. Second, run-time extension of the hierarchical structure, i.e. the DEXTER augmentation, is incorporated into the algorithm. In this section we present the basic dynamic terrain extension to ROAM. In Section 6 we present the modification to the terrain grid representation and to the ROAM algorithm in order to incorporate DEXTER.

5.1 A Brief Review of ROAM

Real-time Optimally Adapting Meshes (ROAM), first presented by Duchaineau et al. [6], is a terrain visualization algorithm that adaptively generates right isosceles triangle meshes to render the underlying regular terrain grid.

The hierarchical structure of ROAM is a binary tree of right isosceles triangles, which is established during the preprocessing stage. Each non-leaf triangle has two children, obtained by splitting the triangle with an edge that links its apex vertex to the midpoint of its base edge. Figure 2 shows how a bintree of four levels is formed by recursively splitting the triangles of higher levels. The root triangle (v_a, v_0, v_1) has a midpoint v_m at its base edge, and its two children, (v_m, v_a, v_0) and (v_m, v_1, v_a), are called its left child and right child, respectively.

To represent a square region, a pair of triangle bintrees is needed. The two root triangles (a *diamond* in ROAM terminology) should be of the same size, and share the base edge.

As in other hierarchical models, a trimming of the tree is required to obtain a mesh representation of the terrain. A view-dependent error metric is used as the criterion for trimming. During each frame, the trimming result from the previous frame is adjusted by moving the trim line further down toward the leaf nodes at some places and up toward the root at some others. Intuitively, some triangles in the previous mesh are replaced by its descendents in the bintree, and some others are replaced by their an-

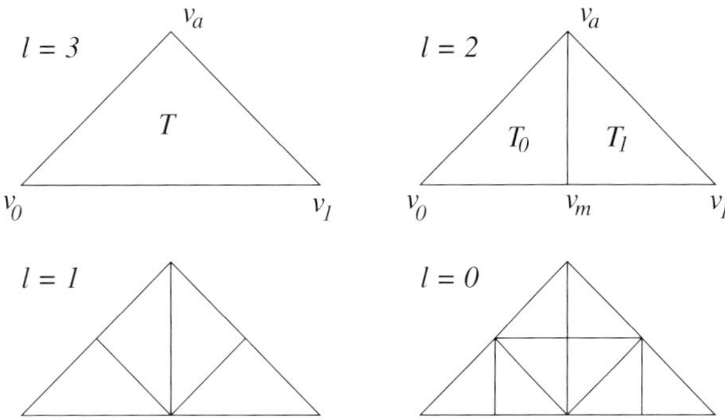

Figure 2: A triangle bintree of four levels.

cestors. Such adjustments are achieved by a sequence of *split* and *merge* operations on triangles. A *split* operation replaces a triangle with its two children in the bintree, while a *merge* operation replaces two siblings in the bintree with their parent. Figure 3 shows the effects of *split* and *merge* in aspects of both triangulation and trimming of the bintree. It is clear that a *split* is the reversal of a *merge*, and vice versa.

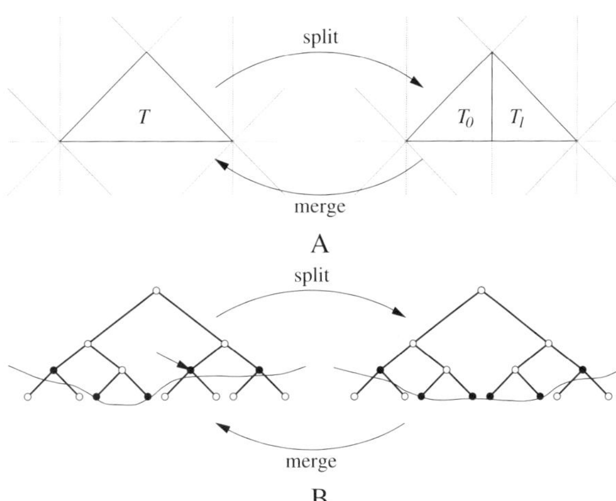

Figure 3: split *and* merge *operations: A. effects on triangle mesh; B. effects on triangle bintree trimming. Solid nodes in B represent the triangles selected for the approximation mesh.*

ROAM-based visualization is free of "crack" problems; mesh continuity is maintained by keeping track of the neighbors of each triangle, executing appropriate recursive *split* and *merge* operations.

5.2 Dynamic Terrain ROAM

The ROAM algorithm uses a pair of triangle bintrees as its data-independent hierarchy. Therefore, the basic structure of the bintrees does not need to be altered when the terrain is modified. However, the world space errors of the mesh elements – the triangles – need to be updated during each iteration. In the original ROAM algorithm, the computation of the world space errors is done in a bottom-up fashion. Therefore their updating needs to be performed bottom-up as well. Although the world space errors are associated to triangles, not vertices, they are derived from the geometry of the vertices. Which triangles are affected can be easily determined by checking which vertices have been modified. Update flags are therefore added to the data structure for the vertices, but not to that for the triangles. During the error updating procedure, the errors of leaf triangles remain zero, but leaf triangles with modified vertices need to notify their parents, whose errors need to be recomputed. This notification is passed on until the root triangles, and the error of every notified triangle is recomputed. Details of world- and screen-space error management for our algorithm are given in [10].

The vertices of the mesh triangles also need to be updated, e.g. the change of elevation, etc. In our implementation, the vertices are posts in the terrain cells (see Section 6.1), and the triangles in the bintrees use pointers to refer to them. Therefore by updating the posts, the vertices of the mesh triangles are automatically updated as well.

6 DEXTER Extension to ROAM

ROAM uses regular terrain grid as the basis of its triangle bintree structure. In order to accommodate DEXTER, the terrain grid representation needs to be modified. We introduce *terrain cells* to enhance the grid representation, and then discuss transition zones required to maintain mesh continuity after local extensions to the mesh hierarchy.

6.1 Terrain Cells

Starting from a uniform-resolution regular terrain grid, we can modify it to accommodate DEXTER. DEXTER allows the resolution to be extended at the deformed region of the terrain, therefore the grid resolution across the terrain may become non-uniform after such extensions. We divide the terrain surface into patches, each allowed to have its own grid resolution. To make the algorithm efficient, we restrict the shape of the patches to axis-aligned rectangles. We call these rectangles *cells*. The data structure for a cell should include its location, size, and grid resolution. The uniform resolution terrain grid can be considered as a special case – a grid with a single cell.

To extend the resolution of the terrain representation at designated regions, new cells that contain a terrain grid with desired resolution are created to cover those regions. Newly created cells overlap existing lower resolution cells, and consistency must be maintained among terrain posts common to multiple cells. The properties of the new grid posts can be obtained from the input surface. If the input surface is simply represented by the initial terrain grid, an interpolation on that initial grid can be performed to get the properties for the new posts.

In our implementation, the terrain is initially represented by a single cell that covers the complete region. As terrain deformation takes place, new cells with higher grid resolution are created dynamically to cover the modified regions. The dynamic cells are all aligned to a cell grid and have uniform sizes. Furthermore, in the implementation demonstrated in this paper, the dynamic cells all have the same grid resolution. The grid resolution of dynamic cells is that of the initial cell times a user-specifiable power of two, so that the hierarchical structure in ROAM – the triangle bintrees – can be extended accordingly, which uses the grid posts of the cells as the vertices of the mesh triangles. Figure 4 shows a dynamic cell that doubles the initial grid resolution partially overlapping the initial terrain cell. The dynamic cells can be organized using a simple two-dimensional array.

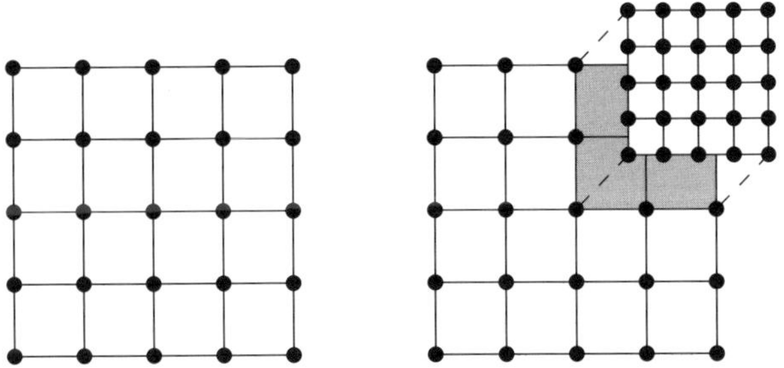

Figure 4: A dynamic cell overlaps the top right quadrant of the initial terrain cell.

The grid resolution may be increased by different amounts at different places. Different kinds of terrain modifiers produce shapes of various details. For example, footprints and tire tracks might require higher resolution representation than bulldozer tracks. This is easily supported - terrain cells form a hierarchy of multiple levels, where a dynamic cell may be partially coveredy by further even-high-resolution dynamic cells - but was not included in the implementation demonstrated on the accompanying video.

6.2 Extending ROAM's Mesh Hierarchy

As mentioned in Section 6.1, the triangle bintrees in ROAM are tightly associated with the terrain cells. As dynamic cells with a high grid resolution are created, the triangle bintrees are extended accordingly. The extension is achieved by recursively subdividing the leaf triangles of the initial bintrees whose areas of coverage are inside the area covered by the newly created cells. The number of levels of triangles that should be added to the bintrees are determined by the extent to which the grid resolution is increased via dynamic terrain cells. Suppose the grid resolution of the dynamic cells is 2^n times the initial resolution, then $2n$ levels of triangles should be added. Figure 5 shows the creation of a dynamic terrain cell matched by the extension of the triangle bintrees.

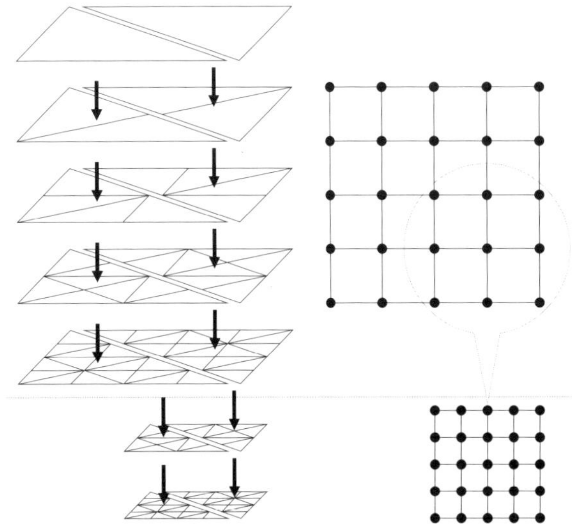

Figure 5: A 5×5 initial terrain grid is matched by a pair of triangle bintrees with 5 levels. The creation of a dynamic cell that doubles the grid resolution leads to the extension of the bintrees by 2 levels.

6.3 Transition Zones

After extending the mesh hierarchy, the triangle bintrees are no longer complete binary trees (except in the special case where the mesh was extended over the whole terrain). There are more levels of approximation available for the regions covered by triangles added to the bintrees at run time than for the rest of the terrain. This could cause problems in mesh continuity, as shown in Figure 6, where the mesh contains cracks around the two circled vertices. Here, the error criteria determine that triangles from newly added levels are needed to approximate the top left quadrant, but no triangles outside that quadrant can match them.

To preclude mesh discontinuities, *transition zones* are introduced. Given terrain region $\mathcal{R}_1$, where the highest grid resolution among all terrain cells that cover it is δ_1, and an adjacent region $\mathcal{R}_2$, whose highest grid resolution is δ_2, a transition zone is defined along the boundary between $\mathcal{R}_1$ and $\mathcal{R}_2$, in $\mathcal{R}_2$, if $\delta_1 > \delta_2$ and the higher

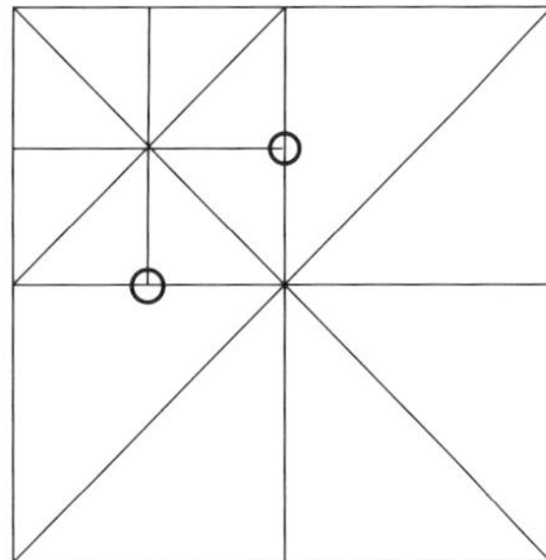

Figure 6: Mesh discontinuity caused by high level-of-detail mesh patches that cannot be matched elsewhere.

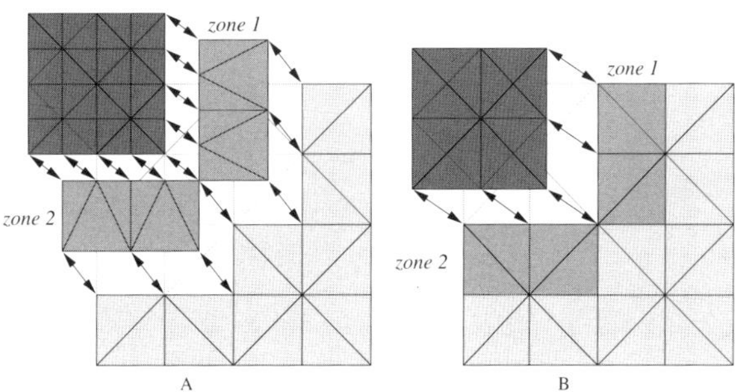

Figure 7: Possible transition zones between regions of different resolutions. Note that although they do preserve continuity, they use special non-right-triangles, and are not the form of triangulation used in our algorithm.

resolution $\mathcal{R}_1$ meshes cannot be matched by $\mathcal{R}_2$ meshes. This transition zone offers the basis for constructing special mesh patches that will match the higher resolution meshes for $\mathcal{R}_1$ with the highest resolution mesh available for $\mathcal{R}_2$. The transition zone needs to have the same high resolution as $\mathcal{R}_1$. In essence, the transition zone is the expansion of $\mathcal{R}_1$, and a simple way to do it is to expand the highest resolution cell that covers $\mathcal{R}_1$ to cover the transition zone as well, and at the same time expand the higher resolution meshes to include the special matching patches for the transition zone. In Figure 7, the top left quadrant of the terrain is of higher resolution than the rest, and two more levels of mesh are available there. Two transition zones are assigned outside the top left quadrant. In this particular case, a special mesh is necessary only to match the highest LOD mesh in the top left quadrant with the highest LOD mesh elsewhere, as shown in Figure 7.A; the second highest LOD mesh in the top left quadrant matches the highest LOD mesh outside perfectly, as in Figure 7.B. The result is, the highest LOD mesh for the top left quadrant is expanded to cover the transition zone, while the second highest LOD mesh is not.

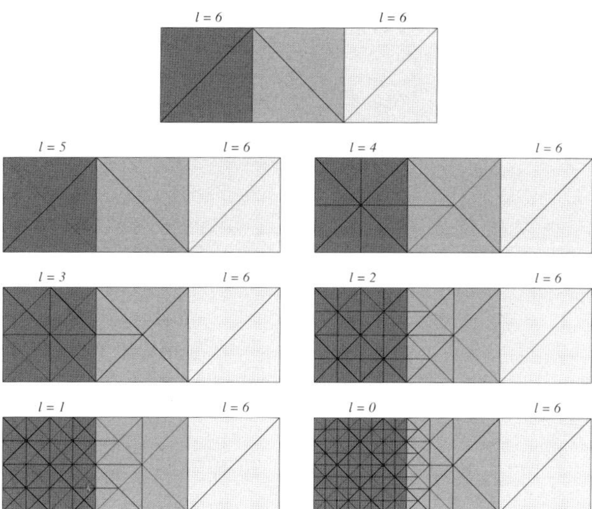

Figure 8: The high resolution meshes of six new levels of detail in the darkest region, from level 0 to level 5, are connected to the mesh in the lightest region with help from the meshes in the transition zone.

The transition zones shown in Figure 7 contain triangles that are not right isosceles triangles; this is not the way we prefer to extend ROAM. Instead, the special transition zone meshes can be constructed in the same fashion as the newly added high resolution mesh patches.

Consider the example shown in Figure 8. The six triangles in the first mesh of the sequence are from the lowest level mesh of an initial mesh hierarchy. They form three diamonds. The region covered by the leftmost diamond is now deformed, and its grid resolution is extended to be 2^3 times the original, thus introducing 6 new levels of detail in the triangle bintree. These 6 levels of detail are not available at the rightmost diamond. But as we can see, if we assign the region covered by the middle diamond as the transition zone, and extend it too by six levels, mesh continuity can be maintained no matter which of the six newly added levels of detail is used to approximate the region covered by the leftmost diamond. Not all triangles in the six levels of meshes in the transition zone are needed to maintain mesh continuity. However, it is simpler to extend the bintree fully there as well. Besides, it is likely that the transition zone will become a high resolution zone later and require the full expansion.

One may observe that in the above example the transition zone is made of just one pair of leaf triangles from the original bintree. In fact, if the resolution is extended by 2^n times, no matter how large n is, the transition zone always only needs to be as wide as a diamond made of a pair of original leaf triangles. Figure 8 shows the case for $n = 3$. The case for $n = 1$ is just the first three meshes;

$n = 2$, the first five. To prove the claim for any n, use mathematical induction. The claim is true for $n = 1$ as demonstrated in Figure 8. Assume the claim is true for $n = k$. For $n = k + 1$, extend the bintree by two more levels in the transition zone than in the case of $n = k$ to match the high resolution region. Next construct a mesh in the transition zone that connects the level 2 mesh in the high resolution region with the lowest level mesh available in the low resolution region. Here, that level is 2^{k+1}. The mesh detail near the boundary between the high resolution region and the transition zone is shown in Figure 9.A. Now split triangles T_1, T_2 and their base neighbors, and we get the mesh in Figure 9.B, which remains continuous. One can now notice that the highlighted region has the same configuration as the first graph in Figure 8, and edge (a, b) corresponds to the boundary between the transition zone and the low resolution region in Figure 8. Lowering the mesh level in the high resolution region to 1 and 0 are just like the second and third meshes in Figure 8, as shown in Figure 9.C and Figure 9.D. In both cases, in order to maintain mesh continuity, the refinement of the mesh in the transition zone can be limited to the left of (a, b). Therefore, the transition zone for $n = k$ is also sufficient for $n = k + 1$.

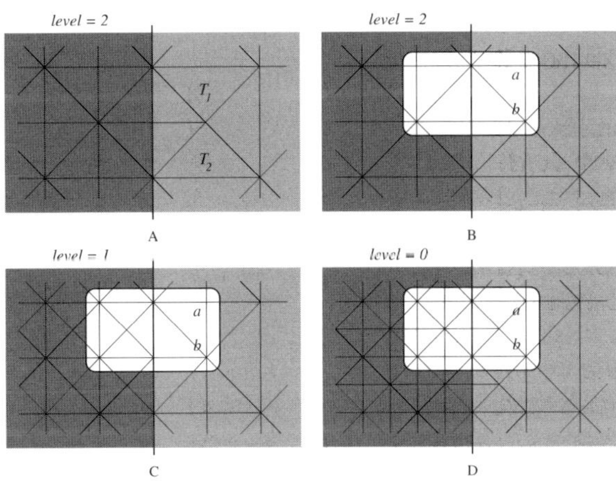

Figure 9: Mesh details near the boundary between the high resolution region on the left and the transition zone on the right.

Since transition zones surround a rectangular region, some occur at corners. These yield different transition trianglations but are still handled easily (see [10] for details).

Note that no special code needs to be implemented for the transition zones. The zones' high resolution combined with error values of zero ensure that the proper transition triangulation will be created as a natural part of the trimming process.

6.4 Updating Triangle Errors

World space errors need to be assigned to triangles added due to bintree extension. The errors of existing triangles can change when the underlying grid resolution is increased and the triangle bintrees extended. Most significantly, some leaf triangles in the initial bintrees now have descendents, so they are no longer part of the finest mesh available, and their errors are generally no longer zero. So, the errors of affected triangles need to be recomputed after hierarchy extension. A bottom-up approach is adopted, similar to the way the world space errors are computed during initialization.

New higher-resolution triangles in transition zones simply have zero error, since the terrain has not been (yet) been modified and the original coarser triangles still have zero error. Some of the high resolution triangles will ultimately be selected into a displayed mesh based not on their error values but because of the component of the algorithm that maintains mesh continuity.

6.5 DEXTER Algorithm Outline

Following is a general multiple LOD dynamic terrain visualization algorithm with DEXTER, applicable to all DEXTER methods that use terrain cells and transition zones[1].

```
   begin
1.    Initialize terrain cells
2.    Initialize mesh hierarchy
3.    while no exit signal do
      begin
4.       deform terrain
5.       add high resolution cells to deformed regions
           if necessary
6.       assign transition zones around new cells
7.       update mesh hierarchy, recompute errors
8.       trim mesh hierarchy to obtain approximation
           mesh for the complete terrain
9.       render the approximation mesh
      end
   end
```

7 Implementation Results

The accompanying video shows DEXTER with ROAM running smoothly in real time on an 866MHz Pentium III with a GeForce2 graphics card and 384MB of RAM. Figures 10, 11, 12, and 13 show screenshots from the same application.

[1]Some multiple LOD terrain visualization methods do not require terrain cells or transition zones when extended with DEXTER, e.g certain methods that do not use regular grids or vertex hierarchy methods that perform triangulation at run time.

The algorithm was implemented as a research prototype with no code tuning or low-level code optimization. Some basic timing results are included in the following paragraphs. The results were recorded from identical 1800 frame portions from the middle of runs using the same vehicle path and scene shown in the video. The error tolerance, τ, was .04 in each case. The terrain for the test runs is perfectly flat at the start. Thus, no loss of detail occurs in representation of the initial unmodified terrain, eliminating differences in the number of triangles that would result from different basic terrain grid sampling resolutions for the regular ROAM and the DEXTER version. Note that the average frame rates include significant non-visualization-related simulation time.

Run 1: ROAM without DEXTER

.

The grid size was 513-by-513, so the finest mesh consists of $512*512*2 = 524,288$ triangles, while the triangle hierarchy has $2+4+8+...+524,288 = 1,048,574$ triangles.

```
Error threshold tau = 0.04
Total time:                         51.47s
 - rendering:                       25.92s
 - DT rep. and error update:        11.43s
 - vehicle/soil simulation:         14.12s
Avg. tri count:                 4140
Avg. frame rate:                35.0
```

Run 2: ROAM with DEXTER

.

The initial grid size was 129-by-129, and the maximum grid size, through DEXTER, was 513-by-513, the same as in Run 1 without DEXTER. In this case, however the initial hierarchy has only $2+4+8+...+128*128*2 = 65,534$ triangles, $1/16th$ that of Run 1.

```
Error threshold tau = 0.04
Total time:                         52.18s
 - rendering:                       25.45s
 - DT rep. and error update:        10.61s
 - vehicle/soil simulation:         16.12s
Avg. tri count:                 4131
Subtrees created:               2186
Avg. frame rate:                34.5
```

2186 subtrees created means a total of $2186 * 30 = 65,580$ triangles were added to the hierarchy, leaving the final total to be $65,534 + 65,580 = 131,114$. Compare this to $1,048,574$ in ROAM without DEXTER.

The two runs result in nearly identical visual appearances, and the triangle counts are also very close. This is expected because the resolution of the regular ROAM and the maximum resolution of the DEXTER version are the same, and the same error threshold is used. The frame rates are also very similar, which means the extra work on the DEXTER version only accounts for a small portion of the total computation.

Run3: ROAM with DEXTER

.

In this run the initial grid size was again 129-by-129. However, the maximum grid size is increased to 1025-by-1025. The error threshold is kept at 0.04.

```
Error threshold tau = 0.04
Total time:                         86.65s
 - rendering:                       49.47s
 - DT rep. and error update:        22.51s
 - vehicle/soil simulation:         14.67s
Avg. tri count:                 9681
subtrees created:               2186
Avg. frame rate:                20.8
```

As expected, the triangle count increases and the frame rate drops, when compared to the previous two runs. But the detail available in the tire tracks is much higher because highest resolution triangles are smaller than before, and are therefore better equipped to represent the curves along the tracks. The number of subtrees created was the same as in Run 2 because the vehicle path is identical. The subtrees are taller than in Run 2, though, so a total of $21,886 * 126 = 275,436$ triangles were added. Still, the final total of $65,534 + 275,436 = 340,970$ is much smaller than Runs 1's 1,048,754. And, the maximum resolution of the grid is four times higher. The test runs clearly exemplify significant reduction in data size without a large speed penalty.

8 Conclusion and Continuing Work

We described methods that enable practical real-time visualization of on-line dynamic terrain. Our approach provides multiresolution view-dependent representation and display of dynamic terrain by extending ROAM with efficient hierarchy updates as terrain deforms, and using DEXTER to provide only-where-needed memory efficient resolution extension.

This paper directly addressed only the geometric aspects of dynamic terrain. Interesting additional research problems remain in dynamic terrain representation and visualization, particularly related to color and texture issues. Error measures in view-dependent multiresolution techniques have largely concentrated on geometric error, but can account for color and texture as well. Like the situation with geometry, however, they are more difficult to handle (and perhaps even more important) in a dynamic terrain setting. Some possible solutions and additional research directions are discussed in He[10].

It is clear that our approach is quite effective for applications, such as off-road driving simulation, that require only small localized terrain updates. We have not yet carefully assessed the method's practical effectiveness for applications involving larger deformations of more extensive terrain areas.

Acknowledgements

This work was supported in part by Automotive Research Center Contract Number DAAE07-98-3-0022.

References

[1] J. Cremer, Y. He, and Y. Papelis. Dynamic terrain for real-time ground vehicle simulation. In *Proceedings of the Image 2000 Conference*, pages 98–105, July 2000.

[2] M. de Berg and K. T. G. Dobrindt. On levels of detail in terrains. Technical Report UU-CS-1995-12, Department of Computer Science, Utrecht University, 1995.

[3] L. De Floriani. A pyramidal data structure for triangle-based surface description. *IEEE Computer Graphics and Applications*, 9(2):67–78, March 1989.

[4] L. De Floriani, P. Magillo, and E. Puppo. Efficient implementation of Multi-Triangulations. In *Proceedings IEEE Visualization '98*, October 1998.

[5] L. De Floriani, P. Marzano, and E. Puppo. Multiresolution models for topographic surface description. *The Visual Computer*, 12(7):317–345, August 1996.

[6] M. Duchaineau, M. Wolinsky, D. E. Sigeti, M. C. Miller, C. Aldrich, and M. B. Mineev-Weinstein. ROAMing terrain: real-time optimally adapting meshes. In *Proceedings IEEE Visualization '97*, pages 81–88, 1997.

[7] M. Garland and P. S. Heckbert. Fast polygonal approximation of terrains and height fields. Technical Report CMU-CS 95-181, Department of Computer Science, Carnegie Mellon University, 1995.

[8] M. Garland and P. S. Heckbert. Surface simplification using quadric error metrics. *Computer Graphics (SIGGRAPH '97 Proceedings)*, pages 209–216, 1997.

[9] M. H. Gross, R. Gatti, and O. Staadt. Fast multiresolution surface meshing. In *Proceedings IEEE Visualization '95*, July 1995.

[10] Y. He. *Real-time visualization of dynamic terrain for ground vehicle simulation*. PhD thesis, The University of Iowa, December 2000.

[11] P. S. Heckbert and M. Garland. Survey of polygonal surface simplification algorithms. In *Multiresolution surface modeling (SIGGRAPH '97 Course notes #25)*. ACM SIGGRAPH, 1997.

[12] H. Hoppe. Progressive meshes. *Computer Graphics (SIGGRAPH '96 Proceedings)*, pages 99–108, 1996.

[13] H. Hoppe. View-dependent refinement of progressive meshes. *Computer Graphics (SIGGRAPH '97 Proceedings)*, pages 189–198, 1997.

[14] H. Hoppe. Smooth view-dependent level-of-detail control and its application to terrain rendering. In *Proceedings IEEE Visualization '98*, October 1998.

[15] P. Lindstrom, D. Koller, W. Ribarsky, L. Hodges, N. Faust, and G. Turner. Real-time, continuous level of detail rendering of height fields. *Computer Graphics (SIGGRAPH '96 Proceedings)*, pages 109–118, 1996.

[16] P. Lindstrom and V. Pascucci. Visualization of large terrains made easy. In *Proceedings IEEE Visualization '01*, pages 363–370, October 2001.

[17] D. Luebke. A survey of polygonal simplification algorithms. Technical Report TR97-045, Department of Computer Science, University of North Carolina at Chapel Hill, 1997.

[18] D. Luebke and C. Erikson. View-dependent simplification of arbitrary polygonal environments. *Computer Graphics (SIGGRAPH '97 Proceedings)*, pages 199–208, 1997.

[19] J. Rossignac and P. Borrel. Multi-resolution 3D approximations for rendering complex scenes. In B. Falcidieno and T. Kunii, editors, *Modeling in Computer Graphics: Methods and Applications*, pages 455–465. Springer-Verlag, Berlin, 1993.

[20] L. Scarlatos and T. Pavlidis. Hierarchical triangulation using cartographic coherence. *CVGIP: Graphical Models and Image Processing*, 54(2):147–161, March 1992.

[21] W. J. Schroeder, J. A. Zarge, and W. E. Lorensen. Decimation of triangle meshes. *Computer Graphics*, 26(2):65–70, July 1992.

[22] A. Shamir, V. Pascucci, and C. Bajaj. Multiresolution dynamic meshes with arbitrary deformations. In *Proceedings IEEE Visualization '00*, pages 423–430, October 2000.

[23] The National Advanced Driving Simulator. URL: http://www.nads-sc.uiowa.edu.

[24] J. Xia and A. Varshney. A dynamic view-dependent simplification for polygonal models. In *Proceedings IEEE Visualization '96*, pages 327–334, 1996.

Figure 10: ROAM without DEXTER. Resolution 513×513, on $44m \times 44m$ square region.

Figure 12: ROAM with DEXTER. Basic resolution 129×129, extended 2049×2049, on $44m \times 44m$ square region.

Figure 11: ROAM with DEXTER. Basic resolution 129×129, extended 2049×2049, on $44m \times 44m$ square region.

Figure 13: ROAM with DEXTER. The triangles shown in yellow are from cells added to extend the initial hierarchy.

Compressing Polygon Mesh Connectivity with Degree Duality Prediction

Martin Isenburg
University of North Carolina at Chapel Hill
isenburg@cs.unc.edu

Abstract

In this paper we present a coder for polygon mesh connectivity that delivers the best connectivity compression rates meshes reported so far. Our coder is an extension of the vertex-based coder for triangle mesh connectivity by Touma and Gotsman [26]. We code polygonal connectivity as a sequence of face and vertex degrees and exploit the correlation between them for mutual predictive compression. Because low-degree vertices are likely to be surrounded by high-degree faces and vice versa, we predict vertex degrees based on neighboring face degrees and face degrees based on neighboring vertex degrees.

Key words: Connectivity coding, graph coding, mesh compression, non-manifold meshes, degree duality.

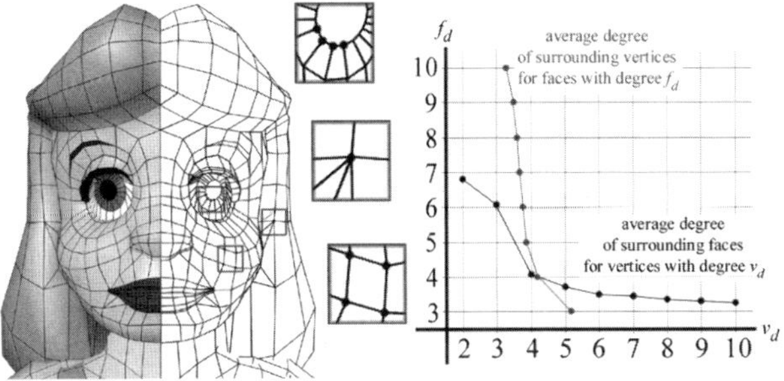

Figure 1: On the left is a close-up of the cupie mesh. Notice that low-degree vertices are likely to be surrounded by high-degree faces and vice-versa. On the right are two plots confirming this. They report the average degree of surrounding faces (vertices) for vertices (faces) of degree d for our example models.

1 Introduction

A polygon mesh is the most widely used primitive for representing three-dimensional geometric models. Such polygon meshes consists of mesh *geometry* and mesh *connectivity*, the first describing the positions in 3D space and the latter describing how to connect these positions together to form polygons that describe a surface. Typically there are also mesh *properties* such as texture coordinates, material attributes, etc. that describe the visual appearance of the mesh at rendering time.

The standard representation of a polygon mesh uses an array of floats to specify the positions and an array of integers containing indices into the position array to specify the polygons. A similar scheme is used to specify the various properties and how they are attached to the mesh. For large and detailed models this representation results in files of substantial size, which makes their storage expensive and their transmission slow.

The need for more compact representations has motivated researchers to develop efficient mesh compression techniques. Most of these efforts have focused on connectivity compression [4, 25, 26, 21, 9, 22, 18, 11, 3, 12, 19, 23, 1]. There are two reasons for this: First, this is where the largest gains are possible, and second, the connectivity coder is the core component of a compression engine and usually drives the compression of geometry [4, 25, 26, 15], of properties [4, 24, 3], and of how properties are attached to the mesh [24, 12, 13].

In this paper we introduce a connectivity coder for polygon meshes that achieves the best compression rates reported so far. Our *Degree Duality coder* extends Touma and Gotsman's triangle mesh compression scheme [26] to polygon meshes and borrows ideas from a paper by Alliez and Desbrun [1] to improve the compression rates. The scheme by Touma and Gotsman codes the connectivity of triangle meshes as a sequence of vertex degrees. Our scheme codes the connectivity of polygon meshes as a sequence of vertex degrees *and* a sequence of face degrees. Furthermore it exploits the correlation between neighboring vertex and face degrees for mutual predictive compression. Low degree vertices are more likely to be surrounded by higher-degree faces and vice versa as illustrated in Figure 1. We predict vertex degrees based on the degree of neighboring faces and we predict face degrees based on the degree of neighboring vertices[1].

2 Coding Mesh Connectivity

Representing the connectivity of a mesh with a list of position indices requires at least $kn \log_2 n$ bits, where n is the total number of positions and k is the average number of times each position is indexed. For pure triangular

[1]A similar coder was developed independently and during the same time period by a group of researchers at CalTech and USC [17].

meshes, k tends to be around 6, while for polygon meshes is closer to 4. The problem with this representation is that the space requirement increases super-linearly with the number of positions, since $\log_2 n$ bits are needed to index a position in an array of n positions.

Efficiently encoding mesh connectivity has been subject of intense research and many techniques have been proposed. Initially most of these schemes were designed for fully triangulated meshes [4, 25, 26, 21, 9, 22, 11, 23, 1], but more recent approaches [18, 12, 19, 17] handle arbitrary polygonal input. These schemes do not attempt to code the position indices directly—instead they only code the *connectivity graph* of the mesh.

If a polygon mesh is *manifold*, then every face (i.e. every edge loop) of its connectivity graph corresponds either to a polygon or a hole. Furthermore, every vertex of the graph has a corresponding position in 3D space. This implies that for representing mesh connectivity, it is sufficient to specify (a) the connectivity graph of the mesh and (b) which of its faces are polygons/holes. The mapping from graph vertices to positions can be established with an order derived from the graph connectivity.

Hence, mesh connectivity is compressed by coding the connectivity graph (plus some additional information to distinguish polygons from holes) *and* by changing the order in which the positions are stored. They are arranged in the order in which their corresponding graph vertex is encountered during some deterministic graph traversal. Since encoding and decoding of the connectivity graph also requires a traversal, the positions are often reordered as dictated by this encoding/decoding process.

This basically reduces the number of bits needed for storing mesh connectivity to whatever is required to code the connectivity graph. This is good news: the connectivity graph of a polygon mesh with sphere topology is homeomorphic to a planar graph. It well known that such graphs can be coded with a constant number of bits per vertex [27] and exact enumerations exist [28, 29]. If a polygon meshes has handles (i.e. has non-zero genus) its connectivity graph is not planar. Coding such a graph adds a logarithmic number of bits per handle [22], but most meshes have only a very small number of handles.

Unfortunately only the connectivity of manifold polygon meshes can be coded this way. A mesh is *manifold* if all vertices of its connectivity graph have a neighborhood homeomorphic to a disk or a half-disk. Polygonal models that describe solid objects tend to have this property. However, when generated from other surface representations (e.g. trimmed NURBS) non-manifoldness is often introduced by mistake. Also hand-authored content is frequently non-manifold, especially if the artist tried to optimize the mesh (e.g. minimize its polygon count).

Optimally coding non-manifold graphs directly is hard and there are no efficient solutions yet. Most schemes either require the input mesh to be manifold or use a preprocessing step that cuts non-manifold meshes into manifold pieces [7]. A notable exception is the layering scheme proposed by Bajaj et al. [3], but this seems quite complicated to implement. Cutting a non-manifold mesh replicates all vertices that sit along a cut. Since it is generally not acceptable to modify a mesh during compression, the coder needs to describe how to stitch the mesh pieces back together. Guéziec et al. [6] report how to do this in an efficient manner. Our Degree Duality coder implements a much simpler stitching scheme at the expense of less compression. For typical meshes with few replicated vertices the use of a simpler scheme is sufficient.

3 Coding Manifold Connectivity Graphs

A planar graph with v vertices, f faces, and e edges can be partitioned into two dual spanning trees. One tree spans the vertices and has $v - 1$ edges, while its dual spans the faces and has $f - 1$ edges. Summing these edge counts results in Euler's relation $e = (v-1)+(f-1)$ for planar graphs. Turan [27] observed that this partition can be used to encode planar graphs. He gave an encoding that used 12 bits per vertex (bpv). Improving on Turan's work, Keeler and Westbrook report a 9.0 bpv encoding for planar graphs, which they can specialize to a 4.6 bpv encoding if the graph is fully triangulated [16].

Taubin and Rossignac were first to use these graph coding techniques for compressing the connectivity of triangle meshes. Their Topological Surgery [25] method run-length encodes both spanning trees and adds a few bits per handle for non-planar connectivity graphs, which results in bit-rates of around 4 bpv in practice.

All recent connectivity compression schemes [26, 9, 21, 22, 5, 12, 19] code this information by following the same *region growing* approach: An iterative process encodes edges/faces adjacent to the already processed region (one at a time) and produces a stream of symbols that describe (a) the degree of each processed face and (b) the adjacency relation between a processed edge/face to the processed region. These schemes maintain one or several boundary loops that separate a single processed region from all unprocessed regions. The edges and vertices on the boundary are called *boundary edges* and *boundary vertices* and they are considered *visited*. Each boundary encloses an unprocessed region. The edges, faces, and vertices of this region are called *unprocessed*. If the connectivity graph has handles, then boundaries can be nested, in which case an unprocessed region is enclosed by more than one boundary. Each boundary has a distinguished edge called the *focus*. The algorithm works on

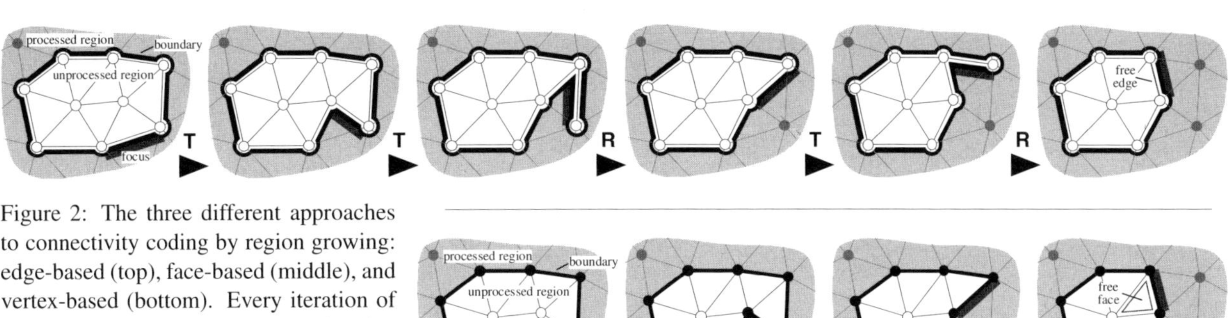

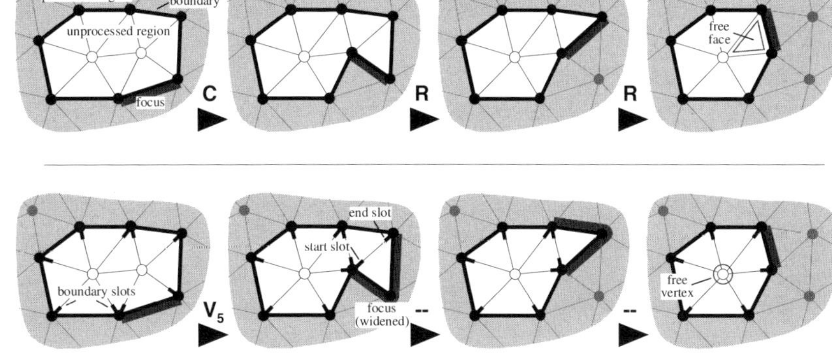

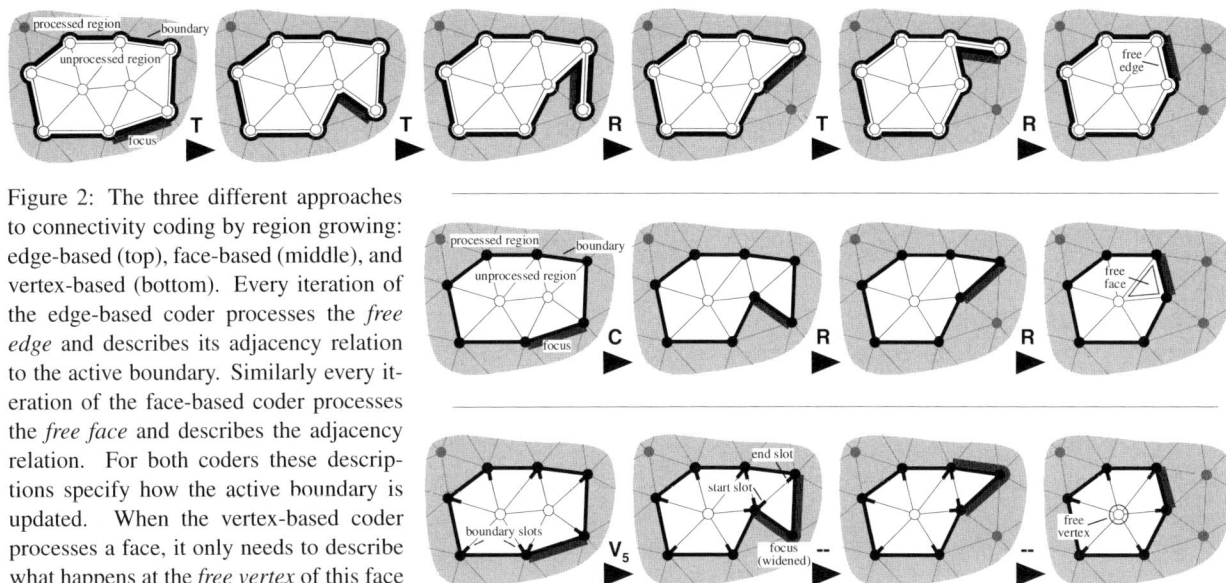

Figure 2: The three different approaches to connectivity coding by region growing: edge-based (top), face-based (middle), and vertex-based (bottom). Every iteration of the edge-based coder processes the *free edge* and describes its adjacency relation to the active boundary. Similarly every iteration of the face-based coder processes the *free face* and describes the adjacency relation. For both coders these descriptions specify how the active boundary is updated. When the vertex-based coder processes a face, it only needs to describe what happens at the *free vertex* of this face to specify the boundary update.

the focus of the *active boundary*, while all other boundaries are kept in a stack.

The adjacency relation between an edge or a face and the already processed region can be described in terms of its adjacency relation to the active boundary. For the case of non-zero genus meshes there will be one situation per handle in which this relation involves a boundary from the stack. The characterizing difference between the compression schemes mentioned earlier is: (a) how the boundaries are defined, (b) how processing an edge or a face updates the boundaries, and (c) with which graph elements the description of the update is associated. Depending on the latter the compression schemes can be classified as *edge-based*, *face-based*, and *vertex-based*.

We will now highlight the exact difference between these three classes of coders. First we do this for the case of pure triangular connectivity. Because all faces are triangles (i.e. have degree three) there is no need to record face degrees. Then we show how each class of coder extends to code arbitrary polygonal connectivity. To simplify this classification we temporarily assume a mesh of sphere topology without boundary, so that we can ignore how to deal with holes and handles.

Edge-based schemes [20, 10] describe all boundary updates per edge. The boundaries are loops of half-edges that separate the region of processed edges from the rest. Each iteration grows the processed region by the edge adjacent to the focus of the active boundary (see Figure 2). This *free edge* is either adjacent to an unprocessed triangle or to the active boundary (in one of four different ways). Triangle Fixer [10] describes the boundary updates corresponding to these five configurations using the symbols T, R, L, S, or E. The Dual Graph method [20] does the same but replaces each pair of symbols S and E by a symbol S_j. Its associated offset j represents a distance in number of edges along the boundary.

Face-based schemes [9, 22, 5] describe all boundary updates per face. The boundaries are loops of edges that separate the region of processed faces from the rest. Each iteration grows the processed region by the face adjacent to the focus of the active boundary. This *free face* can be adjacent to the active boundary in one of five ways. Edgebreaker [22] describes the boundary updates corresponding to these five configurations using the symbols C, R, L, S, or E. Again, each pair of symbols S and E can be replaced by a symbol S_j as done by the Cut-Border Machine [9]. The lowest guaranteed worst-case bounds for coding triangular connectivity have been established for face-based schemes [8].

Vertex-based schemes [26] describe all boundary updates per vertex. The boundaries are loops of edges that separate the region of processed faces from the rest. Furthermore, they store for every boundary vertex the number of *free degrees* or *slots*, which are unprocessed edges incident to the respective vertex. Each iteration grows the processed region by the face adjacent to the *widened focus* of the active boundary. The focus often needs to be widened such that there is a *start slot* and an *end slot* for the face. Only if the processed face has a *free vertex* that is not part of the widened focus, the boundary update needs to be described. Two scenarios are possible: either the free vertex has not been visited, in which case its degree is recorded, or is has been visited, in which case a its distance in slots along the active boundary is recorded and the active boundary is split.

Under the assumption that no splits occur the resulting code sequence contains the degree of every vertex. A result by [2] that was published in [1] shows that the entropy of this sequence asymptotically approaches the number of bits needed to encode an arbitrary triangulated planar graph as found by Tutte's enumeration [28]. However, while it is possible to significantly reduce the number of splits using a sophisticated region growing strategy as proposed by [1], we will later show that such heuristics cannot guarantee to avoid splits completely.

The extension of edge-based schemes to polygon meshes is simple [21, 12]. Whenever the free edge is adjacent to an unprocessed face, its degree d is recorded. For the Face Fixer scheme [12] symbol T is simply replaced with symbol F_d. The extension of face-based schemes to polygon meshes is more complex [18, 19]. The number of possible configurations in which a face of degree d can be adjacent to the active boundary equals the Fibonacci number $F(2d-1)$ [18]. For a quadrilateral face, for example, there are 13 possible configurations. The lowest guaranteed worst-case bounds for coding pure quadrangular meshes have been established for face-based schemes by using a *splitting-rule* [18]. It splits each quadrilateral into two triangles such that the probability for the 13 possible Edgebreaker label combinations can be exploited for compression.

Previously proposed vertex-based schemes only handle triangular connectivity. In this paper we propose the extension to polygonal connectivity.

4 Coding with Face and Vertex Degrees

The vertex-based coder by Touma and Gotsman [26] codes the connectivity graph of a manifold triangle mesh as a sequence of vertex degrees. We now describe how to extend their approach to code the connectivity graph of a manifold *polygon* mesh using a sequence of vertex degrees *and* a sequence of face degrees. Like for triangle meshes, occasionally a split or a merge operation is needed instead of a vertex degree.

Encoding: Starting with a connectivity graph of v vertices and f faces, the encoder produces two symbol sequences: one is a sequence of $f-1-s+m$ face degree symbols F_d, the other is a sequence of $v+s+m$ symbols which consists of v vertex degree symbols V_d, s split operation symbols S_j with associated offset j, and m merge operation symbols $M_{i,k}$ with associated index i and offset k. The connectivity graph can be reconstructed by simultaneously processing both symbol sequences.

The coder maintains one or several loops of *boundary edges* that separate a single processed region from all unprocessed regions. Furthermore, it stores for every *boundary vertex* the number of *free degrees* or *slots*, which are unprocessed edges incident to the respective vertex. Each of these *boundaries* encloses an unprocessed region; its faces, vertices, and edges are called *unprocessed*. In the presence of handles one boundary can contain another, in which case they enclose the same unprocessed region. Each boundary has a distinguished boundary edge called *focus*. The algorithm works on the focus of the *active boundary*, while the other boundaries are kept in a stack.

The initial active boundary is defined counterclockwise around an arbitrary edge, one of its two boundary edges is defined to be the focus. Each iteration of the algorithm processes the face adjacent to the focus of the active boundary. This involves recording its degree and processing its *free vertices* as illustrated by the three examples in Figure 3. Since including a face consumes two boundary slots we sometimes need to widen the focus until there is a *start slot* and an *end slot* for the face. The number of *focus vertices* is called the *width* of the focus. In scenarios **A**, **B**, and **C** of Figure 3 the focus has a width of 3, 2, and 4 respectively. The *free vertices* are those that are not part of the widened focus.

The free vertices are then processed in counterclockwise order starting from the start slot. Three different cases can arise. According to the original reference [26] we call them *add*, *split*, and *merge* (see Figure 3). By far most the frequent case is *add*, which happens whenever the free vertex has not been previously visited. In this case we record the vertex degree d for which we will use the symbol V_d. However, when we encounter a free vertex that has already been visited we either have a *split* or a *merge*. The latter occurs only for meshes with handles (e.g. with non-zero genus). In this case the free vertex is on a stack boundary, which causes the active boundary to *merge* with the respective stack boundary. We record the index i of that boundary in the stack and the number of slots k between the focus of the stack boundary and the merge slot, denoted by symbol $M_{i,k}$. In the other case the free vertex is on the active boundary, which causes the active boundary to *split* into two. We push one part on the stack and record the number of slots j between the new stack focus and the split slot, denoted by symbol S_j.

After processing all free vertices we exit the face and move to the next focus (see Section 6). This repeats until all faces have been processed. Notice that for each boundary we do not need to record the degree of its last face. At this point a boundary has no slots left and wraps around this face. Therefore the number of recorded face degrees F_d equals at most the number of faces f minus

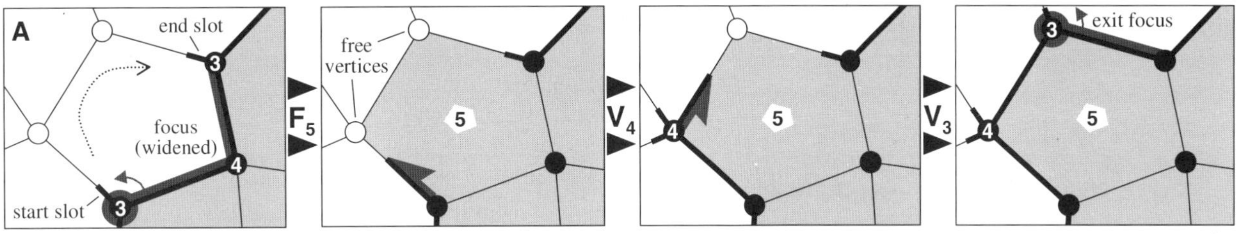

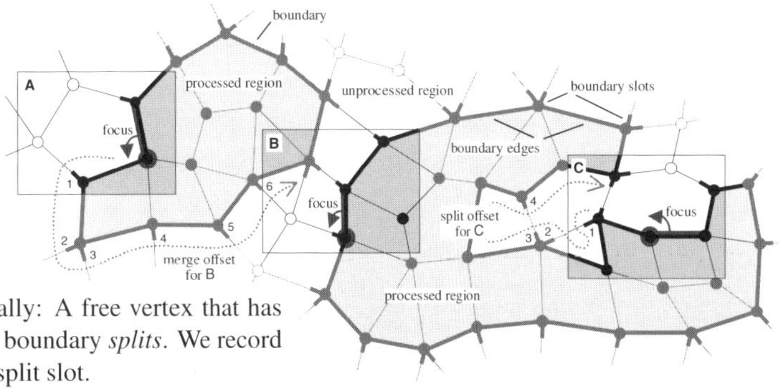

Figure 3: The three frame sequences **A**, **B**, and **C** illustrate different scenarios that can arise when processing a face. **A** is the most common one: The free vertices of the face have not been visited before, we *add* them to the boundary and record their degree. **B** only occurs for meshes with handles: A free vertex that has already been visited is on a boundary in the stack. The active boundary *merges* with this stack boundary. We record its stack index and the number of slots between the stack focus and the merge slot. **C** happens occasionally: A free vertex that has already been visited is on the active boundary. The active boundary *splits*. We record the number of slots between the new stack focus and the split slot.

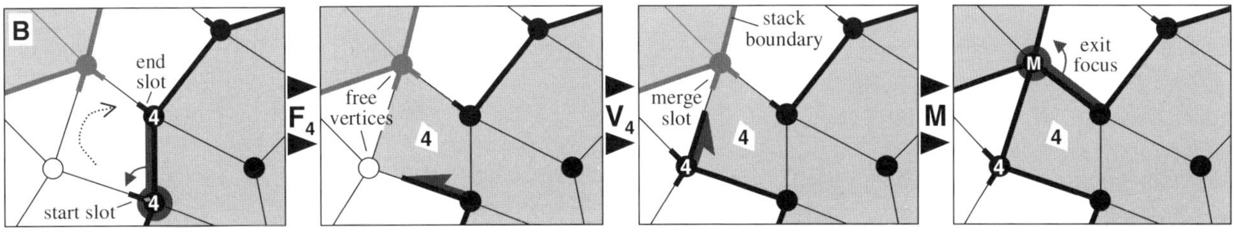

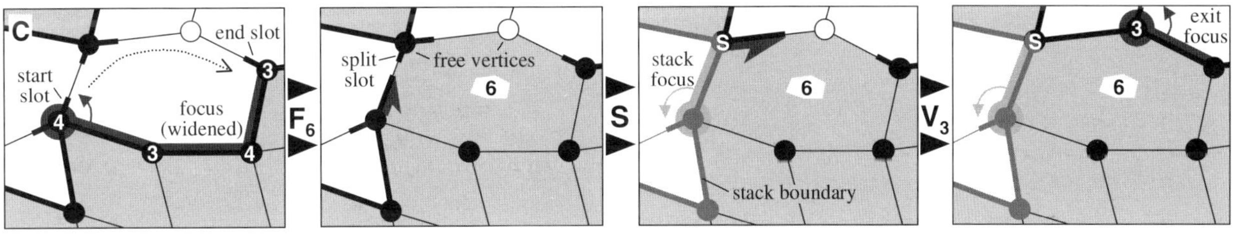

one. Each split increases and each merge decreases the number of boundaries by one. Thus the exact number of face degrees recorded, given we have s split and m merge operations, is $f - 1 - s + m$ (see also Section 8).

Decoding: The decoder exactly replays what the encoder does by performing the boundary updates described by the two symbol sequences. A step by step example run of the decoding process is shown in Figure 4.

Complexity: We assume that the mesh genus is a small constant, so that there are only a constant number of merge operations. Each face is processed once. The cost of processing a face is proportional to its degree plus the cost for processing its free vertices. The sum of all face degrees is linear and each vertex is added once. This leaves us with the split operations. They are the critical ones, because they require to walk the offset along the boundary. Since we always know the length of the boundary we can always walk the shorter way. Thus, in the worst case the boundary consists of all v vertices and is recursively split into half, resulting in a time complexity of $O(v \log_2(v))$.

5 Compressing with Duality Prediction

The two symbol sequences are compressed into a bitstream using a adaptive arithmetic coding [30]. Given sufficiently long input, the compression rate of such a coder converges to the entropy of the input. The entropy for a sequence of n symbols is $-\sum_n \left(p_i \log_2(p_i)\right)$, where the ith symbol occurs with probability p_i.

Whenever a face is processed we need to specify if it represents a polygon or a hole in the mesh. Using the arithmetic coder we code this with two symbols. Similarly whenever a free vertex is processed we need to specify if an add, a split or a merge operation was used. We distinguish between the frequently occurring adds and the other two with three different symbols.

What remains is compressing the face degrees, the vertex degrees, and the offsets and indices associated with split and merge operations. The basic idea is to exploit the fact that high-degree faces tend to be surrounded by low-degree vertices, and vice versa, for predictive compression. For every vertex we know the degree of the face that introduces it. For every face we know the degrees of all vertices of the (widened) focus. We found that using four different predictions each way captures the correlation in the duality of vertex and face degrees quite well. Offsets and indices, on the other hand, are compressed with the minimal number of bits needed based on their known maximal range.

5.1 Compressing Face Degrees

When a face is processed the degrees of all vertices on the (widened) focus are known. The lower their average degree, the more likely this face has a high degree and vice-versa (see Figure 1). This can be exploited by using different contexts for entropy coding the face degrees, dependent on this vertex degree average. In practice the use of four such *face-degree contexts* seems to capture this correlation quite well. We have different contexts for an average vertex degree (a) below 3.3, (b) between 3.3 and 4.3, (c) between 4.3 and 4.9, and (d) above 4.9. These numbers were first chosen based on the plot in Figure 1 and then corrected slightly based on experimental results.

Each of the four face-degree contexts contains 4 entries: The first three entries represent face degrees 3, 4, and 5 and the last entry represents higher degree faces. These are subsequently compressed with a special *large-face-degree context*. This special context is also used for faces that correspond to holes in the mesh. All contexts are initialized with uniform probabilities that are adaptively updated. Four bits at the beginning of the code specify face degrees that do not occur in the mesh. Their representing entry is disabled in all contexts. For our set of example meshes, this predictive coding of face degrees improves the bit-rates on average by 12.2 %.

There is another small improvement possible: The minimal degree of the face equals the width of the focus. If the focus is wider than 3 we can improve compression further by disabling those entries of the chosen context that represents *impossible* degrees. Although this improves the compression rates by only 1 or 2 percent, it was simple to integrate into the arithmetic coder.

5.2 Compressing Vertex Degrees

When a free vertex is processed, the degree of the respective face is known. The lower its degree, the more likely this vertex has a high degree and vice-versa. Again we exploit this for better compression by using four different contexts. We switch the *vertex-degree context* depending if the face is a triangle, a quadrangle, a pentagon, or a higher degree face.

Each of the four vertex-degree contexts contains 9 entries: The first eight entries represent vertex degrees 2 to 9 and the last entry represents higher degree vertices. These are subsequently compressed with a special *large-vertex-degree context*. All contexts are initialized with uniform probabilities that are adaptively updated. Nine bits at the beginning of the code specify vertex degrees that do not occur in the mesh. Their representing entry is disabled in all contexts.

For our set of example meshes, this predictive coding of vertex degrees improves the bit-rates on average by 6.4 %. Predictive coding of vertex degrees does not improve the compression rates as much as predictive coding of face degrees, because we use less information for each prediction. While each face degrees is predicted using an average of two or more vertex degrees, each vertex degree is only predicted by a single face degree.

5.3 Compressing Offsets and Indices

An integer number that is known to be between 0 and n can be encoded with exactly $\log_2(n+1)$ bits. We use this for compressing the offsets and indices associated with the split and the merge operation. Whenever a split offset j, a merge index i, or a merge offset k is encoded or decoded, the maximal value of this number is known. For the split offset j it equals the number of slots on the active boundary, for the merge index i it equals the size of the stack, and for the merge offset k it equals the number of slots on the indexed boundary in the stack.

6 Reducing the Number of Splits

After processing a face, we could continue with the exit focus as the next focus. This is the strategy of the original vertex-based coder for triangle meshes proposed by Touma and Gotsman [26]. However, Alliez and Desbrun [1] propose a more sophisticated strategy for picking the next focus that significantly reduces the number of splits. This is beneficial, because split operations are expensive to code: On one hand we need to specify where in the sequence of vertex degrees they occur and on the other hand we need to record their associated split offset.

Since the decoding process has to follow this strategy, the quest for this better focus can only use information that is available to the decoder. Alliez and Desbrun [1] suggest to move the focus to the boundary vertex with the lowest number of slots. In case there is more than one such vertex, they choose the least dense region by averaging over a wider and wider neighborhood. This strategy makes keeping track of the next candidate an expensive

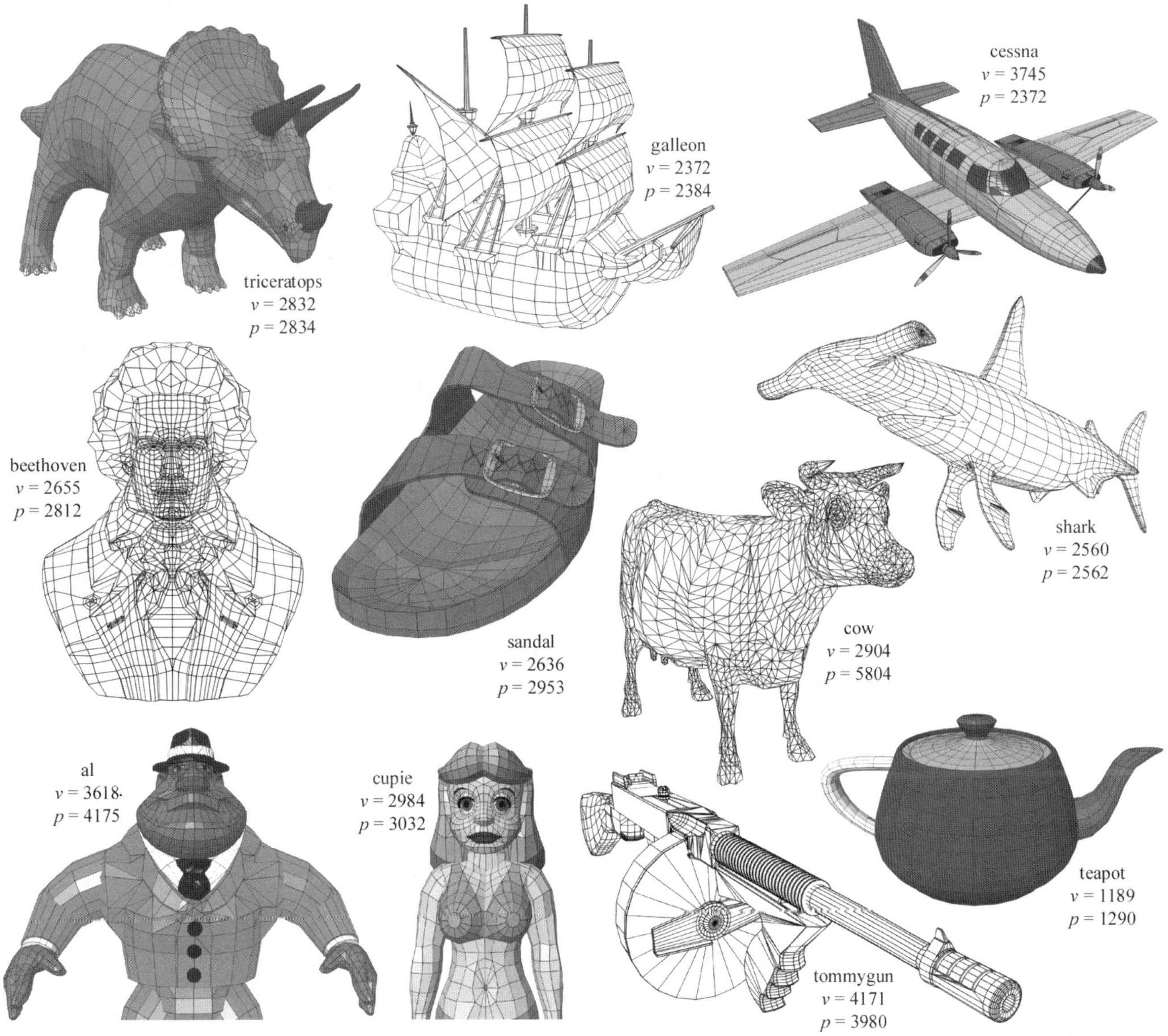

triceratops
$v = 2832$
$p = 2834$

galleon
$v = 2372$
$p = 2384$

cessna
$v = 3745$
$p = 2372$

beethoven
$v = 2655$
$p = 2812$

sandal
$v = 2636$
$p = 2953$

shark
$v = 2560$
$p = 2562$

cow
$v = 2904$
$p = 5804$

al
$v = 3618$
$p = 4175$

cupie
$v = 2984$
$p = 3032$

teapot
$v = 1189$
$p = 1290$

tommygun
$v = 4171$
$p = 3980$

mesh	vertex degree distribution									face degree distribution				holes /		bpv		coding
name	2	3	4	5	6	7	8	9	>9	3	4	5	>5	handles		ff	dd	gain
triceratops	–	8	2816	8	–	–	–	–	–	346	2266	140	82	–	–	2.115	**1.189**	43.8 %
galleon	7	430	1595	270	66	4	1	–	–	336	1947	40	61	–	–	2.595	**2.093**	19.3 %
cessna	8	642	2470	384	178	41	18	1	3	900	2797	180	50	–	–	2.841	**2.543**	10.5 %
beethoven	21	279	1925	295	99	20	14	–	2	680	2078	44	10	10	–	2.890	**2.102**	27.3 %
sandal	–	280	1857	329	95	18	7	12	38	961	1985	7	–	14	12	2.602	**2.115**	18.7 %
shark	–	–	2560	–	–	–	–	–	–	188	2253	83	38	–	–	1.670	**0.756**	54.7 %
al	2	538	1999	720	268	69	15	1	6	1579	2505	44	47	–	–	2.926	**2.429**	17.0 %
cupie	16	272	2405	234	37	12	8	–	–	384	2506	114	28	–	–	2.307	**1.640**	28.9 %
tommygun	–	1557	2002	395	152	21	18	8	18	992	2785	84	119	–	6	2.611	**2.258**	13.5 %
cow	–	7	87	514	1796	364	98	23	15	5804	–	–	–	–	–	2.213	**1.781**	19.5 %
teapot	2	14	1022	125	18	5	1	–	2	215	1070	3	2	–	1	1.669	**1.127**	32.5 %

Table 1: The vertex count v and the polygon count p for the example models is reported above. The table also gives the vertex and face degree distribution for each of these models. We compare the connectivity compression rates (*bpv*) of the Face Fixer coder (*ff*) to those of the proposed Degree Duality coder (*dd*) and report the improvement in percent.

operation. Using a dedicated priority queue, for example, would require $O(\log(b))$ per boundary update, where b is the number of vertices on the active boundary.

The obvious question is whether it is possible to avoid the split operations all together. We can prove that splits cannot be avoided by using a strategy that only uses the already encoded/decoded part of the mesh. Given any such strategy we can always construct a mesh that is guaranteed to result in a split.

First of all, the connectivity of a non-zero genus mesh will require at least as many splits as the mesh has handles. But also for meshes without handles a split operation can occur: Imagine your favorite mesh of torus topology. The encoder eventually has to use the merge operation to code the handle. Every merge operation is preceded by a split operation. In the moment this split operation is performed, we stop the encoding process, perform an edge cut in the unprocessed region such that it opens the handle, insert two large polygons or holes into the cut, and continue the encoding process on the mesh (which now has sphere topology). The coder did not notice what happened, because the edge cut was performed in the region it has not yet seen. But now the coder has produced a split for a mesh of genus zero.

Nevertheless, to reduce the number of splits is especially important in the polygonal case, because here a split operation can pinch off parts of the boundary that do not enclose any unprocessed vertices and that can be as small as a single unprocessed face. This does not happen in the pure triangular case. Inspired by Alliez and Desbrun [1] we suggest a similar, but simpler heuristic to pick the next focus. Most importantly, our strategy does not affect the asymptotic complexity of the decoder.

The focus is moved to the boundary vertex with the smallest number of slots in counterclockwise direction as seen from the current focus. This current focus is usually the exit focus of the face processed last or the stack focus if a new boundary was just popped of the stack. However, we only move the focus if the smallest number of slots is 0 or 1, otherwise the focus remains where it is. Table 2 reports the success of this strategy in reducing the number of splits and the bit-rate.

Starting a brute-force search along the boundary for the vertex with the smallest number of slots would mean a worst-case time complexity of $O(n^2)$. Instead we keep track of the next 0 and the next 1 slot by organizing all of them into two cyclic linked lists. In both lists we always point to the slot that is closest in counterclockwise direction and perform the necessary updates as the boundary changes. This data structure can be maintained without affecting the asymptotic complexity of the decoder.

mesh	current		0 or 1 slot		coding
name	# splits	bpv	# splits	bpv	gain
triceratops	53	1.311	**25**	**1.189**	9.3 %
galleon	78	2.309	**18**	**2.093**	9.4 %
cessna	172	2.882	**28**	**2.543**	11.8 %
beethoven	99	2.431	**15**	**2.102**	13.5 %
sandal	85	2.295	**25**	**2.115**	7.8 %
shark	24	0.818	**13**	**0.756**	7.6 %
al	92	2.616	**14**	**2.429**	7.1 %
cupie	56	1.786	**15**	**1.640**	8.2 %
tommygun	131	2.449	**32**	**2.258**	7.8 %
cow	154	2.313	**13**	**1.781**	23.0 %
teapot	10	1.167	**3**	**1.127**	3.4 %

Table 2: The number of splits and the resulting bit-rate using the *current* focus compared to moving the focus to the next 0 *or* 1 *slot* and the coding improvement in percent.

7 Coding Non-Manifold Meshes

Compared to Guéziec et al. [6] our Degree Duality coder implements a much simpler stitching scheme to recover non-manifold connectivity, that allows a robust, minimal-effort implementation at the expense of less efficiency. However, the number of non-manifold vertices is typically small, which justifies the use of a simpler scheme.

Whenever a free vertex is processed by an add operation we simply specify if this indeed is a new position or not using arithmetic coding. If it is a new position we increment the position counter. Otherwise it is an old position and its index needs to be compressed as well. We can do this with $\log_2(n)$ bits where n is the number of positions already encoded/decoded.

8 Counts and Invariants

The sum of all v vertex degrees and the sum of all f face degrees both equal twice the number of edges e. That means the two sums are equal.

$$\sum_{k=1}^{f} deg(\mathrm{f}_k) = \sum_{k=1}^{v} deg(\mathrm{v}_k) = 2e \qquad (1)$$

If we know all vertex degrees and all face degrees but one we can compute it as the one completing the equality.

$$\mathrm{f}_f = \sum_{k=1}^{v} deg(\mathrm{v}_k) - \sum_{k=1}^{f-1} deg(\mathrm{f}_k) \qquad (2)$$

Furthermore we have the following invariants: The sum of degrees of all unprocessed faces minus the number of all boundary edges b equals twice the number of unprocessed edges u. And also the sum of degrees of all unprocessed vertices plus the number of all boundary slots s equals twice the number of unprocessed edges u.

$$\sum_{f_k \subset \mathcal{B}} deg(f_k) - b = \sum_{v_k \subset \mathcal{B}} deg(v_k) + s = 2u \quad (3)$$

where $\subset \mathcal{B}$ means unprocessed (or enclosed by some boundary). Furthermore, this invariant is true for the face and vertex degree count of every unprocessed regions together with edge and slot count of the respective boundaries that enclose it. In the moment a split occurs, one such equation $\mathcal{E}$ is split into two new equations $\mathcal{E}'$ and $\mathcal{E}''$ that are related with $s = s' + s''$, $b = b' + b''$, $u = u' + u''$, and the correspondingly *split* sums of unprocessed face and vertex degrees. The offset associated with the split operation specifies s'' and b''. Together with the two degree sequences they specify implicitly when each boundary end. This explains why we can omit one face degree for every split operation—it creates a new equation just like (2) that can be solved for a single face degree.

9 Summary and Discussion

We have described coder for polygon mesh connectivity that delivers the best connectivity compression rates meshes reported so far. On our example models the compression rates improve between 10 % to 55 % over those of the Face Fixer coder [12] with an average improvement of 26 %. Furthermore, we provide a web page [14] containing a prototype implementation of the decoder in pure java that proves the bit-rates reported in Table 1.

Our main contribution is (a) the extension of vertex-based coding to polygonal connectivity using a sequences of vertex degrees *and* a sequence of face degrees (b) the observation that the correlation in the duality of the degrees can be used for mutual predictive compression.

Khodakovsky et al. [17] extend a result by [2] that was published in [1] to show that summed entropies of the face degree sequence and of the vertex degree sequence converges to Tutte's bound on the enumeration of planar graphs [29]. This seems to suggest that degree coding is optimal in the sense that it uses not more bits to encode a connectivity than needed to distinguish it among all possible connectivities with the same number of vertices.

This does not mean that degree coding always outperforms other coders. We can construct pathologic examples where other coders perform better. Using the cow model from Table 1 we generated a triangle mesh and a quadrangle mesh that demonstrate this. We generated the triangle mesh by placing a new vertex into every triangle of the original mesh and by connecting it to its three vertices. All new vertices have degree three, while the degree of every vertex of the original mesh doubles. This connectivity compresses to 0.988 bpv using Edgebreaker [22], whereas the Degree Duality coder needs 1.569 bpv. Similarly we generated the quadrangle mesh by placing a new vertex into every original triangle and by connecting it to the three new vertices that are placed on every original edge. All new vertices have either degree three or degree four, while the degree of the original vertices remains unchanged. This connectivity compresses to 1.376 bpv using Face Fixer [12], whereas the Degree Duality coder needs 1.721 bpv. However, such pathological cases rarely occur in practice.

The author thanks Jack Snoeyink for helpful comments and thorough reviews of the manuscript.

10 References

[1] P. Alliez and M. Desbrun. Valence-driven connectivity encoding for 3D meshes. In *Eurographics'01*, pages 480–489, 2001.

[2] P. Alliez, M. Desbrun, S. Gumhold, M. Isenburg, and C. Gotsman. *personal communication*, March 2001.

[3] C. Bajaj, V. Pascucci, and G. Zhuang. Single resolution compression of arbitrary triangular meshes with properties. In *Data Compression Conference'99 Conference Proc.*, pages 247–256, 1999.

[4] M. Deering. Geometry compression. In *SIGGRAPH'95 Conference Proceedings*, pages 13–20, 1995.

[5] L. de Floriani, P. Magillo, and E. Puppo. A simple and efficient sequential encoding for triangle meshes. In *Proc. of 15th European Workshop on Computational Geometry*, pages 129–133, 1999.

[6] A. Guéziec, F. Bossen, G. Taubin, and C. Silva. Efficient compression of non-manifold polygonal meshes. In *Visualization'99 Conference Proceedings*, pages 73–80, 1999.

[7] A. Guéziec, G. Taubin, F. Lazarus, and W.P. Horn. Converting sets of polygons to manifold surfaces by cutting and stitching. In *Visualization'98 Conference Proceedings*, pages 383–390, 1998.

[8] S. Gumhold. New bounds on the encoding of planar triangulations. Technical Report WSI-2000-1, Tübingen, March 2000.

[9] S. Gumhold and W. Strasser. Real time compression of triangle mesh connectivity. In *SIGGRAPH'98*, pages 133–140, 1998.

[10] M. Isenburg. Triangle Fixer: Edge-based connectivity compression. In *Proceedings of 16th European Workshop on Computational Geometry*, pages 18–23, 2000.

[11] M. Isenburg and J. Snoeyink. Mesh collapse compression. In *SIBGRAPI'99 Conference Proceedings*, pages 27–28, 1999.

[12] M. Isenburg and J. Snoeyink. Face Fixer: Compressing polygon meshes with properties. In *SIGGRAPH'00*, pages 263–270, 2000.

[13] M. Isenburg and J. Snoeyink. Compressing the property mapping of polygon meshes. In *Pacific Graphics'01*, pages 4–11, 2001.

[14] http://www.cs.unc.edu/~isenburg/degreedualitycoder/

[15] Z. Karni and C. Gotsman. Spectral compression of mesh geometry. In *SIGGRAPH'00 Conference Proc.*, pages 279–286, 2000.

[16] K. Keeler and J. Westbrook. Short encodings of planar graphs and maps. In *Discrete Applied Mathematics*, pages 239–252, 1995.

[17] A. Khodakovsky, P. Alliez, M. Desbrun, and P. Schroeder. Near-optimal connectivity encoding of 2-manifold polygon meshes. *to appear in Graphic Models*, 2002.

[18] D. King, J. Rossignac, and A. Szymczak. Connectivity compression for irregular quadrilateral meshes. Georgia Tech, TR–99–36.

[19] B. Kronrod and C. Gotsman. Efficient coding of non-triangular meshes. In *Proc. of Pacific Graphics*, pages 235–242, 2000.

[20] J. Li and C. C. Kuo. A dual graph approach to 3D triangular mesh compression. In *Proceedings of ICIP'98*, 1998.

[21] J. Li, C. C. Kuo, and H. Chen. Mesh connectivity coding by dual graph approach. Technical report, March 1998.

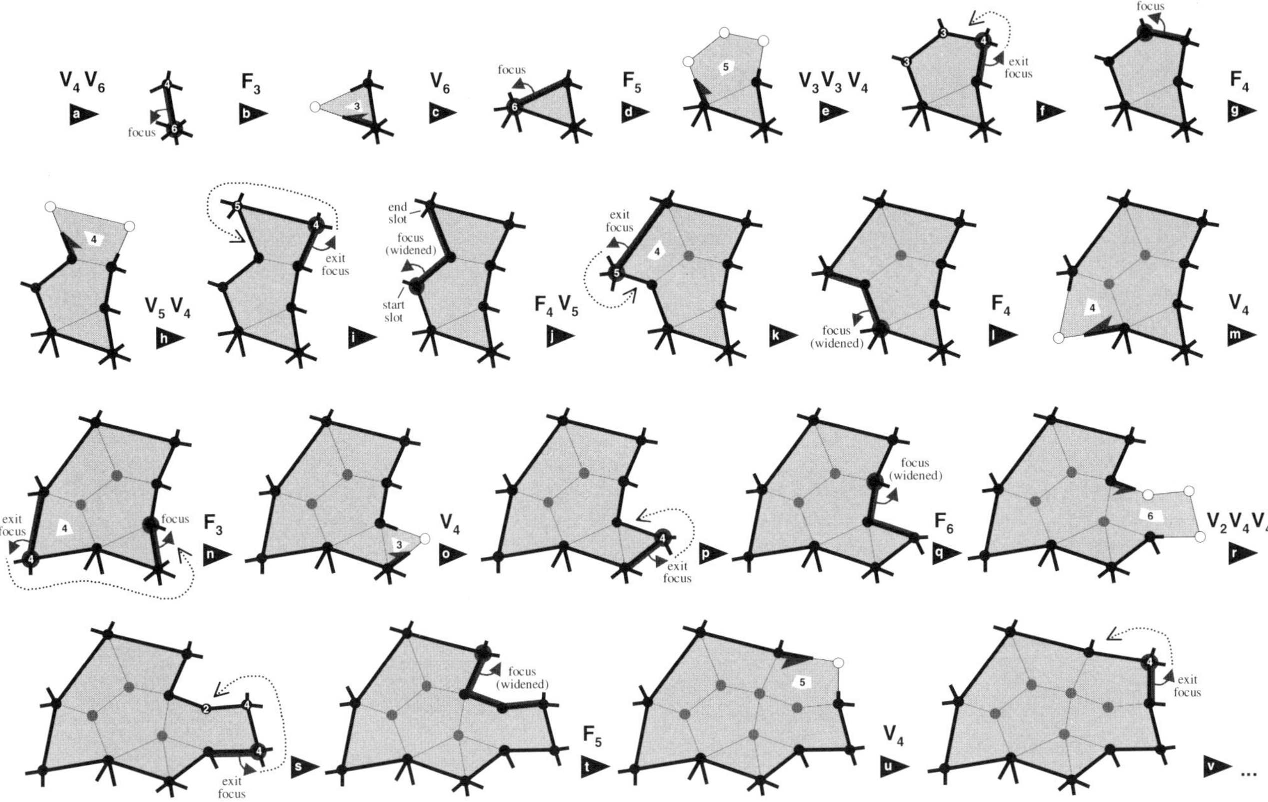

Figure 4: This is an example run of the decoding algorithm. It is an exact replay of the boundary updates performed during encoding: **(a)** The decoder creates the initial boundary by uncompressing the first two vertex degrees. Encoder and decoder use their order to agree on the initial focus. **(b)** Uncompress the first face degree. The average focus vertex degree of 5.0 determines which *face-degree context* the arithmetic decoder uses. **(c)** Uncompress the degree of the free vertex. The face degree of 3 determines which *vertex-degree context* the arithmetic decoder uses. The focus remains at the exit focus, because there is no vertex on the active boundary that has 0 or 1 slots. **(d)** Uncompress the next face degree. The average focus vertex degree that determines the face-degree context is again 5.0. **(e)** Uncompress the degrees of the three free vertices. Now the face degree that determines the vertex-degree context is 5. **(f)** The focus moves in counterclockwise direction along the boundary to the next boundary vertex with the lowest number of slots, which is 1 in this case. **(g)** Uncompress the next face degree. Use average focus vertex degree of 3.5 to determine the face-degree context (e.g. $fdc = 3.5$). **(h)** Uncompress the degrees of the two free vertices. Use face degree 4 to determine the vertex-degree context (e.g. $vdc = 4$). **(i)** The focus is moved in counterclockwise direction to the lowest number of slots, which is 0 in this case. Then the focus is widened such that there is a start slot and an end slot for the next face to process. **(j)** Uncompress the next face degree ($fdc = 3.6$) and uncompress the degree of its free vertex ($vdc = 4$). **(k)** Move the focus in counterclockwise direction to the vertex with 0 slots and widen the focus. **(l)** Uncompress the next face degree ($fdc = 4.6$). **(m)** Uncompress the degree of its free vertex ($vdc = 4$) and move the focus. **(n)** Uncompress the next face degree ($fdc = 5.0$). **(o)** Uncompress the degree of its free vertex ($vdc = 3$). **(p)** Move and widen the focus. **(q)** Uncompress the next face degree ($fdc = 4.0$). **(r)** Uncompress the degree of its three free vertices ($vdc = 6$). **(s)** Move and widen the focus. **(t)** Uncompress the next face degree ($fdc = 3.5$). The focus has a width of 4, therefore the face degree is also at least 4. We disable the entry of the chosen context that represents the *impossible* degree 3. **(u)** Uncompress the degree of its free vertex ($vdc = 5$). **(v)** And so on ...

[22] J. Rossignac. Edgebreaker: Connectivity compression for triangle meshes. *IEEE Transactions on Visualization and Computer Graphics*, 5(1), pages 47–61, 1999.

[23] A. Szymczak, D. King, and J. Rossignac. An Edgebreaker-based efficient compression scheme for connectivity of regular meshes. In *Proc. of 12th Cnd. Conf. Comp. Geom.*, pages 257–264, 2000.

[24] G. Taubin, W.P. Horn, F. Lazarus, and J. Rossignac. Geometry coding and VRML. *Proc. of the IEEE*, 86(6):1228–1243, 1998.

[25] G. Taubin and J. Rossignac. Geometric compression through topological surgery. *ACM Trans. on Graph.*, 17(2):84–115, 1998.

[26] C. Touma and C. Gotsman. Triangle mesh compression. In *Graphics Interface'98 Conference Proc.*, pages 26–34, 1998.

[27] G. Turan. Succinct representations of graphs. *Discrete Applied Mathematics*, 8:289–294, 1984.

[28] W.T. Tutte. A census of planar triangulations. *Canadian Journal of Mathematics*, 14:21–38, 1962.

[29] W.T. Tutte. A census of planar maps. *Canadian Journal of Mathematics*, 15:249–271, 1963.

[30] I. H. Witten, R. M. Neal, and J. G. Cleary. Arithmetic coding for data compression. *Comm. of the ACM*, 30(6):520–540, 1987.

Efficient Bounded Adaptive Tessellation of Displacement Maps

Kevin Moule Michael D. McCool

Computer Graphics Lab
Department of Computer Science
University of Waterloo

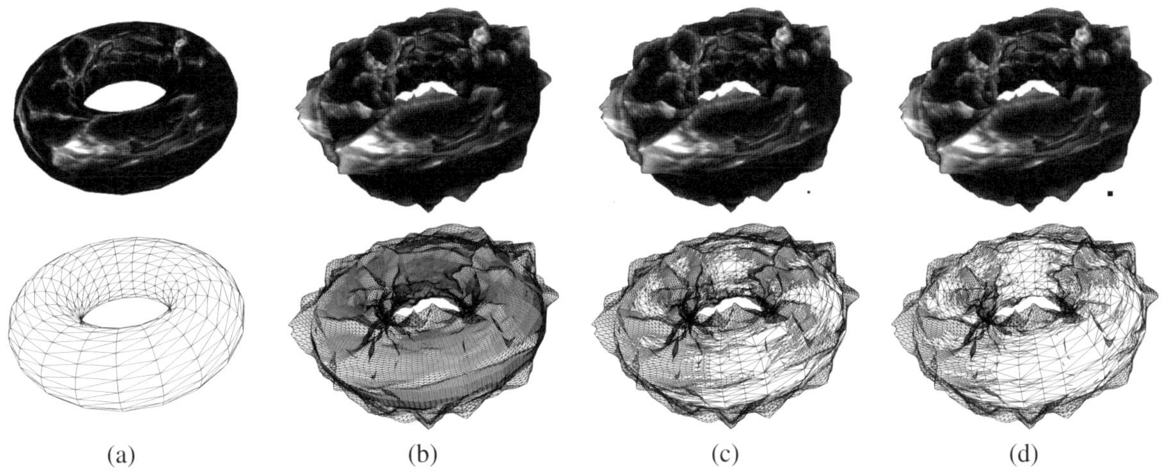

Figure 1: (a) Bump-mapping only (882 triangles), (b) Uniform tessellation (56448 triangles), (c) Adaptive tessellation with a tolerance of 5 pixels (34377 triangles), (d) Adaptive tessellation with a tolerance of 10 pixels (21521 triangles).

Abstract

Displacement mapping is a technique for applying fine geometric detail to a simpler base surface. The displacement is often specified as a scalar function which makes it relatively easy to increase visual complexity without the difficulties inherent in more general modeling techniques. We would like to use displacement mapping in real-time applications. Ideally, a graphics accelerator should create a polygonal tessellation of the displaced surface on the fly to avoid storage and host bandwidth overheads.

We present an online, adaptive, crack-free tessellation scheme for real-time displacement mapping that uses only local information for each triangle to perform a view-dependent tessellation. The tessellation works in homogeneous coordinates and avoids retransformation of displaced points, making it suitable for high-performance hardware implementation. The use of interval analysis produces meshes with good error bounds that converge quickly to the true surface.

Key words: Hardware acceleration. Bump mapping. Displacement mapping. Adaptive tessellation.

1 Introduction

Displacement mapping is a technique for adding surface detail to a base surface. The base surface is moved along its normal at each point on the surface. The distances moved, called the displacements, are generated either by a function defined procedurally or are interpolated from a 2D array. Rendering displacement maps has traditionally been either space-inefficient or computationally expensive (or both). Many techniques neither map onto hardware implementations nor fit within the standard hardware pipeline.

We propose a technique for rendering displacement maps that is targeted towards real time rendering using hardware acceleration. Our technique is not targeted at current accelerators; instead, it is an algorithm *suitable* for implementation in future hardware. However, the technique is simple and efficient enough that a high-performance implementation can be obtained using a software implementation along with the use of a standard accelerator as a back end.

Several restrictions are imposed in the context of hardware accelerated rendering. Firstly, the nature of the graphics pipeline is such that geometric primitives are processed one at a time without any knowledge of the primitive that came before or will come after. Secondly, memory systems in graphics accelerators are specialized for access to coherent data structures. Storing information in general linked structures is usually avoided since variability in access time would adversely effect the rest of the pipeline. This implies that we cannot use or manipulate a complete representation of the geometry, but should design a technique that operates locally.

Under these restrictions we will present a technique that can render displacement mapped surfaces in real-time on current graphics hardware but that is also suitable for direct implementation in future hardware. The technique performs an online adaptive tessellation which tries to minimize the complexity of the resulting mesh. A brute-force technique could also be used. We chose to pursue an adaptive technique so that displacement mapping would produce fewer primitives on average, would access less memory on average, and also to support a simple form of adaptive geometry suitable for terrains, characters, etc.

Our technique uses a hierarchical array structured data representation based on interval analysis as a representation of the displacement function. The extra hierarchical bounding information is used to guide a recursive tessellation process. In hardware, a stack would be used to implement the recursion. At each stage of the recursion, an oracle is used to determine if a given triangle is a sufficient approximation of the displaced surface using an interval error metric. We use a view-dependent, division-free error metric that bounds error in screen space. We also combine displacement with bump-mapped per-pixel lighting. This hides changes in tessellation that would be objectionable under Gouraud shading.

In Section 2, we will define displacement mapping more precisely. Section 3 describes the recursive adaptive tessellation scheme we use. Then, in Section 4 we describe our hierarchical displacement map representation, which provides an efficient interval extension of texture mapping. Section 5 defines an oracle which can efficiently and accurately determine the need for additional mesh subdivision. We evaluate the quality and performance of our algorithm in Section 6. Finally, we summarize our results in Section 7.

2 Displacement Mapping

Displacement mapping is a general technique for applying fine geometric detail to a simpler base surface and can be formulated in many ways. A common approach uses scalar displacement values and the normals at each base surface point to generate the displaced surface (Figure 2). Given a surface $\mathbf{s}(u, v)$ parameterized by u and v the displaced surface $\mathbf{s}_d(u, v)$ can be defined as

$$\mathbf{s}_d(u,v) = \mathbf{s}(u,v) + d(u,v)\hat{\mathbf{n}}(u,v) \quad (1)$$

where $\hat{\mathbf{n}}(u, v)$ is the unit base surface normal and $d(u, v)$ is the scalar displacement function. The displacement function can be defined procedurally or interpolated from samples stored in an array (a displacement texture).

In the context of hardware based triangle rasterization the displaced surface can be approximated by displacing the vertices of a sufficiently dense subdivision of the base surface. Image-based warping techniques can also be used, but these provide fewer opportunities for backward-compatible deployment on older accelerators.

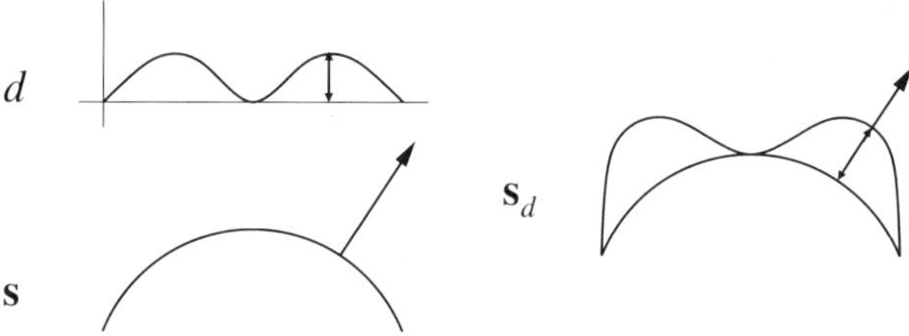

Figure 2: Displacement Mapping.

Displacement mapping was first introduced by Cook in the context of Shade Trees [2] and later in the REYES architecture [3]. The REYES architecture uses sub-pixel micro-polygons for rendering. These micro-polygons are simply displaced at their vertices and this provides a very dense tessellation which gives sufficient accuracy. The REYES architecture is not targeted towards real-time rendering and this micro-tessellation scheme is overkill for real-time application.

Displacement mapping has also been applied in ray-tracing. Early approaches used an inverse technique [10, 11] to warp the base surface to flatten it; the warp curves the ray. This curved ray is then intersected with the displacement map as if it were a height field. Recent techniques have explored direct ray tracing using techniques such as affine arithmetic [7], sophisticated caching schemes [13] and grid base intersections [15].

Alternatively, both image warping [14] and volume rendering [8] techniques have been explored. However, warping techniques require special hardware support (and so would not be backward compatible with existing accelerators), while volumetric techniques require a large texture bandwidth and fill rate.

Recently a few hardware-oriented algorithms for tessellation-based displacement mapping have been proposed. Gumhold and Hüttner [6] proposed a technique that produces a uniform tessellation based on the screen space projection of each base triangle. The technique also tessellates in the z-direction generating triangles where bump mapping would suffice. Doggett and Hirche [5] proposed a technique similar to ours that performs an adaptive tessellation. Their technique uses a combination of two heuristics to guide the tessellation, a point sampled normal variation test and an average height test based on summed area tables. Independently, neither test is sufficient but the combination of the two produces good results. However, their heuristic test is not guaranteed. In particular, the use of average displacement rather than maximum displace can result in the omission of small features with large displacement. The view dependent element of their approach is limited to edge length in screen space, the nature of the displacement on the untessellated interior of the triangles is not considered. Doggett, Kugler and Strasser [4] proposed a multiple pass technique that first renders the geometry on a coarse screen space displacing the coarse pixels. The coarse pixels are then re-meshed into new triangles which are used in the final rendering. The technique is not adaptive and the memory requirements would be comparable to the stack space needed for our approach.

There are also indications that industry support is growing for real-time displacement mapping. A recent paper from NVIDIA proposes displacement mapped subdivision surfaces as a general modeling technique [9]. In a recent presentation by Microsoft on DX9 displacement mapping was mentioned, although in a simple form: a data stream synchronized to the vertex stream can be provided to vertex shaders. This approach is limited to the displacement of the original vertices.

3 Adaptive Tessellation

Displacement mapping can always be implemented by displacing a uniform subdivision of the base surface. However, adaptive tessellation will produce fewer triangles than brute force tessellation and, especially if view-dependent, will make more efficient use of the rasterization units.

If the base surface is approximated using a triangular mesh with vertex normals, adaptive tessellation can be implemented on a triangle by triangle basis. As an input triangle is processed, a local decision can be made as to whether the triangle needs to be split into several triangles to approximate the displaced surface to sufficient accuracy. If the triangle is split, the resultant sub-triangles are then handled in a recursive fashion [1, 5].

Our tessellator is based on this concept. An input triangle has three edges, E_1, E_2 and E_3. Each of these edges is tested independently using an *oracle*. The oracle is a function which takes an edge and information attached to the vertices at the ends of that edge as input, and returns 0 if the edge does not need to be split and 1 otherwise. Triangle edges are always split at their midpoints, introducing new vertices whose properties are set by interpolating the properties of the endpoints of the edge. Given the results from oracle evaluations for all three triangle edges a three bit code can be constructed. This code is used to select one of eight tessellation patterns (Figure 3) to generate a new set of sub-triangles combining the old and new vertices. The resultant sub-triangles are evaluated and possibly further tessellated recursively. Three of the tessellation patterns produce a quadrilateral that needs to be split into two triangles. We have chosen to split the quadrilateral in an arbitrary but consistent fashion. A more intelligent choice could be made by using the displacement data to drive the split but this would incur extra computation and in our tests did not have a huge impact on the resultant tessellation.

Since the tessellation is based on edge splitting, a crack free tessellation can be guaranteed provided the oracle is deterministic and vertex symmetric, that is, it returns exactly the same result given exactly the same edge. This permits input triangles that share edges to be specified and processed in any order. The information provided to the oracle *must* be local to the edge (such as position and texture coordinates) and should not include any information unique to the triangle (such as the triangle normal). Under these conditions two triangles that share an edge will provide the same information to the oracle and the algorithm will generate the same tessellation on either side of the edge. This scheme is not guaranteed to generate an optimal tessellation. It is, however, online, local, robust (with a suitable oracle) and simple enough for hardware implementation.

A naive implementation of this approach requires redundant computation. As the recursion proceeds from one level to the next any edges generated in the interior of the input triangle will produce two sub-triangles that share a common edge. In the naive approach the oracle for this edge would need to be evaluated for both sub-triangles that share it even though the result will be identical. Splitting this common edge will also require the vertex position and any associated parameters to be interpolated twice. As an example, if a triangle is split into four at every step and the recursion depth is four then only 150 unique vertices are generated but 255 oracle evaluations and edge splits are performed.

To reduce the number of redundant calculations we can restructure the recursion such that the oracle evaluations and interpolations are done one step ahead of time. The evaluation work needed at level i is done at level $i-1$ and is shared across all triangles at level i. Likewise, level i pre-calculates the evaluation for level $i+1$ and passes this information on. This technique requires a larger stack since up to nine extra oracle evaluations and interpolated vertices need to be stored. However, oracle results take only a small amount of space: one bit each. Also, we would want to allocate memory in advance for the worst case stack size anyway. Interpolation computations for edge splits are computed regardless of the results of the oracle, but are put into effect only if the oracle evaluations return true. Our results have shown that this pre-calculation technique greatly improves the performance of a software implementation despite the "wasted" oracle and interpolation computations. In a hardware context, we might want to employ multiple arithmetic units for evaluating the worst-case number of oracles and interpolations in parallel. In the case of multiple evaluation units, avoiding a single oracle evaluation or interpolation would not save any time. However, we might want to *only* precompute the oracles, to save space on the stack.

Similar schemes to the one we present here have been used previously for tessellating parametric surfaces [1] and displacement maps [5]. On the one hand, hardware supporting the algorithm proposed here could be extended to the tessellation of procedurally generated parametric surfaces in a future accelerator (supporting generative modeling [16], for instance). This would require only programmable vertex-position functions and interval evaluation of those functions, which is not completely out of the question. However, to keep things simple, we have focussed on displacement mapping. The differences between our technique and the prior use of a similar scheme for adaptive tessellation of displacement maps [5] lie in our oracle and our representation of the displacement map. Our approach is both more robust (it will not miss small features) and operates in homogeneous coordinates. The latter property means we can operate in device space and so do not have to re-transform the vertices generated by the algorithm.

4 Displacement Map Representation

In addition to evaluation of the displacement at a point our oracle requires an upper and lower bound on the range of the displacement function given an area of its domain. In other words, our algorithm is based on interval analysis and we need an interval extension of the displacement function.

More formally, given a displacement function $d(u,v)$ we define its interval extension $D(U,V)$ as follows:

$$\begin{aligned} U &= [u_L, u_H], \\ V &= [v_L, v_H], \end{aligned}$$

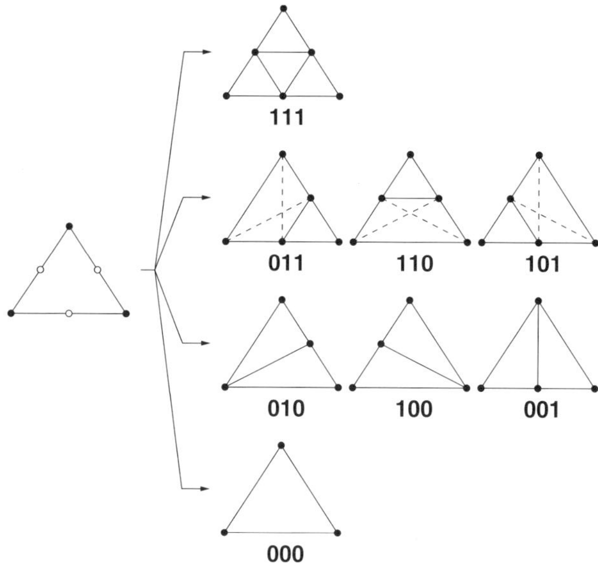

Figure 3: Tessellation patterns. Each pattern has a corresponding three bit code.

$$\begin{aligned} d_L(U,V) &= \min\{d(u,v)|u \in U, v \in V\}, \\ d_H(U,V) &= \max\{d(u,v)|u \in U, v \in V\}, \\ D(U,V) &= [d_L(U,V), d_H(U,V)]. \end{aligned}$$

If the displacement function is defined procedurally then interval arithmetic techniques can be used [16]. This approach was used by Heidrich [7] (using affine interval arithmetic) for ray tracing procedural displacement shaders. If the displacement function is tabulated in the form of a 2D array (as a texture map), or if a texture is used as part of a procedural displacement shader, then an interval extension of the texture lookup operator is needed.

4.1 Bounding a Tabulated Displacement Function

Upper and lower bounds could easily be calculated from a tabulated displacement function by iterating over the desired area, $[u_L, u_H] \times [v_L, v_H]$, to find d_L and d_H. This provides the tightest bound but unfortunately the computational cost is far too high. Instead we use a data structure, similar to MIP-maps, that stores precomputed bounds over predetermined areas.

For our representation, a hierarchy of arrays is built containing $\lg(r)$ levels where r is the resolution of the initial array. Usually, as in MIP-maps, we would start with a square array whose dimensions are a power of two. Each level is a quarter of the size of the previous level, obtained by reducing each dimension by a factor of two. However, unlike MIP-maps, the coarser levels are populated with the *interval* that bounds the corresponding area in the next finer level. Given a particular entry (i, j) at level ℓ, the entry will be populated with the interval over the area $[2^\ell i, 2^\ell(i+1)] \times [2^\ell j, 2^\ell(j+1)]$. The entries can be calculated using the initial tabulated data. Alternatively the entire hierarchy can be constructed in a recursive fashion where entries for level i are calculated using four entries from level $i-1$. A one-dimensional example hierarchy is shown in Figure 4.

The storage requirements for this representation are similar to MIP-maps. The quarter reduction in size of each subsequent level leads to a storage overhead of one third the original size. The interval bound requires an upper and lower value, doubling the size of the hierarchy which results in two thirds the original size.

In our experience, 8-bit displacements are too coarse and at least 16-bit precision is required. However, 8-bit precision can be used for the upper and lower bounds in the internal nodes of the interval hierarchy if outward (conservative) rounding is used. If this is done, then each such interval would take as much space as one original 16-bit sample. This means that a displacement map would take exactly as much space as a single-channel 16-bit MIP-map.

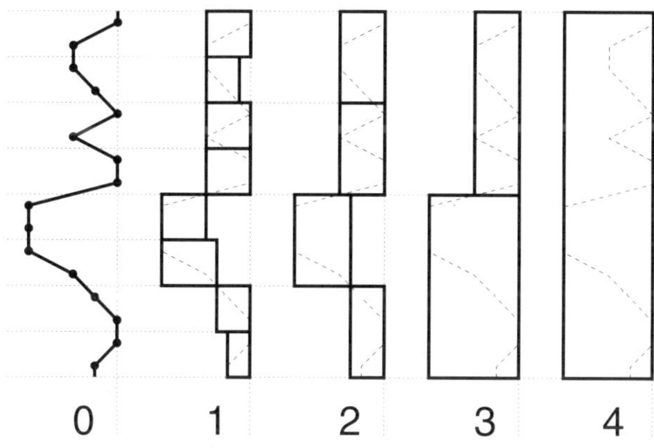

Figure 4: Example interval hierarchy.

The naive approach to acquire an interval bound using the hierarchy is to simply use the entry that completely encompasses the desired area $[u_L, u_H] \times [v_L, v_H]$. This can be accomplished by finding the level ℓ_u that encompasses $[u_L, u_H]$, and the level ℓ_v that encompasses $[v_L, v_H]$, and use $\ell = \max(\ell_u, \ell_v)$. Define the integer representations of u as $i = \lfloor Nu + 0.5 \rfloor$ and v as $j = \lfloor Nv + 0.5 \rfloor$, where N is the number of samples in the finest level of the hierarchy. The level ℓ_u is the number of low-order bits that must be removed from i before $(i_L \gg \ell_u) = (i_H \gg \ell_u)$, and likewise for ℓ_v (where $\gg$ is the right bit shift operator). The appropriate entry in level ℓ can then be found by indexing a 2D array using $(i_L \gg \ell)$ and $(j_L \gg \ell)$.

This approach tends to produce very loose bounds compared to the optimal (exhaustive search) method because the entry selected usually corresponds to an area much larger than the desired one. In particular, if one of the dimensions of the desired area has an integer representation of its interval bounds that are identical in only the topmost bits then the resultant level may be arbitrarily large. This leads to poor convergence and unnecessary tessellation concentrated near the power of two areas in the displacement map. This can be seen in Figure 6(c).

A better approach is to take the interval union of several entries from the hierarchy to construct a tighter bound. We use up to four entries. The possible configurations of the entries is shown in Figure 5. Other configurations and methods for obtaining tighter bounds are possible but in our experiments this set provides sufficiently tight bounds while still being straightforward to calculate.

First, for each dimension an appropriate level is found. The initial level estimate for a given dimension is found using *only* the width of the interval in that dimension, rounded up to the nearest power of two. Without loss of generality we will consider only u, in which case the level estimate would be

$$w_u = \lceil \lg(i_H - i_L + 1) \rceil.$$

Define

$$\begin{aligned} a_u &= (i_L \gg (w_u - 1)), \\ b_u &= (i_H \gg (w_u - 1)). \end{aligned}$$

If $b_u - a_u > 1$, then $\ell_u = w_u$. Otherwise, $\ell_u = w_u - 1$. The initial estimate w_u is sufficient to encompass i_L and i_H. The values a_u and b_u are the entry indices if $w_u - 1$ were used. If b_u and a_u are consecutive entries then $w_u - 1$ would suffice, otherwise w_u is necessary. After finding ℓ_v in the same way, we compute $\ell = \max(\ell_u, \ell_v)$.

Second, once the level ℓ is found each of i_L, i_H, j_L and j_H are right shifted ℓ bits. Due the way ℓ is constructed there are four cases into which the shifted values fall:

1. If $(i_L \gg \ell) = (i_H \gg \ell)$ and $(j_L \gg \ell) = (j_H \gg \ell)$, then only one entry is needed (Figure 5(a)).
2. If $(i_L \gg \ell) = (i_H \gg \ell)$ and $(j_L \gg \ell) < (j_H \gg \ell)$, then two vertical entries are needed (Figure 5(b)).
3. If $(i_L \gg \ell) < (i_H \gg \ell)$ and $(j_L \gg \ell) = (j_H \gg \ell)$, then two horizontal entries are needed (Figure 5(c)).
4. If $(i_L \gg \ell) < (i_H \gg \ell)$ and $(j_L \gg \ell) < (j_H \gg \ell)$, then four entries are needed (Figure 5(d)).

The computational and bandwidth cost of this approach is higher than the naive approach, especially when four entries are combined, which is in fact the predominant case. However, our results have shown that although the cost of the multi-sampling oracle is higher the tighter bounds and better convergence leads to an overall performance that is significantly higher than the naive approach. The lookup cost of the multi-sampling oracle is comparable to bilinear interpolation in ordinary 2D texture mapping (which also requires four samples).

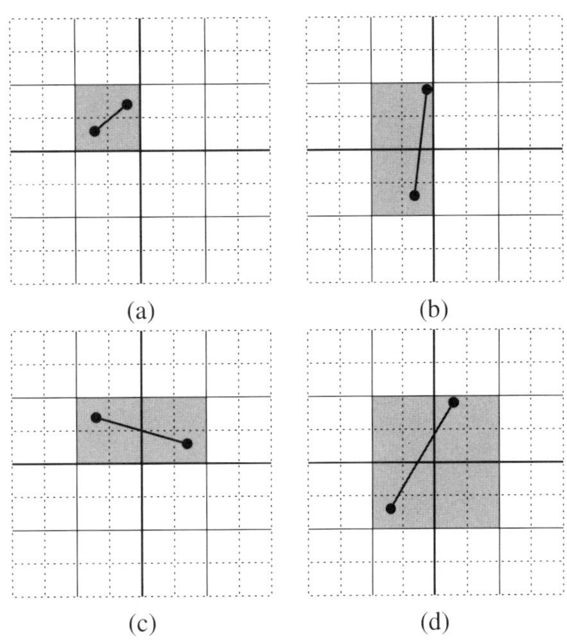

Figure 5: Examples of bounding an edge by combining several intervals.

A comparison of the optimal technique, the naive approach, and our approach are shown in Figure 6. Our approach is significantly closer to the optimal approach, focusing on the areas that require tessellation without excessive over-tessellation in unimportant areas.

5 Oracle

Our oracle function attempts to bound the maximum error within an *area* enclosing an edge. Using the texture coordinates of the two world space coordinate endpoints, $\mathbf{p}_1$ and $\mathbf{p}_2$, we can define an area in texture space (Figure 7). Over this area an interval, D, is found which bounds the displacement using the method described in Section 4. The union of the areas for the three edges that define an input triangle will be guaranteed to cover the interior of the triangle. This guarantees that even though the oracle is evaluated over an edge any displacement details contained on the interior of the triangle will be incorporated into one of the three oracle evaluations.

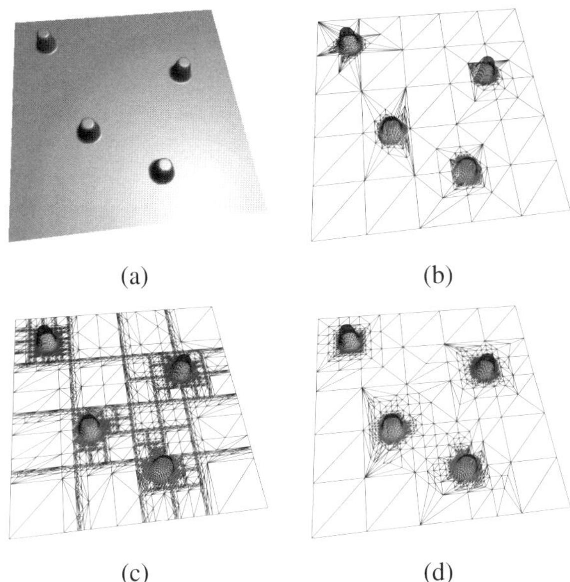

Figure 6: Comparison of interval lookup techniques. (a) Reference rendering, (b) Optimal (exhaustive search), (c) Naive (enclosing interval), (d) Proposed technique (four interval samples).

Using the interval bound D and an edge defined between points $\mathbf{p}_1$ and $\mathbf{p}_2$ with normals $\hat{\mathbf{n}}_1$ and $\hat{\mathbf{n}}_2$, we can find the position of the maximum displacement along the edge as follows:

$$\begin{aligned} \mathbf{p}(t) &= \mathbf{p}_1 + t\,(\mathbf{p}_2 - \mathbf{p}_1), \\ \vec{\mathbf{n}}(t) &= \hat{\mathbf{n}}_1 + t\,(\hat{\mathbf{n}}_2 - \hat{\mathbf{n}}_1), \\ \mathbf{p}_L(t) &= \mathbf{p}(t) + d_L \vec{\mathbf{n}}(t) \\ \mathbf{p}_H(t) &= \mathbf{p}(t) + d_H \vec{\mathbf{n}}(t) \\ t^* &= \arg\max_{t \in [0,1]} (||\mathbf{p}_L(t) - \mathbf{p}_H(t)||) \end{aligned} \tag{2}$$

Given t^*, the location of the maximum width, we decide if the edge should be split by comparing the width of this interval point against a user-defined threshold, ϵ.

$$||\mathbf{p}_L(t^*) - \mathbf{p}_H(t^*)|| < \epsilon. \tag{3}$$

In world space coordinates the left hand side of Equation 3 reduces to $||D||$, the width of the interval. This can be used to obtain a fixed world space tessellation.

However, in screen space with the distance measured in x and y only a view dependent tessellation can be performed. In screen space the maximum width will occur at one of the end points, whichever is closer to the eye. To determine if an edge needs to be split we can evaluate

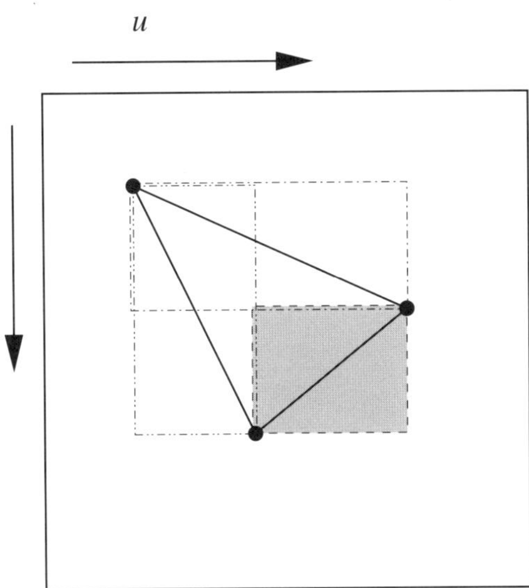

Figure 7: Areas defined by edges in texture space. The displacement is bounded over each of these areas when evaluating the oracle for the corresponding edge.

Equation 3 at $t = 0$ and $t = 1$. If both values are smaller than ϵ the edge need not be split and the oracle returns 0; otherwise the oracle returns 1 and the edge is split. Problems do arise when the edge crosses the eye plane, the maximum displacement will occur at the crossover point. This condition can be easily detected by inspecting the signs of the homogeneous w coordinates of $\mathbf{p}_1$ and $\mathbf{p}_2$. If the signs are different then the edge cross the eye plane and a split is automatic. In the following consider only the case where the signs of the w values are equal.

Using the homogeneous components of $\mathbf{p}_L(t)$ and $\mathbf{p}_H(t)$,

$$\begin{aligned}\mathbf{p}_L(t) &= (x_L, y_L, z_L, w_L), \\ \mathbf{p}_H(t) &= (x_H, y_H, z_H, w_H).\end{aligned}$$

Equation 3 reduces to

$$\sqrt{\left(\frac{x_H}{w_H} - \frac{x_L}{w_L}\right)^2 + \left(\frac{y_H}{w_H} - \frac{y_L}{w_L}\right)^2} < \epsilon.$$

After some further manipulation, this reduces to

$$\begin{aligned}(w_L x_H - w_H x_L)^2 &+ \\ (w_L y_H - w_H y_L)^2 &< (w_H w_L \epsilon)^2.\end{aligned} \tag{4}$$

This form of the oracle will not generate subdivisions when the displacement is directly towards the eye (since bump-mapping alone suffices in that case). It might be interesting to include the $\frac{z}{w}$ term, for example if bump-mapping is not used or the geometry for a shadow map is needed. The nonlinear encoding of z would need to be considered, in particular the interpretation of the ϵ threshold would need to be reconsidered.

6 Results

This algorithm has been implemented as a C library. The library sits on top of OpenGL and exposes an OpenGL-like API extended with displacement mapping functionality. An 866 Mhz Pentium III machine with an NVIDIA GeForce3 running Linux was used to render the images and collect timing information. Bump mapping was implemented in all cases using the NVIDIA texture shader extensions.

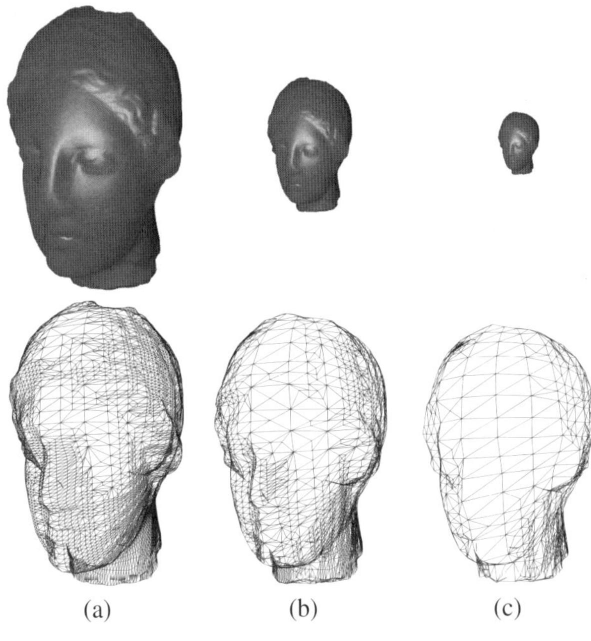

Figure 8: Venus example. Rendering at various distances from the eye with a magnified wire-frame: (a) 21959 triangles at 20fps, (b) 9269 triangles at 30fps and (c) 2516 triangles at 85fps.

Figure 8 shows the venus bust modeled as a displacement mapped sphere. The displacement map was generated using a ray-tracing method similar to the one described by Lee *et al* [9]. In Figure 8 the model is rendered at various distances from the eye. The adjacent wire-frame shows the adaptive tessellation in close-up. As the model moves farther away the oracle decides that more and more edges do not need to be split. This results in significantly reduced tessellation while preserving visual quality. The wire-frame images also demonstrate that the face itself requires less tessellation since it is fairly smooth and relatively perpendicular to the viewing direction. However, the silhouette and the neck require more tessellation to maintain visual quality and henceforth a higher tessellation level in these regions is apparent at all distances.

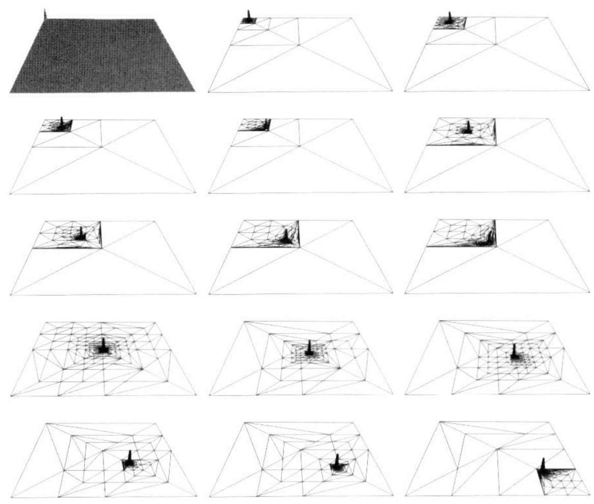

Figure 9: Spike example: average of 700 triangles, frame rate of 1000fps+.

Figure 9 demonstrates that the algorithm does not miss details. The displacement map corresponds to a small spike with a large displacement and no displacement elsewhere. The initial model used is a plane consisting of two large triangles. Several displacement maps are used with the spike positioned at different locations along the diagonal. Although the amount of tessellation differs depending on the location of the spike, the spike is never missed. The variation seen in the tessellation is due to interaction between the spike position, the interval hierarchy, and the initial tessellation. In particular, the interval hierarchy is sensitive to power of two boundaries.

Since our tessellation splits triangle edges only at their midpoints, the convergence to specific features in the displacement map may be slower than that of more flexible schemes. This is particularly noticeable when a displacement map has discontinuities. Figure 10 shows several displaced rectangles each rotated at a different angle (the oracle used here uses produces a fixed, world space tessellation). In the first few images the displacement map has a sampling pattern that coincides with the underlying model and the tessellation produces good visual results. As the rectangle is rotated further, more tessellation is required to capture the discontinuity. The fixed recursion depth in this example causes small "braiding" artifacts to appear when the underlying geometry and the displacement map discontinuities conflict.

We point out these limitations of our algorithm only for comparison purposes. It is important, however, to remember the specialized constraints under which our algorithm operates. Also, it should be noted that our algorithm does *not* fail in the presence of these difficult cases; but does generate additional tessellation.

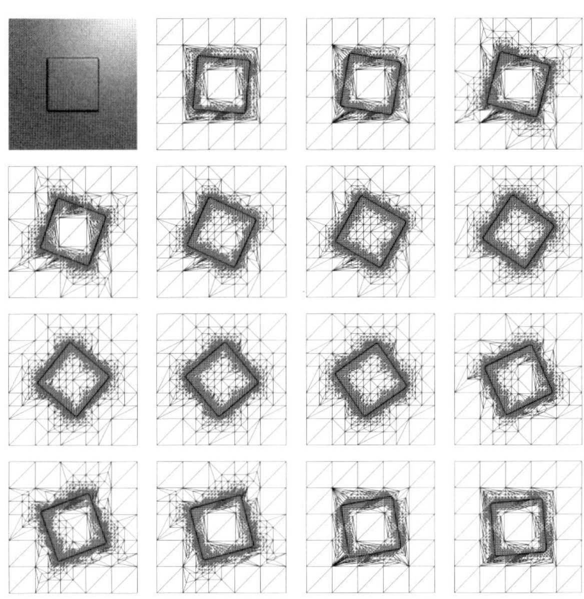

Figure 10: Spin example: average of 2100 triangles, frame rate of 380fps.

Name	Oracle	# Tris	FPS
Torus (Figure 1(b))	True	56448	14
Torus (Figure 1(c)	Adaptive	34377	21
Venus (not shown)	True	51200	12
Venus (Figure 8(a))	Adaptive	21959	20
Venus (Figure 8(b))	Adaptive	9269	30
Venus (Figure 8(c))	Adaptive	2516	85
Earth (Figure 11(c))	True	204800	4
Earth (Figure 11(b))	Adaptive	31374	20

Table 1: Run-time statistics. The "True" in the Oracle column refers to an oracle that always returns 1, giving a uniform tessellation to the maximum depth. The "Adaptive" oracle is the one described in Section 5 using the screen space distance measured in x and y.

7 Conclusions

Implementation of displacement mapping in hardware would lower bandwidth requirements for complex models and would also permit simple adaptive tessellation of complex models to be performed without software sup-

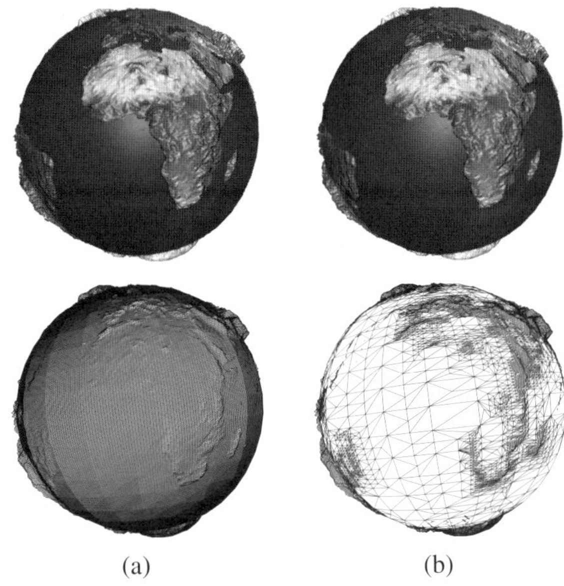

Figure 11: Earth example: (a) uniform tessellation and (b) adaptive tessellation.

port. We have presented an algorithm for implementing displacement mapping, using adaptive tessellation and hierarchical interval bounding of the displacement function. Our interval-based subdivision oracle is more robust than previous approaches that did not consider variation of the displacement over the interior of the input triangles.

Our approach is simple enough to run in real time in software, but would also be suitable for hardware implementation. Since the software implementation runs in real time, it could be added to a driver. Adoption of such an architecture would permit eventual adoption of a hardware displacement unit, while permitting partial hardware acceleration even on current architectures. A conceptual model of the pipeline including the displacement unit is shown in Figure 12. The vertex shading unit would need to be placed ahead of the displacement unit. The displacement unit generates a potentially different set of output vertices each frame. Shading these continuously changing output vertices could possibly produce frame-to-frame shading artifacts.

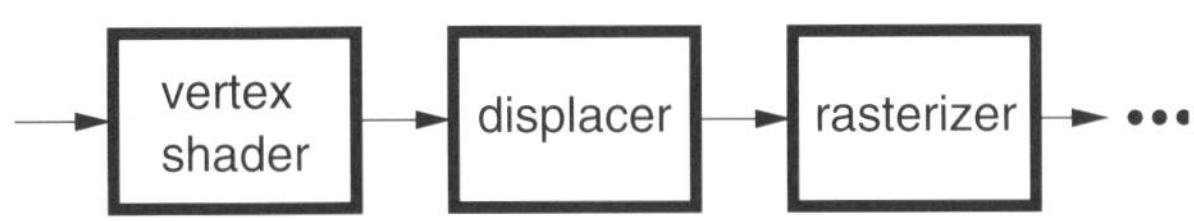

Figure 12: Location of displacement unit in pipeline.

Our approach could be extended in various ways. We only consider splitting edges at their midpoints. This leads to a simple interpolator and a symmetric edge split, but splitting at other than the midpoint might lead to higher convergence rates. It might be interesting, for instance, to perform edge detection on the displacement map and perform edge splits near locations of known discontinuities. Also, as stated in the introduction, it should be possible to extend our scheme to the adaptive tessellation of arbitrary procedural parametric geometry [16], by simply adding a unit to perform programmable interval analysis of "geometry shader" functions. This should probably be performed using affine arithmetic, which would require compiler support for efficient implementation, but would not require a radically new shader processing architecture. It might also be interesting to extend the representation of tabulated displacement functions to a form suitable for affine arithmetic, by storing slope information as well as bounds. Finally, if information could be attached to edges rather than just vertices it might be possible to come up with better oracles that use, for instance, the dihedral angle between adjacent faces.

Acknowledgements

This research was sponsored by research grants from the Natural Sciences and Engineering Research Council of Canada (NSERC), Communications and Information Technology Ontario (CITO), Canadian Foundation for Innovation (CFI), Ontario Innovation Trust (OIT) and Bell University Labs (BUL). We also gratefully acknowledge NVIDIA's hardware donations and the ever helpful members of the Computer Graphics Lab.

References

[1] A. J. Chung and A. J. Field. A simple recursive tessellator for adaptive surface triangulation. *Journal of Graphics Tools*, 5(3):1–9, 2000.

[2] Robert L. Cook. Shade tress. *Proceedings of SIGGRAPH 84*, pages 223–231, 1984.

[3] Robert L. Cook, Loren Carpenter, and Edwin Catmull. The reyes image rendering architecture. *Proceedings of SIGGRAPH 87*, pages 95–102, 1987.

[4] M. Doggett, A. Kugler, and W. Strasser. Displacement mapping using scan conversion hardware architectures. *Computer Graphics Forum*, 20(1):13–26, 2001.

[5] Michael Doggett and Johannes Hirche. Adaptive view dependent tessellation of displacement maps. *2000 SIGGRAPH / Eurographics Workshop on Graphics Hardware*, pages 59–66, 2000.

[6] Stefan Gumhold and Tobias Hüttner. Multiresolution rendering with displacement mapping. *1999 SIGGRAPH / Eurographics Workshop on Graphics Hardware*, pages 55–66, 1999.

[7] Wolfgang Heidrich and Hans-Peter Seidel. Ray-tracing procedural displacement shaders. *Graphics Interface '98*, pages 8–16, 1998.

[8] Jan Kautz and Hans-Peter Seidel. Hardware accelerated displacement mapping for image based rendering. *Graphics Interface 2001*, pages 61–70, 2001.

[9] Aaron Lee, Henry Moreton, and Hugues Hoppe. Displaced subdivision surfaces. *Proceedings of SIGGRAPH 2000*, pages 85–94, 2000.

[10] J. R. Logie and J. W. Patterson. Inverse displacement mapping in the general case. *Computer Graphics Forum*, 14(5):261–273, 1995.

[11] J. W. Patterson, S. G. Hoggar, and J. R. Logie. Inverse displacement mapping. *Computer Graphics Forum*, 10(2):129–139, 1991.

[12] Hans Køhling Pedersen. Displacement mapping using flow fields. *Proceedings of SIGGRAPH 94*, pages 279–286, 1994.

[13] Matt Pharr and Pat Hanrahan. Geometry caching for ray-tracing displacement maps. *Eurographics Rendering Workshop 1996*, pages 31–40, 1996.

[14] Gernot Schaufler and Markus Priglinger. Efficient displacement mapping by image warping. *Eurographics Rendering Workshop 1999*, pages 175–186, 1999.

[15] Brian Smits, Peter Shirley, and Michael M. Stark. Direct ray tracing of displacement mapped triangles. *Rendering Techniques 2000: 11th Eurographics Workshop on Rendering*, pages 307–318, 2000.

[16] John M. Snyder. *Generative Modeling for Computer Graphics and CAD: Symbolic Shape Design Using Interval Analysis*. Academic Press, 1992.

[17] Xiaochuan Corina Wang, Jérome Maillot, Eugene Fiume, Victor Ng-Thow-Hing, Andrew Woo, and Sanjay Bakshi. Feature-based displacement mapping. *Rendering Techniques 2000: 11th Eurographics Workshop on Rendering*, pages 257–268, 2000.

Automatic Generation of Subdivision Surface Head Models from Point Cloud Data

Won-Ki Jeong Kolja Kähler Jörg Haber Hans-Peter Seidel

Max-Planck-Institut für Informatik, Stuhlsatzenhausweg 85, 66123 Saarbrücken, Germany

{jeong,kaehler,haberj,hpseidel}@mpi-sb.mpg.de

Abstract

An automatic procedure is presented to generate a multiresolution head model from sampled surface data. A generic control mesh serves as the starting point for a fitting algorithm that approximates the points in an unstructured set of surface samples, e.g. a point cloud obtained directly from range scans of an individual. A hierarchical representation of the model is generated by repeated refinement using subdivision rules and measuring displacements to the input data. Key features of our method are the fully automated construction process, the ability to deal with noisy and incomplete input data, and no requirement for further processing of the scan data after registering the range images into a single point cloud.

Key words: range scans, subdivision surface, facial animation, point cloud fitting

1 Introduction

In the task of modeling human heads from real individuals for facial animation we are usually confronted with two conflicting goals: one is the requirement for accurate reproduction of facial features, the other is the demand for an efficient representation which can be animated easily and quickly. Additional difficulties are brought in by limitations of current range scanning technology: the data is often noisy and has "holes" due to shadowing effects or bad reflection properties of the scanned surface. Some data, like the part of the lips on the inside of the mouth, cannot be captured at all. To create a triangle mesh that is suitable for real-time animation, extensive manual post-processing of the scanned geometry is often necessary, followed by mesh simplification to reduce the complexity of the mesh. Unfortunately, mesh decimation techniques cannot exert enough control over the connectivity of the mesh to obtain an optimal mesh for animation: the distribution of vertices and alignment of edges should correspond to the basic symmetry of the face and the potential deformations of the mesh, which are not easily derived from the static shape. With low-polygon models, a single misplaced edge can destroy the visual impression of a smooth surface. Resorting to higher resolution meshes is nonetheless undesirable due to the additional computational load for the animation system.

We chose to use a subdivision surface representation in our facial animation environment. Subdivision surfaces have become increasingly popular due to their ability to bridge the gap between polygon meshes and higher-order surfaces. Since they are constructed by repeated refinement of triangle meshes up to an arbitrarily close approximation to their smooth limit surface, they also provide an effective means to control accuracy and efficiency in a systematic manner. By constructing the surface from a control mesh of known topology, we can also avoid the instabilities that are incurred by animating an irregular triangle mesh.

In this paper, we present our approach for generation of multiresolution head model geometry from sampled surface data. The method takes as input an unstructured point cloud that is obtained from range scans of an individual. A fully automatic procedure is used to fit a hand-designed generic control mesh to this point cloud, taking special care to match facial features such as ears and mouth. A hierarchical structure of displaced subdivision surfaces is then constructed, which approximates the input geometry with increasing precision, up to the sampling resolution of the input data. Our method generates useful models from noisy and incomplete input data, with no requirement for further processing of the scan data except for registration into a single point cloud. Figure 1 shows the main stages of our method.

Since we use an interpolating subdivision scheme, displacing a vertex of the subdivision control mesh corresponds directly to the local change of the surface. In our physics-based facial animation system, we interpret the vertices and edges of the control mesh as point masses and springs which are reacting to forces applied by virtual muscles. Animating this very coarse spring mesh is computationally efficient, while the level of detail for rendering the geometry is controlled separately. For a given refinement level, the support of a vertex in the control mesh is known, and thus we can achieve efficient animation by only locally updating the mesh structure.

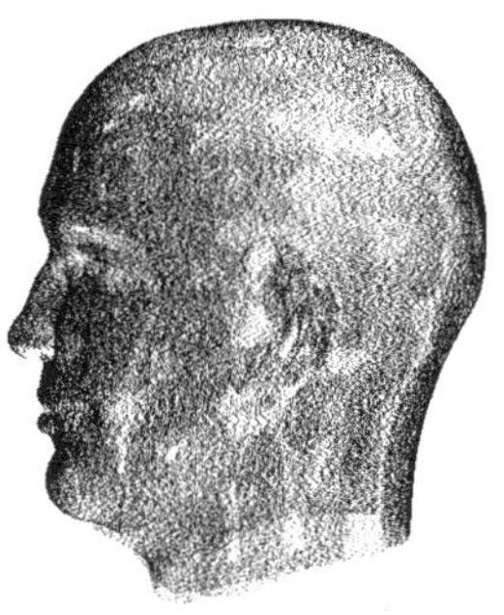  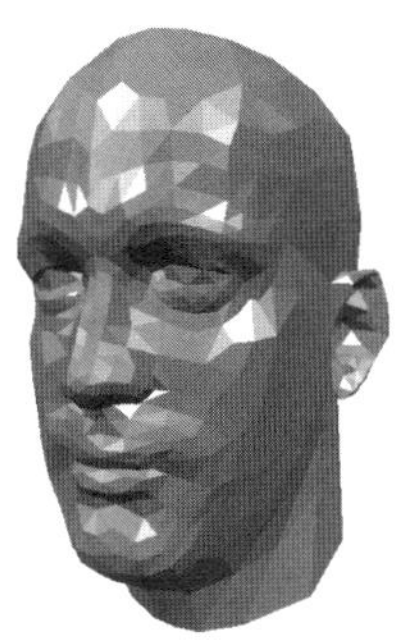 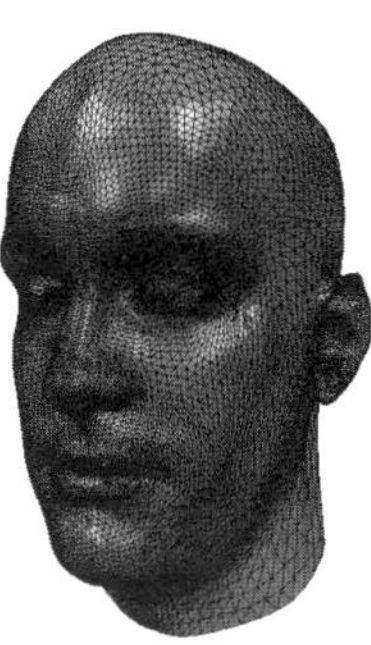

Figure 1: The main stages of head model construction. From left to right: a) a dense set of surface samples obtained directly from a range scanner (thinned in this image for visualization); b) generic mesh; c) deformed mesh used as subdivision control mesh; d) subdivision surface fitted to range data.

2 Previous Work

The literature on surface representations used in modeling and animation is vast. Since we are interested in constructing multiresolution models for real-time facial animation, we focus here on triangle mesh-based structures, because of their conceptual simplicity and the availability of efficient graphics hardware for rendering.

Adaptive refinement of arbitrary triangle meshes is an active topic in multiresolution editing [26, 11]. While these methods provide powerful tools for mesh deformations, the computational complexity is still considerably too high for real-time applications.

In physics-based animation, the vertices of a deformable mesh surface are often interpreted as nodes of a spring mesh [13, 22]. Adaptively refining such a mass-spring system is non-trivial [7]. An efficient method to smooth polygonal geometry proposed by VOLINO *et al.* [23] can be applied to the deformed geometry that results from a mass-spring simulation to improve visual quality. The technique uses on-the-fly refinement of polygons, where additional vertex positions are computed from the vertex normals of the original mesh. The resulting surface has smoother appearance, but does not contain additional geometric detail.

Subdivision surfaces have been successfully used in computer animation [3]. A wide range of subdivision schemes exists today, basically structured by the type of the control mesh (quadrilateral or triangular), the order of continuity they can achieve (usually C^1 or C^2) and whether they approximate or interpolate the control mesh after refinement [24]. While most subdivision schemes apply the subdivision operator uniformly to the surface, some recent results demonstrate adaptive refinement [26, 10]. The algorithms become considerably more complex in these cases.

PIGHIN *et al.* [18] have used an approach based on radial basis functions to match a generic head mesh to several photographs of a head simultaneously. Their approach doesn't need additional hardware besides a low-cost still camera, but requires the manual specification of facial features in all of the views. Animation is limited, because each expression needs to be captured in advance. An optimization process proposed by BLANZ *et al.* [2] generates close approximations to even only a single photograph. This technique draws from a large database of several hundred scanned faces. The resulting model has the same resolution as the scanned faces and cannot be readily animated.

In the context of medical imaging, SZELISKI *et al.* [21] minimize the distance between two surfaces obtained from volume scans of human heads by applying local and global deformations in a hierarchical manner. The deformations are modelled by a combination of global polynomial deformations and local free-form deformations [20]. The method does not require specification of corresponding features on the geometries.

The goal in the method presented by LEE *et al.* [13] is the automated construction of animatable head models from range scans. They adapt a generic face mesh with embedded muscle vectors to range scans of human heads. This process is largely automated, but relies on the inherent automatic registration of the texture to the range data. The model created from the scan data is fully animatable. The generated mesh approximates the input geometry well on a rather coarse detail level.

MARSCHNER *et al.* [17] match a subdivision surface to geometry measured by a range scanner. They use Loop subdivision rules [16] and a fitting algorithm based on the work of HOPPE *et al.* [5]. A continuous optimization process alters vertex positions to minimize an energy functional. For rendering, the surface is subdivided to the desired level. Due to the approximating nature of Loop subdivision, the coarser levels of the subdivision hierarchy do not resemble the scanned geometry everywhere.

Motion of the face is specified by varying positions of sample points on the surface and computing the corresponding control vertex displacements.

3 Overview

In our approach, facial geometry is acquired from real humans using a range scanner. The individuals are captured with a closed mouth and neutral expression. No triangulation or further post-processing such as hole-filling is performed on the scan data. The result of the acquisition stage is an unstructured, dense point cloud, possibly with infrequent large holes due to missing or bad data.

Given the generic head model as shown in Figure 1 b), we deform this mesh to approximate the point cloud in a three-step procedure, which runs automatically without user intervention:

1. **Initial alignment:** This step automatically computes an affine transformation (rotation, translation and non-uniform scaling) that minimizes the difference between the silhouette of the generic head model and the outer hull of the point cloud. This procedure uses an iterative optimization technique, and we exploit graphics hardware for evaluating the current match to achieve fast convergence.

2. **Local fitting:** Due to individual differences in facial proportions, the global affine transformation does usually not result in good registration of the prominent features of the face. Thus, we apply another optimization to the regions containing the ears, nose, and mouth, which are marked in the prototype mesh. Here, a local rigid transformation is found that minimizes the distance from the point samples to the mesh surface. The transformation is applied directly to the mesh regions and blended into the surrounding parts of the mesh to achieve smooth transitions.

3. **Global fitting:** The deformed prototype mesh is now well-aligned to the facial features of the sample data. The final fitting step reduces the distance from the point cloud to the mesh by global energy minimization. The employed energy functional is essentially the same as used by HOPPE *et al.* [6] and MARSCHNER *et al.* [17]. In addition to minimization of the distance between point cloud and mesh, the function accounts for smoothness and constraints defined on the generic mesh.

All three steps of this fitting procedure are explained in detail in Section 4. Provided the deformed generic mesh, we proceed with the construction of the subdivision hierarchy, using the interpolating Modified Butterfly scheme [25]. On the base level and on each level of refinement, the vertices are displaced along triangle normal direction to lie on the surface sampled by the point cloud. In this manner, a hierarchy of surfaces is generated with locally encoded details, similar to normal meshes [4]. The construction process is detailed in Section 5. For animation, we rebuild the surface in the changed areas, such that the local detail will follow the deformation properly, see Section 6.

4 Fitting the Control Mesh

For the following discussion we need some notation. We define a triangle mesh $\mathcal{M}$ as a tuple $(\mathcal{V}_\mathcal{M}, \mathcal{E}_\mathcal{M}, \mathcal{T}_\mathcal{M})$, denoting the vertices, edges and triangles of the mesh, respectively. We refer to the initial generic mesh as $\mathcal{G}$. This mesh will be deformed over the three fitting stages by updating its vertex positions, but leaving the connectivity unchanged. The sample data is given as a set of points $\mathcal{P}$. All points and mesh vertex positions are given as 3D coordinates and will be written in bold face: $\mathbf{p} \in \mathbb{R}^3$. For convenience, for a vertex $v \in \mathcal{V}_\mathcal{M}$, $\mathbf{v}$ will denote its position. We write $star(v)$ for the set of vertices directly connected to v via an edge, and $valence(v)$ for the number of these adjacent vertices.

4.1 Initial alignment

In the initial step of the subdivision surface fitting process, we approximately align the generic head model $\mathcal{G}$ to the point cloud using an affine transformation T. Throughout this section, $\mathcal{G}$ will mean the transformed version of the generic mesh using the current T, which is used – after convergence – as the input for the next step described in Section 4.2. The parameters for T are determined fully automatically by exploiting graphics hardware to perform a silhouette-based geometry fitting. Our approach thus extends the idea of the 2D silhouette-based texture mapping technique presented in [14, 15] to three-dimensional geometry.

To evaluate the current T, we render both $\mathcal{G}$ and $\mathcal{P}$ into a common frame buffer for one of the three canonical viewing directions along the coordinate axes. The frame buffer is initialized to black. Next, we render the point cloud with a white color, an identity modelview matrix, and no further lighting or depth test. We then set the OpenGL logical fragment operation to XOR and render the generic head model with the modelview matrix set to T and identical rendering parameters. Now the frame buffer contains those pixels in white that are covered by only one of the two geometric objects $\mathcal{G}$ and $\mathcal{P}$. The frame buffer image can thus be interpreted as the silhouette-based difference between $\mathcal{G}$ and $\mathcal{P}$ for the chosen viewing direction[1]. Finally, the number of white pixels in the frame buffer is evaluated using the `glGetHistogram` function. It is a measure of how well the objects $\mathcal{G}$ and $\mathcal{P}$ are aligned in their image space projection. This process is repeated for all three different viewing directions in turn and their difference measures are summed up. The resulting *total difference* D is used to control an iterative optimization process to determine T.

We initialize the scaling and translation parameters of T such that the bounding boxes of the point cloud and the generic head model have the same size and center point. Since we know from our range scanner that the point cloud is roughly oriented in such a way that the face looks along the z-axis and the up-vector coincides with the y-axis, we set the initial rotation parameters of T accordingly. For the optimization process, we apply Powell's method [19, Sec. 10.5] to the set of parameters of T. The function to be minimized is given by the total difference D. Figure 2 shows three silhouette-based difference images (according to three orthogonal viewing directions) both after the initialization step and after convergence of the optimization process.

In addition, we have to take into account that the part of the point cloud $\mathcal{P}$ representing the neck of the head might be longer or shorter than the corresponding part of the generic head model $\mathcal{G}$. To avoid artificial "difference pixels" due to these non-corresponding parts of $\mathcal{P}$ and $\mathcal{G}$, we introduce a clipping plane in the world coordinate system (i.e. the location of the clipping plane is independent of T) to cut away those unwanted parts of $\mathcal{P}$ and $\mathcal{G}$. Also, the back of the head can often not be captured appropriately due to difficulties with structured light scanners in hair-covered head regions, so we add another clipping plane that removes this part in $\mathcal{P}$ and $\mathcal{G}$ as well. We provide a generic position and orientation for each of these planes based on the initial T, which may have to be modified by the user before the fitting process is started, according to the specifics of the range scan data.

Further optimization of the process can be achieved by initially rendering the point cloud once for each viewing direction and storing the resulting frame buffer images in three textures. During the optimization process, we then only need to render one textured quad for each viewing direction instead of rendering the full point cloud.

4.2 Adaptive Local Alignment

The initial alignment step gives an optimal fit for the generic mesh using an affine transform. Since individual faces are of different proportions, the main facial features like ears, nose and mouth are generally not registered well in the transformed generic mesh and the point cloud, which prohibits a direct execution of the global distance minimization procedure (section 4.3). Hence, we apply local deformations to the mesh in four areas of the generic model (one for each ear, the nose and the mouth).

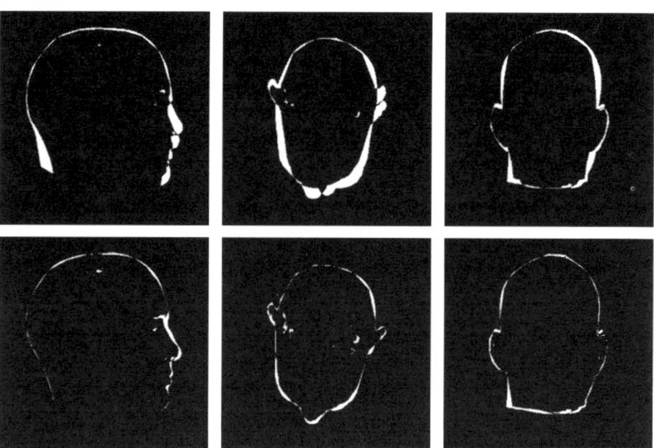

Figure 2: Silhouette-based geometry fitting: white pixels indicate the difference between the silhouettes of the generic head model and the point cloud. Top row: initial difference images for three orthogonal viewing directions. Bottom row: difference images after optimization process.

For this purpose, a set of bounding boxes $\mathcal{B}$ enclosing each feature is predefined for the generic mesh, as shown in Figure 4. The bounding boxes are chosen large enough to ensure that after the initial alignment the sample points belonging to the respective feature on the point cloud are also included in the box. In the following, we write $\mathcal{G}^b$ for the part of the generic mesh $\mathcal{G}$ that is enclosed in bounding box $b \in \mathcal{B}$. Similarly, $\mathcal{P}^b$ is the portion of the point cloud enclosed in box b.

For each bounding box, we now minimize the energy functional $E_{local} = E_{dist} + E_{stretch}$ by optimizing the position of the mesh vertices included in the box. E_{dist} is minimized as the distance from every point in the point cloud to the mesh becomes smaller:

$$E_{dist}(\mathcal{G}^b) = \sum_{\mathbf{p} \in \mathcal{P}^b} (\|\Pi(\mathcal{G}^b, \mathbf{p}) - \mathbf{p}\|^2),$$

where $\Pi(\mathcal{G}^b, \mathbf{p})$ is the projection of point $\mathbf{p}$ onto the nearest surface point on the mesh $\mathcal{G}^b$.

$E_{stretch}$ penalizes changes in length of edges in the generic mesh after transformation, and is defined as

$$E_{stretch}(\mathcal{G}^b) = \sum_{e \in \mathcal{E}_{\mathcal{G}^b}} \frac{1}{2} k |l_e - r_e|^2,$$

[1]If the point cloud does not contain enough data points to result in a fully covered silhouette during rendering, we repeat this step with `glPointsize` set to a slightly higher value.

where k is a spring constant, l_e is the current length, and r_e the rest length of edge e. Including this term prohibits large changes in the position and orientation of the feature, and thus keeps the optimization from converging to a solution too far from the initial configuration.

To find an affine transformation that minimizes the non-linear function E_{local}, we employ Powell's algorithm, as in Section 4.1. Since the optimization is performed only locally over the mesh region $\mathcal{G}^b$, it can be carried out quickly.

After the energy minimization procedure has converged, we apply the transformation found for each bounding box to the contained geometry and perform a gradual blend with the surrounding area, similar to the method used in [1]. For blending, we use a set $L = \{\mathbf{l}_1, \dots, \mathbf{l}_n\}$ of n landmarks defined on the undeformed generic mesh, which are contained in the above mentioned boxes. In practice, we use three landmarks for each ear, and four for the nose and the mouth, see Figure 4. The transformation found for each box is also applied to the contained landmarks, resulting in the transformed landmark set $\tilde{L} = \{\tilde{\mathbf{l}}_1, \dots, \tilde{\mathbf{l}}_n\}$. The displacement vectors for all the landmarks are used to update the subset $\overline{\mathcal{V}^b} := \mathcal{V}_\mathcal{G} \setminus \{\mathcal{V}_{\mathcal{G}^b}\}_{b \in \mathcal{B}}$ of vertices of $\mathcal{V}_\mathcal{G}$ that are not contained in any box. The displacements are weighted by an exponential fall-off function according to the distance between landmark and mesh vertex:

$$\forall v \in \overline{\mathcal{V}^b} : \mathbf{v} \leftarrow \mathbf{v} + \sum_{i=1}^{n} \exp(-\tfrac{1}{k}\|\mathbf{v} - \mathbf{l}_i\|)(\tilde{\mathbf{l}}_i - \mathbf{l}_i)$$

We initialize the constant value k to 1/30 of the diagonal length of the bounding box of the given point set. This parameter controls the size of the region influenced by the blending.

4.3 Global Control Mesh Fitting

Given the generic mesh $\mathcal{G}$ with locally aligned facial features, we can now perform straightforward global optimization by iteratively minimizing the distance from the points of the sample data set to the mesh surface. We perform least squares minimization of the energy functional

$$E_{global} = E_{dist} + \lambda E_{smooth} + \mu E_{binding} + \nu E_{constraint}.$$

Optimization stops, when the difference of the previous and current E_{global} drops below a user-specified error threshold. E_{dist} is just the same functional as used in Section 4.2, but this time applied to all vertices in $\mathcal{G}$. The user-specified weights λ, μ, and ν balance the additional terms against E_{dist}. To enforce local flatness of the mesh, E_{smooth} measures the deviation of mesh vertices to the centroid of their respective one-neighborhood:

$$E_{smooth}(\mathcal{G}) = \sum_{v \in \mathcal{V}_\mathcal{G}} \left\| \frac{\sum_{w \in star(v)} \mathbf{w}}{valence(v)} - \mathbf{v} \right\|^2,$$

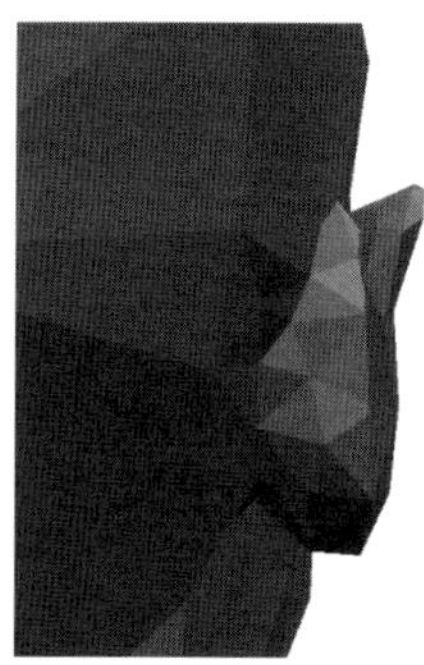

Figure 3: Improving definition of facial features in the fitted control mesh with imperfect scan data. Left: without using binding energy, the upper area behind the ear is flattened due to lack of data in the input sample set. Right: by use of binding edges the shape of the ear is improved.

Because the numerical value of E_{dist} increases with the local density of the points in the scan data set, E_{smooth} has only a comparatively small influence in the regions where data is present. In regions of the scan data set where there is no data, the smoothing term leads to a shrinking effect, since here the distance minimization does not act as a counter-force. We thus introduce additional constraint terms $E_{binding}$ and $E_{constraint}$ into the energy function.

$E_{binding}$ is used to minimize the length of a set of edges, which we call *binding edges*. This constraint helps to keep features in the face from flattening out due to lack of data, as is frequently the case behind the ears: our triangulation scanner cannot measure data in these regions due to shadowing between light source and projector. Since there are no data samples that the surface could approximate, the smoothing term eventually removes concavities. If we define binding edges in these regions, the flattening of that area is effectively prevented:

$$E_{binding}(\mathcal{G}) = \sum_{e \in \mathcal{E}^b} l_e^2,$$

where $\mathcal{E}^b$ is the set of binding edges and l_e is the length of edge e. These edges are for the most part defined by a subset of edges from $\mathcal{E}_\mathcal{G}$. Additionally, some vertices of $\mathcal{G}$ that are not actually connected by edges in $\mathcal{E}_\mathcal{G}$ are bound together in $\mathcal{E}^b$ (see Figure 4). These additional edges are used to keep corresponding vertices of the upper and lower lips together: unconstrained, the shrinking effect of the smoothing term leads to the introduction of a gap between the lips, which should remain closed as in the generic model $\mathcal{G}$. Figure 3 demonstrates the effect of the binding energy term.

Finally, we constrain vertices to their original positions by $E_{constraint}$. This constraint helps to keep the shape of

the inner part of the lips of the mesh model, which would otherwise be flattened onto the outside in the process of minimizing the distance to the point cloud (see Figure 4).

$$E_{constraint}(\mathcal{G}) = \sum_{v \in \mathcal{V}_{\mathcal{G}}^c} \|\mathbf{v} - \tilde{\mathbf{v}}\|^2,$$

where $\mathcal{V}_{\mathcal{G}}^c$ is the set of constrained vertices defined on $\mathcal{G}$, and $\tilde{\mathbf{v}}$ denotes the original position of vertex v before the optimization.

As described in [17], a sparse linear system can be built expressing the function E_{global}, which can be solved using the conjugate gradient method [19]. To be able to set up a linear system, E_{dist} has to be linearized, which can be done as shown in [5, 17].

5 Generation of the Multiresolution Model

We employ the Modified Butterfly subdivision scheme [25] to construct the subdivision hierarchy on top of the base mesh resulting from the fitting process described in the previous section. This scheme guarantees C^1 continuity everywhere and has the advantage of interpolating the vertices of the previous refinement levels, so that coarser levels of refinement serve as an approximation to the head geometry, which is not necessarily the case with approximating subdivision schemes [17].

After fitting, the surface of the deformed generic mesh approximates the point cloud in a least squares sense, i.e. the distance between the points and the surface is minimized. The control mesh vertices are *not* necessarily lying on the point cloud. Before refining the mesh using the Butterfly subdivision rules, we measure the distance from each vertex along normal direction to the nearest point on the point cloud and store this value as an additional displacement. The displacements are then applied to the vertices and the updated mesh is refined. On each level of the resulting hierarchy, we thus obtain a triangle mesh with vertices interpolating the original point cloud after the respective displacements have been applied. In areas of the point cloud with no data we cannot measure displacements, but the subdivision operator generates a smooth surface in these regions. This construction technique is similar to *normal meshes* [4], but we sample displacements to a set of sample points instead of to another mesh. By storing only one scalar displacement value per vertex introduced on each level, we achieve a storage-efficient hierarchical mesh structure [4, 12].

6 Animating the Surface

During animation, the control mesh vertices of the subdivision surface are displaced via simulated muscle contraction [9]. Since the subdivision hierarchy is built using an interpolating scheme, each refinement level including the control mesh can serve as an approximation to the limit surface for rendering. Depending on the available computation time per frame and quality requirements, an appropriate refinement level can be picked for display. Since the mesh topology is completely determined by the topology of the base mesh and the subdivision scheme, the area of change to the refined mesh induced by movement of a control mesh vertex is known a priori and is determined by the support of that vertex [8, 26]. In the Butterfly scheme, the support includes at most the three-neighborhood of a control mesh vertex. When a control mesh vertex is animated, we apply the subdivision rules and displacements only to this area. Thus, we can achieve fast updates of the refined geometry, without having to include the detailed geometry into the simulation task of the physics-based animation engine. Figure 5 shows snapshots from an animation of the head geometry.

7 Results

We have applied our surface generation method to scans of male and female individuals, see figures 1 and 6. With our structured light scanner, the scans show defects in large regions due to shadowing effects and bad reflective properties of the surface, especially on hair. Nonetheless, our algorithm generates subdivision models consistent with the range data, complementing it in a plausible manner in areas with no data. User intervention was not necessary, the only initial requirement being that both scan data and generic head model are looking roughly down the same axis in world coordinates.

The silhouette-based geometry fitting approach converges quite quickly in 8–14 iterations of Powell's optimization method. However, each iteration performs about 250–300 evaluations of the "function" to be minimized, i.e. counting the number of white pixels using `glGetHistogram` calls. For each of these calls, we have to read back and draw the framebuffer using `glCopyPixels` to retrieve the results of the histogram. Unfortunately, such framebuffer read-backs are still quite expensive on current PC graphics boards: using a 256×256 framebuffer, the optimization process takes about 6–10 min on a 1.7 GHz PC with a GeForce3 graphics board while completing within 90–150 sec on an `sgi` Octane with a 300 MHz R12k processor. Increasing the resolution of the framebuffer to 512×512 results in a slightly better alignment and a (relative) convergence speed-up of 1–2 iterations. Due to the larger amount of data that is read from and drawn into the framebuffer, the whole process takes about 20–30 min on the PC and 5–8 min on the Octane in this case.

In the current implementation, we have to reduce the input complexity for the local and global fitting steps to handle large data sets. On the PC, with a dataset of 50k points subsampled from the initial 300k points, the local fitting process runs for approx. 5 minutes, performing about 35 iterations per bounding box. The global fitting process performs 100 iterations in approx. 40 minutes until convergence. The multiresolution mesh is then built using the complete set of point samples with no subsampling. Even though the processing takes up considerable time even on a fast PC, this does not impair usability to a large extent due to the full automation. Not counting times for the simulation and rendering parts in our facial animation system, updating the animated mesh on the second refinement level requires about 40–50ms on the PC, corresponding to a rate of 20–25 fps.

For the models shown in Figure 6, the following table shows the development of the mean and maximum distances from the point cloud to the current control mesh after each of the three steps of the algorithm. The last column shows the distance to the final subdivision surface with displacements applied. The values are normalized to "percent of the point cloud bounding box diameter". The maximum distance to the final surface reflects the "noisiness" of the input data: outliers in overlapping regions of the range scans are not interpolated.

	initial alignment	local fitting	global fitting	subdiv. surface
male / mean	1.51	1.42	0.11	0.04
male / max.	13.13	13.13	1.28	1.30
female / mean	1.09	0.91	0.12	0.08
female / max.	11.35	10.26	1.55	1.55

8 Future Work

Apart from geometric similarities, we would like to employ texture information to improve the accuracy of feature matching. Also, instead of simply generating a smooth surface in areas with no data, it would be interesting to generate artificial surface detail to make the surface match the surrounding areas. For the animation system, we are planning the automatic insertion of separate components representing eyes, teeth, and tongue.

References

[1] T. Akimoto, Y. Suenaga, and R. S. Wallace. Automatic creation of 3d facial models. *IEEE Computer Graphics & Applications*, 13(5):16–22, September 1993.

[2] V. Blanz and T. Vetter. A Morphable Model for the Synthesis of 3D Faces. In *Computer Graphics (SIGGRAPH '99 Conf. Proc.)*, pages 187–194, 1999.

[3] T. DeRose, M. Kass, and T. Truong. Subdivision Surfaces in Character Animation. In *Computer Graphics (SIGGRAPH '98 Conf. Proc.)*, pages 85–94, 1998.

[4] I. Guskov, K. Vidimce, W. Sweldens, and P. Schröder. Normal Meshes. In *Computer Graphics (SIGGRAPH '00 Conf. Proc.)*, pages 95–102, 2000.

[5] H. Hoppe, T. DeRose, T. Duchamp, M. Halstead, H. Jin, J. McDonald, J. Schweitzer, and W. Stuetzle. Piecewise Smooth Surface Reconstruction. In *Computer Graphics (SIGGRAPH '94 Conf. Proc.)*, pages 295–302, 1994.

[6] H. Hoppe, T. DeRose, T. Duchamp, J. McDonald, and W. Stuetzle. Mesh Optimization. In *Computer Graphics (SIGGRAPH '93 Conf. Proc.)*, pages 19–26, 1993.

[7] D. Hutchinson, M. Preston, and T. Hewitt. Adaptive Refinement for Mass-Spring Simulation. In *7th EG Workshop on Animation and Simulation*, pages 31–45, 1996.

[8] I. P. Ivrissimtzis and M.A. Sabin. On the support of recursive subdivision. *submitted for publication*, 2001.

[9] K. Kähler, J. Haber, and H.-P. Seidel. Geometry-based muscle modeling for facial animation. In *Graphics Interface2001 Conf. Proc.*, pages 37 – 46, 2001.

[10] L. Kobbelt. $\sqrt{3}$-Subdivision. In *Computer Graphics (SIGGRAPH '00 Conf. Proc.)*, pages 103–112, 2000.

[11] L. Kobbelt, S. Campagna, J. Vorsatz, and H.-P. Seidel. Interactive Multi-Resolution Modeling on Arbitrary Meshes. In *Computer Graphics (SIGGRAPH '98 Conf. Proc.)*, pages 105–114, 1998.

[12] A. Lee, H. Moreton, and H. Hoppe. Displaced Subdivision Surfaces. In *Computer Graphics (SIGGRAPH '00 Conf. Proc.)*, pages 85–94, 2000.

[13] Y. Lee, D. Terzopoulos, and K. Waters. Realistic Modeling for Facial Animations. In *Computer Graphics (SIGGRAPH '95 Conf. Proc.)*, pages 55–62, 1995.

[14] H. P. A. Lensch, W. Heidrich, and H.-P. Seidel. Automated Texture Registration and Stitching for Real World Models. In *Proc. Pacific Graphics 2000*, pages 317–326, 2000.

[15] H. P. A. Lensch, W. Heidrich, and H.-P. Seidel. A Silhouette-based Algorithm for Texture Registration and Stitching. *Graphical Models*, 2001. (to appear).

[16] C. T. Loop. Smooth Subdivision Surfaces Based on Triangles. Master's thesis, University of Utah, Department of Mathematics, 1987.

[17] S. Marschner, B. Guenter, and S. Raghupathy. Modeling and Rendering for Realistic Facial Animation. In *Rendering Techniques 2000 (Proc. 11th EG Workshop on Rendering)*, pages 231–242, 2000.

[18] F. Pighin, J. Hecker, D. Lischinski, R. Szeliski, and D. H. Salesin. Synthesizing Realistic Facial Expressions from Photographs. In *Computer Graphics (SIGGRAPH '98 Conf. Proc.)*, pages 75–84, 1998.

[19] W. H. Press, S. A. Teukolsky, W. T. Vetterling, and B. P. Flannery. *Numerical Recipes in C: The Art of Scientific Computing*. Cambridge University Press, Cambridge, MA, 2nd edition, 1992.

[20] T. W. Sederberg and S. R. Parry. Free-Form Deformation of Solid Geometric Models. In *Computer Graphics (SIGGRAPH '86 Conf. Proc.)*, pages 151–160, 1986.

[21] R. Szeliski and S. Lavallée. Matching 3-D Anatomical Surfaces with Non-Rigid Deformations using Octree-Splines. *International Journal of Computer Vision*, 18(2):171–186, 1996.

[22] A. Van Gelder. Approximate Simulation of Elastic Membranes by Triangulated Spring Meshes. *Journal of Graphics Tools*, 3(2):21–41, 1998.

[23] P. Volino and N. Magnenat-Thalmann. The SPHERIGON: A Simple Polygon Patch for Smoothing Quickly your Polygonal Meshes. In *Proc. Computer Animation '98*, pages 72–79, 1998.

[24] D. Zorin and P. Schröder. Subdivision for Modeling and Animation. *Computer Graphics (SIGGRAPH '00 Course Notes)*, 2000.

[25] D. Zorin, P. Schröder, and W. Sweldens. Interpolating subdivision for meshes with arbitrary topology. In *Computer Graphics (SIGGRAPH '96 Conf. Proc.)*, pages 189–192, 1996.

[26] D. Zorin, P. Schröder, and W. Sweldens. Interactive Multiresolution Mesh Editing. In *Computer Graphics (SIGGRAPH '97 Conf. Proc.)*, pages 259–268, 1997.

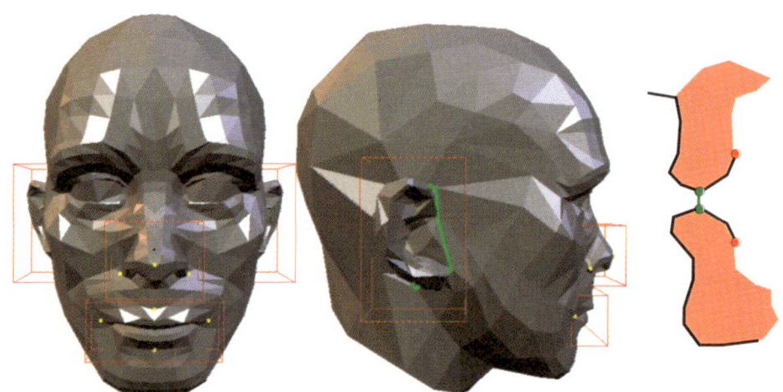

Figure 4: Extra information stored with the generic head model: Left and center: four bounding boxes (red) around ears, nose and mouth; edges to which binding energy constraint is applied (green lines); landmarks on the boxed features (yellow dots). Right: cross-section of the mouth region. The binding energy term is applied to virtual edges connecting upper and lower lip vertices (green line and dots). The inner part of the lips is kept in shape by constraining vertices to their positions (red dots).

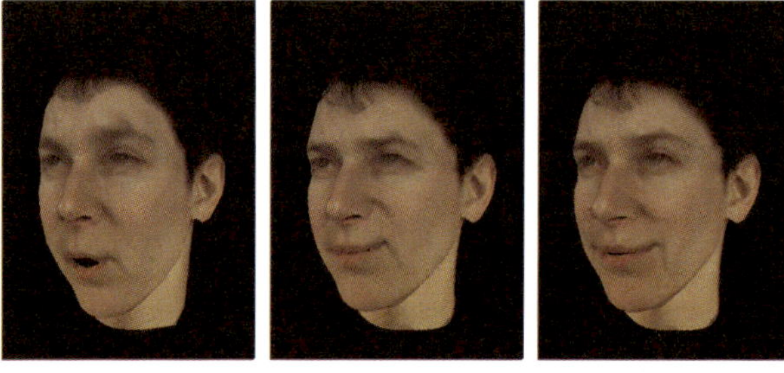

Figure 5: Displaced subdivision surface head model showing different expressions.

Figure 6: Two more point sample sets and the head models generated from them, shown at 2 levels of refinement of the base mesh. Left: female scanned with a bathing cap to enable our scanner to capture data on the back of the head. Right: scan of a male, exhibiting lack of sample data in the hair-covered region.

A BRDF Database Employing the Beard-Maxwell Reflection Model

Harold B. Westlund[a] Gary W. Meyer[b]

Department of Computer and Information Science
University of Oregon · Eugene, Oregon · U.S.A.

Abstract

The Beard-Maxwell reflection model is presented as a new local reflection model for use in realistic image synthesis. The model is important because there is a public domain database of surface reflection parameters, the Nonconventional Exploitation Factors Data System (NEFDS), that utilizes a modified form of the Beard-Maxwell model. Additional surface reflection parameters for the database can be determined because a measurement protocol, using existing radiometric instruments, has been specified. The Beard-Maxwell model is also of historical significance because it predates many computer graphics reflection models and because it includes several features that are incorporated into existing local reflection models. The NEFDS is described and a special shader is developed for use with NEFDS. The shader makes use of the alias method for determining random variates from discrete probability distributions. Realistic images are synthesized from the existing database and from samples that were characterized using the measurement protocol.

Key words: BRDF, local illumination

1 Introduction

Computer graphics has made great progress in the simulation of object appearance. Reflection models have been developed that characterize both the spectral and the spatial distributions of light reflected from an object's surface. Image synthesis systems have been constructed that use Monte Carlo techniques to evaluate these reflection models and simulate the objects in the context of globally illuminated environments. With sufficient processing time, these programs are capable of producing individual photorealistic images. Recent developments in the area of real-time shading have made it possible to utilize sophisticated reflection models in interactive programs [18, 20]. These advances in real-time rendering are likely to bring renewed attention to the subject of surface reflection modeling.

Unfortunately, the accurate synthesis of object appearance is currently limited by the small amount of readily available surface reflectance data. Many sophisticated computer graphics reflection models have been proposed. The best of these models characterize both the spectral and the spatial distributions of reflected light and are therefore appropriate for modeling object appearance. These models have a sound theoretical foundation and often contain measurable surface reflection parameters. Regrettably, measurement protocols and actual measured data are seldom available for the models. This situation is in contrast to object shape information where polygon data is now commercially available.

This paper presents the Beard-Maxwell [30] reflection model which has not been discussed in the computer graphics literature even though a large database of measurements exists for the model. The model is of historical importance because it predates many of the current computer graphics reflection models and foreshadows several of the features that have been incorporated into these models. The model has practical significance because the public domain Nonconventional Exploitation Factors Data System (NEFDS) [1] utilizes a modified version of the Beard-Maxwell model and contains over 400 materials for which the parameters of the modified Beard-Maxwell model have been measured. Furthermore, the NEFDS can be extended because a measurement protocol exists, using standard radiometric instruments, to acquire model parameters for additional materials.

The paper also describes a rendering system that has been developed for use with NEFDS. The Radiance software package [2] has been modified so that it can be employed to make pictures with data taken from NEFDS. Since the Beard-Maxwell model is not an invertible function, this necessitated the use of a probability mass function (the discrete counterpart of the probability density function) and the alias method for generating random variates. The research discussed in this paper also includes an attempt to add additional material to the database. The measurements that were necessary to ac-

[a]Current address: Radical Entertainment, Vancouver, BC, Canada. hwestlund@radical.ca

[b]Current address: Department of Computer Science and Engineering, University of Minnesota, Minneapolis, MN, U.S.A. meyer@cs.umn.edu

complish this are described, and the quality of the approximation provided by Beard-Maxwell and NEFDS is evaluated.

This paper is divided into four major sections. In the next section, a brief review is done of existing computer graphics reflection models. The following section introduces the complete Beard-Maxwell model and shows how it has been modified for use in the NEFDS. An overview of the NEFDS is given in the penultimate section and example renderings that were made using the data are discussed in the last section. These pictures were made using a modified version of a public domain rendering program and data from both NEFDS and from new measurements made using the NEFDS measurement protocol. The paper concludes with a summary of the work and suggestions for further research.

2 Background

2.1 BRDF

In order to create a realistic image of an object, the light reflection properties of the object's surface must be specified. The most common means of quantifying surface reflection of light is by utilizing the bi-directional reflectance distribution function (BRDF). The BRDF, ρ, is defined as the ratio of differential reflected radiance to differential incident irradiance:

$$\begin{aligned}\rho(\Theta_i;\Theta_r;\lambda) &= \frac{dL_r(\Theta_i;\Theta_r;\lambda)}{dE_i(\Theta_i;\lambda)} \\ &= \frac{dL_r(\Theta_i;\Theta_r;\lambda)}{dL_i(\Theta_i;\lambda)\cos\theta_i d\omega_i} \qquad (1)\end{aligned}$$

where the subscripts i and r denote incident and reflected respectively, $\Theta = (\theta, \phi)$ is the direction of light propagation, λ is the wavelength of light, L is radiance, E is irradiance, and $d\omega$ is an element of solid angle [31]. This surface reflection geometry is shown in Figure 1.

2.2 Physics Based BRDFs

Over the past century, a wide variety of analytical reflection models have been created to represent the physics of light reflection off surfaces. They have been developed in the fields of physics and engineering accompanying the development of radio transmission, radar, heat transfer theory, remote sensing, astronomy, and many other areas of research. A few relevant models are presented here.

In 1963, Beckman and Spizzichino [6] developed a model of reflection based upon wave optics. Their reflection model was derived through the use of the Kirchhoff approximation of the Helmholtz boundary conditions. Also in 1963, Hapke [15] developed a reflection model which predicted the light reflection off the lunar surface using scattering theory. He was able to account for both forward and backward scatter through his selection of the scattering function.

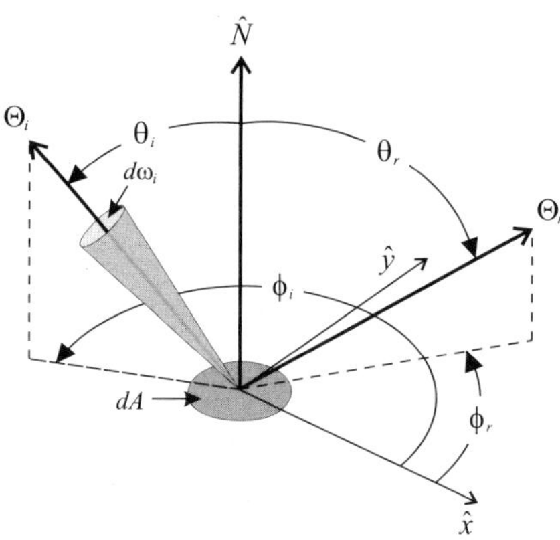

Figure 1: Light reflection geometry

Torrance and Sparrow [37], in 1967, created an analytical reflection model based on a surface composed of small, randomly distributed, mirror-like facets. These micro-facets were distributed using a Gaussian based distribution, which was in correspondence to the measured surface reflection. Their model was novel in its inclusion of a term for representing the shadowing and masking of neighboring facets which helped to predict the measured off-specular peak.

2.3 Physics Based BRDFs in Computer Graphics

The work of Torrance and Sparrow was first introduced to computer graphics by Blinn [7] who extended it by utilizing the facet distribution proposed by Trowbridge and Reitz [38]. This distribution is built on the assumption that the facets are ellipsoids of revolution. Another adaptation of Torrance and Sparrow's reflection model to computer graphics was offered by Cook and Torrance [10]. They incorporated the Fresnel term into the model to capture the wavelength dependency of first surface reflection. Recently Ashikhmin et al. [5] have shown how to produce BRDFs from very general micro-facet distributions by using a model with a simple shadowing term.

Blinn [8] utilized the work of Hapke to develop a reflection model for use in the simulation of the rings of Saturn. He utilized several functions to represent the phase function of light off the scattering particles, including the Henyey-Greenstein [19] function and a function of Rayleigh scattering. Blinn also discussed the extension of the model to account for shadowing and multiple scattering.

He et al. [16] utilized the work of Beckman and Spizzichino in addition to the work of Torrance and Sparrow to generate a model which accounted for many physics derived attributes. Their model utilized polarization of light, directional Fresnel effects and a more complex distribution of micro-facets. It was the first model to provided a unified means of predicting scatter from surfaces with autocorrelation distances much smaller, on the same order, or much greater than the wavelength of incident light. Beyond He et al., Stam [36] is one of the few to have attempted the development of more general physics based BRDFs in computer graphics.

2.4 Empirical BRDFs in Computer Graphics

As pointed out by Ward [29] the very complexity that gives these physics based BRDFs validity also hampers their general use in computer graphics. In Ward's paper he presented a reflection model using an elliptical Gaussian based formula which is ideally suited for fitting to measured data. Ward demonstrated its validity through measurement of several surface BRDFs which were fit to his reflection model.

Lafortune et al. [26] presented a BRDF model built upon sums of cosine lobes specifically constructed to fit measured BRDF data. The number, orientation, and shape of the cosine lobes are variable, allowing for a convincing fit to a wide variety of BRDF distributions.

Dana et al. [11] fit measured data to both the Oren-Nayer model [32] and the Koenderink et al. decomposition [22]. Oren and Nayer built a model of diffuse reflection based on direct and indirect reflections off diffuse micro-facets. Koenderink et al. decomposed the BRDF into a variable-order vector of coefficients, fit to data.

2.5 BRDF Storage Representations in Computer Graphics

Fitting measured data to a BRDF model is avoided if the data rather than the model parameters is stored. Gondek et al. [14] utilized this technique with an adaptive subdivision scheme over the sampled reflection hemisphere. Schröder and Sweldens [35] as well as Lalonde and Fournier [27] offer an efficient method of storing and utilizing BRDFs using spherical wavelets. Cabral et al. [9] and Westin et al. [47] offered the same using spherical harmonics.

3 A New Reflection Model

The modified Beard-Maxwell model presented in this paper incorporates the best attributes of physical and empirical BRDFs. It is a physics based model capturing subtle BRDF characteristics required in realistic image synthesis. Its empirical measurements are themselves built upon the physical model, providing a means to set the required parameters accurately with relatively little effort. Since only a minimal set of defining parameters are used, the model requires minimal storage space.

3.1 Beard-Maxwell Reflection Model

The Beard-Maxwell model presented by Maxwell et al. [30] was originally used to describe the reflection properties of rough, painted surfaces displaying Fresnel effects and later was applied to a wider variety of surfaces. Their model is built on the assumption that the material surface is a three dimensional terrain of micro-facets of varying orientation. In this model, reflected light is the result of only two physical occurrences. Light is reflected off one of the micro-facets (first surface reflectance) and light is scattered out of the surface after having first entered the sub-surface medium (volumetric reflectance). The Beard-Maxwell reflectance model thus takes the form

$$\rho(\Theta_i;\Theta_r) = \rho_{fs}(\Theta_i;\Theta_r) + \rho_{vol}(\Theta_i;\Theta_r) \tag{2}$$

where ρ_{fs} and ρ_{vol} are the first surface and volumetric reflectance functions respectively. For the sake of notational clarity the wavelength of this wavelength dependent reflectance function is not listed as an explicit parameter. We will take this same liberty to hide other functional parameters which are tangential to current discussions.

First surface reflection causes light to be reflected in the specular direction (i.e., mirror reflection) off each individual micro-facet as determined by the micro-facet's normal rather than the macro-surface normal. Therefore the distribution of the first surface reflectance is determined by the distribution of the micro-facet normals which in turn is driven by the density function $\Xi(\Theta)$, the relative density of micro-facet normals (per steradian) in direction Θ. Maxwell et al. calculated the first surface reflectance to be

$$\rho_{fs}(\Theta_i,\Theta_r) = \frac{R(\beta)\Xi(\hat{H})}{4\cos\theta_i\cos\theta_r}\mathrm{SO} \tag{3}$$

where $\hat{H}$ is the half angle vector, β is the bistatic angle (i.e., the angle between either the incident or reflected direction and the half angle vector), $R(\beta)$ is the Fresnel reflectance and SO is a shadowing and obscuration[1] term. Figure 2 is a diagram of the geometry used by the Beard-Maxwell model.

The shadowing and obscuration term in (3), SO, accounts for the height distribution of the micro-facets. Shadowing and obscuration are due to intersections between the other surface facets and the incident and reflected light rays respectively. Torrance and Sparrow [37] accounted for the light ray intersections with a purely analytical function derived from theory. Blinn [7] and Cook

[1] Obscuration is often termed masking in the literature, but we will use obscuration here to follow the original discussion in both Maxwell et al. [30] and the NEFDS documentation [4].

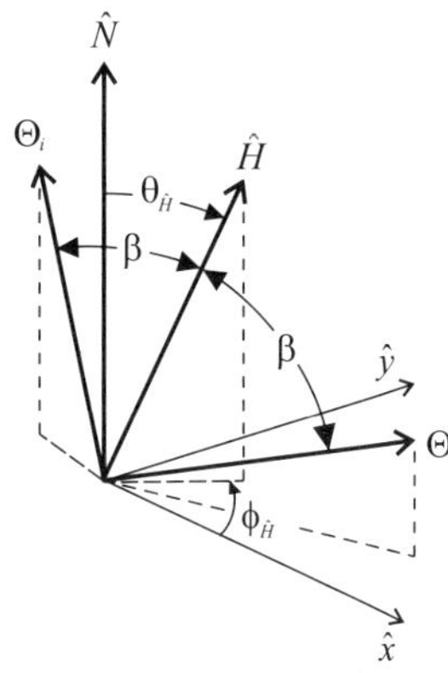

Figure 2: Beard-Maxwell BRDF model geometry

and Torrance [10], who were the first to introduce shadowing and obscuration in computer graphics, also used a purely analytical function. Beard and Maxwell chose to create a function with free parameters set using empirical data. This function, which has a maximum value of one for both specular reflection ($\theta_{\hat{H}} = 0$) and pure backscatter ($\beta = 0$), is defined as

$$\mathrm{SO} = \frac{1 + \frac{\theta_{\hat{H}}}{\Omega} e^{-2\beta/\tau}}{1 + \frac{\theta_{\hat{H}}}{\Omega}} \left(\frac{1}{1 + \frac{\phi_n}{\Omega} \frac{\theta_i}{\Omega}} \right) \quad (4)$$

where the free parameters Ω and τ modify the falloff of SO in the forward-scattered and back-scattered directions respectively, and ϕ_n is a parameter computed from geometry which affects the rate of change of SO [30]. The process of gathering empirical data used to set the equivalent free parameters in the modified Beard-Maxwell model is discussed below in Section 3.2.

Rather than attempting to measure Ξ of (3) directly, Maxwell et al. replaced it with the measured zero-bistatic ($\beta = 0$) first surface reflectance at the half angle, $\rho_{fs}(\hat{H}, \hat{H})$. SO $= 1$ when $\beta = 0$, so (3) can be rewritten as

$$\Xi(\hat{H}) = \frac{4\rho_{fs}(\hat{H}, \hat{H}) \cos^2 \theta_{\hat{H}}}{R(0)}. \quad (5)$$

This is simplified further by their assumption that the surface is isotropic. In that case to generate reflectance values for all incident and reflected directions, $\rho_{fs}(\hat{H}, \hat{H})$ needs only be sampled at the angles $0 \leq \theta_{\hat{H}} \leq \frac{\pi}{2}$ and $\phi = 0$.

Light reflected from the first surface is assumed to maintain its original polarization (i.e., incident and reflected light are of like polarization) while any light reflected through volumetric scattering is assumed to be totally depolarized. In this way, separation of the first surface reflectance from the volumetric reflectance can easily be performed by using a polarized illuminant and then measuring the like and cross polarized light. The first surface reflectance can be expressed in measurable quantities by using the four combinations of polarization, $\rho_{\perp\perp}$, $\rho_{\perp\|}$, $\rho_{\|\perp}$, and $\rho_{\|\|}$[2]:

$$\rho_{fs} = (\rho_{\perp\perp} - \rho_{\perp\|}) + (\rho_{\|\|} - \rho_{\|\perp}). \quad (6)$$

Similarly, the volumetric reflectance can be expressed in measurable quantities:

$$\rho_{vol} = 2\rho_{\perp\|} + 2\rho_{\|\perp} \quad (7)$$

The volumetric reflectance of (2), ρ_{vol} is represented by either Lambertian reflectance, ρ_D, or directional diffuse reflectance, ρ_{ddif}:

$$\rho_{vol} = \begin{cases} \rho_D \\ \rho_{ddif} = \frac{2\rho_v f(\beta) g(\theta_{\hat{N}})}{\cos\theta_i + \cos\theta_r} \end{cases} \quad (8)$$

where ρ_v is the base directional diffuse reflectance when both θ_i and θ_r are zero and where $f(\beta)$ and $g(\theta_{\hat{N}})$ are empirically determined functions that characterize differential subsurface scattering and substrate reflection respectively. The directional diffuse component accounts for any subsurface directional scattering and is selected only if there is any directional reflection unaccounted for by the first surface reflectance. The Lambertian reflectance is selected if the first surface reflectance accounts for all directional reflectance. The directional diffuse component of (8) is based on a model of a subsurface of finite thickness built on a reflective base. Maxwell et al. found that in practice surfaces were well represented by using a constant valued scattering function and by modeling the surface as having infinite thickness. With these simplifications, f and g can be both set to unity and the volumetric reflectance becomes:

$$\rho_{vol} = \begin{cases} \rho_D \\ \rho_{ddif} = \frac{2\rho_v}{\cos\theta_i + \cos\theta_r} \end{cases} \quad (9)$$

3.2 Modification to Beard-Maxwell

The NEF uses a modified form of the Beard-Maxwell reflection model to characterize the reflection properties of surfaces in the NEF database. The NEF Beard-Maxwell (NEF-BM) model includes changes in an attempt to more accurately represent surfaces other than paint, the original target of the Beard-Maxwell model. Additionally, fixed radiometric measurements are introduced which can be

[2]We follow the same notation as in Maxwell et al. to denote polarized reflectance by $\rho_{\alpha_i \alpha_r}$, where the orientations of α_i and α_r indicate the polarization of the incident and reflected light respectively. The polarization state of the incident light is either parallel ($\|$) or perpendicular ($\perp$) to the plane of incidence. The polarization state of the reflected light is described in the same way, but with respect to the reflectance plane.

used to determine appropriate values for the model's free parameters.

In the Beard-Maxwell model, only one volumetric component was utilized, either the Lambertian reflectance or the directional diffuse reflectance. In the NEF-BM model *both* are used. The volumetric Lambertian reflectance is referred to as simply diffuse reflectance and is attributed to multiple first surface reflections. The volumetric directional diffuse reflectance is itself referred to as volumetric reflectance, ρ_{vol}, and is attributed to all the reflectance due to subsurface light interaction.

The NEF-BM model uses a simplified form of (4) for its shadowing and obscuration function:

$$\mathrm{SO} = \frac{1 + \frac{\theta_{\hat{N}}}{\Omega} e^{-2\beta/\tau}}{1 + \frac{\theta_{\hat{N}}}{\Omega}}.$$

The model also uses the simplified form of directional subsurface scattering from (9). So the complete NEF-BM BRDF can be written

$$\rho(\Theta_i;\Theta_r) = \frac{R(\beta)}{R(0)} \frac{\rho_{fs}(\theta_{\hat{H}},0;\theta_{\hat{H}},0)\cos^2\theta_{\hat{H}}}{\cos\theta_i\cos\theta_r} \left(\frac{1 + \frac{\theta_{\hat{H}}}{\Omega} e^{-2\beta/\tau}}{1 + \frac{\theta_{\hat{H}}}{\Omega}}\right) + \rho_D + \frac{2\rho_v}{\cos\theta_i + \cos\theta_r} \quad (10)$$

As in the BM model, the NEF-BM performs the zero-bistatic BRDF measurements at all four combinations of polarization using (6) and (7) to generate the first surface reflection parameters as well as the diffuse and volumetric coefficients. Additionally the NEF-BM utilizes two other series of radiometric measurements.

The first additional set of measurements is a series of specular BRDF measurements for parallel polarized source and receiver over $10\,\mathrm{deg} \leq \theta_i \leq 80\,\mathrm{deg}$ with $\phi_i = 0\,\mathrm{deg}$ and $\phi_r = 180\,\mathrm{deg}$. For each sampled incident direction, the receiver direction is varied about the mirror direction in the plane of incidence by $\theta_i - 5\,\mathrm{deg} \leq \theta_r \leq \theta_i + 5\,\mathrm{deg}$. Data obtained from these measurements provides a means of calculating the complex index of refraction components, n and k which are required for computing the Fresnel reflection coefficient, R. Determination of n and k is performed by utilizing Brewster's angle, the angle of minimum reflectance of parallel-polarized light [17, 4].

The second series of measurements uses a fixed source direction and varying receiver direction, in the plane of incidence, over $-90\,\mathrm{deg} \leq \theta_r \leq 90\,\mathrm{deg}$. These measurements offer means to select the shadowing and obscuration parameters, τ and Ω, in order to reduce the error away from the forward-scattered and back-scattered directions. The values of τ and $Omega$ are set using a least square fit of the modeled BRDF, with shadowing and obscuration, to this measured data. This second series of measurements also provides a good verification of the previously selected model parameters.

We now introduce the dependency of the BRDF on the wavelength of light which has hitherto been considered constant. The naive method of characterizing spectral dependency would be to perform all required measurements at a sufficiently dense sampling of wavelengths. However this would undermine one of the primary motivations of the NEF-BM model which is to represent the BRDF using relatively few measurements.

The solution was found in the observation that for many surfaces, the BRDF at one wavelength is similar in shape, but not necessarily magnitude, to the BRDF of the surface at nearby wavelengths. To utilize this information, the measurements detailed above are only performed at key reference wavelengths and intermediate values are linearly interpolated. The interpolated values are then scaled by directional hemispherical reflectance (DHR) [31] values, $\rho_d(\lambda)$, measured at a dense sampling of wavelengths. The full spectral dependent BRDF then is:

$$\rho(\bar{\Theta};\lambda) = \rho_d(\lambda) \left[\frac{\rho(\bar{\Theta};\lambda_j)}{\int\int \rho(\bar{\Theta}_{DHR};\lambda_j)\cos\theta_i d\theta_i d\phi_i}\left(\frac{\lambda_k - \lambda}{\lambda_k - \lambda_j}\right) + \frac{\rho(\bar{\Theta};\lambda_k)}{\int\int \rho(\bar{\Theta}_{DHR};\lambda_k)\cos\theta_i d\theta_i d\phi_i}\left(\frac{\lambda - \lambda_j}{\lambda_k - \lambda_j}\right)\right] \quad (11)$$

where j and k are the indices of the reference wavelengths bounding λ, $\bar{\Theta}$ is the arbitrary geometry $(\Theta_i;\Theta_r)$, and $\bar{\Theta}_{DHR}$ is the geometry of DHR measurement $(\Theta_i;\Theta_{DHR})$.

This method offers the additional benefit of increased accuracy. DHR measured values are typically more accurate than the corresponding integrated values of measured BRDFs. Scaling the BRDFs to ensure their integrated values match the DHR values corrects propagated measurement errors.

3.3 Limitations of the Model

These measurements generate a reflection model which faithfully represents the actual reflection behavior of many target surfaces. However, a model is an approximation; there are limitations to the types of BRDFs it can accurately represent. Some surface BRDFs simply cannot be accurately approximated with the NEF-BM model using any combination of parameter values. For a model which was initially constructed to represent simple paint reflection, it covers a broad range quite accurately, but care must be used in applying it to new BRDFs.

Another limitation of the NEF-BM model is its inaccuracy at grazing angles. The model was created primarily for remote sensing. Because remote sensing involves interpreting imaged data from aircraft or satellites, accuracy at grazing angles was not a large concern. For use in computer graphics, however, grazing angles are to be expected in every scene.

The problem lies in the fact that the NEF-BM BRDF at grazing incidence, Θ_{gi}, integrated over the reflected hemisphere, results in values greater than one:

$$\int_{\Omega_r} \rho(\Theta_{gi};\Theta_r)d\Omega_r = \int_{\Omega_r} \rho_{fs}(\Theta_{gi};\Theta_r)d\Omega_r + \int_{\Omega_r} \rho_D d\Omega_r + \int_{\Omega_r} \frac{2\rho_v}{\cos\theta_{gi} + \cos\theta_r} d\Omega_r = 1 + \pi\rho_D + 4\pi\rho_v$$

Consequently, light incident at grazing angles will result in more energy reflected than was incident. In practice this has not been a problem mainly because of the foreshortening of incident energy at grazing angles.

4 NEFDS

The NEFDS allows those working in the area of remote sensing to perform complex radiometric calculations while taking into consideration the properties of the target material, the material background, the measuring sensors, and the atmospheric environment. At the heart of this system, and of particular interest to researchers in the field of computer graphics, is the BRDF database. This database contains the BRDFs of hundreds of surfaces from a dozen different categories. In this section, we will present a discussion of the BRDFs available and offer an overview of the relevant portions of the NEFDS.

4.1 Available Material Types

There are currently over 400 materials available in the NEFDS. These materials correspond to a wide variety of objects ranging from dirt to tree canopies. The materials fall into 12 different categories: asphalt, brick, camouflage, composite, concrete, fabric, water, metal, paint, rubber, soil and wood.

Although the number of materials is large and the variety is wide, the selection is limited by two key conditions. One requirement for the inclusion of a material in the database is that the BRDF of the material must be well represented by the NEF-BM BRDF model. For example, the BRDF should not be characterized by extreme anisotropy since the NEF-BM BRDF model only works with isotropic data. (There are in fact some materials included in the NEFDS which are anisotropic. To represent anisotropic material using the NEF-BM model, the material's BRDF is averaged to isotropy.)

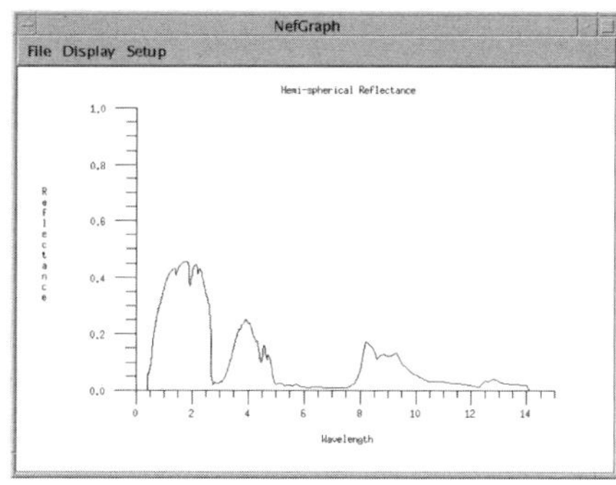

Figure 3: Spectral reflectance function for material 0221, red dirt

The second condition is a result of the data's origin. As mentioned before, the main use of the NEFDS has been in the area of remote sensing. Because of this, the materials in the database were selected on the basis of applicability to that field of work. They include objects which would be viewed from a remote sensor (e.g., a satellite). This still offers a potential wealth of BRDF data for use in computer graphics but is currently constrained to this one area. This however does not restrict future measurement and the inclusion of other materials having more direct applicability to computer graphics.

4.2 Operational Modes

NEFDS can be accessed either through the XWindows interface, *NefMenu*, or by using command line control. A discussion of the full control offered by NEFDS is beyond the scope of this paper (see the NEF Users Guide for detailed discussion [1]). Instead a brief overview will be given.

The model parameter data files used to specify the NEF-BM models are located in the material and groups files [3]. These data files can be viewed interactively through *NefMenu*, providing fully titled and organized fields. *NefMenu* also allows a convenient means of browsing the materials, organized within intuitive groups.

Most interactive programs in NEFDS are available both through the XWindows interface and by command line control. For example, the spectral distribution of hemispherical reflectance can be graphed either through *NefMenu* or through the program *NefPlot*. Such a plot of material number 0221, red dirt, is shown in Figure 3.

The NEFDS may be queried for BRDF values of materials or material groups at ranges of wavelengths for any given geometry. The XWindows control offers interactive control over these parameter settings allowing the user to quickly determine key reflection attributes. The command line counterpart, *BRDF* allows BRDF values to be obtained through a batch process. This is the technique utilized for the BRDF sampling used to generate BRDF tables for rendering discussed in the next section.

5 Rendering data

In this section, BRDF data obtained from NEFDS was used to render synthetic images. NEFDS was queried and the discretely sampled BRDFs were stored in data files. These files were then used as lookup tables to determine BRDF data during the execution of the rendering program. The program was selected based on the physically accurate global illumination solution that it produces. In addition, the program was extended to efficiently execute Monte Carlo integration over the sampled BRDFs.

5.1 The Alias Method

The inverse method is used in some rendering systems to generate random variates of the probability density function (PDF) corresponding to the BRDF. In general analytically generating random variates of arbitrary PDFs is not possible. However, there are techniques available to create the random variates of an arbitrary probability mass function (PMF), the discretized counterpart to the PDF. Gentle [13] and Knuth [21] both offer a nice overview and discussion of the many methods available. For this article, the alias method proposed by Walker [40, 41, 42] was selected because it generates random variates in constant time.

Many variations of Walker's original model have been proposed offering advantages in one way or another [12, 23, 24, 25, 33, 39]. The modification by Vose [39] was chosen because it allows for initialization in $\mathcal{O}(n)$ time versus the original paper's time of $\mathcal{O}(n \log n)$. Vose also presents several optimizations for memory and execution time although they are not used here.

The alias method is most easily viewed as a form of the rejection method in which the rejected values are recycled into usable data. It requires an initial setup which need only be performed once. After the setup is complete, random variates are created by transforming variates of a uniform distribution.

Consider the random variate $\mathbf{X}$ which can take on any of the t values,

$$X = \{x_1, x_2, ..., x_t\} \tag{12}$$

with corresponding probability

$$P = \{p_1, p_2, ..., p_t\}. \tag{13}$$

Ensure that the probabilities form a valid PMF by requiring that $\sum_{c=1}^{t} p_c = 1$.

In the setup process, the alias method creates two new lists, the rejection list and the alias list. The rejection list is a list of probabilities,

$$R = \{r_1, r_2, ..., r_t\}, \tag{14}$$

whose elements r_i determine whether or not an alias is to be used. Each probability r_i in the rejection list forms its own PMF together with its complement, $1 - r_i$. The alias list,

$$A = \{a_1, a_2, ..., a_t\}, \tag{15}$$

consists of t indices which each may take on integer values 1 through t, representing the index of the alias. The setup process is performed only once.

After the setup has been completed, selection of the random variate $\mathbf{X}$ is performed by choosing two uniformly distributed variates, $\mathbf{u} \sim \mathrm{U}(0,1)$ and $\mathbf{i} \sim \mathrm{U_d}(1,t)$, where $\mathrm{U_d}(1,t)$ is a discrete uniform distribution over the integers 1 through t. $\mathbf{X}$ is given the value $x_\mathbf{i}$ if $\mathbf{u} \leq r_\mathbf{i}$ ($\mathbf{u}$ was not rejected). $\mathbf{X}$ is given the value $x_{a_\mathbf{i}}$ if $\mathbf{u} > r_\mathbf{i}$ ($\mathbf{u}$ was rejected so the alias was used). The time required to generate this random variate is equal to the total time required to generate $\mathbf{u}$, perform a comparison, and then lookup the final value. Assuming these three actions can be performed in constant time, so can the generating step.

Consider a BRDF discretely sampled at s reflected directions $\{\Theta_{r,1}, \Theta_{r,2}, ..., \Theta_{r,s}\}$, and for each reflected direction, t incident directions, $\{\Theta_{i,1}, \Theta_{i,2}, ..., \Theta_{i,t}\}$, for a total of st samples. The samples each have a representative solid angle $\Delta\omega_{i,n}$ and a representative projected solid angle $\Delta\Omega_{i,n} = (\Theta_{i,n} \cdot \hat{N})\Delta\omega_{i,n}$ corresponding to $\Theta_{i,n}$, where $1 \leq n \leq t$.

The continuous PDF, $h_{\Theta_{r,m}}$, associated with the reflected direction $\Theta_{r,m}$ then becomes the PMF, $g'_{\Theta_{r,m}}$, by

$$\begin{aligned} g'_{\Theta_{r,m}}(\Theta_{i,n}) &= \int_{\Delta\Omega_{i,n}} h_{\Theta_{r,m}}(\Theta_i) d\Omega_i \\ &\approx h_{\Theta_{r,m}}(\Theta_{i,n})\Delta\Omega_{i,n} \end{aligned}$$

where $1 \leq m \leq s$ and $1 \leq n \leq t$. The approximation is valid for sufficiently small $\Delta\Omega_{i,n}$ and will be used in generating the random variates in the following section. However, it does require a renormalization to ensure that the sum of each PMF is 1. When renormalized and applied to the BRDF, the PMF becomes

$$\begin{aligned} g_{\Theta_{r,m}}(\Theta_{i,n}) &= \frac{h_{\Theta_{r,m}}(\Theta_{i,n})\Delta\Omega_{i,n}}{\sum_{c=1}^{t} h_{\Theta_{r,m}}(\Theta_{i,c})\Delta\Omega_{i,c}} \\ &= \frac{\rho(\Theta_{i,n};\Theta_{r,m})\Delta\Omega_{i,n}}{\sum_{c=1}^{t} \rho(\Theta_{i,c};\Theta_{r,m})\Delta\Omega_{i,c}} \end{aligned} \tag{16}$$

We are now ready to define the lists from (12) and (13) required to generate random variates of the discretely sampled BRDF. For generating random variates of the incident directions corresponding to reflected direction $\Theta_{r,m}$ use

$$X = \{\Theta_{i,1}, \Theta_{i,2}, \ldots, \Theta_{i,t}\}$$

and

$$P = \{g_{\Theta_{r,m}}(\Theta_{i,1}), g_{\Theta_{r,m}}(\Theta_{i,2}), \ldots, g_{\Theta_{r,m}}(\Theta_{i,t})\}$$

5.2 The Rendering Program

The Radiance Lighting Simulation and Rendering System (Radiance) [28, 44] was used to generate the synthetic images in this work. Radiance is a suite of programs built around an advanced distributed raytracer designed for realistic image synthesis. It was selected because it is a physics based rendering system designed to accurately model the light behavior of a scene using physical units [44]. Using such a system reinforces the validity of the results obtained by this physics based BRDF. Additionally, the source code to Radiance is publicly available [2] and the program is currently in wide use, aiding future work.

Radiance is a distributed ray tracer which utilizes Monte Carlo importance sampling. The direction of the ray is stochastically selected so that the distribution matches the corresponding distribution function associated with the reflection model. This requires an inversion of the distribution function to map a uniformly random number to the desired distribution. Ward's implementation uses the relatively straightforward implementation of the Gaussian inversion to achieve this. That is, Ward's reflection model is based on the Gaussian function which provides easy inversion and thus a straightforward method of Monte Carlo integration. This method, however, is not compatible with the BRDFs generated by NEF-BM which are not of a Gaussian nature.

A new shader,[3] called iBRDF was built for Radiance using the alias method described in the preceding section. This provides a means for discretized versions of arbitrary isotropic BRDFs to be used in the creation of synthetic images.

Uniform sampling is used to discretize the BRDF. The BRDF is separated into M, N, and R divisions of the reflected θ, incident θ, and incident ϕ respectively. Since the BRDF is isotropic we define the coordinate system so that $\phi_r = 0$. For most of the BRDFs generated using NEFDS, uniform sampling was found to be sufficient. Good results were obtained by sampling at 40 values of θ_i and θ_r between 0 and $\pi/2$ and at 80 values of ϕ_r between 0 and π [4]. For some BRDFs containing greater variation in the reflectance lobe, a larger number of samples was required.

The iBRDF data is accessible via two different functions. The first is a direct lookup of the BRDF values given incident and reflected directions. This lookup requires only constant time since the sample grid consist of fixed divisions of θ_i and ϕ_i. For this function, tri-linear interpolation is used to interpolate between the three sampled axes. The second function creates random variates distributed as g_{Θ_i} in (16) using the alias method. Interpolation is performed using a stochastic version of linear interpolation for both the selection of the sampled ϕ_r and the selection of the incident direction within the selected $\Delta\omega_i$.

Radiance separates the BRDF into two components, diffuse and specular. The diffuse component refers only to pure Lambertian while specular refers to the remainder of the BRDF. The advantage of this separation is that the diffusely reflected radiance is slowly varying across the surface. Radiance utilizes this by caching the diffusely reflected radiance values and interpolating between those cached results whenever possible [46, 45]. Additionally, since the diffuse reflectance is pure Lambertian, the cached values are valid for all reflected angles. The above two functions provide the required BRDF information for specular reflectance. The diffuse reflectance is easily obtained by finding the minimum reflectance value of the BRDF for each Θ_r and using this as the diffuse portion of the BRDF, ρ_d. The specular portion of the BRDF used in the alias method is then the difference

$$\rho_{specular}(\Theta_i; \Theta_r) = \rho(\Theta_i; \Theta_r) - \rho_d(\Theta_r).$$

Radiance requires that all spectra be reduced to an RGB tristimulus equivalent, and it performs separate illumination calculations for each of the R, G, and B components. This limits the circumstances under which the color calculations will be exact to those where light reaching the viewing plane has struck only a single colored object (or that object and other spectrally neutral surfaces in the scene). Three separate iBRDF data sets are produced, one for each of the three axes of the RGB color space used in Radiance.

5.3 Rendering NEFDS material

Sampled BRDFs (at $\lambda = 550\text{nm}$) of several NEFDS materials were used to generate images in the modified rendering program. Figure 4 shows three vases modeled with the NEFDS materials Bare Construction Lumber, Gloss Paint on Metal, and Scored Aluminum. Figure 5 is rendered using the same materials and additionally the NEFDS materials Cement, and Weathered Concrete along with the addition of a texture map.

The variance in the reflected light over these five sampled BRDFs is shown even clearer in viewing the BRDFs directly. Figures 6 and 7 show the BRDFs of cement and lumber respectively. Notice the significant difference in geometry that can be characterized by the NEF-BM

[3]Radiance uses the term material type rather than shader.

[4]Another consequence of isotropic reflection is the need to only sample half the hemisphere. The other half (i.e., $\pi < \phi_r < 2\pi$) can be determined using the laws of reciprocity.

Figure 4: Vases with NEF materials (left to right) Bare Construction Lumber, Gloss Paint on Metal, and Scored Aluminum. Image from [43].

Figure 5: Cubes with textured NEF materials (top row) Cement, Gloss Paint on Metal, (bottom row) Bare Construction Lumber, Scored Aluminum, and Weathered Concrete. Image from [43].

model. This strength (the ability to capture a wide variety of BRDF distributions) coupled with the systematic method of measurement make for a very powerful rendering tool.

5.4 Fitting New Models to NEF-BM

Not only does NEFDS offer hundreds of pre-existing materials, it also allows new materials to be added. The measured BRDF values of two metallic paint samples were used to create two new modeled BRDFs using the NEF Beard-Maxwell model. The two samples, termed fine and coarse, were respectively dominated by small and large metallic flakes. The paint with a greater number of fine flakes had a larger diffuse component due to more edge scattering. This is easily captured by the NEF-BM model as can be seen in the rendered image of Figure 8. Measurements were performed at the National Institute of Standards and Technology (NIST) using the reference spectrogoniophotometer, the Spectral Tri-function Automated Reference Reflectometer (STARR) [34].

The first measurement[5] discussed here is the near zero-bistatic BRDF measurement. This measurement is used to derive the distribution of micro-facets, which are responsible for the first surface reflection in the Beard-Maxwell model. Measurement of the near zero-bistatic BRDF is performed in a single plane, from the surface normal to grazing angles. Source and detector are held at a fixed six degree separation (near zero) in this plane of measurement.

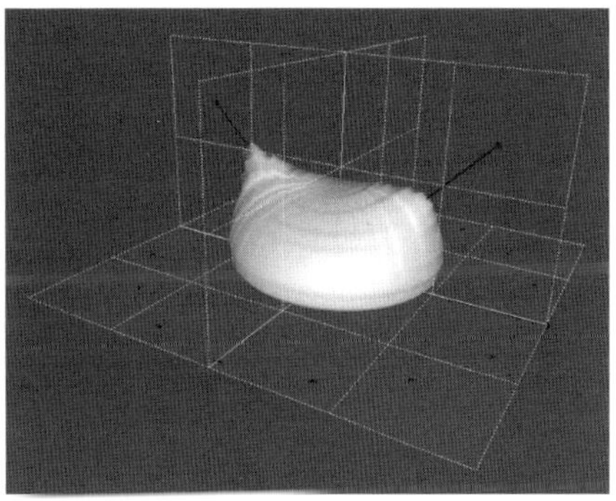

Figure 6: BRDF of Cement

Figure 9 shows the measured versus modeled BRDF values at the near zero-bistatic angles for the fine and coarse metallic paint samples. As can be seen there is a very good fit to the measured data at the points outside the specular peak. The crossover point at about 18 degrees is matched for both measured and modeled data.

In addition to the near zero-bistatic measurements, the specular BRDF measurements were performed using parallel polarized source and receiver over $10\,\mathrm{deg} \leq \theta_i \leq 80\,\mathrm{deg}$ with $\phi_i = 0\,\mathrm{deg}$ and $\phi_r = 180\,\mathrm{deg}$. As mentioned earlier, for each sampled incident direction, the receiver direction was varied about the mirror direction in the plane of incidence by $\theta_i - 5\,\mathrm{deg} \leq \theta_r \leq \theta_i + 5\,\mathrm{deg}$. This provided the means by which the complex index of refraction was determined, used in determining the Fresnel reflection. Lastly, the shadowing and obscuration

[5]Measurements were performed in the four polarization states, $\rho_{\perp\perp}$, $\rho_{\perp\parallel}$, $\rho_{\parallel\perp}$, and $\rho_{\parallel\parallel}$. Unless noted otherwise, the measured values listed are the calculated unpolarized values, computed from these measured polarized values.

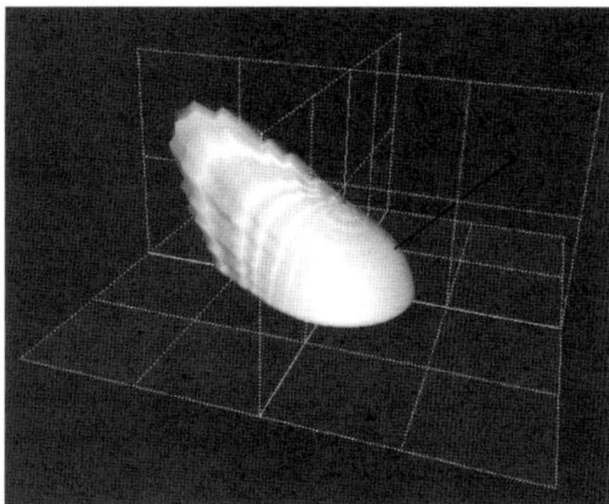

Figure 7: BRDF of Bare Construction Lumber

Figure 8: Coarse and fine metallic paint on vases

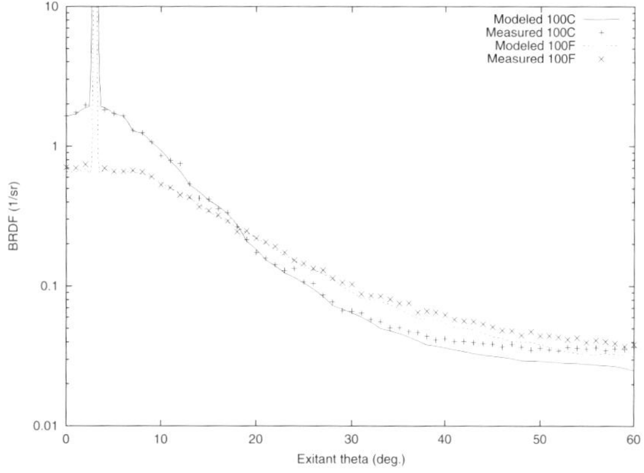

Figure 9: Comparison of measured and modeled six degree bistatic angle BRDF values

Table 1: Comparison of measured versus modeled out-of-plane BRDF values for coarse metallic flake sample.

θ_i (degs.)	θ_r (degs.)	ϕ_r (degs.)	Coarse metallic flake BRDF Measured (1/sr)	Coarse metallic flake BRDF Modeled (1/sr)
-30	45	45	0.269	0.255
-30	45	90	0.0635	0.0698
-30	45	135	0.0389	0.0405
-45	45	45	0.207	0.223
-45	45	90	0.0469	0.0499
-45	45	135	0.0331	0.0332
-60	45	45	0.150	0.173
-60	45	90	0.0401	0.0469
-60	45	135	0.0325	0.0316

Table 2: Comparison of measured versus modeled out-of-plane BRDF values for fine metallic flake sample.

θ_i (degs.)	θ_r (degs.)	ϕ_r (degs.)	Fine metallic flake BRDF Measured (1/sr)	Fine metallic flake BRDF Modeled (1/sr)
-30	45	45	0.254	0.321
-30	45	90	0.1023	0.1001
-30	45	135	0.0627	0.0622
-45	45	45	0.210	0.295
-45	45	90	0.0727	0.0769
-45	45	135	0.0479	0.0454
-60	45	45	0.179	0.240
-60	45	90	0.0581	0.0641
-60	45	135	0.0386	0.0377

terms, τ and Ω, were determined with the fixed source, varying receiver measurements.

The model parameters for the NEF Beard-Maxwell reflection model are selected on the basis of in-plane BRDF measurements only. In order to verify that the NEF Beard-Maxwell model is in fact an appropriate model to represent the BRDF of the surface, validation of out-of-plane BRDF values should be performed. Out-of-plane measurements were made at a variety of incident and reflected directions for both coarse and fine metallic flake samples—the results are listed in Tables 1 and 2. As can be seen from these figures, there is a very good correspondence between the measured and modeled BRDF values, indicating that the NEF Beard-Maxwell model is appropriate for representing these metallic surfaces.

6 Conclusion

The NEFDS provides a collection of surface reflection data that can be useful for work in realistic image synthesis. Although the database was developed for application in the remote sensing field, it contains materials of importance to computer graphics researchers. The database has a good user interface, it is well documented, and it can be extended with additional measurements. The protocol for performing these measurements is well defined and it makes use of existing radiometric instruments.

The NEFDS incorporates a modified form of the Beard-Maxwell reflection model. This is a physics based reflection model that can be fit to measured data. This gives it the advantage of a first principles physics derivation coupled with a measurement scheme for determining the model parameters. The key insight in the model is that all first surface reflectances can be calculated by measuring zero-bistatic first surface reflectances. The principal limitation of the model is its inaccuracy at grazing angles.

The acceptance of sophisticated reflectance models in computer graphics depends upon the availability of data necessary to use of the models. Rendering systems such as Radiance are capable of producing photo realistic pictures. With the addition of real-time shading techniques, even personal computers can make acceptable interactive pictures of surfaces with complex reflectance properties. Just as the need for geometric data has spawned a 3D modeling industry, databases containing the reflectance characteristics of common materials will be of increasing importance in computer graphics. NEFDS is an example of such a database.

7 Acknowledgments

The authors would like to acknowledge the significant contributions made by one of the original co-developers of the NEF-BM model and the NEF database, Michael Metzler of ISciences LLC. Metzler wrote software that allowed us to directly access the data in the NEF database without going through the user interface. Metzler was also instrumental in specifying the protocol that was employed to make the measurements as well as performing the parameter estimation from the measurement data described in Section 5.4. Maria Nadal of the National Institute of Standards and Technology (NIST) acquired the data, some of which is shown in Figure 9, that allowed us to synthesize pictures of the metal flake samples. The scenes shown in Figures 4 and 5 were modeled and rendered by Peter Walker. Funding for this research was provided by NIST under the program administration of Fern Hunt.

8 References

[1] *NEF User Guide*, 9.1 edition. http://math.nist.gov/~FHunt/appearance/nefds.html, Accessed March 20, 2002.

[2] Radiance home page. http://radsite.lbl.gov/radiance. Accessed March 20, 2001.

[3] *NEF Specifications*, July 1996. ORD 258-96, http://math.nist.gov/~FHunt/appearance/nefds.html, Accessed March 20, 2002.

[4] *Nonconventional Exploitation Factors (NEF) Modeling*, August 1996. ORD 257-96, http://math.nist.gov/~FHunt/appearance/nefds.html, Accessed March 20, 2002.

[5] Michael Ashikhmin, Simon Premoze, and Peter S. Shirley. A microfacet-based brdf generator. *Computer Graphics (Proceedings of SIGGRAPH 2000)*, pages 65–74, July 2000.

[6] Petr Beckmann and André Spizzichino. *The Scattering of Electromagnetic Waves from Rough Surfaces*. Pergamon Press, Oxford, England, 1963.

[7] James F. Blinn. Models of light reflection for computer synthesized pictures. *Computer Graphics (Proceedings of SIGGRAPH 77)*, 11(2):192–198, July 1977.

[8] James F. Blinn. Light reflection functions for simulation of clouds and dusty surfaces. *Computer Graphics (Proceedings of SIGGRAPH 82)*, 16(3):21–29, July 1982.

[9] Brian Cabral, Nelson Max, and Rebecca Springmeyer. Bidirectional reflection functions from surface bump maps. *Computer Graphics (Proceedings of SIGGRAPH 87)*, 21(4):273–281, July 1987.

[10] Robert L. Cook and Kenneth E. Torrance. A reflectance model for computer graphics. *Computer Graphics (Proceedings of SIGGRAPH 81)*, 15(3):307–316, August 1981.

[11] Kristin J. Dana, Bram van Ginneken, Shree K. Nayar, and Jan J. Koenderink. Reflectance and texture of real-world surfaces. *ACM Transactions on Graphics*, 18(1):1–34, January 1999.

[12] George S. Fishman and L. Stephen Yarberry. Generating a sample from a k-cell table with changing probabilities in $O(\log_2 k)$ time. *ACM Transactions on Mathematical Software*, 19(2):257–261, 1993.

[13] James E. Gentle. *Random Number Generation and Monte Carlo Methods*. Springer-Verlag New York, Inc., New York, U.S.A, 1998.

[14] Jay S. Gondek, Gary W. Meyer, and Jonathan G. Newman. Wavelength dependent reflectance functions. *Computer Graphics (Proceedings of SIGGRAPH 94)*, pages 213–220, July 1994.

[15] Bruce W. Hapke. A theoretical photometric function for the lunar surface. *Journal of Geophysical Research*, 68(15):4571–4586, 1963.

[16] Xiao D. He, Kenneth E. Torrance, François X. Sillion, and Donald P. Greenberg. A comprehensive physical model for light reflection. *Computer Graphics (Proceedings of SIGGRAPH 91)*, 25(4):175–186, July 1991.

[17] Eugene Hecht. *Optics*, chapter 4: The Propagation of Light, pages 85–147. Addison Wesley Longman, Inc., third edition, 1998.

[18] Wolfgang Heidrich and Hans-Peter Seidel. Realistic, hardware-accelerated shading and lighting. *Computer Graphics (Proceedings of SIGGRAPH 99)*, pages 171–178, August 1999.

[19] L. Henyey and J. Greenstein. Diffuse reflection in the galaxy. *Journal of Astrophysics*, 93:70–77, 1941.

[20] Jan Kautz and Michael D. McCool. Interactive rendering with arbitrary brdfs using separable approximations. *Tenth Eurographics Workshop on Rendering*, pages 281–292, June 1999.

[21] Donald E. Knuth. *Seminumerical Algorithms*, volume 2 of *The Art of Computer Programming*. Addison-Wesley Longman, Reading, Massachusetts, U.S.A., second edition, 1998.

[22] J. J. Koenderink, A. J. van Doorn, and M. Stavridi. Bidirectional reflection distribution function expressed in terms of surface scattering modes. *European Conference on Computer Vision*, pages 28–29, 1996.

[23] R. A. Kronmal and A. V. Peterson. The alias and alias-rejection-mixture methods for generating random variables from probability distributions. In *Proceedings of the 1979 Winter Simulation Conference*, pages 269–280. Institute of Electrical and Electronics Engineers, 1979.

[24] R. A. Kronmal and A. V. Peterson. On the alias method for generating random variables from a discrete distribution. *The American Statistician*, 33:214–218, 1979.

[25] R. A. Kronmal and A. V. Peterson. A variant of the acceptance-rejection method for computer generation of random variables. *Journal of the American Statistical Association*, 76:446–451, 1981.

[26] Eric P. F. Lafortune, Sing-Choong Foo, Kenneth E. Torrance, and Donald P. Greenberg. Non-linear approximation of reflectance functions. *Computer Graphics (Proceedings of SIGGRAPH 97)*, pages 117–126, August 1997.

[27] Paul Lalonde and Alain Fournier. A wavelet representation of reflectance functions. *IEEE Transactions on Visualization and Computer Graphics*, 3(4):329–336, October–December 1997.

[28] Greg Ward Larson and Rob Shakespeare. *Rendering with Radiance, The Art and Science of Lighting Visualization*. Morgan Kaufmann Publishers, Inc., San Francisco, U.S.A, 1998.

[29] Gregory J. Ward Larson. Measuring and modeling anisotropic reflection. *Computer Graphics (Proceedings of SIGGRAPH 92)*, 26(2):265–272, July 1992.

[30] J. R. Maxwell, J. Beard, S. Weiner, and D. Ladd. Bidirectional reflectance model validation and utilization. Technical Report AFAL–TR–73–303, Environmental Research Institute of Michigan (ERIM), October 1973.

[31] F. E. Nicodemus, J. C. Richmond, J. J. Hsia, I. W. Ginsberg, and T. Limperis. Geometric considerations and nomenclature for reflectance. Technical Report MN-160, U.S. Department of Commerce, National Bureau of Standards, October 1977.

[32] Michael Oren and Shree K. Nayar. Generalization of the lambertian model and implications for machine vision. *International Journal of Computer Vision*, 14:227–251, 1995.

[33] A. V. Peterson and R. A. Kronmal. On mixture methods for the computer generation of random variables. *The American Statistician*, 36:184–191, 1982.

[34] James E. Proctor and P. Yvonne Barnes. Nist high accuracy reference reflectometer-spectrophotometer. *Journal of Research of the National Institute of Standards and Technology*, 101(5):619–627, September–October 1996.

[35] Peter Schröder and Wim Sweldens. Spherical wavelets: Efficiently representing functions on the sphere. *Computer Graphics (Proceedings of SIGGRAPH 95)*, pages 161–172, August 1995.

[36] Jos Stam. Diffraction shaders. *Computer Graphics (Proceedings of SIGGRAPH 99)*, pages 101–110, August 1999.

[37] K. E. Torrance and E. M. Sparrow. Theory for off-specular reflection from roughened surfaces. *Journal of Optical Society of America*, 57(9):1105–1114, 1967.

[38] T. Trowbridge and K. Reitz. Average irregularity representation of roughened surfaces. *Journal of the Optical Society of America*, 65(5):531–536, 1975.

[39] Michael D. Vose. A linear algorithm for generating random numbers with a given distribution. *IEEE Transactions on Software Engineering*, 17:972–975, 1991.

[40] A. J. Walker. Fast generation of uniformly distributed pseudorandom numbers with floating point representation. *Electronics Letters*, 10(41):553–554, 1974.

[41] A. J. Walker. New fast method for generating discrete random numbers with arbitrary frequency distribution. *Electronics Letters*, 10(8):127–128, 1974.

[42] A. J. Walker. An efficient method for generating discrete random variables with general distributions. *ACM Transactions on Mathematical Software*, 3:253–256, 1977.

[43] Peter Andrew Walker. A visualization system for bidirectional reflectance distribution functions. Master's thesis, University of Oregon, 1999.

[44] Gregory J. Ward. The radiance lighting simulation and rendering system. *Computer Graphics (Proceedings of SIGGRAPH 94)*, pages 459–472, July 1994.

[45] Gregory J. Ward and Paul S. Heckbert. Irradiance gradients. In *Proceedings of the Third Annual Eurographics Workshop on Rendering*, pages 85–98, Bristol, U.K., 1992. Springer-Verlag.

[46] Gregory J. Ward, Francis M. Rubinstein, and Robert D. Clear. A ray tracing solution for diffuse interreflection. *Computer Graphics (Proceedings of SIGGRAPH 88)*, 22(4):85–92, August 1988.

[47] Stephen H. Westin, James R. Arvo, and Kenneth E. Torrance. Predicting reflectance functions from complex surfaces. *Computer Graphics (Proceedings of SIGGRAPH 92)*, 26(2):255–264, July 1992.

Coherent Bump Map Recovery from a Single Texture Image

J.M. Dischler [(a)] K. Maritaud [(b)] D. Ghazanfarpour [(b)]

(a) LSIIT (UMR 7005 CNRS ULP), Pôle API, Bvd S. Brant, 67400 Illkirch Cedex
(b) Laboratoire MSI, ENSIL, 16 rue Atlantis, 87068 Limoges Cedex

Abstract

In order to texture surfaces realistically with texture images (e.g. photos), it is important to consider the underlying relief. Here, a method is proposed to recover a coherent bump map from a single texture image. Different visual zones are first identified using segmentation and classification. Then, by linearly separating the relief into a noise-like small-scale component and a smooth "shape-related" large-scale component, we can automatically deduce the bump map as well as an "unshaded" color map of the texture. The major advantage of our approach, compared to sophisticated measurement techniques based on *multiple* photos or specific devices, is its practical simplicity and broad accessibility, while it allows us to obtain very easily, via basic bump mapping or displacement mapping, rendering results of good quality.

Key words: texturing, shape from shading, texture segmentation, bump mapping.

1 Introduction

Texturing synthetic 3D surfaces using a single texture image obtained from a real-world surface (e.g. using a photograph) is clearly desirable, because of its simplicity. However, it raises a number of difficult practical problems. One of them is related to the fact that most textures are not limited to color variations. Bump mapping [1], 3D and geometric textures [7], bi-directional texture functions [3, 4, 10], polynomial textures [11] and relief texture mapping [12] outline this well. With conventional texture mapping [2] or with straight texture analysis and synthesis [19, 20, 21], only the color information is considered and reproduced on surfaces. Therefore, rendered surfaces still look smooth and flat, instead of looking rough and bumpy. In order to obtain more realistic rendering results, it is important to also consider the underlying geometry.

Many approaches [3, 10, 11, 16, 17, 18] have been investigated in recent years for acquiring the relief and reflectance from real-world surfaces. These approaches all consist in performing a sort of "real" data measurement by using specific devices and/or multiple photos taken under precise or arbitrary lighting conditions and viewpoints. But, multiple photos with different viewpoints and different lighting conditions are not always easily available. Practical manipulations can be complicated, such as for more or less large, outdoor, natural surfaces (ocean waves, sand dunes, tree bark, etc.). The same applies for specific devices and tools, which are not always available, affordable and accessible to users. In addition, measurement devices such as laser scanners do generally not span all orders of geometric scales, e.g. from microscopic relief (a few microns) to macroscopic relief (several miles), which further limits the domain of application.

In parallel to these practical limitations, users might want to take profit of the numerous texture databases on commercial CD-ROMs, free web pages, photo-albums, etc. providing thousands of individual texture images usually shot under completely arbitrary and unknown lighting conditions. This enormous and easily available texture diversity seems, in our opinion, worth to be "better" exploited by computer graphics by adding – at least – the missing bump maps for relief sensation recovery.

In computer vision, a large number of *shape from shading* (SFS) techniques have been investigated; the goal of these techniques being to recover a bump map from a single view under some precise conditions. The works of Horn and Brooks [9] as well as Zhang et al. [22] give a relatively complete overview of the domain. Unfortunately, these methods still fail with "complex" natural textures [22]. Shadows, specular highlights, hue, different roughness scales, and so forth, still strongly disturb their effectiveness. The inherent mathematical difficulty of extracting relief (and eventually reflectance), from a single image – not even necessarily in an accurate way, but at least in a visually consistent way –

certainly explains the absence, until now, of efficient methods in computer graphics applications.

This paper proposes an approach based on image segmentation and filtering to resolve, under some not too constraining conditions of lighting and types of texture, the problem of bump map recovery from a single texture image. Figure 1 summarizes the principles of our approach. We use segmentation to divide the texture into basic visual components (sets of pixels). On one hand, we identify different color zones, including shadows and specular highlights, using color quantization; and, on the other hand, we identify "texture elements" with a specific signification such as spots, bricks, grains, etc. by grouping some color zones. Then, the classified structures are analyzed in order to recover the desired underlying components: relief and "unshaded" color. Therefore, we simply adapt the actually very general SFS problem to the particular case of "bump-like" textures. To simplify the problem, we linearly separate the relief into two distinct scales (large-scale and small-scale), which actually turns out to be valid for many natural textures. In the case of a brick wall for example, the large-scale relief corresponds to the bricks shapes (how they come out of the wall), while the small-scale relief corresponds to the rough nature of the bricks (small, but yet visible, noise-like asperities). The small-scale relief is addressed using a filter computed according to the light source direction. The large-scale relief is addressed by using the identified texture structures. Our method is mostly automatic, since the user only needs to quickly provide some minimal "external" information, such as structures and apparent light source direction.

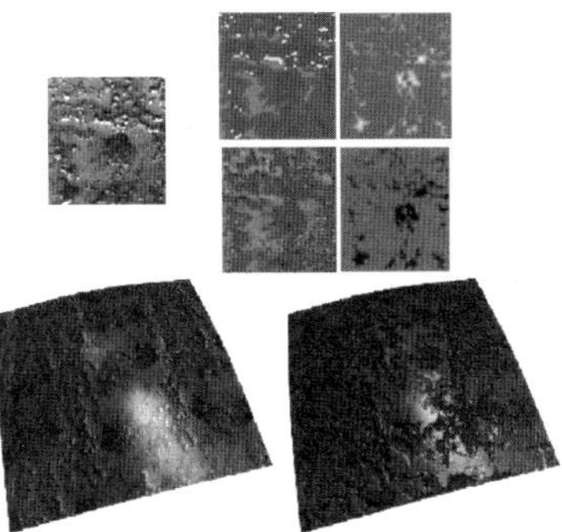

Figure 1: Method overview. Top left: the user provides a single texture image (here, rusty metal) with unknown relief. Top right: Segmentation (upper-left) into color zones to identify color components; and (upper-right) into "semantic" zones to identify the "structures" of the texture. Just below: extraction of color (left) and relief (right) by using the previous segmentation and classification. Bottom left: lapped texture mapping using the original image. Bottom right: result from our method, using the extracted color and relief.

The remaining parts of this paper are organized as follows: section 2 states the mathematical problem and the assumptions that our method makes. Sections 3 and 4 respectively concern small-scale and large-scale relief recovery. Section 5 explains how to combine the elements of the two previous sections. Graphical results are shown in section 6. Finally, we conclude the paper and discuss some future directions.

2 Texture and lighting conditions

In order to simplify the difficult mathematical problem of relief recovery from a single image, we make a certain number of assumptions concerning the texture, its image and the lighting condition. However, we wish to avoid too drastic constraints as generally demanded by SFS [9] to be able to process a wide range of photos of diverse real-world textures.

The most basic assumptions firstly concern the image and the lighting condition. We suppose that the lighting is uniform over the entire image; so, the natural surface should be locally a plane. One white light source is assumed dominant and sufficiently far away to retrieve a constant lighting direction. Inter-reflections and secondary light sources will be approximated by using a constant "ambient" term (scalar value). Hence, a unique vector L_i, plus a single scalar coefficient, can characterize the entire lighting condition. The observer is assumed perpendicular to the image plane, located at a certain distance on the line passing approximately through the center of the image. This line will correspond to the z-axis of the recovered height map (bump map) of the texture. These basic assumptions are common to almost all the usual SFS techniques.

The next assumptions concern the nature of the texture itself. We assume that the relief can be entirely characterized by a height map. This means that fur, wicker, cloth, and so forth are excluded. The reflectance is approximated by a "Phong-like" function; i.e. a diffuse Lambert part, plus a specular part, which we will disregard for relief recovery. We further assume that there are no visible environment reflections on the texture. This excludes highly specular surfaces like mirrors. However, we allow localized specular highlights. Finally, we assume that the texture is composed of individual arbitrarily shaped bumps, which may have different tints, such as bricks in brick walls, "scales" in bark, grooves in stones, etc. Unlike most SFS techniques, we will consider a number of important effects: shadows, specular highlights, different hues and more or less important roughness characteristics. In practice, we distinguish two roughness scales: a small-scale relief that has a relatively small amplitude, which corresponds to noise-like irregularities. Because of this small amplitude, we can assume, without restricting the efficiency of our method, that there are no (or negligible) self-shadowing effects related to this relief (the amplitude may even be null for smooth surfaces). The large-scale relief has a relatively large amplitude, therefore it may also produce self-shadows as well as local specular highlights. We will assume that this type of relief can be characterized by a single elevation curve (1D). Though this seems to be a drastic simplification, many natural textures do verify this condition, including the examples shown in this paper. The use of a single elevation curve has some similarities with the generalized cylinders approach used by Dischler and Ghazanfarpour [6] for reconstructing 3D shapes from two views. Our approach, however, is different, since we do not consider "full" 3D shapes.

Now, let $T(i,j)$, $(i,j)\in[1,n]^2$, be the texture image. With the previous assumptions, we can rewrite our relief recovery problem as the following equation:

$$T(i,j) = K_d C(i,j) L_i N(i,j) + K_s (L_i V(i,j))^p + K_a C(i,j)$$

where, C represents the "unshaded" color map, N the normal vectors and V the median line between N and the observer direction. Both, N and V depend on the texture relief H; e.g. $N = (\partial H(i,j)/\partial i, \partial H(i,j)/\partial j)$. The coefficient p represents the cosine power of the Phong reflectance model, L_i the light source direction, K_d, K_s and K_a the other coefficients of the Phong shading model. K_a is constant over the image. In the remaining parts, we will ignore specular highlights, which can be easily identified with our color-based segmentation. They will be reconsidered once the relief and "unshaded" color have been recovered.

Since we separate large-scale and small-scale relief, H can be written as $H=H_l+H_s$. The problem is now to find coherent values for our unknowns, e.g. for H_l, H_s, and C. K_d does not need to be explicitly recovered since it only influences the global brightness of the texture. For example, a user-defined K_d, lower than the actual K_d of the texture, will darken the texture. K_a is recovered by using the average brightness of shadow zones. If there are no shadow zones, we assume this value to be zero.

3 Small-scale relief recovery

Before dealing with the general case mentioned above, we will first consider the simpler case of small-scale relief. Let us assume first that there are no shadows, no specular highlights, that the color is constant (e.g. gray) and that there are no specific large-scale visual structures. These conditions are typically met by noisy textures. There have been a number of successful investigations in the past for synthesizing "noisy patterns" using an analysis of histograms and wavelet and/or Fourier transforms [5, 8]. Their success comes from the fact that such patterns are characterized by low order statistics, which can be well captured by the frequency domain. In fact, two "noisy patterns" can be considered as visually similar if spatial histograms and frequency distributions are similar.

We will now exploit this principle of visual similitude for relief recovery (not accurately but in a visually coherent and consistent way). Therefore, we assume that the "shading" due to a light source corresponds to a linear filtering of the bump map. Figure 2 illustrates three examples of synthetic bump maps, obtained using Perlin's [13] noise function. On the left, we show the original bump map where the darkest pixels are the deepest. Next, we show the respective frequency domains (note that Perlin's noise produces some important frequencies along the axes, which is a known phenomenon). Then, we show a shaded image using a directional light source (without computing interreflections), plus the corresponding frequency domains. It is visible that the shading has modified the frequency domains in two ways. Firstly, some directional frequencies (the direction matches the light source direction, rotated by $\pi/2$) have been filtered out. Secondly, high frequencies have been introduced. The right-most images in Figure 2 show the results that we obtain by applying a "reverse shading" filter (described below) and the corresponding frequency domains.

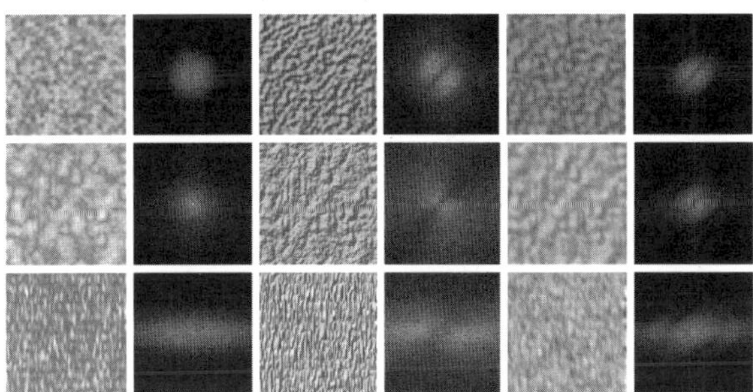

Figure 2: Three examples of synthetic bump maps and their corresponding frequency domains. (left) the original bump maps, (middle) the shaded bump maps using a directional light source, (right) applying a "reverse shading" filter, as described in this paper.

We can design a simple filter-based technique in order to recover a consistent bump map from a shaded image by using the two previous assumptions:

(1) noisy textures are visually alike if they have similar low order statistics (similar frequency domains);
(2) the shading due to a unique directional light source modifies in two ways the frequency domain of the original bump map.

We simply need to filter out some high frequencies and augment the amplitudes of the frequencies in the direction perpendicular to the light source direction.

In practice, the removal of high frequencies can be done using a low-pass filter (e.g. Gaussian), while the increasing of the other frequencies can be done with an anisotropic filter for which the direction matches the perpendicular direction of the light source. Figure 3 shows such filters for different directions (combined with the Gaussian filter). We need to make the height (value) of the directional filter depending on how grazing the light direction is with respect to the bump map, since we experienced that the amplitude of the "groove", caused by the shading in the frequency domain, diminishes when the light direction becomes vertical. The tangent to the angle of the light source direction with respect to the plane of the bump map can be used to obtain a filter depending on the light source direction. At strongly grazing angles, the value of the filter is infinite, while, with a vertical light direction, the height is 1 (e.g. frequencies are not modified and the filter is simply a Gaussian one). Indeed, in the latter case, there is no longer any visible groove, but high frequencies remain.

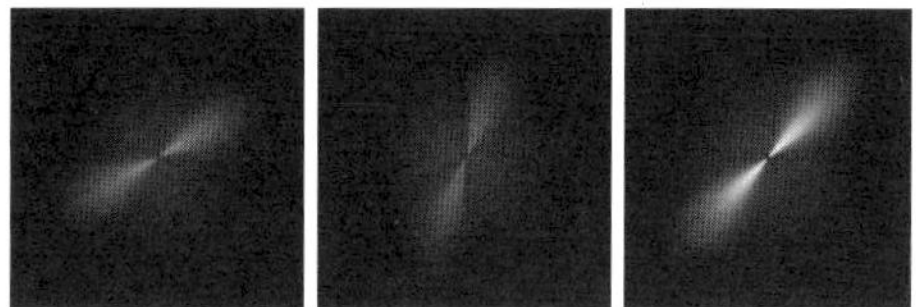

Figure 3: Examples of filters in the frequency domain. (Note: in the frequency domain, filtering is obtained by multiplication, while, in the spatial domain, it is obtained by convolution).

Once the filter has been designed, it is possible to obtain, by inverse Fourier transform, a convolution mask for filtering images of bumpy textures in the spatial domain. In practice, we use finite impulse response filters with very small sizes (3x3, or at most 7x7), firstly because of efficiency but also because the zones that we filter are usually small. The right-most part of Figure 2 illustrates the results of the filtering process, which we call "reverse shading filtering". The small size of the discrete filters explains that in our case the filtering produces some artifacts visible on Figure 2 (we do not recover exactly the original frequency domain). For example, it is visible that all the frequencies in the light source direction could not be restored (they were augmented but not "fully").

But, in spite of these artifacts, we experienced that the filtering process was yet already sufficient to restore coherent and consistent bump maps well, especially in the case of "noisy" textures. Figure 4 demonstrates this. We show the three previous synthetic bump maps applied to tori using lapped textures [14] that we extended to bump mapping. Note that the middle tori "naively" use the shaded image as a bump map (i.e. the middle images of Figure 2). This implies that each bump has become a smaller bump and a cavity and, thus, clearly introduces too high frequencies, as well as directional artifacts. Using filtering (Figure 2, right), we obtain results of much better quality (though not completely correct because of a slight "over-blurring" effect). Visible discontinuities on these images may be related to the lapped textures technique, which tends to produce seams on low frequency texture regions.

Figure 4: Applying the synthetic bump maps of Figure 2 to tori. The left-hand tori show the references, the middle ones show the results obtained using a "naive" method consisting in directly applying the shaded images as bump maps, the right-hand ones show the results obtained using our filtering technique.

4 Large-scale relief recovery

Natural texture images seldom meet the restrictive conditions that we set for small-scale relief. So, we will also need to consider shadows, specular highlights, hue, etc. Indeed, most textures are made of areas of different colors; and their shadows and highlights are mostly due to the large-scale structure of the texture.

4.1 Identifying large scale structures

The first step consists in identifying different color zones in the supplied texture image. For segmentation, we adopted a technique based on training sets, almost similar to the one used by Premoze et al. [15] for segmenting satellite images. With this technique, the user provides a training set, based on a few selected pixels. Figure 5 illustrates the segmentation of an image representing a synthetic bumpy texture composed of two different colors. Therefore, we obtained two zones after segmenting and the training set was composed of only two selected pixels, one for each color zone. Once the image has been segmented into k color zones, we can associate to each pixel a color index c_k. Each color zone can be composed of one or multiple connected components, which we will call "color structures" (dots in the case of Figure 5).

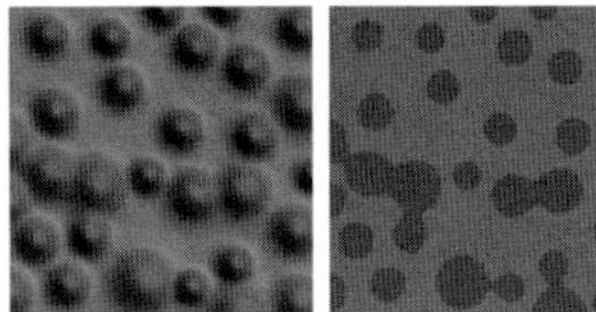

Figure 5: An example of synthetic bump-texture image. (Left) the image. (Right) the segmented image.

We now want to identify the "bumps" of the input image. To simplify the problem, we will assume that the bumps match the color structures. However, this does not mean that each bump is necessarily composed of a single color structure. On the contrary, one bump is often a composition (union) of multiple color structures. Grouping and classifying color structures requires users to click only on a few pixels.

We obtain two types of segmentation. The first corresponds to color structures, the second to the bump shapes. To compute the relief, we will now ignore specular highlights and shadows. These particular color zones can be easily identified since specular highlights generally correspond to the brightest color zone, while shadows generally correspond to the darkest zone. But, since not all images have specular highlights and/or shadows, we let users set a Boolean value for each. If the value is true, the system selects the brightest, respectively darkest zones as highlights respectively shadow. Otherwise, it assumes that there are none.

We assume that the relief of the bump structures is related to their shapes and, thus, it can be characterized by a single elevation curve. So, for all bump structures, we compute a discrete distance transform, based on erosion (this is a morphological operator). Figure 6 (left) illustrates this, in the case of the synthetic texture of Figure 5. The distance transform $D(B_s)$ provides for each bumpy structure B_s a value between 0 and 1, where 0 means: "on the border"; and 1: "on the innermost part of the structure" (the innermost pixels can be considered as a sort of skeleton).

We are interested in finding the normal $N(i,j)$ on each pixel of each bumpy structure. The normal is defined with polar coordinates as:

$$\begin{cases} N_x = \cos(\alpha)\cos(\beta) \\ N_y = \sin(\alpha)\cos(\beta) \\ N_z = \sin(\beta) \end{cases}$$

Angle α is obtained using the previously computed distance transform. In fact, for each pixel of the bump, we can compute a closest "innermost" corresponding pixel (a pixel on the "skeleton"), which defines the direction (see Figure 6, middle part).

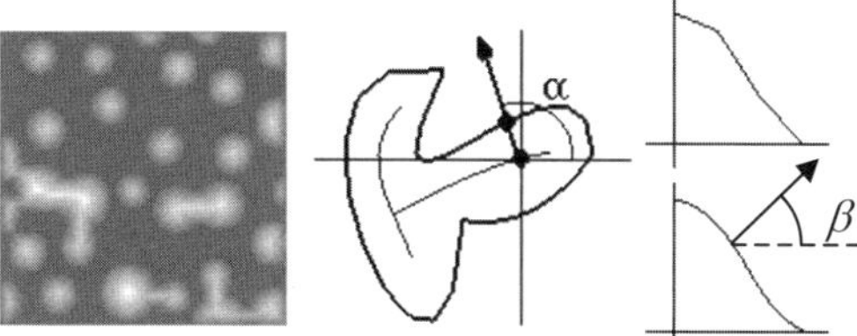

Figure 6: (Left) erosion is used to provide a distance transform for each bumpy structure. (Middle) computing the normal direction using the skeleton; (right) smoothing the elevation curve.

Now, we must compute the angle β (see Figure 6, right-hand part). Angle β is computed by using the shading information given by the texture image $T(i,j)$. β is constant for pixels at the same distance D, e.g. for all pixels p_i, p_j, such that $D(p_i)=D(p_j)$. For a diffuse reflector, we have:

$$C(i,j)N(i,j)L_i = T(i,j). \qquad (1)$$

The color $C(i,j)$ depends on the color zone obtained by segmentation. We assume that the tint (hue and saturation) of pixels is rather constant inside one color zone and that the color variations are essentially due to the brightness, which depends on the relief. To obtain the constant color of each zone, we simply keep the color of the brightest pixel inside that zone (specular highlights are excluded), since on this particular pixel the light source direction approximately matches the normal (the cosine value is maximal, i.e. close to 1). Let us call max_k the brightest color of the zone with index c_k. Now, in Equation 1, we can replace $C(i,j)$ by max_k. The remaining unknown in this equation is β. By noticing that $\sin^2+\cos^2=1$, we obtain an equation system of the second order that can be straightforwardly solved. Unfortunately, this system provides two solutions, among which we have to make a choice. The choice will be motivated by the following two statements. (1) The large-scale relief varies smoothly, so that, from one pixel to another, the normal only changes slightly. (2) On the skeleton, the normal is vertical. Now, we can compute one angle β for each pixel by starting with the innermost pixels (skeleton) and by moving away to the border (on constant distance D levels). Note that this procedure has some similarity with traditional SFS, for which the brightest pixels are also assumed oriented towards the light source. Each β is chosen to minimize the difference with the previous one (i.e. on the previous distance level). For each level, we obtain a collection of angles β, i.e. for all pixels with the same distance D. Theoretically, all should be equal, but due to irregularities in the relief (natural textures are rarely perfectly smooth) and discretization errors, all are generally different. So, we must compute an average to reduce noise. The same is done for all bump structures, which provides us with angle series that are again averaged. We finally obtain, for each distance level D, a certain mean angle β, which can be used to determine a discrete elevation curve (see right part of Figure 6). When β equals $\pi/2$, the elevation is null, otherwise we move up or down, proportionally to the cosine of β (which can be negative). The obtained curve, often still noisy, can be further smoothed to obtain a continuous elevation variation according to the distance D.

Once we have an elevation curve, for the bumpy structures, we can compute a large-scale bump map $H_l(i,j)$ simply using the distance transform.

Figure 7 illustrates the relief we obtained for the synthetic bump texture of Figure 5 (in this case there is no small-scale relief). A rendering on a mushroom is also shown (visible discontinuities are due to the lapped textures). We obtain a result that matches well the "real" relief. The only noticeable problem is that the discrete distance transform has introduced edges on connected dots. This is because the dots are very small in terms of pixels. Thus, errors concerning the computation of β are high, especially close to the skeleton (there is an increasing error on , as pixels come closer to the skeleton).

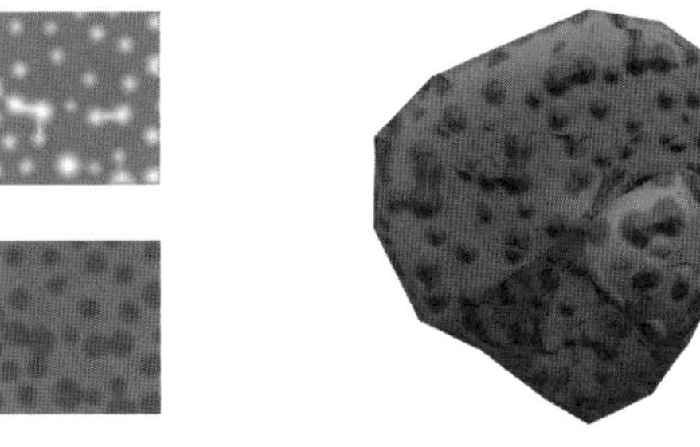

Figure 7: Left: a recovered bump map (top) and an "unshaded" color map (bottom). Right: applying the texture to a mushroom (viewed from below). The result is consistent with the original image of Figure 5.

4.2 Computation of an "unshaded" color map

The last step consists in computing an "unshaded" color map. It is easy to compute since we assumed that color variations are only due to the relief (except for user specified zones, which are simply ignored, as for Figure1). However, instead of using directly the segmented image as a color map, we blur it to avoid visible discontinuities. Finally, the areas corresponding to the specular highlights and shadows are filled with consistent patterns, either with a constant mean color or by a texture analysis and synthesis technique [20].

5 Combining large-scale and small-scale relief

As described in the previous chapters, the small-scale bump map represents all the details of a texture and the large-scale bump map represents its macrostructure. Very noisy textures with low amplitudes (which implies no cast shadows) only require a small-scale bump-map while textures made of large and very smooth parts only require a large-scale bump map. But, these kinds of textures are not the majority. In fact, most of the natural textures have a visible macrostructure made of large parts, which contain small details. Therefore, it is necessary to combine both large-scale (H_l) and small-scale (H_s) bump maps.

The resulting bump map (H) is simply computed by a weighted sum of both normalized bump maps, like this:

$$H = C_{mix}\,\mathrm{norm}(H_s) + (1 - C_{mix})\,\mathrm{norm}(H_l)$$

where C_{mix} is a coefficient of blending from 0 to 1; 0 giving more importance to H_l and 1 giving more importance to H_s. Function norm(x) normalizes the bump map given as parameter so that its depth levels vary from 0 to 1.

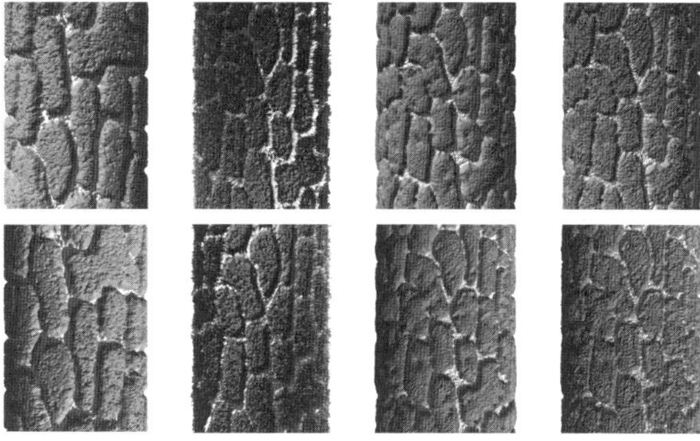

Figure 8: Combining large scale and small-scale. From left to right: the accurate bump texture (reference image), the "naive" approach, our method with C_{mix}=25%, then C_{mix}=50%.

Thus, the user simply chooses a value for C_{mix} corresponding to the provided texture image, whether it is rather structured and smooth or noisy. Figure 8 illustrates an example with a synthetic texture. We compare the reference (obtained with known synthetic bump and color maps) with a "naive" approach that simply uses the gray-scale image as bump map and with our method using different values for C_{mix}, (25%, and 50%). Images have been rendered with two different light directions. Here, even a novice user could reckon intuitively that a good value for C_{mix} is around 40% by observing closely the original texture. Note that the last three sets of color and bump maps were extracted from an image of the reference texture rendered on a plane.

6 Results

We first tested the small-scale relief recovery in the case of "real" textures. Figure 9 illustrates some results for leather, bark and roughcast. On the left, we show the input image; in the middle, the straight utilization of this image as height field ("naive" approach) and on the right, the result after "reverse shading filtering". As for the synthetic examples of Figure 4, the straight use of the images introduces excessive noise. The results "look" more correct with the filtering approach even though, in these cases, we cannot compute reference images, since the relief information is not available.

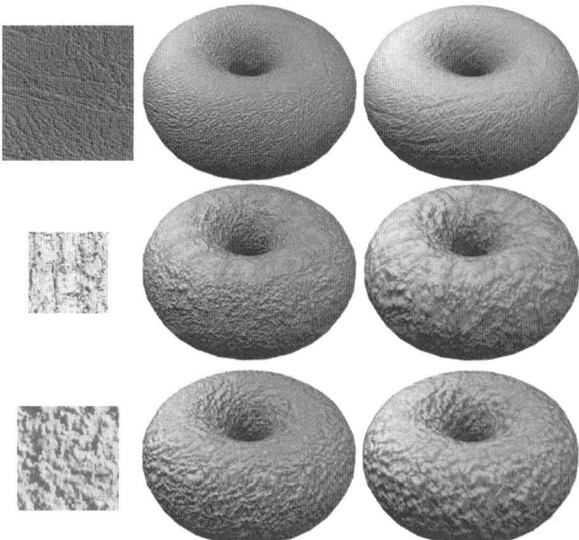

Figure 9: Small-scale relief recovery for natural textures. From top to bottom: leather, bark and roughcast.

While Figure 1 only illustrates large-scale relief recovery, Figure 10 and Figure 11 show the results achieved by combining the bump maps obtained with both large-scale and small-scale analysis. In all cases, we obtained consistent rendering results improved compared to conventional texture mapping and compared to a "naive" approach, which is too "noisy".

However, for texturing the trees of Figure 11 more realistically, we used displacement mapping instead of bump mapping. We also note that we did not use an "unshaded" color map on the trees. We used the original image instead, because too many colors were hard to distinguish from shading effects, especially for the second bark texture. Also, the dark cracks of the first bark texture were not only due to shadows. As a consequence, there is a slight "double shading" effect.

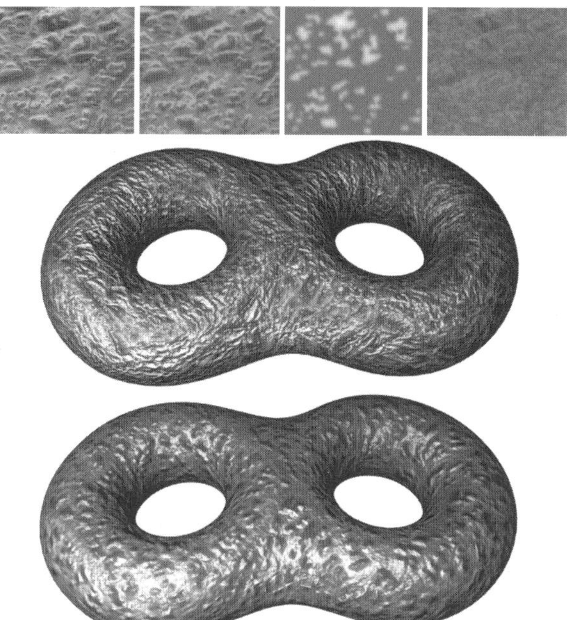

Figure 10: An example of bumpy surface applied to some object. Top (from left to right): input image; "unshaded" color map; H_l; H_s. Middle: result with "naive" method. Bottom: result with our method.

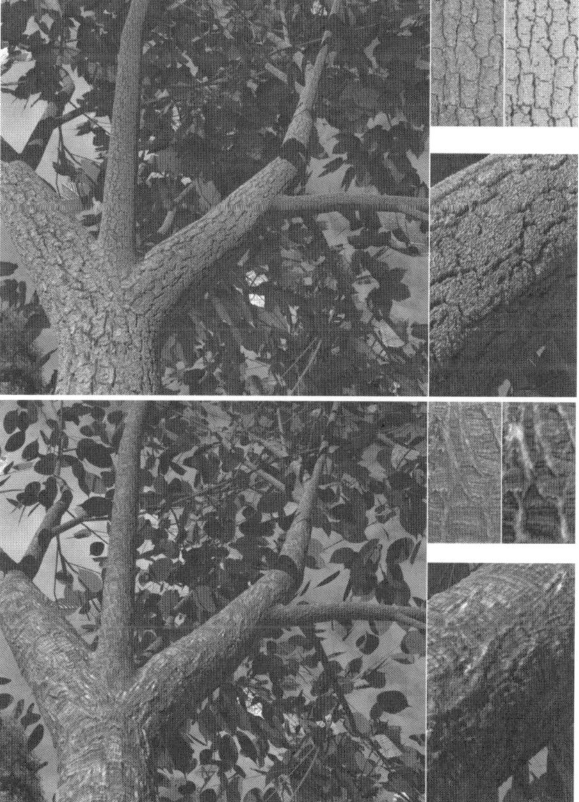

Figure 11: Two examples of trees with bark textures applied to their limbs, using displacement mapping.

7 Conclusions and future directions

Recovering a coherent relief from a single image is a difficult problem. In this paper, we have proposed a solution that consists in recovering the small-scale and large-scale relief separately. We used a filter-based method plus segmentation and classification. This works for many different types of textures, while users provide only some limited information (light source direction and training sets for segmentation and classification). This avoids a lot of empirical and manual work. In parallel, the use of a single image makes this method broadly accessible, in particular for collections of texture images available in diverse databases.

The method also computes an "unshaded" color map, which is satisfying when most of the details are given by the relief, rather than the colors. Otherwise, the original image should be used, though.

Nevertheless, due to the difficulty of the "shape from shading" problem, we had to make several simplifications. The most constraining is that we assumed that the large-scale relief could be characterized by a single curve. Though this is valid for many textures, it represents a restriction in some cases. So, we will need to improve the method on this point in our future works. A secondary problem is that, currently, our method cannot be used for reflectance recovery, since it does not provide an accurate relief, but only a visually consistent one. However, it should be possible to determine automatically the light source direction since the shading effect appears in the frequency domain. Some other information is given by shadows. The goal of further improvements would be to achieve a completely automatic method, for which the user would no longer have to provide any information at all.

References

[1] J. F. Blinn. Simulation of wrinkled surfaces. In Computer Graphics (Proceedings of Siggraph'78), 12(3), pages 286-292, 1978.

[2] E. Catmull. A subdivision algorithm for computer display of curved surfaces. In *PhD thesis, Dept. of CS, University of Utah*, 1974.

[3] K. J. Dana, B. van Ginneken, S. K. Nayar, J. J. Koenderink. Reflectance and texture of real-world surfaces. In *ACM TOG*, 18(1), pages 1-34, 1999.

[4] J.M. Dischler. Efficiently rendering macro-geometric surface structures using bi-directional texture functions. In *Rendering Techniques'98 (Proceedings of Eurographics Workshop on Rendering)*, 1998.

[5] J.M. Dischler, D. Ghazanfarpour, R. Freydier. Anisotropic solid texture synthesis using orthogonal 2D views. In *Computer Graphics Forum*, 17(3), pages 87-95, 1998.

[6] J.M. Dischler, D. Ghazanfarpour. Interactive image-based modeling of macrostructured textures. In *IEEE CG&A*, 19(1), pages 66-74, 1999.

[7] J.M. Dischler, D. Ghazanfarpour. A survey of 3D texturing. In *Computers and Graphics*, 25(10), pages 135-151, 2001.

[8] D. J. Heeger, J. R. Bergen. Pyramid-based texture analysis/synthesis. In *Computer Graphics (Proceeding of Siggraph'95)*, pages 229-238, 1995.

[9] B. K. P. Horn, M. J. Brooks. Shape from shading. In *MIT Press*, 1989.

[10] X. Liu, Y. Yu, H.Y. Shum. Synthesizing Bidirectional Texture Functions for real-world surfaces. In *Computer Graphics (Proceedings of Siggraph'01)*, pages 97-106, 2001.

[11] T. Malzbender, D. Gelb, H. Wolters. Polynomial texture maps, In *Computer Graphics (Proceedings of Siggraph'01)*, pages 519-528, 2001.

[12] M. M. Oliveira G. Bishop, D. McAllister. Relief texture mapping. In *Computer Graphics (Proceedings of Siggraph'00)*, 2000.

[13] K. Perlin. An image synthesizer. In *Computer Graphics (Proceeding of Siggraph'85)*, 19(3), pages 287-296, 1985.

[14] E. Praun, A. Finkelstein, H. Hoppe. Lapped textures. In *Computer Graphics (Proceedings of Siggraph'00)*, pages 465-470, 2000.

[15] S. Premoze, W. Thompson, P. Shirley. Geospecific rendering of alpine terrain. In *10th Eurographics Rendering Workshop*, pages 115-126, June 1999.

[16] Rocchini C., Cignoni P., Montani C., Multiple textures stitching and blending on 3D objects, In *10th Eurographics Rendering Workshop*, pages 127-138, June 1999.

[17] H. Rushmeier, G. Taubin, A. Guéziec. Applying shape from lighting variation to bump map capture. In *Rendering Techniques'97 (Proceedings of Eurographics Workshop on Rendering)*, 1997.

[18] Y. Sato, M. D. Wheeler, K. Ikeuchi, "Object shape and reflectance modeling from observation", In *Computer Graphics (Proceedings of Siggraph'97)*, pages 379-387, 1997.

[19] G. Turk. Texture synthesis on surfaces. In *Computer Graphics (Proceedings of Siggraph'01)*, pages 347-354, 2001.

[20] L. Wei, M. Levoy. Texture synthesis over arbitrary manifold surfaces. In *Computer Graphics (Proceedings of Siggraph'01)*, 2001.

[21] L. Ying, A. Hertzmann, H. Biermann, D. Zorin. Texture and shape synthesis on surfaces, In *EuroGraphics Workshop on Rendering*, 2001.

[22] R. Zhang, P.S. Tsai, J. E. Cryer, M. Shah, Shape from shading : a survey. In *IEEE Transactions on PAMI*, 21(8), pages 690-706, 1999.

Interactive Lighting Models and Pre-Integration for Volume Rendering on PC Graphics Accelerators

Michael Meißner
Viatronix Inc., Stony Brook, USA

Stefan Guthe
WSI/GRIS, Univeristy of Tübingen

Wolfgang Straßer
WSI/GRIS, Univeristy of Tübingen

Abstract

Shading and classification are among the most powerful and important techniques used in volume rendering. Unfortunately, for hardware accelerated volume rendering based on OpenGL, direct classification was previously only supported on SGI platforms and shading could only be approximated inaccurately, resulting in artifacts mostly visible in darkening.

In this paper, we present a novel approach for accurate shading of complex lighting models using multitexturing, dependent textures (e.g. cube maps), and register combiners. Additionally, we present how different material properties can be integrated as a per voxel property to allow for more realistic image synthesis. Furthermore, we present a new technique circumventing the shading artifacts of previous approaches by pre-integrating an interpolation weight. Finally, we discuss how texture compression can be integrated to reduce the memory bandwidth required for relatively large volumes.

Key words: Volume Rendering, Texture Mapping Hardware, Multi-Texturing, Dependent Textures, Phong Shading, Classification, Pre-Integration.

1 Introduction

Due to the large amount of data, computations, and tremendous bandwidth requirements, software approaches are usually limited and far from interactive frame updates. One well known exception might be the ShearWarp algorithm [10], which can achieve interactivity taking advantage of optimizations such as run length encoding (pre-processing). However, each time the classification changes a new run length encoding needs to be calculated, and hence, for a fully occupied dataset with semi-transparent classification, no interactivity can be achieved on a desktop machine.

To overcome the inherent large amount of computation and the extreme bandwidth, texture mapping hardware has evolved to become the best known practical volume rendering method for rectilinear grid datasets. Despite the wide availability, texture mapping based volume rendering has some severe limitations: classification is a key technique in volume rendering interpreting the volume data as color, opacity, and material properties. To enable classification in texture mapping based volume rendering, a lookup is needed right after the texture mapping stage. Unfortunately, such a lookup was previously only available on a few platforms and is limited to the assignment of color and opacity but no further material properties can be integrated. Shading is yet another key technique to add further visual cues to the rendered images and enables a better interpretation of the images. In contrast to polygon rendering where a normal is a vertex property, a gradient is a voxel property. When using texture mapping for rendering volume data, no gradient estimation is supported in hardware. To circumvent this limitation, one can store the pre-calculated gradient together with the volume data as first proposed by Westermann et al. [19]. Despite the fact that many improved techniques have been proposed based on this approach, the subsequent shading operations of all of them [19, 15, 17] are based on not normalized interpolated gradients, resulting in shading artifacts and requiring that pre-normalized gradients are stored in the texture memory.

In this paper, a new approach for integrating lighting models into texture mapping based volume rendering on PC graphics hardware is presented. Furthermore, a new technique accomplishing the integration of classification for RGBA and material properties without the need of regenerating the entire texture nor requiring a second volumetric texture is described. Moreover, we present how the shading quality can be improved significantly when using pre-integrated classification, circumventing the artifacts of previous approaches.

1.1 Related Work

3D texture mapping hardware is recognized as a very efficient acceleration technique for volume rendering, since the first SGI RealityEngine [1] has been shipped. Cabral et al. [2] render datasets of 256^3 voxels at interactive frame-rates on a four Raster Manager SGI RealityEngine

Onyx with a single 150 MHz CPU. Similar results are presented by Cullip and Neumann [3]. The major drawback of the general texture mapping approach is the absence of shading functionality for volume data. To circumvent this, Van Gelder et al. [7] propose a 3-4 parameter lookup which is used to classify and shade the data. Unfortunately, no direct hardware support for such a lookup is available. Therefore, each time the viewing or classification changes, an entire new 3D texture needs to be generated.

Westermann et al. [19] store density values and corresponding pre-computed and pre-normalized gradients in texture memory and extensively exploit OpenGL and extensions for unshaded volume rendering and shaded isosurface rendering. Meißner et al. [15] extend this approach combining classification and diffuse shading for semi-transparent rendering of volume data. While both approaches use a matrix multiplication to obtain the diffuse shading intensity, Rezk-Salama et al. [17] use register combiners as available on the NVIDIA GeForce2. Despite of the impressive visual results, all these approaches [19, 15, 17] are based on not normalized interpolated gradients which result in shading artifacts, as explained later in this paper. Similarly to Westermann [19], Dachille propose to use the available hardware for efficient sample computation and possibly for blending [4]. Shading is performed on the host to ensure high quality rendering, thus avoiding the problem of non normalized gradients but interactivity is sacrificed.

Alternatively, the VolumePro board can be used to accomplish real-time frame-rates [16] but despite its superior performance, it offers less programmability than texture mapping and pre-integration is not feasible since dependent texturing is limited to a 1D lookup.

The remainder of this paper is organized as follows: Section 2 briefly summarizes the state-of-the-art in texture mapping based volume rendering, Our new artifact free shading approach for texture mapping based volume rendering is presented in Section 3. Section 4 presents a novel method for combining shading and pre-integrated classification, circumventing artifacts by pre-integrating an interpolation weight for the gradients. The necessary texture configuration is described in Section 5 and the results are summarized in Section 6. Finally, we conclude our paper and outline future work.

2 Texture Mapping Revisited

The shipment of the first SGI RealityEngine made 3D texture mapping hardware an available interactive feature. With respect to volume rendering, slicing planes parallel to the viewing plane are put through the volume in back to front order, see Figure 1(a). When using perspective projection, this becomes more complicated since one needs to account for the correct blending. Opacity values represent the volumetric absorption along a unit length and hence, one would need to use spherical shells [11] or either recompute the opacity values (see formula 4) or use dependent textures to correct the opacity which would suffer form the limited texture resolution (8 bit).

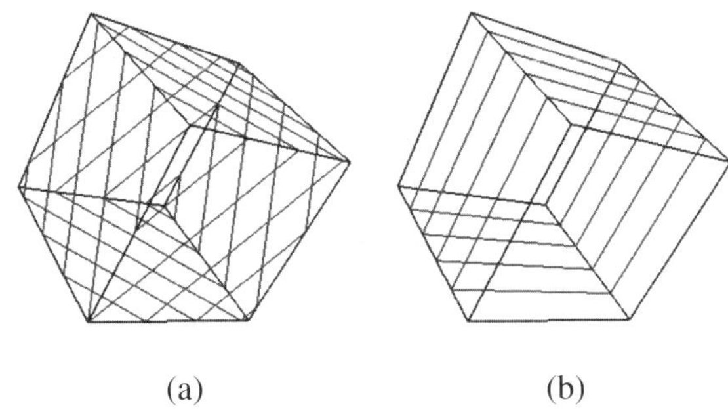

Figure 1: While in 3D texture mapping (a) arbitrary planes can be positioned in the volume, 2D texture mapping (b) requires a texture stack for each major viewing direction and the one most perpendicular to the actual viewing is selected.

Previously, the limited availability of 3D texture mapping prevented this approach from being widely used. Therefore, an alternative method — derived from the ShearWarp algorithm — has become popular. Three stacks of 2D textures are used, one for each major axis (see Figure 1(b)). Depending on the viewing vector, the stack most perpendicular to the viewing direction is used. To account for accurate volumetric absorption, opacity values need to be corrected depending on the viewing angle. Due to performance issues of 3D textures, this approach is still worth to be used when applicable.

2.1 Classification

Classification after resampling the volumetric data can be realized using post texturing lookup tables. Earlier, this could only be realized on mid- and high-end SGI platforms applying SGI's GL_TEXTURE_COLOR_TABLE_SGI. Exploiting multi-pass rendering, classification can also be accomplished using pixel textures, as presented in [15]. Unfortunately, pixel textures are not available on all platforms and due to the nature of multi-pass, the performance is reduced significantly. Another approach uses two volumetric textures and multi-texturing hardware, accomplishing classification in a single-pass [17]. Nevertheless, the approach requires two volumetric textures significantly increasing the memory requirements even if paletted textures are used. Furthermore, this approach can not be combined with tri-linear interpolation based on two bilinear interpolations and register combiners. Other recent approaches make use of dependent texturing to accomplish classification [6, 9]. So far, only RGBA values are provided but no material properties.

2.2 Shading

As mentioned in the introduction, there has been a number of publications presenting shading of interpolated sample values within the context of texture mapping based volume rendering [19, 15, 17, 6]. Despite the fairly reasonable shading effects, all these approaches pre-compute the voxel gradient which is normalized, scaled, and biased in order to obtain gradient values of range $[0, 1]$. The gradient components are then stored in the RGB channels of an RGBA texture and the density value goes into the A channel. Using traditional texture mapping hardware, the gradient components and density value are interpolated and the scalar product is computed using using register combiners [17, 6, 9]. The severe drawback of all of these approaches is that they compute the scalar product using not normalized interpolated gradients. Thus, resulting in severe shading artifacts, mostly noticeable as darkening of the images. Furthermore, this also occurs for fairly smooth non binary datasets because the gradients at grid position need to be pre-normalized which again can introduce big differences of the gradient values of neighboring voxels, e.g. $(1, 0, 0)$ and $(0, 1, 0)$ enclose a 90 degree angle and in the worst case, the interpolated gradient will not be of length one but $\sqrt{0.5}$ causing the earlier mentioned darkening artifacts.

2.3 Gradient Magnitude Modulation

Using the gradient magnitude to suppress data which resides within homogeneous areas of a dataset is a very powerful feature for enhancing material boundaries [12]. Besides the magnitude of the first derivative, also the magnitude of the second derivative can be used to accomplish better visualizations of features within the dataset [8, 9].

Generally, when applying gradient magnitude modulation, the quality of the boundary enhancement depends mainly on the quality of the used gradient filter. While the intermediate and central difference gradient filters are prone to artifacts — since they result in non symmetric gradients —, the Sobel operator is the gradient operator of choice and used throughout this paper. Figure 7(d), (e), (f), and (k) show images using gradient magnitude modulation.

2.4 Pre-Integration

Pre-integrated classification is a technique used in volume rendering when classification is applied after interpolation [14, 6]. Following the Nyquist theorem, one can generally ensure that the reconstruction of the volumetric function along the rays is accurate. However, a non continuous transfer function, e.g. binary classification with infinite frequencies, introduces well-know slicing artifacts, as shown in Figure 2(a) and (c)).

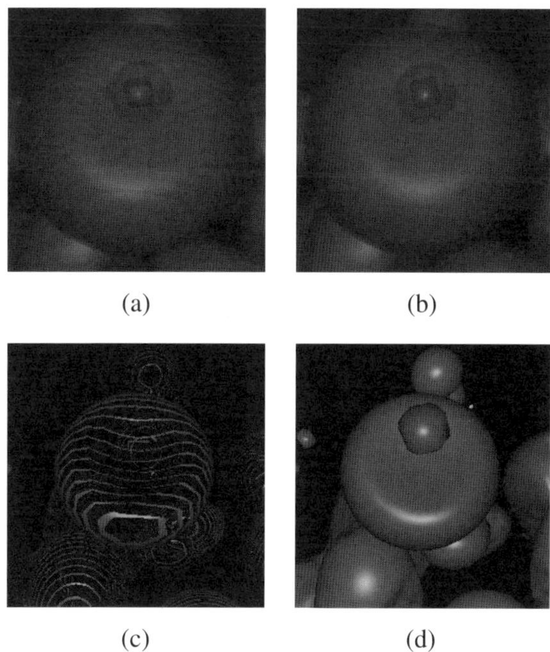

Figure 2: Pre-integrated volume rendering: Sample distance is 0.5 using plain ray casting without ((a) and (c)) and with pre-integration ((b) and (d)). The high frequencies of the iso-surface-like transfer function in (c) can be realized using pre-integrated sample intervals (d).

To circumvent this, pre-integration assumes a certain behavior of the volumetric function along the cast ray, e.g. linear. Based on the conventional 1D classification table, each interval between two samples can be pre-integrated and stored in a 2D table. During rendering, two consecutive sample values are used as indices for the 2D table, instead of classifying each individual sample assuming the color to be constant for the distance to the next sample along the ray. The advantage of pre-integrated volume rendering is that even precise iso-surfaces can be rendered without any additional cost during ray casting, see Figure 2(b) and (d). While Max et. al [14] pre-integrated opacity only, Engel et al.[6] extended this to RGBA but yet no material properties were considered. Generally, pre-integration suffers from shading artifacts when using more than one iso-surface or semi-transparent rendering, as explained in more detail in Section 4.

One of the main draw-backs of pre-integrated volume rendering is its incompatibility with gradient magnitude modulation. Since the color is pre-integrated based on the voxel value only, no gradient magnitude modulation is possible, unless using a 4D function which would prevent interactivity. Solving this is still topic of research.

3 Lighting Models

Phong illumination is the most commonly used illumination model in volume rendering applications. The local illumination is split into three independent components and can be written as:

$$\begin{aligned} C^\lambda &= k_a * \sum_{i=0}^{n} L_i^\lambda + k_s * \sum_{i=0}^{n} (\vec{N}\vec{R})^{n_s} * L_i^\lambda \\ &+ k_d * \text{Class}^\lambda(v) * \sum_{i=0}^{n} *(\vec{N}\vec{L_i}), \qquad (1) \end{aligned}$$

where C^λ is the resulting color of wavelength λ, k_a, k_d, and k_s are the ambient, diffuse, and specular material properties, L_i is the color of lightsource i, v is the density value, Class^λ is the classified color, $\vec{N}$ is the gradient, $\vec{R}$ is the reflected eye vector, $\vec{L}$ is the vector to the light-source, and n_s is the exponential factor to determine the size of the specular highlight.

Evaluating the Phong illumination requires normalized vectors in order to obtain the correct scalar products. However, when using pre-computed gradients stored in the volumetric texture, the length of the interpolated gradients is ≤ 1. The only approach to correctly solving this issue in the graphics pipeline is the use of cube-maps.

3.1 Cube-Maps

Generally, cube-maps are used to map the information contained in the scene onto the faces of a unit cube. During rendering, this information can be retrieved from the cube-map and projected onto the rendering primitive. One intuitive application of this are environment maps were the cube-map contains the projected RGB information of the scene, thus allowing glossy objects to reflect the environment without the need of sampling the real environment during rendering.

The same approach can be used to perform shading. Instead of projecting the colors of the objects of a scene onto the cube-map, the light sources can be projected onto the cube-faces and during rendering true shading for any number of light sources can be accomplished. This approach can also be extended to reflected components but requires the computation of the reflected vector [18]. Fortunately, the computation of the reflected vector recently became available in graphics accelerators since it is needed for bump- and environment-mapping. Thus, true Phong shading can be accomplished, e.g. on the NVIDIA GeForce3 or the ATI Radeon 8500.

For the application of shading in volume rendering, the interpolated gradient can be used to access a diffuse cube-map and compute the reflected vector to access a reflectance map containing the specular components [5]. Figure 3 (a) and (b) illustrate the diffuse and the specular cube-map for a single light-source. To support light

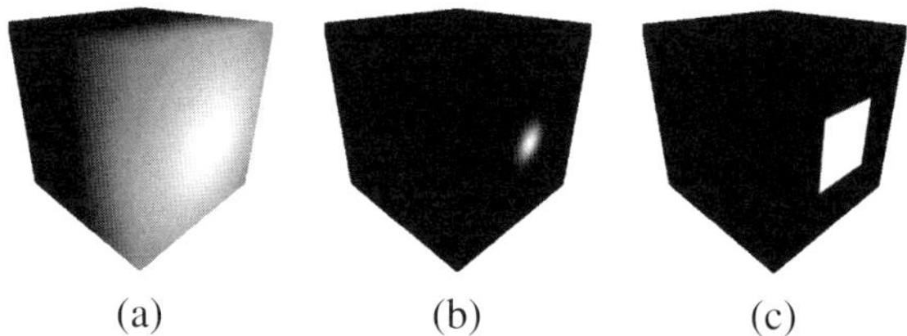

(a) (b) (c)

Figure 3: Cube-maps for one light source: (a) Diffuse cube-map. (b) Specular cube-map using a phong exponent of 50. (c) Specular cube-map of a squared light source.

sources of different color, the specular cube-map needs to be of format RGB, resulting in images as shown in Figure 7(c). With the diffuse and specular light intensity, one can evaluate the Phong illumination using register combiners. The advantages of cube-maps are the available hardware support and the fact that they only need to be rebuilt when the light sources change the position relative to each other. For each light source it takes approx. 20 ms to build the corresponding cube-map which can easily be done interactively. Generally, the generation of the cube-maps is fill-rate limited but sizes larger than 64^2 do have a significant performance issue, presumably because they exceed what can be residing within the texture cache besides the 3D textures.

3.2 Different lightsources

Generally, any type of light source that can be represented in a cube-map can be realized. Thus, besides conventional point light sources also squared or arbitrary shapes of light sources are feasible. Our current implementation supports squared and rectangular shaped light sources as well as point light sources, possibly residing within the volume. The specular cube map for a squared light source is given in Figure 3(c) and the resulting rendering of the Neghip is shown in Figure 7(b).

4 Pre-Integration And Shading

Pre-integrated classification of ray intervals prevents artifacts due to the use of non continuous transfer functions. While pre-integration works well for opaque iso-surface or non-shaded volume rendering, it can not be combined correctly with semi-transparent volume rendering or when visualizing more than one iso-surface. This

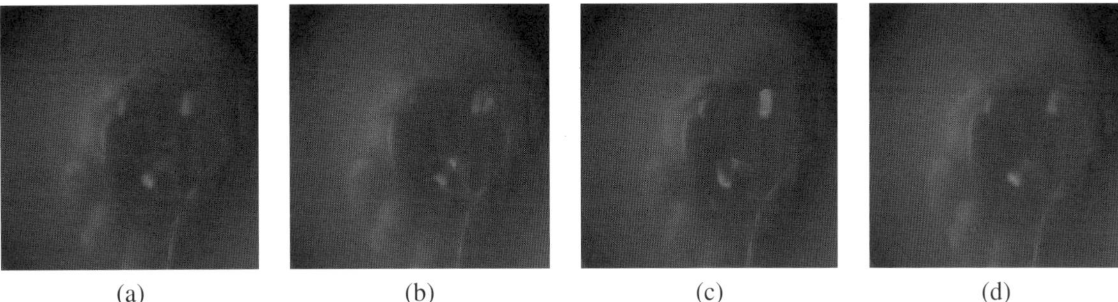

(a) (b) (c) (d)

Figure 4: Pre-integrated classification and sample based shading in a software implementation. Blue material is opaque and highly specular while green material is semi-transparent and mainly diffuse: (a) Ray casting using 0.01 sample distance (b) Pre-integrated ray casting (sample distance 0.5) using the gradient and material properties of the first sample for shading. (c) Same as (b) but using the gradient and material properties of the second sample. (d) Ray casting using a pre-integrated weight to linearly interpolate the gradient used for shading.

is due to the fact that the color is pre-integrated for a given interval but the shading is performed on the fly at discrete ray sample positions. For any given voxel interval $[v_l, v_r]$, the two gradients at sample location are available but in most cases neither of the two allows for correct shading of this interval.

Engel et al.[6] approached this problem by correspondingly weighting the two gradients based on a global iso-surface value. Consequently, the offset of this iso-surface value v_i within the interval is computed during rendering and divided by the voxel interval length. The resulting weight

$$w = (v_i - v_l)/(v_r - v_l) \tag{2}$$

is used to perform a linear interpolation and the interpolated gradient is used to perform shading. While this approach correctly reveals the illumination for a single iso-surface v_i (see Figure 5(a)), it can fail when displaying more than one iso-surface (b) and generally fails for semi-transparent classification (c); e.g, in case of two iso-surfaces (v_i, v_j) being present, the method will fail for all intervals where the iso-surface v_i is behind the second iso-surface v_j which is orientation dependent. As a result, the gradient of the occluded iso-surface v_i is used for shading the visually contributing iso-surface v_j. The problem becomes worse for more than two iso-surfaces or for semi-transparent classification.

As a natural extension to pre-integration, we propose a new method solving this problem by pre-integrating an interpolation weight that matches the location of iso-surfaces within the interval. Thus, no global iso-value is required and for each interval always the gradient of the closest iso-value can be used for shading. The weight w is pre-integrated, weighting it with the remaining transparency.

Figure 5: Shading of a pre-integrated color interval of a ray showing the sample location and the sample gradients. Left is voxel value v_l and right is v_r. (a) Single iso-surface being present. (b) Two iso-surfaces being present. (c) Semi-transparent classification along the interval.

$$w_{[v_l,v_r]} = \sum_{i=v_l}^{v_r} \frac{(v_i - v_l)}{(v_r - v_l)} \prod_{j=v_l}^{i-1} (1 - \alpha(v_j)) \tag{3}$$

To account for the correct remaining transparency in dependence of the interval length, the opacity $\alpha(v_j)$ needs to be corrected for each pre-integrated interval [13].

$$\alpha(v_j) = 1 - \sqrt[n]{1 - \alpha(v_j)} \tag{4}$$

where $n = \frac{d}{v_r - v_l}$ is the individual interval length and d being the actual sample distance along the ray.

Pre-integrating the gradient interpolation weight ensures that for any number of iso-surface being present in any interval, the corresponding gradient of the closest iso-surface is used for shading. Furthermore, for semi-transparent classification, it allows to weight the two sample gradients to match best the opacity distribution within each interval.

Figure 4 summarizes the issues of pre-integrated color values and shading being performed on a discrete sample base. The images show a zoomed view of the Neghip dataset and were generated using $< k_a, k_d, k_s >$ = $< 0.1, 0.6, 0.3 >$ for the green material and $< 0.1, 0.3, 0.6 >$ for the blue material. The reference image was generated using a sample distance of 0.01 and conventional point based classification, see Figure 4(a). For the other images, a sampling distance of 0.5 and a 2D pre-integrated classification table was used. Figure 4(b) shows the result of using the gradient at sample location v_l and (c) was generated using the gradient at v_r. In both cases, the obtained shading effects are wrong, especially the reflected highlights. In contrast, using the pre-integrated interpolation weight to obtain the gradient representing the interval best (see 4(d)), hardly any difference to (a) can be distinguished.

It should be mentioned that when using different material properties for each voxel, the k_d factor needs to be pre-integrated together with the diffuse color to account for correct shading. In addition, k_a and k_s need to be pre-integrated for the interval such that the specular and ambient term are correctly representing the entire interval.

$$k_{a,[v_l,v_r]} = \sum_{i=v_l}^{v_r} \frac{(v_i - v_l)}{(v_r - v_l)} \prod_{j=v_l}^{i-1} k_a(v_j) \quad (5)$$

$$k_{s,[v_l,v_r]} = \sum_{i=v_l}^{v_r} \frac{(v_i - v_l)}{(v_r - v_l)} \prod_{j=v_l}^{i-1} k_s(v_j) \quad (6)$$

In summary, weighting the gradient based on the opacity distribution across the pre-integrated interval allows to accomplish high image quality while performing the shading /computation only once per interval $[v_l, v_r]$.

5 Texture Setup

Setting up the texture and shading environments for either the NVIDIA GeForce3 or the ATI Radeon 8500 to achieve interactive frame rates is not a trivial task. Due to the limited hardware resources of the GeForce3, we first describe the implementation on the Radeon 8500 and subsequently describe the differences for the GeForce3.

For both, the gradient magnitude modulation and pre-integrated volume rendering, two 2D classification textures are used. One contains the diffuse color of the sample and the other the material properties and the opacity. Depending on the mode used, these classification textures are either addressed using the voxel and the norm of the gradient (gradient magnitude modulation mode) or by using two voxels (pre-integrated classification). Corresponding to the mode, the textures are initialized accordingly. In case additional lighting is enabled, two cube-maps are used as described earlier (see Section 3).

For gradient magnitude modulation, the 3D texture contains the voxel value, the norm of the gradient, and possibly the norm of the second order derivative to support higher dimensional transfer functions as recently presented in [9]. In order to support additional lighting, a second 3D texture is needed containing the pre-computed Sobel gradients since there is no texture format with more than four channels available. Without gradient magnitude, one GL_RGBA texture suffices.

For pre-integrated volume rendering, two instances of one volumetric texture containing the voxel and the gradient components are needed to provide the two sample values for the 2D lookup. Note that the volume is stored only once on the graphics card but two texture units use the same 3D texture.

For either of the two modes, pre-integration or gradient magnitude modulation in combination with illumination, a total of six texture operations is needed. Thus, on the ATI Radeon 8500 both approaches can be realized in a single pass due to its six independent texture units. With respect to programming the fragment shaders, the same program can be used for both modes since the setup for gradient magnitude modulation:

- 3D texture with voxel, gradient norm, etc.
- 3D texture with gradient
- 2D texture for material properties and opacity
- 2D texture for diffuse color
- Cube-map for diffuse light intensity
- Cube-map for specular light intensity

and the setup for pre-integrated volume rendering:

- 3D texture with voxel and gradient
- 3D texture with voxel and gradient
- 2D texture for (pre-integrated) material properties and opacity
- 2D texture for (pre-integrated) diffuse color
- Cube-map for diffuse light intensity
- Cube-map for specular light intensity

are very similar, using the same addressing scheme. In the first texture lookup the voxel and the gradient are extracted. The gradient is rotated into the coordinate system of the light sources and the texture coordinates for addressing the classification textures are set up. It is worth to be mentioned that since we do a per-pixel matrix multiplication to rotate the gradients into the coordinate system of the light source, we are also able to implement point light sources residing within the volume. In the second texture lookup, the voxel colors and the lighting intensities are obtained and combined in the final fragment shader step.

To achieve a higher lighting quality for pre-integrated rendering, as mentioned in Section 4, the gradient components need to be interpolated based on the pre-integrated interpolation weight. Due to the additional dependency, a second rendering pass is currently unavoidable but this might change with upcoming new graphics accelerators.

In contrast to the Radeon 8500, the implementation on the GeForce3 is either limited to lighting only or we have to use multiple rendering passes. The gradient magnitude modulation as done in a single pass on the Radeon 8500, has to be split into a total of four passes to allow for our general lighting model. This can be reduced to three passes when using a uniform color for either the diffuse or the specular cube map. However, the pre-integration approach without weighted gradients requires five passes while the additional interpolation of the gradient using the pre-integrated weight can not be implemented, due to the 8 bit quantization in the pipeline. While this appears to be very advantageous for the Radeon 8500, this might be quite different once the next generation graphics chips are released.

5.1 Texture Compression

One of the main drawbacks when using texture mapping hardware for volume rendering including shading is the need for storing an RGBA texture containing the pre-computed gradients. This is necessary because there is no support for extracting gradients directly from the density volume, as e.g. done in VolumePro [16]. Thus, a significant amount of texture memory is required to store the additional gradient information. For 8 bit voxel values and a 256^3 volume, the memory requirements are increased from 16 MBytes to 64 MBytes. Thus for a graphics card with 64 MBytes of memory (texture and framebuffer memory), and a volume that is much larger than the available texture memory, the volume needs to be partitioned into bricks which are transfered from main memory to the graphics card when needed. Even with an AGP bus, this significantly reduces the overall performance and real-time frame-rates are beyond feasibility.

Recently, the Architecture Review Board (*ARB*) of OpenGL released an extension for texture compressions named ARB_texture_compression and supported on many PC graphics cards (Voodoo5, Radeon, GeForce). The compression is based on the s3tc algorithm and accomplishes a constant compression rate of four by packing 4×4 texels into a compact bit stream. Thus, datasets which are much larger than the available texture memory of the graphics card can still be rendered at interactive frame-rates. However, image quality is potentially sacrificed due to the lossy compression algorithm and the missing adaption scheme for gradient compression. Figure 6 illustrates the difference in image quality for a full (a,b) and a close-up view (c,d) of the engine dataset. While the global information and structure is still present,

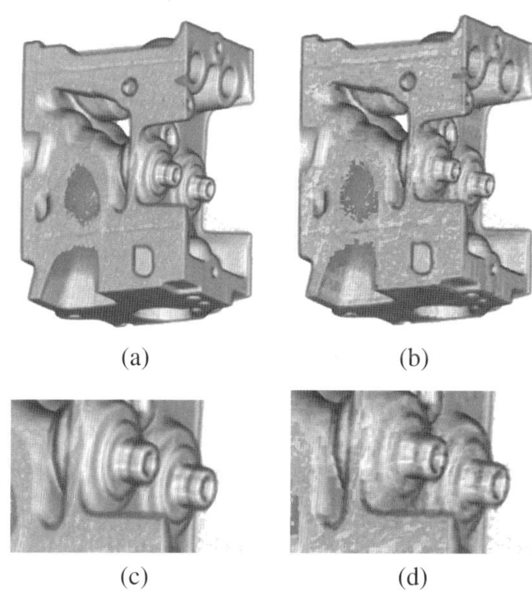

Figure 6: Texture compression applied to the engine dataset: (a,c) Without compression. (b,d) With compression.

fine detail is lost. Thus, one might want to implement a hybrid renderer, using compressed textures only during motion. Additionally, one can subdivide the volume into bricks and render from compressed textures only for the bricks being further away from the observer. However, such a hybrid rendering would require two different volumes which compete for residency on the graphics card.

6 Results

Several different datasets available on the volvis web page (http://www.volvis.org/) were used for rendering. The resulting images are shown in Figure 7 and clearly demonstrate the high quality of the presented techniques.

More interesting than the actual quality is the timing analysis. While all renderings can be accomplished on the NVIDIA GeForce3 and on the ATI Radeon 8500, the performance shows significant differences. This is due to the different hardware resources available on these systems. While the GeForce3 has four texture units, the Radeon 8500 provides six and has less restrictions when using cube-maps. E.g. when using 3D textures, shading, and classification, three passes are needed to accomplish the rendering on the GeForce3 while the Radeon 8500 is capable of handling this in one pass. While this is likely to constantly change with new upcoming graphics accelerators, the following results were measured on the ATI Radeon 8500.

We investigated several issues and their impact onto the overall rendering speed. First, the size of the viewport and the dataset determine the amount of tri-linear samples that need to be generated. Second, enabling or disabling shading because there are more textures to be used per polygon. Third, the size of the cube-maps which is a trade-off between quality and cache efficiency and last but not least, the impact of compression. For all measurements, the slice distance was chosen to be one and the size of the diffuse and specular cube-map were 16^2 and 64^2 respectively. Increasing the diffuse cube-map to 64^2 reduced the performance by 10% without further increasing the image quality.

Table 1 illustrates the timing using a viewport of 200×200 pixels. Simply slicing the density volume and applying a dependent 2D texture for classification is in the range of 3.6 to 82.9 frames. When slicing a density and gradient texture and applying the cube-maps including classification, the frame rate drops strongly. This is mainly due to the utilization of two volumetric textures per sample for pre-integration (halfing the performance) as well as applying the cube-map which competes for texture cache. In case of *no-light*, we are using the same RGBA texture containing the gradients and the performance can be improved by a factor of two using a GL_ALPHA texture. With the currently released drivers we were not able of getting cube-maps to run with a 256^3 dataset but this is likely to change and could be circumvented using bricking.

Data size	no-light	cube-map	compression
64^3	82.8	36.1	40.1
128^3	18.4	12.8	19.6
$256^2 \times 128$	8.2	4.6	8.4
256^3	3.6	-	4.7

Table 1: Frames per second for a 200×200 viewport.

Enabling ARB_TEXTURE_COMPRESSION increases the rendering performance but not so much for the small datasets than for the larger datasets. The reason for this is that for larger datasets the memory bandwidth of the graphics card is the limitation and due to the compression, the cache efficiency is increased. However, for smaller datasets, the cache efficiency is already high and thus, texture compression can not significantly accelerate the rendering because the actual limitation here is the cube-map lookup.

Finally, table 2 shows the same timings for a viewport of 400×400 pixels. In comparison to Table 1, all timings are reduced by a factor of 2 to 2.9 due to the four times enlarged viewport. The factor reveals the increase in texture cache efficiency allowing a higher pixel fill-rate.

Data size	no-light	cube-map	compression
64^3	37.3	12.7	12.4
128^3	11.4	5.5	6.4
$256^2 \times 128$	5.0	2.5	3.9
256^3	2.3	-	2.5

Table 2: Frames per second for a 400×400 viewport.

On the Radeon 8500 3D textures are a factor of two to three slower than 2D textures and their performance varies depending on the viewing direction (linear memory access problems). However, true 3D textures are mandatory for pre-integrated classification because the pre-integration is based on a fixed interval length. Thus, when using 2D textures the interval length depends on the viewing direction and would need to be recomputed for every frame which is not possible at interactive framerates unless only iso-surface rendering is of interest.

7 Conclusions

In this paper, we presented a novel approach for accomplishing artifact free shading of volumetric data using cube-maps. This approach allows to not only support directional light sources but also any complex lighting situation. Additionally, the presented approach allows to specify material properties on a per sample base.

Furthermore, we presented how pre-integrated classification can be combined with shading by additionally pre-integrating an interpolation weight used to interpolate the two respective gradients at sample location.

The presented results were generated on a ATI Radeon 8500 using OpenGL but most of them could also be accomplished on a NVIDIA GeForce3 using multi-pass rendering due to the limited hardware resources. Besides its high throughput, the Radeon 8500 offers highest possible flexibility within the texturing and the rasterization stage. As demonstrated, this flexibility can be efficiently exploited to enable and combine the most important and valuable techniques of volume rendering at interactive frame rates.

A topic of future work is to investigate the impact of the limited frame-buffer accuracy onto the image quality as well as investigating how pre-integrated classification and gradient magnitude modulation can be combined. Using a 4D table (v_s, v_e, gm_0, gm_1) would allow to handle this correctly but the table could not be computed interactively and other solutions are necessary.

References

[1] K. Akeley. RealityEngine Graphics. In *Computer Graphics*, Proc. of ACM SIGGRAPH, pages 109–116, August 1993.

[2] B. Cabral, N. Cam, and J. Foran. Accelerated Volume Rendering and Tomographic Reconstruction Using Texture Mapping Hardware. In *Workshop on Volume Visualization*, pages 91–98, Washington, DC, USA, October 1994.

[3] T. J. Cullip and U. Neumann. Accelerating Volume Reconstruction with 3D Texture Mapping Hardware. Technical Report TR93-027, Department of Computer Science at the University of North Carolina, Chapel Hill, 1993.

[4] F. Dachille, K. Kreeger, B. Chen, I. Bitter, and A. Kaufman. High-Quality Volume Rendering Using Texture Mapping Hardware. In *Proc. of Eurographics/SIGGRAPH Workshop on Graphics Hardware*, pages 69–76, Lisboa, Portugal, August 1998.

[5] S. Dominé and J. Spitzer. OpenGL Texture Shaders. *Technical document, available from http://www.nvidia.com/*, 2001.

[6] K. Engel, M. Kraus, and T. Ertl. High-quality pre-integrated volume rendering using hardware-accelerated pixel shading. In *Proc. of Eurographics/SIGGRAPH Workshop on Graphics Hardware*, Los Angeles, CA, USA, August 2001.

[7] A. Van Gelder and K. Kim. Direct Volume Rendering With Shading via Three-Dimensional Textures. In *Symposium on Volume Visualization*, pages 23–30, San Francisco, CA, USA, October 1996.

[8] G. Kindlmann and J. W. Durkin. Semi-automatic generation of transfer functions for direct volume rendering. In *Symposium on Volume Visualization*, pages 79–86, Research Triangle Park, NC, USA, October 1998.

[9] J. Kniss, G. Kindlmann, and C. Hansen. Interactive volume rendering using multi-dimensional transfer functions and direct manipulation widgets. In *Proc. of IEEE Visualization*, pages 255–262, San Diego, CA, USA, October 2001. IEEE Computer Society Press.

[10] P. Lacroute and M. Levoy. Fast Volume Rendering Using a Shear-Warp factorization of the Viewing Transform. In *Computer Graphics*, Proc. of ACM SIGGRAPH, pages 451–457, July 1994.

[11] E. LaMar, B. Hamann, and K. Joy. Multiresolution Techhniques for Interactive Hardware Texturing-based Volume Visualization. In *Proc. of IEEE Visualization*, pages 355–361, San Franisco, CA, USA, October 1999. IEEE Computer Society Press.

[12] M. Levoy. Display of surfaces from volume data. *Ph.D. Dissertation, Department of Computer Science, The University of North Carolina at Chapel Hill*, May 1989.

[13] B. Lichtenbelt, R. Crane, and S. Naqvi. *Introduction to volume rendering*. Hewlett-Packard Professional Books, Prentice-Hall, Los Angeles, USA, 1998.

[14] N. Max, P. Hanrahan, and R. Crawfis. Area and volume coherence for efficient visualization of 3d scalar functions. pages 27–33, San Diego, CA, USA, nov 1990.

[15] M. Meißner, U. Hoffmann, and W. Straßer. Enabling Classification and Shading for 3D Texture Mapping based Volume Rendering using OpenGL and Extensions. In *Proc. of IEEE Visualization*, pages 207–214, San Franisco, CA, USA, October 1999. IEEE Computer Society Press

[16] H. Pfister, J. Hardenbergh, J. Knittel, H. Lauer, and L. Seiler. The VolumePro Real-Time Ray-Casting System. In *Computer Graphics*, Proc. of ACM SIGGRAPH, pages 251–260, Los Angeles, CA, USA, 1999.

[17] C. Rezk-Salama, K. Engel, M. Bauer, G. Greiner, and T. Ertl. Interactive volume rendering on standard pc graphics hardware using multi-texturing and multi-stage rasterization. In *Proc. of Eurographics/SIGGRAPH Workshop on Graphics Hardware*, pages 109–118, Interlaken, Switzerland, August 2000.

[18] D. Voorhies and J. Foran. State of the art in data visualization. In *Computer Graphics*, Proc. of ACM SIGGRAPH, pages 163–166, July 1994.

[19] R. Westermann and T. Ertl. Efficiently Using Graphics Hardware in Volume Rendering Applications. In *Computer Graphics*, Proc. of ACM SIGGRAPH, pages 169–177, Orlando, FL, USA, August 1998.

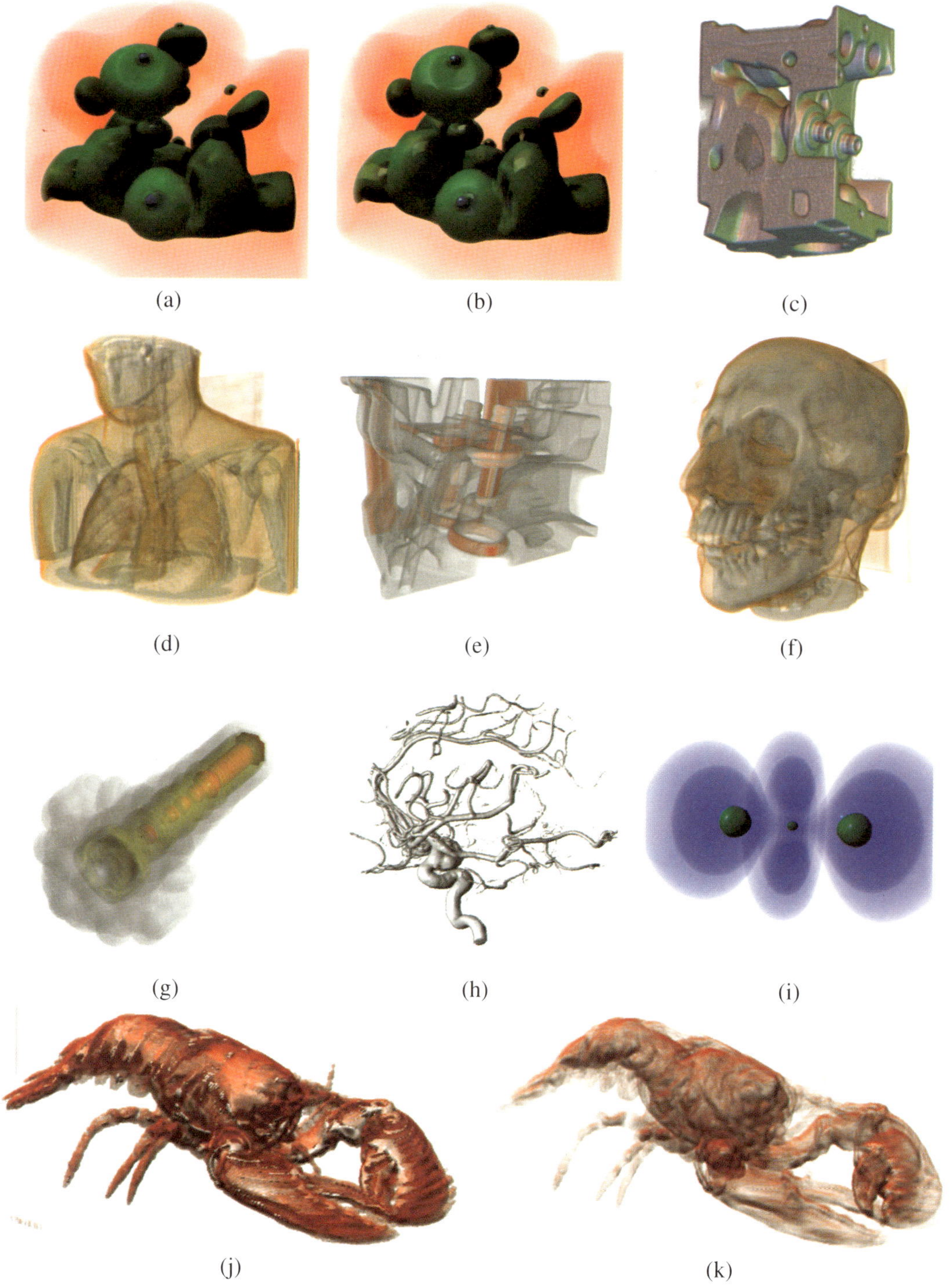

(a) (b) (c)

(d) (e) (f)

(g) (h) (i)

(j) (k)

Figure 7: Color plates: gm *denotes gradient magnitude modulation and* mp *denotes different material properties. (a) Neghip using a point light source and mp. (b) As (a) using a squared light source. (c) Engine using differently colored light sources. (d) Visible human using gm. (e) Engine using gm and mp. (f) Head using gm. (g) Fuel using mp. (h) Aneurysm. (i) Hydro using mp. (j) Lobster. (k) as (j) using gm.*

Single Sample Soft Shadows using Depth Maps

Stefan Brabec Hans-Peter Seidel
Max-Planck-Institut für Informatik

Abstract

In this paper we propose a new method for rendering soft shadows at interactive frame rates. Although the algorithm only uses information obtained from a single light source sample, it is capable of producing subjectively realistic penumbra regions. We do not claim that the proposed method is physically correct but rather that it is aesthetically correct. Since the algorithm operates on sampled representations of the scene, the shadow computation does not directly depend on the scene complexity. Having only a single depth and object ID map representing the pixels seen by the light source, we can approximate penumbrae by searching the neighborhood of pixels warped from the camera view for relevant blocker information.

We explain the basic technique in detail, showing how simple observations can yield satisfying results. We also address sampling issues relevant to the quality of the computed shadows, as well as speed-up techniques that are able to bring the performance up to interactive frame rates.

1 Introduction

One of the most problematic tasks in computer graphics is the accurate and efficient computation of soft shadows caused by extended light sources. Although there have been enormous efforts in this specific area, only a small subset of algorithms are really appropriate for interactive rendering applications.

In this paper we will present a way of computing soft shadows using only sampled images taken from the view of a point light source. This soft shadow algorithm can be seen as an extension of the classical shadow map algorithm for calculating hard shadows. Instead of computing only a binary value (shadowed or lit) for each pixel seen by the camera, our algorithm processes the neighborhood of the corresponding depth map entry to gather information about what the shadow might look like in the case of an area light source.

Even though the input data contains no information about the characteristics of an area light, the resulting shadows are yet of very good quality and give the impression of a physically plausible computation. Using only a minimal amount of input data and a very compact algorithm, we can achieve extremely high computation speed. This way we can also utilize graphics hardware and specialized processor instruction sets.

2 Previous Work

Since a vast number of hard and soft shadow methods exist for general and very specific situations, we will only briefly discuss some methods here, focusing on those suitable for interactive and real-time applications, as well as on algorithms which are related to our method. As a good starting point we recommend Woo's survey on shadow algorithms [21].

In the field of hardware accelerated, interactive rendering, shadow algorithms are mainly categorized by the space in which the calculation takes place. One of the fundamental shadow algorithms, Crow's shadow volumes [5], processes the geometry of the scene. By extending occluder polygons to form semi-infinite volumes, so called shadow volumes, shadowed pixels can be determined by simply testing if the pixel lies in at least one shadow volume. A hardware-accelerated implementation of Crow's shadow algorithm was later proposed by Heidmann [10]. McCool [15] presented an algorithm that reduces the often problematic geometry complexity of Crow's method by reconstructing shadow volumes from a sampled depth map. Complexity issues were also addressed by Chrysanthou and Slater [4]. They propose the use of BSP trees for efficient shadow volume calculations in dynamic scenes. Brotman and Badler [3] came up with a soft shadow version of Crow's algorithm where they generated shadow volumes for a number of light source samples and computed the overlap using a depth buffer algorithm. Discontinuity Meshing, e.g. [14], is another exact way for computing soft shadows in object-space. Here surfaces are subdivided in order to determine areas where the visible part of the area light source is constant.

William's shadow map algorithm [20] is the fundamental idea of most methods working on sampled representations of the scene. The depths of visible pixels are computed for the view of the light source and stored away in a so called depth or shadow map. In the final rendering pass, pixels seen by the camera are transformed to the light source coordinate system and tested against the precomputed depth values. A hardware-based shadow map technique was presented by Segal et al. [18].

William's original work suffered from sampling artifacts during the generation of the shadow map as well as when performing the shadow test. Reeves et al. [17] proposed a filtering method called percentage closer filtering which solved these problems and generates smooth, antialiased shadow edges. Reeves' approach is also often used to approximate penumbra regions by varying the filter kernel with respect to the projected footprint. This is somewhat similar to our approach but in general requires a very high resolution depth map in order to obtain soft shadows with reasonable quality.

Brabec et al. [2] showed how Reeves' filtering scheme can be efficiently mapped to hardware. Hourcade and Nicolas [12] also addressed the shadow map sampling problems and came up with a method using object identifiers (priority information) and prefiltering.

To compute soft shadow textures for receiver polygons, Herf and Heckbert [9] combined a number of hard shadow images using an accumulation buffer [7]. Although this method uses graphics hardware, it still requires a large number of light source samples to achieve smooth penumbra regions.

An approximative approach to soft shadowing was presented by Soler and Sillion [19] using convolution of blocker images. On modern hardware this method can utilize specialized DSP features to convolve images, leading to interactive rendering times. The main drawback of the method is the clustering of geometry, as the number of clusters is directly related to the amount of texture memory and convolution operations.

Heidrich et al. [11] showed that soft shadows for linear light sources can be computed using only a minimal number of light source samples. Depth maps are generated for each sample point and processed using an edge detection step. The resulting discontinuities are then triangulated and warped to a so called visibility map, in which a percentage visibility value is stored. Although the method works very well for linear lights, it can not directly be applied to the case of area light sources.

Keating and Max [13] used multi-layered depth images (MDIs) to approximate penumbra regions. This method is related to our algorithm because MDIs are obtained from only a single light source sample. However, in contrast to this multi-layer approach, our algorithm operates just on a single depth map taken from the view of the light source sample.

Agrawala et al. [1] efficiently adopted image-based methods to compute soft shadows. Although their coherence-based ray tracing method does not perform at interactive rates, they also presented an approach using layered attenuation maps, which can be used in interactive applications.

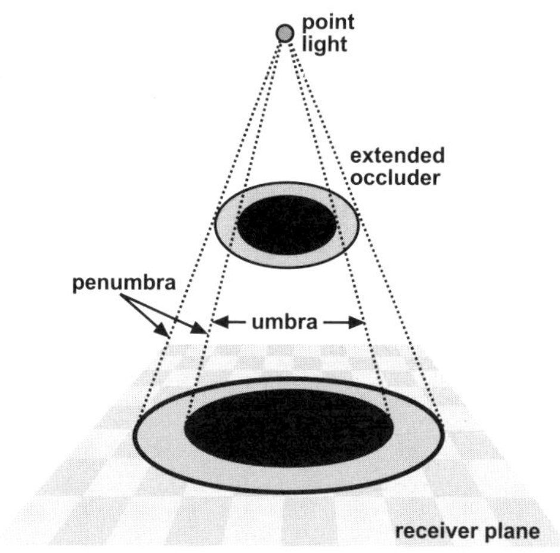

Figure 1: Computing penumbrae for a point light source.

A fast soft shadow method, especially suited for technical illustrations, was proposed by Gooch et al. [6]. Here the authors project the same shadow mask multiple times onto a series of stacked planes and translate and accumulate the results onto the receiver plane.

Haines [8] proposed a method for approximating soft shadows by first generating a hard shadow image on the receiver plane and then compute penumbra regions using distance information obtained from the occluder's silhouette edges. This paper is related to our work since it is also based on the work of Parker et al. [16], which will be explained in detail in Section 3.1. Drawbacks of Haines' method are that receivers need to be planar and that penumbra regions are only generated for regions outside the initial hard shadow.

3 Soft Shadow Generation using Depth Maps

3.1 Single Sample Soft Shadows

Parker et al. [16] showed how soft penumbra regions can be generated by defining an extended hull for each possible occluder object. By treating the *inner* object as opaque and having the opacity of the *outer* object fall off towards the outer boundary one can dim the contribution of a point light source according to the relative distances of light, occluder and receiver. Figure 1 illustrates this scheme.

In order to avoid light leaks occurring for adjacent objects the size of the inner object needs to be at least as large as the original occluder geometry. Since this causes relatively large umbra regions, which would not occur in a physically correct shadow computation, the approximation still produces reasonably looking shadows as long as the occluder objects aren't too small compared to the simulated light source area. Parker et al. implemented this scheme using standard ray tracing. In this case, it is a comparatively easy task to compute the extended hulls for primitives like spheres and triangles, and ray intersection directly calculates the distances to the outer and inner boundaries, which are used to compute a corresponding attenuation factor.

Although it was shown that the algorithm only introduces about 20% of computation overhead (compared to normal ray tracing), it is still far from being suitable for interactive rendering. Especially when it comes to more complex scenes, too much computation is spent on extending the geometric primitives and computing attenuation factors that later will be discarded.

In the following sections we will show that this method can be adopted to work on sampled data (depth maps) in a much more efficient manner, while still achieving good shadow quality.

3.2 A Sampling Based Approach

Just like the traditional shadow map algorithm presented in [20], we start with the computation of two depth images, one taken from the view of the point light source and one taken from the camera. To compute hard shadows we simply have to compare the transformed z value of each frontmost pixel (as seen by the camera) to the corresponding entry in the light source depth map, according to the following algorithm:

```
foreach(x,y) {
  P = (x,y,depth_camera[x,y])
  P' =warp_to_light(P)
  if(depth_light[P'_x, P'_y] < P'_z)
    pixel is blocked
  else
    pixel is lit
}
```

To modify this method to add an *outside* penumbra region, we have to extend the `else` branch of the shadow test to determine if the pixel is really lit or lies in a penumbra region. According to the ray tracing scheme explained in the previous section, we have to trace back the ray from the surface point towards the light source and see if any outer object is intersected. If we consider the light source depth map as a collection of *virtual layers*, where each layer is a binary mask describing which pixels between the light and the layer got blocked by an occluder inbetween (hard shadow test result), we can simulate the intensity fall-off caused by an area light source by choosing the nearest layer to P'_z that is still in front, and compute the distance between (P'_x, P'_y) and the nearest blocked pixel in that specific layer. This is in a sense similar to Parker's method since finding the minimum distance corresponds to intersecting the outer hull and computing the distance to the inner boundary. The main difference is of course that we use a sampled representation containing all possible occluders rather than the exact geometry of only one occluder.

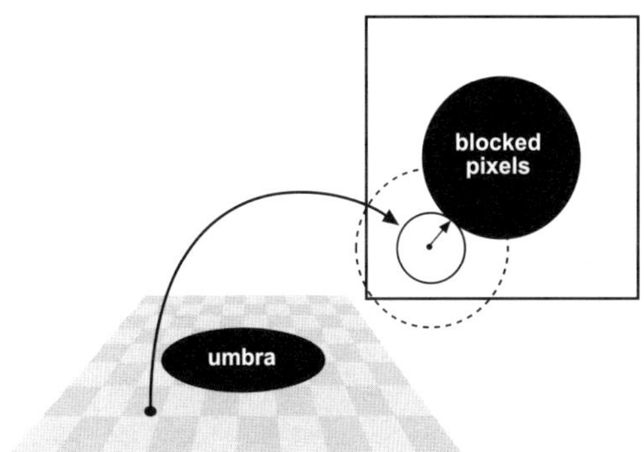

Figure 2: Projecting and searching for the nearest blocker pixel.

Figure 2 illustrates the search scheme using a very simple setup consisting of the umbra generated by an ellipsoid as an occluder and a ground plane as the receiver polygon. For a given point P which does not lie inside the umbra, we first warp P to the view of the light source (P'). Since the original point P was somewhere near the umbra, we find the transformed point P' in the neighborhood of the blocker image which causes the umbra. To calculate an attenuation factor for P, we start searching the neighborhood of P' till we either find a blocked pixel or a certain maximal search radius r_{max} is exceeded. The attenuation factor f is now simply the minimal distance r (or $r = r_{max}$ if no blocking pixel is found) divided by the maximal radius r_{max}. So $f = \frac{r}{r_{max}}$ rises up from 0 (no illumination) to 1 (full illumination) as the distance to the blocker increases.

In other words, we can now generate smooth shadow penumbra regions of a given maximal extent r_{max}. To simulate the behavior of a *real* area light source, we now have to define which properties affect the size of the penumbra and how these can be realized with our search scheme. As widely known, the following two distances mainly define the extend of the penumbra[1]:

- the distance between occluder and receiver, and
- the distance between receiver and light source.

For our search scheme the distance between receiver and light source can be integrated by varying r_{max} according to the distance between a given surface point P and the light source position. Assuming a fixed occluder,

[1] Apart from other properties like orientation of receiver and light source etc.

a receiver far away from the light source will get a larger penumbra whereas a receiver near to the light source will have a smaller r_{max} assigned.

Taking into account the distance between occluder and receiver is a little bit tricky: Since finding an appropriate occluder is the stop criterion for our search routine, we do not know in advance what this distance will be. What we do know is that the occluder has to be inside the region determined by the maximal extend, which is computed using the distance between receiver and light source.

In other words, the final r_{max} may be less the initial search radius. For our search routine this means that we first search the maximal extend since an occluder pixel is found and then re-scale the initial search radius by a factor computed using the distance between the surface point P and the found occluder pixel and use this r_{max} as the denominator for computing f (attenuation factor).

Assuming that the position of the point light in light source space is located at $(0, 0, 0)$ and that the light direction is along the z axis, we set the inital search radius

$$r_{max} = r_{scale} * |P'_z| + r_{bias} \quad ,$$

where r_{scale} and r_{bias} are user defined constants describing the area light effect[2]. Since shadow maps are usually generated for the very limited cut-off angle of spotlights, the difference of using P'_z instead of computing an euclidean distance is negligible. We can now rewrite the hard shadow algorithm to produce soft shadows by simply adding this search function:

```
foreach(x,y) {
  P = (x,y,depth_camera[x,y])
  P' =warp_to_light(P)
  if(depth_light[P'_x, P'_y] < P'_z)
    pixel is blocked
  else
    f = search(P')
    modulate pixel by f
}
search(P') {
  r = 0
  r_max = r_scale * |P'_z| + r_bias
  while(r < r_max) {
    if ∃(s,t) : ||(P'_x, P'_y) - (s,t)|| = r ∧
        depth_light[s,t] < P'_z {
      r_max *= r_shrink * (P'_z - depth_light[s,t])
      return clamp_{0,1}(r/r_max)
    }
    else
      increase r
  }
  return 1.0
}
```

[2] r_{bias} can be used to force a certain penumbra width even for receivers very near to the light source.

In the first loop we iterate over all frontmost pixels as seen by the camera performing the hard shadow test. For each lit pixel we start a search routine where we search in the light source depth map in order to find a suitable blocker pixel at a minimal distance to the transformed surface point. If a blocker pixel is found we then re-scale the inital r_{max} by a factor computed using the distance between the surface point and the occluder pixel. An user-defined scaling factor r_{shrink} is used to give additional control on the effect of this distance.

As can be seen in the pseudo code the described *virtual layers* are implicitly selected by processing only those pixels in the depth map where a blocker lies in front of the potential receiver (depth_light$[s,t] < P'_z$).

Up to now we have restricted ourselves to a very simple setup where the receiver was parallel to the light source image plane. This has the effect that P'_z remains constant during the soft shadow search, or in other words, the search takes place in a constant virtual layer. This is no longer the case if we consider an arbitrary receiver as depicted in Figure 3.

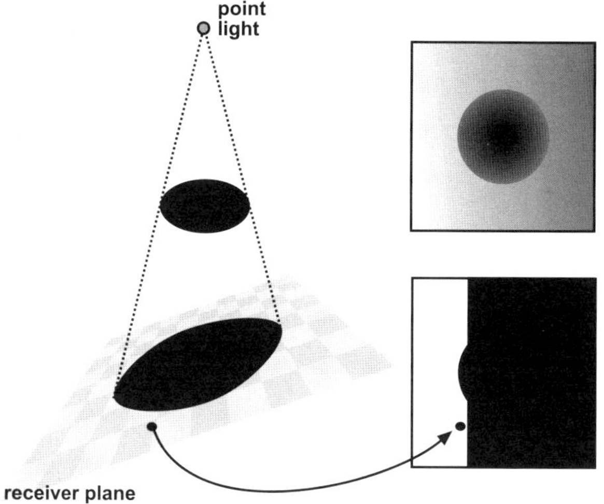

Figure 3: Wrong self shadowing due to layer crossing.

If we performed a search on the constant layer $z < P'_z$ we would immediately end up in the receiver's own shadow since the receiver plane may cross several of the virtual layers. This can be seen in the virtual layer image in Figure 3 where about two thirds of the layer contain blocked pixels belonging to the receiver polygon.

To solve this problem, we either have to divide the scene into disjunct occluders and receivers[3], which would make the algorithm only suitable for very special situations, or we need to supply more information to the

[3] Which is e.g. suitable for games where a character moves in a static environment.

search routine. To define an additional search criterion, which gives the answer to the question "does this blocker pixel belong to me?", we follow Hourcade's [12] approach and assign object IDs. These IDs are identification numbers grouping logical, spatially related, objects of the scene.

It must be pointed out that all triangles belonging to a certain object in the scene must be assigned the same object ID, otherwise self shadowing artifacts would occur if the search exceeded the projected area of the triangle belonging to P. Of course there are situations where also the ID approach fails, e.g. if distinct objects are nearly adjacent, but for most real-time applications there should exist a reasonable grouping of objects.

3.3 Handling of Hard Shadow Regions

Up to now we have concentrated on the computation of the *outer* part of the hard shadow region and simply assumed that the hard shadow region is not lit at all. In the case of an area light source, which we would like to simulate, this is of course an indefensible assumption. What we would like to obtain is of course a penumbra region which also smoothes this *inner* region. This can be easily achieved if we apply the same search technique for pixels that are initially blocked by an occluder. Instead of searching for the nearest blocker pixel within a given search radius we now have to search for the nearest pixel that is lit by the light source.

To combine this with the *outer* penumbra result we assume that *outer* and *inner* regions meet at an attenuation value of 0.5 (or some user defined constant). The final algorithm (including the object ID test) that produces penumbra regions can then be implemented according to the following pseudo code:

```
foreach(x,y) {
  P = (x,y,depth_camera[x,y])
  P' =warp_to_light(P)
  P'_ID =id_camera[x,y]
  inner = depth_light[P'_x,P'_y] < P'_z
  f = search(P',inner)
  modulate pixel by f
}
search(P',inner) {
  r = 0
  r_max = r_scale * |P'_z| + r_bias
  while(r < r_max) {
    if inner
      if ∃(s,t) : ||(P'_x,P'_y) - (s,t)|| = r  ∧
           depth_light[s,t] >= P'_z  ∧
           id_light[s,t] == P'_ID
        r_max* = r_shrink * (depth_light[s,t] - P'_z)
        return 0.5 * clamp_0,1(r/r_max)
    else
      if ∃(s,t) : ||(P'_x,P'_y) - (s,t)|| = r  ∧
           depth_light[s,t] < P'_z  ∧
           id_light[s,t] ≠ P'_ID
        r_max* = r_shrink * (P'_z - depth_light[s,t])
        return 1.0 - 0.5 * clamp_0,1(r/r_max)
    increase r
  }
  return inner ?  0.0 :  1.0
}
```

3.4 Discussion

The presented algorithm is capable of producing perceptually pleasing, rather than physically correct soft shadows using a total of four sampled images of the scene (two object ID maps, two depth maps). The behavior (extent) of the area light can be controlled by user defined constants. Using unique object IDs to group primitives into logical groups, soft shadows are computed for every occluder/receiver combination not sharing the same object ID.

4 Implementation

4.1 Generating the Input Data

Since our algorithm relies on sampled input data, graphics hardware can be used to generate the input data needed for the shadow computation. In a first step we render the scene as seen by the light source and encode object IDs as color values. For very complex scenes we either use all available color channels (RGBA) or restrict ourselves to one channel (alpha) and assign object IDs modulo 2^n (n bits precision in the alpha channel). This gives us the depth map (z-buffer) and the object IDs of the frontmost pixels according to the light source view, which we transfer back to the host memory. We then repeat the same procedure for the camera view. If only the alpha channel is used for encoding the object IDs, we can combine this rendering pass with the rendering of the final scene (without shadows).

In cases where 8 bits are enough we could also use a special depth/stencil format available on newer NVIDIA GeForce cards. With this mode we simply encode IDs as stencil values and obtain a packed ID/depth map (8 bits stencil, 24 bit depth) using only one frame buffer read. Another benefit of this format is that memory accesses to id/depth pairs are more cache friendly.

4.2 Shadow Computation

The actual shadow computation takes place at the host CPU. According to the pseudo code in Section 3.3, we iterate over all pixels seen by the camera and warp them to the light source coordinate system. Next we start searching for either the nearest blocker pixel (*outer* penumbra

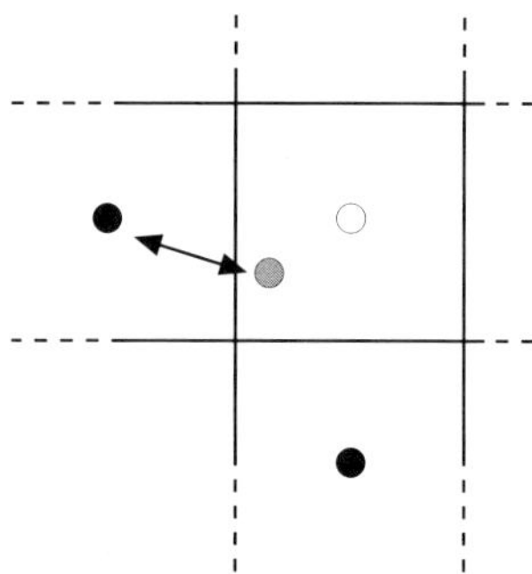

Figure 4: Computing distances at subpixel accuracy.

region) or the nearest pixel that is lit (*inner* penumbra region).

Since memory accesses (and the resulting cache misses) are the main bottleneck, we do not search circularly around the warped pixel but search linearly using an axis aligned bounding box. Doing so we are actually computing more than needed but this way we can utilize SIMD (single instruction, multiple data) features of the CPU, e.g. MMX, 3DNow, or SSE, which allows us to compute several r in parallel. If an appropriate blocking pixel is found (object ID test, minimal distance), we store the resulting attenuation factor for the given camera space pixel. If the search fails, a value of 1.0 or 0.0 is assigned (full illumination, hard shadow).

At the end, the contribution of the point light source is modulated by the attenuation map using alpha blending.

4.3 Improvements

Subpixel Accuracy

When warping pixels from camera to light there are two ways to initialize the search routine. One would be to simply round (P'_x, P'_y) to the nearest integer position and compute distances using only integer operations. While this should give the maximum performance, the quality of the computed penumbrae would suffer from quantization artifacts. Consider the case where pixels representing a large area in camera screen space are warped to the same pixel in the light source depth map. Since all pixels will find the same blocker pixel at the same distance, a constant attenuation factor will be computed for the whole area. This can be avoided by not rounding to the nearest integer but performing the distance calculation at floating point precision. As depicted in Figure 4, we compute the distance of the warped pixel (grey) to the next blocker pixels, which lie at integer position. Quantization artifacts can be further reduced if we also slightly jitter the integer position of the blocker pixels. In practice we observed that the latter is only needed for very low resolution depth maps.

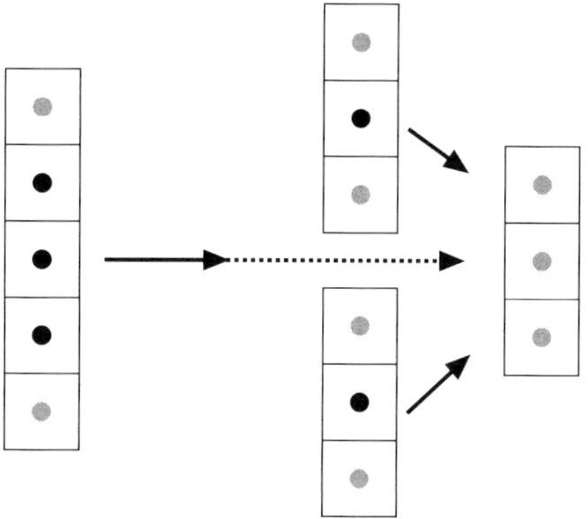

Figure 5: Subdivision and interpolation.

Adaptive Sampling

Up to now we only briefly discussed the cost of searching the depth map. Consider a scene where only 5% of the frontmost pixels are in hard shadow. To compute accurate penumbra regions we would need to perform neighborhood searches for 95% of the pixels in the worst case[4]. So for all completely lit pixels we have searched the largest region (r_{max}) without finding any blocker pixel. Even with a highly optimized search routine and depth maps of moderate size it would be very difficult to reach interactive frame rates.

Instead we propose an interpolation scheme that efficiently reduces the number of exhaustive searches needed for accurate shadowing. The interpolation starts by iterating over the columns of the camera depth map. In each iteration step, we take groups of 5 pixels and do the hard shadow test for all of them. Additionally, we also store the corresponding object IDs of the blockers, or, in the case of lit pixels, the object ID of the receiver pixel. Next, we perform a soft shadow search for the two border pixels in this group. As a criterion for the inner pixels we check if

- the object IDs are equal and
- the hard shadow test results are equal.

If this is true, we assume that there will be no dramatic shadow change within the pixel group and simply linearly interpolate the attenuation factors of the border pixels across the middle pixels. If the group test fails we refine by doing the soft shadow search for the middle pixel and subdivide the group into two three pixel groups for which we repeat the group test, interpolation and subdivision.

Figure 5 shows an example of such an interpolation step. Let us assume that the object ID of pixel 3 differs from the rest. In the first phase we perform hard shadow

[4] Worst case occurs when all pixels are in the view of the light source.

tests for all pixels and soft shadow searches for the two border ones. Since the interpolation criterion fails (IDs not equal), the pixel group is refined by a soft shadow search for pixel 2 and subdivided into two groups. Pixel group $(0, 1, 2)$ fulfills the criterion and an interpolated attenuation factor is assigned to pixel 1, whereas for pixel group $(2, 3, 4)$ we need to compute the attenuation by search. As we will later also need object IDs for interpolated pixels, we simply use the object ID of one interpolant in that case. We repeat this for all pixel groups in this and every 4th column, leaving a gap of three pixel in horizontal direction.

Having linearly interpolated over the columns we now process all rows in the same manner and fill up the horizontal gaps. This bi-linear interpolation mechanism is capable of reducing the number of expensive searches. In the best case, the searching is only done for one pixel in a 16 pixel block. Since this case normally occurs very often (e.g. in fully illuminated areas), we can achieve a great speed-up using the interpolation. On the other hand, quality loss is negligible or non-existent because of the very conservative refinement.

The size of the pixel group used for interpolation should depend on the image size. In experiments we observed that blocks of 4×4 pixels are a good speed/quality tradeoff when rendering images of moderate size (512×512, 800×600 pixels), whereas larger block sizes may introduce artifacts due to the non-perspectively correct interpolation.

5 Results

We have implemented our soft shadow technique on an Intel Pentium 4 1.7GHz computer equipped with an NVIDIA GeForce3 graphics card. Since the generation of depth and ID maps is done using graphics hardware, we get an additional overhead due to the two frame buffer reads needed to transfer the sampled images back to host memory.

Figure 7 shows the results of our soft shadow algorithm for a very simple scene consisting of one torus (occluder) and a receiver plane. We rendered the same scene three times varying only the position and orientation of the occluder.

All images in Figure 7 were rendered using an image resolution of 512×512 pixels and a light depth/ID map resolution of 256×256 pixels. By default, we always use the full image resolution when computing the depth and ID map for the camera view. Frame rates for this scene are about $10 - 15 fps$. Computing only the hard shadows (shadow test done on the host CPU) the scene can be rendered at about $30 fps$.

In the left image r_{max} was set to 20 (20 pixel search

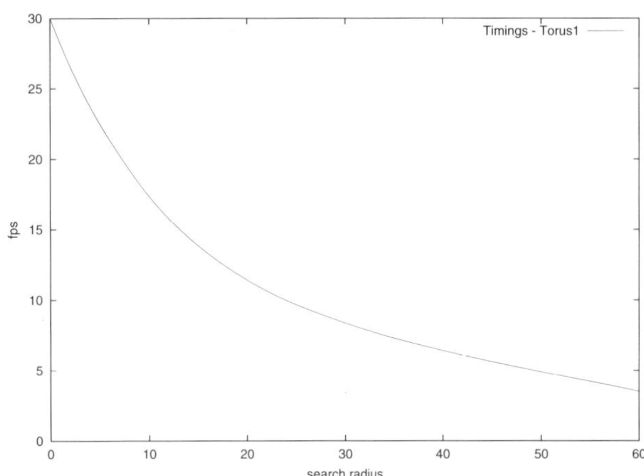

Figure 6: Frame rates for the torus test scene (Figure 8)

radius) for the inner and outer penumbra. The receiver plane does not reach this maximum (due to the distance between receiver and light source). The average search radius for pixels on the receiver plane is about 16 pixels. The effect of increasing or decreasing r_{max} for this scene is plotted in Figure 6. It must be pointed out that the distance between occluder and receiver does not affect the inital search radius. Therefore the cost of computing soft shadows for the three images in Figure 7 is nearly constant.

In the left image artifacts can be seen (ring), where the inner and outer penumbra meet. This is because the attenuation factors for inner and outer regions are computed in a slightly different way (see Section 3.3). Theoretically this transition should be smooth.

Figure 8 (left) shows a more crowded example scene with objects placed at various heights. It can be seen that objects very near to the floor plane cast very sharp shadows, whereas the shadows from the three tori are much smoother. The other two images in Figure 8 show the scene with hard shadows and hard shadows with outer penumbra. Since our soft shadow algorithm is based on the shadow map technique, we are independent of the scene geometry, which means we can generate soft shadows for arbitrary geometry. There is no distinction between receiver and occluder objects (apart from the missing self shadowing due to the ID test).

Figure 9 shows two more complex scenes where we used our soft shadow algorithm for penumbra generation. In order to assign reasonable object IDs we simply group polygons using the tree structure obtained when parsing the scene file. This way all polygons sharing the same transformation and material node are assigned the same object ID. Both images were taken using a low-resolution light depth/ID map of 256×256 pixels and an image resolution of 512×512 pixel. In the right image we choose a very large cutoff angle for the spotlight which would normally generate very coarse hard shadows. Here the subpixel accuracy explained in Section 4.3 efficiently smoothes the shadows. Both images can be rendered at interactive frame rates ($\approx 15fps$).

Note that all the timings strongly vary with the size of the penumbra, so changing the light position or altering r_{max} may speed up or slow down the computation, depending on the number of searches that have to be performed. When examining the shape of the penumbrae, one can observe that they do not perfectly correspond to the occluder shape. This is due to the circular nature of the search routine, which rounds off corners when searching for the minimal distance.

6 Conclusions and Future Work

In this paper we have shown how good-looking, soft penumbra regions can be generated using only information obtained from a single light source sample. Although the method is a very crude approximation it gives a dramatic change in image quality, while still being computationally efficient. We showed how the time consuming depth map search can be avoided for many regions by interpolating attenuation factors across blocks of pixels. Since the algorithm works on sampled representations of the scene, computation time depends mostly on the shadow sizes and image resolutions and not on geometric complexity, which makes the method suitable for general situations.

In it is current state the algorithm still relies on a number of user parameters (r_{max}, r_{shrink}, etc.) which where introduced *ad-hoc*. As future work we would like to to hide these parameters and compute them based on one intuitive parameter (e.g. the radius of a spherical light source, defined in the scene's coordinate system). This way it would also be possible to compare our method to more accurate algorithms.

With real time frame rates as a future goal, another focus will be on more sophisticated search algorithms that work on hierarchical and/or tiled depth maps as well as investigating methods of pre-computed or cached distance information. Further speed improvements could also be achieved by using graphics hardware, e.g. interleaved frame buffer reads, as well as on the host CPU by using special processor instructions sets.

Another research direction will be the quality of shadows. Up to now we simply used a linear intensity falloff, which of course is not correct. Assuming a diffuse spherical light and an occluder with a straight edge (similar to Parker's original algorithm), a better approximation would be a sinusoid as the attenuation function.

Finally, we have only slightly addressed aliasing issues that occur when working on sampled data. Our algorithm can work on very low-resolution image data since the search technique efficiently smoothes blocky hard shadows. However, we expect an additional improvement of quality by using filtering schemes that also take into account the stamp size of the warped pixel or work on super-sampled depth maps.

Acknowledgements

We would like to thank Prof. Wolfgang Heidrich of the University of British Columbia, Canada, and the anonymous reviewers for valuable discussions and comments on this topic.

References

[1] Maneesh Agrawala, Ravi Ramamoorthi, Alan Heirich, and Laurent Moll. Efficient image-based methods for rendering soft shadows. *Proceedings of SIGGRAPH 2000*, pages 375–384, July 2000. ISBN 1-58113-208-5.

[2] Stefan Brabec and Hans-Peter Seidel. Hardware-accelerated rendering of antialiased shadows with shadow maps. *To appear in: Computer Graphics International 2001*, 2001.

[3] L. S. Brotman and N. I. Badler. Generating soft shadows with a depth buffer algorithm. *IEEE Computer Graphics and Applications*, 4(10):71–81, October 1984.

[4] Yiorgos Chrysanthou and Mel Slater. Shadow volume bsp trees for computation of shadows in dynamic scenes. *1995 Symposium on Interactive 3D Graphics*, pages 45–50, April 1995. ISBN 0-89791-736-7.

[5] Franklin C. Crow. Shadow algorithms for computer graphics. In *Computer Graphics (SIGGRAPH '77 Proceedings)*, pages 242–248, July 1977.

[6] Bruce Gooch, Peter-Pike J. Sloan, Amy Gooch, Peter S. Shirley, and Rich Riesenfeld. Interactive technical illustration. In *1999 ACM Symposium on Interactive 3D Graphics*, pages 31–38. ACM SIGGRAPH, April 1999. ISBN 1-58113-082-1.

[7] Paul E. Haeberli and Kurt Akeley. The accumulation buffer: Hardware support for high-quality rendering. In *Computer Graphics (SIGGRAPH '90 Proceedings)*, pages 309–318, August 1990.

[8] E. Haines. Soft planar shadows using plateaus. *Journal of Graphic Tools*, 6(1):19–27, 2001.

[9] Paul Heckbert and Michael Herf. Simulating soft shadows with graphics hardware. Technical Report CMU-CS-97-104, Carnegie Mellon University, January 1997.

[10] T. Heidmann. Real shadows real time. *IRIS Universe*, 18:28–31, November 1991.

[11] Wolfgang Heidrich, Stefan Brabec, and Hans-Peter Seidel. Soft shadow maps for linear lights. *Rendering Techniques 2000: 11th Eurographics Workshop on Rendering*, pages 269–280, June 2000. ISBN 3-211-83535-0.

[12] J. C. Hourcade and A. Nicolas. Algorithms for antialiased cast shadows. *Computers & Graphics*, 9(3):259–265, 1985.

[13] Brett Keating and Nelson Max. Shadow penumbras for complex objects by depth-dependent filtering of multi-layer depth images. In *Rendering Techniques '99 (Proc. of Eurographics Rendering Workshop)*, pages 197–212, June 1999.

[14] Daniel Lischinski, Filippo Tampieri, and Donald P. Greenberg. Discontinuity meshing for accurate radiosity. *IEEE Computer Graphics & Applications*, 12(6):25–39, November 1992.

[15] Michael D. McCool. Shadow volume reconstruction from depth maps. *ACM Transactions on Graphics*, 19(1):1–26, January 2000.

[16] Steven Parker, Peter Shirley, and Brian Smits. Single sample soft shadows. Technical Report UUCS-98-019, Computer Science Department, University of Utah, 1998. Available from http://www.cs.utah.edu/vissim/bibliography/.

[17] William T. Reeves, David H. Salesin, and Robert L. Cook. Rendering antialiased shadows with depth maps. In *Computer Graphics (SIGGRAPH '87 Proceedings)*, pages 283–291, July 1987.

[18] Marc Segal, Carl Korobkin, Rolf van Widenfelt, Jim Foran, and Paul Haeberli. Fast shadow and lighting effects using texture mapping. In *Computer Graphics (SIGGRAPH '92 Proceedings)*, pages 249–252, July 1992.

[19] Cyril Soler and François X. Sillion. Fast calculation of soft shadow textures using convolution. In *Computer Graphics (SIGGRAPH '98 Proceedings)*, pages 321–332, July 1998.

[20] Lance Williams. Casting curved shadows on curved surfaces. In *Computer Graphics (SIGGRAPH '78 Proceedings)*, pages 270–274, August 1978.

[21] Andrew Woo, Pierre Poulin, and Alain Fournier. A survey of shadow algorithms. *IEEE Computer Graphics & Applications*, 10(6):13–32, November 1990.

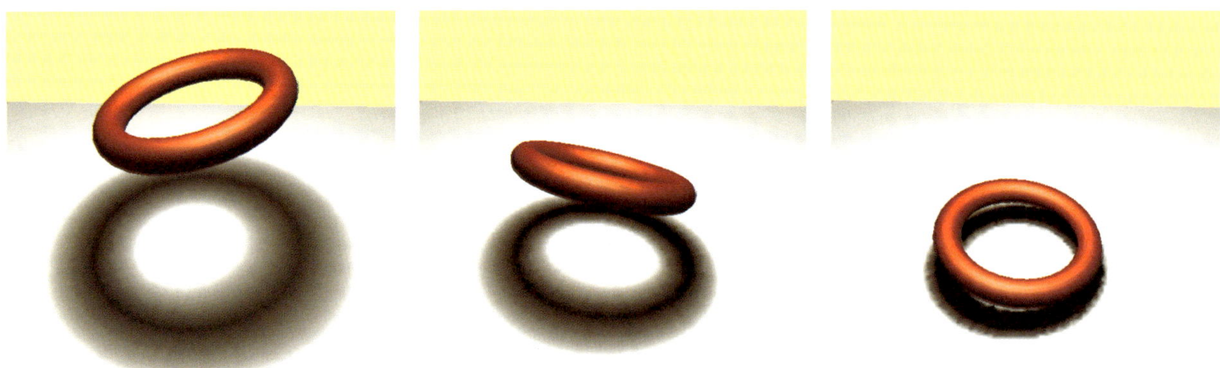

Figure 7: A simple test scene showing the effect of varying distance between receiver and occluder.

Figure 8: A more *crowded* scene. Left: soft shadows, middle: hard shadows, right: hard shadows with outer penumbra.

Figure 9: Two more complex scenes rendered with our soft shadow algorithm.

Video Games: What the heck?

John W. Buchanan
Electronic Arts Canada

The video game industry is growing up. Over the last 7 years the content delivery media for games has gone from 64 megabytes to 9 gigabytes. The processors and associated graphics cards have increased in power. It is now feasible to render fairly realistic characters. It is also realistic to render cartoon characters. In short we can now focus on the story and the experience rather than on the technology. We can start to answer the question, what is an intelligent avatar?

It used to be the case that the game engine was the crucial part of a game. This is no longer the case; the task of building an efficient game engine is well understood. The primary task before a game team is now content production. Thus the engineering task in game building is focused on tools for the artist and the art pipeline that bakes the data for the game. What are the tools that we need? Well, we basically need the same tools that the movie industry needs, and then some. We need to manage transition trees between animations that may have 10000 transitions in them. We need to blend between arbitrary frames on animations. We need our artist to be able to instantly see his/her work on the target platform.

In this talk I give a historical perspective of the games industry. I talk about the changes that have occurred over the last 7 years and I talk about our future directions and what our biggest technical challenges are.

Rapid Prototyping of Physical User Interfaces

Saul Greenberg

Department of Computer Science
University of Calgary
Calgary, Alberta, Canada T2N 1N4
+1 403 220 6087
saul@cpsc.ucalgary.ca

In the last few years, researchers have embraced human-computer interface designs that include physical user interfaces augmented by computing power. These began with Weisser's vision of ubiquitous computing and calm technology [8], and continued to notions of pervasive computing [1], tangible user interfaces [6], information appliances [7], ubiquitous media and reactive environments [2], interactive art installations (e.g., see SIGGRAPH Art Galleries), ambient displays [3], and context-aware computing [4]. The area is so new that we are still entranced by breakthrough examples of physical user interfaces. Indeed, many papers and proceedings are speckled with beautiful exhibits illustrating what can be done.

While this is an exciting new area, everyday programmers face considerable hurdles if they wish to create even simple physical user interfaces. Most lack the necessary hardware training. Those willing to learn will find themselves spending most of their time building and debugging circuit boards, firmware and low-level wire protocols rather than building their physical user interface designs.

The problem is that we have not provided programmers with adequate building blocks for rapidly prototyping physical user interfaces. This leaves them in a position similar to early GUI researchers who had to build their widgets from scratch, or to early graphics researchers who had to build their 3D environments by brute force using primitives such as 'DrawPixel' and 'DrawLine'. Given this onerous situation, it is no wonder that papers on physical user interfaces mostly come from top researchers at major university and industrial research laboratories.

Magnetic Desert by Kari Basaraba is an ambient display that moves metal bearings around a dish at a rate that varies with the amount of motion detected in the room. It is constructed from steel ball bearings, sand, a Plexiglas dish, and (behind the scenes) magnets.

Marble Mail by Shannon Goodman is a physical representation of your email box. The top bowl acts as a storage area representing potential email. As email arrives, a marble drops to the middle bowl containing unopened messages. As email is read, a marble drops into the last bowl containing read messages.

As a consequence of these problems, I and my collaborators made a concerted effort to think about how we could package physical devices and their software for easy development of physical user interfaces. Our goals were to create devices:

simple enough so that developers can concentrate on the overall use, modification and recombination of devices into a physical user interface instead of low-level device construction and implementation;

easy enough for the average programmer to program and extend.

Our solution was to develop physical widgets, or *phidgets*, whose use is almost directly analogous to how graphical user interface (GUI) widgets are packaged and 'dropped into' software applications [5]. Our primary belief is:

> ...just as widgets make GUIs easy to develop, so could phidgets make the new generation of physical user interfaces easy to develop.

Through the phidget hardware and software, it becomes very easy to control various output devices by computer: servo motors, LEDs, 112 volt power bars, variable power to DC components (motors, lights, etc.), solenoids, and so on. It is just as easy to gather input from physical buttons, toggle switches, potentiometers, light sensors, force sensors, heat sensors, motion detectors, accelerometers, and a host of other input components.

I gave phidgets to undergraduate students with no hardware expertise to see what they could do with them. These typically took the form of a short two week assignment. The results were remarkable. While some students replicated examples of physical user interfaces reported by other researchers, most produced their own innovative designs [5]. Several of the more recent student projects are documented on the following pages. I should emphasize that these examples are typical of what students did!

My main message is that packaging devices as physical widgets greatly simplifies their programming and construction, which in turn empowers designers to craft physical user interfaces rather than waste their time on low-level implementation details.

Acknowledgements. Chester Fitchett, a graduate student who loves hardware, was the mastermind behind the phidget toolkit. Hats off to my students in CPSC 581 who produced projects far beyond my expectations in a ridiculously short amount of time.

Software and hardware is available from www.phidgets.com or www.cpsc.ucalgary.ca/grouplab/.

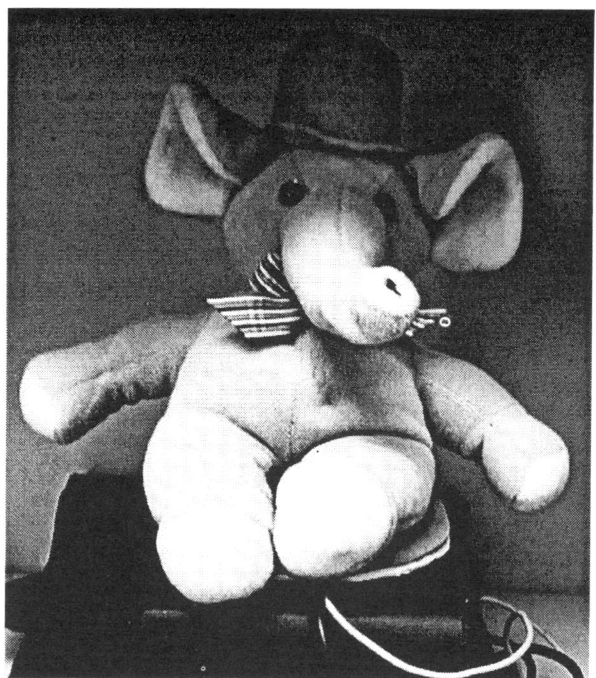

Ele-Phidget by Shivaughan Warwaruk is an ambient notification for an audio chat program. When you receive a message, the elephant turns around and faces you. You push the elephant's stomach to listen to the message, When no messages are left, the elephant turns away. To record a message, you squeeze the elephant's head and speak into the elephant's trunk. A second squeeze sends the message.

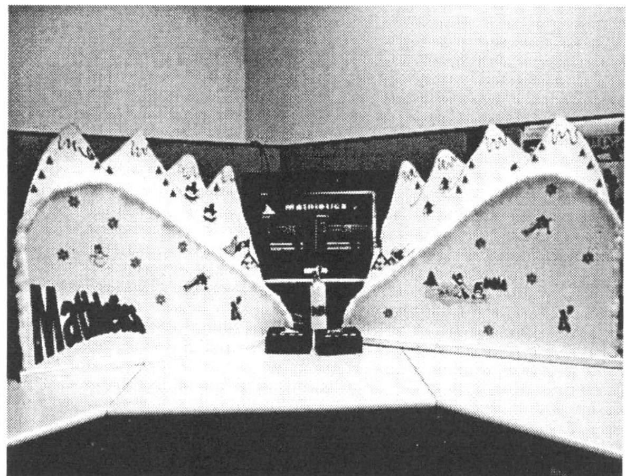

Mathletics by Russel Kruger is a game for children to learn their multiplication tables. Multiple-choice questions appear on the screen, and each child enters the answer to their questions using a controller. As one answers a question correctly, a skier skies partway down the mountain. The first child to correctly answer 10 questions wins, at which time their figure reaches the bottom of the mountain, and the lights on their mountain light up.

REFERENCES

[1] Ark. W. and Selker, T. A look at human interaction with pervasive computers. *IBM Systems Journal* 38(4), 1999.

[2] Buxton, W. Living in Augmented Reality: Ubiquitous Media and Reactive Environments. In K. Finn, A. Sellen & S. Wilber (Eds.). *Video Mediated Communication*, Erlbaum, 363-384, 1997.

[3] Dahley, A., Wisneski, C. and Ishii, H. Water Lamp and Pinwheels: Ambient projection of digital information into architectural space. *Summary of CHI '98*, 269-270, 1998.

[4] Dey, A. K., Salber, D., and Abowd, G. A conceptual framework and a toolkit for supporting the rapid prototyping of context-aware applications. *Human-Computer Interaction*, Vol 16, 2001.

[5] Greenberg, S. and Fitchett, C. Phidgets: Easy Development of Physical Interfaces through Physical Widgets. *Proc ACM UIST'01*, 209-218, 2001.

[6] Ishii, H. and Ullmer, B. Tangible bits: Towards seamless interfaces between people, bits and atoms. *Proc. ACM CHI'97,* 234-241, 1997.

[7] Norman, D.A. *The Invisible Computer*. MIT Press, 1998.

[8] Weiser, M. and Brown, J. Designing calm technology, *Powergrid Journal,* v1.01, July, 1996.

Monster Phidget by Edward Tse greets people as they walk by e.g., "hey, how's it going" or "good day sir". If someone stops in front of Monster, he responds with something like "cool, you're hanging out eh?" and then tells jokes (laughs and drum rolls included). When the person leaves, monster says something like "catch ya later". If someone pulls on Monster's mouth, it responds with a short phrase from the Monsters Inc. movie.

Disharmony by Mike Polowick is an abstract conglomeration of loosely-related themes designed for provoking thought in the viewer. All parts were crafted with deliberate intention, but there is no specific meaning; any interpretation is correct. Depending on how one moves a pieces on a chess board (not shown), bubbles disturb real fish in their fish bowl, lights blink, a disk spins, and so on.

Messenger Frame by Michael Hornby-Smith is a physical notification device attached to MSN Instant Messenger. As a person appears online or changes his activity status, that person's photo is lit up and a sound cue is generated. One can send a message directly to that person by touching his photo.

How Long can Graphics Chips Exceed Moore's Law?

David Kirk
NVIDIA

A few short years ago, single-chip PC 3D graphics solutions arrived on the market at performance levels that rivaled professional workstations with multi-chip graphics pipelines. Since then, graphics performance has grown at a rate approaching doubling every 6 months, far exceeding Moore's Law. How is this possible? Will it be sustainable? There is evidence that this geometric performance growth is not only possible, but inevitable.

Author Index